World Economic and Financial Surveys

WORLD ECONOMIC OUTLOOK
October 2000

Focus on Transition Economies

International Monetary Fund

Production: IMF Graphics Section
Cover and Design: Luisa Menjivar-Macdonald
Figures: Theodore F. Peters, Jr.
Typesetting: Choon Lee and Joseph A. Kumar

World economic outlook (International Monetary Fund)
World economic outlook: a survey by the staff of the International
Monetary Fund.—1980– —Washington, D.C.: The Fund, 1980–

v.; 28 cm.—(1981–84: Occasional paper/International Monetary Fund
ISSN 0251-6365)
Annual.
Has occasional updates, 1984–
ISSN 0258-7440 = World economic and financial surveys
ISSN 0256-6877 = World economic outlook (Washington)
1. Economic history—1971– —Periodicals. I. International
Monetary Fund. II. Series: Occasional paper (International Monetary
Fund)

HC10.W7979   84-640155
                          338.5'443'09048--dc19
                                          AACR 2 MARC-S

Library of Congress   8507

Published biannually.
ISBN 1-55775-975-8

Price: US$42.00
(US$35.00 to full-time faculty members and
students at universities and colleges)

Please send orders to:
International Monetary Fund, Publication Services
700 19th Street, N.W., Washington, D.C. 20431, U.S.A.
Tel.: (202) 623-7430   Telefax: (202) 623-7201
E-mail: publications@imf.org
Internet: http://www.imf.org

recycled paper

CONTENTS

Boxes

Tables

Figures

ASSUMPTIONS AND CONVENTIONS

A number of assumptions have been adopted for the projections presented in the *World Economic Outlook*. It has been assumed that real effective exchange rates will remain constant at their average levels during July 18–August 15, except for the currencies participating in the European exchange rate mechanism II (ERM II), which are assumed to remain constant in nominal terms relative to the euro; that established policies of national authorities will be maintained (for specific assumptions about fiscal and monetary polices in industrial countries, see Box A1); that the average price of oil will be $26.53 a barrel in 2000 and $23.00 a barrel in 2001, and remain unchanged in real terms over the medium term; and that the six-month London interbank offered rate (LIBOR) on U.S. dollar deposits will average 6.8 percent in 2000 and 7.4 percent in 2001. These are, of course, working hypotheses rather than forecasts, and the uncertainties surrounding them add to the margin of error that would in any event be involved in the projections. The estimates and projections are based on statistical information available through the end of August 2000.

The following conventions have been used throughout the *World Economic Outlook*:

. . . to indicate that data are not available or not applicable;

— to indicate that the figure is zero or negligible;

– between years or months (for example, 1997–98 or January–June) to indicate the years or months covered, including the beginning and ending years or months;

/ between years or months (for example, 1997/98) to indicate a fiscal or financial year.

"Billion" means a thousand million; "trillion" means a thousand billion.

"Basis points" refer to hundredths of 1 percentage point (for example, 25 basis points are equivalent to ¼ of 1 percentage point).

In the main text, shaded areas of figures and tables indicate IMF staff projections. In the Statistical Appendix, projections are shown in white.

Minor discrepancies between sums of constituent figures and totals shown are due to rounding.

As used in this report, the term "country" does not in all cases refer to a territorial entity that is a state as understood by international law and practice. As used here, the term also covers some territorial entities that are not states but for which statistical data are maintained on a separate and independent basis.

FURTHER INFORMATION AND DATA

This report on the *World Economic Outlook* is available in full on the IMF's Internet site, *www.imf.org*. Accompanying it on the website is a larger compilation of data from the WEO database than in the report itself, consisting of files containing the series most frequently requested by readers. These files may be downloaded for use in a variety of software packages.

Inquiries about the content of the *World Economic Outlook* and the WEO database should be sent by mail, electronic mail, or telefax (telephone inquiries cannot be accepted) to:

World Economic Studies Division
Research Department
International Monetary Fund
700 19th Street, N.W.
Washington, D.C. 20431, U.S.A.
E-mail: weo@imf.org   Telefax: (202) 623–6343

PREFACE

The projections and analysis contained in the *World Economic Outlook* are an integral element of the IMF's ongoing surveillance of economic developments and policies in its member countries and of the global economic system. The IMF has published the *World Economic Outlook* annually from 1980 through 1983 and biannually since 1984.

The survey of prospects and policies is the product of a comprehensive interdepartmental review of world economic developments, which draws primarily on information the IMF staff gathers through its consultations with member countries. These consultations are carried out in particular by the IMF's area departments together with the Policy Development and Review Department and the Fiscal Affairs Department.

The country projections are prepared by the IMF's area departments on the basis of internationally consistent assumptions about world activity, exchange rates, and conditions in international financial and commodity markets. For approximately 50 of the largest economies—accounting for 90 percent of world output—the projections are updated for each *World Economic Outlook* exercise. For smaller countries, the projections are based on those prepared at the time of the IMF's regular Article IV consultations with those countries or in connection with the use of IMF resources.

The analysis in the *World Economic Outlook* draws extensively on the ongoing work of the IMF's area and specialized departments, and is coordinated in the Research Department under the general direction of Michael Mussa, Economic Counsellor and Director of Research. The *World Economic Outlook* project is directed by David Robinson, Assistant Director of the Research Department, together with Tamim Bayoumi, Chief of the World Economic Studies Division.

Primary contributors to the current issue include John H. Green, Maitland MacFarlan, Peter Sturm, Cathy Wright, Luis Catão, Mark De Broeck, Luca Ricci, Ranil Salgado, and Torsten Sløk. Other contributors include Martin Cerisola, Ximena Cheetham, Markus Haacker, Oleh Havrylyshyn, Prakash Loungani, Christian Mumssen, Ramana Ramaswamy, Thomas Richardson, Julius Rosenblatt, Kevin Ross, Ratna Sahay, Alessandro Zanello, and Harm Zebregs. Mandy Hemmati, Bennett Sutton, Siddique Hossain, and Yutong Li provided research assistance. Gretchen Byrne, Nicholas Dopuch, Toh Kuan, Olga Plagie, Di Rao, and Anthony G. Turner processed the data and managed the computer systems. Lisa Nugent, Marlene George, and Jemille Tumang were responsible for word processing. Jeff Hayden and Jacqueline Irving of the External Relations Department edited the manuscript and coordinated production of the publication.

The analysis has benefited from comments and suggestions by staff from other IMF departments, as well as by Executive Directors following their discussion of the *World Economic Outlook* on August 30 and September 1, 2000. However, both projections and policy considerations are those of the IMF staff and should not be attributed to Executive Directors or to their national authorities.

CHAPTER I

PROSPECTS AND POLICY CHALLENGES

The outlook for the global economy has continued to strengthen, with GDP growth projected to increase in all major regions of the world. This improvement has been led by the continued strength of the U.S. economy, a robust expansion in Europe, and a nascent—albeit still fragile—recovery in Japan. In emerging markets, economic fundamentals in most countries have strengthened, aided by the consolidation of the recovery in Asia, rebounds from last year's slowdowns in Latin America and the Middle East, and improved activity in Africa. Nevertheless, economic and financial imbalances in the three main currency areas remain large, posing a continued risk to the global expansion, and higher oil prices have become an increasing concern.

The main themes developed in this issue of the World Economic Outlook *include:*

- *The need to continue policies designed to rebalance growth and demand across the major currency areas in an orderly manner;*
- *The progress that has been made in developing market-oriented economies and the necessary supporting institutional structures in the transition economies of Europe and Asia, and the reform agenda for the future; and*
- *The role that greater integration in the global economy—for instance, through accession to the European Union or the World Trade Organization—can play in supporting the reform effort in transition economies.*

The global economic expansion has continued to gain strength, with global output growth now projected at 4.7 percent in 2000, 0.5 percentage points higher than expected in the May *World Economic Outlook* (Figure 1.1 and Table 1.1). Growth is projected to increase in all major regions of the world (Figure 1.2), led by the continued strength of the U.S. economy; the robust upswing in Europe; the consolidation of the recovery in Asia; and a rebound from last year's slowdowns in emerging markets in Latin America and the Middle East and Europe. Activity in Africa is projected to rise further, and the countries in transition are expected to register a second year of solid growth, underpinned by a much better-than-expected performance in Russia. Nevertheless, a number of countries continue to experience serious economic problems—in some cases due to natural disasters and adverse movements in commodity prices—while

the HIV/AIDS pandemic poses a severe human and economic threat, particularly in sub-Saharan Africa and parts of Asia.

The slowdown in global activity in 1998 was shallower than previous troughs and has been followed by a rapid recovery (Figure 1.3). This partly reflects the fact that the slowdown originated in emerging market economies, while previous slowdowns were driven by developments in advanced countries accounting for a more substantial share of global activity. However, the rebound also owes much to the concerted efforts of policymakers across the globe. Among the advanced countries, the continued strong expansion in the United States played a critical role in supporting global activity at the height of the crisis, and policies to strengthen growth in both Europe and Japan also supported the recovery. Among most crisis countries, the determined adjustment efforts pursued by policymakers contributed to an early restoration of macroeco-

Figure 1.1. Global Indicators[1]
(Annual percent change unless otherwise noted)

The global recovery continues to strengthen, while inflation remains subdued.

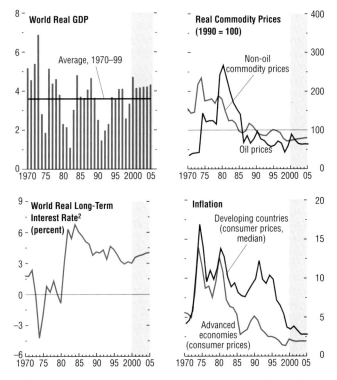

[1]Shaded areas indicate IMF staff projections. Aggregates are computed on the basis of purchasing-power-parity weights unless otherwise indicated.
[2]GDP-weighted average of 10-year (or nearest maturity) government bond yields less inflation rates for the United States, Japan, Germany, France, Italy, the United Kingdom, and Canada. Excluding Italy prior to 1972.

nomic stability and a steady improvement in external confidence. The pursuit of sound macroeconomic policies in other major developing countries also played an important role in preventing the crisis from spreading further.

With many advanced economies now growing at rates at or above potential, most central banks have continued to raise policy interest rates. Although headline inflation rates have risen in response to higher energy prices—and inflationary pressures are a concern in some cyclically advanced countries, including the United States and the faster-growing countries in Europe—underlying inflation in most advanced economies remains relatively subdued. In part this reflects the continued margins of slack in some regions of the world, notably Japan and to a lesser extent continental Europe (Figure 1.4), but other factors, including fiscal consolidation and regulatory and technological changes, have also played a role. Inflation is projected to decline in most regions of the developing world, as well as in the transition economies.

While the overall outlook is encouraging, there are significant risks and uncertainties. First, as recent issues of the *World Economic Outlook* have discussed in some detail, a number of economic and financial imbalances continue to exist in the global economy. These include the uneven pattern of GDP and demand growth among the three major currency areas, and the associated imbalances in their external current accounts, including a record deficit in the United States, and surpluses in Japan and in some other major countries (Table 1.2); the apparent misalignments among major currencies, particularly the euro and the U.S. dollar; and the still high level of equity market valuations in the United States and some other countries. Some progress has been made toward resolving these imbalances over the past six months through, among other things, the continued expansion in Europe, some easing of demand pressures in the United States, and a modest decline in stock market valuations in some countries from recent peaks, but the possibility that these imbalances may unwind in a disorderly fashion remains a risk to the global expansion.

Table 1.1. Overview of the *World Economic Outlook* Projections
(Annual percent change unless otherwise noted)

	1998	1999	Current Projections		Difference from May 2000 Projections[1]	
			2000	2001	2000	2001
World output	**2.6**	**3.4**	**4.7**	**4.2**	**0.5**	**0.3**
Advanced economies	2.4	3.2	4.2	3.2	0.6	0.2
Major industrial countries	2.5	2.9	3.9	2.9	0.6	0.2
United States	4.4	4.2	5.2	3.2	0.8	0.2
Japan	−2.5	0.2	1.4	1.8	0.5	—
Germany	2.1	1.6	2.9	3.3	0.1	—
France	3.2	2.9	3.5	3.5	—	0.4
Italy	1.5	1.4	3.1	3.0	0.4	0.2
United Kingdom	2.6	2.1	3.1	2.8	0.1	0.8
Canada	3.3	4.5	4.7	2.8	1.0	0.1
Other advanced economies	2.0	4.7	5.1	4.2	0.6	0.1
Memorandum						
Industrial countries	2.7	3.0	3.9	3.0	0.5	0.2
Euro area	2.7	2.4	3.5	3.4	0.3	0.2
Newly industrialized Asian economies	−2.3	7.8	7.9	6.1	1.3	—
Developing countries	3.5	3.8	5.6	5.7	0.2	0.4
Africa	3.1	2.2	3.4	4.4	−1.0	−0.1
Asia	4.1	5.9	6.7	6.6	0.5	0.7
China	7.8	7.1	7.5	7.3	0.5	0.8
India	6.3	6.4	6.7	6.5	0.4	0.4
ASEAN-4[2]	−9.3	2.6	4.5	5.0	0.5	0.6
Middle East and Europe	3.1	0.8	4.7	4.1	0.1	0.1
Western Hemisphere	2.2	0.3	4.3	4.5	0.3	−0.2
Brazil	−0.1	1.0	4.0	4.5	—	—
Countries in transition	−0.8	2.4	4.9	4.1	2.3	1.1
Central and eastern Europe	2.0	1.3	3.1	4.2	0.1	—
Excluding Belarus and Ukraine	2.0	1.8	3.8	4.6	0.2	—
Russia	−4.9	3.2	7.0	4.0	5.5	2.6
Transcaucasus and central Asia	2.5	4.6	5.3	4.5	0.4	0.8
World trade volume (goods and services)	**4.3**	**5.1**	**10.0**	**7.8**	**2.1**	**0.6**
Imports						
Advanced economies	5.7	7.6	10.3	7.9	2.5	0.8
Developing countries	0.3	—	10.0	9.0	0.2	0.5
Countries in transition	2.5	−2.9	12.4	8.4	6.3	1.5
Exports						
Advanced economies	3.9	4.8	9.9	7.6	2.7	0.8
Developing countries	3.7	3.5	8.8	7.1	−0.9	−1.2
Countries in transition	6.5	5.0	10.1	6.0	4.2	0.4
Commodity prices						
Oil[3]						
In SDRs	−31.2	36.5	52.0	−13.0	15.5	6.4
In U.S. dollars	−32.1	37.5	47.5	−13.3	12.4	5.9
Nonfuel (average based on world commodity export weights)						
In SDRs	−13.5	−7.8	6.4	4.8	0.4	1.9
In U.S. dollars	−14.7	−7.1	3.2	4.5	−1.7	1.3
Consumer prices						
Advanced economies	1.5	1.4	2.3	2.1	0.4	0.1
Developing countries	10.1	6.6	6.2	5.2	0.5	0.5
Countries in transition	21.8	43.8	18.3	12.5	−1.2	−1.7
Six-month London interbank offered rate (LIBOR, percent)						
On U.S. dollar deposits	5.6	5.5	6.8	7.4	—	0.3
On Japanese yen deposits	0.7	0.2	0.3	0.5	0.1	0.1
On euro deposits	3.7	3.0	4.6	5.1	0.5	0.2

Note: Real effective exchange rates are assumed to remain constant at the levels prevailing during July 18–August 15, 2000.
[1]Using updated purchasing-power-parity (PPP) weights, summarized in the Statistical Appendix, Table A.
[2]Indonesia, Malaysia, the Philippines, and Thailand.
[3]Simple average of spot prices of U.K. Brent, Dubai, and West Texas Intermediate crude oil. The average price of oil in U.S. dollars a barrel was $17.98 in 1999; the assumed price is $26.53 in 2000 and $23.00 in 2001.

Figure 1.2. World Industrial Production[1]
(Percent change from a year earlier; three-month centered moving average)

A strong recovery in industrial production is under way in all major regions.

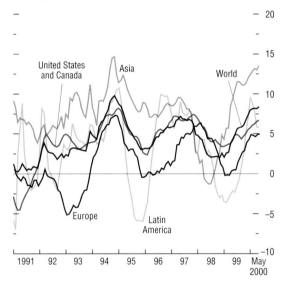

Sources: IMF, *International Financial Statistics*; OECD; and WEFA, Inc.
[1]Based on manufacturing data for 32 advanced and emerging market economies representing about 75 percent of world output. Data through 1994 exclude Indonesia.

Second, oil prices have been significantly higher than previously expected, due to both supply constraints in producing countries and the continued strength of global demand. Following the announcement of further supply increases at the OPEC meeting in June, as well as indications that some oil producers would be willing to boost supply further, the oil price fell back within the OPEC target band of $22–$28 per barrel in July. However, since early August prices have rebounded significantly, and as of early September were over 20 percent above the baseline used for the *World Economic Outlook* forecast for the last quarter of 2000 and beyond. At the OPEC meeting on September 10, Ministers agreed to increase production by 800,000 barrels per day (equivalent to 1 percent of global supply). However, in the immediate aftermath of the announcement, prices rose further. While the outlook remains highly uncertain, with many oil producers close to capacity and stocks relatively low, there may still be upside risks to prices in coming months.

A $5 per barrel increase in oil prices (about 20 percent above the *World Economic Outlook* baseline) raises net oil imports by advanced countries by about $40 billion annually compared to the level projected in this *World Economic Outlook*, matched by a corresponding increase in trade balances of oil exporters, mainly in the Middle East. The aggregate impact on other developing country regions—a mix of oil exporters and importers—would be small, but many individual developing countries would be seriously affected, with trade balances deteriorating by more than ½ percent of GDP. Higher oil prices would also have a direct impact on global activity and inflation. Estimates using MULTIMOD, the IMF's econometric model, suggest that a $5 per barrel increase would reduce GDP growth in industrial countries by 0.2 percentage points in 2001, accompanied by higher inflation and interest rates. Output in many developing countries would also be adversely affected, particularly in Asia, which is relatively dependent on imported oil (see Chapter II for a more detailed discussion).

Third, the amount of monetary tightening that may be needed to control inflationary pres-

sures in the United States and some other countries remains unclear, especially if the recent increase in oil prices is sustained.

Fourth, as recent experience has shown, the
imbalances described above—combined with recent reductions in the depth and liquidity in financial markets—could generate further volatility in mature financial markets.[1] This could in
turn spill over to emerging markets, notwithstanding their generally strengthening economic
fundamentals. During the recent period of market volatility from March to May, spreads on
emerging market debt increased, especially for
countries with larger financing needs, and there
was a slowdown in gross capital flows (see Chapter
II). These pressures appear to have eased, in part
reflecting growing evidence of a slowdown in the
United States, but further volatility cannot be
ruled out, especially if U.S. interest rates to were
rise higher than presently expected.

The IMF staff's baseline scenario, which envisages a modest slowdown in global GDP growth
to 4.2 percent in 2001, followed by continued
strong growth at about the same rate thereafter,
is predicated on the assumption that the imbalances in the global economy are resolved in an
orderly fashion. Thus, the growth of GDP and
demand in the United States are projected to
slow rapidly toward potential output growth,
while the expansion in Europe continues and
Japan's recovery gathers strength; and there is
no disorderly correction in equity or foreign exchange markets. This realignment of growth
and demand across the major currency areas
would facilitate a smooth adjustment in external
current account balances, while maintaining
continued strong growth for the world as a
whole.[2] Given the risks noted above, however, a

---

[1]See Chapter II, *International Capital Markets—Developments, Prospects, and Policy Issues* (Washington: IMF, 2000).
[2]While the baseline scenario shows that present levels
of current account surpluses would broadly stabilize during 2001–05, this is partly because the projections—like
those of many other forecasters, including the OECD—
assume that real effective exchange rates remain unchanged. Allowing for the elimination of currency misalignments, current account imbalances would be
significantly reduced over the projection period.

**Figure 1.3. A Comparison of Global Growth in Recent
Slowdowns[1]**
(Percent)

The slowdown in activity during the recent crisis has been shallower
than in previous episodes and followed by a relatively rapid recovery.

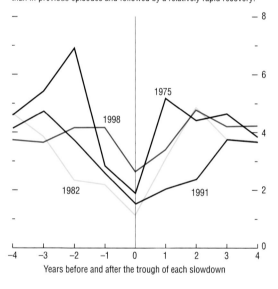

Years before and after the trough of each slowdown

[1]The year zero corresponds to the trough (1975, 1982, 1991, and 1998)
in world growth during previous and current world slowdowns.

Figure 1.4. Major Industrial Countries: Output Gaps[1]
(Actual less potential output, as percent of potential)

Output is above potential in the United States, and to a lesser extent the
United Kingdom and Canada, but slack remains in continental Europe and Japan.

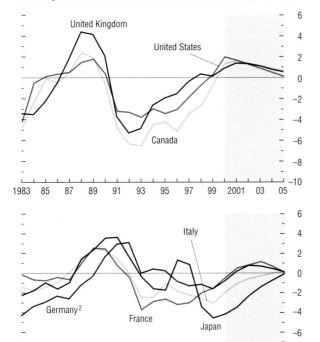

[1]Shaded areas indicate IMF staff projections. The estimates of output gaps are
subject to a significant margin of uncertainty. For a discussion of approaches to
calculating potential output, see Paula R. De Masi, "IMF Estimates of Potential Output:
Theory and Practice," in *Staff Studies for the World Economic Outlook* (Washington:
IMF, December 1997), pp. 40–46.
[2]Data through 1991 apply to west Germany only.

less benign outcome remains possible. In particular, were investors to revise significantly their
views about future U.S. growth and corporate
earnings, there would be the possibility of a
much more abrupt adjustment in equity markets; such an adjustment could make the United
States less attractive to international investors
and could lead to a sharp decline in the value
of the U.S. dollar. Such a scenario could be triggered either by an unexpected increase in U.S.
interest rates in response to rising inflationary
pressures—along the lines of the alternative scenario in the last *World Economic Outlook*—or by
other factors (such as a reassessment of the extent of U.S. labor productivity growth generated
by the "new economy"). As described in an alternative scenario in Appendix I, such a disorderly adjustment could lead to a substantial reduction in demand in the United States,
resulting in a sharp slowdown in growth that
would spill over—to a lesser extent—to other industrialized countries. It could also have a significant effect on developing countries, particularly those dependent on commodity exports or
which have substantial external financing needs
(see Chapter II).

To protect against such a scenario, the major
currency areas will need to continue to pursue
policies directed at achieving an orderly rebalancing of growth and demand. While the United
States will need to restrain the growth of domestic demand, Europe and Japan will need to ensure that domestic demand grows rapidly. To illustrate this, Appendix I also sets out a second
alternative scenario assuming that, as a result of
more rapid structural reforms, Europe and
Japan grow ½ percentage point faster for a
decade, driven by a combination of higher labor
participation and stronger productivity growth
(along the lines experienced recently in the
United States—see Chapter II). Higher growth
rates and increased demand in Europe and
Japan would help to support global activity and
reduce existing imbalances, thereby promoting a
stronger and more sustainable recovery in global
output, including in developing countries, particularly in Africa and Asia.

The primary instrument to help facilitate an orderly rebalancing of growth and demand remains the implementation of an asymmetric approach to monetary policy across the three main currency areas. In the United States, monetary policy may need to be tightened somewhat further to restrain demand and inflationary pressures, while pressures to relax fiscal policy should be resisted. In the euro area, the central challenge is to seize the opportunity afforded by the current expansion and to accelerate growth-enhancing fiscal and structural reforms. On the macroeconomic side, fiscal policies will need to focus on faster consolidation during the upswing. Monetary policy should remain flexible, responding appropriately both to risks arising from diminishing margins of slack and potential inflationary pressures from rising oil prices and the weak euro, and remain alert to the possibility of an eventual substantial appreciation of the euro that could unduly tighten the monetary stance. In Japan, where consumer confidence remains weak and deflationary pressures persist, monetary policy should be highly accommodative until clear signs that the recovery has become self-supporting emerge. The government will also need to introduce an early supplementary budget to mitigate the withdrawal of fiscal stimulus coming from a sharp fall off in public investment starting in the second half of the year. As in Europe, continued structural reform is critical to support sustainable long-term growth.

In emerging markets, economic fundamentals have generally continued to improve; external current account positions are projected to strengthen in all major geographical areas (except Asia, which is already running a substantial surplus) and are being increasingly financed by equity rather than debt. Nevertheless, a number of countries—particularly in Latin America—continue to face large gross financing needs, and the ongoing tightening of global financial conditions could make financing for emerging market countries more difficult. Thus, these countries need to take advantage of the economic upswing to continue to strengthen economic fundamentals and reduce vulnerabilities

Table 1.2. Selected Economies: Current Account Positions
(Percent of GDP)

	1998	1999	2000	2001
Advanced economies				
United States	−2.5	−3.6	−4.2	−4.2
Japan	3.2	2.5	2.6	2.6
Germany	−0.2	−0.9	−0.2	−0.0
France	2.7	2.7	2.7	3.4
Italy	1.7	0.7	1.0	1.3
United Kingdom	−0.0	−1.2	−1.5	−2.0
Canada	−1.8	−0.4	1.4	1.0
Australia	−5.0	−5.7	−4.8	−4.9
Austria	−2.3	−2.8	−2.0	−1.8
Finland	5.7	5.2	5.6	5.3
Greece	−3.0	−4.1	−4.9	−4.9
Hong Kong SAR	1.8	5.9	6.9	6.8
Ireland	2.0	0.3	−0.6	−0.9
Israel	−0.9	−2.6	−2.2	−2.9
Korea	12.8	6.1	2.3	0.4
New Zealand	−5.1	−8.1	−6.2	−5.3
Norway	−1.3	3.9	14.3	13.3
Portugal	−7.0	−8.8	−10.4	−10.5
Singapore	25.4	25.0	23.6	22.8
Spain	−0.2	−2.2	−2.2	−1.9
Sweden	2.9	2.6	2.6	2.5
Switzerland	9.1	11.3	10.0	10.3
Taiwan Province of China	1.3	2.5	2.1	2.2
Memorandum				
Euro area[1]	1.3	0.6	0.9	1.3
Developing countries				
Algeria	−1.9	0.0	12.6	10.3
Argentina	−4.8	−4.4	−3.7	−3.6
Brazil	−4.3	−4.6	−3.9	−3.5
Cameroon	−2.7	−4.3	−2.4	−2.8
Chile	−5.7	−0.1	−2.4	−3.1
China	3.1	1.6	1.6	1.3
Côte d'Ivoire	−3.9	−4.0	−5.4	−4.0
Egypt	−3.1	−2.0	−1.8	−1.8
India	−1.7	−0.6	−1.2	−1.3
Indonesia	4.2	3.7	3.7	1.3
Malaysia	12.9	15.8	13.6	7.4
Mexico	−3.8	−2.9	−3.5	−3.7
Nigeria	−8.7	−11.0	2.4	−3.0
Pakistan	−2.7	−3.8	−2.2	−1.5
Philippines	2.4	9.4	8.0	3.8
Saudi Arabia	−10.2	−1.2	6.6	1.6
South Africa	−1.6	−0.4	−0.7	−1.3
Thailand	12.7	9.1	7.2	5.9
Turkey	1.0	−0.7	−3.1	−2.4
Uganda	−5.6	−7.4	−7.9	−7.9
Countries in transition				
Czech Republic	−2.4	−2.0	−3.4	−3.3
Estonia	−9.2	−6.1	−5.9	−6.1
Hungary	−4.9	−4.3	−4.5	−4.4
Latvia	−10.1	−9.7	−8.6	−7.7
Lithuania	−12.1	−11.2	−7.4	−6.9
Poland	−4.4	−7.5	−7.4	−7.0
Russia	0.4	11.3	13.4	7.9
Slovak Republic	−10.4	−5.7	−4.7	−3.9
Ukraine	−3.1	−0.1	−2.1	−1.6

[1]Calculated as the sum of the balances of individual euro area countries.

to external shocks. In Latin America, the priorities include further fiscal consolidation and reform, supported by measures to improve the operation of labor markets. In Asia, the countries farthest along in the recovery will need to take gradual steps toward a more neutral macroeconomic policy stance, and it will be essential to continue with bank and corporate sector restructuring. A substantial agenda of fiscal and structural reforms also remains in the transition economies, accompanied by the need to develop the institutions and institutional framework required to support a market economy.

Despite the strength of the global recovery, many countries continue to face deep-seated economic problems, and 1.2 billion people still subsist on less than $1 per day. Thus, as noted in a recent United Nations report, "poverty in all its forms is the greatest challenge to the international community."[3] A sustained reduction in poverty requires stronger growth, achieved in a fashion that benefits the poor. The poorest countries will need to focus on improving macroeconomic stability, addressing governance problems, harnessing market forces for development, and promoting domestic ownership of the reform agenda, but much stronger support from the international community is also required.[4] In this connection, the main priorities are to fully fund the enhanced initiative for Heavily Indebted Poor Countries (HIPCs), to allow debt relief to be delivered to the poorest countries in a way that achieves poverty reduction; to reform trade policies discriminating against the poorest countries (especially for agricultural trade); and to reverse the declining trend in some advanced countries' official development aid. Additional international assistance will also be needed to help address the HIV/AIDS pandemic, which has infected more than 20 percent of the adult population in some African countries.

The assessment of global economic conditions continues to be complicated by the global current account discrepancy, which—according to preliminary data—increased sharply in 1999 (see Appendix II for a more detailed discussion). Although the discrepancy is projected to decline in 2000, the staff's projections, in common with those of other forecasters, suggest that it will widen significantly thereafter. To the extent that this reflects an underestimation of future export growth, there could be potential upside risks to global growth in the staff's baseline scenario, particularly in 2001–02.

Can the United States Achieve a "Soft Landing"?

In the *United States*, the current economic expansion has continued apace (Figure 1.5). Following very rapid growth of 7 percent (annualized) in the second half of 1999, GDP growth moderated to 5 percent in the first half of 2000, accompanied by some signs of an easing in domestic demand growth. Fixed investment has remained buoyant, underpinned by strong business confidence and an ongoing drive to invest in new technologies, but consumption growth fell sharply in the second quarter, largely reflecting a decline in durables purchases. Recent economic reports show a mixed picture; housing starts are turning down and employment growth has moderated, but personal consumption expenditures have risen again.

The strength of domestic demand relative to output growth over the past two years has been reflected primarily in a sharp widening of the current account deficit, which has risen from 1¾ percent of GDP in 1997 to 3¾ percent of GDP in 1999 and to 4¼ percent in the first quarter of 2000. With the fiscal surplus increasing, this has entirely reflected the emergence of a large deficit in private sector net savings, reflecting both high

---

[3]See *A Better World For All*, coauthored by the United Nations, the World Bank, the International Monetary Fund, and the Organization for Economic Cooperation and Development; available on the websites of each organization as well as at www.paris21.org/betterworld.

[4]See "How Can the Poorest Countries Catch Up?," Chapter IV in the May 2000 *World Economic Outlook*, for a detailed analysis.

investment but also a sharp decline in household savings to a record low. Headline inflation has been gradually trending upward, reaching 3½ percent in July, mainly due to higher energy prices; core inflation has risen slightly, dampened by modest wage increases and strong growth in labor productivity, as well as by earlier declines in non-oil import prices. However, there have been signs of underlying price and wage pressures, and non-oil import prices have begun to rise. Business surveys also point to exceptionally tight labor markets and increasing evidence that enterprises are beginning to raise prices.

The U.S. expansion's remarkable strength and record longevity have owed much to the consistent pursuit of sound macroeconomic policies, as well as to the flexibility of the country's product and labor markets. Since 1995, this strong performance has been underpinned by strong growth in labor productivity, partially linked to rising investment in high technology, which has led some observers to conclude that the United States is now experiencing a "new economy," in which technology gains allow for an increase in productivity growth. This strong growth in productivity—and the expectation that it will continue—has helped attract substantial capital inflows into the United States, thereby contributing to the appreciation of the U.S. dollar and the widening current account deficit, and has underpinned the high level of equity market valuations, which in turn is associated with the decline in household saving. At this juncture, however, it remains unclear how long higher productivity growth can be sustained; the recent increase may in part reflect a onetime jump in the level of productivity associated with capital deepening, rather than an underlying increase in productivity growth. The evolution of market expectations of the future path of productivity and growth will have important implications for how the imbalances in the U.S. economy are unwound, as well as for the conduct of monetary policy (discussed in more detail in Chapter II).

Despite the uncertainties associated with the new economy, it is clear that over the past three years both demand and supply have grown above

Figure 1.5. United States: Rapid Growth, But Rising Imbalances
(Percent change from four quarters earlier unless otherwise noted)

The record economic expansion in the United States has continued, underpinned by strong labor productivity growth. However, there are some signs of inflationary pressures and substantial imbalances persist.

Sources: Bloomberg Financial Markets, LP; and WEFA, Inc.

Table 1.3. Advanced Economies: Real GDP, Consumer Prices, and Unemployment
(Annual percent change and percent of labor force)

	Real GDP				Consumer Prices				Unemployment			
	1998	1999	2000	2001	1998	1999	2000	2001	1998	1999	2000	2001
Advanced economies	**2.4**	**3.2**	**4.2**	**3.2**	**1.5**	**1.4**	**2.3**	**2.1**	**6.7**	**6.3**	**5.9**	**5.7**
Major industrial countries	2.5	2.9	3.9	2.9	1.3	1.4	2.2	1.9	6.2	6.0	5.7	5.8
United States	4.4	4.2	5.2	3.2	1.6	2.2	3.2	2.6	4.5	4.2	4.1	4.4
Japan	-2.5	0.2	1.4	1.8	0.6	-0.3	-0.2	0.5	4.1	4.7	5.0	5.3
Germany	2.1	1.6	2.9	3.3	0.6	0.7	1.7	1.5	9.0	8.3	7.9	7.6
France	3.2	2.9	3.5	3.5	0.7	0.6	1.5	1.1	11.7	11.3	9.8	8.8
Italy	1.5	1.4	3.1	3.0	1.7	1.7	2.5	1.6	11.8	11.4	10.7	10.1
United Kingdom[1]	2.6	2.1	3.1	2.8	2.7	2.3	2.0	2.4	4.7	4.3	3.9	4.0
Canada	3.3	4.5	4.7	2.8	1.0	1.7	2.3	2.1	8.3	7.6	6.6	6.5
Other advanced economies	2.0	4.7	5.1	4.2	2.4	1.3	2.4	2.6	8.1	7.3	6.2	5.7
Spain	4.0	3.7	4.1	3.5	1.8	2.2	3.1	2.4	18.8	15.9	14.0	12.6
Netherlands	3.7	3.6	3.9	3.5	2.0	2.0	2.4	3.5	4.1	3.2	2.3	2.0
Belgium	2.7	2.5	3.9	3.0	0.9	1.1	2.2	1.4	9.5	9.0	8.3	7.7
Sweden	3.0	3.8	4.4	3.4	-0.1	0.4	1.4	1.8	6.5	5.6	4.6	4.0
Austria	2.9	2.2	3.5	2.9	0.8	0.5	1.9	2.1	4.7	4.4	3.5	3.5
Denmark	2.5	1.7	2.1	2.1	1.8	2.6	2.9	2.5	6.4	5.6	5.4	5.5
Finland	5.5	4.0	5.0	4.0	1.3	1.3	2.7	2.5	11.4	10.3	9.0	8.2
Greece	3.7	3.5	3.5	3.9	4.5	2.2	2.5	2.8	10.8	11.7	11.5	11.3
Portugal	4.2	3.0	3.4	3.5	2.2	2.2	2.5	2.3	5.0	4.4	4.1	4.0
Ireland	8.9	9.9	8.7	6.9	2.2	2.5	4.8	3.5	7.4	5.6	4.5	4.0
Luxembourg	5.0	5.2	5.1	5.0	1.0	1.0	1.6	1.4	3.3	2.9	2.7	2.3
Switzerland	2.1	1.7	3.0	2.6	0.1	0.8	1.7	1.7	3.9	2.7	2.0	1.9
Norway	2.0	0.9	3.0	2.4	2.3	2.3	3.0	2.5	2.4	3.2	3.6	3.6
Israel	2.2	2.2	4.0	4.0	5.4	5.2	2.1	3.0	8.5	8.9	8.4	8.2
Iceland	4.7	4.5	4.0	2.1	1.7	3.4	4.9	3.5	2.9	1.9	1.8	1.8
Korea	-6.7	10.7	8.8	6.5	7.5	0.8	2.2	3.0	6.8	6.3	4.2	3.5
Australia[2]	5.2	4.4	4.0	3.4	0.9	1.5	4.8	3.3	8.0	7.2	6.7	6.6
Taiwan Province of China	4.7	5.7	6.5	6.0	1.7	0.2	1.6	2.3	2.7	2.9	2.5	2.3
Hong Kong SAR	-5.1	2.9	8.0	4.8	2.8	-4.0	-2.5	2.0	4.7	6.1	4.0	3.1
Singapore	0.4	5.4	7.9	5.9	-0.3	0.1	1.4	2.1	3.2	3.5	2.9	2.5
New Zealand[2]	-0.2	3.4	4.0	3.2	1.6	1.1	2.3	3.3	7.5	6.8	6.4	6.4
Memorandum												
European Union	2.7	2.4	3.4	3.3	1.4	1.4	2.1	1.9	9.5	8.8	8.0	7.5
Euro area	2.7	2.4	3.5	3.4	1.1	1.2	2.1	1.7	10.8	9.9	9.0	8.3

[1]Consumer prices are based on the retail price index excluding mortgage interest. Unemployment rate on a claimant count basis.
[2]Consumer prices excluding interest rate components; for Australia, also excluding other volatile items.

the upper end of reasonable assessments of potential output growth. Against this background, between mid-1999 and early 2000, the Federal Reserve raised interest rates by a cumulative 1¼ percentage points, followed by a further ½ percentage point increase in May 2000; the Federal Open Market Committee did not raise rates at its June or August meetings, but noted that the risks to the outlook continued to be weighted mainly toward conditions that may generate inflationary pressures. Given the lags with which monetary policy affects the economy, and the boost to output and demand provided by the recent rise in equity prices, the bulk of the past monetary tight-

ening has yet to be felt. At the same time, the real appreciation of the U.S. dollar over the past 18 months, as well as higher oil prices, should also exert a contractionary effect on activity. For 2000 as a whole, real GDP growth is projected to average 5.2 percent, falling to about 3.2 percent in 2001 (Table 1.3). Given the ongoing recovery in other regions of the world, this slowdown would be consistent with an orderly resolution of outstanding imbalances without serious disruption to world growth.

Nevertheless, with indicators pointing to continued strong momentum in the U.S. economy, and labor markets still tight, a further increase in interest rates may be needed in the future to dampen inflationary pressures and to reduce the growth of domestic demand below that of potential output. The extent of such additional tightening, however, remains subject to considerable uncertainty, and it remains to be seen whether, and by how much, the recent slowdown in domestic demand growth will be sustained. Since May, in response to signs that the economy was slowing, markets have substantially marked down estimates of future interest rate increases; there has also been some recovery in equity markets and a decline in mortgage and corporate bond yields. It is possible, however, that these developments could themselves add to pressures on growth and demand later in the year, at a time when labor markets are still very tight. Also, earlier temporary factors that have held down prices—such as declining non-oil import prices—have begun to unwind. In such circumstances, a further tightening of monetary policy might later be needed to restrain inflationary pressures.

To address these concerns, fiscal policy should remain consistent with efforts to reduce demand. Following the substantial fiscal consolidation in recent years, the surplus is projected to increase to 1½ percent of GDP in 2000 (Table 1.4), which will further restrain demand pressures. In the short term, the current fiscal stance should be maintained—and to the extent possible, strengthened—by resisting calls for tax reductions or additional expenditures. Over the longer term, the authorities' intention to substantially preserve the fiscal surpluses in prospect, and to pay down the public debt, will help support national savings, as well as prepare for the coming long wave of unfunded liabilities associated with the retirement of the baby boom generation.

In *Canada*, following a temporary slowdown as a result of the Asian financial crisis, the economy has continued to rebound strongly, aided by buoyant U.S. demand, rising commodity prices, and a competitive exchange rate. GDP grew by 5.1 percent (annualized) in the first half of 2000, driven by booming growth in exports and fixed investment. With most indicators suggesting that the economy still has considerable mo-

mentum, GDP growth is projected at 4.7 percent in 2000, before easing to 2.8 percent in 2001 due to the tightening of monetary policy and the anticipated slowing in U.S. growth. Unemployment is projected to decline below 6¾ percent, the lowest level since the mid-1970s, and the external current account is expected to move into modest surplus.

Given the strength of demand, as well as signs that the economy may be rapidly approaching capacity limits, the Canadian authorities have appropriately sought to preempt inflationary pressures by raising interest rates in parallel with U.S. rates so far this year. Even though core inflation is at the lower end of the 1 percent to 3 percent target range and wage increases remain modest relative to productivity growth, slack in the economy is being absorbed quickly; a further moderate tightening of policy may therefore be needed in the future, although this would depend on conditions in Canada, and not necessarily on developments in U.S. rates. On the fiscal side, Canada maintains the largest structural surplus among major industrial countries. Over the medium term, prospective fiscal surpluses should be used to reduce the still high level of public debt and to support ongoing tax reduction.

Maintaining the Expansion in Europe

The expansion in the *euro area* has gathered strength, with GDP growth rising to 3¾ percent (annualized) in the second half of 1999 and continuing at a similar rate in the first quarter of 2000. This rise has been aided by resurgent export growth due to the strengthening global recovery and a highly competitive currency. During the remainder of the year, the expansion is expected to be sustained by high consumer and business confidence and the favorable external environment. For the year as a whole, GDP growth is projected at 3½ percent, with all countries registering above-potential growth rates. The pickup in activity has been accompanied by a substantial decline in unemployment. However, with some slack still remaining in area-wide labor and product markets, underlying

Table 1.4. Major Industrial Countries: General Government Fiscal Balances and Debt[1]
(Percent of GDP)

	1983–93	1994	1995	1996	1997	1998	1999	2000	2001	2005
Major industrial countries										
Actual balance	−3.8	−4.2	−4.1	−3.5	−2.0	−1.4	−1.1	−0.3	−0.3	0.3
Output gap	−0.7	−2.4	−2.5	−2.0	−1.5	−1.5	−1.2	0.1	0.3	0.1
Structural balance	−3.4	−3.1	−3.1	−2.5	−1.3	−0.7	−0.5	−0.6	−0.5	0.2
United States										
Actual balance	−4.9	−3.8	−3.3	−2.4	−1.3	—	0.7	1.4	1.5	1.6
Output gap	−1.2	−3.1	−3.5	−3.1	−1.9	−0.8	0.2	1.9	1.6	—
Structural balance	−4.6	−2.7	−2.1	−1.4	−0.6	0.3	0.6	0.8	0.9	1.5
Net debt	46.0	60.1	59.6	59.2	57.1	53.4	48.8	43.9	40.2	27.1
Gross debt	60.1	72.8	72.9	72.8	70.3	66.6	63.2	57.0	52.1	35.1
Japan										
Actual balance	0.1	−2.3	−3.6	−4.2	−3.3	−4.7	−7.4	−8.2	−6.3	−2.6
Output gap	0.3	−1.6	−1.7	1.3	0.9	−3.4	−4.5	−4.1	−3.4	−0.1
Structural balance	0.2	−1.7	−2.9	−4.5	−3.5	−3.3	−5.5	−6.5	−4.9	−2.5
Net debt	18.2	7.7	13.0	16.4	17.9	30.6	38.2	46.3	51.5	61.0
Gross debt	69.0	82.2	89.7	94.4	99.2	114.2	125.6	136.0	141.7	149.4
Memorandum										
Actual balance excluding Social security	−3.0	−5.1	−6.5	−6.8	−5.9	−6.8	−9.2	−9.5	−7.3	−4.0
Structural balance excluding Social security	−3.3	−4.5	−5.8	−6.9	−5.9	−5.8	−7.9	−8.3	−6.3	−3.8
Germany										
Actual balance[2]	−2.0	−2.5	−3.4	−3.5	−2.7	−2.1	−1.5	1.6	−1.2	−1.2
Output gap	−1.3	0.3	0.2	−0.9	−1.4	−1.2	−1.7	−0.9	0.1	—
Structural balance[3]	−1.0	−2.5	−3.4	−2.7	−1.6	−1.2	−0.6	−0.4	−1.2	−1.2
Net debt[4]	22.0	40.6	49.4	51.1	52.2	52.0	52.3	49.8	48.3	44.4
Gross debt	41.8	50.2	58.3	59.8	60.9	60.7	61.0	58.5	57.0	53.1
France										
Actual balance[2]	−2.0	−5.5	−5.5	−4.2	−3.0	−2.7	−1.8	−1.2	0.3	—
Output gap	0.3	−3.0	−2.7	−3.3	−3.1	−2.1	−1.6	−0.6	0.4	—
Structural balance[3]	−2.4	−3.9	−4.0	−2.4	−1.4	−1.6	−0.7	−0.8	−1.3	—
Net debt	21.6	40.5	45.9	48.1	49.4	49.6	48.8	48.3	48.3	41.4
Gross debt	32.7	48.5	54.6	57.1	59.0	59.3	58.6	58.0	57.0	52.5
Italy										
Actual balance	−10.9	−9.1	−7.6	−7.1	−2.7	−2.8	−1.9	−1.3	−0.9	0.2
Output gap	0.1	−2.5	−1.1	−2.0	−2.3	−2.7	−3.1	−2.0	−1.2	—
Structural balance	−10.9	−7.9	−7.0	−6.0	−1.5	−1.5	−0.3	−0.3	−0.3	0.2
Net debt	79.8	117.2	116.6	115.7	113.4	110.1	108.8	105.1	102.8	90.0
Gross debt	87.1	123.8	123.2	122.2	119.8	116.3	114.9	111.0	108.5	95.0
United Kingdom										
Actual balance[2]	−2.4	−6.8	−5.8	−4.1	−1.6	0.2	1.6	3.6	0.8	−0.9
Output gap	−1.1	−2.7	−2.0	−1.6	−0.4	0.3	0.1	0.8	1.3	0.5
Structural balance[3]	−1.1	−4.2	−4.2	−2.9	−0.9	0.3	1.5	0.9	0.2	−1.2
Net debt	30.8	31.2	37.0	37.6	39.6	40.3	38.3	34.3	31.8	29.7
Gross debt	45.0	48.5	52.0	52.1	50.1	47.4	44.7	40.8	38.2	36.1
Canada										
Actual balance	−7.0	−6.7	−5.4	−2.8	0.2	0.2	2.2	3.0	2.9	1.9
Output gap	−1.9	−4.6	−4.4	−5.3	−3.5	−2.8	−0.8	1.2	1.5	0.5
Structural balance	−5.6	−3.9	−2.9	—	2.1	1.7	2.6	2.4	2.2	1.6
Net debt	38.2	68.7	70.2	69.8	65.2	61.9	75.3	66.7	60.8	43.1
Gross debt	70.4	99.4	102.2	101.9	97.3	95.1	111.6	100.3	92.8	70.2

Note: The budget projections are based on information available through August 2000. The specific assumptions for each country appear in Box A1.

[1]The output gap is actual less potential output, as a percent of potential output. Structural balances are expressed as a percent of potential output. The structural budget balance is the budgetary position that would be observed if the level of actual output coincided with potential output. Changes in the structural budget balance consequently include effects of temporary fiscal measures, the impact of fluctuations in interest rates and debt-service costs, and other noncyclical fluctuations in the budget balance. The computations of structural budget balance are based on IMF staff estimates of potential GDP and revenue and expenditures elasticities (see the October 1993 *World Economic Outlook*, Annex I). Net debt is defined as gross debt less financial assets of the general government, which include assets held by the social security insurance system. Debt data refer to end of year. Estimates of the output gap and the structural budget gap and of the structural budget balance are subject to significant margins of uncertainty.

[2]Includes mobile telephone license receipts equivalent to 2.5 percent of GDP in 2000 for Germany, 1.3 percent of GDP in 2001 for France, and 2.4 percent of GDP in 2000 for the United Kingdom.

[3]Excludes mobile telephone license receipts.

[4]For net debt, the first column refers to 1987–93. Beginning in 1995, the debt and debt-service obligations of the Treuhandanstalt (and of various other agencies) were taken over by general government. This debt is equivalent to 8 percent of GDP, and the associated debt service is equivalent to ½ to 1 percent of GDP.

price pressures have been muted. The headline CPI increased to 2.4 percent by midyear, due largely to rising oil prices and exchange rate pass through. Core inflation, at about 1.3 percent, has remained subdued, aided by moderate wage settlements, falling utility prices as deregulation and privatization take effect, and, in some countries, cuts in indirect taxes.

Since the last *World Economic Outlook*, the euro has been quite volatile, hitting record lows against the U.S. dollar and most other major currencies in mid-May, and again in early September. By early September, the euro had depreciated over 15 percent in nominal effective terms since its inception in 1999, and is below the level that could be justified by medium-term fundamentals. In part, this has reflected the relative cyclical position of the euro area, with growth still considerably slower than in the United States; in addition, relative interest rate differentials and market perceptions of differences in the underlying climate for investment across countries may have played a role (Box 1.1). Given buoyant activity, money and credit developments, rising oil prices, and the weakness of the euro, the European Central Bank has raised interest rates by a cumulative 2 percentage points since late 1999, most recently through a ¼ percentage point increase in late August, to forestall potential pressures on wages and prices. While monetary policy needs to adjust gradually to a less accommodative stance as the recovery proceeds, it will need to remain flexible, responding appropriately to risks arising from diminishing margins of slack and potential inflationary pressures from rising oil prices and the weak euro, but also remaining alert to the possibility that the euro could eventually appreciate substantially from current levels, which could unduly tighten the monetary stance and slow the expansion.

During 1999, growth rates among individual countries in the euro area have continued to differ markedly, which—since monetary policy must be set on the basis of conditions in the euro area as a whole—has posed challenges for

policymakers, particularly in the small and faster-growing economies. Over the coming year, differences in growth rates are projected to decline as the recovery in *Italy* and *Germany* catches up with that in *France* and some of the cyclically advanced countries.[5] Nevertheless, substantial differences in underlying cyclical positions are likely to persist for a period. Most of the cyclically advanced countries continue to experience higher than average inflation, rapid growth in domestic credit, sharply rising property prices, and, in *Portugal*, a large current account deficit. In some cases, particularly *Ireland* and possibly the *Netherlands*, relatively clear signs of overheating have emerged. While budgetary positions in these countries are in most cases in surplus, every effort should be made to save the fiscal windfalls arising from higher growth in order to avoid fuelling demand pressures.

The central challenge in the euro area is to take advantage of the present cyclical upturn to decisively accelerate fiscal and structural reforms. Since 1993, spurred by the convergence requirements under Economic and Monetary Union (EMU), fiscal deficits have been substantially reduced in all euro area countries, and the IMF staff projects that the area as a whole will be close to overall balance by 2003 (Figure 1.6). This is a commendable achievement, but progress has slowed recently, and fiscal consolidation in some countries is not keeping up with the pace of the expansion. At the same time, most countries continue to face heavy tax burdens and high debt stocks, and are ill-prepared to deal with the coming demographic shock from aging populations. Although fiscal situations vary, countries that have high domestic debt or that anticipate a continued structural fiscal deficit in 2003 need to step up deficit reduction. In this connection, a more ambitious deficit reduction path in France would be desirable; and while Italy has announced a welcome strengthening of the fiscal deficit target for 2000, it has left the medium-term deficit targets essentially unchanged. In almost all countries,

---

[5]The cyclically advanced countries are Finland, Ireland, the Netherlands, Portugal, and Spain.

Figure 1.6. Euro Area: A Strengthening Expansion Will Allow Accelerated Reform[1]
(Percent change from four quarters earlier unless otherwise noted)

A solid expansion is under way, aided by rising exports, and unemployment has fallen significantly. This provides an opportunity to accelerate fiscal reform, given still high revenue and domestic debt ratios.

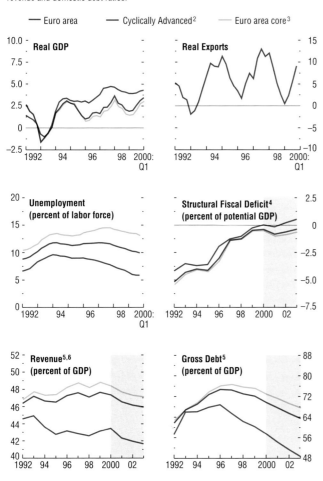

Sources: European Central Bank; OECD; and WEFA, Inc.
[1]Shaded areas indicate IMF staff projections.
[2]Finland, Ireland, Netherlands, Portugal, and Spain.
[3]Austria, Belgium, France, Germany, Italy, and Luxembourg.
[4]Excludes Luxembourg.
[5]General government.
[6]Excluding mobile telephone license receipts for France and Germany.

however, the central fiscal challenge is to build on ongoing efforts to reduce the tax burden, which remains very high by international standards and undermines incentives and long-term growth prospects. The recent income tax reform in Germany is a major step forward; and the package of tax cuts announced in France is also welcome. Such reforms, however, will need to be undertaken without weakening the underlying fiscal position, underscoring the need for further efforts to reduce noninterest expenditures, supported by reforms of pension and health systems to deal with the pressures from aging populations. Windfall gains, such as from the sale of mobile telecommunication licenses, should be used to reduce domestic debt.

In the past, recoveries in Europe have tended to be choked off at an early stage as entrenched economic rigidities kindled inflationary pressures, requiring early monetary tightening and leading to a steady ratcheting up of unemployment. While this is not an immediate risk, structural reforms to address these rigidities—building on the recent agreements at the Lisbon Summit—are critical to sustain the present expansion over the medium-term. In recent years, many countries have made significant progress in privatization, liberalizing telecommunications and electricity, introducing active labor market programs, and facilitating part time work; there has also been an increase in corporate restructuring, prompted in part by the introduction of the euro. Much remains to be done, however, including eliminating administrative barriers that inhibit competition and business formation and encouraging labor supply (lower labor utilization and participation rates explain the bulk of the difference between per capita GDP in Europe and the United States). Measures to ensure greater wage differentiation, reform social and unemployment benefits, and reduce labor taxation are of particular importance.

In the *United Kingdom,* GDP growth is projected to pick up to 3.1 percent in 2000 from 2.1 percent last year, reflecting a smaller deterioration of the trade balance and continued strong domestic demand growth, bolstered in part by

Box 1.1. Why Is the Euro So Undervalued?

As of early September 2000, the euro has depreciated by over 15 percent in nominal effective terms and by over 20 percent against the U.S. dollar since the start of stage three of Economic and Monetary Union (EMU) on January 1, 1999, defying market expectations and becoming a source of concern for European policymakers. Indeed, on many measures the euro has sunk below earlier historical lows reached in the mid-1980s by its synthetic counterpart.[1]

The extent of the euro's depreciation is difficult to fully explain. From the point of view of medium-term fundamentals, the current level of the euro appears to be significantly misaligned, especially against the U.S. dollar, but also against the yen. A number of short-term factors appear to be contributing to the euro's current undervaluation:

The comparative cyclical positions of the euro area and the United States. The less advanced cyclical position of the euro area relative to the United States appears to have contributed to the weakness of the European currency. Certainly, the depreciation of the euro has coincided with a widening of private sector estimates of the differential in growth in 2000 between the euro area and the United States (first Figure). This may partly reflect the impact on markets' expectations of the future path of interest rates on either side of the Atlantic.

Euro area–U.S. interest rate differentials. In a world of high capital mobility, interest rate differentials play an important role in determining the path of exchange rates, as investors shift funds internationally. Over the period through June 1999, the long-term interest rate differential moved in a manner that would tend to weaken the euro against the U.S. dollar, with the differential peaking at about 160 basis points (second Figure). Subsequently, however, long-term interest rate differentials have narrowed by about half, while the euro has remained weak.

[1]Both the real and nominal effective exchange rate of the euro have fallen below the historical low of its (synthetic) counterpart recorded in late 1984. When measured against the U.S. dollar, however, the euro has remained above its low in 1985.

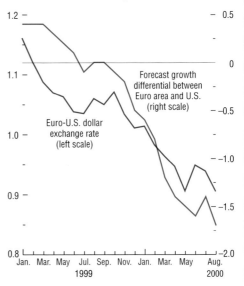

Rolling Forecast for 2000 GDP Growth and the Euro-U.S. Dollar Exchange Rate

Sources: Consensus Economics; and IMF staff calculations.

Relative medium- and long-term growth prospects. The strong macroeconomic performance of the U.S. economy over recent years associated with new technology and relatively more flexible product and labor markets has lowered assessments of the medium- to long-term growth potential of the euro area compared to the United States, reducing the attractiveness of the single currency.[2] Large financial outflows, especially foreign direct investment, from the euro area to the United States support the view that the United States is perceived as a more desirable destination for capital investment.

Foreign participation in the euro bond markets. A fourth potential reason for the euro's weakness

[2]See European Commission, Directorate General for Economic and Financial Affairs, "ICT Take-up in Europe and the Prospects for Future Growth" (Brussels: European Commission, 1999); and Paul Schreyer, "The Contribution of Information and Communication Technology to Output Growth: A Study of G-7 Countries," STI Working Paper 2000/2 (Paris: Organization for Economic Cooperation and Development, 2000).

Box 1.1 *(concluded)*

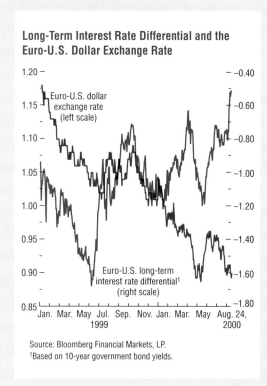

Long-Term Interest Rate Differential and the Euro-U.S. Dollar Exchange Rate

Source: Bloomberg Financial Markets, LP.
[1]Based on 10-year government bond yields.

is the elevated participation of nonresident issuers as the size of the euro area bond market increased following the introduction of the single currency. The share of euro-denominated bonds in global bond issues rose from an average of around 30 percent in 1995–98 to about 45 percent in 1999. Nonresident issuers—who accounted for about half of the new issues—contributed greatly to such an increase. To the extent that these issuers have switched the proceeds into other currencies, particularly U.S. dollars, this would create downward pressure on the euro. The unwinding of long positions acquired by foreigners in the run-up to stage three of EMU may have also contributed to selling pressure.

Market participants' evaluation of euro area policymaking. A final factor often cited by market analysts in explaining the weakness of the euro is adverse perceptions of euro area policymaking. Notwithstanding regular press briefings, some analysts argue that the European Central Bank's communication strategy has lacked clarity. Others express concern that progress on needed structural reforms is still relatively slow, particularly given the constraints in monetary policy implied by a single currency, such that the euro area does not provide as attractive a business environment as the United States.

Euro Area Policies: Potential Costs and Implications

Although the weak euro has helped to jump-start an export-led recovery in the euro area in the aftermath of the 1998 slowdown, a sustained period of currency misalignment would have a number of adverse effects. First, it would cause resources to shift toward the now more profitable traded goods sectors in the euro area and away from such sectors elsewhere. When the exchange rate finally corrected, a corresponding—and possibly costly—reallocation of resources would be required. In addition, by reducing competition in the traded goods sector, a depreciated exchange rate could also reduce the pressure on firms to restructure. Second, prolonged weakness of the euro would hamper adjustment of the existing current account imbalances across the three major currency blocs, which could increase the prospects of a disorderly adjustment in exchange rates, and could fuel a rise in protectionist pressures.

The depreciation of the euro has also significantly complicated the conduct of monetary policy. In the short run, the depreciation of the currency provides a direct boost to the price level through its impact on import prices, and—to the extent it feeds through into wages—may also have a second-round impact on inflation. In addition, by increasing competitiveness, it loosens overall monetary conditions (the IMF's monetary conditions index for the euro area indicates that the depreciation of the currency since the start of 1999 is equivalent to about a 2 percentage point reduction in real short-term interest rates). Given the potential for a future rapid appreciation in the value of the euro, which would correspondingly tighten monetary conditions, monetary policy will therefore need to remain flexible in the period ahead.

the planned expansion in government consumption. Inflation has remained below the Bank of England's 2.5 percent target, owing to subdued wage pressure, falling price-cost margins, and the strength of sterling. Nevertheless, labor market conditions remain tight with the unemployment rate (on a claimant count basis) below 4 percent. Following a cumulative 1 percentage point increase since mid-1999, the Bank of England has left policy rates on hold from February to early September. Further tightening may prove necessary if domestic demand continues to strengthen, or if further depreciation of sterling appears likely to lead to inflationary pressures.

In *Sweden*, GDP growth is projected to rise to 4½ percent in 2000, driven by strengthening domestic demand and a firming up of net exports. Nevertheless, some slack still remains in the economy, wage increases have been moderate, and core inflation is well below the 2 percent midpoint of the target zone. The present stance of monetary policy appears appropriate, but the authorities will need to remain alert to inflation pressures, especially given strong increases in property prices in major cities. Following the remarkable fiscal consolidation in recent years, attention should now focus on reducing the tax burden—among the highest in industrial countries—and on further labor market reform to underpin possible entry to EMU in the future. Activity has also remained strong in *Greece*, which—aided by a stability-oriented economic policy and more recently some recourse to administrative measures to reduce inflation—has successfully met the EMU convergence requirements and will join in 2001. With interest rates falling sharply as EMU entry approaches, and monetary policy losing its potency, Greece needs to strengthen its fiscal position to avoid a resurgence in price inflation and to reduce the very high public debt. This should be accompanied by a bolder and more comprehensive liberalization and deregulation and effective labor market reform.

A solid recovery is also under way in *Denmark, Norway,* and *Switzerland,* all of which experienced among the lowest growth rates in Europe in 1999. In Norway and Denmark, where the slowdown partly reflected policy measures to address overheating, the ensuing rebound has been led by rising exports (for Norway, aided by higher oil prices). Domestic demand is projected to pick up in both countries during 2000, as fiscal policies have now returned to a broadly neutral stance. In *Switzerland,* the recovery has been driven by both exports and domestic demand, aided by an accommodative monetary stance. As the strength of the recovery became apparent, the central bank appropriately moved to tighten monetary conditions, while allowing the franc to appreciate against the euro.

Regaining the Confidence of Japan's Consumers

In *Japan*, following two quarters of output decline, GDP growth rose by 4 percent (annualized) in the first half of 2000. Given the deficiencies in the national accounts, these data must be interpreted cautiously (Box 1.2); analysis of a broad range of indicators suggests that activity may not have been as weak as reported in the second half of 1999, while a significant proportion of the strong first half growth is transitory in nature. Overall, it appears that a modest recovery is under way, supported by strengthening corporate profitability and investment, particularly in the high technology sector. Over the coming year, the recovery is expected gradually to gather momentum, with GDP growth projected at 1.4 percent in 2000 and 1.8 percent in 2001.

The emerging recovery has led to increasing pressure to roll back the exceptional macroeconomic measures that were introduced during the past two years. In August, the Bank of Japan ended the zero interest rate policy, increasing the overnight call rate to 0.25 percent; however, since this was broadly anticipated by the market, there has been only a small increase in short- and long-term market rates. With the fiscal deficit approaching double digit levels and public debt very high, there have also been pres-

Box 1.2. Risky Business: Output Volatility and the Perils of Forecasting in Japan

How good are forecasters at predicting developments in the economy? The simple answer, based on recent research, is that the track record leaves much to be desired.[1] For *year-ahead* forecasts, the average error in forecasting real GDP growth during the 1990s for a large sample of industrial countries was 1.5 percent. Actual real GDP growth over this same period was 2.3 percent. For *current-year* forecasts made as late as October, the average error declined only to 0.6 percent. Furthermore, only two of the 60 recessions that occurred over this period were predicted a year in advance; two-thirds remained undetected in the April of the year in which the recession occurred.

The forecasts for Japan are even more off the mark than those for other countries, perhaps not surprisingly as the economy has sailed in uncharted waters over much of the 1990s. Among the Group of Three (G-3) countries, for instance, the forecast errors for Japan in the 1990s have been almost twice as large as those for Germany and the United States (see the Figure). There has also been much greater discord among forecasters in their predictions of Japanese growth. The standard deviation of the year-ahead GDP predictions published in the *Consensus Forecast* in April was about 50 percent higher in Japan than in either the United States or Germany, while the standard deviation of current-year output projections made in April was twice as large as in the United States or Germany.

The greater dispersion among forecasters of the Japanese economy is not necessarily an adverse phenomenon if it reflects independent thinking or genuine uncertainty about where the economy is headed. However, it may also be due to the poorer quality of information on which forecasts have to be made. There are also delays involved in procuring data on the Japanese economy—the quarterly national accounts are released about a full month after they come out in the United States, although the delay in relation to Germany is smaller. The higher degree of discord (relative to the other

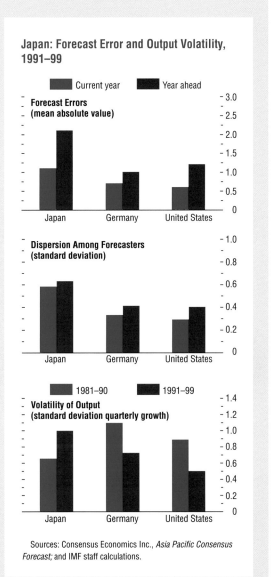

Japan: Forecast Error and Output Volatility, 1991–99

Sources: Consensus Economics Inc., *Asia Pacific Consensus Forecast;* and IMF staff calculations.

G-3) for current-year Japanese forecasts than for the year-ahead forecasts may reflect the difficulties of procuring timely and reliable data.

Another, less well-known, phenomenon that has complicated forecasting of the Japanese economy has been the large increase in the volatility of output in Japan during the 1990s. Volatility, as measured by the standard deviation of the growth in quarterly GDP, rose over a half in Japan, from 0.65 in the 1980s to unity in the

[1]Prakash Loungani, "How Accurate Are Private Sector Forecasts? Cross Country Evidence from Consensus Forecasts of Output Growth," IMF Working Paper 00/77 (Washington: International Monetary Fund, 2000).

1990s. On the same basis, volatility of output fell significantly in Germany and the United States (see the Figure). Because of this high volatility (caused in part by technical factors, discussed below), forecasters tend to be more split as to whether data movements reflect genuine turning points in demand or are more transient.

Why has volatility of output increased so dramatically in Japan in the 1990s? The answer is a complex one, combining aspects of the way policies, particularly fiscal policies, were formulated and implemented, technical factors relating to the measurement of the national accounts statistics, as well as macroeconomic shocks such as the Asian crisis, the financial turmoil induced by the banking crisis during 1997–98, and the impact of constraints on monetary policy as interest rates approached their zero bound.

There is now a broad consensus that the systematic implementation of stabilization policies in the postwar period reduced output volatility in advanced economies significantly.[2] As in other countries, stabilization policies in Japan also proved successful in reducing output volatility in the postwar period. However, a structural break appears to have occurred in the 1990s when fiscal policy was used aggressively to support domestic demand. Such fiscal activism appears to have contributed to volatility, as public investment fluctuated significantly from quarter-to-quarter and temporary tax cuts were introduced at various times. The preannounced hike in consumption taxes in April 1997 also contributed to output volatility by generating intertemporal substitution of consumption. The effects of the financial turmoil following the failures of some major banks and securities firms during 1997–98 also exacerbated volatility through an impact on precautionary savings.

Measurement problems associated with the Japanese national accounts (and other economic statistics) have also contributed to the volatility of GDP in the 1990s, particularly for private consumption and public investment. In the case of

private consumption, seasonal adjustment procedures have failed to take adequate account of a structural shift related, in part, to changes in the pattern of bonus payments—an increasing part of the traditional December bonuses have tended in recent years to spill over into the January of the subsequent year. Consequently, measured private consumption has tended to fall sharply in the last quarter of the year and rise sharply in the first quarter of the subsequent year. Sampling procedures used for computing private consumption have also had a role in explaining the recent discrepancies between the stronger outlook provided by supply-side data compared with demand-side data—the quarterly national accounts in Japan are calculated almost exclusively from the expenditure side. The Household Survey, which is used as the main ingredient for computing private consumption excludes big-spending, single-person households, while the proxy measure used for incorporating such households tends to underweight them. The quarterly path of public investment is computed mainly from the statistics on public construction works, which are often revised substantially, thereby further aggravating the volatility of measured public investment.[3] Finally, the failure of seasonal adjustment procedures to take account of leap year effects has also contributed to volatility—including in the first quarter of this year. In response to these problems, the Japanese authorities have taken a number of steps recently to improve sampling and seasonal adjustment procedures to better reflect underlying trends in the economy.

The problems relating to the quality of Japanese data are not just statistical issues of only technical concern. They constitute another element that exacerbates output volatility by forcing economic decisions to be made under incomplete or misleading information. Furthermore, they make forecasting an even more difficult task in Japan than it is in other countries, introducing a higher level of uncertainty into decisions that have to be based on predictions of the future, creating in turn the potential for a vicious circle.

[2]For a more detailed discussion of the evidence and issues, see Christina D. Romer, "Changes in Business Cycles: Evidence and Explanations," *Journal of Economic Perspectives,* Volume 13 (Spring 1999) pp. 23–44.

[3]See OECD, *Economic Outlook,* (Organization for Economic Cooperation and Development, June 2000).

Figure 1.7. Japan: Modest Recovery But Consumption Still Weak
(Percent change from four quarters earlier unless otherwise noted)

A modest recovery is under way, led by rising business investment. But households remain reluctant to spend, due to declining incomes and to precautionary savings in response to higher unemployment.

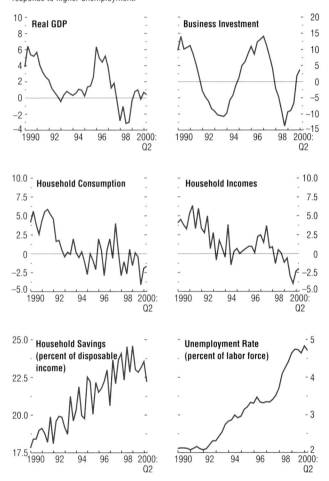

Source: Nikkei Telecom.

sures for fiscal consolidation. At the same time, however, the recovery remains fragile and subject to downside risks, particularly beyond mid-year, after which—in the absence of additional measures—public investment is expected to fall off sharply. A critical element remains the near-term outlook for private consumption, which has remained weak due to declining household income, and high savings rates in response to ongoing corporate restructuring and high unemployment (Figure 1.7). With retail sales sluggish and only a modest gain in consumer confidence, a sustained recovery in consumer demand is still not assured and could be derailed by adverse macroeconomic developments.

Against this background, it is important that macroeconomic policies remain highly supportive until a self-sustaining recovery is under way. On the fiscal side, timely implementation of a supplementary budget to support public investment beyond mid- 2000 will be important to assure continued recovery. Thereafter, the fiscal stance will need to be flexible, adapting to evolving economic conditions. However, given Japan's high public debt and the future burden of the aging population, the government will need to start laying out the main elements of a flexible fiscal consolidation strategy, with the broad aim of stabilizing and then reducing the debt-GDP ratio over a five- to ten-year horizon; in this context, continued efforts to improve fiscal transparency, including through regular publication of medium-term fiscal projections, are desirable. With a continued large output gap, and deflationary risks not yet dispelled, monetary policy should remain accommodative, and it will be important that the ending of the zero interest rate policy is not seen as foreshadowing an accelerated series of rate increases, which could undermine sentiment and the still fragile recovery.

Structural reform remains essential to ensure a durable economic recovery. Over the past two years, the authorities have taken important steps toward strengthening the banking system, and a number of megamergers have been announced.

However, few banks have yet put forward credible plans to restore core profitability, which remains very low; banks may also be adversely affected by the recent decline in equity prices, and vulnerable to capital losses when long-term bond rates eventually rise. Further efforts to restructure the credit cooperatives and some regional banks, and address remaining gaps in the regulatory and supervisory framework are also needed to allow a smooth transition to partial deposit insurance. Efforts are also urgently needed to strengthen the financial position of life insurers, which has continued to deteriorate.

The restructuring of Japan's corporate sector remains a key to revitalizing the economy and the financial system. Over the last year, a substantial number of corporate restructuring plans have been announced, encouraged by tax and other incentives under the Industrial Revitalization Law and more transparent accounting standards, and takeover and merger activity has substantially increased. Nevertheless, there has been only limited progress in strengthening corporate balance sheets and disposing of nonproductive assets, and it will be critical to avoid backsliding as macroeconomic conditions begin to improve. Early introduction of consolidated corporate taxation, removal of tax impediments for mergers and spin-offs, strengthened corporate governance, and continued progress with regulatory and product market reforms—especially in the telecom sector—are also required.

A number of observers have expressed concern that the continuation of accommodative macroeconomic policies could adversely affect progress with restructuring. For instance, low interest rates could encourage imprudent borrowing and reduce pressures on firms to downsize; at the same time, government credit guarantee programs and public works spending could help prop up economically nonviable enterprises. These are genuine risks, and—especially with regard to bank lending—need to be closely monitored by the authorities; there may also be scope to improve the efficiency and effectiveness of public investment. At the same time, modest macroeconomic tightening seems unlikely to reverse these adverse incentives, while the impact on demand could do further damage to already weak balance sheets. At the present juncture, the dangers arising from a premature withdrawal of macroeconomic support appear greater, especially in view of Japan's gloomy recent history of economic recoveries aborted by macroeconomic shocks.

Latin America and the Caribbean: Recovery and Divergence

Latin America and the Caribbean are continuing to recuperate from the emerging market crises of 1997–98. Growth is being fueled by buoyant exports (particularly to the United States), as well as a recovery in consumer confidence and spending that is occurring despite recent falls in stock prices (see Chapter II). Real GDP, which was basically flat in 1999, is expected to expand by a healthy 4¼ percent in 2000 and 4½ percent in 2001, while inflation is projected to remain quiescent and in single digits in most countries (Table 1.5). The current account deficit for the region (as a ratio of GDP) is expected to narrow somewhat in 2000, reflecting healthy export volumes and some improvement in the terms of trade coming from higher commodity prices. These aggregate trends, however, mask important differences across countries. Several countries, such as Brazil, Mexico, and Chile, are exhibiting more rapid growth than other countries in the region, particularly those where economic and political uncertainties are most acute.

The region's needs for external funds remain sizable, particularly once debt amortization and the relatively closed nature of many of the economies are taken into consideration, although vulnerability indicators have improved, in part because of increases in (relatively stable) foreign direct investment flows, and reserves are not currently under pressure (Figure 1.8). The high level of volatility of capital flows to emerging markets (again, see Chapter II) amplifies the attendant uncertainties. The most important ex-

Table 1.5. Selected Western Hemisphere and Asian Countries: Real GDP, Consumer Prices, and Current Account Balance
(Annual percent change unless otherwise noted)

	Real GDP				Consumer Prices[1]				Current Account Balance[2]			
	1998	1999	2000	2001	1998	1999	2000	2001	1998	1999	2000	2001
Western Hemisphere	**2.2**	**0.3**	**4.3**	**4.5**	**10.2**	**9.3**	**8.9**	**7.0**	**−4.5**	**−3.1**	**−2.9**	**−3.1**
Argentina	3.9	−3.1	1.7	3.7	0.9	−1.2	−0.7	0.5	−4.8	−4.4	−3.7	−3.6
Brazil	−0.1	1.0	4.0	4.5	3.2	4.9	7.5	5.0	−4.3	−4.6	−3.9	−3.5
Chile	3.4	−1.1	6.0	6.8	5.1	3.3	3.2	3.5	−5.7	−0.1	−2.4	−3.1
Colombia	0.5	−4.5	3.0	3.8	18.7	10.9	11.2	8.8	−5.3	−1.1	−1.1	−2.0
Dominican Republic	7.3	8.3	8.4	6.5	4.8	6.5	7.5	8.4	−2.1	−2.9	−5.7	−3.2
Ecuador	0.4	−7.3	0.5	3.5	36.1	52.2	100.6	30.0	−11.0	7.0	3.2	−2.4
Guatemala	5.1	3.5	3.6	3.0	6.6	5.3	7.0	7.6	−5.5	−5.6	−4.7	−4.4
Mexico	4.9	3.5	6.5	4.8	15.9	16.6	9.5	8.2	−3.8	−2.9	−3.5	−3.7
Peru	0.3	3.8	4.0	6.0	7.3	3.5	3.9	3.5	−6.0	−3.6	−3.9	−4.6
Uruguay	4.6	−3.2	2.0	4.0	10.8	5.7	5.2	4.5	−2.1	−2.9	−2.5	−2.0
Venezuela	−0.1	−7.2	2.5	3.0	35.8	23.6	17.0	16.0	−2.7	4.4	7.3	4.7
Asia	**4.1**	**5.9**	**6.7**	**6.6**	**7.5**	**2.4**	**2.4**	**3.3**	**2.2**	**2.0**	**1.6**	**0.9**
Bangladesh	5.0	5.2	5.0	4.5	8.0	6.2	5.8	7.1	−1.2	−1.5	−1.2	−1.2
China	7.8	7.1	7.5	7.3	−0.8	−1.4	0.5	1.2	3.1	1.6	1.6	1.3
India	6.3	6.4	6.7	6.5	13.2	4.7	5.6	6.5	−1.7	−0.6	−1.2	−1.3
Indonesia	−13.0	0.3	4.0	5.0	58.0	20.8	3.2	5.2	4.2	3.7	3.7	1.3
Malaysia	−7.4	5.6	6.0	6.0	5.3	2.8	3.2	3.6	12.9	15.8	13.6	7.4
Pakistan	2.6	2.7	5.6	5.3	7.8	5.7	3.6	5.5	−2.7	−3.8	−2.2	−1.5
Philippines	−0.6	3.3	4.0	4.5	9.7	6.7	5.0	5.9	2.4	9.4	8.0	3.8
Thailand	−10.2	4.2	5.0	5.0	8.1	0.3	1.7	2.6	12.7	9.1	7.2	5.9
Vietnam	3.5	4.2	4.5	5.4	7.8	4.2	0.5	5.6	−3.9	4.4	2.5	0.5
Memorandum												
Newly industrialized Asian												
economies	**−2.3**	**7.8**	**7.9**	**6.1**	**4.5**	**0.0**	**1.4**	**2.6**	**8.3**	**6.7**	**4.8**	**3.9**
Hong Kong SAR	−5.1	2.9	8.0	4.8	2.8	−4.0	−2.5	2.0	1.8	5.9	6.9	6.8
Korea	−6.7	10.7	8.8	6.5	7.5	0.8	2.2	3.0	12.8	6.1	2.3	0.4
Singapore	0.4	5.4	7.9	5.9	−0.3	0.1	1.4	2.1	25.4	25.0	23.6	22.8
Taiwan Province of China	4.7	5.7	6.5	6.0	1.7	0.2	1.6	2.3	1.3	2.5	2.1	2.2

[1]In accordance with standard practice in the *World Economic Outlook*, movements in consumer prices are indicated as annual averages rather than as December/December changes during the year, as is the practice in some countries.
[2]Percent of GDP.

ternal uncertainty for the region is the potential impact of interest hikes in the United States. Historically, activity in Latin America has been particularly susceptible to U.S. monetary policy, reflecting the close economic and financial links with the north and the appetite for external loans. Tighter U.S. monetary policy affects the region through several channels whose importance varies across countries:

- *Higher cost of international borrowing.* Hikes in the federal funds rate are generally magnified in emerging markets, as tighter global monetary conditions reduce the appetite for risk and widen spreads, particularly for higher-risk borrowers. This effect is amplified if the hike in U.S. rates is not anticipated (Box 2.1 of Chapter II).

- *Higher domestic interest rates.* This effect is direct in countries whose exchange rates are pegged to the dollar, most notably Argentina. Other central banks may feel a need to hike rates to counter downward pressure on the currency as capital flows diminish, although this may be mitigated by the inflation-targeting framework now in place in several countries—including Brazil and Mexico—and associated gains in policy credibility.

- *Fewer exports.* As U.S. activity slows, consumers in the U.S. will lower their demand for foreign goods, particularly from close economic partners such as Mexico.

Appendix I to this Chapter reports an alternative scenario that illustrates the consequences of a harder landing in the United States brought on by greater-than-expected inflationary pressures and tighter monetary policies.

Growth in *Brazil* continues to recover, led by exports, which surged as a result of the depreciation in early 1999. But rising consumer spending and investment have also contributed more recently. Real GDP is now projected to rise by 4 percent in 2000 and 4.5 percent in 2001, while the current account deficit should fall significantly. *Chile* is also experiencing a recovery, supported by buoyant consumer spending. In both countries, confidence has been maintained by responsible macroeconomic policies, including inflation-targeting regimes. In Brazil, this year's targeted public sector primary surplus of 3¼ percent of GDP is expected to be achieved. The budget for 2001 targets a primary surplus of 3 percent of GDP, which is expected to be consistent with a further decline in public debt relative to GDP. In Chile, the government has suggested giving legal status to the objective of maintaining a structural fiscal surplus of 1 percent of GDP.

Mexico's economy continues to expand at a healthy pace, as it has been doing since 1995, backed by prudent monetary policy, as well as higher oil prices, rapid growth in the United States, buoyant consumer spending, and healthy demand for investment goods. Growth is forecast to accelerate to almost 6½ percent in 2000 before falling back slightly in 2001, while inflation is projected to continue to decline as monetary policy is tightened. Higher oil prices are supporting the external position and the fiscal balance; however, procyclical fiscal policy, resulting in a deterioration in the non-oil fiscal balance, is of concern. Progress in needed banking system restructuring has taken place in the last few months, including the passage of new bankruptcy laws, successful asset sales and debt refinancing, and important steps to recapitalize the banking system (through, among other actions, consolidation and associated capital infusions). The new administration is continuing to address remaining vulnerabilities of the banking system, including the high proportion of illiquid assets in banks' balance sheets.

Figure 1.8. Selected Latin American Countries: Financial Developments

Inflation targets in Brazil, Mexico, and Chile have generally resulted in higher short-term interest rates and greater fluctuations in exchange rates. In most countries, reserves have been relatively stable.

Short-Term Interest Rates[1]
(percent)

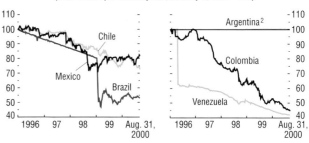

Bilateral U.S. Dollar Exchange Rates
(U.S. dollars per currency unit; January 5, 1996 = 100)

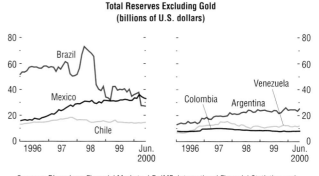

Total Reserves Excluding Gold
(billions of U.S. dollars)

Sources: Bloomberg Financial Markets, LP; IMF, *International Financial Statistics*; and WEFA, Inc.
[1]Three-month interbank rate.
[2]Pegged to U.S. dollar.

After a severe recession in 1999, the *Argentine* economy has begun to recover at a still gradual pace that, in the absence of external shocks, is expected to accelerate in 2001. Slower-than-expected recovery has adversely affected government revenue. Earlier this year, the authorities introduced a fiscal package that reduced planned government outlays to minimize the overshoot compared to the targeted deficit. This helped moderate concerns in international capital markets about fiscal slippages, although on average financial conditions remain tighter than in the latter part of 1999. Against these headwinds, real GDP is projected to grow by under 2 percent in 2000 and the current account deficit is anticipated to decline significantly. Continued structural reform in the fiscal area remains a high priority, including passing laws tightening tax administration, modifying revenue sharing arrangements with provinces, and reforming the social security system.

The Andean region, outside of Chile and Peru, was particularly hard hit by the 1998–99 recession. Activity is expanding again, but political uncertainties may slow progress on needed reforms and create pressures to relax macroeconomic policies. Business confidence remains weak in *Colombia,* in part due to continuing internal armed conflict, and the currency has fallen to record lows against the U.S. dollar, while in *Venezuela* the fiscal benefits of higher oil prices are being partially offset by increased spending. *Ecuador* plunged into a major economic and financial crisis in 1999, caused by serious policy slippages and the weakening of oil prices. Real output fell by 7¼ percent, inflation soared, and there was severe damage to the banking system. The government's rehabilitation strategy involves promoting monetary stability through dollarization, strengthening the fiscal position, restructuring household and corporate debt, and recapitalizing the banking system. The shift to dollarization appears to be succeeding, although substantial structural reform will be required to sustain it, and output is projected to rise moderately in the second half of 2000.

In the Caribbean, strong demand for tourism from the United States has helped to support activity. Growth remains strong in *Trinidad and Tobago,* partly reflecting some diversification of the economy into sectors such as manufacturing and services, while *Jamaica* is beginning to recover from a lengthy recession caused by financial sector difficulties and a severe drought. A major issue over the medium term is the appropriate recent moves to increase scrutiny of offshore financial centers, as the financial industry is an important part of the regional economy, particularly for *the Bahamas* (where 20 percent of employment is associated with financial services), *St. Vincent,* and *St. Kitts and Nevis.*

Asia: Continuing Strong Expansion

The rebound from the crisis of 1997–98 is continuing in Asia, with growth projected to rise from 6 percent in 1999 to more than 6½ percent in 2000 and 2001 (see Table 1.5). The rapid recovery of output in 1999 was fueled by continuing monetary and fiscal stimulus, as well as external demand, supported by a recovery in prices of electronics—Asia is now the world's largest supplier of such equipment. Continuing demand for information technology goods is expected to help underpin the expansion, but private domestic demand is projected to become a more important force propelling regional growth in 2000, particularly in the countries most advanced in recovery, where fixed investment is increasing rapidly (Figure 1.9). Activity also continues to be buttressed by continuing robust growth in the region's two most populous economies, China and India.

The recovery of activity in the countries most affected by the 1997–98 crisis is expected to continue, with growth in the countries where the recovery is least advanced still below that in their more advanced counterparts. Despite concern in financial markets about the pace of structural reforms, and more recent political uncertainties, growth in *Indonesia* is expected to accelerate to 4 percent in 2000 and 5 percent in 2001, supported by firm oil prices, while activity in *Korea* is projected to moderate from its recent rapid pace to 8¾ percent in 2000 and 6½ percent in 2001. Fiscal policies have been generally supportive of activity, but are appropriately beginning to move to a more neutral stance. This process, which has already started in Korea, is being initiated in the Philippines this year, while elsewhere it is planned to start in 2001.

The export-led nature of the recovery has led to strong current account positions throughout the region, although surpluses are beginning to fall in response to domestic recovery and higher oil prices (except in Indonesia). External surpluses are helping to insulate parts of the region from some of the financial impact of tighter global monetary conditions, although again the distinction between the cyclically advanced and less advanced is important. Intervention continues to be used to limit the upward pressure on the exchange rate in Korea, and a further appreciation of the won would reduce the burden on interest rate policy in dampening inflationary pressures. In *Malaysia,* which maintains a fixed exchange rate, reserves continue to be strong. With inflation relatively quiescent and economic slack still present, domestic monetary policy remains accommodative in both countries, providing support for activity and assisting balance sheet restructuring in the banking and corporate sectors. By contrast, in economies where there are doubts about the authorities' commitment to structural reform, recoveries have been delayed, real interest rates are higher, and exchange rate pressures have been felt in recent months.

The key to ensuring that the vigorous recovery continues is to maintain the momentum of structural reforms and the attendant recovery in confidence and fixed investment. Although progress is being made in restoring fragile banking systems and restructuring corporate balance sheets, particularly in Korea and Malaysia, bank retrenchments have contributed to slow credit growth. In *Thailand,* about 35 percent of bank loans remain nonperforming and market sentiment has been depressed, reflecting concerns about the pace of debt restructuring as well as

Figure 1.9. Selected East Asian Countries: Real GDP Growth and Its Composition¹
(Annual percent change)

In the countries most affected by the Asian crisis, growth rates are projected to converge as the recovery in fixed investment broadens.

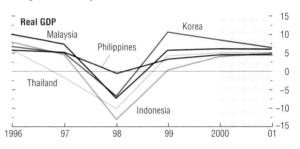

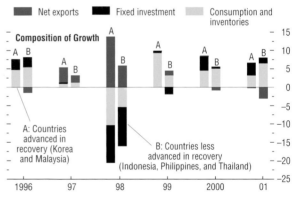

¹Data for 2000 and 2001 reflect IMF staff projections.

uncertainty related to the upcoming elections. In Indonesia, legal and political obstacles continue to slow the pace of restructuring, as demonstrated by the annulment of the government takeover of the bankrupt Bank Bali by IBRA, the government's restructuring agency.

Recent data indicate that *China*, the world's most populous economy, continues to grow at a robust pace. Real GDP growth is projected to increase to 7½ percent in 2000, supported by stronger private consumption and exports, and deflationary pressures are projected to diminish. Monetary policy is expected to remain accommodative. On the fiscal side, the authorities have announced a package of additional expenditures; however, buoyant revenues caused by strong activity are shifting policy to a more neutral stance. China's entry into the World Trade Organization (WTO), which will increase external competition in many areas (Box 1.3), underscores the need to accelerate reforms of state-owned enterprises and the banking system, whose financial situations remain difficult. A key element in this effort will be to ensure that the enterprises taken over by asset management companies are effectively restructured. Given that the Chinese economy is undergoing major structural changes, including the prospective WTO accession, a more flexible implementation of the current exchange rate arrangement (possibly involving a wider band) will be desirable at an appropriate time. The growth rate in *Hong Kong SAR* is expected to slightly exceed that in the mainland in 2000, as consumption and investment continue to recover despite continuing high levels of real interest rates caused by broad-based deflation of goods and asset prices.

India's economic performance has been remarkable in recent years, despite the adverse effects of the regional crisis on exports and the more recent hike in world oil prices, and growth is projected to rise to around 6¾ percent this year, reflecting continued strength in the information technology sector and a rebound in agricultural production. Nonetheless, significant policy challenges need to be addressed in order to sustain high growth and facilitate poverty reduction over the medium term. The fiscal situation has deteriorated markedly in recent years—with the overall public sector deficit estimated to exceed 11 percent of GDP in fiscal year 1999/2000—crowding out private sector investment and constraining funds for infrastructure and social programs. Against this backdrop, the central government's fiscal year 2000/01 budget, signs of continued fiscal stress among the states, and delays in bringing fuel prices to import parity suggest the risk of little or no fiscal adjustment in the coming year. The large government borrowing requirement has complicated the conduct of monetary policy, and the central bank raised interest rates in July in the face of exchange rate weakness and a rebound in inflation. Structural reforms in the agricultural and industrial sectors are also needed to reduce the role of government and allow the private sector to reap the full benefits of the growing globalization of goods and capital markets. In *Pakistan*, nonagricultural activity continues to be weak, and disappointing levels of tax revenue have put pressure on the fiscal position. The external sector remains fragile; reserves have continued to decline from already low levels and the Pakistani rupee has come under significant pressure following the depreciation of other regional currencies. As in India, unshackling the economy from government regulation and moving ahead forcefully with structural reform would help promote export-led growth and increase confidence both at home and abroad.

In *Australia* and *New Zealand*, the monetary policy tightening launched in late 1999 has contributed to a slowing of domestic demand. The momentum in these economies, however, is expected to be maintained by rising external demand, supported by depreciated exchange rates, accelerating growth in the rest of the world, and a pickup in some commodity prices. The rebalancing of demand from domestic to external sources and the recovery of commodity prices is expected to reduce large existing current account deficits—in New Zealand the current account deficit reached a record high of 8 percent

Box 1.3. China's Prospective WTO Accession

After 14 years of negotiations, China has reached bilateral agreements on the terms of its entry to the World Trade Organization (WTO) with most of the trade partners participating in accession negotiations, including the United States and the European Union. Over the past two decades, the opening up of the external sector has been a key element of China's economic reforms, which have now entered a critical stage, with a focus on the interlinked reforms of the state-owned enterprise and financial sectors. WTO accession could prove to be a watershed for reform. It promises to increase foreign direct investment, remove protection from inefficient industries, and spur the development of the legal and regulatory framework necessary for a market economy. It will also serve as an impetus to domestic banks to accelerate their restructuring efforts and improve efficiency. To meet the challenges of international competition, a further acceleration of reform—accompanied by a strengthening of the social safety net and narrowing regional disparities—has become even more urgent.

Content of the China-U.S. Bilateral Agreement

So far, only limited information has become available to assess the economic impact of China's accession to the WTO, but the bilateral agreement with the United States (which has been made public) is widely regarded as the core of the likely final agreement. The main details of the China-U.S. agreement are:
* China will reduce tariffs on nonagricultural products (which account for 95 percent of total imports) from about 17 percent to 9.4 percent by 2005, and lower tariffs on agricultural products to 17 percent by January 2004;[1]

[1]There is some uncertainty with regard to the tariff reductions implied by WTO accession, because the base rate of applied tariffs is not known with certainty, nor is it clear whether the new tariff levels are simple or weighted averages. For the calculations of the economic impact of WTO accession, the following World Bank estimates of weighted average tariffs in 1998 are used: 20 percent for agricultural products and 18½

eliminate quotas and nontariff restrictions on industrial products by 2005; introduce a tariff rate quota system in agriculture; and provide full trading and distribution rights to foreign firms.
* China will significantly expand market access in the services sector, including by eliminating geographic and other restrictions in most key sectors by 2005; increasing foreign ownership limits in telecommunications (50 percent by 2002), life insurance (50 percent on accession), and securities (49 percent by 2003); and giving full national treatment to foreign banks (within five years after accession). Some of these phase-in periods were reportedly accelerated in the EU negotiations.
* The United States will eliminate quotas on China's textile imports under the WTO Agreement on Textiles and Clothing (previously known as the Multi-Fiber Arrangement) by 2005, subject to anti-surge provisions, which are yet to be specified) through 2008, and give China Permanent Normal Trade Relations (PNTR) status.

It is possible that WTO accession could take place in 2000, but to complete the accession process China needs to conclude a few more bilateral agreements, finish multilateral negotiations consolidating all the bilateral agreements into a single protocol of accession, and modify its laws and regulations to be consistent with its obligations under the WTO and the protocol of accession. It is therefore likely that the economic impact of China's entry to the WTO will not begin to be felt until 2001.

Potential Economic Impact

The IMF staff's projections—while subject to large uncertainties—suggest the macroeconomic impact of accession should be manageable in the near term, and that there will be considerable long-term gains. With the affected sectors accounting for only a small portion of output and

percent for manufactures (corresponding simple averages are estimated to be 18 percent and 17½ percent, respectively).

Box 1.3 *(concluded)*

China: Differences Between WTO and Non-WTO Scenarios

	2001	2002	2003	2004	2005
	(Deviation in percentage points)				
Real GDP growth	−0.3	0.1	0.6	0.6	0.8
	(Deviation in billions of U.S. dollars)				
Current account balance	0.2	−5.7	−12.4	−21.0	−10.5

Source: IMF staff estimates.

trade, the initial adverse impact on GDP growth and the external current account should be small. Indeed, the structure of China's trade suggests that WTO accession is likely to affect only about 40 percent of present trade flows, since the remaining 60 percent is processing trade, which is largely exempt from tariffs. (Trade, defined as the sum of exports and imports, is about 40 percent of output.) Nevertheless, between 2000 and 2004, the external current account could weaken—relative to a baseline scenario in which China does not accede—as tariff reductions will result in higher import demand (see the Table). In 2005, however, this trend should begin to be reversed as the quota elimination under the WTO Agreement on Textiles and Clothing will provide a boost to exports of textiles and apparel. Any deterioration in the external current account should be largely offset by higher foreign direct investment—especially in the services sector—so that the overall balance of payments may not be greatly affected and will effectively remain in surplus.

In the immediate future, WTO accession will increase competitive pressures in a number of sectors, including agriculture, automobiles, certain capital intensive sectors (including telecommunications), and the banking system. As the effects of increased competition feed through into efficiency gains, total factor productivity growth should rise, reversing the decline witnessed in recent years. Moreover, from 2005, China's textile sector will benefit significantly from the elimination of quotas.

While output growth is expected to fall only slightly in the first year following accession relative to baseline, labor market pressures—especially in the labor intensive agricultural sector—and income distribution problems could increase in the next few years, underscoring the need to strengthen the social safety net and to develop rural and inland regions. One study estimates that an additional 2 percent of the workforce—comprising 13 million workers in rural areas and about 1¼ million workers in urban areas—will need to be reemployed in other sectors over the next five years.[2] Nevertheless, employment growth should pick up over time, as the positive effects of trade liberalization are felt. Additional challenges will come from the need to address rural/urban and coastal/western income disparities.

Given the size of China's economy, the impact of its entry to the WTO is expected to extend beyond the mainland. The boost in China's exports will benefit Hong Kong SAR, because of its reliance on entrepôt trade to and from the mainland, although, as the mainland ports become more efficient, Hong Kong SAR's entrepôt role is likely to diminish. In addition, structural reforms related to WTO accession will increase the mainland's demand for services (such as financial, accounting, and legal services), which Hong Kong SAR is well positioned to provide. Over the longer term, however, Hong Kong SAR may face increased competition as a financial center from Shanghai.

[2]Shoukang Li and Fan Zhai, "China's WTO Accession and Implications for National and Provincial Economies" (unpublished; People's Republic of China: Development Research Center of The State Council, October 1999).

Table 1.6. Commonwealth of Independent States and Countries on the European Union Accession Track: Real GDP, Consumer Prices, and Current Account Balance

(Annual percent change unless otherwise noted)

	Real GDP				Consumer Prices[1]				Current Account Balance[2]			
	1998	1999	2000	2001	1998	1999	2000	2001	1998	1999	2000	2001
Commonwealth of Independent States	**−2.7**	**2.7**	**5.6**	**3.8**	**25.0**	**70.8**	**22.9**	**16.2**	**−1.6**	**6.8**	**9.2**	**5.2**
Russia	−4.9	3.2	7.0	4.0	27.7	85.9	18.6	13.8	0.4	11.3	13.4	7.9
Armenia	7.2	3.3	4.5	6.0	8.7	0.7	0.8	3.0	−20.6	−14.8	−13.4	−12.3
Azerbaijan	10.0	7.4	5.0	7.9	−0.8	−8.3	2.2	3.0	−32.8	−15.9	−12.6	−21.5
Belarus	11.6	−2.4	−6.3	−0.6	73.0	293.7	156.0	83.0	−5.9	−2.2	−7.6	−6.3
Georgia	2.9	3.3	4.0	5.0	3.6	19.1	4.6	7.5	−15.1	−11.7	−9.9	−6.8
Kazakhstan	−1.9	1.7	5.0	4.0	7.3	8.4	13.2	7.5	−5.6	1.1	4.9	2.2
Kyrgyz Republic	2.1	3.6	4.0	4.2	10.3	35.7	22.7	14.6	−19.8	−16.3	−11.2	−9.8
Moldova	−6.5	−4.4	—	4.0	7.7	39.3	28.5	12.5	−17.3	−1.5	−3.2	−3.1
Tajikistan	5.3	3.7	5.0	5.0	43.2	27.6	17.2	7.3	−9.3	−3.4	−3.2	−4.8
Turkmenistan	5.0	16.0	15.9	6.4	16.8	23.5	13.9	35.0	−27.7	−16.0	−9.7	−30.5
Ukraine	−1.9	−0.4	2.5	3.5	10.6	22.7	26.0	14.7	−3.1	−0.1	−2.1	−1.6
Uzbekistan	4.3	4.4	3.0	3.0	29.0	29.1	26.2	21.6	−0.8	−0.1	−0.3	0.1
European Union accession track	**2.4**	**−0.3**	**4.1**	**4.8**	**35.6**	**25.8**	**23.2**	**10.4**	**−2.9**	**−3.9**	**−4.7**	**−4.3**
Bulgaria	3.5	2.4	4.5	5.0	22.3	2.1	7.9	4.5	−0.5	−5.4	−4.6	−3.9
Cyprus	5.0	4.5	4.8	4.3	2.2	1.8	5.4	5.6	−6.7	−2.6	−2.3	−2.1
Czech Republic	−2.2	−0.2	2.3	3.2	10.6	2.1	4.9	4.1	−2.4	−2.0	−3.4	−3.3
Estonia	4.7	−1.1	4.0	6.0	8.2	3.3	3.0	2.7	−9.2	−6.1	−5.9	−6.1
Hungary	4.9	4.5	5.5	5.0	14.3	10.0	8.3	6.5	−4.9	−4.3	−4.5	−4.4
Latvia	3.9	0.1	4.0	6.0	4.7	2.4	3.5	2.7	−10.1	−9.7	−8.6	−7.7
Lithuania	5.1	−4.1	2.5	4.0	5.1	0.8	1.6	2.1	−12.1	−11.2	−7.4	−6.9
Malta	3.1	3.5	3.2	4.3	2.4	2.5	2.5	2.5	−4.9	−3.7	−3.9	−3.7
Poland	4.8	4.1	5.0	5.5	11.8	7.3	9.5	6.9	−4.4	−7.5	−7.4	−7.0
Romania	−5.4	−3.2	1.3	3.0	59.1	45.8	40.2	19.4	−7.2	−3.8	−3.9	−3.8
Slovak Republic	4.4	1.9	2.4	3.5	6.7	10.7	12.1	6.0	−10.4	−5.7	−4.7	−3.9
Slovenia	3.9	4.9	4.5	4.6	8.0	6.1	7.5	5.0	—	−2.9	−2.3	−2.5
Turkey[3]	3.1	−5.0	4.5	4.8	84.6	64.9	46.5	17.0	1.0	−0.7	−3.1	−2.4

[1]In accordance with standard practice in the *World Economic Outlook*, movements in consumer prices are indicated as annual averages rather than as December/December changes during the year, as is the practice in some countries.

[2]Percent of GDP.

[3]For consumer price inflation, projections for 2000 and 2001 are based on program targets.

of GDP in 1999 and continues to be a concern in currency markets. Key structural policy initiatives in Australia include reforms of the business tax regime, the introduction of a uniform goods and services tax to replace a wide range of indirect taxes, and additional labor market reforms. Following a long period of wide-ranging reforms aimed at increased flexibility, openness, and market-orientation, the new government in New Zealand is contemplating a somewhat different course, including a greater role for industrial policy, increased trade union power, higher income taxes, and a freeze in unilateral tariff reductions.

Commonwealth of Independent States: Will Macroeconomic Improvements Accelerate Structural Reform?

The Russian economy has proved much more buoyant than anticipated, as the benefits from higher world oil prices and a competitive exchange rate have started to be felt in the broader economy. Greater-than-expected Russian domestic demand and (in some cases) higher world energy prices are providing support for most of the rest of the Commonwealth of Independent States (CIS) (Table 1.6). Progress on structural and institutional reforms generally remain well behind

Figure 1.10. Russia: Signs of a Strong Recovery

Rising oil prices and a depreciated exchange rate have strengthened Russia's external position, leading to a recovery in activity. Russia's revival is supporting activity elsewhere in the Commonwealth of Independent States (CIS), but reforms still lag compared to countries being considered for EU membership.

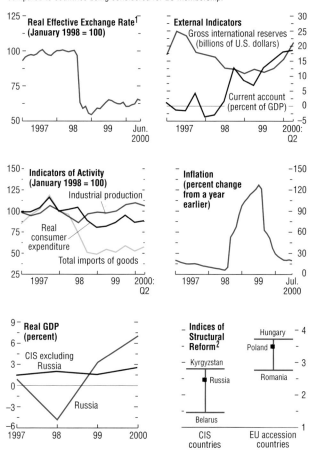

Sources: European Bank for Reconstruction and Development, *Transition Report 1999* (London: EBRD, 1999); IMF, *International Financial Statistics;* and IMF staff calculations.

[1]Defined in terms of relative consumer prices based on 1988–90 trade weights.

[2]This is an average of eight indices of structural reform produced by EBRD, as linearized by the staff. A value of 1 indicates no change from conditions under central planning, while 4⅓ indicates a structure equivalent to a typical advanced economy.

the norm set by central and eastern Europe, although conditions vary across countries (see Chapter III). Improved short-term macroeconomic prospects and the associated increase in government revenues provide an opportunity for more rapid progress on the often costly structural reforms needed to secure longer-term prosperity. Unfortunately, in some cases the opposite result appears to be occurring, with the cyclical upswing reducing the commitment to fundamental change.

The *Russian* economy is continuing its rapid recovery from the financial crisis of 1998 (Figure 1.10). After expanding by 3.2 percent in 1999, real GDP growth accelerated further in early 2000 and is now above pre-1998 crisis levels. Much of the growth in 1999 was driven by favorable terms of trade shocks whose benefits were initially expected to be temporary— namely, rising prices of energy exports and import compression due to the crisis-induced real exchange rate depreciation (real imports fell by almost 30 percent in 1999). In the event, however, improving external earnings seeped through to the domestic economy. Investment and non-oil exports began to strengthen during 1999, followed more recently by increased consumption and imports. Rising real wages, reductions in arrears, and lessening use of barter all point to continued improvements in activity. Real growth is now forecast at 7 percent in 2000 and 4 percent in 2001, much stronger than in the May *World Economic Outlook*.

Higher energy prices, import compression, and increasingly buoyant growth in non-energy exports have resulted in a strong external position. The current account surplus in 1999 was more than 10 percent of GDP and is expected to rise in 2000, and capital flight, while still sizable, appears to be falling. The central bank has been resisting the associated upward pressure on the exchange rate through large-scale intervention, and has found it increasingly difficult to sterilize such interventions. Some further nominal appreciation of the ruble should be considered to deal with the strong balance of payments position and to offset inflationary pressures. On the fiscal front, the buoyancy of output and energy prices has led to a dramatic improvement in the financial position of all levels of government.

Longer-term economic prospects continue to depend upon accelerating the slow pace of structural reform. The new 18-month reform plan of the government has many encouraging features, including measures to accelerate enterprise restructuring, strengthen the investment climate, and a tax policy reform package. However, implementation remains crucial. For example, it will be important to ensure that any net revenue costs of tax reforms are offset by expenditure restraints, particularly as the budget is likely to be burdened by significant reform-related expenditures in the coming years, including the costs of bank restructuring. Little progress has been achieved in shutting down insolvent banks, and the financial review of the government-owned saving bank (Sberbank) has yet to be completed. Other priorities include a revision of the bankruptcy law and measures to reduce barter and arrears caused, at least in part, by the use of the energy sector as a vehicle for off-budget subsidies to loss-making enterprises and underfunded social institutions.

The revival of activity in Russia is particularly benefiting close trading partners, such as *Ukraine*. Indeed, Ukraine is expected to grow for the first time since the start of transition, but progress on structural reform remains slow. It will be important to ensure that the banking system is restructured in an effective manner, cash collection in the energy sector increased, and the privatization program proceeds transparently. The successful completion of a private debt restructuring in April has helped to stabilize the external position, although the outlook remains difficult. Structural reforms are even less advanced in *Belarus*, where macroeconomic stability remains elusive, with inflation projected to remain in triple digits through 2000.

Elsewhere in the region, *Kazakhstan*, *Azerbaijan*, and *Turkmenistan* have received boosts from higher prices of energy and other commodities. In Kazakhstan the consequent improvement in the external position and recent

discovery of significant additional oil reserves has led to significant repayment of external debt (including all obligations to the IMF) and to a diminished appetite for structural reforms. Other countries in the region are less well placed to benefit from higher commodity prices, and many continue to suffer from more fundamental weaknesses. In particular, high levels of external debt and the slow pace of structural reforms continue to hobble economic activity in *Georgia, the Kyrgyz Republic, Moldova,* and *Tajikistan* (see Chapter III).

Sustaining the Momentum in Countries on the European Union Accession Track

Economic activity is expected to strengthen in 2000 and 2001 in the countries on the European Union (EU) accession track, with increasing and positive output growth and declining or moderate (single-digit) inflation in nearly all of the countries (see Table 1.6). The recovery in activity after the crises of the past few years has been bolstered by the upswing in exports to western Europe, as growth has strengthened there, and by better-than-expected performances in Russia and the other CIS countries, which have helped to improve confidence in the region (Figure 1.11). The stronger outlook can also be attributed to generally sound macroeconomic policies and to progress made on structural reforms.

Nevertheless, the relatively large—and in some instances, growing—external current account deficits in most of these countries have raised concerns. In part, these deficits reflect sizable capital inflows that have led to the appreciation of the real exchange rate and made monetary policy more difficult, as well as the rise in oil prices. Accommodative fiscal policies also contributed to the deficits in a few instances. To reduce the vulnerability of these economies to a reversal in financial market sentiment, particularly as capital accounts are liberalized as part of the EU accession process, countries need to ensure fiscal and monetary discipline and continue progress on structural reforms—particularly, in the development of

Figure 1.11. Selected European Countries: Export Market Growth and Real Effective Exchange Rates[1]

Export market growth has accelerated for EU accession countries, many of which face rising real effective exchange rates.

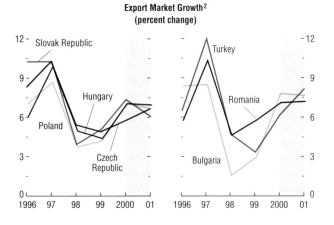

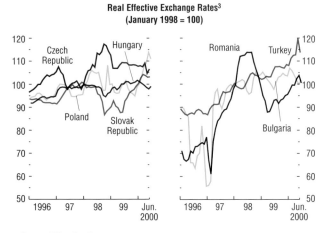

Source: IMF staff estimates.
[1]Shaded areas indicate IMF staff projections.
[2]Growth of partner country goods imports excluding oil.
[3]Defined in terms of relative consumer prices based on 1988–90 trade weights.

the financial sector and other institutions, as well as in privatization, labor market adjustment, and business restructuring. The major medium- and longer-term challenges facing most of the countries as they prepare for full membership in the European Union are discussed further in Chapter IV.

Growth is projected to increase to over 5 percent in Hungary and Poland in 2000 and 2001 after a very mild slowdown in 1999. The stronger-than-expected growth in *Hungary* has been fuelled by exports and investment, as well as by sound macroeconomic policies and substantial progress in structural reforms. The current account deficit has narrowed against a background of strong export growth and a tightening of fiscal policy. Meanwhile, in the face of strong demand, the pace of disinflation has stalled—after the inflation rate had fallen from 14 percent in 1998 to under 10 percent earlier this year. The official objective of achieving annual average inflation of 6 to 7 percent in 2000 is likely to be missed and the authorities may need to tighten monetary conditions through, among other measures, greater exchange rate flexibility, accompanied by fiscal tightening to avoid additional pressure on the external current account.

In *Poland*, output growth has been strong and the current account deficit has remained at 7½ percent of GDP in the first four months of this year, while inflation overshot its end-1999 target by 2 percentage points and the general government deficit exceeded its 1999 target by 1 percent of GDP. In response, the Monetary Policy Council has raised interest rates sharply since late 1999. In April, the central bank removed its exchange rate trading band and allowed the zloty to float freely to maintain its sole focus on inflation targeting. International reserves remain relatively high at more than seven months of imports and 350 percent of short-term debt, and the banking sector, which is largely foreign owned, remains sound. However, with the current account deficit projected to remain above 7 percent of GDP through the end of 2000 and perhaps beyond, the authorities need to follow through on proposed plans to reduce the general government deficit, which was 3¾ percent of GDP in 1999.

In the other accession candidates, where the slowdown in economic activity was more severe in recent years, output growth is expected to rebound in 2000 and generally increase further in 2001. Among these countries, Bulgaria and the Slovak Republic suffered relatively mild slowdowns in 1999, while the Baltic countries suffered sharper, although also short-lived, slowdowns largely because of closer trade ties with Russia. In *Bulgaria*, which is projected to grow almost 5 percent annually in 2000 and 2001, the relatively strong performance reflects substantial macroeconomic reforms since 1997 that have been underpinned by the currency board arrangement and complemented by progress in structural reforms—particularly, wage restraint in state enterprises, enterprise restructuring, and privatization. In the *Slovak Republic*, the slowdown in GDP growth in 1999 was limited by strong export growth—reflecting gains in competitiveness associated with the depreciation of the koruna in the first half of the year and strong productivity growth in exporting industries. With the government deficit likely to increase this year, further tightening of macroeconomic policies may be needed. In the Baltic countries—*Estonia*, *Latvia*, and *Lithuania*—the economic recoveries that generally began in the latter part of 1999 are projected to continue in 2000 and 2001. The slowdown in activity was deeper in Lithuania because of the relatively large appreciation of the exchange rate (which is pegged to the U.S. dollar) in effective terms and greater reliance on trade with Russia, and because an earlier period of expansionary fiscal policies has resulted in the need for greater fiscal adjustment.

After three consecutive years of negative growth, output is also projected to rebound in the Czech Republic and Romania. The recovery in the *Czech Republic* has been aided by accommodative monetary and fiscal policies, although the ongoing restructuring of the banking and traditional corporate sectors continues to act as a drag, partly by contributing to a credit crunch and high unemployment. In *Romania*, the rebound follows a determined adjustment effort in 1999—including large corrections of the fiscal accounts and the exchange rate—that has significantly strengthened the external position. The recent financial sector problems in both of these countries, however, highlight the need to continue to implement structural reforms as well as maintain macroeconomic discipline to ensure lasting and durable recoveries.

Following the recession last year, output growth in *Turkey* is projected to rebound in 2000. The recovery is attributable to several factors, including reconstruction following the earthquakes, stronger growth in exports to western Europe and Russia, a rebound in tourism, falling interest rates, and improving business and consumer confidence. Underpinning many of these factors has been the successful initial implementation of an ambitious IMF-supported stabilization program that has already achieved a higher-than-targeted primary consolidated government surplus, a rapid reduction in real interest rates, and falling inflation.[6] Nonetheless, partly because of rising oil prices, inflation in the first few months of the program was higher-than-targeted and the external current account deficit has widened more rapidly than expected. To mitigate any risks stemming from the higher-than-programmed inflation and from an increasing current account deficit, the government has decided to lock in additional fiscal savings that are projected to arise in 2000 and ensure that primary fiscal expenditures do not increase in real terms in 2001. In addition, the government intends to press forward with the structural reform agenda—including banking sector reform, reduction of agriculture support programs, and privatization of some public enterprises.

---

[6]See Box 2.1, "Turkey's IMF-Supported Disinflation Program," in the May 2000 *World Economic Outlook* for a more detailed description of the program.

Table 1.7. Selected Middle Eastern and African Countries: Real GDP, Consumer Prices, and Current Account Balance

(Annual percent change unless otherwise noted)

	Real GDP				Consumer Prices[1]				Current Account Balance[2]			
	1998	1999	2000	2001	1998	1999	2000	2001	1998	1999	2000	2001
Middle East[3]	**3.1**	**2.8**	**4.8**	**3.6**	**9.3**	**7.9**	**7.4**	**7.1**	**−6.1**	**1.0**	**8.3**	**4.6**
Egypt	5.6	6.0	5.0	4.5	4.7	3.8	2.9	3.0	−3.1	−2.0	−1.8	−1.8
Iran, Islamic Republic of	2.2	2.5	3.4	4.0	20.0	20.4	16.0	13.0	−2.2	5.0	7.7	3.4
Jordan	1.7	1.6	3.0	3.5	3.1	0.6	2.5	3.1	0.3	5.2	3.4	1.5
Kuwait	2.0	−2.4	3.6	2.0	0.5	1.9	1.5	2.5	10.0	16.5	28.7	24.4
Saudi Arabia	1.6	−1.0	3.5	2.9	−0.2	−1.2	1.0	1.9	−10.2	−1.2	6.6	1.6
Africa	**3.1**	**2.2**	**3.4**	**4.4**	**9.1**	**11.8**	**12.7**	**8.6**	**−4.8**	**−3.9**	**−0.8**	**−2.0**
Algeria	5.1	3.3	4.3	4.2	4.9	2.6	1.0	2.0	−1.9	0.0	12.6	10.3
Cameroon	5.0	4.4	4.2	5.3	−0.0	2.9	2.0	2.0	−2.7	−4.3	−2.4	−2.8
Côte d'Ivoire	4.5	2.8	2.2	4.5	4.5	0.7	2.5	2.5	−3.9	−4.0	−5.4	−4.0
Ghana	4.7	4.4	4.0	4.5	19.3	12.4	14.7	10.0	−4.7	−10.6	−8.5	−4.9
Kenya	2.1	1.5	1.6	3.3	6.6	3.5	5.2	5.0	−4.8	−3.2	−4.0	−6.8
Morocco	6.8	−0.7	2.4	5.0	2.7	0.7	2.3	2.0	−0.4	−0.8	−2.3	−1.6
Nigeria	1.9	1.1	3.5	3.6	10.0	6.6	5.1	6.9	−8.7	−11.0	2.4	−3.0
South Africa	0.6	1.2	3.0	4.0	6.9	5.2	4.7	5.9	−1.6	−0.4	−0.7	−1.3
Tanzania	3.3	4.6	5.2	5.6	12.6	7.9	5.7	4.4	−14.2	−14.8	−15.3	−15.4
Tunisia	5.0	6.2	5.0	6.0	3.1	2.7	3.5	3.0	−3.4	−2.0	−3.4	−3.5
Uganda	5.5	7.8	5.0	6.1	5.8	−0.2	6.3	5.6	−5.6	−7.4	−7.9	−7.9

[1]In accordance with standard practice in the *World Economic Outlook*, movements in consumer prices are indicated as annual averages rather than as December/December changes during the year, as is the practice in some countries.
[2]Percent of GDP.
[3]Middle East and Europe *World Economic Outlook* grouping excluding Cyprus, Malta, and Turkey.

Middle East and Africa: Recovering but Vulnerable to Commodity Price Cycles

In recent years, economic developments in many Middle Eastern and African countries have been shaped importantly by external factors, including changes in commodity prices and growth in export markets. During 1999–2000, the rebound in world oil prices, as well as recent increases in OPEC oil production quotas, have boosted economic activity and prospects for most of the oil-producing countries in the Middle East and Africa (Table 1.7 and Figure 1.12). The rise in oil prices and oil output have led to stronger fiscal and external balances in these countries and also to improved confidence and greater domestic demand. Many of the non-oil-producing countries in the region, however, have faced substantial terms-of-trade losses as export prices of nonfuel commodities and other primary goods remain generally depressed, particularly in real terms, while oil import prices have risen (see Chapter II for a more detailed discussion). Nonetheless, growth in a number of these coun-

tries has rebounded in the past year because of appropriate macroeconomic policies and reform efforts that have made economic activity more broad based and allowed these countries to benefit from stronger export market growth. By contrast, in countries that have followed poor policies and in some instances suffered other adverse shocks—including armed conflicts and drought—economic performance has been weak.

The recent fluctuations in commodity prices again highlight the vulnerability of almost all of the countries in the region to changes in prices of primary goods. Reforms continue to be needed to liberalize and diversify these economies and to encourage broad-based, labor-intensive growth led by the private sector, focused on industries in which these countries have a comparative advantage. In addition, in some countries, fiscal policy needs to be conducted in a less procyclical fashion so as not to exacerbate the boom and bust cycles in these commodity-dependent countries.

The international community will need to continue to bolster these efforts through ongoing

Figure 1.12. Africa and the Middle East: Terms of Trade Impact of Commodity Price Changes[1]

Terms of trade have improved substantially for oil-exporting countries but have deteriorated for many other countries, particularly in areas of central Africa that rely on nonfuel commodity exports.

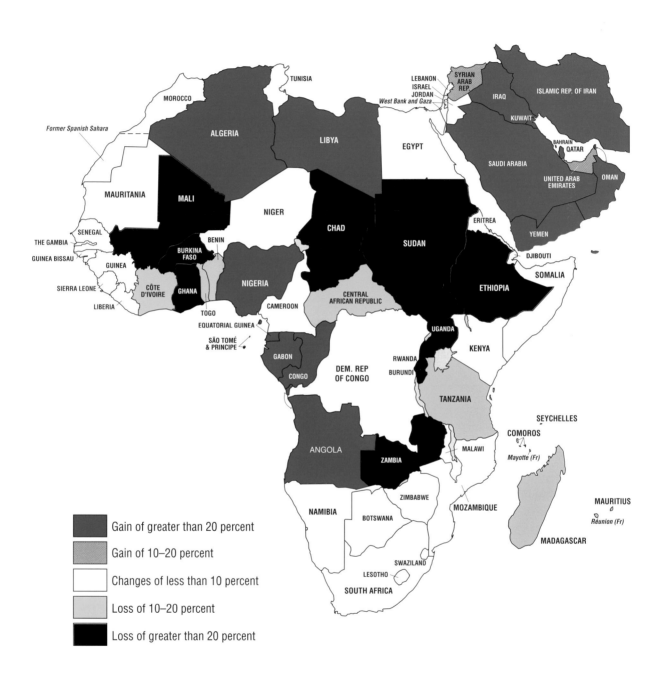

Gain of greater than 20 percent

Gain of 10–20 percent

Changes of less than 10 percent

Loss of 10–20 percent

Loss of greater than 20 percent

[1]Calculated based on the change in commodity prices for 2000 relative to the 1995–97 average, weighted by the commodity's share in total trade.

support for debt relief and the HIPC initiative, as well as increasing efforts to open their markets to the products of poor countries—such as reducing import restrictions on agricultural products and textiles—and to reverse the downward trend in advanced countries' official development assistance. Of growing concern are the potentially catastrophic human and economic consequences of the HIV/AIDS epidemic in Africa (Box 1.4). Government, society, and the international community will need to expand substantially efforts to address the threat from this and other infectious diseases through effective education, health, and other social programs.

In the Middle East, economic growth among the Gulf oil exporters is projected to turn positive in 2000 and remain so in 2001. Despite the improvement in growth prospects, as well as external and fiscal balances, many of these countries are pressing ahead, albeit sometimes slowly, with structural reforms to boost the non-oil private sector that were initiated when much lower oil prices threatened macroeconomic stability. For example, in *Saudi Arabia*, the government is restructuring and corporatizing the telecommunication and utility sectors to make them more attractive to private investment, as well as revising laws and regulations to improve the business environment and attract foreign investment and expertise. In *Kuwait*, a package of structural reforms aimed at laying the foundation for higher private sector-led growth and employment creation has been partially passed by parliament. In the *Islamic Republic of Iran*, although the external and fiscal positions improved sharply owing to the rise in oil prices, output growth remains constrained by structural distortions, and unemployment and inflation remain high. Promised reforms, which are being implemented at a cautious pace, will focus on encouraging private sector investment as the primary source of growth and employment through more market-based exchange rate and interest rate policies and by opening up to foreign investment.

Annual output growth in *Egypt* is projected to slow in 2000 while inflation, currently about 3 percent, remains in check. Until recently, rapid

domestic credit growth and unfavorable external developments—including the appreciation of the effective exchange rate as a result of the de facto peg to the U.S. dollar—had led to pressures on the external accounts, substantial loss of external reserves, and illiquidity in the foreign currency market. With a tightening of fiscal and credit policies and an improved external environment more recently, the pressures on the external accounts have declined somewhat, and the loss of foreign reserves has slowed. A continuation of the recent tightening of monetary and fiscal policies is needed to further ease the pressures on the balance of payments, while progress on structural reforms, which has slowed, will need to be accelerated to support continued rapid growth.

In *Israel*, the modest economic recovery now under way is projected to strengthen further in the next two years, led by exports, particularly from the high technology sector. Growth in private domestic demand is also expected to increase because of improved confidence and lower interest rates, with monetary policy being gradually eased as inflation remains below or near the lower bound of the 3 to 4 percent inflation target. In view of the still high public debt (103 percent of GDP), continued progress with fiscal consolidation is needed.

Annual output growth in Africa is projected at 3½ percent in 2000, rising to 4½ percent in 2001, spurred by rebounds in South Africa and the oil-exporting countries, as well as continued strength in some of the smaller economies. In *South Africa*, the continent's largest economy, the economic recovery, while still fragile, is gaining momentum, with output on track to grow 3 to 4 percent in each of the next two years. The rebound has been supported by a strengthening of public finances, improvements in external competitiveness, and the expansion in world output. The rand has come under some pressure since the beginning of this year largely as a result of the fallout from the turbulence in Zimbabwe and decreased relative bond yields, but progress continues to be made in reducing the net open forward position of the Reserve Bank, which has

Box 1.4. The Economic Impact of HIV/AIDS in Southern Africa

At the end of 1999, 33.6 million people were living with HIV/AIDS, of which some 25 million are in Africa. Within this, the highest rates of infection are in southern Africa. The Joint United Nations Program on HIV/AIDS (UNAIDS) estimates that about 36 percent of the adult population in Botswana, 25 percent in Zimbabwe and Swaziland, and 20 percent in South Africa and Zambia are infected; this compares to a prevalence rate of 8.6 percent for sub-Saharan Africa and 1.1 percent for the world as a whole. By 2010, the U.S. Census Bureau predicts that life expectancy will fall from about 60 years to around 30 years for the worst affected countries, and that the rate of population growth will stagnate or turn negative for several countries in the subregion (see the Table).[1] The social and economic implications will be far reaching and long-lasting, both through the huge toll in human lives and the dislocation of society that will result. In particular, the epidemic is affecting the social structure of local communities by disrupting existing social networks and traditional support mechanisms. It is also creating a generation of orphans—which could reach up to 10 percent of the population in some countries—who may grow up without the support and guidance of adults.

This box briefly discusses the potential macroeconomic implications of the HIV/AIDS pandemic, which will also be extremely serious. As discussed below, there will be substantial effects on a broad range of economic variables, including GDP growth, poverty and income inequality, labor supply, domestic saving, productivity, and human, physical, and social capital.[2] Since HIV/AIDS has a long incubation period, the impact of the disease will be gradual, and its full effects in most countries have yet to be felt.

Initially, the main impact will be felt in the public sector, as health care and other expenditures increase, revenue bases are eroded, and public sector workers are lost. The Table provides estimates of the demand in 1999 (based on local health standards) for HIV/AIDS-related health services in some of the affected countries; these are substantial, accounting for between 20 and 90 percent of health budgets. Even if only a proportion of HIV/AIDS patients are treated, the strains on the health sector as a whole will be severe and will likely lead to increased rationing of treatment for both HIV and non-HIV related illnesses. It is important to note that these estimates do not include the cost of modern combination therapies. If the latter could be made available to even 10 percent of those infected with HIV at an annual cost of $5,000 each, the total cost would range from 1.6 percent of GDP (South Africa) to 14.5 percent of GDP (Mozambique). This could only be financed with considerable outside assistance.

HIV/AIDS will have a number of other direct effects on the public sector. The early loss of qualified employees will result in a decline in productivity and the quality of public services, and countries will find it difficult to replace highly trained public servants such as doctors and teachers who fall victim to HIV/AIDS. In addition, the costs of absenteeism will be significant. In some countries, government employees may take up to one year of sick leave. This is likely to result mainly in a deterioration in the quality of public services, rather than an increase in personnel costs, as staff are not replaced speedily. The impact on public sector pension funds will also be substantial. While fewer government employees will reach retirement age, so pension expenditures will decline—by up to 3 percent of the public sector payroll in the worst affected countries—death-related benefits and pensions for surviving dependents may well rise to 5 percent of the government wage bill.[3] Other social spending will also rise, most importantly for the growing num-

[1]U.S. Bureau of Census, *World Population Profile 2000* (Washington: U.S. Bureau of Census, 2000).

[2]For further details, see Markus Haacker, "The Economic Impact of HIV/AIDS in Southern Africa" (unpublished manuscript; Washington: International Monetary Fund, 2000).

[3]Overall, pension funds report that between 30 percent and 70 percent of payouts have been related to HIV/AIDS.

37

Box 1.4 *(concluded)*

The Economic Impact of AIDS in Southern Africa
(1999, unless otherwise noted)

	HIV Prevalence *(percent of population, age 15–49)*	Estimated AIDS Deaths	Demand for AIDS Health Services[1] *(percent of GDP)*	Health Expenditure 1994–98 *(percent of GDP)*
Botswana	35.8	24,000	1.8	2.0
Lesotho	23.6	16,000	0.9	4.8
Malawi	16.0	70,000	0.8	. . .
Mozambique	13.2	98,000	0.6	1.0
Namibia	19.5	18,000	1.3	3.8
South Africa	19.9	250,000	0.7	3.0
Swaziland	25.3	7,100	0.9	2.3
Zambia	20.0	99,000	1.3	2.8
Zimbabwe	25.1	160,000	1.6	2.2

Sources: UNAIDS, *Report on the Global HIV/AIDS Epidemic* (Geneva: UNAIDS, 2000); and IMF staff estimates.
[1]Estimated cost of treating all AIDS patients at local standards. In practice, costs may be reduced by rationing.

ber of orphans (in Botswana, for example, orphan allowances will exceed 1 percent of GDP by 2010). Over the longer term, there are also likely to be adverse effects on tax revenues, putting further pressure on the fiscal position.

As in the public sector, HIV/AIDS affects the private sector through lower productivity and costs related to labor turnover, a shrinking labor supply, and medical, pension, and death-related benefits. While there are few empirical studies of the impact of HIV/AIDS at the company level, those that are available suggest that AIDS-related absenteeism is very significant, in addition to the costs of training and recruitment and of medical and death-related benefits. Overall, AIDS-related costs corresponding to 50–100 percent of an infected employee's salary seem realistic. Costs tend to be higher in sectors where employees require extensive training and in companies offering generous pension schemes. For example, a study conducted by Metropolitan Life for the manufacturing sector in South Africa suggests that, owing to AIDS, the cost of death-related benefits across all employees will more than double between 1997 and 2007 (from 5.5 percent to 12 percent of total payroll).

The HIV/AIDS epidemic will have a large impact on the supply of labor and human capital. Current estimates suggest that some southern African countries will lose over one-quarter of their skilled and educated population. These losses will result in a decline in productivity and in the effectiveness of public administration. Some evidence also suggests that children of AIDS victims may have to drop out of school, in order to care for sick relatives or because their families can no longer afford schooling. This will affect the supply of human capital in the longer run.

Investment and physical capital may also decrease because of HIV/AIDS, as domestic saving may fall and external saving may decline unless an increase in foreign aid offsets the likely decrease in foreign direct investment. Empirical evidence suggests that domestic saving will fall because of the epidemic.[4] Public saving will likely suffer from an increase in the public deficit (as detailed above) and private non-household saving may suffer from a decrease of business profits (especially due to lower labor productivity). The impact on household saving is less clear, although on balance it may also decline because of the increase in the dependency ratio. Microeconomic studies indicate that households that care for an AIDS patient are dissaving, because of increased medical spend-

[4]An econometric analysis of developing countries by the World Bank shows that the domestic saving rate is negatively correlated with the level of the HIV prevalance rate. See World Bank, "Economic Analysis of HIV/AIDS," Annex 5 in *Multisectoral HIV/AIDS Program* (Washington: World Bank, forthcoming).

ing and decreased income when ill adult family members can no longer work. Precautionary saving may increase, however, in other households because of the increased risk of contracting AIDS-related diseases.

The implications of HIV/AIDS for GDP growth will clearly be substantial, both through the direct impact on labor supply, human capital, and saving, but also through a decline in total factor productivity. Recent studies suggest that annual GDP growth rates may drop by 1–2 percentage points, although the impact will not be uniform across countries and will depend, among other factors, on the health infrastructure, the stock of human and physical capital, and the composition of output.[5] Calculations by IMF staff produce broadly similar results. This analysis suggests that GDP per capita in 2010 may be about 5 percent lower in the worst affected countries than it would be without the impact of HIV/AIDS, although this certainly underestimates the welfare cost because GDP per capita does not account fully for the human, social, and pecuniary costs of HIV/AIDS. Given the extent of the crisis faced by many of the countries—including the danger of macroeconomic instability as the fiscal position deteriorates, the potential disruption to established economic and social relationships, and the adverse impact on internal and external confidence—it is quite possible that the impact will in practice be significantly more severe.

[5]See John T. Cuddington and John D. Hancock, "The Macroeconomic Impact of AIDS in Malawi," *Journal of African Economics*, Vol. 1, pp. 1–28 (May 1995); and Channing Arndt and Jeffrey D. Lewis, "The Macro Implications of HIV/AIDS in South Africa: A Preliminary Assessment" (unpublished; Washington: World Bank, 2000).

Moreover, poverty and income inequality are likely to increase because of HIV/AIDS. The epidemic creates a vicious cycle by reducing economic growth, which leads to increased poverty, which, in turn, facilitates the rapid spread of HIV/AIDS, as household food and health spending declines, thereby reducing resistance to opportunistic infections. In addition to reducing income and wealth in households affected by HIV/AIDS, the epidemic is likely to increase income inequality by increasing the scarcity of skilled labor, leading to relatively higher wages for skilled labor. Wages for unskilled labor are unlikely to rise because of the large pool of unemployed workers and potential migrant workers from rural areas.

The HIV/AIDS problem in southern Africa is already of enormous dimension, and—as noted above—it is clear that these countries will require considerable external assistance to address it. To prevent the situation from deteriorating further, it will be critical to reduce the rate of new infections. The experiences of countries such as Uganda (where the infection rate has declined substantially following extensive efforts by the government) and Senegal (where early public awareness efforts have helped keep the infection rate low) suggest that highly publicized prevention campaigns, supported by strong political commitment, early education programs (particularly for girls), treatment of infected pregnant women with anti-viral drugs just before they give birth, and measures targeted at high-risk groups (such as migrant or sex workers) can be successful in reducing the incidence of new HIV infections. Taking measures to limit the further spread of the disease must therefore be a central priority, both in southern Africa and in other countries, including those that—so far—remain relatively unaffected.

helped reduce the risk premium on South African investments and boost economic activity. Improvements in productivity growth have helped dampen the potential inflationary impact of the economic recovery. Nevertheless,

some cost-push pressures have been evident as a result of the depreciation of the rand, a flood-related surge in food prices, and the rise in oil prices. The Reserve Bank is being careful in ensuring that these developments do not undermine confidence in the inflation-targeting framework. In the longer term, continued implementation of key structural reforms—including in the areas of privatization and labor market practices—will enhance private and foreign investment and promote improvements in productivity so as to raise annual growth to the rate of 5 percent or more that is needed to reduce unemployment significantly.

Algeria and Nigeria, like other oil producers, have benefited from higher oil prices, with significant improvements in fiscal and external balances, along with higher oil-sector output growth. In addition, in *Algeria*, the private industrial sector, which is still relatively small despite extensive liberalization in the mid-1990s, has expanded rapidly in recent years. Unemployment, however, remains high because of, among other things, structural weaknesses in various sectors and rapid labor force growth. The new government plans to accelerate reforms, including restructuring and privatizing public sector companies, restructuring the banking sector, reducing government intervention in the economy, and enacting judicial, housing, and land reforms. In *Nigeria*, the current government has made strides in tackling corruption, restoring macroeconomic stability, and improving relations with creditors. Limited institutional capacity, however, may make the implementation of further structural and governance reforms difficult. Sharply increased fiscal expenditures need to be used productively—in particular for poverty reduction programs such as education and health—and a significant portion of the increased fiscal revenues should be saved. These moves should help avert a real currency appreciation and provide a cushion for when revenues are pressured by lower oil prices.

Output growth is projected to remain strong in *Cameroon, Ghana, Mozambique, Tanzania*, and *Uganda*, as these countries have begun to reap some of the benefits of macroeconomic and structural reforms. In Mozambique, where floods caused substantial damage earlier this year, the government has drawn up a comprehensive reconstruction plan that will be implemented with generous and timely international support, while in Tanzania and Uganda, economic activity has withstood weak prices for their main exports—coffee and cotton for Tanzania and coffee for Uganda. (A food shortage caused by the failure of seasonal rains also hampered Tanzania.) Growth in these countries has remained resilient, despite adverse shocks, largely because output has become more broad based and governments and the international community have been responsive. In addition, Cameroon, as well as a number of other countries in the CFA franc zone, has benefited from depreciation of the exchange rate (which is pegged to the euro) in effective terms.

Elsewhere, by contrast, adverse shocks and, in some instances, poor policies have hurt economic prospects, with activity projected to weaken or remain sluggish in, for example, *Côte d'Ivoire* (adverse shocks include weak cocoa prices and a significant slowdown in disbursements of external assistance, partly the result of the *coup d'etat*), the *Democratic Republic of Congo* (war), *Eritrea* (drought and war), *Ethiopia* (drought and war), *Kenya* (drought and weak export prices), *Morocco* (drought), and *Zimbabwe* (political turbulence). First and foremost, in some of these countries, efforts will need to be made to end and prevent armed conflicts and restore political stability. Reform efforts aimed at macroeconomic stability, improved governance, sound institutional arrangements, openness to trade, and efficient investments in infrastructure, education, and health also will need to be expanded to broaden development and support growth and poverty reduction.[7]

The Transition Process

It has been 20 years since China began the process of reform and opening up to the outside

---

[7]See Chapter IV of the May 2000 *World Economic Outlook* for a more extensive discussion of the challenges in sustaining and promoting income growth and poverty reduction in the poorest countries.

world, and over 10 years since the Berlin Wall came down and economies from Prague to Vladivostok started their transition to market-based systems. This *World Economic Outlook* focuses on the transition process, with Chapter III discussing the overall experience—including that of China and other east Asian transition economies—and Chapter IV focusing on accession to the European Union, the major policy issue for many European transition countries. Much has been achieved since the start of transition, with many of the countries involved now enjoying the benefits of a stable macroeconomic environment. Great strides have also been made in the difficult task of creating the infrastructure for a market economy almost from scratch. Strikingly, distinguishing transition economies from developing countries at similar levels of development can be difficult, although this is less true for the CIS countries.

Outside of east Asia, however, the transition process has generally been more difficult than anticipated. Output fell rapidly in the early years of transition while poverty has increased significantly. By contrast, the rapid growth experienced in the east Asian transition economies has led some to suggest that a more gradual approach to reforms and later sequencing of privatization would have produced better results. However, the more gradualist strategy adopted in east Asia was dependent on the structure of these economies. The difficult task of reforming state-owned enterprises could be delayed because they were a relatively small segment of the economy, while market reforms in the large agricultural sector rapidly increased incomes and provided a pool of labor for new businesses. Such an approach was not available in other transition economies, with their large enterprise sectors in need of rapid reform and agricultural sectors of limited size. In addition, the fastest-growing areas in the east Asian economies—agriculture, exports, and small enterprises—were also the ones in which reforms were most radical. Finally, reforms in east Asia were implemented in a relatively stable political climate, without the disruptions associated with strife and the dissolution of state structures.

That being said, the structural policies that were followed elsewhere in pursuit of transition were not always ideal. The need for creating an institutional infrastructure to support the nascent market economies was recognized from the beginning, but in practice it was not always given the attention it required, particularly if the macroeconomic situation appeared stable. In addition, the evidence from countries outside of east Asia does appear to indicate that the most effective privatization schemes involved ensuring that the sale of large enterprises to the private sector was accompanied by measures to create effective corporate governance structures and competition safeguards.

Another striking feature of the transition process has been the better performance of the countries of central and eastern Europe and the Baltics that are now candidates for accession to the EU compared to the CIS. This partly reflects more favorable starting conditions, proximity to western European markets, and greater progress in structural and institutional reforms, itself reflecting the CIS countries' lesser experience with market institutions and more limited initial access to external financing. In addition, however, in many CIS countries the difficult process of implementing structural and institutional reforms has been slowed by the influence of vested interests. By contrast, in the EU accession candidates the requirements for accession helped create consensus on potentially divisive reforms. In China, WTO entry is performing a similar role. A major challenge for the CIS countries is to find a similarly effective focal point, either external or domestic, to promote needed structural and institutional reforms.

Even with such a focal point, much remains to be done in the transition countries that are being formally considered for EU accession, including continuing progress on building the infrastructure of a market economy and ensuring adequate enforcement and implementation of its essential principles and practices. At the same time, accession also provides challenges for existing EU members, including agreeing to reforms on such contentious issues as revised internal voting procedures and reforming the Common Agricultural Policy. It now seems questionable whether the European Union will admit new members by the end of 2002, as originally planned. Rapid agreement on such reforms would benefit existing members of the European Union, as well as ensuring that entry of qualified accession candidates will not be delayed.

Appendix I: Alternative Scenarios

The baseline forecast in this *World Economic Outlook* contains a scenario in which many of the imbalances currently facing the world economy are gradually eliminated while existing differences in growth rates of potential output are maintained. This appendix reports on two alternative scenarios constructed using MULTIMOD, the IMF's multicountry macroeconomic model, that explore the consequences of different outcomes. The first scenario discusses consequences of a more precipitous elimination of global imbalances (a "harder" landing in the United States).[8] The second scenario examines the effects of an acceleration of growth in Europe and Japan associated with more vigorous structural reforms that reduce current differences in the rate of growth of potential output across the major currency areas.

A "Harder Landing" in the United States

In the baseline forecast, the U.S. monetary authorities are able to engineer a smooth deceleration in activity that gradually brings the economy back to potential while inflation remains contained. While this is an entirely plausible projection, it needs to be acknowledged that forecasters in general have great difficulties in projecting cyclical turning points and also tend to underestimate the size of future movements

in output. In the alternative scenario reported here, it is assumed that greater-than-expected inflationary pressures in the United States lead to a tightening of monetary policy and a fall in stock market prices in the United States and abroad, as well as a depreciation in the dollar, and to slower global growth. It should be recognized, however, that there are other potential triggers of the financial turbulence at the heart of the scenario. For example, a reassessment of the extent of future productivity growth generated by the "new economy" could produce a similar response in asset markets even with no further moves by the U.S. Federal Reserve.

The "harder landing" scenario assumes that the U.S. economy experiences greater-than-expected inflationary pressure in late 2000, and that over the same period growth in U.S. domestic demand is also stronger than in the baseline. This evidence of overheating causes the U.S. Federal Reserve to tighten policy by more than is currently anticipated, to squeeze current and future inflation out of the system.[9] Some time in early 2001, this in turn causes financial markets to fundamentally reevaluate prospects for the U.S. economy, with expectations of the future growth of profits scaled back significantly. As a consequence, the U.S. stock market is assumed to fall by about 20 percent, with significant effects on the confidence of both consumers and producers.

The downgrade in the assessment of U.S. prospects by financial markets has several ramifications for the rest of the world:

- The dollar is assumed to depreciate as the United States becomes less attractive to international investors, reducing the capital flows that have been financing the record current account deficit. Given the weakness of the single European currency (euro) and the existence of significant capital flows

---

[8]This scenario is similar to one reported in the May 2000 *World Economic Outlook*, although the results differ both because of a slightly different formulation of the underlying disturbance and because of changes in MULTIMOD, including a different monetary policy reaction function.

[9]Both scenarios assume that the monetary authorities in the United States and elsewhere target inflation in a forward-looking manner and that the fiscal authorities let automatic stabilizers operate but take no other discretionary actions.

from the euro area to the United States (see Box 1.1), it is assumed that the value of the dollar falls by about a fifth versus the euro, and by about one-tenth versus the yen and the currencies of other industrial countries.

- The fall in the U.S. stock market (and confidence) is assumed to lead to more muted reductions in other advanced countries through international linkages across capital markets.[10] Again, these effects are assumed to be somewhat larger in the euro area (about a half of the size of the impact in the United States) than for Japan—whose stock market appears less correlated with the U.S. markets than countries in Europe—and other industrial countries (about a quarter of the size of the impact in the United States).

The results of this scenario are reported in Table 1.8. After stronger growth in 2000, real GDP growth in the United States—the epicenter of the financial market uncertainties—falls to 1¼ percent, a decline of slightly less than 2 percentage points, relative to baseline, in 2001. The response of domestic demand is somewhat larger, reflecting the impact of lower asset prices. Although initially somewhat limited by the need to contain inflationary pressures, easier monetary policies support a gradual recovery in activity over the next few years. By the end of the simulation, however, domestic demand remains significantly below baseline, reflecting the impact of reductions in wealth and the real value of the dollar, while reduced investment over the intervening period also leads to lower output. The current account improves throughout the simulation, rising by about 1 percent of GDP by 2004 relative to baseline.

The reduction in external demand from the United States depresses output in other advanced economies. By contrast, domestic demand remains relatively stable as the impact of the fall in wealth is offset by monetary easing, although in Japan the zero floor on interest rates

Table 1.8. Alternative Scenario: Harder Landing
(Percent deviation from baseline unless otherwise specified)

	2000	2001	2002	2003	2004
World GDP	**0.1**	**−1.1**	**−1.2**	**−0.7**	**−0.4**
United States					
Real GDP	0.3	−1.9	−2.1	−1.1	−0.7
Real domestic demand	0.4	−2.9	−3.3	−2.2	−1.7
CPI inflation	0.3	0.8	−0.7	−1.0	−0.8
Short-term interest rate	0.7	−0.9	−2.3	−1.8	−1.0
Real effective exchange rate	0.1	−10.4	−9.2	−9.1	−9.3
Current account ($ billion)	−11.5	15.9	81.2	118.2	133.8
Euro area					
Real GDP	0.1	−1.3	−1.4	−1.0	−0.5
Real domestic demand	—	0.2	0.1	0.2	0.4
CPI inflation	—	−1.6	−0.8	−0.9	−1.0
Short-term interest rate	0.1	−2.0	−2.7	−2.6	−2.6
Real effective exchange rate	−0.1	10.2	8.3	7.8	7.6
Current account ($ billion)	4.4	−26.5	−47.5	−58.6	−65.4
Japan					
Real GDP	0.1	−0.8	−0.9	−0.3	−0.2
Real domestic demand	—	−0.4	−0.4	−0.1	—
CPI inflation	—	−0.3	−0.5	−0.5	−0.5
Short-term interest rate	0.1	−0.2	−0.3	−1.0	−0.8
Real effective exchange rate	−0.3	2.6	3.0	2.7	2.4
Current account ($ billion)	3.3	−4.3	−19.1	−30.2	−27.1
Other industrial countries					
Real GDP	0.1	−0.5	−0.5	−0.1	0.1
Real domestic demand	—	0.1	0.4	0.6	0.8
Current account ($ billion)	5.0	−28.5	−39.6	−37.5	−37.3
Developing countries					
Real GDP	0.1	−0.5	−0.7	−0.5	−0.3
Domestic demand	0.2	−1.4	−1.3	−0.7	−0.4
Current account ($ billion)	−1.3	43.7	25.8	10.4	0.1
Memorandum items					
Real domestic demand					
Africa and others[1]	0.1	−1.2	−0.9	−0.3	−0.1
Asia	0.2	−1.3	−1.3	−0.8	−0.4
Latin America	0.2	−2.0	−1.8	−1.0	−0.5
Net creditors	—	−0.2	−0.3	−0.3	−0.3
Real GDP					
Africa and others[1]	—	−0.1	−0.2	−0.2	−0.1
Asia	0.2	−0.6	−0.7	−0.3	−0.1
Latin America	—	−0.4	−0.8	−0.9	−0.8
Net creditors	0.1	−1.0	−0.9	−0.4	−0.1

[1]Includes countries not in other groups.

constrains the degree of the policy response. The euro area experiences the most significant fall in output relative to baseline, reflecting the larger adjustment of the currency against the dollar (which also explains the larger deterioration in the region's current account balance) and domestic asset prices.

[10]See Chapter II of this *World Economic Outlook* and Chapter III of the May 2000 *World Economic Outlook* for a further discussion of this topic.

Developing countries are adversely affected by these developments in the industrial countries through a number of channels. The first is the direct impact of weaker activity in industrial countries on the demand for their exports. This is amplified by a fall in the real price of oil and nonfuel commodities coming from lower demand in the advanced world, which produces a negative terms-of-trade shock that further reduces domestic demand. In addition, financial turbulence and reduced export earnings constrain private external capital flows in the short term, creating more import compression, although over time the beneficial effects of lower borrowing costs due to easier monetary policies in the advanced countries reverse this effect.[11] For developing countries as a whole, the impact on output is relatively limited—real GDP falls by about ¾ percent compared to baseline and then recovers—but the reduction in domestic demand is about twice as large.

The effects of these forces vary by region. The negative impact is largest for Latin America, the region that is most exposed to a deceleration in U.S. activity and the vagaries of international capital flows, as well as having significant exports of commodities.[12] Asia is also affected by a slowdown in the United States through trade linkages, but the region as a whole is better placed to weather the impact of reduced capital inflows because of its stronger external position. Africa is relatively insulated from the direct effects of U.S. activity and private sector capital flows, and indeed benefits slightly from the appreciation of the euro given that Europe is the continent's major trading partner. However, output and demand fall compared to baseline because of the exposure of the continent to lower real commodity prices. Falling real oil prices also help explain the reduction in output in net creditor countries relative to baseline (essentially high income Middle Eastern oil exporters), where adverse movements in the terms of trade reduce activity and demand.

More Buoyant Growth in the Euro Area and Japan

A striking development of the last decade has been the divergence in performance among the major currency blocs. While U.S. growth has generally outperformed expectations, and estimates of the growth rate of potential output have been revised upwards, the opposite has occurred for Europe and Japan.[13] The baseline projection assumes that the rate of growth of potential output in the euro area and Japan stays relatively constant over the forecast period. It remains a distinct possibility, however, that the acceleration in performance seen in the United States over the latter half of the 1990s—based on flexible labor markets and new technologies—could be repeated over the next few years elsewhere. In particular, more aggressive reforms of continental European labor markets and a more conducive environment for Japanese economic restructuring could provide the basis for a sustained increase in the potential growth rate of these regions. Higher potential growth is also assumed in these simulations to lead to a significant appreciation of the euro and the yen, as market participants reevaluate the attractiveness of these regions for investment, leading to greater capital inflows and a deterioration in the external position.

The impact of increasing the rate of growth of potential output in the euro area and Japan from 2001 by ½ percent for 10 years is shown in

---

[11]MULTIMOD does not, however, incorporate the impact of falls in stock markets in advanced countries on domestic capital markets in developing countries.

[12]MULTIMOD only distinguishes between net debtor and net creditor developing countries. Results for separate groups of net debtor countries—Latin America, Asia, and Africa (which includes other countries)—were created by allocating the aggregate impact based on the geographic pattern of trade, the importance of commodities in total trade, and exposure to private capital markets.

[13]See "Growth Divergences in the United States, Europe and Japan: Trend or Cycle?" in the October 1999 *World Economic Outlook* for further discussion of these issues.

Table 1.9. Real output rises at about the new rate of potential growth in these regions, so that by 2004 it is around 2 percent above baseline.[14] Inflationary pressures remain subdued due to the increase in supply, which allows monetary policy to be mildly expansionary. Together with higher asset prices from higher expected growth, this means that domestic demand rises by more than output, particularly in the euro area. These effects continue to accumulate up to and beyond 2004, providing increasing benefits to the two regions.

The benefits to output in other industrial countries coming from faster growth in the euro area and Japan also build steadily over time. The boost comes largely from external demand, reflecting the real depreciation of the U.S. dollar and other currencies that form the counterpart to the appreciation of the euro and the yen. The increases in output compared to baseline are somewhat smaller for the United States than for the other industrial country group, reflecting the closer trade links of industrial economies in Europe and the Asia-Pacific region with the euro area and Japan. On the domestic side, more depreciated exchange rates lead to higher inflation that, in turn, requires somewhat tighter monetary policies and results in a fall in real domestic demand compared to baseline. Finally, more competitive exchange rates in the United States and elsewhere lead to a strengthening of the underlying external position.

Developing countries also benefit from higher growth in the euro area and Japan. Higher output in the industrial countries raises the demand for imports from the developing world, with an additional boost through higher commodity prices, while capital flows to emerging markets are relatively unaffected as higher investment in the euro area and Japan is largely financed domestically or from the other industrial countries. The benefits from faster growth largely accrue to Africa and Asia, with African countries gaining from their relatively close trade contacts to

Europe and higher commodity prices, while growth in developing countries in Asia is boosted by the expansion of activity in Japan. The impact on Latin American developing countries is more limited, reflecting their great sensitivity to U.S. interest rates.

Table 1.9. Alternative Scenario: Faster Growth in Euro Area and Japan
(Percent deviation from baseline unless otherwise specified)

	2000	2001	2002	2003	2004
World GDP	—	**0.2**	**0.5**	**0.8**	**1.0**
United States					
Real GDP	–0.1	0.2	0.3	0.3	0.4
Real domestic demand	–0.1	–0.1	–0.3	–0.4	–0.5
CPI inflation	0.1	0.2	0.3	0.3	0.4
Short-term interest rate	0.3	0.1	0.8	0.9	0.8
Real effective exchange rate	–1.0	–3.1	–4.7	–4.8	–4.7
Current account ($ billion)	2.1	8.2	19.6	31.7	45.2
Euro area					
Real GDP	0.1	0.2	1.1	1.5	1.9
Real domestic demand	0.3	0.7	2.0	2.7	3.2
CPI inflation	–0.2	–0.5	–0.5	–0.4	–0.4
Short-term interest rate	–0.5	–0.4	–0.8	–0.9	–0.6
Real effective exchange rate	1.0	3.4	5.0	5.2	5.2
Current account ($ billion)	–2.6	–4.9	–24.0	–40.1	–52.2
Japan					
Real GDP	0.1	0.3	1.0	1.5	2.0
Real domestic demand	0.2	0.5	1.4	2.0	2.7
CPI inflation	–0.1	–0.2	–0.1	–0.1	—
Short-term interest rate	–0.2	–0.2	–0.2	–0.1	0.2
Real effective exchange rate	0.9	3.1	4.2	4.2	4.1
Current account ($ billion)	3.6	6.8	3.4	–3.2	–11.2
Other industrial countries					
Real GDP	–0.1	0.3	0.3	0.5	0.9
Real domestic demand	–0.2	–0.3	–0.7	–0.8	–0.6
Current account ($ billion)	2.9	6.1	17.0	26.7	32.0
Developing countries					
Real GDP	—	0.1	0.2	0.2	0.3
Domestic demand	—	0.1	0.2	0.3	0.4
Current account ($ billion)	0.2	–6.8	–4.0	–3.6	–4.7
Memorandum items					
Real domestic demand					
Africa and others[1]	—	0.1	—	0.2	0.4
Asia	—	0.1	0.2	0.4	0.6
Latin America	—	0.2	0.2	0.2	0.2
Net creditors	—	—	—	—	—
Real GDP					
Africa and others[1]	—	—	0.1	0.2	0.4
Asia	—	0.1	0.3	0.4	0.5
Latin America	—	—	0.1	0.1	—
Net creditors	—	0.1	0.2	0.2	0.3

[1]Includes countries not included in other groups.

---

[14]There are some limited benefits in 2000, before the increase in potential output occurs, as asset markets anticipate the benefits of higher growth.

Figure 1.13. Global Current Account Discrepancy
(Percent of global imports of goods)

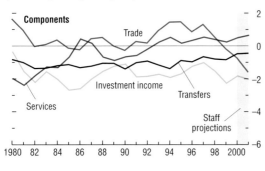

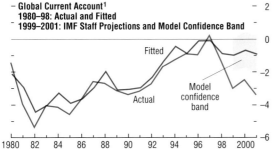

[1]The shaded area reflects the model confidence band for 1999–2001, and IMF staff projections of actual for 2000–01. The fitted values and the model confidence band are based on a paper by Jaime Marquez and Lisa Workman, "Modeling the IMF's Statistical Discrepancy in the Global Current Account." See text and their paper for details.

Appendix II: The Global Current Account Discrepancy

In principle, since the exports of one country are the imports of another, the current account balances of all countries in the world should sum to zero. In practice, however, this is not the case (see Figure 1.13, upper panel). Since the mid-1970s, the sum of all countries' current account balances has—except in 1997—been negative, giving the world in aggregate a measured current account deficit. In 1998, the last year for which complete data are available, this global current account discrepancy was about 1 percent of world imports, but preliminary data suggest that it increased sharply to 3 percent of world imports in 1999. Such a large and variable current account discrepancy is of particular concern at a time when substantial external current account imbalances in the three main currency areas are a major policy issue.

What are the underlying causes of the global current account discrepancy? While this is—by definition—a matter of great uncertainty, some clues can be found from examining the various components of the global current account (each of which should in principle also sum to zero). As Figure 1.13 shows, since the mid-1980s, the largest contributor has been a substantial deficit on the investment income account, with smaller, but still significant deficits on the transfers account. In contrast, the global trade account has been in surplus over much of the period, with the large increase in 1993 reflecting a change in European data collection practices. A recent paper by Jaime Marquez and Lisa Workman at the U.S. Federal Reserve Board, drawing on earlier work of the IMF, finds that the reasons for the measured discrepancies in the various accounts may include the following factors:[15]

---

[15]Jaime Marquez and Lisa Workman, "Modeling the IMF's Statistical Discrepancy in the Global Current Account" (unpublished; Washington: Federal Reserve Board, July 2000); *IMF Committee on Balance of Payments Statistics: 1998 Annual Report* (Washington: International Monetary Fund, 1999); and *Report on the World Current Account Discrepancy* (Washington: International Monetary Fund, 1987).

- *Transportation delays.* Exports can be recorded in one time period while the corresponding imports are recorded in the next because of time spent in shipment. Since the value of trade is generally expanding, this would tend to give rise to a positive discrepancy in the global trade balance.
- *Asymmetric valuation.* The same good or service can be recorded at different export and import values. This can occur when different exchange rates are used to value the same transaction or when exports are recorded at a subsidized price but the corresponding import is recorded at the market price.
- *Data quality.* Trade data quality can vary across countries causing an under reporting of credits or debits and discrepancies in the global accounts for goods, services, and income flows. This may be an especially large problem for transportation services and workers' remittances.
- *Underreporting of investment income.* Investment income is difficult to capture and therefore may go underreported in the balance of payments. The growth of offshore financial centers is making it more difficult for statistical agencies to track financial transactions.

To test these hypotheses, Marquez and Workman developed and estimated a model of the discrepancy for each element of the current account. As the lower panel of Figure 1.13 indicates, the model describes developments through 1998 reasonably well. The reduction in the global current account deficit in the mid-1980s is explained in part by falling interest rates, the rise in U.S. imports (which are thought to be better measured than other countries' imports), and the pickup in world trade growth (proxying the impact of transportation delays). The continued reduction in the global discrepancy after 1992 reflects the change in European data collection methods mentioned above. The apparent sharp deterioration in the current account discrepancy in 1999, however, falls somewhat outside of the model's confidence band (as measured by two standard deviations on each side of the model's expectation). This could suggest that the preliminary data for 1999 overstate the discrepancy, or that other factors that are not captured in the model have become important—for instance, valuation effects associated with exchange rate swings, or possibly changes in the quality of euro area current account data following the introduction of the euro in January 1999.

While the past global current account discrepancy is given, economic forecasters face a difficult challenge in projecting the current account discrepancy in the future. As discussed in past issues of the *World Economic Outlook*, the IMF global economic projections—along with those of most other forecasters—have tended to display a significantly rising discrepancy over time, often attributed to export pessimism. In producing the *World Economic Outlook* projections, the IMF staff follow an interactive procedure, under which a sharply widening global current account discrepancy triggers a reassessment of country projections. Nevertheless, in this *World Economic Outlook*, the projected global current account deficit falls outside of the confidence band of the Marquez–Workman model.[16] This may partly reflect the large and so far unexplained deterioration in 1999. An analysis of the components of the projected discrepancy shows that this is primarily due to the trade account, suggesting that the forecast may continue to exhibit some export pessimism. Correspondingly, there would be upside risks to GDP growth, and—if this export pessimism were in countries that face capacity constraints—to inflation as well. There is also a smaller widening in the projected deficit on the investment income account, which may reflect some underestimation of investment income receipts in creditor countries as a result of rising interest rates.

---

[16]For this exercise, the Marquez–Workman model is simulated over 1999–2001 using IMF staff projections for the necessary exogenous assumptions. These include the world price of oil, interest rates, global imports, and the U.S. share of global imports.

This chapter discusses in further detail some of the key issues facing the world economy (see Chapter I). Much of the chapter focuses on the nexus of increased productivity in the United States and some other countries in the late 1990s, its connection to technology (the "new economy"), and the consequences in terms of equity valuations and capital flows to emerging markets. As noted in Chapter I, these issues are closely linked to the imbalances and risks facing the global economy. In addition, the chapter looks at recent developments in commodity markets, including the oil market, another potential source of significant global risk.

The links between productivity growth and investment in information technology in the advanced economies are discussed first, focusing on the evidence of a "new economy" in the United States, the prospect that this could spread elsewhere, and some implications for the conduct of policies. Next, the consequences of the information technology revolution for asset prices are discussed across a wide range of advanced and emerging markets. The growing importance of the information technology sector has been associated with historically high price-earnings ratios in stock markets, greater equity price volatility, and stronger linkages of stock prices worldwide, implying that a correction of technology stocks would have important implications for both advanced and emerging market countries. The theme of financial stability and balanced economic growth worldwide is then carried forward into a review of recent developments in capital inflows to emerging markets. The implications of recent macroeconomic developments in the advanced economies ("push" factors), including the relationship between cap-

ital flows to emerging markets and developments in advanced countries' asset markets, as well as developments in emerging markets ("pull" factors) have contributed to the recovery in private financing since the Asian crisis.

Finally, the chapter reviews a rather separate issue, namely recent commodity market developments and their consequences for commodity exporting countries. While oil prices have rebounded sharply over the last 18 months, the prices of most non-fuel commodities have not recovered from their post-Asian crisis decline. This has led to large, negative terms of trade shocks for individual countries, particularly those that are heavily dependent on non-fuel commodity exports and must import oil. The hardest-hit countries are concentrated in Africa and are, regrettably, typically very poor, making the necessary adjustments all the more difficult but necessary to restore growth and reduce poverty.

Productivity Growth and IT in the Advanced Economies

Rapid economic growth in the United States over the past five years and the accompanying sharp increase in productivity growth have caused many observers to suggest that fundamental changes are under way in the U.S. economy. Recent evidence suggests that the pickup in productivity growth in the second half of the 1990s has been led by rapid advances in the information technology (IT) sector and the application of these technologies in other areas of the economy. This possibility of a "new economy" has sparked considerable interest in the United States and also in other faster-growing advanced economies, some of which have shown a similar pickup in productivity growth.[1] However, a num-

---

[1]Definitions of the "new economy" are not precise but typically include one or more of the following characteristics: (1) a higher rate of productivity growth related to investment in IT; (2) a rise in total factor productivity growth due to IT

ber of uncertainties remain, in particular whether these recent improvements in performance will spread to other economies that have yet to show new economy phenomena, and how sustainable they ultimately will prove to be.

The "New Economy" in the United States

The rapid pace of U.S. output growth in the second half of the 1990s was made possible—as in many other countries—by both rising labor utilization and accelerating labor productivity (Figure 2.1).[2] Expanding employment added approximately 1¾ percentage points to growth over the period, with this rise reflecting both an increasing labor force (1¼ percent a year) and a decline in the unemployment rate from 6 percent in 1994 to nearly 4 percent by early 1999. Productivity growth in the nonfarm business sector jumped to 2½ percent a year, compared with a relatively stable rate of 1½ percent a year during 1973–95. Since the rise in productivity growth is relatively recent, and given the empirical difficulties in identifying the causes and nature of productivity shocks, most analysts have been reluctant to conclude that there had been a change in trend, despite speculation that advances in IT may have played a role. However, this is starting to change as supporting evidence accumulates.

A rise in productivity growth can be linked to computers and information technology through three channels:

- *Direct productivity gains* in industries that produce information technology goods add to

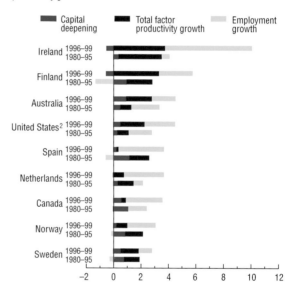

Figure 2.1. Faster-Growing Advanced Economies: Output, Employment, and Productivity Growth in the Business Sector[1]
(Percent)

Labor productivity growth is the sum of capital deepening and total factor productivity growth.

Sources: OECD Analytical Data Bank; and IMF staff estimates.

[1]The advanced economies with average income growth close to or above the median rate for 1996–99. Greece, Iceland, Korea, and Portugal were dropped from the sample because total factor productivity estimates are not available.

[2]Estimates for the United States are based on gross capital stock data to facilitate cross-country comparisons. Estimates in Table 2.1 are based on capital services, a preferred measure in productivity analysis. This difference can affect estimates of capital deepening and TFP growth.

---

utilization across the economy and resulting spillover effects (networking, increasing returns to scale); (3) an increase in factor utilization—for example, a decline in the nonaccelerating inflation rate of unemployment (NAIRU). See Paula R. De Masi, "Does the Pickup in Productivity Growth Mean That There Is a 'New Economy'?" *United States—Selected Issues,* (Washington: International Monetary Fund, 2000).

[2]Figure 2.1 shows average output growth in the business sector, and contributions to it from employment growth, capital deepening, and total factor productivity (TFP). By construction, labor productivity is equal to TFP plus capital deepening.

economy-wide productivity. These gains have driven computer and related equipment prices down, especially on a quality adjusted basis.

- *Capital deepening* increases the capital-labor ratio and therefore labor productivity through investment. Investment in information technologies has been strong, reflecting falling computer prices and new ways technology can help accomplish old tasks with fewer inputs.

- *Spillover* effects occur when returns to an investment increase because others make similar investments. Some positive effect is plausible with IT investment—for example, the returns to an internet-capable computer rise as more consumers and businesses connect to the internet.

An assessment of IT's impact on productivity growth is complicated by serious statistical problems. First, output and investment data for the IT sector are not readily available on a timely basis for many countries (the United States being a key exception), and therefore provide little information on technology's contribution to the recent increases in aggregate productivity. Second, real output in the IT sector may be mismeasured, or at least measured inconsistently across countries. The United States, Canada, and Japan are among the countries that adjust IT equipment price index data for quality improvements—for example, to account for a personal computer today being more powerful than last year's model that sold for the same price or more. To the extent that these new capabilities are incorporated in basic models and are not al-

ways fully used by consumers, however, price declines and real output increases would be overstated. Other countries (such as Germany and Italy) do not make this type of adjustment, and therefore data may understate output gains. Third, estimates of the capital services provided by IT equipment are subject to wide uncertainty because rapid technological progress itself makes it difficult to determine economic depreciation and useful service lives. Finally, the areas where output is likely to have the biggest impact—service industries—are those where output and productivity are the least well measured in the national accounts.

These problems notwithstanding, several new studies have concluded that IT accounted for about ½ to ¾ percentage point of the estimated one percentage point rise in U.S. productivity growth in the second half of the 1990s (Table 2.1).[3] Of this, investment in IT equipment (capital deepening) produced up to a ½ percentage point increase in productivity growth. There is a wider range of reported spillover effects, probably because these cannot be measured directly and are approximated in the studies by total factor productivity (TFP) calculations.[4] For the total economy, TFP is estimated to have contributed between ¼ and 1 percentage point to the increase in productivity growth. Of this, TFP growth in the IT sector itself contributed up to ½ percentage point, while TFP in all other sectors added up to ¾ percentage point to the increase in productivity growth.[5] One study that finds no spillover effects outside of the IT sector attributes ¾ percentage point of the observed productivity growth to cycle effects.[6]

---

[3]The recent studies that identify this link are cited in Table 2.1. Before 1999, the main issue was the lack of evidence linking productivity growth to IT. For example, see Stephen D. Oliner and Daniel E. Sichel, "Computers and Output Growth Revisited: How Big is the Puzzle?" *Brookings Papers on Economic Activity: 2*, Brookings Institution (1994), pp. 273–317.

[4]In the Solow growth accounting framework, TFP is a residual category that can capture spillover effects, and also other phenomena such as mismeasurement of capital and labor service inputs to production and other cyclical effects.

[5]Very high TFP growth rates in the IT sector translate into smaller contributions to growth in the whole economy because the IT sector represents only about 5 percent of total output. Stephen D. Oliner and Daniel E. Sichel, "The Resurgence of Growth in the Late 1990s: Is Information Technology the Story?" FED Working Paper 2000–20 (Washington: Federal Reserve Board, May 2000) estimate TFP growth in computer and semiconductor sectors as 16.6 percent and 45 percent, respectively, over 1996–99.

[6]Robert J. Gordon, "Does the 'New Economy' Measure up to the Great Inventions of the Past?" NBER Working Paper No. 7833 (Cambridge, Massachusetts: National Bureau of Economic Research, 2000).

Table 2.1. United States: Sources of the Acceleration in Labor-Productivity Growth, 1974–99[1]

	Study 1 Jorgenson and Stiroh 1990–95/ 1995–98	Study 2 Oliner and Sichel 1990–95/ 1995–99	Study 3 Whelan 1974–95/ 1996–98	Study 4 Council of Economic Advisors 1973–95/ 1995–99	Study 5 Gordon 1972–95/ 1995–99
Acceleration in labor productivity *Of which:*	0.9	1.0	1.0	1.5	0.7[2]
Capital deepening	0.3	0.5	. . .	0.5	0.3
Information technology sector	0.2	0.5	0.5	. . .	. . .
Other sectors	0.1	0.0	. . .	. . .	. . .
Lab or quality	–0.1	–0.1	. . .	0.1	0.1
Total factor productivity Production of information	0.7	0.7	. . .	0.9	0.3
technology goods	0.2	0.2	0.3	0.2	0.3
Other	0.5	0.5	. . .	0.7	0.0
All other factors	. . .	. . .	0.3	. . .	0.0
Memorandum Percent of acceleration in labor productivity related to information technology	44	64	73	. . .	. . .

Sources: *Study 1:* Dale Jorgenson and Kevin Stiroh, "Raising the Speed Limit: U.S. Economic Growth in the Information Age," *Brookings Papers on Economic Activity* (Washington, D.C., 2000); *Study 2:* Steven D. Oliner and Daniel E. Sichel, "The Resurgence of Growth in the Late 1990s: Is Information Technology the Story?" *Journal of Economic Perspectives* (forthcoming); *Study 3:* Karl Whelan, "Computers, Obsolescence, and Productivity," Board of Governors for the Federal Reserve Working Paper 2000-6 (Washington: Federal Reserve Board, May 2000); *Study 4:* Council of Economic Advisors, *Economic Report of the President* (Washington, D.C.: U.S. Government Printing Office, 2000); *Study 5:* Robert J. Gordon, "Does the 'New Economy' Measure up to the Great Inventions of the Past?" *Journal of Economic Perspectives* (forthcoming). Study 3 looks at computer equipment only. All others incorporate data on communications equipment and software.
[1]In percentage points.
[2]Structural acceleration in labor productivity that eliminates the increases associated with cyclical effects.

Will productivity growth continue at a high rate? There are no clear answers. Over the next few years, it is likely that the recent higher rates of productivity growth will persist as businesses adapt to new technologies such as the Internet. Productivity growth would come through further investment and capital deepening or spillover effects, for example, as workers and managers become increasingly familiar with the new technologies. There are risks, however, that productivity growth could slow in the near term. One set of risks is captured in the harder landing scenario in which greater than expected inflation pressures, tighter monetary policies, and a reevaluation of economic prospects by financial markets cause the U.S. economy to slow (see Appendix 1 to Chapter I). Weaker investment growth in this scenario would slow capital deepening and thus productivity growth. Another possibility is that some part of the recent pickup in productivity growth is cyclical, as noted above. Even though such an acceleration in productivity is not typical in a mature expansion, it is possible that firms have met an uptick in demand by intensifying resource use beyond normal, sustainable levels. If this proves true, productivity growth could slow.

From a longer-term perspective, it is possible that the United States is experiencing a shift in the level of productivity rather than its growth rate. While it is difficult to distinguish the two when productivity is rising, and indeed there may be little practical difference during this period, it is important to note that a permanent productivity pickup implies continuous innovation. But almost by definition, the effects of innovations such as the personal computer, the Internet, and their useful purposes are impossible to predict with certainty.[7] Thus, policymakers face unavoid-

[7]The phenomenal gains in computer technology have fueled IT-related growth. This is captured by Moore's law: that is, computer power doubles every 18–24 months. Some scientists believe that Moore's Law may be in jeopardy because of physical limits to miniaturization. See Paul A. Pakan, "Pushing the Limits," *Science*, Vol. 285, No. 5436 (September 24, 2000), pp. 2079–80.

able uncertainty concerning both near- and longer-term productivity prospects. The implications for the conduct of monetary policies under this uncertainty are discussed in the concluding part of this section; implications for financial markets are discussed in the following section.

What Is the Scope for New Economies Elsewhere?

Several other advanced economies performed as well or better than the United States in terms of economic growth in the second half of the 1990s (see Figure 2.1).[8] In Canada, the Netherlands, and Spain, economic growth appears to have primarily reflected labor market developments, with structural reforms paving the way for strong employment growth. In the remaining countries in Figure 2.1, labor productivity gains owing to TFP or capital deepening contributed to output growth. While very little analytic work has been done on the role of IT in productivity increases, interest is growing. New studies are under way but have not yet reached firm conclusions.[9]

What is the evidence so far? Australia has experienced a pickup in labor productivity through TFP growth and capital deepening while Ireland, Finland, and Sweden have experienced pickups to varying degrees through TFP growth (see Figure 2.1).[10] The extent to which these contributions to growth can be attributed to IT is not clear, however. Capital deepening through investment in IT equipment may be

contributing to the aggregate growth shown in Figure 2.1, as these countries spent at least five percent of GDP on IT equipment in 1997, the most recent year for which data are available (Figure 2.2). The TFP growth for the business sector shown in Figure 2.1 could partly reflect the spillover effects of a new economy, but the magnitudes—especially for Ireland and Finland—are far larger than the IT spillover effects estimated for the United States (up to one percentage point). This suggests that much of the increase in productivity growth is probably coming from other areas. More research is needed to estimate the impact of IT using sector-specific, detailed data.

High productivity growth in the IT sector itself also may be contributing to aggregate productivity gains in some cases. In Finland and Sweden, IT equipment accounts for approximately 4 to 5 percent of output in each economy, well above most other advanced economies. While still a relatively small part of each economy, the IT sector could be adding about ¼ percentage point to economy-wide productivity growth, assuming that productivity growth in the industry is similar to that in the United States.[11] At the same time, not all higher productivity countries have a significant IT producing sector. IT spending as a share of GDP is extremely high in Australia, but production of IT equipment is a small share of total output (see Figure 2.2).[12]

Will the effects of IT spread to industrial countries beyond the United States? The answer

---

[8]The comparison periods 1980–95 and 1996–99 reflect data limitations and the pickup in U.S. economic growth. They are therefore somewhat arbitrary for other advanced economies.

[9]Paul Schreyer, "The Contribution of Information and Communication Technology to Output Growth: A Study of the G-7 Countries," OECD Working Paper 2000/02 (Paris: Organization for Economic Cooperation and Development, 2000).

[10]Capital deepening in Ireland and Finland lowered business sector output growth somewhat. This is because capital deepening reflects changes in the capital-labor ratio, which fell in these countries over the period because of very strong employment growth.

[11]This should be seen as a very rough estimate, and depends on the relative share of IT production in the economy and the share of IT production going to intermediate inputs (which in theory do not add directly to GDP productivity) or final consumption or investment goods (which do add to GDP productivity). The Swedish Ministry of Finance has estimated that productivity growth in the IT sector has contributed about ½ percentage point to aggregate labor productivity growth in recent years.

[12]Ranil Salgado, "Australia: Productivity Growth and Structural Reform," *Australia: Selected Issues and Statistical Appendix,* IMF Staff Country Report No. 00/24, (Washington: International Monetary Fund, March 2000), pp. 3–33, finds that reforms in Australia's trade and product markets are important in explaining the observed improvement in productivity growth.

is almost certainly yes, but the speed and scope are uncertain. Spending on IT equipment is a significant share of business sector output in most of these economies, and in principle there is no reason why IT should not play a role similar to that in the United States, with the exception in many cases of the contribution of the IT equipment sector. The timing will depend on several factors, however, including a high rate of investment in IT capital and a supportive environment.[13] Some studies indicate that productivity gains lag IT investment because of the learning needed to use the new technology efficiently.[14] The learning process could explain why IT did not boost productivity before the 1990s in the United States and why more definitive signs are not seen elsewhere. In this connection, structural reforms to ensure dynamic and mobile labor markets, available capital for start-ups, and entry into the telecommunications sector are an important part of fostering profitable IT investment. IT is also likely to have an impact on other advanced and emerging markets—some of which have very large IT sectors (see Figure 2.2)—provided the structural conditions just listed are in place.

New Economy Uncertainties and Policy Responses

Faster productivity growth is clearly a welcome development that raises living standards. The uncertainties related to a possible change in pro-

Figure 2.2. Advanced Economies: Expenditure and Production of Information and Communication Technology, 1997[1]
(Percent of GDP)

Spending on information and communication technologies exceeded 5 percent of total economy output in most countries. Production varied considerably.

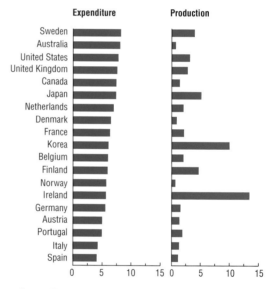

Sources: OECD Analytical Data Bank; and *OECD Information Technology Outlook 2000* (Paris: Organization for Economic Cooperation and Development, 2000).
[1]Data not available for Hong Kong SAR, Iceland, Israel, Luxembourg, Singapore, and Taiwan Province of China.

---

[13]The impact of IT investment on productivity growth will depend on the relative share of IT equipment in the total capital stock and thus the past path of IT spending. Schreyer, "The Contribution of Information and Communication Technology to Output Growth," estimates that as of 1996, the share of IT equipment (including communications) in the nominal productive capital stock was in the 2 to 3 percent range in France, western Germany, Italy, and Japan; around 5 percent in Canada and the United Kingdom; and 7½ percent in the United States.

[14]Jeremy Greenwood and Mehmet Yorukoglu, "1974," *Carnegie-Rochester Conference Series on Public Policy*, Vol. 46 (June 1997), pp. 49–95. Also see Michael T. Kiley "Computers and Growth With Costs of Adjustment: Will the Future look like the Past," FED Working Paper 1999–36 (Washington: Federal Reserve Board, July 1999).

Figure 2.3. Illustrative Country Scenario: New Economy Uncertainty and Monetary Policy[1]

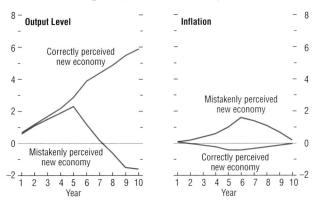

Identifying a Productivity Shock is Initially Difficult
(percent, deviations from baseline)

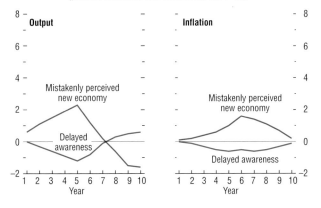

Consequences of Perception Errors[1]
(percent, deviations from productivity scenarios)

Source: IMF MULTIMOD simulations.
[1]The "correctly perceived" and "mistakenly perceived" simulations are compared to the *World Economic Outlook* baseline. The "delayed awareness" simulation is compared to a special baseline in which productivity growth increases by ½ percentage point a year starting in 2000. This increase is correctly perceived by both the central bank and the private sector. The deviations in output show the variability due to the central bank mistake.

ductivity growth, however, pose two related challenges for policymakers, namely identifying a shock when it occurs and determining how to respond to the uncertainties inherent when the growth rate of productivity is changing. Three simulations using the IMF's global macroeconomic model, MULTIMOD, are used to illustrate these challenges.[15]

In the first simulation, the central bank and the private sector correctly perceive that productivity growth has increased by ½ percentage point a year starting in 2000. The higher rate of productivity growth raises the private sector's expectations of returns to investment and future wealth and in consequence domestic demand and output increase (Figure 2.3, the "Correctly Perceived New Economy," in the upper panel). Inflationary consequences are absent because higher productivity growth raises aggregate supply. This outcome can be compared with a simulation in which the central bank and the private sector mistakenly perceive a positive productivity shock of the same size ("Mistakenly Perceived New Economy"). In the first few years, demand and output rise in a very similar manner to the first scenario, through the same expectations channels described above. After a few years, however, the inflationary consequences of the mistake in productivity expectations begin to emerge as the economy's potential supply does not increase as expected, providing a signal that productivity expectations may be incorrect. Hence, in the short term, it may be quite difficult to identify a "true" productivity increase. After five years, when it is assumed that people realize that productivity growth has not increased, output declines, falling significantly below the baseline scenario as earlier excess investment and consumption are reversed.

Given that identifying a "true" productivity increase may be difficult, it is also useful to examine the costs of the central bank making an in-

[15]See Tamim Bayoumi and Benjamin L. Hunt, "New Economy or Not: What Should the Monetary Policy Maker Believe?" (unpublished; Washington: International Monetary Fund, May 2000).

correct assumption about the productivity growth rate. The lower panel of Figure 2.3 reproduces the "Mistakenly Perceived New Economy" scenario discussed above in which both the central bank and the private sector mistakenly believe in higher productivity growth. This is compared with a "Delayed Awareness" scenario that illustrates the economic costs when the central bank fails to recognize a true rise in productivity growth of ½ percentage point. The central bank's error in this case (which is not shared by the private sector) causes it to run an inappropriately tight monetary policy that in the short term reduces wealth, domestic demand, and output relative to the alternative situation in which the productivity growth increase is correctly perceived by all parties. After five years, when the central bank is assumed to become aware of its mistake, interest rates are lowered and demand increases as the private sector makes up for lost investment and consumption opportunities. The scenarios indicate that these mistakes lead to relatively similar amounts of macroeconomic instability, and that this instability rises rapidly over time, thereby putting a premium on recognizing any policy error at the earliest possible moment.

The policy lesson from this analysis is that, in a situation when future productivity growth is highly uncertain, the costs of maintaining an inappropriate policy rise rapidly with time. Hence, when facing a potential shift in productivity growth, central banks should be particularly flexible and make use of a wide range of analytic tools in assessing the policy stance.[16] In particular, it is important to operate in a pragmatic fashion when exploring the limits to noninflationary growth, including placing weight on a wide range of direct indicators of economic performance and less emphasis on constructs such as the output gap (which depends on assumptions about trend productivity growth).

Developments in Global Equity Markets

Recent Trends

Fuelled by robust economic growth in the United States, an improved macroeconomic outlook for the world economy, and favorable liquidity conditions around the Year 2000 (Y2K) transition, stock prices staged a worldwide rally in the second half of 1999 through February 2000 (Figure 2.4).[17] Reflecting continuing upbeat sentiment about the growth prospects of the IT sector, the rally was especially pronounced for IT stocks, with the benchmark indicator of market developments in the sector—the U.S. NASDAQ stock index—rising by 80 percent between end-June 1999 and its mid-March 2000 peak.[18]

With Y2K transition fears behind, oil prices climbing up, and robust economic growth in the United States continuing into the first quarter of 2000 *pari passu* with expectations of faster growth in the euro area, inflation concerns have been intensifying and monetary conditions in advanced countries have tightened since March. In an environment where price-earnings ratios were at record highs, interest rate increases by the U.S. Federal Reserve and the European Central Bank triggered a downward revision in stock valuations. Stock prices fell sharply between mid-March and late May and, despite some recovery since, by early September most indices remained below their early 2000 peaks. In the United States and other advanced countries, the drop was largely felt in the IT sector. Because this sector's stock market capitalization has increased markedly in recent years, the decline in several stock indices in advanced economies largely reflected the drop in IT stock prices. Among emerging markets, stock prices also fell generally during March–May and, while staging a partial recovery in some countries, stock prices remain well below early 2000 peaks

---

[16]Similar arguments are made in Lars P. Hansen and Thomas J. Sargent, "Wanting Robustness in Macroeconomics," presented at the Ninth International Conference at the Bank of Japan (July 2000) and Tiff Macklem, "Discussion of Wanting Robustness in Macroeconomics," presented at the same conference.

[17]For evidence on the positive relationship between global liquidity and stock prices, see Chapter II, "The Ongoing Recovery in Emerging Market Economies" in the May 2000 *World Economic Outlook*.

[18]The IT sector includes telecommunications and media technologies.

Figure 2.4. Equity Price Indices
(1995 = 100)

Stock prices rallied between late 1999 and early 2000, but have come down since in most countries.

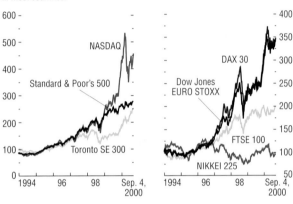

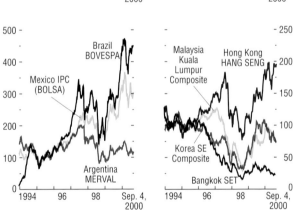

Source: Primark Datastream.

in other countries. This is notably the case in a few Asian economies where the IT sector has grown briskly over the past year.

While the differential behavior between stock prices in the IT and non-IT (or "traditional") sectors has received much attention recently, this phenomenon has in fact been under way since the mid-1990s, and has not been exclusive to the United States or even to advanced countries.[19] Figure 2.5 shows the extent of the price bifurcation between IT and "traditional" stocks in a number of advanced and developing countries, scaled by earnings.[20] The prospect of faster earnings growth associated with the diffusion of the internet and the development of new telecommunication technologies, combined with expectations that the bulk of these earnings will come on stream farther into the future, have led prices of IT stocks to rise far more rapidly than the prices of non-IT stocks and, indeed, than current earnings in the IT sector itself. This has produced price-earnings (P/E) ratios several times higher than those of traditional stocks.[21] Partly because of this much faster growth in IT stock prices, and partly because some IT firms have gained market share at the expense of older incumbents, the share of the IT sector in total stock market capitalization has risen markedly in advanced countries as well as in some emerging economies (Table 2.2).

[19]The empirical analysis in the remainder of this chapter is based on the breakdown between IT versus non-IT sectors provided by Datastream Primark. The definition and coverage of the IT sector may differ somewhat from other individual country sources. However, the use of a single source for all countries is better suited to the type of cross-country comparative analysis conducted here. See Table 2.2 for the list of industries included under the respective definition of IT stocks.

[20]A similar picture emerges if stock prices alone (i.e., without scaling by earnings) are plotted. This is not presented here to avoid duplication. The advantages of focusing on P/E ratios will become clearer in the subsequent discussion.

[21]Although P/E ratios in the IT sector have come down since March, they remain far higher historical averages in most countries. In the United States, for instance, the average P/E ratio for the S&P 500 in the post-war period is about 16, having risen to an all-time high of 32 at end-1999. In contrast, the average P/E ratio for the NASDAQ peaked at 186 in March 2000.

Table 2.2. Market Capitalization of Information Technology Stocks as a Share of Total Market Capitalization[1]

	1990	1995	1999
North America	18.3	21.6	33.1
Canada	18.3	17.9	27.9
United States	18.3	21.8	33.3
Europe	8.5	10.4	19.4
Belgium	0.2	0.3	3.8
France	10.7	8.8	19.8
Germany	3.5	6.2	22.9
Ireland	2.1	3.2	9.1
Italy	11.7	16.2	27.7
Netherlands	5.2	13.9	12.6
Spain	9.3	10.2	17.2
United Kingdom	12.0	12.9	18.8
Finland	8.7	40.2	71.3
Asia	10.4	12.6	22.3
China	. . .	. . .	4.3
Hong Kong SAR	16.0	10.9	18.0
India	0.2	8.4	19.9
Korea	0.4	5.1	18.2
Malaysia	2.9	12.8	12.1
Thailand	3.0	25.5	14.8
Singapore	3.9	28.9	27.0
Japan	11.1	12.4	23.9
Latin America	. . .	17.0	29.3
Argentina	. . .	31.8	28.4
Brazil	. . .	14.7	39.7
Chile	14.4	8.6	11.2
Mexico	25.5	23.4	25.2

[1]IT stocks are defined to include stocks issued by enterprises that provide the following goods and services: computer hardware, semiconductors, telecom equipment, computer service, Internet, software, telecom fixed line, telecom wireless, broadcasting, cable and satellite, media agencies, publishing, and printing. Because of differences of coverage, the ratios reported in this table may differ from those obtained using other indices.

Behind these aggregate national figures on IT market capitalization, there are substantial regional differences in sector composition. While the IT sector in Asia largely consists of computer (hardware and software) technology and internet firms, the IT sector in the emerging countries of the Western Hemisphere and Europe is dominated by a few large firms operating in the telecommunications and media subsector (Table 2.3). Moreover, in some of the Asian countries, IT firms are primarily engaged in the production and export of semi-conductor technology and computer equipment, whereas Western Hemisphere telecom and media companies that issue equity cater largely to domestic markets.

Figure 2.5. Price-Earnings Ratios for Information Technology (IT) vs. Non-IT Sector
(Percent)

Stock prices have gone up much faster than earnings in the information technology sector.

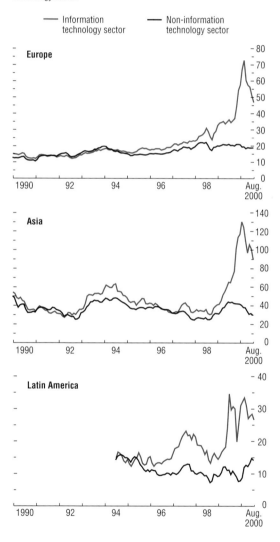

Figure 2.5 *(concluded)*

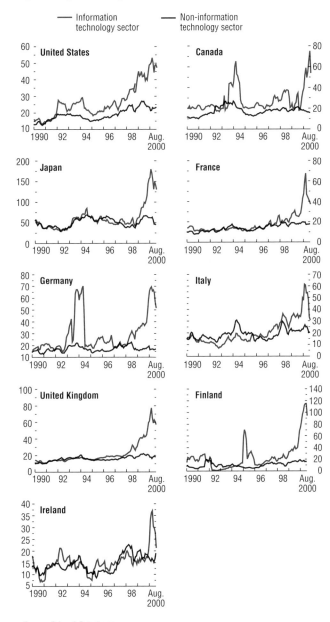

Source: Primark Datastream.

Table 2.3. Decomposition of the IT Sector into Telecommunications and Computer Subsectors
(Percent of total market capitalization)

	December 1997	December 1998	December 1999	June 2000
Computer Software, Hardware, and Internet				
North America	10.8	14.3	20.2	24.5
Europe[1]	1.7	2.0	3.2	5.0
Asia	4.9	5.2	10.9	11.9
Latin America	0.0	0.0	0.1	0.1
Telecommunications				
North America	9.6	12.1	16.2	16.8
Europe[1]	8.7	12.3	19.8	21.8
Asia	9.1	10.5	18.1	16.2
Latin America	16.4	29.7	31.0	30.1

Source: Datastream Primark.
[1]European Union member countries plus Switzerland.

The stock price bifurcation between IT and non-IT sectors, and the rising market capitalization of the technology sector worldwide, has been accompanied by growing international correlation of IT stock prices. Indeed, the growing internationalization of capital markets over the past decade has raised crossborder correlations of stock prices in general, and tech stocks in particular. Simple correlation measures between IT stock prices in the United States—the leading country in the new information technology— and in three other geographical areas (Asia, Europe, and Latin America) show that, over the past two and a half years, changes in IT stock prices have been more correlated internationally than those of non-IT stocks. More strikingly, this correlation has increased since early 1999, while the correlation for non-IT stocks has generally decreased (Table 2.4).

Within individual countries, IT stocks have also been more volatile than traditional stocks, in some cases by a substantial margin (Figure 2.6). This volatility appears to be on the rise, particularly since mid-1999. Thus, in addition to a bifurcation in terms of price *levels* and price-earnings ratios, recent years have witnessed a bifurcation in the stock price volatilities between the two sectors. The increased weight of IT stocks in national stock market indices helps explain some of the rise in aggregate stock market volatility worldwide.

Table 2.4. International Correlations of Stock Price Changes[1]

IT stocks (January 1995-May 2000)

	United States	EU	Asia	Latin America
United States	1			
EU	0.77	1		
Asia	0.59	0.50	1	
Latin America	0.44	0.50	0.56	1

Non-IT stocks (January 1995-May 2000)

	United States	EU	Asia	Latin America
United States	1			
EU	0.78	1		
Asia	0.40	0.39	1	
Latin America	0.43	0.46	0.44	1

IT stocks (January 1999-May 2000)

	United States	EU	Asia	Latin America
United States	1			
EU	0.85	1		
Asia	0.75	0.62	1	
Latin America	0.54	0.60	0.62	1

Non-IT stocks (January 1999-May 2000)

	United States	EU	Asia	Latin America
United States	1			
EU	0.54	1		
Asia	0.35	0.44	1	
Latin America	0.26	0.24	0.38	1

Source: Datastream Primark and staff estimates.
[1]Based on monthly data in U.S. dollars. EU figures include data for Switzerland.

Possible Causes of Stock Market Bifurcation

These developments raise three main questions. First, as the new information and communications technology becomes increasingly available to both new and older firms, why is there a marked bifurcation in stock valuations between these two groups? Second, why have IT stocks been more volatile than traditional stocks? Third, what explains the closer international correlation of IT stock prices relative to the non-IT stocks?

Although there is no established view on the matter, recent research has shed useful light on these questions. It has been argued, for instance, that the IT "revolution" favors new (and often smaller) firms, since old incumbents have a comparative disadvantage in adopting the new tech-

Figure 2.6. Selected Regions: Equity Price 12-Month Volatility
(Percent)

Stock price volatility has increased since the mid-1990s, particularly in the information technology sector.

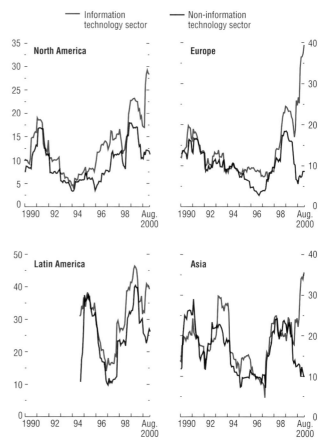

Sources: Primark Datastream; WEFA, Inc.; and IMF staff estimates.

nology due to high "sunk" costs.[22] Also, times of major technological change may tend to favor younger entrepreneurs who are better equipped to cope with the uncertainties of implementing a new technology.[23] The fact that old management practices die hard and well-established interest groups in older firms tend to be less receptive to radical changes in the production process also helps explain why younger firms tend to profit more from new technologies. Although, in principle, takeovers should gradually help eliminate less efficient firms and do away with this source of price bifurcation, institutional barriers to takeovers make the process much slower in practice.[24]

Arguments derived from the literature on technological change and industrial organization also help explain why the price volatility of new IT stocks is larger than that of traditional stocks. Once it is accepted that the commercial implementation and diffusion of new technologies are inherently riskier, it follows that earnings in the sector will often turn out to be disappointing, and tend to be more volatile in general. Indeed, while earnings in the IT sector as a whole in the United States turned positive after 1995, their volatility has increased despite the relative stability of aggregate demand growth and the decline in earnings volatility in the tradi-

tional sector. Since stock prices tend to respond sharply to "bad news," and given historical evidence that the short-run elasticity of stock prices to actual earnings growth is significantly greater than one,[25] higher volatility of earnings tends to produce an even greater volatility of stock prices. Moreover, corporate performance in the sector has been highly heterogeneous. As the IT sector is comprised of a few large firms alongside a large number of small firms operating in a fiercely competitive environment, survival rates tend to be lower. And insofar as small firms tend to be financially more fragile than well-established conglomerates and more dependent on capital markets for financing their current operations, both earnings prospects and survival rates of IT firms tend to be more vulnerable to macroeconomic shocks and changes in investors' appetite for risk.[26]

It is possible that these factors, which seem to account for the high volatility of IT stock prices relative to traditional stocks in the United States, may also help explain the volatility of IT stock prices at a global level. While more research is needed in this area, it is plausible that with falling barriers to the international diffusion of new technology, technology-intensive sectors in different countries are now more influenced by shocks in one country than in the past.[27] With

[22]This "sunk cost" argument has been widely developed in the context of vintage capital growth models. For a brief discussion and useful references on the topic, see Bart Hobijin and Boyan Jovanovic, "The Information Technology Revolution and the Stock Market: Evidence," NBER Working Paper No. 7684, (Cambridge, Massachusetts: National Bureau of Economic Research, May 2000).

[23]See Thomas Holmes and James Schmitz, "A Theory of Entrepreneurship and its Application to the Study of Business Transfers," *Journal of Political Economy,* Vol. 98, No. 2 (April 1990), pp. 265–294.

[24]This argument is developed in Hobijin and Jovanovic, "The Information Technology Revolution and the Stock Market."

[25]Using U.S. data since 1880, Barsky and De Long (1993) show that a 1 percent growth in dividends (or equivalently earnings) is typically associated with a 1.5 percent increase in stock prices in the short run. See Robert Barsky and J. Bradford De Long, "Why Does the Stock Market Fluctuate?" *Quarterly Journal of Economics,* Vol. 108 (May 1993), pp. 291–311.

[26]A recent econometric study using post-war U.S. data finds that small firms' stock returns are not only more cyclical than those of large firms but also the dispersion of small firms' earnings is higher during cyclical contractions than during cyclical expansions. This implies that the imminence of a slowdown in economic activity tends to raise the risk premia for those firms (or equivalently, lower their stock returns), and vice versa. See Gabriel Perez-Quiros and Allan Timmermann, "Firm Size and Cyclical Variations in Stock Returns," *Journal of Finance,* forthcoming. Evidence on the greater financial vulnerability of the IT sector can be gauged from the fact that several major Internet companies depend on frequent access to capital markets to finance their current operations.

[27]Empirical analysis of the breakdown of country versus industry-specific effects on stock returns indicates that country effects loom significantly larger. See Steven L. Heston and K. Geert Rouwenhorst, "Industry and Country Effects in International Stock Returns," *Journal of Portfolio Management,* Vol. 21 (Spring 1995), pp. 53–58. However, this and other studies dating back to the mid-1990s do not provide a breakdown of country versus industry-specific effects between IT and non-IT industries, which could possibly tilt the balance of their findings in the opposite direction.

the United States taking a leading role in IT, it follows that most such shocks will tend to stem from the U.S. market. Moreover, the fact that the United States is the home country of most IT companies operating internationally also tends to induce investors in the IT sector in other countries to be guided by market developments in the United States. In sum, to the extent that fluctuations in IT stock prices in the United States are viewed as indicating the industry's future prospects in other regions, this will tend to produce the high cross-country correlations in the price of IT stocks observed in the data.

Some Implications

The discussion above highlighted the growing importance of the IT sector and its association with historically high P/E ratios in stock markets around the globe, greater volatility of equity prices, and stronger international linkages of stock prices worldwide. As will be discussed in the next section, there is also evidence that a higher proportion of international capital flows is being influenced by such price fluctuations. These trends have some potentially important macroeconomic implications for both advanced and emerging countries.

In advanced countries, despite some drop in recent months, P/E ratios for IT remain very high relative to both historical standards and P/E ratios in emerging markets. Although it is hard to establish the extent to which this represents an overvaluation of such stocks relative to fundamentals, high P/E ratios have been historically associated with lower future stock returns and, often, with sharp market corrections.[28] Thus, to the extent that the growing bifurcation in stock markets since the late 1990s has been as-

sociated with very high P/E ratios, it raises the risk of a large market correction.[29] The macroeconomic implications of such a correction would tend to be more severe in the United States, where stock market capitalization is higher and the wealth effects are deemed to be larger, but far from negligible in other advanced countries (see Table 2.4).[30]

Regarding emerging markets, one obvious implication of the continuing diffusion of the technology sector is to increase emerging market exposure to fluctuations in IT prices originating in the developed world. Such an impact, however, is bound to differ significantly across the different countries, as the ratio of IT stock market capitalization to GDP varies widely (Figure 2.7). Moreover, it has been seen that the composition of the IT sector differs substantially across regions, being comprised mainly of Internet and computer hardware and software companies in Asia, and of telecoms and media companies in Western Hemisphere emerging markets. For the most part, Asia leads the latter region in the diffusion of new technology, explaining the higher correlation between IT stock price fluctuations in Asia and the United States (see Table 2.4). This suggests that a steep downward correction in tech stock prices in the advanced world is likely to have a more significant negative impact on the stock market and output in Asia than in other regions. Since a higher share of output and investment in Asia is stock market financed, the impact would also tend to be significant via domestic investment and balance-of-payments channels, with capital inflows into IT industries tending to slow and the export price of semiconductors and computer equipment declining.

Despite these near-term risks, the rapid expansion of IT sectors in emerging markets has the

---

[28]See John Y. Campbell, "Asset Prices, Consumption, and the Business Cycle," in *Handbook of Macroeconomics,* edited by John Taylor and Michael Woodford (New York: Elsevier, 1999).

[29]See Chapter III in the May 2000 *World Economic Outlook* and the September 2000 *International Capital Markets Report.*

[30]Estimates typically indicate that wealth effects arising from the stock market are in the order of 3 to 5 cents on the dollar for the United States, and somewhat lower in other advanced countries. It is possible, however, that the magnitude of wealth effects may be changing with greater stock market bifurcation but the direction is not clear. On the one hand, changes in IT stock prices may lead to smaller wealth effects than changes in the price of traditional stocks, if volatile changes in IT stock prices are viewed as temporary rather than permanent. On the other hand, as a larger portion of IT stocks are bought on margin calls, their wealth effects will tend to be higher.

Figure 2.7. Market Value of Information Technology Stocks, 1999
(Percent of GDP)

The weight of the information technology sector in the economy has varied widely across countries and regions.

North America and Europe

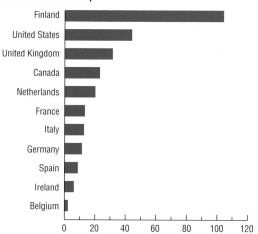

Asia and Latin America

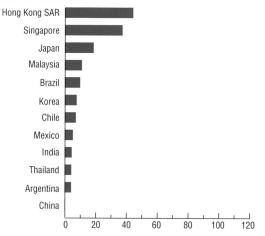

Sources: Primark Datastream; and IMF staff estimates.

potential to yield sizable longer-term benefits. One is related to the capacity of IT industries to finance their investment needs through the stock market, as witnessed by recent developments in the developed world as well as in some emerging economies in Asia. Wherever stock market capitalization is low and the banking system is less efficient in allocating resources to investment, the expansion of the IT sector may be instrumental in boosting savings and fostering financial deepening more generally, even though at first IT firms may be held back by similar institutional barriers that hampered equity financing for traditional sectors and caused stock market capitalization to be very low in some of these countries. At the same time, the higher productivity of IT industries, if maintained and spread further, will tend to raise potential output worldwide, benefiting both advanced and emerging countries. Finally, as documented in the next section, expanding IT sectors have been associated with higher equity capital inflows to emerging markets. Provided that such investment is fairly priced (and not mainly the result of a bubble in IT valuations), a higher share of IT-related investment in total emerging market financing may contribute to the longer-term financing of current account deficits in the emerging world and a more efficient allocation of world savings.

International Capital Flows to Emerging Markets

Recent Developments

Following robust growth earlier in the decade, capital flows to emerging markets fell sharply between mid-1997 and end-1998, in the wake of the financial crises that hit Asia and Russia. The recovery from the trough in the last quarter of 1998—when gross private financing to emerging markets had fallen to nearly a third of the level just prior to the Asian crisis—has been uneven. After remaining relatively subdued through 1999, gross private sector financing to emerging markets boomed in the first quarter of 2000, before dropping again in the second quarter (Table 2.5). Moreover, this volatility has been

Table 2.5. Gross Private Financing to Emerging Market Economies
(Billions of U.S. dollars)

	1997	1998	1999	1999 Q1	1999 Q2	1999 Q3	1999 Q4	2000 Q1	2000 Q2	2000 Apr.	2000 May	2000 Jun.
Total	292.5	150.2	173.2	32.6	53.1	34.7	52.8	73.0	55.2	16.1	8.8	30.3
Asia	128.6	35.0	62.9	11.9	17.1	17.4	16.5	29.6	25.3	10.8	3.2	11.3
Europe	37.7	35.9	26.0	3.2	7.9	5.1	9.8	9.5	9.5	2.8	0.9	5.8
Middle East and Africa	30.9	13.1	20.1	4.4	6.0	2.4	7.2	7.7	6.4	0.3	1.1	5.0
Western Hemisphere	95.3	66.1	64.2	13.2	22.0	9.8	19.3	26.2	14.0	2.2	3.6	8.2
Bond issues	133.2	80.2	87.0	21.8	27.5	15.9	21.8	36.4	16.0	2.6	3.7	9.8
Asia	45.5	12.4	24.1	7.0	6.3	6.2	4.7	8.7	4.0	1.3	0.6	2.1
Western Hemisphere	59.0	40.2	42.2	10.8	14.1	6.9	10.5	18.7	6.6	1.0	2.4	3.2
Other regions	28.7	27.6	20.6	4.1	7.1	2.9	6.5	9.1	5.4	0.4	0.6	4.4
Other fixed income	19.7	1.0	0.0	0.0	0.0	0.0	0.0	0.0	0.0	0.0	0.0	0.0
Asia	9.8	0.5	0.0	0.0	0.0	0.0	0.0	0.0	0.0	0.0	0.0	0.0
Western Hemisphere	0.0	0.0	0.0	0.0	0.0	0.0	0.0	0.0	0.0	0.0	0.0	0.0
Other regions	9.8	0.5	0.0	0.0	0.0	0.0	0.0	0.0	0.0	0.0	0.0	0.0
Loan commitments	123.2	60.0	63.0	8.4	18.9	12.6	23.0	27.6	26.2	12.3	3.7	10.2
Asia	58.9	17.7	20.5	3.5	5.1	5.9	5.9	14.2	11.9	9.1	1.4	1.5
Western Hemisphere	30.9	25.7	21.3	2.2	7.9	2.7	8.4	6.2	5.2	0.9	1.0	3.3
Other regions	33.4	16.6	21.3	2.7	5.9	4.0	8.7	7.2	9.1	2.4	1.3	5.5
Equity issues	26.2	9.4	23.2	2.4	6.7	6.1	8.0	8.9	12.9	1.2	1.5	10.3
Asia	14.4	4.5	18.3	1.4	5.7	5.3	5.8	6.7	9.3	0.4	1.2	7.7
Western Hemisphere	5.4	0.2	0.8	0.2	0.0	0.3	0.3	1.3	2.2	0.3	0.2	1.7
Other regions	6.4	4.8	4.2	0.8	1.0	0.5	1.9	0.9	1.3	0.4	0.1	0.9

accompanied by considerable dispersion in the composition of these flows, both across regions and countries, as well as by type of instrument.

Asia has led the recovery in 1999, with gross portfolio flows into the region nearly doubling in the year through the first half of 2000, despite the slowdown in the second quarter. Within this, loan commitments jumped sharply, but almost entirely due to two very large loans (to the infrastructure sector in Taiwan Province of China and to a major IT company in Hong Kong Special Administrative Region), which together accounted for two-thirds of such flows. Bond issues declined slightly, while equity financing more than doubled in the first half of 2000 from a year earlier, with Asia alone accounting for about three-quarters of emerging markets' external equity placements. A substantial part of portfolio equity flows has been directed toward IT firms, reflecting their brisk growth over the past year and investors' upbeat sentiment about the sector, at least until very recently (see previous section). Reflecting the growing importance of the IT sector and its relatively high market capitalization in

Asia, gross equity financing flows to Asia appear to have been sensitive to fluctuations in IT stock prices worldwide. As the demand for IT stocks retreated and prices dropped worldwide during March-May 2000, equity capital flows to Asia slowed accordingly; together with the decline in bond issuance during April and May, this caused total gross financing to Asia to drop in the second quarter, despite some recovery in June.

Compared with Asia, gross private financing to other regions remained relatively subdued through most of 1999 but, as in Asia, it rose sharply in the first quarter of 2000. First quarter gross flows into the Western Hemisphere were particularly strong, led by a boom in sovereign and other public sector placements. Gross private flows into emerging Europe, the Middle East, and Africa also rose, driven by large sovereign bond placements by a handful of individual countries. This boom in sovereign and other public sector issuance from all regions came to a virtual halt, however, in April and May 2000. As emerging market bond spreads widened (Figure 2.8), new issuance was postponed, with some

Figure 2.8. Emerging Markets: Bond Spreads[1]
(Percentage points)

Emerging market bond spreads narrowed through the first quarter of 2000, but widened in the second quarter.

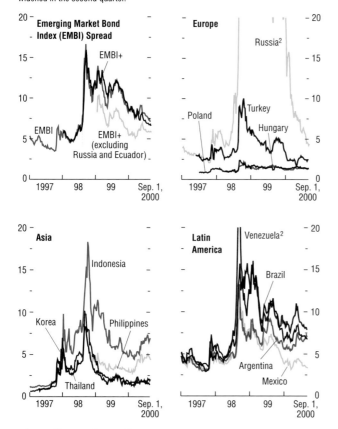

Sources: Bloomberg Financial Markets, LP; Reuters; and IMF staff estimates.

[1]Secondary market yield spreads on U.S. dollar-denominated bonds over comparable U.S. Treasury securities. The J.P. Morgan's EMBI+ tracks total returns for traded external debt instruments in the emerging markets. The instruments include external-currency-denominated Brady bonds, loans, and Eurobonds, as well as U.S. dollar local market instruments.

[2]The Russian Eurobond spread reached 67.3 percentage points in the first week of September 1998. The Venezuela EMBI+ spread reached 25.4 percentage points in the fourth week of July 1998.

governments resorting more heavily to domestic capital markets to meet their borrowing needs, thus contributing to the marked drop in total external financing flows; as in Asia, however, there was some recovery in June.

While gross private financing has picked up, *net capital flows* have continued to decline, reflecting sizable debt repayments by a few large economies and a large reduction in banks' external exposure (particularly in Asia). Net capital flows are not projected to increase until 2001 and, even then, to levels well below those just before the Asian crisis (Table 2.6). Within these, the level of direct foreign investment has been steady, slowing down through the crisis episodes of mid-1997 to early 1999, but forging ahead through the entire 1992–2000 period. Other net capital flows, including notably bank loans, have been considerably more volatile. Bank loans fell steeply during the 1997–98 Asian crisis—as international bank loans to the region were sharply curtailed—and continued to drop in net terms thereafter. This has resulted mainly from Asian banks accelerating foreign loan repayments and seeking to reduce their external exposure, as well as from the positive impact of higher oil prices on liquidity in Middle Eastern countries. Net portfolio investment has also been significantly more volatile than foreign direct investment, having risen rapidly in the early 1990s, before declining sharply during the 1997–98 financial crises and recovering afterwards. The greater volatility of portfolio flows relative to foreign direct investment is all the more apparent when looking at fluctuations across regions.[31]

[31]For instance, flows into the Western Hemisphere fell steeply during the 1995 "Tequila" crisis that followed the sharp devaluation of the Mexican peso in December 1994, to bounce back in 1996 and remain positive during the Asian and Russian crises of 1997–98. In contrast, net portfolio flows to Asia continued to grow rapidly through 1994–95 amidst financial turbulence in the Western Hemisphere, but plunged into negative territory in 1998 before recovering in 1999 and early 2000. For an analysis of the links between large swings in foreign portfolio investment and regional financial contagion, see the May 1999 *World Economic Outlook*.

Table 2.6. Emerging Market Economies: Net Capital Flows[1]
(Billions of U.S. dollars)

	1992	1993	1994	1995	1996	1997	1998	1999	Proj. 2000	Proj. 2001
Total										
Private capital flows, net	106.9	128.6	142.3	211.4	224.7	115.2	66.2	67.4	36.4	116.0
Private direct investment, net	35.7	57.9	81.0	95.8	119.5	141.3	151.6	154.6	141.9	140.5
Private portfolio investment, net	62.7	76.8	105.0	41.4	79.6	39.4	0.3	4.8	17.3	31.8
Other private capital flows, net	8.5	−6.1	−43.7	74.2	25.6	−65.6	−85.6	−91.9	−122.8	−56.4
Official flows, net	25.0	48.7	4.8	15.7	2.0	52.7	55.3	13.0	19.9	9.9
Change in reserves[2]	−58.0	−62.7	−67.9	−117.5	−110.6	−62.9	−32.3	−64.0	−97.2	−108.1
Memorandum										
Current account[3]	−79.3	−119.5	−74.2	−93.3	−94.7	−65.2	−55.9	22.7	65.5	−3.3
Africa										
Private capital flows, net	−1.7	1.1	7.5	7.9	7.8	12.1	6.8	10.3	9.0	7.9
Private direct investment, net	1.0	2.2	2.5	2.2	4.7	8.2	6.6	9.0	8.0	8.8
Private portfolio investment, net	2.0	0.9	3.4	3.1	2.6	7.0	6.5	8.7	4.5	4.6
Other private capital flows, net	−4.7	−2.0	1.6	2.6	0.6	−3.1	−6.4	−7.4	−3.5	−5.5
Official flows, net	9.0	6.1	7.8	8.9	3.2	2.1	6.0	3.8	0.9	4.4
Change in reserves[2]	0.9	2.9	−6.0	−3.1	−9.2	−10.6	1.3	−2.9	−14.3	−7.9
Memorandum										
Current account[3]	−10.6	−11.6	−11.9	−16.8	−6.7	−7.9	−20.4	−16.8	−3.6	−9.1
Asia[4]										
Crisis countries[5]										
Private capital flows, net	21.4	22.5	33.6	53.9	67.4	−15.6	−28.2	2.9	−22.4	10.6
Private direct investment, net	6.3	6.7	6.5	8.8	9.8	9.8	10.3	13.1	9.1	9.0
Private portfolio investment, net	12.4	18.3	12.0	18.8	25.5	8.4	−8.2	12.8	13.2	3.3
Other private capital flows, net	2.7	−2.5	15.1	26.3	32.0	−33.8	−30.4	−23.0	−44.6	−1.7
Official flows, net	2.1	1.4	0.6	0.7	−6.1	15.7	19.5	−6.7	5.0	−2.1
Change in reserves[2]	−18.2	−20.6	−6.1	−18.5	−5.6	39.5	−47.0	−38.8	−19.2	−30.6
Memorandum										
Current account[3]	−16.1	−13.5	−23.2	−40.4	−53.0	−25.0	69.7	61.7	44.3	23.2
Other Asian emerging markets										
Private capital flows, net	−7.4	20.8	36.0	38.3	52.6	22.3	−12.5	−0.6	4.6	13.0
Private direct investment, net	8.4	26.3	38.2	39.3	44.4	45.3	49.6	41.1	38.4	38.9
Private portfolio investment, net	3.4	0.9	7.0	2.6	3.9	−0.1	−7.2	−8.9	−8.0	−0.2
Other private capital flows, net	−19.2	−6.4	−9.2	−3.5	4.3	−23.0	−54.8	−32.8	−25.8	−25.8
Official flows, net	8.9	8.1	2.0	−3.8	−7.6	−8.3	−1.1	−0.1	−8.1	−4.2
Change in reserves[2]	−7.7	−14.9	−51.7	−26.2	−43.1	−46.8	−16.9	−20.9	−16.4	−30.8
Memorandum										
Current account[3]	14.1	−8.2	18.9	9.2	16.3	50.4	41.4	36.7	34.9	34.1
Middle East and Europe[6]										
Private capital flows, net	36.7	26.8	16.6	14.3	13.4	22.5	10.1	1.1	−18.3	1.2
Private direct investment, net	1.9	3.4	5.4	7.5	8.4	7.4	8.2	5.4	8.2	9.7
Private portfolio investment, net	12.1	2.6	2.7	−0.4	−5.4	−5.8	−16.7	−10.1	−7.0	−3.3
Other private capital flows, net	22.8	20.8	8.4	7.1	10.4	20.9	18.6	5.7	−19.5	−5.2
Official flows, net	−1.3	4.0	0.8	2.5	2.7	1.5	8.5	5.6	3.1	1.7
Change in reserves[2]	−8.6	1.6	−3.1	−8.6	−21.0	−21.3	12.5	−4.7	−17.0	−15.0
Memorandum										
Current account[3]	−26.8	−31.9	−8.0	−6.8	4.5	2.9	−30.7	1.2	41.6	18.3
Western Hemisphere										
Private capital flows, net	53.4	35.5	39.9	46.0	64.0	67.6	61.7	40.4	47.5	65.1
Private direct investment, net	13.9	13.4	23.1	25.0	39.4	53.4	56.5	65.3	56.6	50.6
Private portfolio investment, net	32.8	45.4	62.5	2.7	38.3	19.2	19.8	9.3	6.3	18.2
Other private capital flows, net	6.7	−23.4	−45.7	18.2	−13.6	−5.0	−14.6	−34.2	−15.4	−3.7
Official flows, net	3.4	29.9	7.3	13.3	5.3	15.5	16.0	10.6	19.5	10.6
Change in reserves[2]	−22.9	−20.7	4.3	−23.4	−29.4	−14.1	18.9	10.3	−9.6	−9.5
Current account[3]	−34.8	−46.1	−52.2	−37.1	−38.9	−65.1	−89.5	−56.3	−58.7	−66.5

Table 2.6 *(concluded)*

	1992	1993	1994	1995	1996	1997	1998	1999	Proj. 2000	Proj. 2001
Countries in transition										
Private capital flows, net	4.6	21.9	8.6	51.1	19.3	6.2	28.4	13.4	16.0	18.2
Private direct investment, net	4.2	6.0	5.3	13.0	12.8	17.2	20.3	20.7	21.7	23.5
Private portfolio investment, net	0.1	8.7	17.3	14.6	14.7	10.6	6.0	−7.1	8.3	9.2
Other private capital flows, net	0.3	7.3	−14.0	23.4	−8.1	−21.6	2.0	−0.3	−14.0	−14.6
Official flows, net	3.0	−0.8	−13.7	−5.9	4.6	26.2	6.5	−0.2	−0.5	−0.6
Change in reserves[2]	−1.7	−11.0	−5.3	−37.7	−2.2	−9.5	−1.1	−7.1	−20.7	−14.4
Memorandum										
Current account[3]	−5.1	−8.1	2.2	−1.4	−16.8	−20.4	−26.4	−3.8	6.9	−3.4

[1]Net capital flows comprise net direct investment, net portfolio investment, and other long- and short-term net investment flows, including official and private borrowing. Emerging markets include developing countries, countries in transition, Korea, Singapore, Taiwan Province of China, and Israel. No data for Hong Kong SAR are available.

[2]A minus sign indicates an increase.

[3]The sum of the current account balance, net private capital flows, net official flows, and the change in reserves equals, with the opposite sign, the sum of the capital account and errors and omissions.

[4]Includes Korea, Singapore, and Taiwan Province of China. No data for Hong Kong SAR are available.

[5]Indonesia, Korea, Malaysia, the Philippines, and Thailand.

[6]Includes Israel.

To gain further insight into the recent fluctuations of emerging market external financing and better assess the risks and prospects for their continuing recovery, it is useful to separate the determinants of these flows into "push" factors (which stem from developments in advanced countries) and "pull" factors (due to developments in emerging markets). Among "push" factors, there is evidence that gross external financing to emerging markets has been importantly influenced by monetary conditions in advanced countries, particularly in the United States. Periods of tighter (looser) liquidity conditions in advanced countries—brought about, for instance, by contractionary (expansionary) monetary policy stances—have tended to be associated with widening (narrowing) sovereign spreads and lower capital flows into Asia and Latin America (Box 2.1). Moreover, given the forward-looking nature of bond markets, greater uncertainty about the course of monetary policy in the United States, the European Union, and Japan, and prospects of additional tightening ahead, also appear to weigh down on emerging market bond prices, as witnessed by developments during March–May 2000.

Stock market developments in advanced countries have constituted another important "push" factor behind capital inflows to emerging markets.[32] As discussed above, there has been a positive and apparently growing correlation between changes in stock prices in advanced countries and those in emerging markets, particularly in the IT sector, as witnessed by the impact of the sharp losses in the NASDAQ on emerging market equity returns earlier this year.[33] Such a positive correlation between stock price changes in these two groups of countries implies that periods of high stock price volatility in advanced

[32]While changes in stock prices in advanced countries are clearly influenced by the monetary policy in these countries, the correlation between stock prices and monetary policy in advanced countries is not one-to-one. As extensively discussed in the May 2000 *World Economic Outlook*, fluctuations in stock prices in advanced countries also reflect other factors, including investors' sentiment and expected productivity growth, which are not under the control of monetary authorities and therefore constitute a distinct channel through which stock prices in advanced economies affect foreign investment in emerging markets.

[33]Rolling correlations of weekly returns in the NASDAQ and the Dow Jones stock indices and emerging market equity returns by region are provided in IMF, *Emerging Market Financing: A Quarterly Report on Development and Prospects*, second quarter 2000 (Washington: International Monetary Fund, August 2000).

Box 2.1. U.S. Monetary Policy and Sovereign Spreads in Emerging Markets

With the increased integration of global capital markets, changes in U.S. monetary policy are felt by developing countries through effects on the cost and availability of funds, and on their creditworthiness. In addition to the direct impact of changes in U.S. interest rates on rates in developing countries, interest rate spreads move in the same direction as the changes in U.S. interest rates. (Interest rate spreads refer to the differences between yields on sovereign bonds of developing countries and those on U.S. Treasury securities of comparable maturities, which are a proxy for country risk.) This effect on developing country spreads was seen clearly in 1994 when a tightening of U.S. monetary policy was reflected in a substantial widening of spreads, and in 1998 when an easing of U.S. monetary policy following the flight to quality associated with the Russian default and the demise of the hedge fund Long-Term Capital Management helped to reduce spreads somewhat.

The existing empirical literature is less conclusive on *how* U.S. monetary policy affects emerging market sovereign spreads. Most of the specifications adopted so far have proxied U.S. monetary policy by the yields on U.S. Treasury securities. Shocks to Treasury yields do not always imply changes in U.S. monetary policy, however, and the so-called "flight to quality" experienced during the Asian crisis was quite revealing in terms of fluctuations in U.S. Treasury yields in the absence of changes in U.S. monetary policy. The flight to quality also illustrates how changes in U.S. short-term rates affect sovereign spreads in emerging markets. One study has found, for a sample of Latin American and east Asian countries during 1991–95, that a rise in interest rates on U.S. Treasury bills tended to reduce spreads, perhaps because it deterred less creditworthy borrowers from issuing bonds.[1] The study concluded that while the level of sovereign spreads was determined largely by fundamentals, changes in sovereign spreads were also driven significantly by shifts in investor sentiment. Other studies have found a positive but statistically insignificant effect of U.S. Treasury yields on sovereign spreads in selected emerging markets during the mid-1990s.[2]

To examine this issue further, an econometric model for sovereign bond spreads was estimated individually for a group of emerging market countries.[3] The model explains fluctuations in spreads as a function of country-specific macroeconomic variables, the level of the U.S. Federal Funds target rate, and as a proxy for volatility in capital markets, based on estimates of the (variable) standard deviation of the residuals derived from a model of the spread between the three-month U.S. Treasury bill yield and the U.S. Federal Funds target rate. This proxy for market volatility is intended to capture changes in investor sentiment that may be related to expected changes in U.S. monetary policy. The model may also pick up the effects of other market related events, such as the so-called "flight to quality" effects. To provide a sense of overall devel-

[1]See Barry Eichengreen and Ashoka Mody, "What Explains Changing Spreads on Emerging-Market Debt: Fundamentals or Market Sentiment?" NBER Working Paper No. 6408 (Cambridge, Massachusetts: National Bureau of Economic Research, February 1998). Their results might reflect the fact that the analysis was based on spreads for new bond issues of developing countries and not on spreads for bonds actively traded in secondary markets. In addition, their analysis, which covers the period 1991–95, is based on a subperiod (1991–93) when the market for sovereign bonds was developing, and on another subperiod (1994–95) when shocks seriously restricted access to the market for lower quality issuers.

[2]See Kevin Barnes and William Cline, "Spreads and Risk in Emerging Markets Lending," Institute of International Finance, Working Paper No. 97-1 (December 1997), and Steven Kamin and Karsten von Kleist, "The Evolution and Determinants of Emerging Market Credit Spreads in the 1990s," unpublished manuscript (Federal Reserve Board and Bank for International Settlements, 1997).

[3]The model was estimated for Argentina, Brazil, Bulgaria, Colombia, Indonesia, Korea, Mexico, Panama, Philippines, Poland, and Thailand. For further details, see Vivek Arora, Martin Cerisola, and Victor Culiuc, "How Does U.S. Monetary Policy Influence Economic Conditions in Emerging Markets?" *United States—Selected Issues* (Washington: International Monetary Fund, 2000).

Box 2.1 *(concluded)*

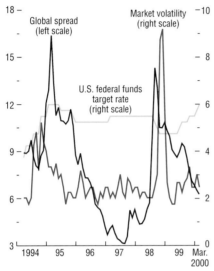

Emerging Market Sovereign Spread, U.S. Federal Funds Target Rate, and Market Volatility
(Percent)

Sources: Merrill Lynch; U.S. Federal Reserve; and IMF staff estimates.

opments, the figure reports the global spread across all emerging markets, the U.S. Federal Funds rate, and the proxy for market volatility over the sample period.

The results suggest that the stance and predictability of U.S. monetary policy is important in explaining fluctuations in developing country interest rate spreads. To the extent that monetary policy actions can be anticipated by market participants, market turbulence would likely be reduced. One important conclusion therefore is that an approach to monetary policy that pro-

vides financial markets with clear indications of the U.S. authorities' intentions is likely to reduce the impact of a U.S. rate increase on developing countries. In particular, the results show that the level of the U.S. Federal Funds target rate has significant positive effects on emerging market spreads, with the estimated coefficient ranging from about ½ to 1.[4] The model also supports the view that increased market volatility related to heightened uncertainty about the expected path of U.S. monetary policy has significant positive effects on spreads across countries and regions.

Nevertheless, a significant proportion of fluctuations in emerging market spreads is driven by country-specific fundamentals. In general, improved macroeconomic fundamentals—such as higher net foreign assets (in terms of GDP or imports), lower fiscal deficits, and lower ratios of debt service to exports and debt to GDP—help to lower sovereign spreads across countries. For example, a higher net foreign asset position contributed to lower spreads in many Latin American and Asian countries (after 1997 in this region)—particularly in those have had in place fixed exchange rate regimes, such as Argentina, Panama, Thailand, and Korea. Foreign indebtedness appears to contribute positively to sovereign spreads, especially in Latin America (particularly Argentina, Mexico, Brazil, Panama), and in the Philippines—countries that underwent comprehensive debt reschedulings in the past.

---

[4]The rise in the level of emerging market interest rates will, however, not necessarily be as large as the sum of the rise in spreads and the rise in the U.S. Federal Funds rate. In the United States, the yield curve tends to flatten as monetary policy is tightened, so that a rise in short-term interest rates tends not to be fully passed through to longer-term rates.

countries tend to be associated with higher volatility of stock prices in emerging markets. This in turn, by increasing investment risk, tends to impact negatively on capital inflows, reducing gross private financing to these countries. The negative relationship between the volatility of

stock returns in emerging markets and the capital inflows they receive is borne out by the data (Figure 2.9).

The links between stock prices in developed countries and gross private financing to emerging markets have not been confined to the equity markets. Stock price volatility in advanced countries also appears to have had a significant impact on emerging market bond spreads. This is substantiated by a positive and relatively high correlation between emerging market bond spreads and stock returns in the Dow Jones and NASDAQ indices.[34] Moreover, as the volatility of those indices is reflected in the volatility of equity returns in emerging markets (as discussed above), periods of high price volatility of local stocks in emerging markets tend to be associated with higher EMBI spreads (see bottom panel of Figure 2.9). These correlations seem to reflect two main factors. First, institutional investors appear to regard most IT (and also a few non-IT) stocks, together with emerging market debt, as high risk assets. Thus, when seeking to reduce overall risk exposure, these investors will tend to cut down on their holdings of both assets; conversely, when appetite for risk is high, demand for both types of securities tends to rise. Second, recent commentary suggests that investors tend to view emerging market debt as liquid relative to its closest competitor asset class (U.S. corporate debt). So, when stock market volatility rises and greater uncertainty motivates investors to reduce their overall risk exposure, they will first reduce holdings of the more liquid class of assets, which includes emerging market debt. Emerging market spreads will thus tend to widen during those periods, causing emerging market borrowers to try to cut down or at least postpone new international issues, leading to a drop in portfolio flows.

On the "pull" side, recent developments suggest that both the volume and the terms of external financing have been quite responsive to domestic macroeconomic conditions and policies in

[34]Since 1994 the correlations between stock returns in the two U.S. indices and EMBI spreads have fluctuated between 0.4 and 0.7, and are statistically significant in a multivariate regression model. See International Monetary Fund, *International Capital Markets: Developments, Prospects, and Key Policy Issues*, September 2000. In recent months, the correlation between the NASDAQ and the average emerging market spread has been rising, while that between the Dow Jones and the EMBI has been falling, though both correlations have displayed considerable ups and downs in the very short run.

Figure 2.9. Emerging Markets: Capital Flows, Bond Spread, and Volatility in Equity Returns
(Percent, unless otherwise indicated)

Stock market volatility has been negatively correlated with gross private financing to emerging markets, and positively correlated with emerging market bond spreads.

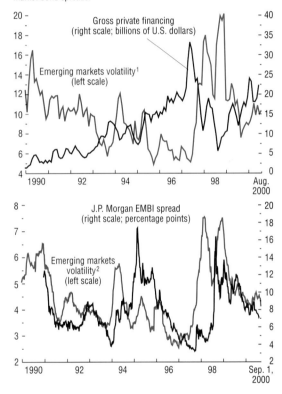

Sources: Capital Data Ltd.; J.P. Morgan; Morgan Stanley Capital International; International Finance Corporation, Emerging Markets Data Base; and Bloomberg L.P.
[1]Rolling 20-week volatility of monthly U.S. dollar equity returns, average for nine emerging markets.
[2]Rolling 20-week volatility of monthly U.S. dollar equity returns, average for 15 emerging markets.

Figure 2.10. Selected East Asian and Latin American Economies: Current Account Balance[1]
(Percent of GDP)

The current account positions of the east Asian economies have improved considerably since the crisis, but those of most Latin American countries remain relatively weak.

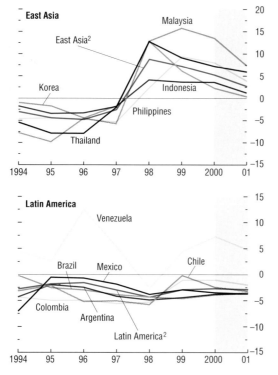

[1]Shaded areas indicate IMF staff projections.
[2]Weighted average.

emerging markets. In general, the decline in emerging market spreads since the 1997–98 financial crises—and more definitely since Brazil's move to a floating exchange rate regime in early 1999—has been associated with a strengthening of macroeconomic fundamentals in most countries. This is witnessed by the general upgrading of emerging market debt by credit rating agencies since early 1999.[35] As discussed in Chapter I, economic growth in Asia accelerated markedly during 1999 and early 2000 while external current accounts continued to post sizable surpluses (Figure 2.10). Although public deficits and external debt in a number of countries in the region are substantially higher than in the pre-1997 period (Tables 2.7 and 2.8), and concerns remain about the pace of structural reforms, progress has been made on both fronts. Consistent with these developments, Asian countries' spreads have declined markedly over the past two years, to a much lower level than elsewhere (see Figure 2.8). The drop in spreads has been larger in those countries where growth has been stronger and macroeconomic management has been more prudent, such as Korea and Malaysia.

Macroeconomic fundamentals have also improved considerably in some large emerging market economies in the Western Hemisphere since early 1999. Growth has been particularly robust in Mexico, and recoveries are firmly under way in Brazil and Chile. The fiscal position has also improved considerably in those three countries, while domestic interest rates have come down and inflation has remained under control. Mexico's debt was upgraded to investment grade in March 2000, contributing to a further decline in its EMBI spread to early 1997 lows and the continued strength of capital inflows (Figure 2.11). On the other hand, spreads in Argentina, Brazil, and Venezuela remain significantly higher than in Mexico. In the first two countries less favorable balance of payments out-

---

[35]A discussion of the impact of credit rating upgrades on emerging market financing is provided in the forthcoming IMF *International Capital Markets* report, Chapter III, Box 3.2.

Table 2.7. General Government Balance

(Percent of GDP)

Country	1994	1995	1996	1997	1998	1999	2000
Argentina	−1.8	−2.3	−3.2	−2.0	−2.1	−4.1	−2.8
Brazil	−3.3	−7.0	−5.9	−6.6	−8.1	−9.8	−3.7
Chile	1.5	3.6	2.6	2.1	−0.1	−2.4	−1.0
Venezuela	−13.2	−6.9	7.2	1.9	−6.8	−1.2	0.3
Mexico	−0.3	−0.8	−0.7	−1.2	−1.7	−1.3	−0.6
Indonesia	0.0	0.8	1.2	−0.7	−1.9	−1.5	−3.6
Korea	1.0	1.3	1.0	−0.9	−3.8	−2.7	−1.6
Malaysia	3.3	2.2	2.3	4.1	−0.4	−3.8	−1.5
Philippines	−1.8	−1.4	−0.6	−0.8	−2.7	−4.4	−3.1
Thailand	1.9	3.0	2.5	−0.9	−2.5	−2.9	−2.4
Of which: central government							
Argentina	−0.5	−1.5	−2.2	−1.1	−1.3	−2.5	−1.8
Brazil	0.1	−2.3	−2.6	−2.6	−5.5	−6.7	−2.2
Chile	1.5	3.6	2.6	2.1	−0.1	−2.4	−1.0
Venezuela	−7.3	−4.3	0.6	1.6	−2.6	−3.0	−4.2
Mexico	−0.5	−1.3	−0.1	−2.8	−1.7	−1.5	−2.6
Indonesia	0.0	0.8	1.2	−0.7	−1.9	−1.5	−3.6
Korea	0.1	0.3	0.0	−1.7	−4.3	−3.3	−2.5
Malaysia	1.4	1.3	1.1	2.5	−1.5	−4.1	−4.3
Philippines	−1.8	−1.4	−0.6	−0.8	−2.7	−4.4	−3.1
Thailand	2.0	2.5	1.0	−1.7	−2.9	−3.7	−2.9

Table 2.8. External Debt

(Percent of GDP)

Country	1994	1995	1996	1997	1998	1999	2000
Argentina	33.3	38.2	40.3	42.6	47.1	51.1	52.6
Brazil	18.2	22.6	23.2	24.9	31.2	44.6	36.3
Chile	42.2	33.3	33.5	35.6	43.6	50.4	49.8
Colombia	27.4	27.9	31.6	31.5	36.0	42.6	44.2
Mexico	33.9	59.0	49.6	38.2	38.4	34.6	30.0
Venezuela	71.3	51.0	53.1	41.1	39.3	36.7	31.8
Indonesia	57.0	56.3	53.4	63.9	149.4	96.5	93.8
Malaysia	39.0	37.6	38.4	43.8	58.8	53.4	49.3
Philippines	61.4	54.9	55.0	61.6	81.7	75.7	78.9
Korea	22.0	26.0	31.6	33.4	46.9	33.4	26.5
Thailand	44.9	49.1	49.8	62.0	76.9	61.4	51.7
Of which: short-term debt							
Argentina	3.5	4.8	5.0	6.5	7.2	6.9	6.5
Brazil	3.5	4.3	4.9	4.6	3.4	5.1	3.8
Chile	10.7	7.9	6.5	4.8	5.4	5.8	9.5
Colombia	5.4	5.8	5.1	4.4	4.6	4.8	4.5
Mexico	3.4	5.4	4.5	3.3	3.1	2.9	2.4
Venezuela	4.3	1.9	2.6	2.7	2.2	1.5	1.9
Indonesia	6.5	8.7	7.5	27.5	76.4	5.9	5.7
Malaysia	7.5	7.2	9.9	11.1	11.7	7.6	6.4
Philippines	8.9	8.3	12.0	14.0	15.6	11.3	7.5
Korea	14.5	14.6	17.9	13.3	9.7	9.3	7.7
Thailand	20.2	24.5	20.7	23.1	21.0	11.4	6.8

looks and sizable public sector financing needs make them more vulnerable to higher volatility in mature markets. In the case of Venezuela, higher spreads appear to be more related to uncertainties regarding political developments and the future course of economic policy. A clear negative correlation between sovereign spreads on the one hand, and macroeconomic fundamentals on the other, is also seen in other economies in the region, sometimes exacerbated by political factors, as in Peru.

Macroeconomic fundamentals also have strengthened elsewhere in the emerging world. With a recovery in economic activity under way in the Czech Republic, Hungary, and Poland, and macroeconomic policies remaining broadly on track, spreads have narrowed and capital inflows have increased (see Figure 2.3). The combination of a recovering economy, improving commodity prices, and the reduction in the South African Reserve Bank's net open forward position in foreign currency has helped boost investors' confidence in South Africa, leading to a fall in spreads between 1999 and early 2000. And while the South African rand has not strength-

ened (largely for external reasons), the flow of foreign investment into the country has been steady. As discussed in Chapter I, improvements in macroeconomic fundamentals have been particularly remarkable in Russia and Turkey, where spreads have fallen the most, and a sharp pickup in external capital inflows is projected for 2000.

Outlook and Risks

To sum up, private financing to emerging markets has recovered from its late 1998 lows, reflecting a combination of improving macroeconomic fundamentals in these economies and favorable liquidity conditions in advanced economies between mid-1999 and February 2000. Sovereign spreads remain well above pre-Asian crisis levels for economies with sizable public sector financing needs and high current account deficits, underscoring the vulnerability of these economies to monetary tightening and other adverse asset market developments in the advanced world. Developments during March–May 2000—when average emerging mar-

Figure 2.11. Selected Emerging Market Economies: Capital Flows[1]
(Billions of U.S. dollars)

Net direct investment has been the most stable component of private capital flows to emerging markets and has grown rapidly in several countries in recent years.

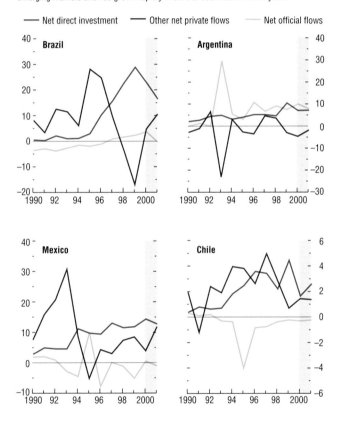

ket spreads widened in response to monetary policy tightening in the United States and the European Union, and higher stock market volatility—clearly illustrated this phenomenon. But the widening was steeper for regions and countries with weaker fiscal and balance-of-payments positions and less favorable growth performance. This suggests that investors are differentiating sharply both between regions and across countries.

Three other main trends in emerging market financing are worth stressing. One is the remarkable stability of foreign direct investment compared with private portfolio flows and crossborder bank loans, highlighting the important stabilizing role of direct investment in the international financial system. Second, the rapid expansion of the IT sector in some regions has been associated with some shift in external financing patterns. This is notably the case in Asia, where international equity issues have been growing faster than bond issues. While bonds and loans together still account for most of the gross portfolio flows into the region, a growing share of such flows is now non-debt creating. As local IT firms expand faster elsewhere and public sector financing needs shrink, a similar change in financing patterns may eventually be observed in other regions as well. Third, there are indications that higher asset market volatility in advanced economies leads to small capital flows into emerging markets. Although further research is needed to identify the different components behind such volatility—which, as discussed earlier, may have been exacerbated by the growing importance of the IT sector in these regions—this seems to underscore the importance of stable macroeconomic and sound structural policies that help minimize equity market volatility in emerging markets.

Over the medium term, the staff's baseline scenario envisages a continuing recovery of capital flows to emerging markets. This primarily reflects the continued strengthening of macroeconomic fundamentals in emerging markets, which will tend to lower sovereign spreads and broaden opportunities for external private sector borrowing, and—more specifically—the conclusion of banks' stock adjustment in exposure to Asia. However, there are three potential risks. First, as both equity prices and bond spreads in emerging markets have been closely related to stock market developments in the United States, a sharp fallout from present valuation levels would likely have a substantial negative impact on portfolio financing to emerging markets. Second, as discussed in Box 2.1, further monetary tightening and/or greater uncertainty about the future course of monetary policy in advanced economies is also bound to impact significantly on the terms and volume of such flows— the impact likely to be mostly felt in countries with larger public sector financing needs and higher current account deficits. Third, a substantial slowdown of U.S. economic growth would adversely affect growth and therefore capital flows to emerging markets with strong trade links with the United States. The impact would be smaller on other emerging markets, however, especially if counterbalanced by further strengthening of economic activity in Europe and Japan.

Commodity Prices and Commodity Exporting Countries

Over the past three years, large swings in commodity prices have greatly affected many countries. After peaking in 1996, commodity prices fell by 30 percent in 1997–98, due to fallout from the Asian crisis as well as favorable harvests of some crops, causing a substantial terms of trade shock for commodity exporting developing countries (Figure 2.12). The oil price rebound in 1999–2000 has reversed these losses for oil exporters, but has substantially worsened the position of most other commodity exporters—many of which are among the poorest countries—especially given the relatively weak outlook for nonfuel commodity prices. In the advanced economies, commodity price developments have generally been helpful from a cyclical perspective, although the most recent rise in

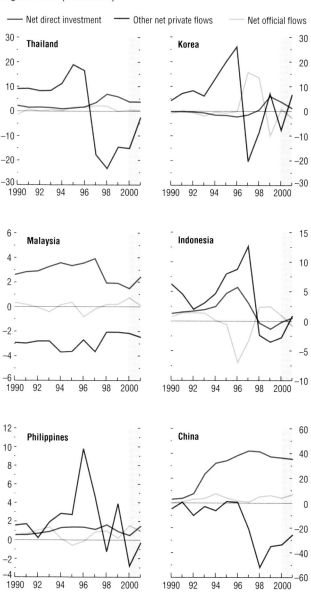

Figure 2.11 *(continued)*

— Net direct investment — Other net private flows — Net official flows

Figure 2.11 *(concluded)*

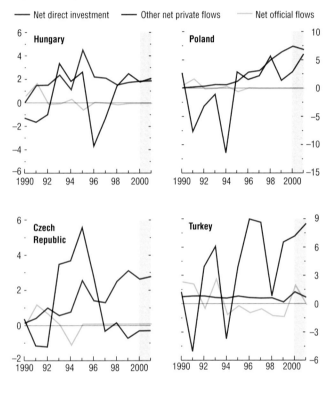

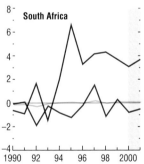

¹Shaded areas indicate IMF staff projections.

oil prices may add to inflationary risks, as well as slow output growth.

The prices of many key commodities have moved relatively independently over the past 12 to 18 months. While fuel prices have increased sharply, prices of nonfuel commodities have staged modest recoveries at best, with agricultural prices being particularly weak, despite rising global demand. In consequence, the IMF's nonfuel commodity index remained about 20 percent below 1995–97 levels through June 2000.[36] The remainder of this section focuses on the outlook in the oil market, the reasons for the underlying weakness of nonfuel commodity prices, and the implications of these developments for commodity exporting and importing countries.

The Oil Market

Oil prices have increased sharply in the last year and a half, rising from under $12 a barrel in the first quarter of 1999 to almost $27 a barrel in the second quarter of 2000, and are now at a 15-year high (excluding the Gulf war period) in both real and nominal terms.[37] The rapid run-up in world oil prices—from historically low levels—initially reflected supply constraints that followed a series of agreements involving major oil exporters beginning in March 1999. More recently, the upward pressure on oil prices has reflected more buoyant current and expected world demand growth as well as the limited capacity of oil producers, apart from a few major members of OPEC, to increase production. In the first half of 2000, prices fluctuated in the $25–$30 a barrel range, and continued to display considerable volatility (with day-to-day changes in spot prices of $1 a barrel not uncom-

[36]From end-June through end-August 2000, the IMF's nonfuel commodity index fell another 4 percent.

[37]Based on a simple average of spot prices for U.K. Brent, Dubai, and West Texas Intermediate. This basket of crude oil is also used to compute the baseline assumptions in the *World Economic Outlook.* It differs from the basket used for the OPEC reference price, which is a simple average of seven crude prices (Saharan Blend, Indonesian Minas, Arabian Light, Dubai, Tia Juana Light, Bonny Light, and Isthmus).

mon). Box 2.2 reviews recent developments in global oil markets, while risks to the projections are outlined below.

As a result of the recent run-up in prices, as of early September, spot oil prices (at more than $33 a barrel) and oil prices futures were over 20 percent higher than projected in the *World Economic Outlook*. Given the announced intention of OPEC members to hold oil prices in a $22 to $28 a barrel range, additional demand pressures could in principle be met through further increases in supply. While non-OPEC exporters are producing close to capacity (see Box 2.2 for details), some estimates indicate that OPEC member countries could increase supply by about 3 million barrels a day. However, this excess capacity is concentrated in a few countries, while an adjustment in supply targets would need to be agreed to by all OPEC members. In an environment of strengthening global demand and low oil inventories, the risks to oil prices would appear to be on the upside. At the OPEC meeting on September 10, OPEC members agreed to raise production by 800,000 barrels a day, about 3 percent of OPEC production or 1 percent of total world production. In the immediate aftermath of the meeting, oil prices continued to rise.

What Keeps Nonfuel Commodity Prices So Weak?

In many nonfuel commodity markets, the surprise has been the lack of larger price movements and consequently a persistence of prices at low levels when compared with pre-Asian crisis prices. From mid-1997 into 1999, the weakness in the prices of most commodities reflected largely the disruptions in demand growth, particularly in Asian markets. More recently, as the global recovery has gained pace, favorable conditions have increased supplies of many commodities and have kept price pressures in check.

The prices of most *agricultural* commodities have been particularly weak, in part because production did not adjust quickly to the slump in demand in 1998–99. For cereals and oilseeds, weather conditions, particularly in the Western

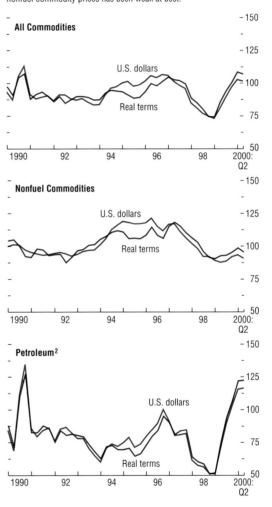

Figure 2.12. Prices of Crude Petroleum and Nonfuel Commodities¹
(1990 = 100)

Oil prices have increased sharply since early 1999, while the recovery in nonfuel commodity prices has been weak at best.

¹Indices in real terms are obtained by deflating the nominal U.S. dollar price series by the unit value of manufactures exported by 20 industrial countries.
²Average Petroleum Spot index of UK Brent, Dubai, and West Texas.

Box 2.2. Developments in the Oil Markets

In March 1999, with oil prices still at their lowest levels since the 1980s, members of the Organization of Petroleum Exporting Countries (OPEC) pledged to cut targeted oil production by a total amount of 1.7 million barrels a day.[1] Some non-OPEC countries (most notably Mexico and Norway) pledged additional cuts in exports of around 0.4 million barrels a day. Compliance with the agreed output cuts was generally high and increasing demand resulting from continued global economic expansion outstripped supply with a corresponding drawdown of inventories, particularly in the United States, the most important market for petroleum and petroleum products. As a result, oil prices rose from little more than $10 a barrel in February 1999 to over $30 a barrel by February 2000.

In March 2000, a new OPEC agreement was announced, which increased targeted crude production by 1.7 million barrels a day in an effort to check the oil price increase. Following this agreement and partly in response to concerns by OPEC members on the long-term effect of high prices, OPEC informally defined a target price band of $22 to $28 a barrel, while Saudi Arabia indicated that it would like to see prices at around $25 a barrel.[2] Prices then declined in April to $23–$24 a barrel, but bounced back and in June exceeded the upper limit of the band, while inventories remained low.

At their June 21 meeting in Vienna, OPEC members (including Iran) agreed to increase output by 708,000 barrels a day as of July 1, followed by commitments by Mexico and Norway to increase production by 75,000 barrels a day and 100,000 barrels a day, respectively. The immediate reaction of the market was a small price increase, as the market had anticipated a larger production increase. With the oil price above $30, Saudi Arabia announced on July 3 that it was prepared to increase output by an additional 500,000 barrels a day. Iran followed the announcement by indicating it would go along with any boost in production, provided there was consensus among OPEC members to do so. (Iran is the second largest OPEC producer after Saudi Arabia—see the table).

During August, spot and futures prices continued rising, and by early September, futures contracts had soared to their highest levels since the Gulf War. On September 10, OPEC agreed to an increase in production of 800,000 barrels a day. With Saudi Arabia already producing significantly above its earlier target, the increase had been largely discounted in the markets, and oil prices initially increased further.

One of the major elements contributing to the uncertainty in the prospects for oil prices is the limited capacity of oil producers, apart from a few major members of OPEC, to increase production. With most OPEC and non-OPEC countries producing close to full capacity, OPEC as a whole has limited incentives to agree to an increase in production intended to reduce prices as earnings would decrease.[3] Low prices during 1998 and the first half of 1999, and the uncertainty of the overall oil market, have also severely limited recent investment aimed at expanding oil output.[4]

[1]OPEC members produce about 40 percent of the world's oil output, and hold over 75 percent of the world's proven oil reserves.

[2]The price band mechanism of $22 to $28 a barrel was set by OPEC with the specification that if the average price for the OPEC crude basket falls below $22 or increases above $28 for 20 market days, OPEC's production would be decreased or increased by 500,000 barrels a day, respectively. The precise formulation of the trigger point was unclear. Some reports had the mechanism triggering after 20 consecutive market days; others made reference to an average price over a period of 20 days. The OPEC basket reference price is the simple average of seven crudes: Saharan Blend, Indonesian Minas, Arabian Light, Dubai, Tia Juana Light, Bonny Light, and Isthmus.

[3]Capacity is defined by Bloomberg as production attainable within 30 days and sustainable for 90 days. Non-OPEC producers typically operate close to capacity. See U.S. Energy Information Agency, *Non-OPEC Fact Sheet*, available via the Internet at http://www.eia.doe.gov (June 2000).

[4]The uncertainties in the oil market include the potential impact of U.N. sanctions on Iraq, including Iraq's threats to temporarily cut down or interrupt exports. Iraq has an estimated capacity of 2.8 million barrels a day or about 4 percent of the world's crude output.

Box 2.2 *(concluded)*

Crude Output and Estimated Capacity
(in thousands of barrels a day as of August 2000)

| | Actual Output, 2000 | | | | | Estimated |
	April	May	June	July	August[1]	Capacity[2,3]
OPEC	27,700	28,220	28,080	28,340	28,800	32,150
Algeria	790	800	810	820	830	950
Indonesia	1,290	1,300	1,300	1,310	1,310	1,400
Iran	3,650	3,680	3,680	3,710	3,720	3,750
Iraq	2,660	2,970	2,650	2,660	2,900	2,950
Kuwait	2,060	2,080	2,110	2,100	2,130	2,600
Libya	1,410	1,410	1,420	1,420	1,430	1,500
Nigeria	2,000	1,960	2,010	2,050	1,980	2,200
Qatar	680	690	700	700	700	750
Saudi Arabia	8,030	8,180	8,230	8,350	8,550	10,500
United Arab Emirates	2,280	2,280	2,280	2,300	2,320	2,500
Venezuela	2,850	2,870	2,890	2,920	2,930	3,050
Non-OPEC	13,138	13,263	13,331	13,610	...	13,610
Mexico	3,041	3,040	3,056	3,100	...	3,100
Norway[4]	3,077	3,153	3,125	3,290	...	3,290
Oman	930	930	935	945	...	945
Russia	6,090	6,140	6,215	6,275	...	6,275
Total OPEC plus Non-Opec	40,838	41,483	41,411	41,950	...	45,760
World (IEA)[5]	76,090	76,350	76,190	76,750	...	...

Sources: Bloomberg Financial Services and *Oil Market Report* (Paris: International Energy Agency, various issues).
[1]Preliminary figures.
[2]Capacity is defined as that which is attainable within 30 days and sustainable for 90 days.
[3]Estimated capacity for non-OPEC producers is taken as their output in the most recent month for which data are available.
[4] The decline in production in June 2000 is associated with maintenance and technical problems.
[5]Includes condensates, Natural Gas Liquids, and oils from non-conventional sources.

The demand for crude is expected to continue to increase in the near term. Estimates by the International Energy Agency (IEA), based on underlying growth assumptions for Organization for Economic Cooperation and Development countries in 2000 that are slightly higher than those in the *World Economic Outlook*, suggest that there will be little change in the demand and supply balance for the remainder of the year. In addition, IEA suggests that increased demand for gasoline both in the United States and in Europe, together with the high gasoline prices and the high cost of inventories, may delay the usual shift from gasoline to heating oil refining. With the arrival of winter in the Northern Hemisphere, low stocks could result in a sharp hike in prices for heating oil.

Hemisphere, have been much more favorable in the late 1990s than in the mid-1990s, and there also was a slowing of the growth in global demand for livestock feed. Commodities such as coffee, cocoa, and sugar carry high fixed costs of planting trees and cane, and therefore downward adjustments to supply typically occur slowly, because it can be profitable to harvest in the short run even if prices are below total production costs. Even for cotton, which unlike the perennials above must be replanted each year, heavy infrastructure and other investment result in a high proportion of fixed costs; these farmers also may choose high production levels even if prices are low. This has resulted in rising stocks in some cases, putting further downward pressure on prices and dimming prospects for a price rebound. *World Economic Outlook* projections assume a moderate price rise for these commodities, but on average prices are not expected to return to 1995–97 average levels in the near term.

The prices of other nonfuel commodities have shown modest increases since early 1999, but still remain well below their 1995–97 averages. The prices of most *metals* and some other industrial inputs have already increased from their lowest levels in mid-1999, but the increases have been less than might be expected, given the rise in global demand. For example, through the end of August 2000, the price of copper remained about 30 percent below its 1995–97 average, in part reflecting, until recently, high stock levels. This continuing weakness is also due to the slow pace at which supplies of these commodities have adjusted to changing market conditions. As with agricultural goods, metals prices are expected to increase but remain below previous peaks, with the exception of nickel, which surpassed its average price in 1995–97.

Implications for Commodity Exporting Countries

The recent movements in commodity prices have significantly impacted a number of commodity exporting countries, particularly those that export only a few commodities. Table 2.9 shows price movements in key commodities through June 2000 compared to a 1995–97 base period. Table 2.10 shows the impact of these changes on the most affected nonfuel commodity exporting countries, defined as those that have experienced a combination of lost export revenues and higher oil import costs amounting to at least 10 percent of total exports compared with 1995–97.[38] Nearly 30 countries have experienced cumulative terms of trade losses of more than 10 percent, and in over 10 countries the terms of trade losses exceed 20 percent. Losses measured as a percent of domestic absorption are also large in many cases. They range from

Table 2.9. Selected Primary Commodities: Recent Price Movements[1]

Commodity	1998	1999	2000 First-half
Commodities with prices in 2000 much higher than in 1995–97			
Crude petroleum	−31	−4	41
Natural gas	−17	−33	16
Nickel	−39	−21	25
Tea	24	21	26
Commodities with prices in 2000 much lower than in 1995–97			
Agricultural commodities			
Wheat	−30	−38	−40
Rice	−5	−22	−31
Soybeans	−14	−30	−24
Fish meal	18	−30	−29
Sugar (free market)	−27	−49	−49
Coffee (arabica)	−13	−33	−37
Coffee (robusta)	−13	−30	−51
Cocoa beans	12	−24	−39
Cotton	−24	−38	−35
Jute	−32	−27	−22
Metals			
Copper	−34	−37	−29
Cobalt	−17	−35	−41
Gold[2]	−24	−28	−26

[1]Percentage change from 1995–97 levels.
[2]Compared with base period 1995–96. Price slide began in 1997.

about 1 percent of domestic absorption (Brazil, Haiti, Rwanda, Tanzania) to more than 8 percent (Guyana, Zambia), and average about 4 percent. Agricultural exporters, particularly exporters of coffee, cocoa, and cotton, and also those that import large amounts of oil relative to total exports, have been hardest hit. Burundi, with its dependence on coffee (70 percent of total exports), and Mali, with its reliance on two exports (cotton and gold), are examples of the first group, while Tanzania and Haiti are two countries where a high oil import dependency resulted in gains in 1998, but losses in 2000.

Regrettably, almost all of the countries hit hardest by falling commodity prices are also among the world's poorest. All but two (Brazil

[38]The base period 1995–97 precedes the commodity demand shock attributed to the Asian crisis. The estimates reflect price changes from the base period and hold trade volumes unchanged from the base period. The loss estimates can be thought of as partial terms of trade effects, expressed as a percentage of base period export earnings. See footnote 2 to the table for details on the underlying calculations.

Table 2.10. Nonfuel Commodity Exporters: Export Dependency and Terms of Trade

Country	Export Dependency[1]		Oil Import Dependency	Change in Terms of Trade[2]		
	Main Export	Other Commodities		1998	1999	2000[3]
	Coffee					
Burundi	70	Tea 8	−24	1	−20	−33
Ethiopia	60	Gold 3	−22	−1	−19	−32
Uganda	56	Cotton 3	−11	−5	−17	−34
Rwanda	45	Tea 12	−29	6	−11	−25
El Salvador	30		−5	−2	−10	−14
Guatemala	19	Sugar 6	−1	−4	−10	−11
Madagascar	22		−9	0	−6	−15
Honduras	19		−11	0	−6	−11
Tanzania	11	Cotton 10, Tea 2	−14	1	−7	−13
Haiti	6		−33	10	−1	−16
	Cotton					
Mali	46	Gold 21	−17	−11	−23	−28
Chad	42		−14	−6	−15	−20
Burkina Faso	39	Gold 7	−23	−4	−16	−25
Benin	38		−7	−7	−14	−16
Uzbekistan	38	Gold 19	4	−15	−20	−17
Togo	20	Coffee 4, Cocoa 3	−8	−2	−9	−14
Sudan	18		−42	9	−5	−23
Pakistan	16	Rice 5	−20	2	−6	−15
Central African Republic	12	Coffee 9	−8	−2	−7	−12
	Cocoa					
Saõ Tomé and Príncipe	44		−27	−14	−10	−28
Côte d'Ivoire	30	Coffee 8, Cotton 3	0	2	−11	−16
	Copper					
Zambia	56	Cobalt 15	−7	−20	−26	−25
Chile	28	Fishmeal 3	−8	−7	−11	−12
Peru	15	Fishmeal 11, Gold 7	−5	−3	−11	−11
	Gold					
Ghana	31	Cocoa 24	−12	−1	−14	−22
Guyana	16	Rice 12	−14	0	−7	−14
	Soybeans					
Brazil	9	Coffee 7, Sugar 3	−9	0	−7	−11
	Jute					
Bangladesh	8		−39	10	0	−17

[1]Export dependency refers to the exports of the specific commodity (averaged over 1995–97) as a percentage of total exports of goods and services (averaged over 1995–97).

[2]The change in the terms of trade is defined as the average price change of each of the commodities listed relative to the 1995–97 base period, weighted by that commodity's share of total exports of goods and services in the base period. Changes are shown as percent of total exports. Countries with terms of trade shocks of 10 percent or more are shown.

[3]Through June 2000.

and Chile) are classified as low-income countries by the World Bank, over half are in sub-Saharan Africa, and sixteen are Heavily Indebted Poor Countries. In addition, average output growth for this group declined in 1998–2000, compared with the base period, consistent with studies that find that heavy dependence on nonfuel com-modity exports is negatively related to output growth.[39] The low incomes and poor perfor-mance of these commodity exporters underscore the importance of export diversification as a longer-term objective, provided diversification comes in areas of comparative advantage and is commercially viable.

[39]Chapter IV of the May 2000 *World Economic Outlook* reviews the developing country growth issues in detail. In particular, Table 4.7 examines the relationships between terms of trade and real growth.

In general, adjustment to a *permanent negative terms of trade shock* requires a reduction in domestic absorption, accompanied by a real exchange rate depreciation particularly when access to international capital markets is limited.[40] This tends to occur because a negative terms of trade shock lowers domestic income (and wealth, if the shock is perceived as permanent) and demand. The demand slowdown may reduce inflation and contribute to a real depreciation, which may be augmented by downward pressure on the nominal exchange rate associated with an initial deterioration in the current account.

In many cases, however, restrictive fiscal policies—and in some cases a flexible exchange rate—are needed to augment market forces and reduce demand. Uganda provides a good example of the needed adjustments. Coffee makes up more than 50 percent of exports in Uganda, which experienced a terms-of-trade loss equivalent to 3½ percent of domestic demand in 1998–99 (close to the group average). By cutting back on planned spending and keeping priority spending mostly on track, Uganda succeeded in offsetting lower government revenues (related in part to the decline in coffee prices and the regional drought). External balances were held in a sustainable range as a depreciation of the Ugandan shilling essentially offset the terms of trade deterioration. Uganda also benefits from debt relief under the Initiative for Heavily Indebted Poor Countries (HIPCs).[41]

Table 2.11 presents similar terms of trade calculations for the countries in which oil exports made up at least 20 percent of total exports in the base period (1995–97). The 22 countries represented include a mix of economies, the majority of which are low income. In the case of Oman, Libya, and Nigeria, where oil exports account for some 90 percent of net exports, the drop in oil prices in 1998 cut export receipts by up to 28 percent, or about 11 to 15 percent of domestic absorption.[42] When the prices rebounded in 1999–2000, fuel exporters more than recouped these losses, and by 2000 all of these countries were showing substantial terms of trade gains—25 percent and more in about one-half of the countries.

The positive terms-of-trade shock to the oil exporters in 1999–2000 has clearly been a benefit and brought relief after the 1998–99 price slump, especially to the lower-income countries. At the same time, the increase in oil prices presents challenges to policymakers who need to ensure that increasing oil revenues are not wasted. For example, Cameroon, where oil accounted for 30 percent of exports in the base period, has responded to the recent rise in oil prices at a time when coffee and cocoa prices remained weak by allowing government spending to increase slightly in the current fiscal year compared with the budget, while devoting the bulk of the unanticipated revenue increase to a reduction in bank borrowing.[43] This approach of partially "sterilizing" revenue surprises and limiting the pass-through to government spending may work well in other low-income countries facing similar demands on resources.

For the higher-income oil exporters, the key policy challenge associated with higher oil prices is both to maintain fiscal discipline and strengthen ongoing structural reforms. Among the members of the Gulf Cooperation Council (GCC), episodes of falling oil prices in the 1980s

---

[40]Temporary terms of trade shocks can be met with a mix of reduced domestic absorption and borrowing, depending on a country's access to external capital markets. Because it is often difficult to distinguish between temporary and permanent shocks *ex ante*, it may be prudent to seek a reduction in absorption at the outset.

[41]See Chapter IV, "How Can the Poorest Countries Catch Up?" of the May 2000 *World Economic Outlook* for a review of progress in HIPCs.

[42]The table assumes unchanged volumes from the 1995–97 base period. Price changes are also measured relative to this base period. See footnote 3 in the table for more details.

[43]This is being accomplished through a framework that allows for price "surprises" to feed partially through to spending and partially to borrowing (or debt repayment) in a symmetric way as oil prices rise and fall. In the medium term, sustained higher oil prices would provide scope to meet pressing human development needs, provided expenditure management is improved.

Table 2.11. Fuel Exporters: Export Dependency and Terms of Trade

Country[3]	Export Dependency[1]		Change in Terms of Trade[2]		
	Oil (Net Exports)	Other Commodities	1998	1999	2000[4]
Nigeria	92		−28	−4	38
Libya	91		−28	−4	37
Oman	90		−28	−4	37
Angola	87		−27	−4	36
Yemen	87		−27	−4	36
Kuwait	85		−26	−4	35
Congo, Republic of	84		−26	−4	34
Saudi Arabia	83		−26	−4	34
Iran, Islamic Republic of	78		−24	−3	32
Gabon	73		−23	−3	30
Equatorial Guinea	72		−22	−3	30
Venezuela	70		−22	−3	29
Syrian Arab Republic	64	Cotton 4	−21	−4	25
Algeria	63	Natural gas 27	−24	−12	30
Qatar	63		−20	−3	26
United Arab Emirates	45	Natural gas 6	−15	−4	19
Brunei Darussalem	37	Natural gas 36	−18	−14	21
Cameroon	30	Coffee 9, Cocoa 9	−10	−6	4
Ecuador	28	Coffee 4, Cocoa 3	−9	−3	9
Bahrain	27		−9	−1	11
Norway	24	Natural gas 4	−8	−3	11
Russia	21	Natural gas 14, Nickel 2	−10	−6	11

[1]Export dependency refers to net oil exports (averaged over 1995–97) as a percentage of total exports of goods and services (averaged over 1995–97).

[2]The change in the terms of trade is the average of the price change of each commodity listed relative to the 1995–97 base period, weighted by that commodity's share of total exports of goods and services in the base period. Changes are shown as a percent of total exports for countries for which oil exports were at least 20 percent of total exports in the base period.

[3]Not including Iraq.

[4]Through June 2000.

through the mid-1990s were addressed by a mix of financing and fiscal adjustment measures—an approach made possible by large official assets and access to international capital markets. In the later part of the decade, many countries in the region undertook fiscal and structural reforms aimed at fostering longer-term sustainability through improved fiscal balances and more diversified economies. It is important that the pace of these reforms does not slow. Indeed, governments in the region could take the opportunity provided by buoyant revenues to speed up the reform process, including trade liberalization, to enhance economic efficiency and bolster investor confidence.

Implications of Higher Oil Prices for the World Economy

As noted above, the *World Economic Outlook* projections of oil prices may be subject to potential upside risk. Indeed, by early September, spot oil prices (at about $33 a barrel) and oil price futures were substantially higher than when the oil price assumptions used in this *World Economic Outlook* were set.[44] This change

[44]Based on closing prices on September 8. Oil price assumptions for the *World Economic Outlook* projections were set in mid-July with average prices for 2000 and 2001 projected to be $26.53 and $23.00 a barrel, respectively. See "Oil Price Assumptions and the World Economic Outlook," Box 1.4 of the October 1999 *World Economic Outlook* for information on methodology used to set the oil price assumption.

Table 2.12. Preliminary Estimates of a First Round Effect of an Oil Price Increase on Oil Importing Developing Countries[1]

Decline in Current Account Balance as Percent of GDP	
0.5 to 1 percent	Greater than 1 percent
Benin	Armenia
Bulgaria	Belarus
Cambodia	Burundi
Chile	Gambia
Croatia	Ghana
Czech Republic	Jamaica
Dominican Republic	Jordan
Ethiopia	Kyrgyz Republic
Georgia	Lao, P.D.R.
Guinea-Bissau	Lithuania
Honduras	Macedonia, FYR
Hungary	Mali
India	Mauritania
Kenya	Moldova
Madagascar	Mongolia
Mauritius	Nepal
Morocco	Slovak Republic
Namibia	Swaziland
Nicaragua	Tajikistan
Pakistan	Ukraine
Philippines	
Rwanda	
Senegal	
Sierra Leone	
Slovenia	
Sri Lanka	
Thailand	
Togo	
Turkey	
Uganda	
Zimbabwe	

[1]Computations are based on an increase of $5 a barrel above the WEO baseline of $26.53 a barrel in 2000. Only countries with population greater than one million are included. These estimates are preliminary and because of data limitations there may be some additional countries where prospective first round effects of a $5 a barrel increase will also have substantial effects on current account balances. In addition, the impact of the oil price increase may be larger because prices of substitutes will also be affected.

Table 2.13. Macroeconomic Impact of a Ten Percent Increase in Oil Prices[1]

(Percentage points)

	Real GDP	Consumer Price Inflation
Major industrial countries		
United States	−0.1	0.2
Japan	−0.1	0.1
Euro area	−0.1	0.2
United Kingdom	—	0.1
Canada	−0.1	0.2
Developing countries[2]		
Africa	—	0.3
Asia	−0.2	0.4
Western Hemisphere	—	0.3

Sources: Major industrial countries: IMF's MULTIMOD simulation; developing country regions: IMF staff estimates.
[1]Deviation from baseline.
[2]Weighted average of the larger economies in each region.

in prices, if sustained, would suggest an upward revision to the oil price baseline of about $2.50 a barrel (or almost 10 percent) in 2000 and almost $5 a barrel (or about 21 percent) for 2001 and beyond.

Higher oil prices affect the world economy through several channels, with the most immediate impact felt through trade balances. Given a sustained $5 a barrel increase in oil prices (and

assuming no change in oil trade volumes), aggregate net oil imports by advanced economies would increase by about $40 billion annually; trade balances among the oil-exporting countries would rise by a corresponding amount, with the bulk of the increase accruing to the Middle East region.[45] In aggregate, the change in the trade balance in dollar terms for other developing country regions would be relatively small. However, a number of developing countries will be seriously affected as trade balances would deteriorate by more than ½ percent of GDP, leading to a sharp contraction in domestic absorption, particularly for countries with large current account deficits or with limited access to external financing. As shown in Table 2.12, these include a number of emerging market countries, as well as many transition and low-income economies (especially in Africa).

Higher oil prices would also have a direct impact on global activity and inflation. In particular, higher oil prices would put upward pressure on prices. This could cause central banks—particularly in the cyclically advanced countries—to raise interest rates, which—along with the direct impact of the terms of trade shock—would lower

---

[45]These calculations do not take account of the potential impact of higher oil prices on other energy substitutes (such as gas).

COMMODITY PRICES AND COMMODITY EXPORTING COUNTRIES

GDP growth. This, in turn, would add to the direct impact of higher oil prices on activity in developing countries.[46] Based on the ready reckoners displayed in Table 2.13, derived using the Fund's MULTIMOD economic model, a sustained $5 a barrel increase in world oil prices (almost 20 percent higher than prices in the first half of 2000) would result in a reduction in output of about 0.2 percentage points in the major industrial countries after one year, while—notwithstanding higher interest rates—consumer price inflation would rise by 0.2 to 0.4 percent-age points (less than in previous episodes since the ratio of oil consumption to GDP has significantly fallen over time).[47] Among the developing country regions, output in Asia—which is relatively dependent on imported oil—would decline by 0.4 percentage points, while there would be little net output impact in Africa and the Western Hemisphere regions because both include a mix of oil importers and producers. However, as discussed above, the impact on some individual countries could be significantly more serious.

[46]Since the oil exporting countries have a lower propensity to consume than do the oil importing countries, higher oil prices also tend to raise global savings and to reduce global growth and trade volumes.

[47]A "ready reckoner" provides a rough idea of the relationship between two variables, in this case relating a percentage change in oil prices to changes in output growth and inflation rates. See "Oil Price Assumptions and the World Economic Outlook," Box 1.4 of the October 1999 *World Economic Outlook,* for a more complete analysis, including the macroeconomic implications for developing countries.

CHAPTER III

TRANSITION: EXPERIENCE AND POLICY ISSUES

The rise and subsequent failure of central planning ranks among the most significant events in the twentieth century, posing major challenges to both economic theory and policy from Prague to Beijing.[1] By the late 1980s the limitations of central planning had become very clear, and, since the fall of the Berlin Wall, countries that had maintained centrally planned economies have been—with the assistance of the major international institutions (including the IMF; Box 3.1)—engaged in a historic transition process to market economies.[2] As a result, both the economic structure and the behavior of consumers and producers have undergone major changes, although progress has been very uneven among the participating countries. While much has been achieved, the process has turned out to be much more difficult than anticipated at the outset, and in retrospect it is clear that policies pursued in transition have not always been ideal. In particular, although the need for an institutional infrastructure to support the nascent market economies was recognized from the beginning, in practice such institution building was not always given adequate attention.

This chapter summarizes the results of the transition process to date, including the reasons why results have varied widely between the different transition countries. While it is still too early to pass a final judgment on many aspects of the transition process, the chapter also reviews the main policy lessons that can be drawn from the experience to date and the policies required to move the transition process forward. Specific attention is paid to the political economy aspects of the transition process and how they help to explain intercountry differences in reform efforts and results. Given the scope of the topic, the chapter is necessarily selective. The issues chosen for discussion and the lessons highlighted are those that, from the perspective of the *World Economic Outlook*, seem most striking and relevant.

Among the many legacies of the now defunct systems of central planning, one of the most detrimental was the absence of an institutional and legal infrastructure underpinning the operation of market-oriented economies.[3] There was an absence of well-defined property rights, commercial legislation regulating the entry and exit of private enterprises, financial markets, a commercial banking system, open labor markets, and a market-oriented system of taxation. By definition, central planning implied massive direct government involvement in economic decision making. The absence of market-generated signals about the relative scarcities of outputs and inputs led to highly distorted relative prices and output structures, while ideological suppression of the profit motive reduced innovation, entailing a growing technology gap between the centrally planned and the advanced market economies. The policy bias toward autarky within the Council of Mutual Economic Assistance (CMEA) disregarded potential gains from global international trade, and, in any case, the absence of a domestic price system that signaled relative scarcity made it difficult for countries to identify their "true" international comparative advan-

[1]See Chapter V, "The World Economy in the Twentieth Century: Striking Events and Policy Lessons," in the May 2000 *World Economic Outlook*.

[2]In China and some other east Asian countries with centrally planned economies, the transition began much earlier, although initially with the prime objective of improving rather than abolishing the planned economy.

[3]The only countries currently holding on to central planning and the predominant state ownership of means of production are North Korea and Cuba.

Box 3.1. The IMF and the Transition Economies[1]

When the 25 countries of central Europe, the Baltics, and the Commonwealth of Independent States (CIS) embarked on the transition process, they sought external assistance from a variety of sources, including the IMF.[2] By the early 1990s, all 25 countries had officially become members of the IMF. Soon thereafter, virtually all requested and received financial assistance from the IMF. Based on the necessarily limited experience of countries confronting similar issues, the appropriate transition strategy was hotly debated within and outside the transition economies, including at the IMF. In the international financial community a general consensus was reached on the desirability of a comprehensive approach to deal simultaneously with the liberalization, stabilization, and structural transformation of the economies. To assist the initial stages of the transition, a new IMF lending facility called the Systemic Transformation Facility (STF) was established for a limited period (1993–95). The STF, which had lower conditionality and access than the more traditional IMF facilities, was designed as a stepping stone to the latter.

Throughout the transition years, international institutions, including the World Bank and the IMF, as well as bilateral donors, extended considerable technical assistance, principally in support of national authorities' efforts to build the economic institutions needed for a well-functioning market economy. The IMF helped to draft legislation and provided technical assistance principally in three areas. In the financial sector, the IMF helped to transform the former monobank into a central bank and a commercial banking system and to introduce new payment systems. It also advised countries on banking supervision and prudential regulations, foreign exchange management, and market-oriented monetary policy tools. In the fiscal area, the IMF helped to set up new treasury and new tax systems and provided guidance on improving tax administration and public expenditure management. In the statistical area, the IMF helped to set up new statistical systems for national accounts and prices, balance of payments, money and banking, and public finance accounts. Over time, the emphasis shifted to improving the quality and reliability of data and its timely dissemination. As the Table shows, all three regions received technical assistance at a fairly early stage of the transition. Among the regions, the CIS countries (which had the weakest institutions) have been the largest beneficiaries, with assistance continuing at a fairly intense pace in the later years.

Economic policy advice was also provided by the IMF from the start of the transition process. In the early years of transition, 18 transition economies received financial assistance from the STF. With the exception of some central and eastern European countries, financial access to the more common IMF facilities came later—for example, programs in more than half the CIS countries began only in 1995. Delays typically occurred because it took time to reach agreement on a common policy framework with the authorities or to ensure that basic elements of a market framework existed before programs were implemented.[3] For these reasons, and to assure the commitment and capacity of the authorities to deliver, IMF programs often had a number of "prior actions" (a standard element of most IMF-supported programs), mainly structural reform measures or enactment of necessary legislation that were expected to be undertaken before disbursements began on an IMF-supported program.

[1]For further reading, see Stanley Fischer and Ratna Sahay, "The Transition Economies After Ten Years," IMF Working Paper 00/30 (Washington: International Monetary Fund, 2000); and Charles Wyplosz, "Ten Years of Transformation: Macroeconomic Lessons," a paper prepared for the Annual World Bank Conference on Development Economics, April 28–30, 1999 (unpublished; Washington: The World Bank, 1999).

[2]This box primarily discusses the role of the IMF in the transition economies of central and eastern Europe and the CIS. It should be noted, however, that the IMF has also provided substantial financial and technical assistance to other transition economies in east Asia.

[3]Other reasons were that, in many countries, new currencies were not introduced until late 1993 or 1994, while in some others civil conflicts precluded stabilization and reform.

Box 3.1 *(continued)*

IMF Assistance in 25 Transition Economies

	Central Europe (10)[1]			Baltics (3)[1]			CIS Countries (12)[1]		
	1989–91	1992–95	1996–99	1989–91	1992–95	1996–99	1989–91	1992–95	1996–99
IMF-supported programs[2]	40	73	60	—	100	83	—	35	71
IMF financial assistance									
In percent of IMF Quota	64.1	27.9	35.7	—	58.9	—	—	47.6	57.4
Billions of U.S. dollars									
(net basis)[3]	2.4	–0.7	–0.1	—	0.5	–0.2	—	12.6	8.8
Technical assistance (person-years)									
Fiscal area	7.1	20.7	13.1	—	7.6	2.8	2.9	57.0	53.9
Financial sector	11.6	25.2	20.1	0.3	9.6	7.6	0.6	66.3	51.5
Statistics	1.2	4.9	4.5	—	5.7	—	0.8	22.1	21.6

Source: International Monetary Fund.
[1]Number of countries in parenthesis.
[2]The percentage of the period during which countries in the group had an IMF-supported program in at least part of the calendar year. Excludes the STF, extended to 18 countries during 1993–95, with a maximum access of 25 percent of their quota.
[3]On a cumulative basis over the indicated period.

The design of IMF-supported programs in the region typically had several common elements, reflecting the fact that all economies were going through similar systemic changes, but at the same time were flexibly designed to suit local conditions. The common elements included the large-scale freeing of price and exchange regimes in tandem with firmer monetary policies, internal and external trade liberalization, demonopolization of large enterprises, rapid privatization of retail trade, encouragement of small businesses, social safety net provisions in the budget, and an overhaul of the tax system. The programs also differed in many important ways, depending on the countries' specific circumstances and the desires of domestic policymakers. For example, "heterodox" programs with wage controls were implemented where wage pressures were a concern. Many countries pegged their exchange rates, while others floated. Privatization programs ranged from voucher schemes to direct sales of enterprises. Subsidies were removed at varying speeds; for example, in the relatively low income countries, energy prices and utility charges were raised more slowly. Occasionally, as in the Baltic countries, fiscal deficits were designed to widen temporarily to accommodate the financing of growth-enhancing reform measures.

As discussed in the main text, there has been considerable heterogeneity in the reform efforts and economic performances of the transition countries during the past decade. Several key factors mainly explain this heterogeneity, especially substantial differences in initial conditions, in the external environment facing different transition countries, and, perhaps most important, in the willingness and ability of national authorities to implement and maintain political support for consistent and sensible policies of economic stabilization and structural reforms—with or without support from the IMF or from the international community more generally. Because these factors were the dominant determinants of the relative success of the transition process in different countries, assessing the contribution of the IMF-supported programs and policy advice is necessarily a difficult and delicate undertaking and one unlikely to lead to consensus or unambiguous conclusions.

Nevertheless, it should be recognized that, operating under IMF-supported programs, virtually all transition countries were able to reduce inflation from three- or four- digit levels fairly rapidly, and this disinflation was generally associated with reductions of fiscal deficits to manageable proportions. These achievements in the area of macroeconomic stability were important in their own right and were at the core of the IMF's areas of responsibility. They were also a critical foundation for broader efforts at structural reform and institution building that are central to the transformation process. Although, among the international financial institutions, the lead in providing advice and assistance in several key areas of structural reform (including the form and sequencing of privatization, enterprise restructuring, design of social safety nets, and reforms of the legal system) was taken by the World Bank and other institutions, IMF-supported programs embodied important elements of structural reform. The structural reforms in IMF-supported programs generally had a longer time horizon for full implementation than the initial efforts targeted at macroeconomic stabilization.

Where reasonable fiscal discipline was maintained and meaningful structural reforms were pursued—generally under the aegis of IMF-supported programs—inflation typically remained well contained, and output recovered more rapidly than in countries where stabilization and reform efforts were less consistent and vigorous. In line with the principles of IMF conditionality, financial support was generally provided with fewer program delays and interruptions to those countries that implemented their stabilization and reform policies with greater consistency and vigor. As discussed in the main text, this group of relatively successful transition countries was primarily (but not exclusively) in central and eastern Europe and the Baltics, where relatively strong domestic commitment to reform was reinforced by prospects of EU accession, and where initial conditions typically were somewhat more favorable. Thus, the relative success of these transition countries cannot be uniquely or mainly attributed specifically to their adherence to IMF-supported programs; but in general terms, if not necessarily in all of their particular elements, these programs would seem to deserve some credit for that relative success.

The case of most of the CIS countries (excluding the Baltics) is more complex. The disintegration of the Soviet state and the associated collapse of trade and of demand for the products of key industries (especially in the military and industrial complex), termination of large implicit transfers from energy rich to energy poor regions, and the outbreak of armed conflicts occurring in some cases made for particularly unfavorable initial conditions. Understanding of the institutions and practices of a market economy was typically quite poor, and political support for implementation of serious policies of stabilization and structural reform—either rapidly or gradually—was usually weak. Perhaps the domestic political balance could have been shifted toward greater support for sensible and sustainable reform and the losses suffered by the general population could have been eased if, as some suggested, massive foreign financial assistance—a new Marshall Plan—had been made available under appropriate conditionality. Such large-scale external assistance, however, was simply not available. IMF lending to most CIS countries was significant, both as a share of countries' quotas in the IMF and in relation to other official creditors. But the potential scale of IMF lending (together with other external assistance) was never such as to be likely to change substantially the domestic political balance or to help countries absorb a major part of the cost of transition.

In the countries where the transition has been less successful, the IMF's role has tended to be more controversial. This is especially so for Russia because of its size and geopolitical importance and because the progress of IMF-supported programs was a subject of intense interest for many key players in the international community. For Russia, IMF-supported programs were associated with some significant successes, especially the reduction of inflation and the enforcement of meaningful fiscal discipline under the 1995 Stand-By Arrangement. In contrast, the Extended Fund Facility agreed in early 1996 was not a success; little progress was made in most key areas of structural reform and the erosion of fiscal discipline culminated in the devaluation and default of August 1998. Aside from these general observations, an assessment of the IMF's role in this critically

Box 3.1 *(concluded)*

important and highly complex case is beyond the scope of this Box.

For countries (including Russia) that have been less successful in the transition process, it is notable that most IMF-supported programs were subject to significant delays and interruptions. This reflected the normal IMF procedure of insisting on prior actions in key policy areas to demonstrate the commitment of the authorities before initiating IMF lending, and of interrupting a program's disbursements if the authorities fail to put forward reasonable efforts to meet a program's agreed objectives. In several cases (e.g., Bulgaria and the Kyrgyz Republic since 1995), this strategy proved effective in reinvigorating the stabilization and reform process. In other cases, success has remained elusive.

Arguably, in these difficult cases, a different approach by the IMF might have worked better. Perhaps the IMF should have been more sensitive both to constraints on the practical administrative capacity and to limits on the willingness or political ability of some national authorities to push through and sustain rigorous stabilization and reform programs, and should have been more accommodating when programs went off track. But in some of these difficult cases where political support for reforms was typically quite weak, it might have been better for the IMF to stand back from financing and wait for a more auspicious environment for meaningful reform. Judgment on these delicate questions is mainly a matter of political economy rather than of the technical economic content of IMF-supported programs. In the end, it is clear that domestic political support and the development of a viable institutional framework are essential to ensure that IMF-supported programs are effective—in the transition economies, as well as in other countries.

tage.[4] After having initially narrowed the gap with advanced market economies through forced industrialization, the relative performance of the centrally planned economies in terms of income per capita and international competitiveness deteriorated increasingly in the postwar period.[5] And incomplete or failed reform efforts aimed at stalling this relative decline led to unsustainable fiscal deficits and a large monetary overhang in many centrally planned economies in the late 1980s.

There was, however, a positive legacy of state socialism as well. Human capital endowment with respect to both health standards and levels of education was and still is relatively high in these countries compared with market-oriented economies at comparable levels of per capita income. And although comparisons in this area are fraught with statistical difficulties, incomes were apparently more evenly distributed than in the capitalist economies. In addition, the social safety net was both comprehensive and universal, guaranteeing work and thus income for everybody. These favorable aspects reflected policy priorities under state socialism. Their implications for successful transition are probably quite dissimilar. High levels of human capital should facilitate transition, but the comprehensive social safety net left people with little experience in dealing with economic uncertainty and adversity (e.g., unemployment), thereby making the transition more difficult. This is especially so in many countries of the Commonwealth of Independent States (CIS), where a lack of reform of enterprise-provided social services and benefits ties workers to chronically loss-making firms.

---

[4]The international specialization that did develop within the CMEA was predominantly based on a central-plan determined division of labor rather than on market-driven comparative advantage.

[5]Apart from entailing large private costs and inefficiencies due to the supression of market mechanisms, the system also led to major environmental problems by neglecting social costs in pursuit of policy priorities with regard to military buildup and energy sector development.

Table 3.1. Selected Characteristics of Transition Countries

Transition Country/Group[1]	Year Transition Began[2]	Starting Date of Stabilization Program[2]	Real Output Ratio 1999/1989	Average Inflation 1989–99	1999 EBRD Average Transition Indicator[3]	PPP GDP per Capita 1999
EU accession countries (excluding Baltics)	**1991**	**Mar–91**	**0.95**	**35.5**	**3.3**	**10,009**
Bulgaria	1991	Feb–91	0.67	68.4	2.9	4,812
Czech Republic	1991	Jan–91	0.94	7.8	3.4	13,408
Hungary	1990	Mar–90	0.99	19.7	3.7	11,273
Poland	1990	Jan–90	1.28	49.2	3.5	8,832
Romania	1991	Jan–93	0.74	76.1	2.8	5,798
Slovak Republic	1991	Jan–91	1.01	14.3	3.3	10,255
Slovenia	1990	Feb–92	1.05	12.9	3.3	15,685
Baltic countries	**1992**	**Jun–92**	**0.68**	**33.5**	**3.2**	**6,850**
Estonia	1992	Jun–92	0.78	24.3	3.5	7,909
Latvia	1992	Jun–92	0.56	35.1	3.1	5,893
Lithuania	1992	Jun–92	0.70	41.0	3.1	6,750
Other southeastern European countries	**1990**	**Jun–93**	**0.77**	**3,331.8**	**2.5**	**3,651**
Albania	1991	Aug–92	0.93	33.4	2.5	2,897
Bosnia and Herzegovina[4]	. . .	. . .	0.93	13,118.0	1.8	1,014
Croatia	1990	Oct–93	0.80	100.0	3.0	6,793
Macedonia, FYR	1990	Jan–94	0.59	75.6	2.8	3,903
Commonwealth of Independent States[5]	**1992**	**Aug–94**	**0.53**	**149.1**	**2.3**	**3,337**
Armenia	1992	Dec–94	0.48	106.5	2.7	2,469
Azerbaijan	1992	Jan–95	0.47	233.2	2.2	2,404
Belarus	1992	Nov–94	0.81	162.4	1.5	6,485
Georgia	1992	Sept–94	0.31	17.9	2.5	3,950
Kazakhstan	1992	Jan–94	0.61	77.3	2.7	4,351
Kyrgyz Republic	1992	May–93	0.61	22.3	2.8	2,419
Moldova	1992	Sept–93	0.31	16.5	2.8	1,847
Mongolia	1990	. . .	0.93	46.5	2.8	1,573
Russia	1992	Apr–95	0.55	88.0	2.5	6,815
Tajikistan	1992	Feb–95	0.29	688.5	2.0	1,045
Turkmenistan	1992	. . .	0.61	4.9	1.4	4,589
Ukraine	1992	Nov–94	0.35	169.4	2.4	3,276
Uzbekistan	1992	Nov–94	0.97	304.5	2.1	2,157
East Asia	**1986**	**. . .**	**1.78**	**17.1**	**2.1**	**2,042**
Cambodia	1990	. . .	1.62	6.3	2.5	1,261
China	1978	. . .	2.52	8.1	2.1	3,709
Lao P.D.R.	1986	. . .	1.85	28.6	1.8	1,385
Vietnam	1986	. . .	1.97	25.4	1.9	1,815

Source: European Bank for Reconstruction and Development, *Transition Report 1999;* IMF staff estimates unless otherwise noted.
[1]Data for country groups are simple averages of group member data.
[2]From Fischer and Sahay, "The Transition Economies After Ten Years," IMF Working Paper 00/30 (Washington: International Monetary Fund, 2000).
[3]Indicator of progress in structural reforms; see the Appendix.
[4]For Bosnia and Herzegovina, inflation over the period 1991–99 for the Federation is used for "Average Inflation 1989–99," and 1999 GDP per capita in U.S. dollars is used for "PPP GDP per Capita 1999."
[5]Data include Mongolia.

The Transition Experience to Date

The countries referred to as "transition economies" and discussed in this chapter comprise 31 countries in Europe and Asia, including all former members of the CMEA (excluding Cuba) and a number of additional countries in east Asia and the Balkan region comprising close to 30 percent of the world's population.[6] They are listed in Table 3.1, together with relevant sta-

[6]Others might spread the net still wider, including countries in Africa and Latin America that embraced some form of central planning at some time. As the impact of socialism on their underlying institutions was, however, quite limited, these countries are not included.

Table 3.2. Transition Economies: Alternative Geographic, Political, and Reform-Effort Groupings[1]
(Boldface denotes radical reformers; italics denotes moderate reformers; all others are slow reformers)

Southeastern Europe	Countries on the European Union Accession Track		Commonwealth of Independent States (CIS)	East Asia
	Baltic countries	Others		
Albania	**Estonia**	*Bulgaria*	*Armenia*	*Cambodia*
Bosnia and Herzegovina	**Latvia**	**Czech Republic**	*Azerbaijan*	*China*
Croatia	**Lithuania**	**Hungary**	Belarus	Lao P.D.R.
Macedonia, FYR		**Poland**	*Georgia*	*Mongolia*
Yugoslavia, Fed. Rep. of		*Romania*	*Kazakhstan*	Vietnam
		Slovak Republic	*Kyrgyz Republic*	
		Slovenia	*Moldova*	
			Russia	
			Tajikistan	
			Turkmenistan	
			Ukraine	
			Uzbekistan	

[1]The reform-effort classification takes as criterion the average level of EBRD transition indicator in 1999, choosing the following thresholds: radical reformers (in bold) with an indicator above 3; intermediate reformers (in italics) with an indicator between 2 and 3; and slow reformers (in plain type) with an indicator below 2. See the Appendix to this chapter for further description of the transition indicator.

tistics characterizing each country's transition process, and can be classified according to a number of geographical, political, and reform-effort criteria that tend to be highly correlated. The most common classification, which will be extensively used in this chapter, partitions the transition countries into five groups, highlighted in Table 3.2: the EU accession countries (which include the Baltic countries);[7] the countries of the CIS; the east Asian transition economies;[8] and the other countries in southeastern Europe (excluding the EU accession countries located in the Balkan region). Some important differences, however, remain between members within groups. In particular, among the EU accession candidates, the three Baltic countries and Romania and Bulgaria differ in important ways from the remaining five central European members of this group, an issue that is addressed in more detail in Chapter IV of this *World Economic Outlook*.[9]

The defining characteristic of the transition countries is their decision to abandon central planning as the principal mode of organizing their economies and to move to market-oriented economies with significant private ownership of the means of production. In most of these countries, the "transition" coincided with major political transformations, and some, but not all, observers include the shift from a one-party autocratic system to a multiparty democracy in their definition of "transition." In China, Vietnam, and the Lao People's Democratic Republic, however, the political system has not been modified significantly during the transition process.[10] In addition to these political differences, transition economies display an enormous diversity in terms of physical and population size, level of development (as measured by GDP per capita), natural resource endowment, and cultural and historical background, greatly complicating intercountry comparison.

The key economic objectives of the transition are to raise economic efficiency and promote

[7]Given the unique position of the three Baltic countries as members of both the former Soviet Union and the EU accession group, they will be presented as a separate group in most tables and figures in this chapter.

[8]Mongolia, which formally belongs in the non-CIS Asia group, will normally be attached to the CIS group, given its former close political and economic association with the Soviet Union, which has heavily influenced its transition experience.

[9]Similarly, Croatia differs significantly from the other countries in the southeastern Europe region.

[10]Whether countries can make a full transition to a market economy without a political transition to a representative democracy remains a bone of contention among social scientists; see European Bank for Reconstruction and Development, *Transition Report 1999* (London: EBRD, 1999), Chapter 5.

growth. The major elements of the transition process comprise macrostabilization, price and market liberalization (including international trade), restructuring and privatizing state enterprises, and redefining the role of the state. As can be seen from Figure 3.1, these elements—and their possible sequencing—were clearly identified early in the transition process, although views on the relative importance of individual components have changed significantly in some instances (Box 3.2).[11] However, despite the similarity of ultimate objectives and basic direction of changes required, countries' actual transition experience has differed enormously, with respect to both policies implemented and results achieved to date. The reasons for the differences include the country's initial conditions, the external environment (notably external shocks), and the specific policies pursued during the transition.

With regard to each of these factors, the situation in the EU accession countries has been more favorable than that in the CIS countries. Proximity to western Europe was associated with more favorable initial conditions, as the imprint of central planning was more limited, while rapid reorientation of trade to the more stable western European markets reduced these countries' exposure to external shocks largely caused by declining trade within the CMEA. The resulting more favorable output performance was generally associated with more ambitious structural and institutional reforms, which in turn seems to have been partly a result of the external anchor provided by potential accession to the European Union. The close correlation among geographic location, initial conditions, and policies complicates the assessment of the role each of these factors played in determining outcomes.

The transition process consists largely of changes in institutions and modes of business conduct—in both the government and private

---

[11]The figure is drawn from Stanley Fischer and Alan Gelb, "The Process of Socialist Economic Transformation," *Journal of Economic Perspectives*, Vol. 5, No. 4 (Fall 1991), pp. 91–105.

Figure 3.1. Key Elements of Reform in Transition

The transition comprises reform in many key areas of the economy, with differing duration and changing intensity over time.

Source: Based on Stanley Fischer and Alan Gelb, "The Process of Socialist Economic Transformation," *Journal of Economic Perspectives*, Vol. 5, No. 4 (Fall 1991), pp.91–105.

Box 3.2. Transition Controversies

While the overall objective of transition—creating functioning market economies—is generally agreed, there has been a vigorous debate on how best to accomplish this goal. The conclusions in the main text are not necessarily shared by all observers, and this box presents alternative views on some of the key issues. Most such discussions take as a reference point the "market-fundamentalism" reform strategy that was followed by most of the transition countries of central and eastern Europe, the Baltics, and the CIS, which reflected the thinking of the majority of political leaders in these countries and was supported by many prominent academic advisers and the international financial institutions, including the IMF. This approach, broadly summarized in Figure 3.1, involved simultaneously initiating and implementing macrostabilization, price and market reform, enterprise restructuring and privatization, and institutional reorganization—the so-called "big bang" approach.[1] The decision to start along many fronts simultaneously reflected a belief that the components of reform were interlinked and complementary, so that partial reforms would lead to unsatisfactory outcomes, and that it was important to make the market reform process irreversible by rapidly initiating a comprehensive transition program in the immediate aftermath of the breakdown of the existing political regime.

The debate over transition strategies has been between four groups. One group consists of the protagonists of the reform strategy actually pursued, who consider that the strategy was essentially sound and generally successful where it was vigorously implemented, and that problems arose primarily as a result of shortfalls in implementation. The other three are: those who agree in principle with the market-fundamental-

ism reform strategy, but disagree with some of the specifics of its implementation; those who believe that the proposed sequencing and speed of reforms were ill-advised; and those who think that the overall strategy was misguided in emphasizing radical reform over gradual institutional development. This debate has intensified recently, fueled by a number of papers that revisit these issues in view of the cumulative evidence from the first decade of transition.[2]

Apart from privatization, dealt with in Box 3.4, the discussion of reform implementation based on market fundamentalism has focused on macroeconomic stabilization. This debate has centered on the adoption of tight fiscal and monetary policies, which, according to the critics, exacerbated the initial output decline and contributed to problems of barter and arrears (Box 3.3).[3] Others argue that the decline in out-

---

[1]For more details see Alan Gelb and Cheryl Gray, "The Transformation of Economies in Central and Eastern Europe," World Bank Policy and Research Series No. 17 (Washington: The World Bank, 1991), and Stanley Fischer and Alan Gelb, "The Process of Socialist Economic Transformation," *Journal of Economic Perspectives*, Vol. 5, No. 4 (Fall 1991), pp. 91–105.

[2]For an overview of the debate see Gérard Roland, *Transition and Economics. Politics, Markets and Firms* (Cambridge, Mass.: The MIT Press, 2000) and also Grzegorz Kolodko, *From Shock to Therapy: The Political Economy of Postsocialist Transformation* (Oxford: Oxford University Press, 2000). A survey sympathetic to the market fundamentalist strategy is contained in Marek Dabrowski, Stanislaw Gomulka, and Jacek Rustowski, "Whence Reform? A Critique of the Stiglitz Perspective," CASE Working Paper (Warsaw: Center for Social and Economic Research, 2000). A more critical review can be found in János Kornai, "Ten Years After the Road to a Free Economy: The Author's Self-Evaluation," a paper presented at the World Bank Annual Conference on Development Economics, April 2000, Washington. An even more critical approach, with an institutionalist flavor, can be found in Joseph Stiglitz, "Whither Reform?" a paper presented at the World Bank Annual Conference on Development Economics, April 1999, Washington, and Joseph Stiglitz, "Quis Custodiet Ipsos Custodies?" paper presented at the World Bank Annual Conference on Development Economics—Europe, June 1999, Paris.

[3]An earlier body of literature argued that tight macroeconomic policies were needed, but that stabilization could have been accomplished sooner through alternative exchange-rate management policies, more international financial support, and greater efforts toward nonmonetary financing of the budget deficit; see Jeffrey Sachs, "Transition at Mid-Decade," *American Economic Review*, Vol. 86, No. 2 (May 1996), pp. 128–133.

put largely reflected initial conditions and external shocks, and that tight macroeconomic policies laid the basis for a faster and more robust recovery subsequently. This argument applies especially to CIS countries, where incipient hyperinflation made stabilization an urgent priority, and external resources were limited. In the event, tight macroeconomic policies—when applied—did succeed in stabilizing the economies concerned, thus meeting a necessary condition for proceeding with the transition process.

The debate on optimal sequencing and speed of reforms has moved beyond the initial emphasis on "gradualism" versus "shock therapy." Critics of the "big bang" approach argue that the emphasis on speed destroyed still-valuable organizational arrangements among existing enterprises and that the resulting "disorganization" contributed significantly to the output collapse. This collapse, when combined with price liberalization and deep cuts in government spending, in turn led to sharp increases in poverty and income inequality. Also, given the uncertainties inherent in transition, some argue that in a number of cases, Russia in particular, badly sequenced reforms led to vested interests becoming entrenched and blocking further reforms. Other researchers, however, dispute these criticisms, noting that output was already beginning to fall before the transition began, that the organizational arrangements inherited from central planning were unsuited to the market, and that privatized firms have in many cases restructured more rapidly than those left in the hands of the state. They also note that the most unequal allocations of wealth and pronounced increases in income inequality and poverty occurred largely in countries where reforms were

implemented only partially, and could be manipulated by vested interests for their own benefit. Finally, they note that the decision to use early "windows of opportunity" to push reforms through rapidly was successful in central and eastern Europe, while the slower recovery of output and continuing disruption in the CIS reflected a failure to implement the strategy with sufficient vigor.

A more basic criticism of market fundamentalism is that it greatly underestimated both the importance and difficulty of creating the institutional infrastructure needed to underpin the operation of market economies. According to this view, creating effective institutions is a lengthy process requiring much trial and error, implying that reform should occur in an evolutionary manner that adapts existing institutions to new needs pragmatically and gradually, as has occurred in China. In this view, market fundamentalism was flawed because it eliminated institutions that could have been useful in the early stages of transition and because it emphasized financial reform and the adoption of new legal frameworks, while underestimating the more lengthy and difficult process of ensuring enforcement of laws, reforming the organization of government, and developing self-enforcing norms that foster entrepreneurship. In the absence of core market-oriented institutions, some argue, other reform efforts often had unintended and negative consequences. Others, however, argue that an evolutionary approach was both inappropriate for the industrial economies of the CMEA region and infeasible given the collapse of central planning and political upheavals associated with the breakdown of Soviet hegemony.

industry—that are difficult to quantify. To facilitate the evaluation and monitoring of progress in transition over time, and to allow a comparison of progress between different countries, analysts have developed quantitative indicators of structural change on the basis of expert judgment, which will be referred to repeatedly in this

chapter. The most frequently used and referred to of these so-called transition indicators are those introduced by the European Bank for Reconstruction and Development (EBRD). The EBRD's indicators range from 1 to 4+, with 1 representing conditions unchanged from those prevailing in a centrally planned economy with

Figure 3.2. Progress in Structural Reform and Output Performance
(Simple country averages for each group)

The extent of structural reform and output performance since the start of transition has differed greatly among countries.

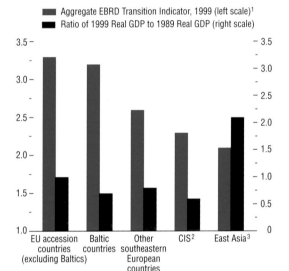

Sources: European Bank for Reconstruction and Development, *Transition Report 1999* (EBRD: London, 1999); and IMF staff estimates for east Asian countries and Mongolia.

[1]Aggregate of eight EBRD transition indicators. For an explanation of these indicators, see the Appendix.

[2]Data include Mongolia, whose EBRD transition indicator is estimated by IMF staff.

[3]EBRD transition indicator estimated by IMF staff.

dominant state ownership of means of production and 4+ for conditions in an advanced market economy.[12] The indicators cover key areas of structural reform and are presented and explained in more detail in the Appendix to this chapter.[13] Key differences among the five groups of transition countries defined above are summarized in Figure 3.2, which juxtaposes average transition indicator scores for each group, as well as real output in 1999 as a multiple of real output in 1989.

Macroeconomic Developments

Macroeconomic developments during the transition process, as reflected in output levels and rates of inflation, are summarized in Figure 3.3 for five country groups.[14] The outstanding feature of this diagram is the difference in output growth across these groups. Even though assessing the precise path of output, including relative performance among countries, is complicated by numerous data weaknesses, the broad features shown in Figure 3.3 are undisputed, including relative performance among country groups.[15] The European and CIS transition economies suffered a substantial output contraction at the start of the transition. The de-

[12]Analysts often linearize the scores by assigning a value of ⅓ to a "+" sign and –⅓ to a "–" sign attached to the integer scores 1 to 4, a practice also followed in this chapter.

[13]Transition indicators for Mongolia and the east Asian countries reported in this chapter are IMF staff estimates.

[14]In this, and all other figures of this type, the data are adjusted for the east Asian countries whose transition began prior to 1989. The first 11 years of transition for these countries cover the following periods: China (1978–89), Lao P.D.R. (1986–97), and Vietnam (1986–97).

[15]For further discussion of data (un)reliability see Mark De Broeck and Vincent Koen, "The Great Contractions in Russia, the Baltics and the Other Countries of the Former Soviet Union: A View from the Supply Side," IMF Working Paper 00/32 (Washington: International Monetary Fund, March 2000); and Simon Johnson, Daniel Kaufman, and Andre Schleifer, "The Unofficial Economy in Transition," *Brookings Papers on Economic Activity: 2*, Brookings Institution, 1997, pp. 159–239.

cline was particularly severe in the CIS countries, where the recovery process also started later and was less vigorous. The Baltic countries' output performance was initially similar to that of the CIS countries, but subsequently started to converge to that of other EU accession countries. Performance in the other countries of southeastern Europe has been erratic, heavily influenced by civil strife and war during much of the transition period. Armed conflict also affected developments in some CIS countries in central Asia and the Caucasus. More generally, almost 10 years after the transition process took off in Europe, only a handful of countries are estimated to have returned to output levels at—or slightly above—those prevailing at the start of transition. In contrast, output growth remained very strong in the transition countries of east Asia following the onset of reforms; it continued throughout the transition period, and output levels now substantially exceed starting point levels in these countries (Figure 3.4).

Except in the east Asian transition countries, employment fell in the early years of the transition, but by much less than output, although both output and employment data are likely to be affected by considerable margins of error. In central and eastern Europe, the return to robust growth in the second half of the 1990s has led to some net employment creation.

Nevertheless, total employment at the end of the decade was still more than 10 percent below its 1989 level because the growth stemmed mainly from efficiency gains. In the CIS countries, where the recovery did not take hold until 1999, employment has continued to decline gradually in recent years. In these countries, the labor hoarding inherited from central planning has intensified during the transition, as the cumulative decline in output has far exceeded that in employment, resulting in widespread involuntary temporary layoffs and part-time work.

In most transition countries prices increased substantially in the initial stage of the transition, as a result of price liberalization and the large monetary overhang inherited from the period under central planning (Figure 3.3, lower

Figure 3.3. Output and Inflation Performance During Transition

The evolution of output and inflation during the transition has differed considerably among countries.

— EU accession countries (excluding Baltics)
— Baltic countries
— Other southeastern European countries
— CIS[1]
— East Asia[2]

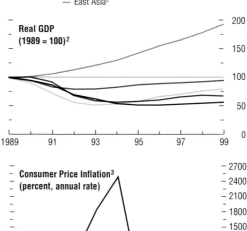

[1]Data include Mongolia.

[2]Chart is adjusted for three east Asian countries whose transitions began prior to 1989. The first 11 years of transition for the following countries are as follows: China (1978–89), Lao P.D.R. (1986–97), and Vietnam (1986–97).

[3]The increase in the EU accession group's inflation, in 1997, is largely accounted for by the hyperinflation experienced in Bulgaria that year.

Figure 3.4. Real GDP Ratio, 2000 to 1989[1]

Only in the east Asian transition economies does the current level of output greatly exceed the level recorded at the start of transition.

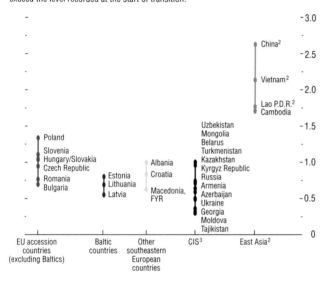

[1]Output projections for 2000 are IMF staff estimates.

[2]Chart is adjusted for three east Asian countries whose transitions began prior to 1989. The first 11 years of transition for the following countries are as follows: China (1978–89), Lao P.D.R. (1986–97), and Vietnam (1986–97).

[3]Data include Mongolia.

panel). The monetization of large budget deficits, arising from output contraction and fiscal restructuring, fueled inflation, which reached four-digit rates in the mid-1990s in a number of CIS countries. As in the case of output, the southeast European countries had an intermediate inflation performance falling between the CIS and the EU accession group. The resulting macroeconomic instability was much more virulent and persistent in the CIS than in east Asian and European countries. As of 2000, however, significant macroeconomic imbalances persisted in only five countries, with either the inflation rate projected to exceed 40 percent annually, or the budget deficit expected to be 5 percent of GDP or more (Figure 3.5); all of these countries belonged to the group of slow or intermediate reformers in the CIS and other southeastern Europe regions.

A serious problem related to fiscal consolidation and macrostability is the persistence of tax arrears and the proliferation of barter trade, a phenomenon particularly prevalent in several CIS countries (Box 3.3 discusses the origins, extent, and implications of this problem in Russia). The persistence of tax arrears and barter trade reflects the failure to carry out or to complete structural reform in several interlocking areas—most importantly enterprise restructuring; the creation of a financial sector that operates on a commercial basis; and public sector reform, especially the collection of tax revenues.

Countries adopted a variety of exchange rate regimes at the start of the transition or at the time when national currencies were introduced. Estonia instituted a currency board, a number of central and eastern European countries (Croatia, the Czech Republic, the former Yugoslav Republic of Macedonia, Hungary, Poland, and the Slovak Republic) introduced a pegged exchange rate regime, and the other central and eastern European and Baltic countries and all CIS countries chose a flexible exchange rate regime. The choice of a flexible regime was often motivated by a lack of sufficient foreign exchange reserves to back a peg, low initial credibility of policies, and severe uncertainty regarding the rate at which the currency should be pegged. Many of the nominally flexible regimes were, however, heavily managed in practice as stabilization programs were implemented. The initial choice of exchange rate regime was often modified in the course of the transition. Flexible exchange rate regimes gave way to a peg in Latvia and to currency boards in Bulgaria and Lithuania. Pegged regimes were replaced by more flexible arrangements in the Czech Republic, Poland, and the Slovak Republic, prompted in part by concerns about potentially destabilizing effects of large capital inflows.

Macroeconomic stabilization was not a smooth process in all countries. Most transition economies succeeded in bringing down the high inflation rates that characterized the start of transition, reaching reasonable price stability by the mid-1990s, but several countries experienced a resurgence of inflation in the second half of the decade. Belarus, Bulgaria, Romania, Russia, and Tajikistan are the countries where this "U-shaped" stabilization pattern has been most conspicuous. While external shocks (e.g., regional war in the Balkan area) played a role in some cases, an important common factor seems to have been the failure to pursue the reform agenda consistently and vigorously. The resulting buildup of bad loans in the banking sector and of government debt eventually led to a loss of confidence among both domestic and external creditors, entailing currency and banking crises in the countries concerned. Among the stabilization setbacks experienced by various countries, the Russian crisis of 1998 was the most serious, caused by a fiscal policy stance that turned unsustainable—especially when combined with an exchange rate policy aimed at nominal exchange rate stability—and exacerbated by the lack of prudence among international lenders.[16]

[16]Causes and consequences of this crisis, which affected several other countries in the area, and—in combination with the Asian financial crisis preceding it—the world economy, have been analyzed in detail in the December 1998 Interim Assessment of the *World Economic Outlook* (Washington: International Monetary Fund, 1998).

Figure 3.5. Macrostabilization: Budget Deficit and Inflation, 2000[1]

Several transition countries have not yet gained macrostability as of 2000.

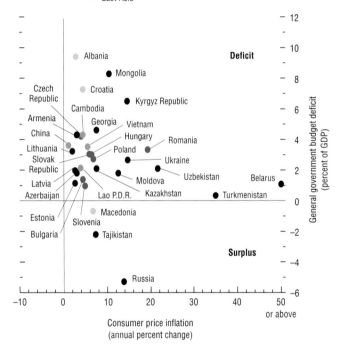

[1]Data for 2000 are IMF staff projections. Belarus, whose annual inflation in 2000 is expected to be 83 percent, appears on the far right side of the graph.
[2]Data include Mongolia.

Box 3.3. Addressing Barter Trade and Arrears in Russia

Widespread enterprise arrears and barter transactions are symptoms of the deep-rooted structural problems affecting the transition process in Russia. The non-monetary share in industrial sector revenues rose from about 10 percent in 1993 to almost 50 percent in 1998, while overdue payables by enterprises rose from below 10 percent to over 35 percent of GDP (see the Figure). Despite a significant decline following the August 1998 crisis, barter and arrears remain prevalent in both state-owned and privatized enterprises and in most subsectors of industry and construction. Many firms that now earn cash on exports still make use of barter trade in their domestic transactions.

The reasons behind the proliferation of barter and arrears are complex, but recent studies provide some tentative explanations.[1] Following the liberalization of prices and trade, industrial firms experienced growing liquidity problems as demand fell and directed credit and subsidies were reduced. Many enterprises responded by resorting to nonpayment and barter to keep afloat rather than embarking on market-oriented restructuring. Crucially, the state sanctioned this attitude by tolerating an increase in non-monetary and late payments for both tax and utility bills and a lax approach to bankruptcy. As noncash tax payments, so-called "tax offsets," tend to overvalue the goods delivered to the state, this practice amounted to a significant infusion of implicit subsidies, which became the key reason for the growth of barter and arrears until 1998. The state, especially subnational governments and public utilities, re-

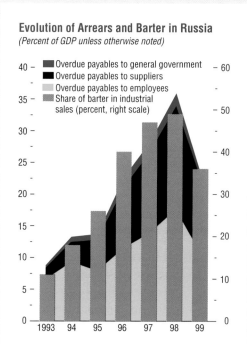

Evolution of Arrears and Barter in Russia
(Percent of GDP unless otherwise noted)

Source: Data communicated by Russian European Center for Economic Policy, Moscow.

mains a central participant in complex chains of late payments and offsets.[2]

Barter and arrears have imposed severe costs on the Russian economy and continue to delay enterprise restructuring. Tax arrears and offsets erode fiscal revenues, and the lack of transparency associated with non-monetary transactions creates opportunities for corruption and fraud. Barter locks firms into trading patterns and networks that tend to discourage innovation and competition. The common practice of mispricing goods in barter and offset transactions obscures financial accounts of enterprises, thus reducing their access to potential outside credi-

---

[1]See, for example, Simon Commander and Christian Mumssen, "Understanding Barter in Russia," European Bank for Reconstruction and Development Working Paper 37 (London: EBRD, 1999); Clifford G. Gaddy and Barry W. Ickes, "Beyond a Bailout: Time to Face Reality About Russia's 'Virtual Economy,'" *Foreign Affairs*, Vol. 77, pp. 53–67; Brian Pinto, Vladimir Drebentsov, and Alexander Morozov, "Give Growth and Macro-Stability in Russia a Chance: Harden Budgets by Dismantling Nonpayments," World Bank Policy Research Working Paper No. 2324 (Washington: World Bank, 2000).

[2]While barter trade is common in other CIS countries as well, transition countries outside the CIS have largely avoided high levels of barter, mainly because firms have generally maintained monetary payments to the state and public utilities. Arrears, however, have also been a problem in several central and eastern European countries.

tors and investors alike. Perhaps the most damaging aspect of the noncash economy is the ad hoc allocation of implicit subsidies, which provides a cushion against market discipline. As large loss makers tend to run up higher arrears and pay more frequently with overvalued output than profitable small and medium-sized enterprises, this amounts to an implicit cross-subsidy from more productive to less productive segments of the economy.

Barter and arrears ultimately reflect a failure of economic policy to promote the restructuring of the ailing industrial sector. Outdated technology, oversized plants, environmental liabilities, high levels of industry concentration, rigid supplier links, and high transport costs are among the many problems inherited from central planning in Russia. The initial market reforms—price liberalization, privatization, and macroeconomic stabilization—were meant to introduce competitive market forces that would kick-start the restructuring process. However, the competitive effects of these reforms were partly offset by the new implicit subsidies channeled through barter and arrears. This has led to a vicious circle of nonpayment and lack of restructuring.

The persistent failure to impose "hard budget constraints" on nonviable enterprises is partly rooted in social considerations, given the importance of large enterprises for the local economy and the absence of an effective national social safety net. However, it also reflects institutional weaknesses, including the absence of clear property rights and the complex nature of the fiscal relations between the federal, regional, and local governments.[3] In addition, the corporate governance structures resulting from Russian privatization tend to inhibit restructuring, and vested interests continue to dominate relations between the state and the large enterprises.

A credible solution to the nonpayment problem in Russia would have to involve a fundamental reform of public finances, including more stringent enforcement of tax and utility pay-

ments, a more effective fiscal transfer system, as well as measures to ensure that budgetary entities pay their own bills in time and in cash. Whereas tax offsets have been virtually eliminated at the federal level and tax arrears reduced, the public utilities and local governments remain important sources of implicit subsidies. The federal government has recently made efforts to improve the fiscal transfer system in a way that provides more incentives to subnational government to collect taxes in cash. In addition, recent initiatives to reform the tax code may facilitate tighter enforcement if they succeed in simplifying the tax system and lowering the overall tax burden on enterprises. The large public utilities have also tried to raise cash collection ratios, but so far with only limited success. Part of the problem is the absence of clear rules on when to cut off nonpayers from the utility service, but there are also corporate governance problems in these utilities, including an unclear separation of commercial and state interests.

While measures to improve payments to the tax authorities and public utilities are necessary to phase out the noncash economy, they may not yield a sustainable solution unless complementary efforts are made to promote enterprise restructuring. An important element would be to establish an effective social safety net for workers who lose their jobs in the process of restructuring. Moreover, the state should use the resources freed by a reduction of tax arrears and offset-based subsidies for explicit support of the restructuring process, by financing redundancy packages for workers, lump-sum grants for municipalities that take on the social responsibilities of large enterprises, and environmental rehabilitation. What is perhaps even more important is to stimulate the creation and growth of new private firms by removing bureaucratic hurdles and addressing corruption. This would help to create employment and shift labor to more productive sectors, thus strengthening domestic product market competition. Combined with more stringent enforcement of tax and utility payments, competition could force loss-making enterprises to restructure more rapidly and thereby reduce barter and arrears, or to go out of business altogether.

---

[3]See Box 3.5 in this chapter and OECD, *OECD Economic Surveys—Russian Federation* (Paris: Organization for Economic Cooperation and Development, 2000).

Figure 3.6. Change in Poverty and Income Distribution
(Simple country averages for each group)

Except for the east Asian transition economies, the incidence of poverty rose in all countries during transition, and income distribution became more uneven.

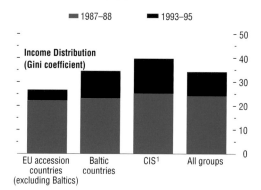

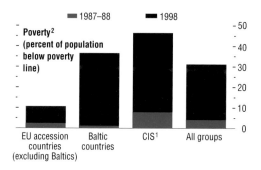

Source: Branko Milanovic, *Income, Inequality and Poverty during the Transition from Planned to Market Economy,* The World Bank Regional and Sectoral Series (Washington: World Bank, 1998).
[1]Data exclude Armenia, Azerbaijan, Georgia, and Tajikistan.
[2]Poverty is defined as having an income of less than four U.S. dollars per day in purchasing-power-parity terms.

The transition process had a major impact on poverty and income inequality (as conventionally measured), which—as noted earlier—under central planning had been generally less pronounced than in other countries at similar levels of income (Figure 3.6). Once again, a full assessment is complicated by data weaknesses. Under central planning, real income was significantly influenced by privileged access to certain goods and services; and given pervasive shortages before the transition, the data in Figure 3.6 are also likely to exaggerate the actual increase in poverty. Also, some increase in inequality could be expected as a result of introducing market incentives and adjustment of relative prices to reflect scarcities. Nevertheless, there is little doubt that inequality has risen substantially and the economic situation for a substantial number of people, particularly those at the lower end of the income scale or whose savings were wiped out by high inflation at the start of transition, has worsened, while in some cases small groups have reaped substantial material benefits from rent-seeking activities.[17]

The deterioration was most pronounced in the countries of the former Soviet Union (particularly the western CIS), where the share of the population living in poverty rose to 60 percent in some instances. It was more limited, but still significant, in some central and eastern European countries, and poverty was still a persistent phenomenon in most transition economies as of 1998. The recorded increases in poverty were sharpest in those countries where the reform process has stalled, stultifying entrepreneurship and new growth opportunities, and where privatization favoring insiders and poor

[17]In the present context, poverty is defined as a daily income of $4 measured at purchasing power parity; income inequality is measured using the Gini coefficient of the distribution of income. For a more comprehensive analysis of social conditions and related indicators in transition economies outside east Asia, see Annex 1.1 in EBRD, *Transition Report 1999,* and Branko Milanovic, *Income, Inequality, and Poverty during the Transition from Planned to Market Economy,* The World Bank Regional and Sectoral Studies (Washington: World Bank, 1998).

targeting of social safety nets have permitted a lopsided accumulation of wealth. Income inequality also increased in the transition economies of Asia, but since output increased rapidly, these countries were still able to achieve impressive reductions in their poverty rates during the transition process.

Structural Reform and Institutional Change

There are two dimensions to the massive changes in the structure of the transition economies witnessed since the start of transition: the wide range of structural and institutional reforms implemented by governments and the resulting changes in economic behavior and institutions. Although considerable progress has been achieved overall, as of 1999 the structural reform process was far from complete, and progress differed greatly across reform areas (Figure 3.7). Reform is most advanced in privatization of small-scale enterprises. The other areas in which reforms are relatively advanced are the liberalization of foreign trade and exchange (although some CIS countries have not started reforms in this area at all) and the elimination of price controls. Structural reforms are least advanced in the regulation and supervision of the banking and financial sector, the development and enforcement of competition policy, the restructuring of large-scale enterprises, and the reform of governance in both the private and the public sector.

Reform progress has also been uneven across countries. Only nine out of the 31 countries listed in Table 3.1 achieved an average transition indicator score above 3, with all but one (Croatia) of these advanced reformers belonging to the EU accession countries (Figure 3.8).[18] The six lowest scores (below 2) are all found outside the group of EU accession countries: three of these slow reformers are members of the CIS (Belarus, Tajikistan, and Turkmenistan),

[18]The only EU accession countries scoring below the threshold (i.e., a score of 3) separating advanced from intermediate reformers are Bulgaria and Romania.

Figure 3.7. Progress in Reform by Area, 1999[1]
(Simple average of all transition economies for each indicator)

Progress in structural reform, measured on a scale from 1 to 4⅓, differs greatly between different reform areas.

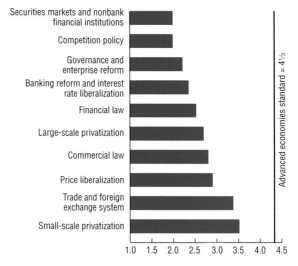

Sources: European Bank for Reconstruction and Development, *Transition Report 1999* (EBRD: London, 1999); and IMF staff estimates.
[1]For an explanation of the indicators, see the Appendix.

and two are located in east Asia (Lao P.D.R. and Vietnam).[19] The bulk of the transition countries (including Russia and China) fall into the group of "intermediate" reformers, with scores ranging from 2 to 3, underlining the need to continue with intensive reform efforts.

The ranking of transition economies according to their aggregate transition indicator score closely matches their ranking in terms of perceived institutional quality, as measured by standardized sample surveys or ratings by commercial agencies. The overall indicator of institutional quality in Figure 3.9 is an aggregate of five component indicators, comprising government effectiveness, extent of regulation, rule of law, the extent of democracy, and graft.[20] At a more detailed level, some interesting differences emerge among countries with respect to the component indicators. CIS countries have excessive regulatory burdens and face significant governance problems, while the EU accession countries are favored by a higher degree of democratization and a more limited degree of public regulation and control (see Table 3.11 in the Appendix).

In response to structural reforms and efforts to stabilize the economy, several important characteristics of the transition countries have changed drastically (Figure 3.10).[21] Most prices are now market determined: in 1997 only three

Figure 3.8. Aggregate EBRD Transition Indicator, 1999[1]

The extent of structural reforms undertaken during transition, measured on a scale from 1 to 4⅓, differs considerably among countries.

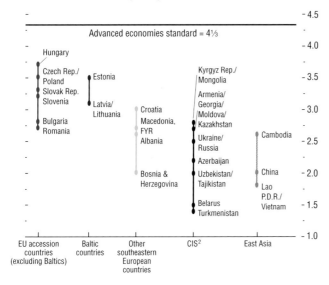

Source: European Bank for Reconstruction and Development, *Transition Report 1999* (London: EBRD, 1999).
   [1]Average of eight EBRD indicators. For an explanation of the indicators, see the Appendix.
   [2]Data include Mongolia.

   [19]The slow reformer group also includes Bosnia and Herzegovina, where the situation is complicated by a continuing *de facto* split of the country into two separate administrative entities, which impedes effective policymaking at a central government level.

   [20]A paper prepared for the *World Economic Outlook* by Beatrice Weder, "Institutional Reform in Transition Economies: How Far Have They Come?" (unpublished; Washington: International Monetary Fund, 2000), provides an extensive survey of the institutional quality of transition economies, using indicators developed by Daniel Kaufmann, Aart Kraay, and Pablo Zoido-Lobatón in "Governance Matters," World Bank Policy Research Working Paper No. 2196 (Washington: World Bank, 1999) and "Aggregating Governance Indicators," World Bank Policy Research Working Paper No. 2195 (Washington: World Bank, 1999). These indicators are explained in more detail in the Appendix.

   [21]See EBRD, *Transition Report 1999*, Chapter 4, for a more detailed overview of progress in structural adjustment.

transition countries (all members of the CIS) administered more than 30 percent of the prices of basic goods. The excessive industrialization that characterized all but the transition countries of east Asia has also been reduced, as is evident from the falling share of industry in total employment in all but the east Asian transition economies.[22] This was partly a result of a rapid expansion—in both absolute and relative terms—of the service sector, which had been severely neglected under central planning. And the public sector dominance in economic activity was replaced by a remarkable pickup in private sector activity: the private sector share of GDP rose to an average of 70 percent in the EU accession countries in 1998 and to 50 percent in CIS countries. This adjustment was achieved via both the privatization of old state-owned enterprises and the emergence of new private firms and activities. Although privatization generally boosted firms' productivity, especially when hard budget constraints were imposed, there is some evidence that productivity in both new domestic firms and foreign-owned firms exceeds that in domestic privatized or public firms, suggesting that the process of enterprise restructuring remains incomplete.[23]

An area in which progress differed significantly among transition countries, with important implications for the transition process overall, is the privatization and restructuring of large-scale public enterprises. The transition countries of east Asia, where privatization of large public enterprises is just starting, are at one end of the spectrum, and restructuring of the enterprises concerned still looms large on

---

[22]In terms of output shares, which combine both price and output effects, by 1998 only three countries recorded an industrial share of GDP above 40 percent, as opposed to 12 countries in 1990.

[23]See "Enterprise Response to Reforms," Part III in EBRD, *Transition Report 1999;* Simeon Djankov and Peter Murrell, "Enterprise Restructuring in Transition: A Quantitative Survey," (unpublished; Washington: World Bank, 2000); and Simon Commander, Mark Dutz, and Nicholas Stern, "Restructuring in Transition Economies: Ownership, Competition, and Regulation" (unpublished; Washington: World Bank, 1999).

Figure 3.9. Index of Institutional Quality, 1997–98[1]

The differences in "institutional quality" among countries, measured on a scale from –20 to 12.6, are very similar to differences in the extent of structural reform.

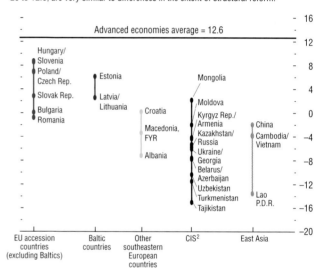

Source: Beatrice Weder, "Institutional Reform in Transition Economies: How Far Have They Come?" (unpublished; Washington: International Monetary Fund, 2000).
[1]For an explanation of the indicators, see the Appendix.
[2]Data include Mongolia.

Figure 3.10. Progress in Structural Adjustment

In response to wide-ranging structural reforms, all transition economies have undergone significant structural change.

— EU accession countries (excluding Baltics)
— Baltic countries
— Other southeastern European countries
— CIS[1]
— East Asia[2]

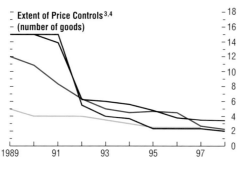

Extent of Price Controls[3,4]
(number of goods)

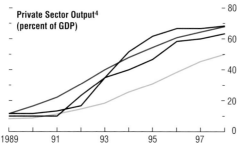

Private Sector Output[4]
(percent of GDP)

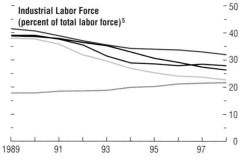

Industrial Labor Force
(percent of total labor force)[5]

Sources: For the extent of price controls: European Bank for Reconstruction and Development, *Transition Report, 1999* (London: EBRD, 2000); for private sector share in GDP, World Bank, *World Development Indicators*; for industrial labor force, national authorities; and IMF staff estimates.

[1]Data include Mongolia.

[2]Chart is adjusted for three east Asian countries whose transitions began prior to 1989. The first 11 years of transition for the following countries are as follows: China (1978–89), Lao P.D.R. (1986–97), and Vietnam (1986–97).

[3]Number of goods with administered prices in the basket of 15 basic goods constructed by the EBRD.

[4]Simple average.

[5]Countries within group weighted by their total labor force.

the policy agenda. At the opposite end of the spectrum are the majority of the advanced EU accession countries, where most large-scale public enterprises have been privatized and where restructuring is proceeding apace. Most CIS countries occupy an intermediate position: many large public enterprises have been privatized, but restructuring has made little progress for a number of reasons (see Box 3.4, which also reviews the policy debate regarding the speed and sequencing of privatization and restructuring public enterprises).

The development of the financial sector has been marked by the elimination of the central bank monopoly in credit allocation, as virtually all transition countries have by now established a two-tier banking system. However, in many countries, the extent of intermediation by the banking sector—especially in terms of credit extended to the private sector and deposit taking from households—has remained limited. Banks often have made little progress in developing a capacity for prudent lending and sound risk management, and they continue to lend to affiliated enterprises or, under official pressure, to loss-making, state-owned enterprises. As a result, these banks are burdened by large amounts of nonperforming loans and they remain vulnerable to systemic crises. Although the core elements of a proper legal and regulatory framework for the banking sector have been put in place in most countries, implementation and enforcement problems remain widespread, in part owing to the weakness and lack of independence of the regulatory authorities. Development of the nonbank financial institutions, including insurance companies and securities markets, is even more limited than that of the banking sector.

Transition in the External Sector

The process of reintegrating the transition economies into the world economy through trade flows has made major progress. Before the transition, most transition economies were locked in excessive and inefficient trade relations with other CMEA members, often due to

Box 3.4. Privatization in Transition Economies

The privatization of state-owned companies has been a central element of the transition in central and eastern Europe, the Baltics, and the CIS. A larger private sector, which would harness profit motives, was expected to result in better allocation of resources and improved economic efficiency. The scale and pace of private sector development—both in terms of privatization and establishment of new enterprises—have been remarkable. The EBRD estimates that in 1999 the private sector produced over half of GDP in 20 of the 26 transition countries monitored.[1] Small-scale privatization is virtually complete in all but five countries, while the privatization of medium-sized and large enterprises is nearing completion in about 10 countries.

Has privatization yielded the expected benefits? A number of empirical studies have examined the impact of privatization at the enterprise level, using various measures of enterprise performance and restructuring, such as changes in the workforce, revenue growth, profitability, and productivity.[2] Although it is difficult to assess to what extent this research is affected by selection bias (i.e., good firms are privatized before bad firms), a number of fairly robust conclusions have emerged:

- In central and eastern Europe and the Baltic countries, privatized firms have generally restructured more quickly and performed better than comparable firms that remained in state ownership; partly this is due to extensive involvement of foreign investors in the privatization process and a relatively sound business environment.
- Privatization has often failed to boost restructuring and better performance of enterprises

in most of the CIS countries, partly as a result of the poor corporate governance structures in many privatized firms and partly because of the persistence of "soft budget constraints," including implicit subsidies from the state.
- Post-privatization ownership is an important determinant of firm-level restructuring and performance. Across the whole region, the best performers have been firms that were acquired by foreign strategic investors. Similarly, firms with concentrated ownership (insider and outsider) have generally performed better than firms with dispersed ownership.
- The method of privatization has been important for the speed and perceived equity of the process. However, since many countries applied a combination of methods (vouchers, management-employee buyouts, and direct sales), there has not been a clear relationship between privatization method and post-privatization ownership and restructuring.

These stylized facts suggest that privatization has not always been effective in bringing about enterprise restructuring. Although private ownership activates profit motives, private ownership alone is not sufficient to make firms efficient—complementary conditions are required to make privatization lead to effective restructuring.[3] This has significant policy implications:
- Privatization risks producing perverse results in the absence of hard budget constraints and competition. When privatized firms continue to receive subsidies, especially implicit support in the form of soft credit and tax arrears, they tend to focus their efforts on rent seeking rather than on restructuring. When barriers to international trade and entry of new firms remain high, incumbent large firms continue to operate as quasi-monopolists, with little incentive to restructure. These factors are among the reasons why privatization in cen-

[1]See European Bank for Reconstruction and Development, *Transition Report 1999* (London: EBRD, 1999). The east Asian transition countries are excluded from this sample.

[2]For a review of this research, see Oleh Havrylyshyn and Donal McGettigan, "Privatization in Transition Countries: A Sampling of the Literature," forthcoming in *Post-Soviet Affairs,* as well as Simeon Djankov and Peter Murrell, "Enterprise Restructuring in Transition: A Quantitative Survey" (unpublished; Washington: World Bank, April 2000).

[3]See, for example, Jeffrey Sachs, Clifford Zinnes, and Yair Eilat, "The Gains from Privatization in Transition Economies: Is 'Change of Ownership' Enough?" CAER Discussion Paper No. 63 (Cambridge, Mass.: Harvard Institute for International Development, Consulting Assistance on Economic Reform, 2000).

Box 3.4 *(concluded)*

tral and eastern Europe and the Baltics has worked much better than in the CIS.

- Privatization that results in widely dispersed ownership structures can work well only in countries with effective standards of corporate governance. In many transition countries, managers with relatively small ownership stakes wield considerable power without being effectively controlled by shareholders, which provides incentives for asset stripping and self-dealing. Concentrated ownership, such as in firms owned by foreign strategic investors or in small and medium enterprises fully owned by managers, has generally yielded the best results.

- The benefits of privatization are larger in countries with an effective legal framework and secure property rights. In many transition economies, especially those in the CIS, the business environment remains marred by corruption, weak courts, and overbearing bureaucracy, as well as by complex and unfair tax systems. These conditions generally undermine enterprise efficiency and long-term investment incentives.

The first decade of transition thus suggests that privatization does not work equally well in all circumstances. Indeed, there is a view that privatization should have been implemented much more gradually, with enterprise restructuring and improvements in the institutional framework preceding privatization.[4] Yet, building effective legal institutions and good corporate governance generally takes a long time and there is no guarantee that in the meantime state firms are run any better than privatized firms, especially if the general business environment remains influenced by vested interests.[5] On balance, it is clear that strong emphasis on financial discipline and competition early on in the reform process (as

was the case in Poland, but not Russia) is an important complement to privatization.

Looking ahead, the question is what can be done with the large number of dysfunctional privatized firms, especially in the CIS countries. Strengthening the effectiveness of legal, regulatory, and fiscal institutions is without doubt desirable. However, this process takes time, and the existing shortcomings in corporate governance may require more immediate action.

Some observers have suggested that re-nationalization may be a way to prevent continuing abuses by rogue managers.[6] In countries with widespread corruption, however, reversion to state ownership may make matters even worse. Moreover, a process of re-nationalization and subsequent re-privatization is likely to be hijacked by precisely those vested interests that have undermined the initial privatization process. A more promising route would be to dilute the ownership stake of managers in those firms that have failed to restructure and have run up large arrears, with creditors converting the firm's debts and arrears into new stock and selling the company to strategic investors. This is essentially a case-by-case approach, however, especially considering the limited number of willing investors.

Perhaps the most effective way to promote restructuring at this stage of transition is to foster competition and hard budget constraints to force even badly run enterprises to adapt or go out of business. This would require further opening up of international trade, reducing bureaucratic hurdles to entry, tightening payment discipline, improving bankruptcy procedures, promoting a healthy financial sector, and phasing out implicit subsidies. "Starting all over" by re-nationalization and re-privatization is unlikely to be a realistic or desirable option. Accelerating reform to foster competition and hard budget constraints seems a more effective, if difficult, way forward.

[4]See, for instance, Joseph Stiglitz, "Whither Reform? Ten Years of the Transition," paper presented at The World Bank Annual Conference on Development Economics, April 1999, Washington.

[5]This point is made, for example, by John Nellis, "Time to Rethink Privatization in Transition Economies?" *Finance and Development*, Vol. 36, No. 2 (June 1999), pp 16–19.

[6]This may come about automatically if the original privatization is legally challenged. However, instances of revoking privatization have been very rare despite frequent complaints about cronyism and corrupt privatization practices in the past.

political and strategic considerations rather than economic criteria. But extensive trade liberalization has helped to bring the geographical and commodity composition of trade more in line with countries' comparative advantage. The central and eastern European countries in particular have reallocated trade flows away from other centrally planned economies toward the European Union, while transition countries in east Asia, especially China, strongly penetrated world markets. As of 1997, more than 70 percent of exports from the EU accession and other southeastern European countries were directed to non-transition economies, but this share rose only to 30 percent in CIS countries, partly reflecting geographic location. Despite these gains, reintegration into the world economy has not been completed. According to EBRD calculations, intraregional trade among transition economies (excluding east Asia) in 1997 remained well above normal levels as computed by a gravity model (Figure 3.11). This legacy of excess intraregional trade is still particularly prevalent in CIS countries.

With the exception of China and Russia, a major commodity exporter, the opening to external trade has been accompanied by rising current account deficits. In central Europe, current account deficits remained moderate as a share of GDP in the first years of the transition, reflecting contractions in domestic demand, real exchange rate undervaluations that occurred at the beginning of the transition, and external financing constraints. Current account deficits in central Europe have widened since 1996, however, as the regional pickup in growth and investment has been associated with rapidly rising imports of both consumption and investment goods. In the Baltics and the CIS countries other than Russia, current account balances, measured as a percentage of GDP, increased considerably between 1992 and 1998. Several factors contributed to this development. Many of these countries experienced large terms of trade losses, as prices for energy imports from former CMEA trade partners moved to market-determined levels. Moreover, these countries ran high

Figure 3.11. Adjustment Gap of Regional Export Structure[1]
(Percentage point deviation from "norm")

Although the foreign trade of most transition countries has been largely liberalized, the regional structure of exports is still affected by the legacy of directed trade under central planning.

■ Difference between actual and predicted trade with the European Union
■ Difference between actual and predicted trade with other transition economies
■ Difference between actual and predicted trade with the rest of the world

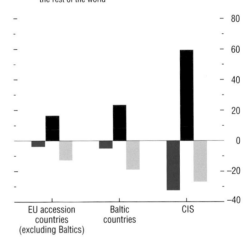

Source: European Bank for Reconstruction and Development, *Transition Report 1999* (London: EBRD, 1999).
[1]The "norm" is the hypothetical share of regional exports in total exports, computed from a gravity model of export structure.

Figure 3.12. Current Account Deficit and Foreign Direct Investment, 1999
(Percent of GDP)

In most transition countries the current account deficit greatly exceeds foreign direct investment, increasing these countries' external vulnerability.

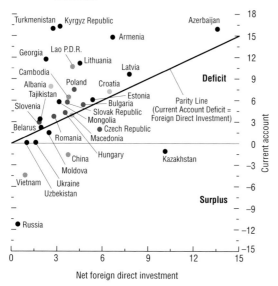

¹Data include Mongolia.

fiscal deficits, as the authorities tried to absorb the revenue and expenditure pressures associated with sharp falls in national income and fiscal restructuring. Finally, as a result of slow progress in building a competitive and diversified export sector, trade liberalization early on mainly stimulated imports of consumer goods and services. External adjustment policies introduced in the wake of the Russian crisis have narrowed the current account deficits in this group of countries, but in many cases the deficits still remain high—sometimes above 10 percent of GDP (Figure 3.12).

In part prompted by the need to cover sizable current account deficits, the transition countries have required substantial external financing since the early 1990s. The amounts and composition of such financing have varied markedly (Figure 3.13). In the EU accession countries official flows, which accounted for most of the financing in the initial transition years have been replaced by private inflows as the main financing source. Foreign direct investment to these countries increased sharply from the mid-1990s in response to improved economic performance, deeper policy reforms, and prospects of EU membership. In most of these countries short-term capital inflows have also picked up. These flows have at times complicated the conduct of monetary policy. Foreign direct investment in China and Vietnam rose very rapidly in recent years, aided by—in the case of China—the establishment of free trade zones in coastal areas. China has also gained increasing access to other private financing flows, foreign bank loans in particular.

In contrast, the CIS countries have had relatively little access to private capital flows. During the early 1990s, their financing needs were often met in a disorderly manner. In the framework of the common ruble zone, which existed until the middle of 1993, the Central Bank of Russia was an important source of financing, as was the accumulation of arrears on payments for energy imports. Following the breakdown of the ruble zone, Russia continued to provide financing to other CIS countries on commercial terms, but in several cases the resulting debt was not serviced and arrears on payments for energy imports continued.[24] Since the mid-1990s, however, the role of such exceptional financing has diminished, and most CIS countries with current account deficits have relied increasingly on multilateral loans as the main financing source. During 1996–97, some CIS countries, including Kazakhstan, Moldova, and Ukraine, also turned increasingly to private market financing, but these efforts suffered a major setback following the 1998 Russian crisis. Also, with the exception of oil-rich Azerbaijan and Kazakhstan, the CIS countries have received little foreign direct investment.

The high current account deficits registered throughout the transition in a number of CIS countries have led to rapid increases in external debt and debt service. The initial debt position in the CIS countries other than Russia was favorable, as they concluded agreements under which Russia inherited all external debt obligations for the entire former Soviet Union to official and private creditors.[25] Following the breakdown of the ruble zone in the course of 1993, arrears and obligations to the Central Bank of Russia incurred by other CIS countries were converted into government debt at commercial terms. As the public sector in many of these countries, including subnational governments and state enterprises, continued to resort to external borrowing to cushion the impact of the transitional recession, the median external debt to GDP ratio increased further, to around 45 percent by 1999, reflecting both the rise in debt and the decline in output. Most of the external debt is owed to or guaranteed by the government, and

[24]For an analysis of how the disorderly financing of substantial external imbalances contributed to the macroeconomic instability and high inflation in the CIS countries during 1992–94, see Patrick Conway, *Crisis, Stabilization and Growth: Economic Adjustment in Transition Economies* (Boston: Kluwer Academic Publishers, forthcoming).

[25]Russia, in return for taking over the debt of the former Soviet Union, inherited the Union's external assets. It also received a debt relief package from official creditors under the auspices of the Paris Club and debt referrals by commercial bank creditors.

Figure 3.13. Composition of Net Capital Flows
(U.S. dollars per capita)

Net capital flows to transition economies varied considerably between different countries and over time.

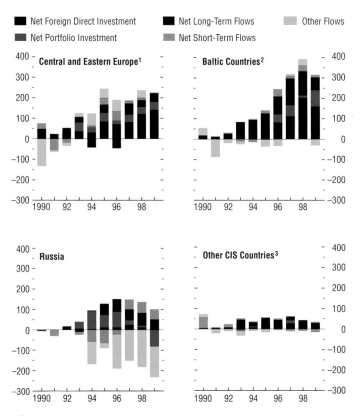

[1]Central and eastern Europe excluding Belarus, Estonia, Latvia, Lithuania, and Moldova.
[2]Estonia, Latvia, and Lithuania.
[3]Commonwealth of Independent States excluding Russia.

Table 3.3. Foreign Indebtedness, 1999
(In percent)

Country Group[1]	Ratio of Debt to GDP	Ratio of Debt to Exports	Ratio of Short-Term Debt to Total Debt	Ratio of Debt Service to Exports
EU accession countries (excluding Baltics)	46.3	110.3	13.5	13.2
Baltic countries[2]	29.8	56.9	26.2	14.4
Commonwealth of Independent States[3]	62.7	150.3	12.8	15.5
High-debt CIS countries[4]	86.8	192.5	10.4	20.9
Low-debt CIS countries[5]	34.5	101.0	15.5	9.2
Other southeastern European countries	38.8	149.0	17.1	43.2
East Asia[6]	76.3	212.9	4.8	8.3

Sources: European Bank for Reconstruction and Development; and IMF staff estimates.
[1]Data for country groups are simple averages of group member data.
[2]Baltic countries data are from the European Bank for Reconstruction and Development.
[3]Data include Mongolia.
[4]Countries with debt to GDP ratios above 60 percent.
[5]Countries with debt to GDP ratios below 60 percent.
[6]Excluding Lao P.D.R. and Vietnam, which are Heavily Indebted Poor Countries, the debt to GDP ratio would drop to 43.2 percent and the debt to exports ratio would fall to 143.9 percent.

therefore it constitutes a future budget obligation. Moreover, a high proportion of the debt—including most borrowing from multilateral sources—has been contracted on market (or near market) terms, and poor debt management practices have exacerbated the debt burden. In some cases, key debt indicators, including fiscal indicators, are approaching levels that may be difficult to sustain, similar to those in many of the economies currently defined as Heavily Indebted Poor Countries in the late 1980s. With the exception of these CIS countries, and also of Bulgaria—which continues to carry a heavy debt legacy from the central planning era—the external debt burdens of the transition countries remain moderate (Table 3.3).

Comparing Transition Economies with the Rest of the World

With the transition process now under way for over 10 years, it is legitimate to ask how far the reform process has advanced and whether transition economies are still distinct from other countries. Across a range of characteristics, the answer appears to be that the transition countries as a group are difficult to distinguish from other countries with similar levels of per capita income, although the CIS countries continue to exhibit some significant differences.[26] The quality of institutions actually appears to be higher in the advanced EU accession countries than in upper-middle income developing countries, but lower in the CIS and some Balkan countries than in lower-middle income developing countries; for most Balkan and east Asian countries the quality of institutions is comparable with that of countries at similar income levels (Table 3.4).[27]

The overall comparison gives essentially similar results when the attractiveness and the competitiveness of the business environment is evaluated on the basis not only of institutions, but also by using indicators of openness, governance, financial sector development, infrastructure quality, state of technology, and labor market flexibility.[28] The EU accession countries are

---

[26]For an international comparison of the status of institutional development, see Weder, "Institutional Reform," and Daniel Gros and Marc Suhrcke, "Ten Years After: What Is Special About Transition Countries," Hamburg Institute of International Economics Discussion Paper No. 86 (Hamburg: HWWA, 2000).

[27]Table 3.4 ranks the countries on the basis of the overall index of institutional quality and provides a quintile allocation of countries. The table is meant to provide a rough comparison rather than a precise ranking, given the lack of precision of the underlying data.

[28]See Jeffrey Sachs, Clifford Zines, and Yair Eilat, "Benchmarking Competitiveness in Transition Economies," CAER II Discussion Paper 62 (Cambridge, Massachusetts: Harvard Institute for International Development, February 2000).

Table 3.4. Countries' Institutional Quality: Quintiles, 1997–98

Highest Quintile	Second Quintile	Third Quintile	Fourth Quintile	Lowest Quintile
Switzerland	Costa Rica	Fiji	Senegal	Albania
Netherlands	Poland	Western Samoa	Ecuador	Korea, Dem. People's Rep. of
Finland	Malawi	Comoros	Macedonia, FYR	Cameroon
New Zealand	Czech Republic	Bahrain	Turkey	Syrian Arab Republic
Denmark	Israel	Croatia	Uganda	Chad
Norway	Bahamas, The	Cape Verde	Venezuela	Belarus
Sweden	Greece	Bolivia	Cuba	Indonesia
United Kingdom	Estonia	Bulgaria	Papua New Guinea	Azerbaijan
Luxembourg	Trinidad and Tobago	India	Sri Lanka	Kenya
Singapore	Uruguay	Brazil	Madagascar	Mauritania
Canada	Botswana	El Salvador	Vietnam	Yemen, Republic of
Australia	Qatar	Jamaica	Bangladesh	Guinea-Bissau
Ireland	Belize	Gambia, The	Cambodia	Maldives
Austria	Oman	Mexico	Central African Republic	Sierra Leone
Germany	Namibia	Romania	Colombia	Bosnia and Herzegovina
Iceland	Korea, Republic of	Lebanon	Nicaragua	Nigeria
United States	New Caledonia	Mali	Kyrgyz Republic	Burundi
Portugal	Kuwait	Dominican Republic	Honduras	Niger
Solomon Islands	Jordan	Ethiopia	Armenia	Congo
Spain	Argentina	Tanzania	Swaziland	Uzbekistan
France	Tunisia	Ghana	Djibouti	Liberia
Cyprus	Slovak Republic	Egypt	Mozambique	Yugoslavia, Fed. Rep. of
Hong Kong SAR	Brunei	Malaysia	Guatemala	Haiti
Puerto Rico	Latvia	Peru	Zimbabwe	Turkmenistan
Japan	Lithuania	Côte d'Ivoire	Kazakhstan	Angola
Italy	United Arab Emirates	Moldova	Gabon	Rwanda
Belgium	West Bank and Gaza	China	Iran, Islamic Republic of	Bhutan
Taiwan Province of China	Mongolia	Zambia	Russian Federation	Equatorial Guinea
Chile	Philippines	Suriname	Guinea	Algeria
Hungary	Morocco	Saudi Arabia	Paraguay	Sudan
Malta	Thailand	Lesotho	Ukraine	Lao P.D.R.
	Guyana	Burkina Faso	Pakistan	Tajikistan
Barbados	Panama	Benin	Georgia	Somalia
São Tomé and Príncipe	South Africa	Nepal	Togo	Zaire

Group Identification				
EU accession (excluding Baltics)	Baltic countries	Other southeastern European countries	CIS[1]	East Asia

Source: Beatrice Weder, "Institutional Reform in Transition Economies: How Far Have They Come?," (unpublished; Washington: International Monetary Fund, 2000).

[1]Data include Mongolia.

the most "competitive," but could gain by increasing their openness. The Baltic countries had even lower tariff barriers than the advanced economies (on average) in 1998–99, but are still afflicted by poor quality of physical infrastructure and low labor market flexibility. The CIS countries were the least competitive, with the western member countries scoring higher than those in central Asia on almost all fronts.

Some structural distortions inherited from central planning are still present in the eco-

nomic structure of the transition countries, while some positive legacies also persist. On the one hand, government size (as measured by revenue and expenditure ratios to GDP) in transition economies of middle income levels is generally larger than in market economies at similar levels of income (Figure 3.14). Also, even after controlling for income and other pertinent economic indicators, the extent of trade among the former CMEA countries (excluding Vietnam) and the size of the industrial sector

Figure 3.14. Government Revenue and Expenditure, 1999
(Percent of GDP)

Transition economies with per capita incomes above $5,000 still have a relatively large public sector; their ratios of government revenue and expenditure to GDP systematically exceed the average ratios in non-transition economies.

- EU accession countries (excluding Baltics)
- Baltic countries
- Other southeastern European countries
- CIS[1]
- East Asia

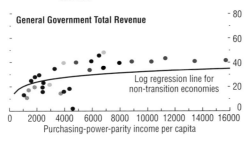

General Government Total Revenue

Log regression line for non-transition economies

Purchasing-power-parity income per capita

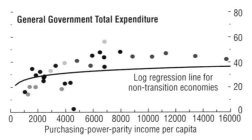

General Government Total Expenditure

Log regression line for non-transition economies

Purchasing-power-parity income per capita

[1]Data include Mongolia.

are generally still larger than market economy benchmarks.[29] On the other hand, human capital endowment was and remains high by international standards in the transition economies, even though its skill mix may not always correspond optimally to the requirements of a market economy. Despite a temporary negative effect of the transition process—particularly in western CIS countries, where indicators of life expectancy and adult mortality have worsened since the onset of transition—health and education conditions are generally still favorable compared with other countries at similar levels of income (Table 3.5).

The financial system is still underdeveloped by international standards, based on measures of financial maturity that have recently been developed and appear to be linked to growth and development.[30] On the one hand, the provision of credit by private banks relative to that by the central bank is by now close to the norms observed in market economies at comparable levels of income (Figure 3.15, upper panel).[31] The east Asian transition countries and the EU accession countries are somewhat above this benchmark, and most CIS countries are below it. On the other hand, the depth of the financial system and the degree of financial intermediation to the private sector are still more limited than in traditional market economies. For most transition economies (with the notable exception of

[29]Jarko Fidrmuc and Jan Fidrmuc, "Integration, Disintegration and Trade in Europe: Evolution of Trade Relations During the 1990s," paper presented at the fifth Dubrovnik conference on Transition Economies, Croatia, June 23–25, 1999, published as Working Paper B3 (Bonn: Center for European Integration Studies, 2000), and Gros and Suhrcke, "Ten Years After."

[30]For the link between financial intermediation and growth, see Ross Levine, Norman Loyaza, and Thorsten Beck, "Financial Intermediation and Growth: Causality and Causes," World Bank Policy Research Working Paper No. 2059 (Washington: World Bank, February 1999).

[31]The data in Figure 3.15 on financial markets in transition countries were specially constructed for the *World Economic Outlook*; see William Branson and Ben Sutton, "Financial Maturity in Transition Economies" (unpublished; Washington: International Monetary Fund, 2000).

Table 3.5. Proxy Measures of Human Capital
(Average across years)

Country Group[1]	Primary School Enrollment (gross) 1995–99	Life Expectancy at Birth (years) 1998–99	Infant Mortality Rate per 1,000 Live Births 1998–99	Adult Illiteracy (percent of people aged 15 and over) 1998–99	*Memorandum* Purchasing Power Parity GDP per Capita 1998–99
EU accession countries (excluding Baltics)	99.9	72.2	10.4	1.1	9,837
Baltic countries	94.0	70.3	11.1	0.4	6,737
Other southeastern European countries	92.9	72.4	16.5	9.3	4,514
Commonwealth of Independent States[2]	93.8	68.4	21.8	7.0	3,278
East Asia	115.6	61.5	65.5	35.2	1,987
Other Economies					
Advanced economies	101.9	77.5	5.2	4.8	23,278
Developing countries[3]	93.7	60.5	61.3	30.2	4,435
Low income	78.0	52.3	89.1	45.0	1,401
Lower middle income	101.2	66.9	42.2	19.9	4,305
Upper middle income	102.8	69.4	26.6	13.3	9,287

Sources: World Bank; IMF staff estimates.
[1]Data for country groups are simple averages of group member data.
[2]Data include Mongolia.
[3]Data exclude Cambodia, China, Lao P.D.R., Mongolia, and Vietnam.

China), indicators such as the ratio of private credit to GDP and liquid bank liabilities to GDP are well below the average of other countries with similar levels of income, with the EU accession countries being generally closer to the benchmark than the CIS countries (Figure 3.15, middle and lower panels).

Explaining Differences in Performance and Resulting Policy Lessons

Among the major differences in performance among transition economies are the evolution of output and inflation following the start of the transition process (Figure 3.3). Empirical research suggests that this divergent performance can be explained in terms of four main factors: differences in inherited economic structures; po-

litical developments—including civil strife and war in some countries in southeastern Europe and the CIS; reform strategies; and macroeconomic policies.[32] In particular, the much larger output contraction experienced initially by the CIS and Baltic countries compared to the central European transition economies owed much to worse initial conditions in terms of larger price and trade distortions (Table 3.6), as these implied a more extensive reorganization of resources and structural adjustments.[33] In contrast, some countries in southeastern and central Europe (especially the successor states to the former Republic of Yugoslavia, but also Hungary and Poland) had made significant progress with reform before, particularly in terms of public controls of prices, ownership of small firms, and the structure of external trade.[34] Given the dis-

[32]Stanley Fischer and Ratna Sahay, "The Transition Economies After Ten Years," IMF Working Paper 00/30 (Washington: International Monetary Fund, 2000); Charles Wyplosz, "Ten Years of Transformation: Macroeconomic Lessons," CEPR Discussion Paper No. 2254 (London: Centre for Economic Policy Research, 2000); Jànos Kornai, "Ten Years After The Road to a Free Economy: The Author's Self-Evaluation," paper presented at the World Bank Annual Bank Conference on Development Economics held in Washington, D.C. on April 18–20, 2000.

[33]Martha De Melo, Cevdet Denizer, Alan Gelb, and Stoyan Tenev, "Circumstances and Choices: The Role of Initial Conditions and Policies in Transition Economies," World Bank Policy Research Working Paper No. 1866 (Washington: World Bank, 1997), and Peter Murrell, "How Far Has The Transition Progressed?" *Journal of Economic Perspectives*, Vol. 10, 1996, pp. 25–44.

[34]The liberalization index for the transition economies of east Asia for the year 1989 is also relatively high, as these countries started the reform process earlier.

Figure 3.15. Financial Maturity Indicators, 1994–99
(Simple country averages)

Two-tier banking systems have been established in almost all transition countries, but the extent of financial intermediation is generally still limited when compared with other economies.

- EU accession countries (excluding Baltics)
- Baltic countries
- Other southeastern European countries
- CIS[1]
- East Asia

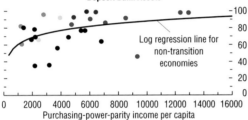

Ratio of Deposit Bank Assets to Central Bank Assets and Deposit Bank Assets

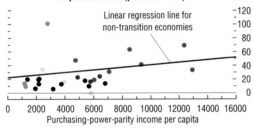

Liquid Liabilities (percent of GDP)

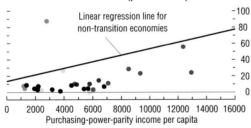

Total Private Credit (percent of GDP)

[1]Data include Mongolia.

torted structure of industry and trade, the collapse of the CMEA in 1991 resulted in a severe demand shock, particularly for countries of the former Soviet Union and Mongolia (Figure 3.16), where—with the exception of Russia, which had a somewhat more diversified geographic composition of trade—intra-CMEA trade accounted for as much as 80–90 percent of total trade (some 30–40 percent of GDP). In addition, many of the CIS countries were severely affected by the loss of fiscal transfers through the former Union budget, by 16 price increases on energy deliveries from Russia, and by the large output falls in Russia—their principal trading partner.[35] However, recent empirical evidence shows that the impact of initial conditions faded gradually over time: the macroeconomic performance at the beginning of the transition process was heavily influenced by the initial conditions, but the subsequent path of recovery was closely associated with the strength of the reform efforts.[36]

The slower output recovery in CIS countries, compared to the EU accession countries, has been mostly associated with less vigorous and more limited structural and institutional reforms, as well as less successful stabilization policies, entailing greater macroeconomic instability following the onset of transition. A wide body of research suggests that countries with deeper and wider reforms experienced an earlier resumption of output growth and a faster reduction in inflation, while delaying key structural reforms or stabilization measures did not prevent output declines. The countries that implemented more ambitious structural reform programs were also the ones that were more successful in achieving macroeconomic stabili-

[35]See Robert A. Mundell, "The Great Contractions in Transition Economies," in *Macroeconomic Stabilization in Transition Economies,* ed. by Mario I. Blejer and Marko Skreb (Cambridge: Cambridge University Press, 1997).

[36]See de Melo and others, "Circumstances and Choices," and Elisabetta Falcetti, Martin Raiser, and Peter Sanfey, "Defying the Odds: Initial Conditions, Reforms, and Growth in the First Decade of Transition" (unpublished; London: EBRD, 2000).

Table 3.6. Initial Conditions

Transition Country/Group[1]	Share of Industry in GDP 1990	Liberalization Index 1989	Repressed Inflation 1987–90[2]	Black Market Premium 1990 (%)	Years Under Central Planning[3]	Purchasing Power Parity Income per Capita (U.S. Dollars) 1989	Council of Mutual Economic Assistance Trade (percent of GDP) 1990	Natural Resource Endowment
EU accession countries								
(excluding Baltics)	**0.52**	**0.16**	**5.5**	**339**	**43**	**6,547**	**8.3**	
Bulgaria	0.59	0.13	18.0	921	43	5,000	16.1	poor
Czech Republic	0.58	0.00	−7.1	185	42	8,600	6.0	poor
Hungary	0.36	0.34	−7.7	47	42	6,810	13.7	poor
Poland	0.52	0.24	13.6	277	41	5,150	8.4	moderate
Romania	0.59	0.00	16.8	728	42	3,470	3.7	moderate
Slovak Republic	0.59	0.00	−7.1	185	42	7,600	6.0	poor
Slovenia	0.44	0.41	12.0	27	46	9,200	4.0	poor
Baltic countries	**0.45**	**0.05**	**25.7**	**1,828**	**51**	**7,973**	**35.9**	
Estonia	0.44	0.07	25.7	1,828	51	8,900	30.2	poor
Latvia	0.45	0.04	25.7	1,828	51	8,590	36.7	poor
Lithuania	0.45	0.04	25.7	1,828	51	6,430	40.9	poor
Other southeastern								
European countries	**0.38**	**0.27**	**9.4**	**163**	**47**	**3,655**	**6.2**	
Albania	0.37	0.00	4.3	434	47	1,400	6.6	poor
Croatia	0.35	0.41	12.0	27	46	6,171	6.0	poor
Macedonia, Former								
Yugoslav Rep. of	0.43	0.41	12.0	27	47	3,394	6.0	poor
Commonwealth of								
Independent States[4]	**0.41**	**0.04**	**24.3**	**1,795**	**70**	**4,755**	**27.2**	
Armenia	0.55	0.04	25.7	1,828	71	5,530	25.6	poor
Azerbaijan	0.44	0.04	25.7	1,828	70	4,620	29.8	rich
Belarus	0.49	0.04	25.7	1,828	72	7,010	41.0	poor
Georgia	0.43	0.04	25.7	1,828	70	5,590	24.8	moderate
Kazakhstan	0.34	0.04	25.7	1,828	71	5,130	20.8	rich
Kyrgyz Republic	0.40	0.04	25.7	1,828	71	3,180	27.7	poor
Moldova	0.37	0.04	25.7	1,828	51	4,670	28.9	poor
Mongolia	0.41	0.00	7.6	1,400	70	2,100	31.0	moderate
Russia	0.48	0.04	25.7	1,828	74	7,720	11.1	rich
Tajikistan	0.34	0.04	25.7	1,828	71	3,610	31.0	poor
Turkmenistan	0.34	0.04	25.7	1,828	71	4,230	33.0	rich
Ukraine	0.44	0.04	25.7	1,828	74	5,680	23.8	moderate
Uzbekistan	0.33	0.04	25.7	1,828	71	2,740	25.5	moderate
East Asia[5]	**0.36**	**0.50**	**8.7**	**336**	**19**	**882**	**4.1**	...
Cambodia	...	...	...	...	15	894	...	...
China[5]	0.49	0.46	2.3	208	29[6]	800	1.0	moderate
Lao People's Democratic								
Republic[5]	...	...	...	...	11	736	...	...
Vietnam[5]	0.23	0.53	15.0	464	11/32[7]	1,100	7.2	moderate

Sources: Martha De Melo, Cevdet Denizer, Alan Gelb, and Stoyan Tenev, "Circumstances and Choices: The Role of Initial Conditions and Policies in Transition Economics" (Washington: World Bank, 1997); Data for Cambodia and Lao P.D.R. are IMF staff calculations.

[1]Data for country groups are simple averages of group member data.

[2] Repressed inflation is calculated as the percent change in the average real wage less the percent change in real GDP over 1987–90.

[3]Until beginning of transition.

[4]Data include Mongolia.

[5]Table is adjusted for three east Asian countries whose transitions began prior to 1989 (China, 1978; Lao P.D.R, 1986; Vietnam, 1986), except for the "Liberalization Index", 1989, which refers to 1989 for all countries.

[6]Data is IMF staff evaluation and different from original source.

[7]South and North Vietnam respectively. IMF staff evaluation, different from original source.

zation.[37] (The special case of east Asian transition economies will be reviewed in the following paragraphs.).

The initial surge in prices in most transition countries was a result of repressed inflation preceding reform, but the subsequent explosion into hyperinflation in several CIS countries was due to ongoing policies failing to maintain macroeconomic stability. In the last years of central planning, most countries allowed a monetary overhang to build up: wages paid to workers exceeded the value of goods produced by state-owned enterprises (whose prices were set artificially low), the excess being financed by money creation. When prices were liberalized, this inflationary pressure generated a one-off jump in prices. A rapid deterioration of the fiscal accounts, coupled with monetary financing of budget deficits in the context of the ruble zone, subsequently generated rapid inflation.[38] The reasons why these adverse developments were so

Figure 3.16. Trade-Weighted Real GDP Growth of Trading Partners

(Annual percent change)

Strong trade links among members of the defunct Council for Mutual Economic Assistance (CMEA) at the start of transition led to the transmission of output shocks within this area, which were largest for the member states of the former Soviet Union.

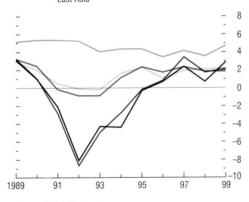

Source: IMF staff estimates.
[1]Data include Mongolia.
[2]Chart is adjusted for three east Asian countries whose transitions began prior to 1989. The first 11 years of transition for the following countries are as follows: China (1978–89), Lao P.D.R. (1986–97), and Vietnam (1986–97).

[37]For the role of structural reforms, see Falcetti, Raiser, and Sanfey, "Defying the Odds"; Oleh Havrylyshyn and others, "Growth Experience in Transition Countries, 1990–98," Occasional Paper No. 184 (Washington: International Monetary Fund, 1999); Andrew Berg and others, "The Evolution of Output in Transition Economies: Explaining the Differences," IMF Working Paper 99/73 (Washington: International Monetary Fund, 1999); Holger Wolf, "Transition Strategies: Choices and Outcomes," *Princeton Studies in International Finance No. 85* (Princeton, New Jersey: Princeton University, June 1999); Peter Christoffersen and Peter Doyle, "From Inflation to Growth: Eight Years of Transition," IMF Working Paper 98/100 (Washington: International Monetary Fund, July 1998); Martha De Melo, Cevdet Denizer, and Alan Gelb, "Patterns of Transition from Plan to Market," *The World Bank Economic Review*, Vol. 10, No. 3., pp. 397–424, and references cited therein. The importance of institutions for growth in transition economies has been documented, among others, by Aymo Brunetti, Gregory Kisunko, and Beatrice Weder, "Institutions in Transition: Reliability of Rules and Economic Performance in Former Socialist Countries," World Bank Policy Research Working Paper No. 1809 (Washington: World Bank, 1997); and Oleh Havrylyshyn and Ron van Rooden, "Institutions Matter, But So Do Policies," IMF Working Paper 00/70 (Washington: International Monetary Fund, 2000).

[38]On fiscal developments, see Vito Tanzi and George Tsibouris, "Fiscal Reform over Ten Years of Transition," IMF Working Paper 00/113 (Washington: International Monetary Fund, 2000).

different in scale among transition economies can only be fully understood by discussing the political economy of reform (see next section).

Unlike the macroeconomic developments in the transition countries in Europe and the CIS, the transition countries of east Asia did not experience an initial output contraction following the initiation of the reform process, and output growth actually rose significantly during transition.[39] The rapid growth experienced by China in particular has led a number of observers to argue that a gradual approach to reform may be more effective.[40] Others, however, have argued that this favorable outcome occurred despite gradualism, not because of it, and that a large part of the difference in performance is explained by differing initial conditions and political stability.[41]

A distinguishing feature of the transition process in China and other east Asian countries is that the process was started by the incumbent governments, with the initial objectives of raising income and growth by introducing incentives, modifying the traditional planning system, and opening up the economy to the outside world. The reform process was therefore inevitably gradualist in nature—although in specific areas it was quite far reaching—and evolved over time.[42] Thus, in contrast with the experience in a number of transition countries in other regions, economic reform efforts were initiated and implemented in a relatively stable political climate, without the disruptive effects associated with civil strife or the dissolution of state structures.

While the debate on the causes of the strong growth in the transition countries of east Asia still continues, specific initial conditions clearly also played an important role. Apart from the political aspects noted above, a central distinction is that the east Asian economies were still largely agricultural, with a large pool of surplus labor. Thus, initial reforms—for instance, permitting greater private sector activity in agriculture and relaxing entry into industry in rural areas—could generate large increases in output. In most other transition countries, where most people were securely employed by large, albeit inefficient, public enterprises, there was no alternative to tackling the problems in the state-owned industrial sector up front, which inevitably resulted in a period of substantial economic dislocation.

In addition, macroeconomic conditions were generally more favorable. In particular, China enjoyed a relatively strong fiscal position when initiating its reform efforts and has succeeded in avoiding major macroeconomic crises.[43] Although the other transition economies in east Asia faced large fiscal deficits and experienced a period of very high inflation at the outset of their transitions, they were able to quickly reduce inflation to more moderate levels by drastically tightening fiscal and monetary policies, and any decline in output was modest and short-lived—mainly because of a strong supply response from agricultural reforms. The transition countries in east Asia also were less affected by trade distortions, having begun to diversify and

---

[39]The transition process in Mongolia is in many ways similar to that of the faster reforming economies in central Europe—see Sanjay Kalra and Torsten Sløk, "Inflation and Growth in Transition: Are the Asian Economies Different?" IMF Working Paper 99/118 (Washington: International Monetary Fund, August 1999).

[40]See Barry Naughton, "What Is Distinctive About China's Economic Transition? State Enterprise Reform and the Overall System Transformation," *Journal of Comparative Economics*, Vol. 18, No. 3, (1994), pp. 470–90; and Thomas Rawski, "Progress without Privatization: The Reform of China's State Industries," in *The Political Economy of Privatization and Public Enterprise in Post-Communist and Reforming Communist States*, ed. by Vedat Milor (Boulder, Colorado: Lynne Rienner, 1994).

[41]See Jeffrey Sachs and Wing Thye Woo, "Structural Factors in the Economic Reforms of China, Eastern Europe, and the Former Soviet Union," *Economic Policy*, Vol. 9 (April 1994), pp. 101–145.

[42]China's present objective of developing a socialist market economy was not formally adopted until 1993, 15 years after the start of the reform process.

[43]However, stabilization in China has taken place in distinct cycles. Typically, reforms led to rising domestic demand and inflationary pressures, which—given the limitations of macroeconomic instruments—prompted the authorities to tighten administrative controls and slow down reforms to maintain macroeconomic stability; see Stefan Erik Oppers, "Macroeconomic Cycles in China," IMF Working Paper 97/135 (Washington: International Monetary Fund, September 1997).

reduce their trade dependency on the CMEA area much earlier; thus when the CMEA collapsed in 1991, the negative external demand shock was less severe.

The strong growth performance in the east Asian transition economies following the onset of the transition may also reflect three key elements of the reform strategies adopted in the region. First, while reforms in the east Asian transition countries have indeed been partial, leaving the large state-owned enterprises and the financial sector until late in the process, they have nevertheless been quite radical in the areas in which growth has been most dynamic, such as agriculture, foreign enterprise entry, and creation of new rural enterprises. Second, the reform process facilitated and encouraged the development of new small and medium-scale enterprises (even though property rights were never well defined). In China, the so-called township and village enterprises grew rapidly, accounting for an increasing share of industrial output and especially exports. However, this approach of allowing small-scale initiatives to thrive while postponing the reform of the large-scale, state-owned industrial enterprises appears to have been possible only where the large-scale, state-owned firms did not constitute a major part of the overall economy. Third, the reform strategy—particularly in China—has been characterized by pragmatism and flexibility, with different reform approaches often allowed to coexist and compete for a period. Given the difficulties of implementing reforms in such a large and diverse country such as China, this approach has helped to build local ownership of reforms, and has yielded important lessons that could then be applied country wide. For example, the development of both the household responsibility system in agriculture, and to some extent of the township and village enterprises, stem from local, rather than central, initiatives and experience.

As noted earlier, the gradual pace of reform in public enterprises and in the financial sector was feasible because of the initial structure of the economy, and it has helped maintain social stability in China and other east Asian transition economies. Such stability has, however, been bought at a price. In China, for example, the lack of reform of state enterprises contributed to a serious deterioration in the firms' financial positions, financed primarily through a substantial buildup of nonperforming loans in the state-owned commercial banks. By the mid-1990s, the situation was no longer sustainable, and since that time financial and enterprise sector reforms have been at the top of the policy agenda. Over the last few years, significant progress has been made—including privatization of the bulk of small-scale enterprises and the reduction of nonperforming loans in state banks—although much remains to be done to restructure large enterprises and to develop a strong and commercially oriented banking system.

Political Economy of Transition

It is tempting to argue that the large differences in stabilization efforts and progress in structural reform are simply a manifestation of different policy objectives and commitment, as revealed by actual reform measures taken and the effectiveness of their implementation. This interpretation, however, begs the important question: why were there such large differences in policy objectives and in countries' success (or failure) in translating the objectives into legislation and then implementing this legislation? To shed more light on this question, it is necessary to complement economic analysis with insights from political economy.[44]

The more successful EU accession countries embarked on vigorous structural reform and dismantled the command economy before the suc-

---

[44]This section relies heavily on the analysis presented in Oleh Havrylyshyn and John Odling-Smee, "The Political Economy of Reform in Transition Countries," *Finance and Development*, Vol. 37, No. 3, September 2000, pp. 7–10; and Gérard Roland, *Transition and Economics—Politics, Markets and Firms* (Cambridge, Massachusetts: MIT Press, 2000); and "The Politics of Economic Reform," Chapter 5 in the EBRD *Transition Report 1999*.

cessor countries to the former USSR. The reason for this is first of all political: Soviet hegemony in the eastern bloc and the resulting Soviet tutelage of the states in eastern Europe had weakened well before the disintegration of the Soviet Union itself. However, not only the timing but also the depth and vigor of reforms to transform their economies was more pronounced among these countries, which, following the breakup of the Soviet Union, came to include the three Baltic states. The major reason for the greater determination and consistency with which these EU accession countries approached the structural reform process is explained by most observers by their underlying historical affinity to western Europe and—with central planning introduced only in the late 1940s—significant understanding of a market-based economy.[45] Consequently, the political upheavals that shook central and eastern Europe toward the end of the 1980s were perceived by these countries as an opportunity to return to a market economy and adopt the institutions that underpin it. The resulting resolve to embrace necessary structural change, and the positive incentive of joining the European Union, accelerated the reform process and helped to prevent opposing coalitions from forming and obstructing it.

In contrast, most of the CIS countries had no obvious alternative model to follow when the Soviet Union disintegrated, and with central planning having existed for close to 70 years, lit-

tle knowledge of the operation of a market-based economy remained. In fact, it can be argued that a market-oriented economy has never existed in the majority of the CIS countries. As noted above, little up-front external financing was made available—relative to needs—to support radical reform in most CIS countries, particularly at the beginning of the process.[46] Together with a lack of clear orientation in the reform process, this in many cases led to a situation where reforms moved relatively slowly.[47] The major exception to this pattern was Russia, which obtained considerable outside support and developed a reform plan early on. However, following some initial radical initiatives, reforms were subsequently slowed by internal opposition in a manner similar to the rest of the CIS.

In a situation where reform was only partial, a variety of opportunities for rent seeking by individuals emerged, including many members of the former governing elite. These "vested interests" benefited from a situation of partial and incomplete reforms, because their ability to influence and modify policies enabled them to generate rents from persistent market distortions, unchecked by either the political system or by competitive markets. Since this situation would have been undermined by a more comprehensive reform, these groups used their economic power to distort or stall the reform process.[48] The success of vested interests in appropriating wealth and income, in combination

---

[45]In corresponding econometric research this explanatory factor is usually proxied by one or more "initial conditions," like time spent under central planning and/or geographical distance from western Europe; for representative examples of such research see Wolf, "Transition Strategies," Fischer and Sahay, "The Transition Economies After Ten Years," and Jeffrey Sachs, Clifford Jinnes, and Yair Eilot "Patterns and Determinants of Economic Reform in Transition Economies: 1990–1998," CAER II Discussion Paper No. 61 (Cambridge, Massachusetts: Harvard Institutue for International Development, February 2000).

[46]A determined comprehensive approach comparable to the Marshall Plan, which supported the reconstruction of western Europe following World War II, never materialized. Much of the financing that did materialize at the early stages of transition was in the form of cumulating arrears, rather than loans or grants dedicated to support an orderly transition process.

[47]In a more nuanced classification, the EBRD distinguishes those CIS countries where the reform process has stalled and another group where little, if any, substantial reform had occurred up to mid-1999 (Belarus, Turkmenistan, and Tajikistan); see "The Politics of Economic Reform," Chapter 5, EBRD, *Transition Report 1999.*

[48]There is a historical parallel between these powerful interest groups (the "oligarchs") in some of today's transition economies and the "robber barons" of early capitalist development in today's market economies; see Mancur Olson, *Power and Prosperity: Outgrowing Communist and Capitalist Dictatorships* (New York: Basic Books, 2000). In Olson's view, overcoming the grip of vested interest groups on the government and the economy in general in either case requires the development of a representative government immune to "capture" by these (or other) interest groups.

with falling aggregate output, led to a significant increase in income inequality and poverty (Figure 3.6). This weakened general public support for the reform process, which often found its expression in the election of parliamentary majorities (or strong minorities) skeptical about the direction of reform, generally resulting in a slowdown in the pace of reform.

Lessons from the Transition Process

The experience accumulated during the last two decades of transition provides important policy lessons not only for the transition countries themselves, but also for reform strategies in other countries—developing and advanced economies alike. The following issues stand out.

Countries that adopted a two-pronged strategy combining macroeconomic stabilization and comprehensive structural reform were, on the whole, more successful in limiting the output losses at the outset of the transition and achieving robust growth subsequently.[49] The two components of the strategy were equally necessary: a measure of macroeconomic stability had to be secured before countries could proceed effectively with enterprise and financial sector reform, and such stability could not be maintained unless the enterprise and banking sectors were subject to financial discipline and competitive pressures.

Delaying certain key structural reforms (price and trade liberalization, and the elimination of soft budget constraints) has typically been associated with higher and more protracted inflation and a less robust recovery from the initial output fall. However, a privatization strategy that starts with a rapid privatization of small-scale enterprises and adopts a more gradual approach for large enterprises, conditional on the introduction of commercial legislation to support viable corporate governance structures and to provide effective competition (or regulation in case of natural monopolies), appears to have been most

effective, provided these enterprises were sold in a transparent way (Box 3.4).

The transition strategy pursued by the east Asian economies has been accompanied by a remarkable acceleration of growth, with close to 400 million people lifted out of poverty in China since 1978 according to World Bank estimates. In China, this has owed much to the authorities' ability to develop a reform strategy that took advantage of the specific conditions they faced—such as the large agricultural sector and rural labor surplus—and generated rapid growth without adversely affecting social stability, thereby creating the domestic support for further reforms. However, just as in other countries, the fastest growth seems to have taken place in the sectors where reforms were most comprehensive. Moreover, delays in reforming large enterprises and the financial sector have been costly, and constitute a major challenge for the future.

The importance of institutional reform was recognized at the beginning of the transition, but in practice it was given too little attention relative to macroeconomic developments by both policymakers and advisors alike, probably because the difficulties of implementing these reforms had been underestimated and there was a lack of experienced personnel. The necessary reforms may also have been insufficiently prioritized, especially in view of the limited administrative capacity in many countries. Building an effective institutional and legal infrastructure in support of the market and private sector activity, while essential to the ultimate success of transition, is inevitably time-consuming and complex, as it also requires adjustments in the social practices and behaviors of both government officials and private sector agents. The experience of the EU accession countries strongly suggests that an external political anchor can greatly assist institution building and implementing governance reform.

The extensive trade liberalization measures that were adopted in almost all transition coun-

---

[49]As the example of the Baltic states demonstrates, such a strategy could be pursued and was successful even in cases where unfavorable initial conditions or the negative impact of external shocks had to be overcome.

tries have helped to redress the distortions inherited from central planning and to bring the geographical and commodity composition of trade more in line with each country's specific resources and comparative advantage. And proximity to the European Union has helped the central and eastern European countries in particular to reallocate trade flows away from other centrally planned economies toward western Europe. The more successful reformers have been able to gain rapid access to foreign capital markets, as well as to attract rising foreign direct investment, thereby quickly reducing reliance on official and multilateral financing. The less successful reformers were less able to do so—and in some cases, such as Russia, faced capital flight—which significantly hindered the reform effort.

The role of exchange rate regimes, which was hotly debated during the initial phase of the transition process, has not turned out to be a crucial determinant of success or failure during the stabilization phase of the transition. Countries at both extremes of the exchange rate regime spectrum (e.g., currency boards in Baltic countries and floating exchange rates in the CIS) were able to bring inflation down rapidly, as long as they kept the money supply and related fundamentals under control. Whenever monetary or fiscal policies were not supportive, however, using exchange rate policies to combat inflation was not successful, as exemplified by the Russian crisis of 1998. Pegging the exchange rate served as a monetary anchor initially for several countries, but most of these have now shifted to a more flexible exchange rate (e.g., Poland) to maintain policy independence in the presence of high capital mobility.

Finally, the political economy argument that policy mistakes in sequencing reform and half-hearted implementation allowed insiders to form coalitions aimed at stalling the reform process has been largely validated in central and eastern Europe and the CIS.[50] In several transition countries, the political decision making process, which determines the nature and pace of structural reforms, has been captured by vested interests that engage in rent-seeking activities and maximize their economic benefits—at least in the short run—at an intermediate stage of reform. Such vested interests, once firmly entrenched, are difficult to dislodge. The costs they inflict can be very high, as such groups may succeed in blocking the development of the institutional infrastructure that underpins the operation of market economies, thus stalling the transition process. This underscores the need for carrying out and sequencing further structural reform in such a way as to minimize the interference of vested interest with the policymaking process.

Policy Agenda for the Future

The transition economies, particularly those that have finally overcome the transition recession, face the key challenge of achieving sustained and robust economic growth and catching up with the living standards in market economies. Further restructuring and elimination of inefficiencies inherited from central planning and the absorption of new technology through trade and financial integration with the advanced economies can help these countries to realize their substantial potential for growth and convergence. Indeed, a number of transition economies in central and eastern Europe and the Baltic countries have already embarked on the path of sustained robust growth. They are expected to gradually close the remaining GDP per capita gap with comparator market economies through more rapid productivity growth, in tandem with the rebuilding of the physical capital stock and the adoption of new technologies and management practices. This convergence process is discussed in more detail in Chapter IV.

To catch up, transition economies need to both pursue sound macroeconomic policies and

---

[50]Oleh Havrylyshyn and John Odling-Smee, "The Political Economy of Reform in Transition Countries," and EBRD, Chapter 5, *Transition Report 1999*.

to make progress toward completing structural reforms and building the institutions required to underpin a market economy, while recognizing realistic constraints on their implementation capacity. A well-focused policy agenda is especially important for countries that have not yet managed to embark on a path of sustained growth and convergence. In these countries, the challenge is to reinvigorate the reform process in the face of limited institutional capacities, the existence of vested interests, serious governance problems, and, in some cases, widespread arrears and fiscal problems. Unless reform efforts are focused and strengthened, these countries face the prospect of remaining in an incomplete transformation trap, where low domestic saving and investment, a lack of enterprise restructuring and concomitant inefficiencies, pervasive problems with barter and arrears, lack of competition, limited foreign direct investment, and capital outflows create a vicious circle depriving them of the opportunity to achieve higher growth, bring down inflation, and reduce their dependency on official external financing.

Macroeconomic Policy Challenges

Many transition countries now enjoy the benefits of macroeconomic stability, which is needed for successful growth and convergence. This is particularly true in the EU accession countries, whose macroeconomic challenges are discussed in Chapter IV. Elsewhere in the transition economies, however, the legacies of central planning, and of the transition process, have continued to complicate macroeconomic policies. The rudimentary nature of financial systems often have limited the ability to conduct monetary policies. [51] The most important macroeconomic challenges, however, relate to fiscal policy. High levels of government expenditure—both on and off budget—and lack of an effective tax collection system generate pressures for large fiscal deficits. This problem is further complicated by the non-transparent and quasi-fiscal nature of much government spending, often associated with implicit subsidies for existing enterprises. The transition process has itself created fiscal pressures, as both output declines and tax system reform led to revenue reductions, and structural reform measures generated additional spending, which, when combined, exceeded revenues from privatization.[52]

The legacies of central planning are particularly important for those countries least advanced in structural and institutional reform—Belarus, Tajikistan, Turkmenistan, and Uzbekistan—that continue to maintain large subsidies for enterprises, extensive price controls, and restrictive capital controls. In these countries, central bank support for the budget, banking system, and enterprises continues to fuel rapid growth in the money supply and high inflation. The resulting macroeconomic instability is unlikely to disappear without fundamental structural reform.

Many of the low-income transition economies in the CIS and other countries of southeastern Europe also face significant structural budget deficits, often associated with the desire to cushion the impact of steep falls in output that were deeper and have lasted for longer than originally anticipated. The counterpart to these fiscal deficits has generally been foreign borrowing. The need to service the resulting external debt is putting pressure on fiscal positions, and, in some cases, the limited capacity to raise revenue is a significant constraint on external debt serv-

---

[51]However, many transition countries, particularly those starting central banks from scratch, have in the meantime moved to establish independent monetary authorities, and the quality of their institutional arrangements are now often comparable with those in advanced economies. See Helmut Wagner, "Central Banking in Transition Countries," IMF Working Paper 98/126 (Washington: International Monetary Fund, 1998); and Tonny Lybek, "Central Bank Autonomy, and Inflation and Output Performance in the Baltic States, Russia, and Other Countries of the Former Soviet Union, 1995–97," IMF Working Paper 99/4 (Washington: International Monetary Fund, 1999).

[52]Such spending is associated with restructuring enterprises, recapitalizing banks, creating government social insurance for the unemployed, and replacing social services provided by state enterprises under central planning.

ice (Table 3.3). Further fiscal adjustment is needed to avoid exacerbating these unfavorable debt dynamics, while the international community should consider whether in some cases, as in other low-income countries with high levels of debt, the negative effects of the existing debt overhang require additional measures.[53]

In many transition economies, including Russia, macroeconomic policies are complicated by a variety of structural impediments. Limited spending and revenue management capacities, arrears, and, in some cases, a lack of coordination between central and local governments mean that it is difficult for fiscal policy to respond to shocks, such as large changes in commodity prices, in a discretionary manner. Monetary policy is constrained in many cases by the absence of well-functioning financial institutions and interbank and treasury bill markets. Additional challenges facing the monetary authorities include entrenched inflationary expectations that reflect uneven macroeconomic policy performance in the past, and—most notably in Russia—substantial capital outflows.[54] More generally, the need to import foreign capital to support stronger growth entails the risk of sudden reversals of inflows, while financial imbalances in the enterprise sector and weak financial systems engender a relatively high vulnerability to macroeconomic instability and financial crises.

The central macroeconomic challenge in China and Vietnam, given their rapid growth and low level of inflation, largely relates to the fiscal costs associated with losses in state-owned enterprises and banks, accrued pension liabilities, and the costs of structural reforms. Such liabilities, which also exist in a number of CIS countries, have significant implications for medium-term fiscal sustainability.[55] This underscores the importance of continuing current efforts to strengthen revenue mobilization and further improve budgetary management, combined with comprehensive reform of state-owned enterprises and the banking system.

The Structural Reform Agenda

All transition countries, including those that have advanced most toward meeting the requirements of a well-functioning market economy, continue to face challenges in structural reform and institution building in a broad range of areas (Table 3.7). The need for structural reform and institution building is particularly pressing in those transition economies, including virtually all CIS and some east Asian countries, where reforms have been partial or slow and are in some cases obstructed by special interest groups. The specific reform agenda varies in individual countries, and in most cases reforms will need to be carefully prioritized and sequenced in line with the available administrative and institutional capacity. Three areas that appear particularly critical—and in which countries face common challenges—are restructuring enterprises, building a market-based financial sector, and transforming the role of the state.

Enterprise Restructuring

In most countries outside the EU accession group, continuing inefficiencies and loss-making activities in large-scale enterprises—often the only employer in a single company town—remain a serious drag on the economy. In Russia and other CIS countries, the problem primarily

---

[53]The impact of high levels of debt on low-income developing countries is discussed in "How Can the Poorest Countries Catch Up?" Chapter IV, May 2000 *World Economic Outlook.*

[54]In addition to credibility problems in the conduct of macroeconomic policy, these outflows reflect slow progress in structural reform. Experience in the central and eastern European countries, as well as elsewhere, suggests that sound macroeconomic policies and structural reforms could help eliminate such capital outflows relatively quickly. But, while capital controls can mitigate volatility in short-term flows of external capital, they are largely ineffective at stopping capital flight. See Prakash Loungani and Paolo Mauro, "Capital Flight in Russia," IMF Policy Discussion Paper 2000/05 (Washington: International Monetary Fund, 2000).

[55]See Nicholas R. Lardy, *China's Unfinished Economic Revolution* (Washington: The Brookings Institution, 1998).

Table 3.7. Areas of Remaining Major Reform Backlog[1]

Countries	Large-Scale Privatization	Small-Scale Privatization	Governance & Enterprise Restructuring	Price Liberalization	Trade & Foreign Exchange System	Competition Policy	Banking Reform & Interest Rate Liberalization
EU accession countries (excluding Baltics)							
Bulgaria			■			■	
Czech Republic							
Hungary							
Poland							
Romania			■			■	
Slovak Republic							
Slovenia						■	
Baltic countries							
Estonia							
Latvia							
Lithuania						■	
Other southeastern European countries							
Albania	■		■			■	■
Bosnia & Herzegovina	■	■	■			■	■
Croatia						■	
Macedonia, FYR			■			■	
Commonwealth of Independent States[4]							
Armenia			■			■	■
Azerbaijan	■		■			■	■
Belarus	■	■	■	■	■	■	■
Georgia			■			■	■
Kazakhstan			■			■	■
Kyrgyz Republic			■			■	■
Moldova			■			■	■
Mongolia	■		■			■	■
Russian Federation			■		■	■	■
Tajikistan	■		■			■	■
Turkmenistan	■	■	■	■	■	■	■
Ukraine	■		■			■	■
Uzbekistan			■	■	■	■	■
East Asia							
Cambodia			■			■	
China	■	■	■		■	■	■
Lao P.D.R.	■		■		■	■	■
Vietnam	■	■	■		■	■	■

Source: European Bank for Reconstruction and Development, *Transition Report 1999;* Asian countries not members of the CIS were evaluated by IMF country specialists.
[1]EBRD indicators whose value is less than 2.5 in 1999.
[2]Projected inflation in 2000 exceeds 30 percent.
[3]Projected budget deficit in 2000 exceeds 5 percent of GDP.
[4]Data include Mongolia.

concerns newly privatized enterprises where, due to weak governance structures and persistent soft budget constraints, little restructuring has taken place. In China and Vietnam, in contrast, the problem is centered on state-owned enterprises, which—partly as a result of relatively gradual reforms—are burdened by substantial overcapacity and surplus labor, heavy debt, and a variety of social obligations to employees. In Russia and the CIS, the resulting losses have been financed through rising tax arrears and access to subsidized energy, and in China and Vietnam by borrowing from state-owned banks, resulting in high levels of nonperforming loans.

Securities Markets & Nonbank Financial Institutions	Commercial Law	Financial Regulation Law	Memorandum Macrostabilization Not Achieved	
			Inflation[2]	Budget deficit[3]
■				
■				
■				
■				
■				
■	■	■		■
■	■	■		■
■		■		
■				
■		■	■	
■	■	■		
■	■	■		
■		■		■
■				■
■				
■			■	
■	■	■		
■		■		
■	■	■		
■	■	■		
■	■	■		
■	■	■		

In Russia and the CIS, as discussed in Box 3.3, the most effective way to promote enterprise restructuring now appears to be to foster competition and impose hard budget constraints, through eliminating direct and indirect subsidies from the budget, removing access to subsidized energy, implementing effective bankruptcy laws, and strengthening corporate governance rules (including the rights of minority shareholders and creditors). This is especially important in cases, like Russia, where enterprise control was transferred to insiders, and where the incentive structures to which these insiders respond remain distorted. In China, the authorities are seeking to commercialize and restructure the largest enterprises, most recently by creating four asset management companies to take over nonperforming loans from state banks and to undertake debt equity swaps with qualified enterprises. A key challenge is to ensure that these asset management companies have the necessary legal powers and support to ensure that the enterprises in which they become owners or creditors are appropriately restructured. In both cases, restructuring will need to be accompanied by the development of stronger social safety nets to ease the social costs of adjustment. Since restructuring is necessarily a lengthy process, it is also important to remove obstacles to start up new enterprises, which tend to be the main source of growth and employment creation.

In Russia and the CIS, there is the specific challenge of changing the role of energy and utility companies, which—often under pressure from local authorities or vested interests—are used to support loss-making activities in industry and agriculture, for instance, by charging fees that do not cover costs and accepting barter and arrears (Box 3.3). This practice reflects, in part, lack of progress in corporate restructuring and in providing social safety nets. To reduce the scope for energy and utility companies to be used in this manner, fee collection rates need to be improved and user charges set at levels that reflect costs and eliminate cross-subsidies between different user groups, accompanied by greater competition, privatization, and a general hardening of budget constraints.

Building a Market-Based Financial Sector

The development of a strong and sound banking system that can effectively and efficiently intermediate savings and investment is central to underpin sustainable growth. Once again, the situation varies widely among transition economies. In the EU accession countries—which are discussed in more detail in Chapter IV—the banking system is in most cases starting to intermediate effectively, although it remains relatively underdeveloped by international standards (Figure 3.15). However, considerable restructuring is still required in a number of these countries, and a few—notably Romania—currently face serious systemic problems. In Russia and the other CIS countries, the banking system is very small and underdeveloped, with a number of banks facing serious financial problems, and plays only a limited role in intermediation, which has declined further due to the failure of many private banks in the 1998 banking crisis. Only a small proportion of household saving is placed with the banking sector, and the bulk of new investment is financed through retained earnings or through informal capital markets. In China, in contrast, the banking system is large and intermediates a substantial proportion of household saving. However, as noted above, the bulk of this lending has been directed to state-owned enterprises, resulting in the accumulation of substantial nonperforming loans, while the much more dynamic private sector lacks financing.

In Russia and the CIS countries, developing an action plan to deal with remaining insolvent banks will be important; thereafter, the primary challenge will be to develop the banking system from the present very low base. This will require efforts to stimulate wider private ownership of banks—through privatization of banks that remain state-owned and through new entry—and to foster competition. However, it will be critical that new private and privatized banks are subject to effective corporate governance, as well as proper regulation and supervision to avoid abuses, including insider lending. In addition, accompanying reforms of the legal and regulatory environment—including the accounting framework, collateral rules, and bankruptcy leg-

islation—will also be required. Since this will clearly take time to accomplish, licensing requirements will need to be relatively restrictive so as to encourage entry only by high-quality and well-capitalized institutions. In practice this means that the banking system can only grow gradually, with initial new entrants likely to be primarily foreign banks.

In China, where the assets of the banking system exceed 100 percent of GDP, the challenge is to reform and restructure the existing banks while maintaining financial stability. While the transfer of a substantial proportion of nonperforming loans to asset management companies will substantially improve the financial position of the four state banks, it will be critical to prevent the reemergence of a new bad loan problem. This will require both successful restructuring of the state enterprises—to eliminate ongoing losses—and the development of a commercial credit culture in the banks themselves. As in Russia and the CIS, this will require sustained efforts to strengthen the regulatory and supervisory systems; strengthen banks' internal governance; and ensure that they are free of political interference, particularly from the provinces. The limited entry of new private banks, and the gradual diversification of ownership of state banks, can also play an important role. China's prospective entry to the World Trade Organization—which will give foreign banks full national treatment by 2005 (Box 1.3)—underscores the importance of moving ahead rapidly with restructuring efforts.

Transforming the Role of the State

A key element of transition is the transformation of the role of the government, from directly intervening in economic activities to establishing and enforcing the "rules of the game" for a market economy, while raising revenues in a transparent manner to finance essential public sector activities.[56] In some areas significant progress has been made in this difficult and complex task,

---

[56]Vito Tanzi, "Transition and the Changing Role of Government," *Finance and Development*, Vol. 36, No. 2 (June 1999), pp. 20–24.

notably in setting up some of the key macroeconomic institutions necessary for a market economy. However, in many countries excessive government regulation remains a serious problem, engendering corruption, rent seeking, and a large hidden economy. At the same time, much remains to be done to strengthen the rules and regulations needed to allow markets to function in an orderly and transparent way, and to ensure that rules and legislation are fully and fairly enforced. In particular, a market economy requires clear and well-publicized civil and criminal codes that are fully and impartially enforced by an independent judiciary and an effective police force. In the commercial area more specifically, the reinforcement of collateral and bankruptcy laws, creditor and shareholder protection rules, and accounting and reporting requirements remains of key importance.

In many countries, particularly in the CIS and east Asia, there is a need for continued fiscal reform, focusing on the following key areas:[57]

- *Strengthening the tax system and tax administration.* Tax policies have often left room for negotiation or preferential treatment, which has promoted rent seeking and undermined the ability of the government to raise revenues fairly. Moreover, a tolerance for nonpayment of taxes, in combination with disorderly expenditure compression and spending arrears stemming from budget formulation and implementation problems, has—especially in Russia—contributed to more general nonpayment and arrears cycles throughout the economy (Box 3.3).
- *Improving fiscal transparency and proper accounting for government operations,* off-budget expenditures and contingent liabilities in particular. In a number of countries, off-budget and quasi-fiscal expenditures are substantial, undertaken through extra-budgetary funds (China), subsidies provided by energy and utility companies (Russia and

the CIS), or through the banking system (China, Vietnam, and Lao P.D.R.). Many countries also need to address substantial contingent fiscal liabilities, especially for pensions.
- *Reforming fiscal federalism arrangements,* including in Russia and China (Box 3.5) in particular, to ensure that they are supportive of macroeconomic adjustment and structural reform.
- *Establishing well-functioning public sector institutions,* including government agencies and ministries, and creating the right incentives for those who run these institutions. Progress in this area of reform has been rather slow, reflecting the complexity of the reform agenda, attempts to rebuild rather than replace the old institutions, and weak and inconsistent political commitment to serious reforms. In many cases, inherited organizational and procedural weaknesses and a lack of coordination at the center of government still need to be addressed. Moreover, public sector management practices and the civil service overall need to be strengthened. The rule of law has to apply to all government activities, and government officials need to be held fully accountable for their actions.
- *Continuing expenditure policy reform,* with a focus on phasing out remaining subsidies and on strengthening social expenditure programs. Introducing effective and transparent social assistance programs, facilitating the reallocation of labor by replacing enterprise-provided social benefits and services, and ensuring the financial viability of pension systems are key priorities. In view of the rise in income inequality during the transition, the redesign of tax and expenditure programs may also take into account distribution objectives.

The increase in poverty and income inequality in many countries since the beginning of the

---

[57]The early fiscal reform efforts in the countries in transition are discussed in more detail in Chapter V, "Progress with Fiscal Reform in Countries in Transition," of the May 1998 *World Economic Outlook.*

Box 3.5. Fiscal Decentralization in Transition Economies: China and Russia

A number of advanced and developing countries have experimented with fiscal decentralization over the past two decades, and this trend has extended to the transition countries as well. However, persistent macroeconomic instability in some and the entrenched legacy of socialism and central planning in others have generated additional challenges that are complicating the design of effective fiscal federalism.

The argument for fiscal decentralization is founded mainly on the premise that it facilitates a more efficient delivery of public services. At the same time, because of free-rider problems, decentralization can give rise to significant fiscal and macroeconomic risks. And local government debt can spiral out of control if local officials, and their creditors, believe a central government bailout is likely. The interest in fiscal decentralization has prompted a surge in the literature on its economic consequences. This work focuses on the design of a multi-tier fiscal system, including incentive structures and policy implementation, and emphasizes the importance of good governance, transparency, and elimination of corruption.

There is broad agreement that successful fiscal decentralization is generally based on the following four policy principles:[1] (1) clarity of roles between different levels of government to achieve accountability; (2) a measure of autonomy for both the expenditure and revenue function of subnational governments, accompanied by an efficient system of federal equalization grants; (3) institutional procedures to ensure coordination and cooperation between different levels of government; and (4) institution building, including development of the administrative infrastructure needed by local governments to carry out the tasks assigned to them.

Transition countries must also deal with challenges that are part of the legacy of central planning, including inappropriate location of key industries and that, in most transition countries, health care, education, old age and disability pensions, and often housing were provided through the public enterprise sector. Competitive pressures have led firms to eliminate social overhead expenses, which were usually replaced by transfers and service provision by local rather than central governments. Localities were thus left with large social expenditures that were critical in light of the worsening economic situation, but with little in the way of additional taxing power. While this process began early in the transition period in central and eastern Europe and the countries of the former Soviet Union, it has only recently started to take place in China.

As a result of these transition-related pressures, local governments in many countries face large unfunded obligations, and have been driven to tax competition with central authorities. Uncoordinated rivalry for tax revenues has contributed to excessive tax rates and inefficient tax administration, undermining central government revenue collection. In China, for example, payroll tax rates for the pension system vary from 17 to 29 percent, depending on the province, and until recently some industries had special rates as low as 10 percent, while others paid well over 30 percent. Regional equalization transfers have generally been underfinanced, leaving social safety nets weakest in those regions where they are most needed. Yet without adequate income support for individuals displaced by reform, political pressure to block restructuring has often proven insurmountable.

While transition-related fiscal federalism problems have persisted in a number of countries (Georgia, Kazakhstan, and Ukraine), the two largest transition countries—China and Russia—face remarkably similar problems in this area. Both introduced significant reforms in 1993–94. China, while retaining a unitary state structure, carried out a substantial reform of intergovernmental relations in 1994, aimed in part at increasing the "two ratios"—general government revenue to GDP and the central government's share in total revenue—that were

[1]See Era Dabla-Norris, Jorge Martinez-Vasquez, and John Norregaard, "Fiscal Decentralization and Economic Performance: The Case of Russia, Ukraine and Kazakhstan" (unpublished; Washington: International Monetary Fund, July 2000).

judged to be dangerously low in the early 1990s. The central government revenue share has improved modestly, but general government revenues as a percentage of GDP have continued to decline until recently. Similarly, in 1994 Russia introduced a new constitution that created a federal structure, but powerful local governments especially in resource rich regions were often able to divert revenues collected on behalf of the central government for their own purposes. Several Russian oil-producing regions, notably Tatarstan and Bashkirtostan, won favorable exemptions from the statutory revenue-sharing rules. Current revenue-sharing arrangements also have provided incentives to sub-national authorities to use monetary surrogates, in the form of tax and expenditure offsets in particular, exacerbating Russia's barter and arrears problem (see Box 3.3).

Partly as a result of these developments, central governments in both China and Russia have faced persistent revenue shortages. Moreover, a relatively large share of fiscal transfers has been *discretionary* and subject to negotiation, rather than based on objective criteria that reflect revenue capacity and expenditure need. In both countries, but particularly in China, sub-national governments have extremely limited authority to tax, which has led officials to record some revenues off budget. As a result, the use of authorized extra-budgetary "fees and charges" accounts for over a quarter of general government revenue in China.

China and Russia each face large regional discrepancies in their social safety nets, which are generally financed by payroll taxes that provide the least revenue in precisely those regions where the need for social spending is greatest (because of unemployment and high pension system dependency ratios). This imbalance has at times led to pension and other benefit arrears, in both Russia and China, although in the latter the central government has sporadically provided discretionary transfers to clear them. Furthermore, local pension and unemployment administrations in China have driven payroll tax rates to extremely high levels, particularly for

foreign-funded enterprises, which may undermine job creation and efforts to attract foreign direct investment.

How to reform these systems? In both China and Russia, major revenue sources are shared between central and local governments, giving local officials an incentive to divert central revenue to local coffers. It is important to clarify the assignment of revenue sources to avoid poaching of central government revenues.[2] And once their tax base has been determined, local authorities should be responsible for determining effective tax rates and tax collection to raise revenue in line with needs arising from assigned tasks. Moreover, adverse distribution effects of the regional transfer mechanism should be eliminated in both countries by greater reliance on transparent formula-based grants that reflect spending needs and revenue capacity. Budget processes and tax administration need to be improved at the local level in both countries, including budget reporting, for without adequate data on local public finances, central governments in both countries may face considerable fiscal and macroeconomic risks. Finally, in Russia and especially in China, the expenditure responsibilities of different levels of government need to be clarified so that local governments can focus public resources on areas of responsibility unambiguously assigned to them, including in particular traditionally local public services like schooling and police protection. In the absence of such reforms, in both Russia and China the regional governments most in need of funds will continue to be least able to obtain them at reasonable tax rates. Hence, if the fiscal transfer mechanism is not reformed to ensure that resources go to those localities most in need, financing enterprise restructuring and other structural reforms, including the creation of social safety nets, will be increasingly difficult and could, in turn, slow down the pace of reform.

[2]In 1994 China created separate tax administrations for local governments, to allow the central authority to concentrate on federal taxes.

transition poses an important policy challenge.[58] The best way to alleviate poverty and income inequality in the transition countries will be through robust private sector growth. The benefits of the associated employment opportunities will be made broadly accessible by policies that upgrade human capital by providing equal access to basic health and education services. Policies also need to address the new poverty risks associated with the transition to a market economy, including those stemming from unemployment. Main priorities are to introduce unemployment assistance schemes that are affordable and easy to administer, to streamline pension benefits and ensure their timely payment, and to better target other social assistance programs and utility price subsidies. More generally, and in view of their high dependency on public service provision, the poor have much to gain from efforts to establish a well-functioning legal and judicial system and professional law enforcement and to strengthen the civil service.

Reinforcing the Momentum of Structural and Institutional Reform

The major challenge still facing the transition economies is to reinforce the existing momentum of structural and institutional reform. Building effective market-economy institutions is central to long-term growth prospects in all countries, but is particularly relevant for the transition economies, given the inadequacy of their pre-transition institutional arrangements. Deeper structural reforms in the EU accession group, including the Baltic states that were initially part of the former Soviet Union, compared to Russia and other members of the CIS have led to a superior macroeconomic performance, providing testimony to the importance of such reforms for longer-term welfare. Maintaining the

rapid expansion in the transition economies of east Asia will likewise require continuing efforts to restructure state-owned enterprises and the financial system.

Greater competition—from either domestic or foreign producers—can play a significant role in supporting the reform process. In addition to promoting the efficient use of resources, competition erodes the economic rents associated with particular activities, lowering the benefits to incumbents from the status quo and reducing the resources that they have available to oppose reforms. Domestic competition can be promoted directly by effectively sanctioning anti-competitive behavior, through such actions as banning the formation of cartels and regulating natural monopolies. In addition to promoting competition among existing firms, countries must encourage the entry of new firms, investors, and products that challenge the established market positions of incumbents. This in turn requires providing a favorable business environment for small and medium-size enterprises, removing barriers to foreign direct investment and joint ventures, and developing markets for (re-)sale of equity and control in firms where ownership has been transferred to insiders (incumbent managers and workers).[59]

Another important avenue through which the transition countries can safeguard and nourish the reform momentum is by pursuing further trade and financial integration with the global economy. Among the CIS countries, bilateral trade agreements, cross-border barter, and a tolerance for external payment arrears continue to hamper trade diversification outside the region and should be phased out in favor of most-favored-nation-based trade. Extra-regional trade diversification is not warranted in all cases: restoring and strengthening trade links in regions that in the past have been (and are still prone to be) torn by civil strife

---

[58]These policy challenges are discussed in more detail in World Bank, *Making Transition Work for Everyone: Poverty and Inequality in Europe and Central Asia* (Washington: World Bank, 2000).

[59]The importance of effective competition, in particular by removing obstacles to the entry of new firms—both domestic and foreign—is a theme developed in more detail in Chapters 7 and 8 of the EBRD *Transition Report 1999.*

and ethnic violence can help promote peace and political stability.[60] Advanced economies also have a role to play. Eliminating trade barriers for products such as textiles, steel, bulk chemicals, agricultural products and food stuffs—areas in which the transition countries have a potential comparative advantage—would help stimulate trade linkages. Instead, transition economies that are not yet members of the WTO continue to be subject to more or less arbitrary regulations imposed by importing countries and frequent invocation of antidumping regulations.

International financial integration can also play a major role as an incentive mechanism. Private capital inflows can help to renew and expand the capital stock and close the technology gap with the advanced economies. Foreign direct investment, in particular, is generally considered a stable and effective way to transfer productive capital and technical know how from the advanced economies, and concentrated foreign ownership has been found to consistently outperform other ownership types in producing active enterprise restructuring in the transition countries. Borrowing in international financial markets and the related need to be concerned about creditworthiness and credit ratings can help signal a commitment to honor financial obligations, reinforce domestic financial discipline, and strengthen external debt management practices.

An additional mechanism providing incentives for further structural and institutional reform is linked to membership in supranational organizations (Table 3.8). By establishing a substantial number of policy goals and conditions on which consensus might be difficult to reach, such an "external anchor" helps to focus policy, thereby functioning as an arbitration mechanism in case of differing internal political opinions.[61] The European Union has played this role for the countries of central and eastern Europe and the Baltics, with EU accession providing an objective that continues to promote rapid structural and institutional reforms (see Chapter IV).[62] Indeed, the lure of closer political and economic ties with western Europe was sufficiently powerful that it had an influence on policies in the EU accession group from the beginning of the transition process, well before they became formal candidates for membership in the Union. In east Asia, membership of ASEAN plays a similar role for Vietnam, the Laos People's Democratic Republic, and Cambodia, although given ASEAN's much less stringent membership requirements, it has been considerably less effective in promoting structural and institutional reforms.[63]

The WTO can act in a similar manner for other transition economies, although the range and depth of entrance requirements is much more limited than for EU membership.[64] In particular, WTO membership has been a major

---

[60]Overcoming historical antagonism by strengthening intraregional trade was an important objective in the reconstruction of western Europe following World War II, where it succeeded beyond most peoples' expectations. For similar objectives in today's context, see The World Bank, *The Road to Stability and Prosperity in South Eastern Europe—A Regional Strategy Paper* (Washington: The World Bank, 2000).

[61]See Erik Berglof and Gerard Roland, "From 'Regatta' to 'Big Bang'?—The Impact of the EU Accession Strategy on Reform in Central and Eastern Europe" (unpublished; Washington: IMF, 2000).

[62]The international financial institutions, among them the IMF, also played, and continue to play, a role as an external anchor, in addition to providing technical assistance and financing. In particular, the IMF will continue to promote sound macroeconomic policies and institutional and structural reform to promote sustained growth and convergence and lower vulnerability to financial crises.

[63]ASEAN's most significant contribution has been to advance the liberalization of intraregional trade through the formation of the Asian Free Trade Area (AFTA) in 1992.

[64]While EU accession requires coordination of commercial practices and law, financial cooperation, and adherence to fiscal policy norms, WTO rules and obligations are limited to international trade. A number of transition economies have already become WTO members, and with a few exceptions the remaining transition countries are at present candidates for WTO accession; see Table 3.8. For more details, see Constantine Michalopoulos, "The Integration of Transition Economies into the World Trading System," World Bank Policy Research Working Paper No. 2182 (Washington: World Bank, 1999).

Table 3.8. Transition Economies' Membership in International Organizations
(X represents full membership; O indicates the country has applied for membership)

Country	International Organizations and Treaties										
	Global					Regional				Memorandum	
	IMF/IBRD	WTO	EBRD	OECD	EU	CEFTA[1]	CIS	AFTA[2]	APEC[3]	CMEA[4]	NATO
Albania	X	O	X							X[5]	
Armenia	X	O	X				X			X[6]	
Azerbaijan	X	O	X				X			X[6]	
Belarus	X	O	X				X			X[6]	
Bosnia and Herzegovina	X	O	X							X[7]	
Bulgaria	X	X	X		O					X	
Cambodia	X	O									
China	X	O						X	X		
Croatia	X	X	X							X[7]	
Czech Republic	X	X[8]	X	X	O	X				X[9]	X
Estonia	X	X	X		O					X[6]	
Georgia	X	X	X				X			X[6]	
Hungary	X	X[8]	X	X	O	X				X	X
Kazakhstan	X	O	X				X			X[6]	
Kyrgyz Republic	X	X	X				X			X[6]	
Lao P.D.R.	X	O							X		
Latvia	X	X	X		O						
Lithuania	X	O	X		O					X[6]	
Macedonia, FYR	X	O	X							X[7]	
Moldova	X	O	X				X			X[6]	
Mongolia	X	X								X	
Poland	X	X[8]	X	X	O	X				X	X
Romania	X	X[8]	X		O					X	
Russia	X	O	X				X		X	X[6]	
Slovak Republic	X	X[8]	X	O	O	X				X[9]	
Slovenia	X	X	X		O	X				X[7]	
Tajikistan	X		X				X			X[6]	
Turkmenistan	X		X				X			X[6]	
Ukraine	X	O	X				X			X[6]	
Uzbekistan	X	O	X				X			X[6]	
Vietnam	X	O						X	X	X	

[1]Central European Free Trade Agreement, concluded in 1992 among five central European EU accession candidates.
[2]Asian Free Trade Association, formed in 1992 by the Association of South East Asian countries (ASEAN).
[3]Asia-Pacific Economic Cooperation.
[4]Council for Mutual Economic Cooperation, dissolved in 1991.
[5]Albania became a CMEA member in 1949 but ceased active participation in 1961.
[6]Automatic membership as member of the Soviet Union.
[7]Associated membership as member of the Republic of Yugoslavia.
[8]Member since creation of the WTO in 1995.
[9]Automatic membership as part of Czechoslovakia.

issue on China's policy agenda, providing a potent symbol of the country's continuing "opening up" to the rest of the world. As an external anchor, WTO membership will help to ensure that China's substantial exports of manufactured goods are not discriminated against in foreign markets and that China's important textile sector will benefit from the elimination of the quotas on textiles and clothing administered under the WTO Agreement on textiles and clothings (previously known as the Multi-Fiber Arrangement) from 2005. Providing external competition for domestic firms will also assist in pushing forward needed restructuring of state-owned enterprises and reforming the financial system.

It is tempting to conclude that the WTO (or a free trade arrangement with the European Union) would provide a similarly effective anchor for other transition countries, in particular

Russia and other members of the CIS, but in practice caution is warranted. Although most members of the CIS are either in negotiations for entry into the WTO or are already members, WTO entry seems to play a smaller role in the policy debate in these countries compared to China. One reason is the difference in commodity composition of their exports. The labor-intensive manufactures that constitute the bulk of Chinese exports to advanced economies are more affected by WTO rules than the primary products that dominate exports from Russia and several other CIS members. If an external anchor is not embraced, the need for purely domestically driven reforms and policies that promote competition, entry, and global integration—which could help develop a more broadly based export sector that would in turn be supportive of reform—is correspondingly the greater.

Appendix: Indicators of Structural Reform and Institutional Quality

This appendix documents two indicators of structural reform and the index of institutional quality referred to in Chapter III.

The aggregate transition indicator is the average of eight component transition indicators of structural reforms published in the EBRD *Transition Report*, which measure the extent of enterprise privatization and restructuring (three indicators), market liberalization and competition (three indicators), and financial sector reform (two indicators) (Table 3.9).[65] Three of these indicators have been calculated since 1989, the others since 1994 or 1995.[66] The EBRD indicators range from 1 to 4+, where 4+ indicates that the country's structural characteristics are comparable to those prevailing on average in the advanced economies, and 1 represents conditions before reform in a centrally planned economy with dominant state ownership of means of production. In this *World Economic Outlook* the transition indicators are linearized by assigning a value of $+\frac{1}{3}$ to a "+" sign, and a value of $-\frac{1}{3}$ to a "–" sign. The original indicators are published annually in the EBRD *Transition Report* for all the transition economies discussed in Chapter III, with the exception of the east Asian countries and Mongolia. The transition indicators for these latter transition economies in this *World Economic Outlook* (including in Table 3.9) are IMF staff estimates.

An alternative, widely used indicator of structural reform referred to in Chapter III is the "Liberalization Index", developed by De Melo, Denizer, and Gelb and available yearly from 1989 to 1997 for all countries analyzed in Chapter III, excluding Bosnia and Herzegovina, Cambodia, and the Lao People's Democratic Republic (Table 3.10). [67] The index is a weighted average of three separate indices: domestic market liberalization (weight 0.3), foreign trade liberalization (weight 0.3), and enterprise privatization and banking reform (weight 0.4). The Liberalization Index ranges from 0 to 1, with the boundaries having a similar interpretation to those of the EBRD transition indicators.[68] Given the inherent difficulties in measuring progress made in structural and institutional reforms, the two indices discussed above should be considered only a rough estimate of such progress.

The index of institutional quality used in Chapter III has been developed by Beatrice Weder by aggregating five of the six indicators of

---

[65]European Bank for Reconstruction and Development, *Transition Report* (London: EBRD, 1999 and previous issues).

[66]Since 1998 the EBRD has also published four legal transition indicators, gauging the extensiveness and effectiveness of commercial law and of financial regulation.

[67]Martha De Melo, Cevdet Denizer, and Alan Gelb, "Patterns of Transition from Plan to Market," *The World Bank Economic Review*, Vol. 10, No. 3, pp. 397–424 (Washington: World Bank, September 1996); the index was subsequently updated to 1997 and is available upon request from these authors.

[68]The cumulative liberalization index (the sum of the annual liberalization indices from 1989 to the year under consideration) has sometimes been used as a combined measure of the extent as well as of the duration of reforms.

Table 3.9. EBRD Transition Indicators, 1999[1]

Countries/Transition Groups	Privatization and Restructuring			Market Liberalization and Competition			Financial Markets Reform		Aggregate transition Indicator[2]
	Large-scale privatization	Small-scale privatization	Governance & enterprise restructuring	Price liberalization	Trade & foreign exchange system	Competition policy	Banking reform & interest rate liberalization	Securities markets & nonbank financial institutions	
EU accession countries (excluding Baltics)									
Bulgaria	3.0	3.3	2.3	3.0	4.3	2.0	2.7	2.0	2.9
Czech Republic	4.0	4.3	3.0	3.0	4.3	3.0	3.3	3.0	3.4
Hungary	4.0	4.3	3.3	3.3	4.3	3.0	4.0	3.3	3.7
Poland	3.3	4.3	3.0	3.3	4.3	3.0	3.3	3.3	3.5
Romania	2.7	3.7	2.0	3.0	4.0	2.0	2.7	2.0	2.8
Slovak Republic	4.0	4.3	3.0	3.0	4.3	3.0	2.7	2.3	3.3
Slovenia	3.3	4.3	2.7	3.0	4.3	2.0	3.3	3.0	3.3
Baltic countries									
Estonia	4.0	4.3	3.0	3.0	4.0	2.7	3.7	3.0	3.5
Latvia	3.0	4.0	2.7	3.0	4.3	2.7	3.0	2.3	3.1
Lithuania	3.0	4.3	2.7	3.0	4.0	2.3	3.0	2.7	3.1
Other southeastern European countries									
Albania	2.0	4.0	2.0	3.0	4.0	2.0	2.0	1.7	2.5
Bosnia & Herzegovina	2.0	2.0	1.7	3.0	2.7	1.0	2.3	1.0	1.8
Croatia	3.0	4.3	2.7	3.0	4.0	2.0	3.0	2.3	3.0
Macedonia, FYR	3.0	4.0	2.0	3.0	4.0	1.0	3.0	1.7	2.8
Commonwealth of Independent States[3]									
Armenia	3.0	3.3	2.0	3.0	4.0	2.0	2.3	2.0	2.7
Azerbaijan	1.7	3.0	2.0	3.0	3.3	1.0	2.0	1.7	2.2
Belarus	1.0	2.0	1.0	1.7	1.0	2.0	1.0	2.0	1.5
Georgia	3.3	4.0	2.0	3.0	4.0	2.0	2.3	1.0	2.5
Kazakhstan	3.0	4.0	2.0	3.0	3.0	2.0	2.3	2.0	2.7
Kyrgyz Republic	3.0	4.0	2.0	3.0	4.0	2.0	2.3	2.0	2.8
Moldova	3.0	3.3	2.0	3.0	4.0	2.0	2.3	2.0	2.8
Mongolia[4]	2.0	4.0	2.3	3.3	4.3	2.0	2.3	2.0	2.8
Russian Federation	3.3	4.0	1.7	2.7	2.3	2.3	1.7	1.7	2.5
Tajikistan	2.3	3.0	1.7	3.0	2.7	1.0	1.0	1.0	2.0
Turkmenistan	1.7	2.0	1.7	2.0	1.0	1.0	1.0	1.0	1.4
Ukraine	2.3	3.3	2.0	3.0	3.0	2.0	2.0	2.0	2.4
Uzbekistan	2.7	3.0	2.0	2.0	1.0	2.0	1.7	2.0	2.1
East Asia[4]									
Cambodia	3.3	3.3	2.0	3.3	4.0	1.0	3.0	1.0	2.5
China	1.0	2.3	2.3	2.7	2.3	2.3	1.3	2.0	2.1
Lao P.D.R.	1.7	3.0	2.0	3.0	2.0	1.0	1.0	1.0	1.8
Vietnam	1.0	1.7	2.0	2.7	1.7	2.3	1.3	1.7	1.9

Source: European Bank for Reconstruction and Development, *Transition Report 1999* (London: EBRD, 1999); IMF staff estimates for east Asian countries and Mongolia.

[1]Analysts often linearize the scores by assigning a value of ⅓ to a "+" sign and −⅓ to a "−" sign attached to the integer scores 1 to 4, a practice also followed in this chapter.

[2]Simple average of eight component indicators.

[3]Data include Mongolia.

[4]EBRD transition indicators estimated by IMF staff.

governance developed by Kaufmann, Kraay, and Zoido-Lobatón (Table 3.11). [69] These five component indicators have been developed for the period 1997–98 for some 150 countries by aggregating more than 300 separate indicators from two types of sources: ratings produced by com-

[69]Beatrice Weder, "Institutional Reform in Transition Economies: How Far Have They Come?" (unpublished; Washington: International Monetary Fund, 2000); Daniel Kaufmann, Aart Kraay, and Pablo Zoido-Lobatón, "Governance

Table 3.10. Liberalization Index

Countries/Transition Groups	1989	1990	1991	1992	1993	1994	1995	1996	1997	Cumulative Liberalization Index 1997
EU accession countries (excluding Baltics)										
Bulgaria	0.13	0.19	0.62	0.66	0.66	0.64	0.58	0.65	0.79	4.92
Czech Republic	0.00	0.16	0.79	0.86	0.90	0.90	0.93	0.93	0.93	6.40
Hungary	0.34	0.57	0.74	0.78	0.82	0.86	0.90	0.90	0.93	6.84
Poland	0.24	0.68	0.72	0.82	0.82	0.86	0.89	0.89	0.89	6.81
Romania	0.00	0.22	0.36	0.45	0.58	0.68	0.71	0.72	0.75	4.47
Slovak Republic	0.00	0.16	0.79	0.86	0.83	0.83	0.86	0.86	0.86	6.05
Slovenia	0.41	0.62	0.71	0.78	0.82	0.82	0.85	0.87	0.89	6.77
Baltic countries										
Estonia	0.07	0.20	0.32	0.64	0.81	0.89	0.93	0.93	0.93	5.72
Latvia	0.04	0.13	0.29	0.51	0.67	0.81	0.81	0.85	0.89	5.00
Lithuania	0.04	0.13	0.33	0.55	0.78	0.89	0.89	0.89	0.89	5.39
Other southeastern European countries										
Albania	0.00	0.00	0.24	0.66	0.70	0.70	0.74	0.74	0.78	4.56
Bosnia & Herzegovina	. . .	. . .	. . .	. . .	. . .	. . .	. . .	. . .	. . .	. . .
Croatia	0.41	0.62	0.62	0.72	0.79	0.82	0.85	0.85	0.85	6.53
Macedonia, FYR	0.41	0.62	0.65	0.68	0.78	0.78	0.78	0.82	0.82	6.34
Commonwealth of Independent States[1]										
Armenia	0.04	0.04	0.13	0.39	0.42	0.42	0.49	0.72	0.72	3.37
Azerbaijan	0.04	0.04	0.04	0.25	0.31	0.35	0.44	0.55	0.62	2.64
Belarus	0.04	0.04	0.10	0.20	0.33	0.36	0.48	0.48	0.51	2.54
Georgia	0.04	0.04	0.22	0.32	0.35	0.39	0.49	0.69	0.72	3.26
Kazakhstan	0.04	0.04	0.04	0.33	0.60	0.76	0.82	0.86	0.86	4.35
Kyrgyz Republic	0.04	0.04	0.14	0.35	0.35	0.39	0.61	0.72	0.75	3.39
Moldova	0.04	0.04	0.10	0.38	0.51	0.55	0.68	0.75	0.75	3.80
Mongolia	0.00	0.00	0.44	0.55	0.61	0.67	0.67	0.67	0.83	4.44
Russia	0.04	0.04	0.10	0.49	0.59	0.66	0.77	0.80	0.83	4.32
Tajikistan	0.04	0.04	0.11	0.20	0.26	0.30	0.39	0.42	0.45	2.21
Turkmenistan	0.04	0.04	0.04	0.13	0.16	0.22	0.22	0.32	0.36	1.53
Ukraine	0.04	0.04	0.10	0.23	0.13	0.26	0.51	0.59	0.65	2.55
Uzbekistan	0.04	0.04	0.04	0.26	0.30	0.43	0.58	0.57	0.57	2.83
East Asia										
Cambodia	. . .	. . .	. . .	. . .	. . .	. . .	. . .	. . .	. . .	. . .
China	0.46	0.49	0.49	0.49	0.56	0.59	0.59	0.62	0.66	4.95
Lao P.D.R.	. . .	. . .	. . .	. . .	. . .	. . .	. . .	. . .	. . .	. . .
Vietnam	0.53	0.53	0.56	0.59	0.59	0.62	0.65	0.67	0.68	5.42

Source: Martha De Melo, Cevdet Denizer, and Alan Gelb, "Patterns of Transition from Plan to Market," *The World Bank Economic Review*, Vol. 10, No. 3, pp. 397–424 (Washington: World Bank, September 1996), and subsequently updated to 1997 by the authors.
[1]Data include Mongolia.

mercial risk rating agencies and other organizations, reflecting expert opinions; and surveys of firms and households, compiled by international organizations and other institutions.[70] Weder's institutional quality index is an aggregate of five component indicators related to the extent of

Matters," World Bank Policy Research Working Paper No. 2196 (Washington: World Bank, 1999); and Daniel Kaufmann, Aart Kraay, and Pablo Zoido-Lobatón, "Aggregating Governance Indicators," World Bank Policy Research Working Paper No. 2195 (Washington: World Bank, 1999).

[70]The authors who developed the indicators underlying the institutional quality index warn against precise ranking exercises among the countries for which the index is available, given great data uncertainty and differing degrees of coverage and data availability for different countries.

Table 3.11. Index of Institutional Quality, 1997–98

Countries/ Transition Groups	Voice and Accountability	Political Instability and Violence	Government Effectiveness	Regulatory Burden	Rule of Law	Graft	Simple Average All six Components	Weder[1]
EU accession countries (excluding Baltics)								
Bulgaria	6.0	4.3	−8.1	5.2	−1.5	−5.6	0.1	−0.8
Czech Republic	12.0	8.1	5.9	5.7	5.4	3.8	6.8	6.6
Hungary	12.0	12.5	6.1	8.5	7.1	6.1	8.7	8.0
Poland	10.7	8.4	6.7	5.6	5.4	4.9	7.0	6.7
Romania	4.1	0.2	−5.7	2.0	−0.9	−4.6	−0.8	−1.0
Slovak Republic	7.4	6.5	−0.3	1.7	1.3	0.3	2.8	2.1
Slovenia	10.7	10.9	5.7	5.3	8.3	10.2	8.5	8.0
Baltic countries								
Estonia	7.9	7.9	2.6	7.4	5.1	5.9	6.1	5.8
Latvia	6.2	4.6	0.7	5.1	1.5	−2.6	2.6	2.2
Lithuania	7.7	3.5	1.3	0.9	1.8	0.3	2.6	2.4
Other southeastern European countries								
Albania	−0.1	−10.0	−6.5	−7.0	−9.2	−9.9	−7.1	−6.5
Bosnia & Herzegovina	−9.7	−11.6	−11.1	−12.6	−11.1	−3.5	−9.9	−9.6
Croatia	−3.2	4.1	1.5	2.4	1.5	−4.6	0.3	−0.5
Macedonia, FYR	0.9	−4.0	−5.8	−3.1	−2.6	−5.2	−3.3	−3.2
Commonwealth of Independent States[1]								
Armenia	0.2	−4.5	−6.5	−5.7	−1.5	−8.0	−4.4	−4.3
Azerbaijan	−9.2	−3.6	−8.3	−10.0	−5.6	−10.0	−7.8	−8.6
Belarus	−5.2	−3.7	−6.6	−14.7	−8.8	−6.5	−7.6	−8.3
Georgia	−2.9	−7.6	−5.1	−8.5	−4.9	−7.4	−6.1	−5.8
Kazakhstan	−7.1	2.2	−8.2	−4.0	−5.9	−8.7	−5.3	−6.8
Kyrgyz Republic	−2.5	3.2	−5.8	−7.6	−4.7	−7.6	−4.2	−5.6
Moldova	1.6	−2.0	−4.6	−2.8	−0.2	−3.9	−2.0	−2.0
Mongolia	8.4	3.7	0.2	1.7	0.4	−1.5	2.2	1.8
Russia	−3.1	−6.9	−5.9	−3.0	−7.2	−6.2	−5.4	−5.1
Tajikistan	−15.6	−18.6	−14.2	−15.2	−13.3	−13.2	−15.0	−14.3
Turkmenistan	−14.5	0.0	−12.5	−19.3	−9.7	−12.9	−11.5	−13.8
Ukraine	−0.1	−2.4	−8.9	−7.2	−7.1	−8.9	−5.8	−6.4
Uzbekistan	−13.4	−3.3	−13.0	−14.0	−8.7	−9.6	−10.4	−11.8
East Asia								
Cambodia	−9.1	. . .	. . .	−0.4	−2.3	. . .	−3.9	−2.2
China	−13.0	4.8	0.2	−0.7	−0.4	−2.9	−2.0	−3.4
Lao People's Dem. Rep.	−10.5	. . .	. . .	−18.2	−12.0	. . .	−13.6	−14.6
Vietnam	−14.2	6.5	−3.0	−4.6	−4.4	−3.3	−3.8	−5.9

Source: Beatrice Weder, "Institutional Reform in Transition Economies: How Far Have They Come?" (unpublished; Washington: International Monetary Fund, 2000).
[1]Excludes index of political instability and violence.
[2]Data include Mongolia.

democracy, government effectiveness, extent of regulation, rule of law, and graft, respectively.[71] The index, as well as the component indicators, range from −25 to + 25, and its average value for advanced economies is 12.6.[72] The institutional

quality index is estimated for the period 1997/98 only, and no time series for the index is available.

As can be seen from Table 3.12., the three indices are highly correlated. High correlation be-

---

[71]The component indicator of "Political Instability and Violence" is not included in Weder's institutional quality index.
[72]The original component indicators in Kaufmann and others, "Governance Matters," ranged from −2.5 to +2.5. In Weder's work, these indicators have been multiplied by 10.

Table 3.12. Correlation Among Indices[1]

	EBRD Transition Indicator 1997	Liberalization Index 1997	Institutional Quality Index 1997–98
EBRD Transition Indicator, 1997	1.00	0.95	0.90
Liberalization Index, 1997		1.00	0.85
Institutional Quality Index, 1997–98			1.00

[1]Calculated from a set of 25 transition economies for which all three indices are available.

tween the liberalization index and the aggregate transition indicator reflects the similarity of the concepts measured, while high correlation between these two indicators and the index of institutional quality suggests that countries that have been successful in raising institutional quality were also the ones most successful in implementing structural reforms.

CHAPTER IV

ACCESSION OF TRANSITION ECONOMIES TO THE EUROPEAN UNION: PROSPECTS AND PRESSURES

The first decade of transition for the countries of central and eastern Europe and the Baltics (CEECs) was marked by a substantial reorientation of their economic and institutional focus toward western Europe. A significant milestone during the second decade of transition is likely to be the formal accession, of at least the countries more advanced in the transition process, into the European Union (EU). The EU has accepted as full candidates for accession ten of the transition economies—Bulgaria, the Czech Republic, Estonia, Hungary, Latvia, Lithuania, Poland, Romania, the Slovak Republic, and Slovenia—together with Cyprus, Malta, and Turkey. Detailed negotiations for entry are currently underway in most cases.[1] Although such an enlargement will almost certainly occur in stages, the accession of the ten transition country applicants would increase the population of the EU by more than one-quarter and its surface area by around one-third. The "economic" size of the EU would increase by much less, however, reflecting the much lower levels of income and wealth in the accession countries: GDP on a purchasing-power-parity (PPP) basis would increase by 11 percent, while average GDP per capita would decline by 13 percent.[2]

The goal of EU accession has become one of the key driving forces behind the adjustment and reform efforts that these countries are actively pursuing. Looking beyond EU accession, the prospect of subsequent currency integration through the European Economic and Monetary Union (EMU) provides a further anchor both for monetary policies in the candidate countries and also for their ongoing structural and insti-

tutional reforms. Moreover, for the EU and its current members, enlargement is providing an important opportunity and incentive for their own reforms, so that the EU is ready economically and institutionally to accept new members.

This chapter assesses some of the likely benefits, costs, and risks in the accession and convergence process, looking both at the nearer-term prospect of EU accession and at potential euro area membership over the longer term. In particular, by considering the main institutional, microeconomic, and macroeconomic dimensions of EU and euro area enlargement, the chapter aims to address the following questions:

- *Net gains from accession:* What are the prospects of substantial net economic benefits for the candidates (e.g., from further trade and financial market integration), and also for the EU? Are such benefits likely to occur in the short-term, or are they of a longer-term nature?

- *Potential pressures and risks in the EU and EMU convergence process:* How do financial sector development and supervision in the accession countries compare with standards in the EU? Are the accession countries equipped to implement the extensive legal and regulatory requirements of EU entry? Are concerns about large migration flows from east to west following EU enlargement justified? At what point are these countries likely to be ready to meet the fiscal, inflation, and exchange rate criteria associated with full participation in the euro area, given their need for further economic adjustment and convergence?

- *The accession timetable:* What difficulties could arise if EU accession (and later euro area par-

---

[1]Negotiations with Turkey have not yet begun.

[2]Based on current GDP data. As a point of comparison, the most recent EU expansion in 1995—bringing in Austria, Finland, and Sweden—and also including the reunification of Germany in 1990, led to an 11 percent increase in the EU's population and an 8 percent increase in GDP (on a PPP basis).

ticipation) occurs either too slowly, or too quickly—whether from the perspective of the applicants or of current members? Is the process likely to be prolonged and, if so, would this occur because the candidates are viewed as not ready for the EU or because the EU is not ready for them?

These questions are, in some cases, addressed indirectly. For example, benefits and risks for the applicants could arise from several dimensions of the accession process that are considered in the following sections. A concluding section brings together the main strands of the argument, links these to the questions above, and provides an overall perspective on EU and euro area enlargement.

The coverage of this chapter is necessarily selective, given the complex array of economic, political, and other influences that have some bearing on the proposed enlargement. For the most part, the assessment is forward-looking; however, some background and institutionally-oriented information on EU enlargement is set out in Box 4.1 (see page 144), and some comparisons with past enlargements are presented in Box 4.2 (see page 148). The chapter focuses on the ten transition countries in central and eastern Europe noted above, in keeping with the emphasis of this *World Economic Outlook* on the economics of transition. The other candidates—Cyprus, Malta, and Turkey—are not included in the detailed analysis, given their somewhat different economic and political starting points. Some specific issues concerning Turkey's candidacy are, however, covered in Box 4.3 (see page 152).

Where Do the CEECs Stand on the Road to Accession?

As described in Chapter III, all of the accession countries have made substantial strides since the 1989 fall of the Berlin Wall in moving from centrally planned to market economies, with the private sector now accounting for over half of output (Figure 4.1). Most have also resumed growth with moderate or declining inflation although fiscal and external current ac-

Figure 4.1. Private Sector Share of Output, mid-1999
(Percent of GDP)

The EU accession countries have made substantial progress in moving from centrally-planned to market economies, with the private sector now accounting for more than half of output in each country.

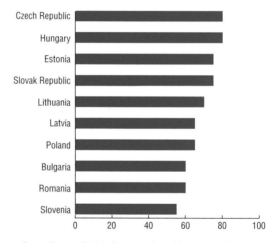

Source: European Bank for Reconstruction and Development, *Transition Report 1999* (London: EBRD, 1999).

Table 4.1. Central and Eastern European Countries: Macroeconomic Indicators

	Real GDP Growth[1]		Inflation[1]		Fiscal Balance[2]		Current Account Balance[2]	
	1997–99	1999	1997	1999	1997–99	1999	1997–99	1999
Bulgaria	–0.4	2.4	1082.2	2.1	–0.7	–1.0	–0.9	–5.4
Czech Republic	–1.2	–0.2	8.5	2.1	–2.9	–3.7	–3.5	–2.0
Estonia	4.6	–1.1	11.2	3.3	–1.1	–4.7	–9.1	–6.1
Hungary	4.6	4.5	18.3	10.0	–4.4	–3.7	–3.8	–4.3
Latvia	4.1	0.1	8.0	2.4	–1.6	–4.2	–8.4	–9.7
Lithuania	2.6	–4.1	8.8	0.8	–5.5	–8.6	–11.2	–11.2
Poland	5.2	4.1	14.9	7.3	–3.4	–3.7	–5.0	–7.5
Romania	–4.9	–3.2	154.8	45.8	–4.2	–3.4	–5.8	–3.8
Slovak Republic	4.3	1.9	6.1	10.7	–4.6	–3.6	–8.8	–5.7
Slovenia	4.5	4.9	8.4	6.1	–0.8	–0.6	–1.0	–2.9

[1]Real GDP growth and inflation are given in annual average percent terms.
[2]Fiscal and current account balances are given as percent of GDP. The fiscal balance refers to the general government balance.

Table 4.2. Selected European Countries: Economic Indicators
(1999)

	Population (Millions)	GDP Level		GDP per Capita		Saving Rate[1,2]	Investment Rate[1]	Broad Money[1,3]
		Billions of U.S. dollars	PPP weight in billions	U.S. dollars	PPP weight			
Central and eastern European countries	**104.6**	**365.1**	**903.8**	**3,490**	**8,638**	**21.5**	**26.9**	**45**
1998 Group	62.4	282.5	635.9	4,524	10,184	23.0	28.4	50
Czech Republic	10.3	53.1	137.6	5,170	13,389	26.9	28.5	77
Estonia	1.4	5.1	11.8	3,585	8,223	21.3	31.0	39
Hungary	10.1	48.4	113.4	4,805	11,256	26.6	31.5	45
Poland	38.7	154.1	342.2	3,984	8,845	20.1	27.6	43
Slovenia	2.0	21.7	31.0	10,981	15,669	24.9	25.2	33
2000 Group	42.2	82.6	267.9	1,958	6,349	17.8	23.3	34
Bulgaria	8.3	12.7	42.5	1,540	5,149	12.6	18.0	30
Latvia	2.4	6.3	14.7	2,593	6,074	20.8	28.9	37
Lithuania	3.7	10.6	25.2	2,885	6,833	11.8	23.0	21
Romania	22.4	34.2	130.3	1,523	5,807	16.1	19.9	23
Slovak Republic	5.4	18.8	55.2	3,491	10,230	28.0	33.8	68
EU-15[4]	**375.3**	**8509.5**	**8371.0**	**22,672**	**22,303**	**20.9**	**20.7**	**69**
Maximum	82.1	2114.8	1940.8	43,467	36,727	25.9	26.6	96
Minimum	0.4	18.7	15.8	11,433	15,207	16.3	16.9	41

[1]Percent of GDP. For aggregates, weighted by purchasing-power-parity GDP.
[2]Excluding Luxembourg.
[3]1998 for the EU-15.
[4]The EU-15 comprise Austria, Belgium, Denmark, Finland, France, Germany, Greece, Ireland, Italy, Luxembourg, the Netherlands, Portugal, Spain, Sweden, and the United Kingdom.

count deficits generally remain high (Table 4.1). Moreover, according to the European Bank for Reconstruction and Development (EBRD) indicators of transition, the CEECs have for the most part successfully liberalized trade and foreign exchange systems and privatized a significant share of both large- and small-scale enterprises (Figure 4.2, and see below). Prices have also been liberalized, although not to the same extent. By contrast, competition policy reforms, governance improvements, enterprise restructuring, and the development of financial institutions have lagged, but to varying degrees.

All of the CEECs have made progress, but they remain a diverse group—with per capita income in 1999, based on market exchange rates, ranging from about $1,500 in Bulgaria and Romania to almost $11,000 in Slovenia (Table 4.2). The more advanced of these countries—the Czech Republic, Estonia, Hungary, Poland,

and Slovenia[3]—began accession negotiations in 1998, and are now approaching some of the current EU countries across a number of economic indicators. On a purchasing-power-parity basis, the average per capita income of the 1998 group (around $10,200) remains less than half of that of the EU ($22,300),[4] although Slovenia has a higher per capita income ($15,700) than the poorest current EU country (Greece, with a per capita income of $15,200). Other than the Slovak Republic, however, each of the countries that began accession negotiations in 2000[5]—also including Bulgaria, Latvia, Lithuania, and Romania—lags behind with lower per capita income than any member of the EU or the 1998 group. The gap between these economies and the EU is also substantially larger than the gap that existed between acceding countries and the EU during prior enlargements (see Box 4.2).

The per capita income differences among the CEECs appear to be related to how advanced the countries are with reform. The 1998 group countries are further along the transition process (as measured by the EBRD transition indicators) than countries in the 2000 group and also generally have a higher private sector share of GDP. In addition, the 1998 group also has a lower agriculture share of value added and a higher services share, consistent with these economies being more advanced along the transition and development process (Table 4.3). It is noteworthy, however, that the Slovak Republic has more similar characteristics—including per capita income, as noted above—to the 1998 group than the 2000 group.

Other indicators also confirm that the 1998 group is not only more advanced than the 2000 group (again with the exception of the Slovak Republic), but also by some measures quite similar to the EU. Saving rates for the 1998 group

Figure 4.2. Indicators of Transition, 1999[1]

All of the EU accession countries have made substantial progress with some dimensions of transition, particularly with liberalizing trade and foreign exchange systems and privatizing both large- and small-scale enterprises. The 1998 group, however, is more advanced than the 2000 group.

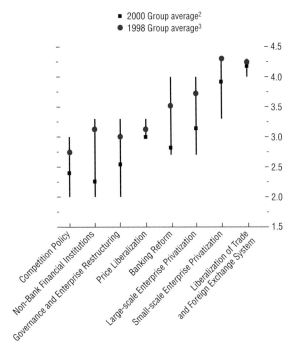

Source: European Bank for Reconstruction and Development, *Transition Report, 1999* (London: EBRD, 1999).

[1]The top and bottom of each line are, respectively, the maximum and minimum for the EU accession countries. Values range from 1 to 4+, with 4+ being the highest rank and set equal to 4.3.

[2]Includes Bulgaria, Latvia, Lithuania, Romania, and the Slovak Republic.

[3]Includes the Czech Republic, Estonia, Hungary, Poland, and Slovenia.

[3]Hereafter, these five countries are called the "1998 group."

[4]These differences are larger when market exchange rates are used.

[5]Hereafter called the "2000 group."

Table 4.3. Selected European Countries: Sectoral Value Added[1]

(Percent share, 1998)

	Agriculture	Industry	Services
Central and eastern European countries[2]	**7**	**34**	**58**
1998 Group[2]	5	34	60
Czech Republic	4	39	57
Estonia	6	27	67
Hungary	6	34	60
Poland	5	32	62
Slovenia	4	39	57
2000 Group[2]	13	35	52
Bulgaria	19	26	56
Latvia	5	29	66
Lithuania	10	33	57
Romania	16	40	43
Slovak Republic	4	32	64
EU-15[2]	**2**	**29**	**69**
Maximum	4	34	72
Minimum	1	26	62

Source: World Bank Development Indicators.

[1]For EU-15, only Austria, Belgium, Finland, France, and the United Kingdom.

[2]Weighted by purchasing-power-parity GDP.

Table 4.4. Selected European Countries: Indicators of Health and Education

	Life Expectancy At Birth (years, 1998)[1]	Secondary School Enrollment (percent, 1997)[2]
Central and eastern European countries[3]	**72**	**86**
1998 Group	73	91
Czech Republic	75	100
Estonia	70	86
Hungary	71	97
Poland	73	87
Slovenia	75	95
2000 Group	70	79
Bulgaria	71	78
Latvia	70	81
Lithuania	72	81
Romania	69	76
Slovak Republic	73	94
EU-15[3]	**78**	**95**
Maximum	79	100
Minimum	75	90

Source: World Bank Development Indicators.

[1]Except 1997 for the Slovak Republic.

[2]Except 1994 for Lithuania and 1996 for the Slovak Republic and Slovenia.

[3]Weighted by population. The EU-15 comprise Austria, Belgium, Denmark, Finland, France, Germany, Greece, Ireland, Italy, Luxembourg, the Netherlands, Portugal, Spain, Sweden, and the United Kingdom.

are in a similar range to those for the EU countries and are actually higher on an average basis. Saving rates in the 2000 group are generally lower than rates for both the 1998 group and the EU countries (see Table 4.2). Investment rates in both CEEC groups are usually higher than in the EU, as would be expected for countries that are catching up and have substantial investment opportunities. The broad money-to-GDP ratio, an indicator of financial deepening, however, is generally lower in both CEEC groups than in EU countries, except in the Czech and Slovak Republics.[6] Indicators of health and education are often used as proxies for the level of human capital.[7] In the CEECs, life expectancy at birth, while relatively high, is somewhat lower than in the EU, and although secondary school enrollment rates among the 1998 group are comparable to those in the EU, they are lower for the 2000 group (Table 4.4).

As the CEEC economies have become more market-oriented, they have also become more integrated with western Europe, with the majority of their trade and capital transactions now occurring with the EU. Nonetheless, looking ahead in particular to euro area membership, the potential vulnerability of the CEECs to asymmetric shocks is suggested by the fact that output growth and inflation in some of these countries are not as yet well correlated with the corresponding indicators in Germany, the largest EU country (Table 4.5). However, because the CEECs are undergoing substantial structural and economic regime changes—including EU accession and subsequently euro area participation itself—it is hard to predict how exposed and vulnerable the CEECs will remain to these shocks

[6]The higher ratio in these two countries, however, may reflect banking sector problems.

[7]For the CEECs, they may be weaker indicators of human capital because many of the workers in the accession economies may have inappropriate skills, gained during a period when these economies were centrally planned and before the structural changes due to transition.

Table 4.5. Selected European Countries: Correlation of Output and Inflation, 1993–99

	Germany		Poland	
	GDP growth	Inflation	GDP growth	Inflation
Central and eastern European countries				
1998 Group				
Czech Republic	0.03	0.84	0.53	0.74
Estonia	0.53	0.98	0.80	0.89
Hungary	0.75	0.43	0.10	0.71
Poland	0.37	0.88	1.00	1.00
Slovenia	0.81	0.98	0.19	0.89
2000 Group				
Bulgaria	0.38	−0.07	−0.41	−0.20
Latvia	0.76	0.96	0.62	0.80
Lithuania	0.50	0.92	0.72	0.70
Romania	−0.11	0.86	0.24	0.57
Slovak Republic	0.74	0.90	0.85	0.70
EU-15[1]				
Average	0.71	0.60	. . .	. . .
Maximum	0.96	0.99	. . .	. . .
Minimum	−0.61	−0.78	. . .	. . .
Euro-11[1]				
Average	0.69	0.69	. . .	. . .
Maximum	0.93	0.99	. . .	. . .
Minimum	−0.61	−0.40	. . .	. . .

Source: IMF staff estimates
[1]EU-15 and Euro-11 data exclude Germany. The other 14 members of the EU-15 are Austria, Belgium, Denmark, Finland, France, Greece, Ireland, Italy, Luxembourg, the Netherlands, Portugal, Spain, Sweden, and the United Kingdom. The other ten members of the Euro-11 are Austria, Belgium, Finland, France, Ireland, Italy, Luxembourg, the Netherlands, Portugal and Spain.

by the time they are fully integrated in the euro area, especially if they follow appropriate complementary policies.[8]

Accession and Convergence: Costs, Benefits, and Risks

EU membership requires applicants to meet a broad set of political, economic, and institutional requirements, as summarized in the EU's Copenhagen criteria set out in Box 4.1. Briefly, the criteria include guarantees for democratic principles and human rights, and the existence of a fully functioning market economy. A key issue that arises in this regard concerns the candi-

dates' ability to adopt and—especially—to enforce the legal and regulatory frameworks that are required not just as part of EU membership but, more generally, as the underpinnings of well-functioning, market-based economies.

Beyond these overall criteria for membership, the conditions for EU and EMU accession can be grouped into two categories. The first involves a number of specific and absolute requirements for membership, where the candidate countries generally have little or no choice as to the form of compliance. The second category covers a broader range of conditions, guidelines, and expectations, often in the form of minimum standards, but where the applicants retain some choice about where they position themselves prior to (and following) accession. Key examples of the former are the common external tariff and associated requirements for the customs union and the full opening of the capital account. In each case, if any derogations from full compliance are permitted, they would likely be of very limited scope and duration. For these issues, the focus is on the extent to which the applicants already meet these EU membership criteria, and the implications of moving to full compliance. A particular question that arises in this regard is whether capital account liberalization is being pursued while the financial sector is at less than full health (raising the same concerns as in the recent financial crisis in Asia). The condition of the financial sector in the accession countries and the quality of supervision are therefore critical issues.

Turning to the second category of accession conditions noted above, a particularly important example concerns labor market policies. Under the *acquis communautaire*, the candidate countries need to follow a range of basic guidelines in such areas as health and safety conditions, protection of worker rights, bargaining arrangements, and so on. But, as indicated by the wide range of regulations and practices among cur-

---

[8]Economic convergence may help to prepare a country for currency union. See Tamim Bayoumi and Barry Eichengreen, "Ever Closer to Heaven? An Optimum-Currency-Area Index For European Countries," *European Economic Review*, Vol. 41 (April 1997), pp. 761–70.

Box 4.1. Formalities and Procedures of EU Enlargement[1]

The formal requirements and procedures underlying EU enlargement have been established largely through a series of resolutions arising from meetings of the European Council (the EU's summit-level, decision-making body). This box sets out briefly, and in approximately chronological order, the main decisions and elements of this process, and summarizes the current state of play regarding the accession proceedings.

Initial cooperation. In the very early stages of their transition, most of the countries of central and eastern Europe and the Baltics (CEECs) declared their interest in joining the EU. Although not initially recognizing accession of these countries as a formal EU objective, the EU nevertheless fostered closer relations with them both through the provision of financial assistance, and especially through trade and cooperation agreements—subsequently transformed into association or Europe Agreements. These bilateral documents provide a detailed legal framework for closer political, economic, and cultural cooperation, including the timing and scope of trade liberalization.

Copenhagen Criteria. In June 1993, the Copenhagen European Council formally agreed that the associated countries would be allowed to join the EU as soon as they were able to "assume the obligations of membership by satisfying the economic and political conditions required"—the so-called Copenhagen Criteria. In particular, membership requires that the "candidate country" has achieved:

- stability of institutions guaranteeing democracy, the rule of law, human rights, and respect for and protection of minorities;

- the existence of a functioning market economy, as well as the capacity to cope with competitive pressure and market forces within the Union;
- the ability to take on the obligations of membership, including adherence to the aims of political, economic, and monetary union."[2]

Application and initial assessment—the Luxembourg Agreement. In mid-1997, the European Commission submitted its assessment of political and economic progress in the economies that had applied for membership, recommending that accession negotiations begin with six—the Czech Republic, Estonia, Hungary, Poland, and Slovenia among the transition economies, together with Cyprus.[3] This recommendation was accepted at the Luxembourg European Council in December 1997, although the Council also left open the possibility that other applicants could subsequently join this "first wave."

Negotiations begin—the acquis communautaire. Accession negotiations opened in March 1998 with these six candidates (referred to as the "1998 group"). The focus of these negotiations is on the *acquis communautaire*—the detailed body of laws and regulations that underpins the EU. The *acquis* is structured into 31 chapters—covering, for example, policies in specific sectors (e.g., agriculture, fisheries, and the financial sector), social policies, the environment, and external relations. One of the chapters also covers economic and monetary union (see below). The bilateral negotiation process works through these different chapters, starting with a screening exercise in which each country sets out its position, including proposed derogations from the *acquis* or transitional periods before full compliance occurs, and then continuing (if necessary) with detailed negotiations.

---

[1]This box draws mainly on material on enlargement available via the Internet on the EU website (http://europa.eu.int/comm/enlargement); on Erik Berglof and Gerard Roland, "From 'Regatta' to 'Big Bang'?—The Impact of the EU Accession Strategy on Reforms in Central and Eastern Europe," unpublished manuscript prepared for this *World Economic Outlook*; and on Heliodoro Temprano-Arroyo and Robert A. Feldman, "Selected Transition and Mediterranean Countries: An Institutional Primer on EMU and EU Accession," *Economics of Transition*, Vol. 7, No. 3 (1999), pp. 741–806.

[2]See the Accession Criteria page of the EU website at http://europa.eu.int/comm/enlargement
[3]The ten associated CEECs submitted formal applications for EU membership during 1994–96. Applications had previously been submitted by Turkey (1987), Cyprus (1990), and Malta (1990, reactivated in 1998).

Helsinki Summit—from "waves" to a more open accession process. The Helsinki meeting of the European Council (December 1999) decided that accession negotiations should begin with the other five transition economy applicants and Malta, and that Turkey should be accepted as a full candidate. As part of this decision, the Council moved away from the "wave" approach to negotiation and eventual accession, to a more open approach. Under the latter, each candidate country's accession prospects would depend on its progress with negotiations through the *acquis.* This decision therefore opened up the possibility for countries to move up or down the accession queue—with original second wave countries, for example, possibly joining or even moving ahead of those placed earlier in the first wave.

What is the status of negotiations and when could enlargement occur?

For the original first wave countries, negotiations have been opened on all chapters of the *acquis,* and provisionally concluded in many cases. Much of the negotiating process has been of an exploratory nature, however. In the areas that pose most problems, notably agriculture, regional policies, and the free movement of labor, substantive negotiations are just beginning and final decisions will depend in part on the EU's own policy reforms in these areas. Negotiations opened in February 2000 with the remaining candidates (apart from Turkey).[4] The initial steps have involved the screening of candidates' positions on individual chapters, followed by the opening of negotiations on selected chapters.

Overall, there are no commitments as to the precise date of accession of any of the candidates. No "accession treaty" is to be signed before the EU-15 have agreed on reforms in the Union's common institutions (discussed in the main text). The European Council concluded in December 1999 that the EU should be in a position to admit new members "from the end of

[4]That is, with Bulgaria, Latvia, Lithuania, Malta, Romania, and the Slovak Republic.

2002," based on the assumption that the intergovernmental conference on reform of EU institutions would be concluded successfully by December 2000, and taking into account that ratification of a treaty usually takes close to two years. The European Union's Commissioner for Enlargement indicated in July 2000 that the "window of opportunity" for accession of the next new members of the EU would be between 2003 and 2005. The countries that are more advanced in the negotiating process have signaled that they plan to be ready for accession by 2003.

What are the linkages between EU accession and participation in the euro area?

While economic and monetary union is one of the negotiating chapters of the *acquis,* the candidate countries are not expected to become full members of the euro area, adopt specific exchange rate regimes, or meet the convergence requirements set out in the Maastricht Treaty on European Union, as preconditions for EU membership (that is, they are likely to enter the EU with derogations regarding these aspects of the *acquis*). As elaborated in the main text, substantial adjustment periods could be required for at least some of the applicants before they are able to meet the Maastricht criteria on a durable basis. Furthermore, the EU recognizes that it would be neither in its own interest nor in that of the applicants to impose on the latter an exchange rate system that might not be credible or sustainable. The Copenhagen Criteria make provision for an adjustment period by referring to the need for candidates to adhere to the *aims* of monetary union, rather than adopt the euro itself. Nevertheless, the EU has decided that new EU members will eventually be required to join the euro area (i.e., there will be no more opt-out clauses) and, under the *acquis,* all EU members are to "treat their exchange rate policy as a matter of common interest." It is not clear precisely what this means in practice. However, the EU has indicated that new members will need to be able to "avoid excessive fluctuations of their exchange rates which could endanger the functioning of the Single Market."

rent EU members, the applicants will still have substantial flexibility about how labor market policies are to be applied domestically once they comply with the minimum standards. Labor as well as product market arrangements need to support these economies' overall adjustment requirements and must be consistent with their macroeconomic policy frameworks.

The EU accession process does not set specific requirements for fiscal and monetary policies in the applicant countries, although assessing the sustainability of macroeconomic policies is clearly a central part of the overall determination of these countries' economic preparedness for entry. The key issue here is the potential pressures that could arise in the fiscal and monetary positions in the lead-up to, and following, EU accession—for example, the implications for public spending of complying with EU legislative requirements, the availability of funding from the EU, and pressures on monetary policy that could arise from increased capital flows.

Macroeconomic requirements are much more precisely defined when it comes to entry into the euro area, although this process cannot begin until EU accession itself has occurred. Under the convergence criteria of the 1993 Maastricht Treaty on European Economic and Monetary Union, countries are required to keep their exchange rates within "normal fluctuation margins" for at least two years in the exchange rate mechanism (ERM); ERM II is based on margins of +/−15 percent against the euro.[9] Also, inflation must remain no more than 1.5 percentage points higher than the average of the three lowest inflation rates in EMU member countries, the fiscal deficit must be below 3 percent of GDP,

and government debt must be below 60 percent of GDP or declining at a satisfactory pace. As noted in Box 4.1, the candidate countries are expected eventually to join the euro area, but they have considerable latitude as to the timing of their full participation. Such decisions will depend in part on the ongoing adjustment and convergence needs of these economies.

Overall Preparedness for EU Accession: Institutional Underpinnings

The importance of *institutions* in economic development has been receiving growing attention in recent years.[10] The evidence from a number of sources is that progress with institution building has contributed to the generally stronger economic performance among the transition economies that are now on the EU accession track compared with those in the Commonwealth of Independent States (CIS). This section looks at just the former group, considering how they compare with the EU and among themselves in terms of institutional progress. Such progress is assessed from two perspectives that correspond closely with the first two Copenhagen criteria outlined in Box 4.1—namely, the degree of *political and civic freedom* in the accession countries, and their progress in establishing the *underpinnings for market-based economic activity*.

Political and Civic Freedom

The European Commission has concluded that all of the transition country applicants fulfill the Copenhagen political criteria.[11] The Commission noted, however, that there was

---

[9]In its Convergence Reports, the European Commission interprets "normal fluctuation margins" as meaning that exchange rate fluctuations should remain within +/− 2¼ percent bands, although breaches of this band should be individually examined to see if they resulted from severe tensions.

[10]See, for example, Oleh Havrylyshyn and Ron van Rooden, "Institutions Matter in Transition, but so do Policies," IMF Working Paper 00/70 (Washington: International Monetary Fund, 2000); Beatrice Weder, "Institutional Reform in Transition Economies: How far have they come?" background paper for this *World Economic Outlook;* Luc Moers, "How Important are Institutions for Growth in Transition Countries?" Tinbergen Institute Discussion Paper (Amsterdam, 1999).

[11]European Commission, "Composite Paper: Reports on progress towards accession by each of the candidate countries" (Brussels, 1999), available via the Internet at http://www.europa.eu.int. In its 1999 review, the Commission cited the particular improvements that had recently been made in the Slovak Republic, which, two years earlier, was the only one of the ten candidates judged to not satisfy the political criteria.

scope for further strengthening of democratic principles and human rights in many of the applicant countries, particularly in their support for minorities and for independence of the media. The Commission's assessment is consistent with indicators compiled by other agencies and researchers. In terms of an indicator of "voice and accountability," based on estimates of political and civic progress compiled by a range of different organizations, most of the applicant countries do not differ significantly from the EU average (Figure 4.3).[12]

Support for Market-Based Economic Activity

More dispersion is apparent among the candidate countries with indicators of economic progress.[13] Following the European Commission's 1999 assessment, based on each applicant's economic framework, policies, and achievements, the Commission concluded that six countries (the Czech Republic, Estonia, Hungary, Latvia, Poland, and Slovenia) could be regarded as having functioning market economies, two (Lithuania and the Slovak Republic) were "close," Bulgaria had made substantial progress from a poor starting point, while the situation in Romania was "very worrying."[14]

There have, however, been important signs of convergence with institutional reform, probably reflecting both the anchoring role of prospective EU membership in domestic reform agendas and also the incentive effects arising from the more open accession process introduced in late 1999,

---

[12]This indicator and the following two indicators (covering the rule of law and graft) are presented in Daniel Kaufmann, Aart Kraay, and Pablo Zoido-Lobatón, "Governance Matters" (unpublished; Washington: World Bank, 1999).

[13]It is also noteworthy that, in terms of the economic indicators discussed in this section, the gap between the accession countries and current EU members closes significantly if the indicators are adjusted for differences in GDP per capita (Weder, "Institutional Reform in Transition Economies").

[14]European Commission, "Composite Paper: Reports on progress towards accession by each of the candidate countries."

Figure 4.3. Indicators of Institutional Development[1]

The more advanced transition economies have largely caught up with the EU in terms of political and civic freedom, but still lag behind in terms of application of laws and freedom from corruption.

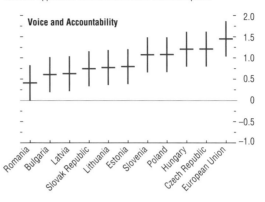

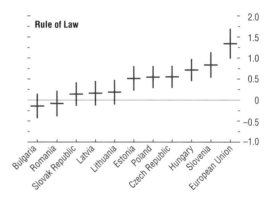

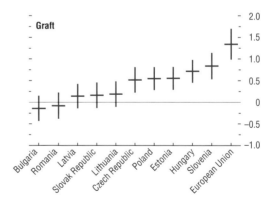

[1]These indicators are from D. Kaufmann, A. Kraay, and P. Zoido-Lobatón, "Governance Matters" (Washington: World Bank, 1999), and are available via the Internet at http://www.worldbank.org/wbi/governance/pubs/govmatters.htm.

The vertical axis measures the number of standard deviations from the global mean for each indicator (constructed to follow a N(0,1) distribution). The horizontal bar for each country shows the mean level of the indicator concerned, and the vertical bars represent 90 percent confidence intervals. With each indicator, a higher score indicates stronger performance (greater freedom and less corruption, etc.).

Box 4.2. Previous EU Enlargements

The accession of the transition economies of central and eastern Europe and the Baltics (hereafter, CEECs) to the European Union (EU) poses distinctive challenges for the Union and the candidate countries, particularly in comparison to past enlargements. Since the Treaty of Rome (in 1957), the EU has expanded on four occasions: Denmark, Ireland, and the United Kingdom in 1973; Greece in 1981; Portugal and Spain in 1986; and Austria, Finland, and Sweden in 1995.[1] Although future expansion will probably not occur all at once, the size of the potential enlargement—in terms of number of countries, population, and land area—is without precedent (see the first table).[2] Moreover, as a group, the CEECs differ from the typical (or average) previous EU candidates (at the time of accession), especially in terms of per capita GDP and inflation relative to the EU, but also in terms of other factors such as openness to trade. However, a few of the previous acceding countries—namely Ireland, Greece, Portugal, and Spain—are more similar to the current applicant group. This box attempts to derive some lessons for the current candidates by examining the past enlargements, particularly the accession of these countries into the Union.

The figure shows a number of economic indicators for these previous candidate countries—Ireland, Greece, Portugal, and Spain—in the 16 years around the year of accession, year t (including five years before and ten years after year t), and for the CEECs in the last six years (with

year t being 1999).[3] Per capita output on a purchasing-power-parity basis in the previous candidates ranged from about half (Portugal in 1986) of the then EU average to over 70 percent (Spain in 1986). By comparison, per capita output in the CEECs currently ranges from about 20 percent (Bulgaria) to almost 70 percent (Slovenia) of the EU average. After accession, the gap in per capita output relative to the EU narrowed in three of the four previous acceding countries—the exception was Greece—during the ensuing five years by at least 1 percent a year and continued to narrow in subsequent years. Indeed, GDP per capita in Ireland now exceeds the EU average, while the gap has narrowed substantially in Portugal and Spain.

These differences in the relative per capita growth performance are reflected in, and perhaps explained by, the differences in other economic variables. Fiscal deficits and the gap in inflation between the acceding countries and the EU decreased in Portugal and Spain and, to a lesser extent, in Ireland (where the fiscal deficit remained large) after accession. Trade and inward foreign direct investment as a percentage of GDP (on a purchasing-power-parity basis) increased—in particular, soon after accession—in these countries.[4] The bilateral real exchange rate (relative to Germany) also increased in the years after accession in these countries, possibly indicating convergence with the rest of the EU. In addition, the correlation of real output growth between the acceding countries and Germany increased after accession both in ab-

[1]The founding members of the Union were Belgium, France, Germany, Italy, Luxembourg, and the Netherlands.

[2]Although in percentage terms relative to the existing EU at the time of each enlargement, the current enlargement is similar to some previous ones in terms of increases in population and area. The non-transition candidates, Cyprus, Malta, and Turkey, would add an extra 65.6 million in population and 787 thousand square kilometers in area.

[3]In the figure, GDP per capita and inflation are compared to these indicators for existing members of the EU when these countries joined the Union. For Ireland, the comparator group includes the founding

members of the Union—namely, Belgium, France, Germany, Italy, Luxembourg, and the Netherlands. For Greece, Portugal, and Spain, the comparator group includes the founding members and Denmark, Ireland, and the United Kingdom.

[4]Previous EU enlargements have tended to be trade creating, although there were trade-diverting effects in the 1973 and 1981 enlargements. See Tamim Bayoumi and Barry Eichengreen, "Is Regionalism Simply a Diversion? Evidence from the Evolution of the EC and EFTA," in *Regionalism Versus Multilateral Trade Arrangements*, NBER—East Asia Seminar on Economics, Vol. 6, edited by Takatoshi Ito and Anne O. Krueger (Chicago: University of Chicago Press, 1997).

EU Enlargements

	Population[1] (millions)	Area[2] (thousands of square kilometers)	GDP Market based (billions of U.S.dollars)	GDP PPP based (billions of U.S.dollars)	GDP/capita Market based (U.S. dollars)	GDP/capita PPP based (U.S. dollars)	Inflation[3] (percent)	Openness[4] (percent of PPP-based GDP)
1973 enlargement (Denmark, Ireland, and the United Kingdom)								
Candidates	64.3	358.2	217.0	267.9	3,374	4,166	9.3	41.5
Existing EU[5]	209.4	1279.8	885.5	854.3	4,229	4,081	8.1	47.2
Candidates/EU (percent)[6]	30.7	28.0	24.5	31.4	79.8	102.1	1.2	−5.6
1981 enlargement (Greece)								
Candidates	9.7	131.9	44.5	55.0	4,575	5,653	24.5	37.8
Existing EU[5]	278.5	1638.0	2528.0	2521.3	9,078	9,054	11.6	61.5
Candidates/EU (percent)[6]	3.5	8.1	1.8	2.2	50.4	62.4	12.9	−23.7
1986 enlargement (Portugal and Spain)								
Candidates	48.5	597.1	275.0	403.2	5,667	8,308	9.2	26.4
Existing EU[5]	290.0	1769.9	3257.3	3497.4	11,232	12,060	2.9	52.1
Candidates/EU (percent)[6]	16.7	33.7	8.4	11.5	50.5	68.9	6.3	−25.7
1995 enlargement (Austria, Finland, and Sweden)								
Candidates	22.0	870.9	605.1	443.7	27,521	20,180	2.1	100.6
Existing EU[5]	350.0	2367.1	8000.1	6780.5	22,856	19,372	3.0	65.7
Candidates/EU (percent)[6]	6.3	36.8	7.6	6.5	120.4	104.2	−0.9	35.0
Current status (1999)								
Candidates (Transition countries)	104.6	1076.9	365.1	903.8	3,490	8,638	11.3	35.3
Existing EU[5]	375.3	3237.9	8509.5	8371.0	22,672	22,303	1.3	63.3
Candidates/EU (percent)[6]	27.9	33.3	4.3	10.8	15.4	38.7	10.0	−28.0

[1]From World Bank Development Indicators.
[2]From *CIA World Factbook 1999*.
[3]IMF, *International Financial Statistics*.
[4]For Greece, exports and imports are from the *International Financial Statistics*.
[5]Members of the EU prior to the enlargement.
[6]Ratio of the candidates to the existing EU, except for inflation and openness where the data refer to candidates minus the existing EU.

solute terms and relative to the corresponding correlations between existing EU members and Germany (see the second table). The picture is more mixed with inflation: only for Ireland (and the 1995 enlargement candidates) does the correlation with Germany increase.[5] By contrast, in

[5]For Portugal and Spain, however, the decrease in the correlation of inflation with Germany after accession may not be due to a lack of convergence. The decrease may instead reflect the relative increase in German inflation during the period of reunification—as underscored by the decreased correlation of German inflation with the rest of the existing EU.

Greece, where macroeconomic and structural reforms were more limited, inflation (relative to the rest of the EU) and the fiscal deficit increased, while trade, inward foreign direct investment, and the output correlation with Germany did not.

These comparisons highlight that convergence occurs in most countries after accession—the exception is Greece, where the gap in per capita GDP remained at about the same level in 1999 as when the country joined the EU. The comparisons also highlight that accession, while providing a key external anchor, does not itself necessarily lead to improved economic perform-

Box 4.2 *(concluded)*

Comparison to Previous EU Enlargements[1]

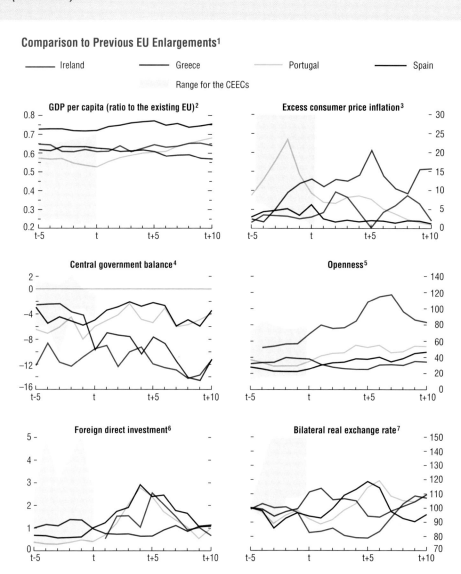

[1]t is the year of accession to the EU, except for the CEECs where t is 1999. For Ireland, t is 1973; for Greece, 1981; and for Portugal and Spain, 1986.

[2]On a purchasing-power-parity basis. The existing EU is the EU prior to the enlargement date.

[3]IMF, *International Financial Statistics* data. Excess inflation (in percentage points) relative to the existing EU prior to the enlargement date. For the CEECs, the maximum excess inflation exceeds 30 percentage points during t-5 to t.

[4]Percent of GDP.

[5]Exports plus imports as a percent of GDP on a purchasing-power-parity basis. For Greece, exports and imports are from the *International Financial Statistics*.

[6]*International Financial Statistics* data. Percent of GDP on a purchasing-power-parity basis.

[7]*International Financial Statistics* data. Indexed to 100 at t-5. Relative to Germany deflated by relative consumer price indices. For the CEECs, the maximum bilateral real exchange rate is above 150 during t-3 to t.

Correlation with Germany around EU Accession [1]

	Real GDP Growth		Consumer Price Inflation	
	Before	After	Before	After
1973 enlargement				
Ireland	0.21	0.46	0.74	0.85
Average for the other candidates	0.32	0.68	0.60	0.60
Existing EU (excluding Germany)[2]	0.44	0.60	0.79	0.73
1981 enlargement				
Greece	0.59	0.42	0.40	0.12
Existing EU (excluding Germany)[2]	0.69	0.23	0.36	0.82
1986 enlargement				
Portugal	0.24	0.59	0.24	0.06
Spain	0.24	0.51	0.41	0.24
Existing EU (excluding Germany)[2]	0.50	0.28	0.79	0.13
1995 enlargement				
Average for the candidates	0.30	0.58	0.21	0.29
Existing EU (excluding Germany)[2]	0.33	0.55	−0.01	0.27

[1]Correlations for ten years before and ten years after the EU enlargement, with the exception of the 1995 enlargement. In the latter case, correlations are for only four years after enlargement because of insufficient data availability.
[2]Members of the EU prior to the enlargement.

ance and integration.[6] Appropriate ancillary policies before and after accession—including macroeconomic stability (through fiscal and monetary policies) and other policies that foster greater openness to trade and an improved cli-

mate for inward foreign investment—are vital, particularly as the current candidates also expect to join the monetary union at some point following EU accession. Although the gap in per capita GDP for most of the CEECs is larger than for countries in previous enlargements, other economic indicators are more similar. As a result, the CEECs are well placed to benefit from further integration with Europe as long as these countries continue to adopt far-reaching—and sometimes difficult—reforms.

[6]See also Erik Berglof and Gerard Roland, "From 'Regatta' to 'Big Bang'?—The Impact of the EU Accession Strategy on Reform in Central and Eastern Europe," unpublished manuscript prepared for this *World Economic Outlook.*

in which all accession candidates are to be considered on an equal footing.[15] In particular, most of the countries left out of the 1998 group appear to have made especially strong efforts to catch up.[16] At the same time, the EU expressed concern at inadequacies in the reform momentum in several

of the 1998 group countries, including institutional strengthening and adoption of the *acquis.* These concerns were consistent with those of outside observers.[17] On balance, the EU's decision to move to a more open approach to accession should reinvigorate the reform process, both for

[15]For a fuller discussion, see Erik Berglof and Gerard Roland, "From 'Regatta' to 'Big Bang'?—The Impact of the EU Accession Strategy on Reform in Central and Eastern Europe," background paper prepared for the October 2000 *World Economic Outlook.*

[16]Reflecting these efforts, the Commission "upgraded" Latvia to functioning market economy status in its 1999 assessment; the implementation of recent reforms in the Slovak Republic and Lithuania were expected to lead to their reaching this status in 2000; and Bulgaria, as noted, was cited as having made remarkable progress since its 1997 economic crisis.

[17]For example, Berglof and Roland, "From 'Regatta' to 'Big Bang'?" also suggest that there were signs of complacency in reform efforts in some of the first wave countries following their selection to be in this group.

Box 4.3. Accession of Turkey to the European Union

Although this chapter focuses on the ten transition countries that are negotiating for EU membership, Cyprus, Malta, and Turkey have also been accepted as candidates for accession. This box presents a few points regarding the candidacy of Turkey—by far the largest of these other three applicants in terms of economic and population size. Turkey's prospects for integration in the European Union took a significant step forward at the 1999 Helsinki European Council meeting, when the Council declared that Turkey is "a candidate State destined to join the Union on the basis of the same criteria as applied to the other candidate States...[and]... will benefit from a pre-accession strategy to stimulate and support its reforms."[1]

Economic size and structure: some indicators and comparisons

Turkey's economy is substantially larger than those of the other EU applicants, with a level of GDP that is about 25 percent larger than that of Poland, the next largest, and a population size that exceeds all of the 1998 negotiating group put together (see the table). GDP per capita (on a purchasing-power-parity basis) is close to the average of the 2000 group, placing Turkey above Bulgaria, Romania, and Latvia, and below Lithuania and the Slovak Republic. In comparison with most of the other EU candidates, apart from Bulgaria and Romania, Turkey's economic structure is weighted relatively heavily toward agriculture: as in Romania, this sector generates around 16 percent of value added and accounts for about 40 percent of employment. The shares of industry and services in value added are close to those of Bulgaria. With around 50 percent of exports going to the EU, Turkey is comparable to Bulgaria and also Lithuania.

Readiness for EU accession

In its 1999 report on progress toward EU accession, the European Commission concluded that Turkey did not yet meet the Copenhagen political criteria (see Box 4.1). Considering eco-

[1]The conclusions of the Helsinki Summit and other material on Turkey's progress toward EU accession are available via the Internet on the EU's website at http://europa.eu.int.

Turkey and Other EU Accession Countries: A Comparison
(1999 data, unless otherwise stated)

	Turkey	1998 Group[1]	2000 Group[2]
Population (millions)	66.1	62.4	42.2
GDP (U.S.$ billions)	191	283	83
GDP (PPP based; U.S.$ billions)	426	636	268
GDP per capita (PPP based; U.S.$)	6,443	10,184	6,349
Sectoral value added:			
Agriculture	16	5	13
Industry	27	34	35
Services	57	60	52
Share of EU in exports	50	68	56

Sources: European Commission; IMF staff estimates.
[1]Czech Republic, Estonia, Hungary, Poland, and Slovenia.
[2]Bulgaria, Latvia, Lithuania, Romania, and Slovak Republic.

nomic readiness for accession, the Commission concluded that Turkey had many of the characteristics of a fully functioning market economy. In particular, the Commission argued that liberalization efforts under way since the late 1980s have given shape to an economy capable of withstanding competition. Moreover, Turkey's industrial sector proved resilient after the opening up of international trade following the signing of the 1995 customs union with the EU. Although progress has been made in achieving macroeconomic stability, the economic reform process nevertheless would need to be consolidated to permanently reduce inflationary pressures and cut public deficits. Furthermore, continuing structural reforms are needed to modernize underdeveloped sectors and regions "in order to ensure that the whole of the economy has the ability to cope with competitive pressure and market forces within the Union."

The Commission also found that, in order to implement and enforce the *acquis communautaire*, Turkey was in need of modernizing its administrative institutions, providing training to its civil servants, and strengthening its judicial capacity. The Commission and Turkey are expected to adopt later in 2000 an Accession Partnership framework that should cover, among other items, the priorities for membership preparation—in particular, adopting the *acquis* and the financial support for that purpose.

Table 4.6. Legal Transition Indicators[1]

	Commercial Law		Financial Regulations	
	Extensiveness	Effectiveness	Extensiveness	Effectiveness
Bulgaria	4	4–	3	2+
Czech Republic	3+	3–	3+	2+
Estonia	3+	4–	4	3+
Hungary	4	4–	4	4
Latvia	4–	3	3	2
Lithuania	4	3	3–	2
Poland	4	3	4	4
Romania	3+	4–	3	3–
Slovak Republic	3+	3	4	3+
Slovenia	4	4	3+	3+

Source: European Bank for Reconstruction and Development.
[1]The scale for these indicators is from 1 to 4+, the latter representing the level reached by the advanced economies.

the original first wave of candidates and for those that were in the second echelon.

The Commission noted that all the candidates needed to further strengthen their legal framework. The most commonly cited concerns included the need to improve bankruptcy proceedings, augment protection of industrial and intellectual property rights, and improve other aspects of the legal environment for business. More broadly, all the applicants were urged to further strengthen their judiciaries, and to tackle what was described as a widespread problem of corruption.

Indicators available from other sources paint a broadly similar picture to that of the Commission. The "rule of law" indicator in Figure 4.3, drawing on around a dozen different sources, reflects perceptions of such factors as the extent of criminality, enforceability of contracts, and general effectiveness of the legal system and judicial authorities. The measure of "graft" reflects outside observers' assessments of the extent of corruption among public officials, attitudes towards corruption, and resulting disruptions to business practices. In each case, there is a sizable shortfall

between the EU average and even the best of the accession countries—more so than in the comparison of political development discussed earlier. Moreover, the five countries in the 1998 group appear to be substantially stronger in terms of these measures of legal development than are countries in the 2000 group. As noted above, the rapid reform efforts pursued by the latter group over the last couple of years may have helped reduce this gap (the indicators are based on data from the 1996–98 period). However, a very similar ranking appears in the latest index of property rights protection published by the Heritage Foundation.[18]

A further perspective comes from indicators of commercial law reform and financial market regulation developed by the EBRD.[19] In each case, experts' views are sought both on the *extensiveness* of reforms—i.e., the extent to which legal rules and standards resemble those of more advanced economies; and on their *effectiveness*—i.e., the clarity of rules and the adequacy of implementation, enforcement, and corrective action.

The latest legal transition indicators reveal four major points (Table 4.6). First, the EU ac-

[18]Available via the Internet at http://www.heritage.org; this index, which is included in the indicator of "rule of law," from Kaufmann, Kraay, and Zoido-Lobatón, "Governance Matters," is one component of the Heritage Foundation/*Wall Street Journal* 2000 Index of Economic Freedom Rankings. In this latest index of property rights, the five first wave countries all received a score of 2 (on a scale of 5), indicating a high level of property rights protection but lax enforcement; Bulgaria, Latvia, Lithuania, and the Slovak Republic received a 3, indicating moderate protection, but some risk of expropriation and the possibility that the judiciary may be influenced by other branches of government; and Romania received a 4, suggesting little legal protection and a poorly functioning judicial system.

[19]European Bank for Reconstruction and Development, *Transition Report 1999* (London: EBRD, 2000).

Table 4.7. Selected European Countries: Trade

	Openness[1] 1999	Openness[2] 1999 (PPP basis)	Tariff Rate 1999 (Percent)	EBRD Index[3] 1999	TRI[4] 1999	WTO (Membership date or status)
Central and Eastern European Countries						
Bulgaria	87.7	26.2	15.1	4+	6	1996
Czech Republic	128.6	49.7	6.8	4+	1	1995
Estonia	186.0	81.1	0.0	4	1	Signed accession protocol
Hungary	137.6	58.8	13.3	4+	5	1995
Latvia	120.6	51.5	5.3	4+	1	1999
Lithuania	89.9	38.0	4.5	4	1	Negotiations ongoing
Poland	48.9	22.0	11.6	4+	2	1995
Romania	62.1	16.3	23.8	4	4	1995
Slovak Republic	134.5	45.9	12.0	4+	2	1995
Slovenia	112.6	78.9	10.6	4+	5	1995
EU-15[5]	74.5	80.6	5.0	. . .	4	

[1]Exports and imports as a percent of GDP using market exchange rates.

[2]Exports and imports as a percent of GDP on a purchasing-power-parity basis.

[3]Trade and foreign exchange liberalization index from the European Bank for Reconstruction and Development. The highest rating is 4+, which means that the countries have achieved the standards and norms of advanced industrial countries, including the removal of most tariff barriers and World Trade Organization membership.

[4]Trade Restrictiveness Index. On a scale of 1–10, 1 is the least restrictive rating. See Appendix I in IMF, *Trade Liberalization in IMF-Supported Programs* (Washington: International Monetary Fund, 1998) for an explanation on the construction of the index.

[5]Unweighted average. The EU-15 comprise Austria, Belgium, Denmark, Finland, France, Germany, Greece, Ireland, Italy, Luxembourg, the Netherlands, Portugal, Spain, Sweden, and the United Kingdom.

cession countries are rated rather highly with respect to the extensiveness of legal reform, probably reflecting in part the influence of (and specific standards derived from) the EU accession process.[20] Second, the effectiveness ratings are usually somewhat lower than those of extensiveness, consistent with the suggestion above that all of these countries need to make further efforts to strengthen the judiciary, improve legal implementation, and reduce corruption. Third, indicators of financial regulation are generally lower than those for commercial law reform. Some countries receive particularly low ratings for the effectiveness of financial measures, reflecting difficulties in such areas as the supply of trained personnel, the conduct of supervision, and timely implementation of corrective measures in the event of financial problems. The

EBRD also notes that, within the financial sector, securities legislation appears to be implemented less effectively than banking laws, a result in part of the relatively new and underdeveloped institutions in the former area. Fourth, regarding the legal transition indicators as a whole, there does not appear to be a clear distinction between the 1998 and 2000 negotiating groups.

Joining the Customs Union

The CEECs have made substantial progress in meeting the trade policy requirements of joining the EU because trade has already been extensively liberalized during the past decade—particularly with the EU.[21] Most of these countries are now relatively open, with trade (import

---

[20]The assigned ratings suggest that most parts of commercial law and financial regulation are reasonably well developed, although with scope for further elaboration and refinement in some areas.

[21]Bilateral agreements with the EU, mainly the Europe Agreements (EAs)—which came into force in all of these countries between 1994 and 1998—have been one of the primary external factors in encouraging trade liberalization, although the General Agreement on Tariffs and Trade (GATT) Uruguay Round, the World Trade Organization, and other special trading arrangements have also played a role. Of course, in the transition from central planning to market economies, the accession countries may have liberalized trade even without these external agreements, although the speed of liberalization may not have been as fast in all countries, the scope not as broad, and the commitment not as deep.

plus export) shares of GDP above the EU average and low tariff rates (Table 4.7).[22] The CEECs also are all either members of the World Trade Organization (WTO) or in the process of WTO accession, rank highly in the EBRD index of liberalization of the trade and foreign exchange system, and are mostly ranked on a comparable or less restrictive level to the EU in the IMF's Trade Restrictiveness Index (TRI). Furthermore, the candidate countries have diversified trade away from other transition countries, and since January 1998, goods exports—other than agricultural goods—from the CEECs to the EU have been duty free (Figure 4.4).[23] The CEECs have also shifted the composition of exports toward expected areas of comparative advantage, such as textiles and natural resources, and some of the leading applicants are experiencing rapid development of FDI-induced, intra-industry trade in such areas as car production and electronics.

Nonetheless, further progress in the candidate countries will be needed in a number of areas. These include removing remaining import restrictions, including non-tariff barriers, on EU exports to the accession countries so as to allow the freedom of movement of goods and services to other EU member states, adopting the Common External Tariff (CET), and ensuring the compatibility of domestic trade policy with the EU's bilateral and multilateral commitments, including extending preferential treatment to third countries.[24] As part of the Europe Agreements, import restrictions on non-agricultural goods from the EU are expected to be

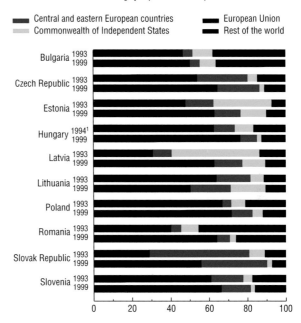

Figure 4.4. Export Markets
(Percent of total exports)

EU accession countries now largely export to the European Union.

Source: IMF, *Direction of Trade Statistics.*
[1]Data unavailable for Hungary in 1993.

---

[22]It should be noted, however, that trade shares of GDP, measured using GDP on a PPP basis, are mostly lower than the EU average.

[23]See also Robert Feldman and others, *Impact of EMU on Selected Non-European Union Countries,* IMF Occasional Paper No. 174 (Washington: International Monetary Fund, 1998).

[24]Non-tariff barriers that exist are generally on imports of consumer products and are more prevalent in Hungary and Poland. See Constantine Michalopoulos, "The Integration of Transition Economies into the World Trading System," paper presented at the Fifth Dubrovnik Conference on Transition Economies, Dubrovnik, Croatia, June 23–25, 1999.

eliminated by 2001. In addition, most of the countries need to continue to lower tariffs (to the level of the CET) for goods imported from third countries, although in some cases—such as Estonia—the process of EU accession is resulting in an increase in tariffs.[25]

The direct effects of further trade integration during the EU accession process should be limited as far as industrial products are concerned, because trade in the CEECs has already been extensively liberalized. However, there is substantial scope for further trade in agriculture (see below), and probably also in services—such as financial services—which are becoming increasingly traded. On balance, accession is likely to be trade creating, largely because tariff rates to third countries will on average continue to fall during the accession process and also as a result of longer-term gains from a larger EU economy and from further falls in non-tariff barriers. Trade diversion is expected to be limited because the EU countries are already the primary trading partners of the CEECs. Moreover, benefits to third countries will include a larger, more uniform export market—particularly for countries that already have preferential arrangements with the EU—for example, the ACP (African-Caribbean-Pacific) countries.

Some trade could be diverted, however, from the CIS countries, which are still substantial trading partners of the CEECs, although these and other countries will gain from larger markets due to increasing income and wealth in the accession countries.[26] It will be incumbent on the EU and the new member states to limit trade diversion that would lead to distorted or suboptimal trade patterns (including among the CEECs if accession does not occur at the same time for all these countries) as trade regimes are brought in line with the European Community regulations, including by adapting policies to allow special trading arrangements to persist and, more importantly, by continuing to expand multilateral and other regional trade relationships.[27] Expansion and diversification of trade from the CEECs into the EU could also be hindered by the administrative costs of implementing and enforcing the *acquis* on the freedom of movement of goods in the member countries—particularly with respect to consumer protection, indirect taxation, health, safety, phyto-sanitary conditions, and mutual recognition of national legislation—given the candidate countries' comparatively lower levels of development.

Capital Account

One of the major challenges for the applicant countries in the next several years will be to manage rising capital inflows while liberalizing the capital account, a requirement of accession. The *acquis* obliges countries to maintain free capital movements with the rest of the EU, although transitory derogations for acceding countries may be provided for certain types of flows (such as short-term ones) and safeguards are provided that allow temporary restrictions on capital movements in the case of balance of payments difficulties. In addition, the Maastricht Treaty requires that countries liberalize capital flows with the rest of the world.

---

[25]Estonia started increasing its tariffs in January 2000.

[26]Gravity models suggest that although trade with the CIS countries has fallen substantially since the breakup of the Council of Mutual Economic Assistance in 1991, it remains higher than what would be expected given the geographic distance between the CEECs and the CIS countries and the size of the CIS market. See, for example, EBRD *Transition Report 1999*, and Jarko Fidrmuc and Jan Fidrmuc, "Integration, Disintegration, and Trade in Europe: Evolution of Trade Relations during the 1990s," ZEI Working Paper (Bonn: Center for European Integration Studies, December 1999).

[27]In part to limit the trade diversion effects of the Europe Agreements, the EU has already encouraged the CEECs to conclude bilateral arrangements to liberalize trade among themselves. Intraregional trade agreements include the Baltic Free Trade Agreement for the three Baltic countries and the Central European Free Trade Association, comprising the other seven accession countries. To reduce potential trade diversion, the EU has also relaxed rules of origin for valued-added content from the CEECs by allowing the accumulation of content among the CEECs and other countries with preferential trade arrangements.

Table 4.8. Central and Eastern European Countries: External Account Liberalization

	Year of IMF Article VIII Acceptance	Indices of Capital Account Liberalization[1]				
		Overall	Direct investment	Real estate investment	Credit operations	Portfolio Flows
Bulgaria	1998	35.3	66.7	50.0	37.5	25.0
Czech Republic	1995	73.7	100.0	50.0	62.5	70.0
Estonia	1994	97.6	100.0	75.0	100.0	100.0
Hungary	1996	59.5	100.0	75.0	75.0	33.3
Latvia	1994	97.6	100.0	75.0	100.0	100.0
Lithuania	1994	85.7	83.3	50.0	62.5	100.0
Poland	1995	55.3	100.0	50.0	75.0	35.0
Romania	1998	12.5	83.3	0.0	0.0	0.0
Slovak Republic	1995	23.7	83.3	50.0	50.0	0.0
Slovenia	1995	40.5	83.3	50.0	37.5	25.0

[1]As of December 31, 1997; from Heliodoro Temprano-Arroyo and Robert A. Feldman, "Selected Transition and Mediterranean Countries: An Institutional Primer on EMU and EU Accession," *Economics of Transition,* Vol. 7, No. 3 (1999), pp. 741–806. The indices can take values between 0 and 100, with 100 representing the maximum degree of liberalization of the capital flows under consideration.

The accession countries have already begun to liberalize external flows (Table 4.8). All have now accepted the obligations of Article VIII of the IMF Articles of Agreement on current account convertibility and have removed most restrictions on foreign direct investment-related transactions. Except in the Baltic countries (and to a lesser extent the Czech Republic), controls on most other capital transactions remain, particularly with regard to portfolio flows and real estate investments. Controls on the latter remain, even in Estonia and Latvia—which have the most open capital accounts—partly because of concerns that foreigners will purchase large portions of the available land. Enforcement of these capital controls in some of these countries, however, is thought to be weak.

In 1999, all but one of the accession countries (the Czech Republic) had external current account deficits larger than 3 percent of GDP, with Lithuania (11¼ percent of GDP), Latvia (9¾ percent of GDP), and Poland (7½ percent of GDP) having the largest (see Table 4.1). The relatively large deficits in most of these countries have raised concerns about their sustainability, particularly since the process of capital account liberalization in an environment of weak financial institutions can lead to large and unsustainable capital inflows—as highlighted by the recent financial crises in east Asia. Sizable external financing currently may be appropriate—because of the investment opportunities offered by transition and convergence and lower than normal domestic saving in some countries on expectations of rising real incomes. But, large current account deficits make countries more vulnerable to reversals in financial market sentiment and thereby can lead to currency and financial crises, and also may be an indicator of other imbalances within an economy.[28]

The method by which a current account deficit is financed may provide some evidence about its sustainability, with foreign direct investment (FDI) generally preferred largely because it is less liquid and generally less volatile than other flows (particularly short-term debt).[29] A large share of capital inflows to the CEECs has been FDI, reflecting the substantial investment opportunities in these countries and early removal of restrictions on FDI inflows (Figure 4.5). Even though privatization in most of the CEECs is almost complete, foreign firms are likely to continue to make greenfield investments partly

[28]See Gian Maria Milesi-Ferretti and Assaf Razin, *Current Account Sustainability,* Princeton Studies in International Finance, No. 81 (Princeton, New Jersey: Princeton University, October 1996) and the May 1998 and May 1999 editions of the *World Economic Outlook.*

[29]Even FDI can be quite volatile, however, if it is based on a few large-scale privatizations.

Figure 4.5. Financing the Current Account Deficit, 1999
(Percent of GDP)

Although mainly financed through foreign direct investment, current accounts deficits in the EU accession countries are high, potentially indicating vulnerability to changes in financial market sentiment.

- ■ Change in reserves[1]
- ■ Other investment (net)[2]
- ■ Foreign direct investment (net)
- ■ Capital account
- ■ Portfolio investment (net)
- ● Current account deficit

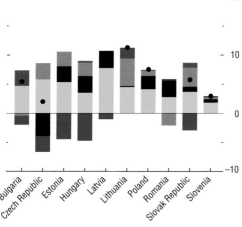

[1]A negative number indicates an increase.
[2]Includes net errors and omissions.

because of expectations of EU accession. Empirical evidence on whether further integration with the EU will increase these flows is mixed, however.[30]

As the CEECs move to further liberalize their capital accounts, several issues warrant consideration. During the liberalization process, appropriate ancillary policies and supporting institutions need to be developed and maintained. In particular, these include fiscal and monetary policies consistent with the exchange rate regime and macroeconomic stability, and policies that help strengthen and deepen financial institutions and capabilities—for example, in regulation, supervision, and risk management. The risk of rapid reversals in financial flows if investor sentiment changes—together with contagion as these countries are grouped more and more together—implies that the accession countries should continue to liberalize longer-term flows first and shorter-term flows only later. More generally, full transparency regarding economic policies and accession prospects is important, to reduce the scope for surprises in financial markets.

Financial Sector Development

Creating liberalized markets and effective institutions in the financial sector has been a significant challenge in transition countries, particularly as market-based banking systems and capital markets have been created from scratch.[31] From a macroeconomic viewpoint, the financial sector is special in four senses, as a number of transition economies have learned to their

[30]See, for example, Paul Brenton, Francesca Di Mauro, and Mathias Lucke, "Economic Integration and FDI: An Empirical Analysis of Foreign Investment in the EU and in Central and Eastern Europe," CEPS Working Document No. 124 (Brussels: Center for European Policy Studies, November 1998) and references therein. See also Box 4.2 for a comparison of FDI inflows following previous EU enlargements.

[31]Detailed individual country presentations can be found in *Capital Market Development in Transition Economies,* OECD Proceedings (Paris: Organization for Economic Cooperation and Development, 1998).

cost.[32] First, a banking crisis can cause sizable fiscal costs. Second, soundness in this sector is crucial to ensure predictable and effective monetary transmission. Third, efficiency of intermediation is key for financing growth. Fourth, risk management in this sector is a crucial safeguard against the problems that could arise from increased levels of debt-creating inflows as capital accounts are progressively opened.

As the accession countries approach the date of EU entry, their experience with financial sector development illuminates three major issues. First, there have been problems with enforcement of banking rules and regulations in most accession countries. Second, there is a threat posed to transparency and standards of disclosure in equity markets, with insider trading presenting particular difficulties in this regard. Third, there is a need for further growth of institutional and retail sectors in securities markets.

In the banking sector, the central and eastern European countries have generally adopted EU regulations, including universal licensing for all banks. Implementing effective banking supervision has in some cases turned out to be difficult, however, because of a lack of trained personnel and supporting infrastructure. As the candidates enter the EU, such differences between banking regulation and supervision standards—in particular enforcement of such standards—could create problems. For example, difficulties could arise if banks located next to each other in the same country were regulated with different degrees of scrutiny in their respective "home" countries.[33] Hence, there is a need for the accession countries not only to adopt the international set of banking standards, but also to apply a similar quality of supervision and enforcement.

In capital market development, above average progress has been achieved by most of the accession countries according to the transition indicators developed by the EBRD. In particular, since the mid-1990s, market infrastructures and market efficiencies have improved and financial markets are now starting to look more similar to those in the current EU countries.[34]

Furthermore, most accession countries now have independent agencies or commissions with an exclusive mandate for market supervision and enforcement (Table 4.9). Even though capital markets are efficient and have developed quickly, however, they often do not yet perform fully the key function of providing an effective alternative to bank funds. Capitalization and liquidity ratios remain relatively small in some of the accession countries, reflecting lack of enforcement of regulations, inadequate financial disclosure, and insufficient transparency of trading. Besides sound monetary and fiscal policies, several measures are still needed to develop an effective cushion against potential contagion effects of financial crises. These include an effective system of bank monitoring and supervision, a lower reliance on debt in relation to equity, and a higher degree of transparency for financial institutions.[35] These will be priorities in the run-up to EU membership and future EMU participation, as investors may want to test the credibility of the prevailing monetary regime; such pressures could be costly in a situation without a sound financial system.

---

[32]Robert Feldman and Maxwell Watson, "From Transition to Membership in the European Union," *Finance and Development*, Vol. 38 (September 2000), pp. 24–27. This paper is based on background work for a forthcoming IMF Occasional Paper on developing policy frameworks in central Europe.

[33]In the case of branch banks, regulatory responsibilities fall on the authorities of the country where the headquarters is located.

[34]Randall Filer and Jan Hanousek, "The Extent of Efficiency in Central European Equity Markets," in *Capital Markets in Central and Eastern Europe*, ed. by Christian Helmenstein (Northampton, Massachusetts: Edward Elgar, 1999). In Peter Christoffersen and Torsten Sløk, "Do Asset Prices in Transition Countries Contain Information About Future Economic Activity?" IMF Working Paper 00/103 (Washington: International Monetary Fund, 2000), evidence is found that asset markets in transition economies display the same leading indicator properties as observed in the current EU member countries.

[35]Lucjan Orlowski, "The Development of Financial Markets in Poland," Center for Social and Economic Research Working Paper Series No. 33 (Warsaw: Central European University, 1999).

Table 4.9. Comparative Market Development Data for Selected Accession Countries: Market Regulation and Supervision

	Independent Securities Commission	Insider Laws and Investor Protection	Disclosure and Compliance Regulation and Enforcement
Czech Republic	Yes, since 1998	Contained in New Securities Law recently approved by Parliament	Enhancement of standards and strengthening of enforcement capabilities needed
Hungary	Capital market and banking supervision integrated into one independent institution under Government supervision	Legal provisions and regulation converging toward International Organization of Securities Commissions (IOSCO) standards	Standards well developed
Poland	Yes, since 1991	Legal provisions and regulation converging toward IOSCO standards	Standards well developed
Romania	Yes, National Securities Commission reports directly to parliament	Certain provisions exist in 1994 Securities Law, but enhancement underway in line with market development	Regulations developed by National Securities Commission and self-regulatory organizations (SROs) but enforcement procedures not in place
Slovenia	Securities Market Agency fully independent from Ministry of Finance	Provision exists in 1994 Law on Securities Market. New law in drafting stage will bring harmonization with EU legislation	Standards developed and enforcement capabilities being strengthened
Slovakia	No, Control Office within Ministry of Finance exercises supervision	The government has approved legislation on the Financial Market Authority which should become effective later in 2000	Standards developed and enforcement capabilities being strengthened

Source: OECD, *Capital Market Developments in Transition Economies* (1998); and IMF staff.

Labor and Product Market Reforms

The accession countries have experienced dramatic changes in their labor and product markets since the beginning of transition. The dismantling of a large part of the public sector and the creation of a private sector is still taking place, and a key requirement for convergence is the ongoing movement of labor to productive, market-oriented, and privately owned companies, including many that can compete successfully with producers in the rest of the EU.

An essential element in facilitating the continued adjustment of the accession economies is labor market flexibility. If labor markets are characterized by low real wage flexibility, low mobility, and a high degree of employment protection such as high costs of firing and hiring, then adjustment is likely to be slow and costly. In some respects, labor markets in the accession countries appear to be more flexible than those among current EU members, although this picture is not entirely consistent across all indicators.[36] In the area of employment protection, for example, the candidates seem to have greater flexibility than the average EU country. The Organization for Economic Cooperation and Development (OECD) has estimated the overall extent of protection using indicators such as the direct costs of dismissal and delays of dismissal for permanent and temporary workers. On a scale from 1 to 6 (with 1 being the least restrictive), the EU average for 1998 was 2.4, whereas Poland, the Czech Republic, and Hungary were significantly lower with values of 1.9, 1.7, and 1.4, respectively.[37]

Table 4.10 examines real wage flexibility during transition for five CEECs—the Czech

[36]Unfortunately, the EBRD transition indicators that are widely used to assess progress with structural reforms do not include the labor market. The wide range of labor market arrangements among current EU members also needs to be noted.

[37]Giuseppe Nicoletti, Stefano Scarpetta, and Olivier Boylaud, "Summary Indicators of Product Market Regulation with an Extension to Employment Protection Legislation," OECD Economics Department Working Paper No. 226 (Paris: Organization for Economic Cooperation and Development, April 2000).

Republic, Hungary, Poland, the Slovak Republic, and Slovenia—and, for the 1990–1998 period, estimates how much employment changed when real wages changed. The table also gives corresponding estimates for France, Italy, Germany, and Spain.[38] The statistical analysis reveals that, in the beginning of transition, the employment response to wage changes in the five CEECS, while statistically significant, was quite modest. This indicates that, in the early phase of transition, there were many factors other than real wages determining labor adjustment. The estimate for the more recent period—although based on fewer observations—is, however, almost identical to the estimate for the current EU members. This simple measure may suggest that labor markets have been through part of their adjustment and are now—at least in some respects—functioning in a similar fashion as in the current EU countries.

The accession countries appear to have generally low mobility across sectors, occupations, and regions, and this has important implications for the pace of adjustment. The evidence shows that overall there are relatively low levels of turnover in the unemployment pools of the accession countries[39] and there is also evidence that there are significant flows from employment to inactivity.[40] Explanations for this low mobility include informational failures, inappropriate skill structure, housing market rigidities, and high costs of moving from public to private enterprises for those with substantial job tenure and labor market experience in the public sector.[41]

Table 4.10. Estimates of Labor Market Flexibility

	Accession Countries[1]		Current EU Countries[2]
	1990–95	1996–98	1990–98
Labor demand elasticity	−0.06 (2.08)	−1.23 (7.88)	−1.22 (3.98)

Source: IMF staff calculations.
Note: t-statistics in parentheses.
[1]Czech Republic, Hungary, Poland, Slovak Republic, and Slovenia.
[2]France, Italy, Germany, and Spain.

The main part of the *acquis* that relates to labor markets is the European Social Charter, which is a range of basic guidelines that accession countries must implement before they can join the EU. The Social Charter sets out minimum standards in areas that are an integral part of almost all well-functioning market economies, including the bargaining system, social welfare, migrant workers' rights, conditions of work, severance protection, protection of workers' claims in the case of bankruptcy, and rights of workers' representatives (Table 4.11). The accession countries have some choice about how far above these minima they pitch their labor market policies. In this regard, several studies have questioned the potential impact of rigorous adoption of the Social Charter on flexibility.[42] In particular, it has been emphasized that, since the accession countries continue to require significant adjustment, labor market policies should rather be defined in the context of what the accession countries need to and can realistically accomplish. Moreover, the enforcement of EU style regulation of labor markets may have adverse consequences on the forma-

---

[38]The fixed effect panel labor demand elasticity that is estimated for the two groups of countries has the following form: $\log(\text{Employment}_{i,t}) = \text{constant} + \alpha \log(\text{Real wage}_{i,t}) + \log(\text{Real income}_{i,t})$, where i denotes country $i = 1,..n$ and t is time.

[39]See Tito Boeri, "Transitional Unemployment," *The Economics of Transition*, Vol. 2 (1994), pp. 1–26. Vit Storm and Katherine Terrell, "A Comparative Look at Labour Mobility in the Czech Republic: Where Have All the Workers Gone?" CEPR Discussion Paper No. 2263 (London: Center For Economic Policy Research, October 1999), however, provides evidence that mobility in the Czech Republic has been relatively higher.

[40]Tito Boeri and Scott Edwards, "Long-term Unemployment and Short-term Unemployment Benefits: The Changing Nature of Non-employment Subsidies in Central and Eastern Europe," *Empirical Economics*, Vol. 23, No. 1/2, (1998), pp. 31–54.

[41]Tito Boeri and Christopher Flinn, "Returns to Mobility in the Transition to a Market Economy" (unpublished manuscript; April 1999). O. Blanchard, S. Commander, and F. Corricelli, eds., *Unemployment, Restructuring, and Labor Markets in Eastern Europe and Russia* (Washington: World Bank, 1995).

[42]Michael Burda, "The Consequences of EU Enlargement for Central and Eastern European Labour Markets," CEPR Discussion Paper No. 1881 (London: Center for Economic Policy Research, 1998), and János Gács, "Accession to the EU: A Continuation of or a Departure from Transition Reforms?" IIASA Interim Report–99–002 (Laxenberg, Austria: International Institute for Applied Systems Analysis, 1999).

Table 4.11. The European Social Charter and the Labor Market[1]

Institutional bargaining system[2]	"Everyone has the right to bargain collectively" and countries should "promote where necessary the machinery for voluntary negotiations between employers and employers' organizations and workers' organizations, with a view to the regulation of terms and conditions of employment by means of collective agreements." In addition, "the right of workers and employers to collective action in cases of conflicts of interest, including the right to strike . . ." should be recognized.
Social welfare[3]	"Everyone has the right to benefit from social welfare services."
Migrant workers' rights[4]	Countries signing the Charter agree "to promote co-operation, as appropriate, between social services, public and private, in emigration and immigration countries" and "to secure for such workers . . . treatment not less favorable than that of their own nationals in respect of . . . a) remuneration and other employment and working conditions; b) membership of trade unions and enjoyment of the benefits of collective bargaining; c) accommodation."
Conditions of work[5]	Countries signing the Charter agree to provide: "reasonable daily and weekly working hours"; "for public holidays with pay"; "for a minimum of four weeks' annual holiday with pay"; "that workers performing night work benefit from measures which take account of the special nature of their work."
Severance protection[6]	Countries signing the Charter agree to recognize: "the right of all workers not to have their employment terminated without valid reasons for such termination connected with their capacity or conduct based on the operational requirements of the undertaking, establishment or service"; "the right of workers whose employment is terminated without a valid reason to adequate compensation or other appropriate relief."
Protection from consequences of bankruptcy[7]	Countries signing the Charter agree to recognize: "that worker's claims arising from contracts of employment or employment relationships be guaranteed by a guarantee institution or by any other effective form of protection."
Rights of workers' representation[8]	Countries agree to undertake that workers' representatives: "enjoy effective protection against acts prejudicial to them, including dismissal based on their status of activities"; "are afforded with such facilities as may be appropriate in order to enable them to carry out their functions promptly and efficiently."

[1]The full text of the European Social Chapter is available on the Internet at http://www.coe.fr
[2]European Social Charter, 1961, article 6.
[3]European Social Charter, 1961, article 14.
[4]European Social Charter, 1961, article 19.
[5]European Social Charter, revised, 1996, article 2.
[6]European Social Charter, revised, 1996, article 24.
[7]European Social Charter, revised, 1996, article 25.
[8]European Social Charter, revised, 1996, article 28.

tion of new firms and industries. High start-up costs may lead to fewer new firms than would otherwise have been the case. And such slower business formation due to excessive costs of hiring, employing, and firing labor may inhibit the transition toward a private sector based economy and may ultimately slow the process of CEEC income levels catching up with those in the EU.

Although concerns about outflows of *skilled* workers (or "brain drain") often appear to predominate when lower income countries integrate with more advanced economic areas, the EU enlargement process has given rise to concerns—especially on the EU side—about possibly large flows of *unskilled* workers from East to West. Indeed, there is some evidence suggesting that there are larger real wage differences between low-skilled workers in the accession countries and the current EU member countries compared with the case of skilled workers.[43] As

[43]These disparities in wage rates for lower-skilled workers may result in part from labor market distortions among EU members that have led to compressed wage differentials and reduced job opportunities for unskilled labor.

discussed below, however, fears of a significant increase in migration flows following accession of the candidate countries may be overstated, particularly in view of the many other factors besides wage differentials that determine migration patterns, including cultural and social influences.

A further key element of EU membership is the existence of competitive markets for goods. Most of the accession countries adopted competition laws at an early stage of transition, and removed product market regulations to intensify competition. In contrast though to some of the labor market indicators, product market deregulation in the most advanced accession countries generally still lags the EU.[44] The OECD has estimated the overall extent of product market regulation in some of these countries using indicators such as state control, barriers to entry, barriers to trade and investment, economic regulation, and administrative regulation.[45] On a scale from 1 to 6 (with 1 being the least restrictive provisions), Hungary's "score" of 1.6 for product market regulation was identical to the average for current EU members, while the Czech Republic and Poland were above the most regulated EU countries (Italy, Greece, and France), with values of 2.9 and 3.3, respectively. It remains possible, however, that product market competition will intensify as trade integration and other economic linkages with the EU deepen. Evidence from the first half of 1999 suggests that foreign competition, as well as improvements in enforcement and institutional effectiveness, has significantly enhanced competition in the transition economies.[46]

Fiscal Implications of EU and EMU Accession

The accession countries face the prospect of both increased public expenditures and in-

creased revenues as a result of the EU accession process. These trends would be occurring in a context where almost all of the applicants already have ratios of public spending and revenue to GDP that are relatively high in comparison with other countries of similar income levels, although not out of line with the EU average (Figure 4.6). The fiscal implications of accession can, to some degree, be divided into those that arise—or at least begin—prior to EU membership, and those that would follow accession. The two largest areas of pre-accession expenditure stem from the costs of complying, first, with the legal and institution building requirements of the *acquis* and, second, with EU environmental standards (e.g., concerning water pollution, air pollution, and waste management). The latter appears to be the most costly area of compliance, although environmental improvements are clearly essential for the long-run development of these countries and increases in their living standards. While the level of expenditure varies substantially among the candidates, estimates in several of the more advanced applicants suggest that the average annual cost of complying with EU environmental standards for the next five years will be around 1.5 percent of GDP per year.[47] An illustration of EU-related spending, in the case of Hungary, is shown in Table 4.12: the costs of both environ-mental development and legal adjustments, as well as other areas of economic development, increased substantially between 1999 and 2000, and total accession-linked spending is now around 2½ percent of GDP.

Not all of this spending falls on domestic budgets, however. The EU has made available a total of €22 billion in pre-accession support for the applicants for the period 2000–06, implying

[44]EBRD, *Transition Report 1999,* Table 2.1, p. 24.

[45]Nicoletti, Scarpetta, and Boylaud, "Summary Indicators of Product Market Regulation with an Extension to Employment Protection Legislation."

[46]Mark Dutz and Maria Vagliasindi, "Competition policy implementation in transition economies: an empirical assessment," EBRD Working Paper No. 47 (London: European Bank For Reconstruction and Development, December 1999).

[47]Dominika Anna Dziegielewska, "How Much Does It Cost to Join the European Union and Who Is Going to Pay for It? Cost Estimates for the Czech Republic, Hungary, Poland and Slovenia, Complying with the EU Environmental Standards," IIASA Interim Report–00–001 (Laxenburg, Austria: International Institute for Applied Systems Analysis, 2000).

Table 4.12. Hungary: EU-Related Spending and Financing
(As percent of Hungary's GDP)

	1999	2000	2001
Legal approximation	0.3	0.8	0.8
Economic development	0.8	1.7	1.6
Key sectors: Agriculture	0.0	0.2	0.3
Transport	0.0	0.2	0.2
Environment	0.7	1.1	1.0
Regional development	0.1	0.3	0.2
Total	1.2	2.5	2.4
Financed by: Central budget	0.7	1.1	1.2
EU assistance	0.2	0.8	0.6
Other[1]	0.3	0.6	0.6

Source: IMF, *Hungary: Selected Issues and Statistical Appendix,* April 2000.
[1]Local governments, nongovernmental organizations, and the private sector.

Figure 4.6. Government Expenditures in Relation to GDP per capita, 1999

General government expenditure (as a share of GDP) in the EU accession countries is relatively high by world standards, but generally comparable with the EU average.

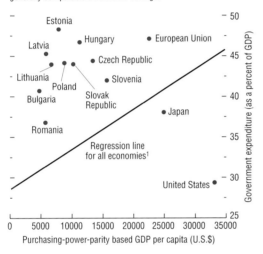

Source: IMF staff calculations.
[1]The regression line is estimated using data from 172 developing, transition, and advanced economies.

annual support averaging around 1 percent of GDP for the candidates. Some of the accession costs—especially those associated with environmental improvements—are expected to be borne by the private sector, such as the polluting companies themselves. However, contingent fiscal risks may also arise in this context as a result of public ownership of some of these companies together with possible pressure for public support for others. Assistance in the form of loans is also available to the applicants—for example, from the European Investment Bank and the EBRD.

Following accession, the new EU members would gain access to a substantial level of EU structural funds and agricultural support although, as considered below, further reforms of these programs will probably make them less generous than in the past. For example, under current rules for Structural and Cohesion Funds, the most advanced accession countries would have gained significantly—a net transfer of more than 7 percent of GDP in the case of Hungary, for instance.[48] But, reflecting in part its concerns about the size and affordability of

[48]Jørgen Mortensen and Sándor Richter, "Measurement of Costs and Benefits of Accession to the European Union for Selected Countries in Central and Eastern Europe," WIIW Research Report No. 263 (Vienna: Institute for International Economic Studies, 2000).

these transfers, the EU has capped structural assistance in any member state at 4 percent of national GDP. Given the need for a new financial perspective after 2006, the levels and forms of future EU assistance are uncertain. On the expenditure side, some of the above increases, including in administrative and environmental costs, would likely continue following full accession of the candidates to the EU. In addition, new members will have to contribute to the EU budget. While the specific level of these contributions—from current as well as prospective members—is subject to ongoing negotiations, the EU budget as a whole is subject to a ceiling of 1.27 percent of EU aggregate GNP.

Several other fiscal implications, both before and after accession, should also be noted. On the one hand, the overall institutional strengthening by EU applicants under the accession process should lead to improvements in the administration of taxes and spending, in procurement practices, and in the general efficiency of the public sector—efforts that should contribute, over the longer run, to improvements in public revenues and to better control over public spending. Interest rates and hence debt servicing costs may well fall, especially as the applicants move closer to euro area membership—as happened with current members—and, indeed, reductions in country risk premia are already evident among some EU applicants. On the other hand, the accession countries are also likely to face several sources of fiscal pressure over the medium term. Some countries still face the need for substantial real and financial sector restructuring, and this may have a significant impact on their public finances. Most of the CEECs also need increased public investment to upgrade aging infrastructure—an area where EU structural funds could continue to make an important contribution. In addition, several of the applicant countries have recently joined the North Atlantic Treaty Organization (NATO), and have committed themselves to higher defense spending in the coming years. As with current EU member countries, all of the transition economies face increased pressure on their public finances as a result of demographic changes. Reforms to pension and social benefit arrangements—including, for example, improved targeting of the latter—will be required if large tax increases or benefit cutbacks are to be avoided.[49]

Overall, while EU assistance may go a long way toward offsetting the costs associated with accession, the fiscal risks and uncertainties facing the applicants argue strongly for them reaching and maintaining conservative fiscal stances. The high public expenditure ratios of almost all the applicants, and the fiscal and debt pressures currently faced by some, imply that the candidate countries generally have little scope for fully accommodating accession-related spending or other fiscal risks. They may therefore need to reduce spending in other areas. Moreover, these countries need to retain substantial fiscal flexibility to help them manage the shocks they are likely to encounter as small, open economies. The need for such flexibility is all the more apparent in the longer-term perspective of euro area membership.

Monetary Convergence

Given the prospect of eventual membership in the euro area, parliaments in most accession countries have already adopted legislation with a view to making monetary arrangements more compatible with the requirements of the Maastricht Treaty.[50] For example, central bank independence has been strengthened, and the enacted limitations of fiscal financing have become more binding. In terms of the formal re-

---

[49]For example, projections for Lithuania based on the current share of people contributing to the pension system show that only 54 percent of the old-age population would be covered by the pension system in 2025. See Svend Erik Hougaard Jensen and others, "Reforming Social Security in a Transition Economy: The Case of Lithuania," unpublished working paper, supported by the European Union's Phare ACE program (June 2000).

[50]Eduard Hochreiter and Tadeusz Kowalski, "Central Banks in European Emerging Market Economies in the 1990s," OeNB Working Paper No. 40 (Vienna: Oesterreichische Nationalbank, April 2000).

Table 4.13. Exchange Rate Arrangements and Anchors of Monetary Policy
(As of July 2000)

Country	Exchange Rate Regime	Monetary Policy Framework	Date Introduced
Bulgaria	Currency board arrangement	Exchange rate anchor (Euro)	1997
Estonia	Currency board arrangement	Exchange rate anchor (Euro)	1992
Lithuania	Currency board arrangement	Exchange rate anchor (U.S. dollar)	1994
Latvia	Conventional fixed peg arrangement (peg to SDR)	Fund-supported or other monetary program	1995
Hungary	Exchange rate within crawling bands	Exchange rate anchor (Euro)	1994
Poland	Managed float with no pre-announced path for exchange rate	Inflation targeting framework	1999
Slovak Republic	Managed float with no pre-announced path for exchange rate	No explicitly stated nominal anchor; rather, the central bank monitors a number of indicators in conducting monetary policy	1998
Czech Republic	Managed float with no pre-announced path for exchange rate	Inflation targeting framework	1997
Slovenia	Managed float with no pre-announced path for exchange rate	Broad money (M3) targeting framework	1991
Romania	Managed float with no pre-announced path for exchange rate	Fund-supported or other monetary program	1997

quirements for euro area membership, the candidates would need to make adjustments to their monetary frameworks in the future. There is, however, no imperative for them to adopt a common strategy for their monetary and exchange rate policies in the near term—particularly in view of the further economic adjustments they are likely to face.[51]

Throughout the transition period, the accession countries have adopted widely different monetary and exchange rate regimes. Currently, Estonia, Bulgaria, and Lithuania are under a currency board arrangement, Latvia has adopted a firm exchange rate peg, Hungary has adopted a narrow crawling band, while the Czech Republic, Poland, Slovak Republic, Slovenia, and Romania have floating exchange rates with different degrees of inflation targeting (Table 4.13).[52] A striking feature of monetary developments in the accession countries is that, inde-

pendently of the choice of exchange rate regime, real exchange rates in most cases have appreciated steadily since the beginning of transition (Box 4.4).

Looking forward, as the accession countries converge with the EU, there will be three main sources of tension for the monetary and exchange rate policy frameworks.[53] First, the changing structure of the financial economy and shifts in money demand will complicate the choice and use of nominal anchors. The transmission mechanism may be unpredictable, affecting, notably, inflation- and monetary-targeting regimes. Second, sizable and possibly volatile capital flows will likely complicate the task of monetary management, whether the exchange rate is fixed or floating. Third, these economies may have difficulty in achieving convergence to very low inflation levels while at the same time achieving exchange rate stability, be-

[51]Robert Corker and others, "Exchange Rate Regimes in Selected Advanced Transition Economies—Coping with Transition, Capital Inflows, and EU Accession," IMF Policy Discussion Paper 00/3 (Washington: International Monetary Fund, April 2000). This study also discusses post-accession issues for the accession countries.

[52]For a discussion of the choice of exchange rate regimes in transition countries, see Michael Mussa and others, *Exchange Rate Regimes in an Increasingly Integrated World Economy,* Occasional Paper No. 193 (Washington: International Monetary Fund, 2000).

[53]Feldman and Watson, "From Transition to Membership in the European Union."

cause of the Balassa-Samuelson effect described in Box 4.4.

The pressures that may arise from high capital inflows and real convergence could present particular challenges for the monetary frameworks of the accession countries as they continue to reform and liberalize their economies. In these circumstances, there is some potential for conflict between, on the one hand, the exchange rate and price level implications of these pressures and, on the other, policy goals of securing very low inflation, nominal exchange rate stability, and hence the degree of real exchange rate stability that would be desirable to secure a fairly smooth path of output and expectations in the economy. [54] Such concerns, however, do not necessarily argue in favor of fundamental changes in the current exchange rate regimes used by the accession countries, at least during the earlier stages of convergence. Instead, the point is that somewhat higher rates of inflation or nominal exchange rate movement among the applicants, compared with the more advanced economies, should be viewed as a normal and expected part of the convergence process. For example, the currency boards and hard pegs used by the Baltic countries and Bulgaria appear to have served these countries well—proving quite robust, for example, in the presence of external shocks (notably the 1998–99 Russian financial crisis).[55] The other countries may well choose to continue with (and, in some cases, strengthen) regimes that give a high weight to inflation objectives while providing substantial exchange rate flexibility, but also allowing policymakers to signal the limits to the variability they are prepared to countenance.

Looking ahead, the adjustments—if any—that the EU accession countries may wish to make in their exchange rate regimes as preparation for integration in the euro area, and the pace of their participation, will depend largely on individual country circumstances, including the extent of convergence with existing members, the state of their banking sectors, and other fiscal and monetary risks. However, when overall convergence has advanced to the point where more formal monetary linkages between the candidate countries and the EU become feasible, notably through the Exchange Rate Mechanism, the further step of full euro area participation should probably follow rather quickly in order to remove the exchange rate risks that these countries could face from stronger capital flows as accession nears—particularly as the credibility of these countries' monetary frameworks is likely to increase during this period.

Challenges for the EU as It Prepares for Enlargement

The accession of the CEECs will entail significant changes and challenges for the EU, increasing the pressure for reforms in several critical areas. While the direct economic impact on the EU may initially be modest, considering that the applicant countries have a relatively small aggregate economic weight and will need considerable time to catch up with current EU members, enlargement will require substantial changes in some key EU institutions and policies. As noted in Box 4.1, the EU has set a target date of year-end 2002 for being ready to accept new members. There have, however, been widespread expressions of concern about the limited progress that has been made so far on the reforms that are required within the EU, and most outside commentators doubt that the end-2002 goal will be achieved. This section focuses on the principal reform requirements and areas of tension within the EU arising from the proposed enlargement, and on the implications of some of the proposed solutions.

[54]Paul Masson, "Monetary and Exchange Rate Policy of Transition Economies of Central and Eastern Europe after the Launch of EMU," IMF Policy Discussion Paper 99/5 (Washington: International Monetary Fund, 1999) examines the choice of monetary framework in the accession countries.

[55]See, for example, Anne-Marie Gulde, Juha Kähkönen, and Peter Keller, "Pros and Cons of Currency Board Arrangements in the Lead-up to EU Accession and Participation in the Euro Zone," IMF Policy Discussion Paper 00/1 (Washington: International Monetary Fund, 2000).

Box 4.4. Convergence and Real Exchange Rate Appreciation in the EU Accession Countries

The degree of over- or undervaluation of a country's exchange rate can be assessed in several ways.[1] One method is to calculate the exchange rate gap between its actual U.S. dollar exchange rate and its purchasing-power-parity-based U.S. dollar exchange rate once the level of development has been taken into account.[2] The relationship between this exchange rate gap and GDP per capita measured at purchasing-power-parity (PPP) for advanced and developing countries is shown in the figure. The bold line, based on a simple linear regression, shows the relationship between these two variables for 149 non-transition countries in the world using 1999 data. The dotted lines in the figure indicate the statistical confidence intervals around the estimated line.[3]

After an initial sharp depreciation of exchange rates in all transition economies in the early 1990s, the exchange rates of the accession countries have since appreciated significantly.[4] The movements from 1993 to 1999 are indicated by the arrows in the figure.[5] The accession countries have moved closer to similar countries elsewhere—the distance from the estimated line

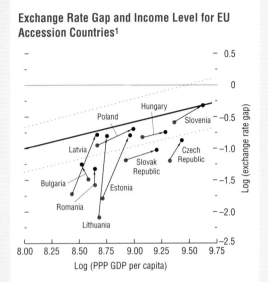

Exchange Rate Gap and Income Level for EU Accession Countries[1]

[1]The bold line shows the estimated relationship between the exchange rate gap (between actual and PPP-based exchange rates) and GDP per capita (in PPP terms) for 149 non-transition countries in 1999. The dotted lines are plus/minus one standard deviation. Arrows indicate movements for the accession countries from 1993 to 1999.

is smaller in 1999 than in 1993. Most of the countries are by now inside the confidence intervals. This indicates that they now have broadly similar exchange rate gaps as market economies at comparable levels of development. Or, put differently, judging from their current positions in the figure, these countries have largely or fully eliminated the exchange rate gap associated with the distortions inherited from central planning.

The narrowing of the exchange rate gap illustrated in the figure can be explained by many factors, including further correction of initial sharp undervaluations of these currencies, and broader improvements in macroeconomic stability and policy credibility. Another contributing influence is likely to have been efficiency improvements experienced in the industrial sectors of the accession countries. Productivity gains in these sectors relative to those in the rest of the world and associated productivity-

---

[1]See, for example, Ronald MacDonald and Jerome Stein, *Equilibrium Exchange Rates,* Kluwer Academic Publishers (Boston, Massachusetts: 1999).

[2]To be precise, the exchange rate gap for each country is calculated as log (actual U.S. dollar exchange rate/purchasing-power-parity-based exchange rate). For further information on the derivation of PPP exchange rates and weights, see *World Economic Outlook,* May 2000, Box A1, and Anne Marie Gulde and Marianne Schulze-Ghattas, "Purchasing Power Parity Based Weights for the *World Economic Outlook,*" *Staff Studies for the World Economic Outlook,* December 1993.

[3]Calculated as plus/minus one standard deviation. For details on these calculations, see Mark De Broeck and Torsten Sløk, "Interpreting Real Exchange Rate Movements in Transition Countries," forthcoming IMF Working Paper.

[4]However, there are several cases where the real exchange rate, calculated using unit labor costs, has depreciated.

[5]The starting year was set to 1993 since by then a major portion of goods prices had moved toward international levels (see also Vincent Koen and Paula R. De Masi, "Prices in the Transition: Ten Stylized Facts," *Staff Studies for the World Economic Outlook,* December 1997).

based wage increases led to more generalized wage and price increases elsewhere in the economy, in line with the so-called Balassa-Samuelson effect.[6] For a given nominal exchange rate, price increases relative to the rest of the world imply an appreciation of the real exchange rate. The higher inflation and associated appreciation of the real exchange rate are not monetary phenomena but are a reflection of an adjustment mechanism involving relative wages and prices. The positive slope seen in the figure indicates that this mechanism also operates in non-transition countries at various income levels, and is a natural part of economic development. The effect is expected to be more pronounced in the transition economies, however, because they started from a situation where liberalization and movements in relative prices led to restructuring and reallocation of resources to more productive, often exporting, sectors.

The slope of the estimated line in the figure also makes it possible to quantify roughly the implications of convergence for inflation in transition economies relative to the rest of the world. Although, as discussed above, the accession countries appear to have largely eliminated the exchange rate gap associated with the distortions inherited from central planning, they are expected to have higher growth rates than in the advanced economies as part of the ongoing convergence in per capita incomes. The slope suggests that "excess" growth of 1 percent (implying convergence with more advanced economies) will lead to a relative increase in price levels of 0.4 percent. Note that this does not imply that there will be no other sources of inflation, including those that are monetary or expectational in nature.[7] But it does imply that, as the accession countries continue to catch up with the EU, they can expect, for example, a 5 percent growth differential with current members to be associated with a 2 percent inflation differential.

---

[6]Bela Balassa, "The Purchasing Power Parity Doctrine: A Reappraisal," *Journal of Political Economy,* Vol. 72 (1964), and Paul Samuelson, "Theoretical Notes on Trade Problems," *Review of Economics and Statistics,* Vol. 46 (1964).

[7]For a discussion of the factors determining inflation in transition, see the papers in Carlo Cottarelli and György Szapáry, eds., *Moderate Inflation: The Experience of Transition Economies* (Washington: International Monetary Fund, 1998).

Institutions

The EU's institutional framework has remained broadly unchanged since its adoption by the original six founding members, despite successive enlargements and increases in the scope of common policymaking. Its reform has been made a precondition for enlargement, on the grounds that an increase in membership with current procedures would stifle the decision-making process. In particular, change is considered a necessity to avoid three problems:

- The European Commission, the EU's executive, might become excessively large. At present there are 20 Commissioners, with the five largest countries appointing two and all others appointing one. The 10 CEECs, with Poland probably qualifying as a large country, plus

Cyprus and Malta, with whom negotiations are also proceeding, would raise this number to 33.

- A larger membership might increase the difficulty of taking decisions owing to the requirement of unanimity in the Council of Ministers in many key areas. Unanimity remains the rule regarding the Union's institutions, membership, economic policy (including controversial matters such as tax harmonization), immigration (from third countries), justice, and foreign policy. As is currently under consideration, the problem might be attenuated by broadening the scope of decisions by qualified majority voting, which is virtually the rule for matters pertaining to the internal market.

- With the present weighting of votes, decisions by qualified majority could be taken in the

Council of Ministers by countries accounting for barely half of the total population, reflecting the number of small countries.[56]

These issues are on the agenda of the EU's intergovernmental conference, which started earlier this year and is due to be concluded in December 2000. More broadly, in recent months a wide-ranging discussion has begun on the longer-term future of the EU's institutions, including allowing groups of member states to embark on closer integration within the EU framework.[57] Many see a more tightly knit institutional framework as an essential requirement for successful common policies. Whatever this may entail in the long run, it should be of little consequence for the accession of the CEECs, as no common views have yet emerged and several member states firmly oppose going beyond the agreed agenda at the present stage.

Labor Markets

Immigration has become an increasingly sensitive issue in the EU, with the opposition often transcending traditional political lines. The possibility that enlargement could lead to large flows of workers from east to west, with attendant risks of job displacement and wage losses for incumbents, has therefore become a matter of concern in some EU countries. However, the free movement of labor is an integral part of EU membership. Whether full integration occurs immediately upon enlargement, or is delayed by means of a transition period, will be determined in the course of negotiations on this part of the *acquis*.

Turning to some of the evidence on this issue, currently available projections suggest that fears of large-scale migration from the CEECs to the EU as a whole are probably ill-founded.[58] For example, a recent comprehensive analysis of this issue suggests that the number of residents from the ten accession countries in the EU could initially increase by around 335,000 people a year following the introduction of free movement of labor, declining to below 150,000 people within a decade.[59] This projected initial inflow is comparable with the peak level of recorded net migration of about 350,000 people a year from the candidate countries to the EU reached in the early 1990s. Since 1993, however, net migration has been negligible (and even negative in some of the applicants), as a result of tighter restrictions placed on such flows by the EU countries. The projected migration would be unevenly distributed, with most migrants moving to the EU nations that are adjacent to the CEECs (such as Austria and Germany), and probably being concentrated in the border regions of these countries. For example, around two-thirds of the initial flows noted above would be to Germany. Migration is expected to exercise some downward pressure on wages at the lower end of the pay scale, owing to the preponderance of less skilled workers among the migrants, but to have only a modest overall impact on labor market conditions.

Based in part on evidence of migration between eastern and western Germany, the most important factors that determine the degree of migration appear to be differences in per capita income, the employment rate in destination

---

[56]Currently, the qualified majority is 71 percent of the votes. In the EU-15, the votes are distributed as follows: France, Germany, Italy, and United Kingdom have 10 votes each; Spain has 8; Belgium, Greece, Portugal, and Netherlands have 5 each; Austria and Sweden have 4 each; Denmark, Finland, and Ireland have 3 each; and Luxembourg has 2. With this weighting of the votes, a decision can be blocked by member states accounting for 12 percent of the population. With a membership of 27 (the EU-15, the CEEC-10, Cyprus, and Malta), this percentage would be lowered to 10.

[57]At present, there is such enhanced cooperation in the case of EMU and the Schengen agreement. Under the latter, all member states except Ireland and the United Kingdom have adopted common rules for visas, asylum rights, and checks at the area's external borders. Iceland and Norway are associated members without voting rights.

[58]Thomas Bauer and Klaus Zimmermann, "Assessment of Possible Migration Pressure and Its Labour Market Impact Following EU Enlargement to Central and Eastern Europe," DFEE Research Report No. 138/139 (London: UK Department for Education and Employment, December 1999) and Tito Boeri and Herbert Brücker, "The Impact of Eastern Enlargement on Employment and Labor Markets in the EU Member States," study for the European Commission (Brussels: European Commission, 2000).

[59]Boeri and Brücker, "The Impact of Eastern Enlargement on Employment and Labor Markets in the EU Member States."

countries, and employment rates in the countries of origin.[60] As emphasized elsewhere in this chapter, policy measures that foster employment growth in the CEECs and rapid convergence of their income levels with those of the EU will therefore be crucial to determining the extent and duration of possible migration pressures. The EU also has an important role to play in this regard. Labor market and other reforms among current members would improve the flexibility of these economies, helping to raise their potential growth rates, add to their employment creation capacity—especially for lower-skilled labor—and hence increase their ability to cope with larger migration inflows.

Intra-EU Solidarity

The EU's budget—which serves to finance the common policies—is currently governed by a "financial perspective," a quantified budgetary framework expressed in real terms, for the period 2000–06. There are ringfenced appropriations for the present member states, together with pre-accession aid and notional appropriations for new members that would become effective upon their accession. From this perspective, then, enlargement would not affect the rights of the present members before 2007.[61]

The negotiation of the next financial perspective may alter these current arrangements. The bulk of budget expenditure is accounted for by structural policy—that is, assistance to areas that are lagging in development—and by the EU's common agricultural policy (CAP). Under current arrangements, structural policy would not necessarily change much on account of enlarge-

ment. Per capita GDP—a chief determinant of assistance—is clearly much lower in the CEECs than in the EU-15, and the EU has estimated that, under unchanged criteria, the population of an enlarged EU that would be eligible for assistance would more than double.[62]

Furthermore, the European Commission noted that the high proportion of population eligible for assistance (60 percent) would "be contrary to the principle of concentration of effort on which the effectiveness of assistance depends."[63] Reflecting these concerns, along with the limited capacity of the candidates to absorb structural funds, the current EU members have decided that structural assistance in the current financial perspective is subject to a ceiling equivalent to 4 percent of GDP (as noted earlier).

Matters are different for agricultural policy. The accession of the ten CEECs will represent a major change for the EU's agricultural sector, with the land devoted to agriculture increasing by close to 50 percent and the number of those employed in the sector more than doubling. Agriculture in the CEECs is already tending toward excess production and has considerable scope for increasing production, given its present relatively low productivity. As farm incomes and prices are low in the CEECs compared to the EU-15, it is feared that production would be given a major boost if new members were to be given the full protection of the EU's CAP—adding to the agricultural surpluses that already exist in the EU. Moreover, a sudden sharp increase in farm incomes might retard economic modernization by drawing resources to the agricultural sector.

The EU's 2000–06 financial perspective includes a steadily increasing amount of agricul-

---

[60]The migration from eastern to western Germany after the unification increased dramatically, but today the net emigration is close to zero. Jennifer Hunt, "Why Do People Still Live In East Germany?" CEPR Discussion Paper No. 2431 (London: Center for Economic Policy Research, April 2000), ascribes this dramatic change to the narrowing of the unemployment and real wage gaps over time.

[61]The financial perspective was drawn up on the assumption that enlargement would begin with a first wave of six countries. It would therefore have to be revised if all twelve recognized active candidates were admitted into the Union before 2006.

[62]In an impact study prepared as part of the Agenda 2000 program in 1997, the European Commission estimated that if the EU were enlarged to include the ten CEECs along with Cyprus, the population eligible for assistance would increase from 94 million to 200 million under the prevailing criteria (European Commission, "Impact Study: The Effects on the Union's Policies of Enlargement to the Applicant Countries of Central and Eastern Europe," Brussels, 1997).

[63]See the Impact Study referred to in the previous footnote.

tural support for new members, starting at €1.6 billion in 2002 and rising to €3.4 billion in 2006 (in constant 1999 prices). By way of comparison, the CAP budget for current members averages €43 billion over this period, out of a total budget of around €90 billion for the EU-15. The EU's agriculture budget for new members is intended to cover only the price and market support components of the CAP, however, while farmers among current EU members also receive "direct" support based on the land area under cultivation and the number of animals. If such support were also extended to new members, this would increase CAP costs by an additional €4.6 billion a year. [64] Although these sums are not large in relation to the total economic size of the EU, extending the full range of agricultural support to the candidates as they joined the EU would imply that the total cost of the CAP—accounting for nearly one-half of the EU budget—would increase by over 14 percent as new members started receiving these funds. Already, costly surpluses have made it necessary to lower the support granted under the CAP. In two reforms, of which the latest entered into force in January 2000, greater sway has been given to market forces by lowering institutional prices and cutting back on intervention purchases, while compensating farmers partly with direct payments.[65]

If new members are to be accepted under the same terms and conditions as incumbents, enlargement is therefore likely to increase pressure for further reform of the CAP. Moreover, the way in which the CAP is reformed and extended to new members could well have spillover effects on the rest of the world, especially in view of the significant distortions that already exist in international agricultural markets.

Conclusions and Policy Implications

This chapter has provided an assessment of the potential benefits, costs, and risks arising from the prospective accession of the transition economies of central and eastern Europe into the EU and, later, into the euro area. The overall picture that emerges is that, in general, the accession countries have made substantial progress with economic liberalization and adjustment, including reorienting their trade to the west, strengthening capital markets, and improving macroeconomic stability. Based on this assessment, it is probably reasonable to conclude that the accession process is being driven forward not so much by the prospect of strong, tangible gains for the applicant countries in the near term, but by the long-term benefits that will arise from the firm economic and political linkages that accession will confirm. For example, these countries have already realized substantial gains from trade in goods with western markets, although benefits from further financial market integration, removal of non-tariff barriers, and increased trade in services may well occur. Although the EU's future policies concerning support for agriculture and allocation of structural funds are still to be determined, funds for new members from these sources will probably be less generous than these programs would have delivered in the past. Nevertheless, structural transfers could still amount to a significant share of the candidate countries' GDP.

Over the longer term, however, the anchoring of the applicants' economic, institutional, and political structures to the group of advanced western European nations is likely to lead to the former countries being viewed as more secure places for doing business. Such a perception should lead to a reduction in the risk premia associated with these countries, and help to foster further investment, stronger trade flows, and other forms of integration that will hasten economic convergence.

The analysis in this chapter has also pointed to several policy directions and priorities that would enhance these longer-term gains from EU

---

[64]Direct support estimates from Goldman Sachs, *Global Economics Weekly* 00/26 (July 2000).

[65]Disposing of new surpluses with the help of export subsidies is not an option, given the limits set in the Uruguay Round Agreement on Agriculture.

and euro area membership, and mitigate the risks. It will be important, for example, for the candidate countries to ensure relatively flexible microeconomic structures, particularly in labor and product markets. All of the applicants still face substantial adjustments—in their mix of occupations and industries (including agriculture), in trade patterns, in the financial sector, and other areas. The changes that are needed will occur more smoothly and at lower economic cost if markets are able to operate efficiently and convey clear price and wage signals.

The candidate countries also need to continue strengthening the institutions that support market activities. The chapter has pointed to several areas of weakness in this regard, particularly in the implementation of laws and regulations: there are concerns, for example, about the functioning of the judiciary, weaknesses in banking supervision, and persistent corruption. Implementation difficulties are probably not surprising, given the rapid pace of legislative development, especially the extensive body of laws that applicant countries need to adopt under the *acquis*. By putting in place a legal framework designed for economically advanced economies, the accession countries have the opportunity to "leap frog" others at a comparable stage of development. But, to fully realize these gains, the transition economies still face a substantial effort to build up the human capital and administrative capacity to ensure that laws are applied and enforced effectively.

As the anchor in the accession process, the EU has a central influence on the form and pace of enlargement. To be ready for new members, its responsibilities include carrying out internal reforms and shaping applicants' expectations about when full membership could occur. In each of these areas, however, substantial progress is still required. The EU needs to tackle critical reforms in such areas as voting procedures, agricultural support, and regional transfers so that it is in a position, both institutionally and fiscally, to include new countries on equal terms with current members. As things stand at present, delays in these reforms have raised substantial doubts about the conditions under

which enlargement will occur, and when full membership can realistically be expected for even the first group of applicants.

These concerns could present significant risks to the accession process: either membership could be delayed, or new members could be placed in some form of transitional status (e.g., with less than full labor mobility, reduced access to EU programs, and so on). Such delays or interim "solutions" may not fundamentally matter—as long as the candidates continue to put in place the reforms that are needed to move them toward the mainstream of well-functioning market economies. But the risk is that slow or incomplete accession would weaken the commitment to and momentum of reforms, erode support for accession (among the applicants or current members), and make the transition economies more susceptible to economic or political shocks that could move them away from the accession track. For example, the sizable current account deficits of most of the applicants underscore the importance of their retaining the support of international investors—support that, to some degree, may be based on expectations of timely EU accession.

The EU therefore faces the urgent responsibility of reforming its institutions and policies in order to be ready for enlargement. In particular, more ambitious progress with its own reforms would help the EU to clarify the terms and conditions of entry, and hence enable a more credible and certain timetable for enlargement to be established. Such progress would then help to anchor the expectations and reform efforts of the applicants. An analogy can be drawn with the Maastricht Treaty criteria for European Economic and Monetary Union. In this case, clear requirements and a firm timetable anchored a process that was able to resist unexpected pressures (including various episodes of financial turbulence), that stimulated reform efforts among the member states—including some that were not originally expected to adopt the euro in the first wave, and led to the desired outcome when the common currency was introduced on schedule.

Turning to macroeconomic policies and, in particular, a longer run look at the prospective path to euro area membership, the transition countries under consideration have in most cases demonstrated a substantial capacity to achieve macroeconomic stability. Moreover, this progress has come about under a range of monetary arrangements and economic pressures. It is noteworthy, for example, that these macroeconomic frameworks proved generally resilient during the recent international financial market turbulence that severely affected other economies in the region. Given these strengths, the applicant countries' desire to secure the even greater degree of monetary stability that would come from adoption of the euro, at some point following their entry into the EU, is understandable and reasonable.

Nevertheless, while the process of EU accession may be occurring "too slowly" from the perspective of a number of candidates, there could be risks for at least some of the applicants if they sought full euro area membership "too quickly." In particular, the inflation and fiscal disciplines of the Maastricht economic convergence criteria could potentially conflict with the real adjustment and convergence requirements that the applicants will continue to face for some time. There is also a risk that, during this convergence process, the types of shocks hitting accession countries and those in the euro area could be asymmetric—as illustrated, for example, by the large impact of the 1998–99 Russian crisis on some of the transition economies—requiring some scope for independence in policy responses.

Four points need to be noted in this context. First, the earlier analysis has shown that initial undervaluations in real exchange rates among the candidate countries have generally been corrected. Further real exchange rate appreciation should be expected, however, as these countries steadily converge with the more advanced economies of the west, requiring that their price levels or nominal exchange rates (or both) be able to adjust. For some applicants, especially those that still face substantial adjustments, the

scope for real convergence could be impaired if rapid euro area accession was their goal, bringing with it the need for very low inflation in the pre-accession period and a tighter currency peg. Moreover, it would not be desirable for these countries to artificially suppress inflation through other means—for example, by slowing the liberalization of regulated prices.

Second, turning to fiscal policy, some potential sources of pressure on the fiscal position and public debt levels also need to be recognized. For example, several of the accession countries still face uncertainties associated with the necessary fiscal accommodation of costs of bank restructuring and recapitalization, compliance with EU environmental and other requirements, and reform of public health and pension systems. While ongoing fiscal discipline is clearly important, it would probably not be appropriate to tie fiscal policy to an external anchor until these underlying pressures have been adequately addressed.

Third, with capital flows to the accession countries potentially increasing as they become more attractive and secure as investment destinations, monetary and fiscal policies would need to work together to counteract any adverse effects associated with the level and volatility of these flows. Such coordination suggests that the countries concerned retain a substantial degree of macroeconomic policy flexibility—in some cases possibly more than would be permitted by early adoption of the Maastricht economic convergence criteria.

Finally, while euro area participation in the near term would not necessarily be desirable for the candidate countries, membership may well provide a key policy target once the more immediate adjustment and convergence pressures have been dealt with. However, full economic convergence with the income levels of western Europe will take years—probably decades in most cases—to accomplish, well beyond any prospective timetable for adoption of the euro. As a result, the importance of microeconomic flexibility again must be emphasized, as a means of providing crucial support for long-term adjustment and convergence.

SUMMING UP BY THE CHAIRMAN

Directors welcomed the continued recovery and strength of the world economy. Global real GDP growth in 2000 is projected to be the strongest in over a decade, and to remain at high levels in 2001. The higher growth rates shown by all major regions of the world are due in large part to the remarkable strength of the United States' economy, supported by a robust expansion in Europe and the countries in transition. Also contributing to world growth are a consolidation of the recovery in Asia, improved activity in Africa, and rebounds from last year's slowdowns in Latin America and the Middle East. Economic activity in Japan is also improving, although the incipient recovery remains fragile. This strong performance owes much to concerted efforts of policymakers across the globe, including determined adjustment efforts in most crisis countries, and sound macroeconomic policies in advanced and developing countries.

While the overall outlook is encouraging, Directors nevertheless observed that risks and uncertainties remain and that there is no room for complacency. In particular, a number of serious economic and financial imbalances persist in the world economy. These include the lopsided pattern of output and demand growth among industrial countries and the associated imbalances in the external current accounts, the misalignments among the major currencies, and the generous level of asset market valuations in the United States and several other countries. The possibility that these imbalances might unwind in a disorderly fashion remains a risk to the global expansion. The recent increase in oil prices, if sustained, will also hamper global growth and increase inflationary pressures in advanced countries, and adversely affect oil-importing developing countries, including many poor countries in sub-Saharan Africa. Nonetheless, Directors noted that the Organization of Petroleum Exporting Countries (OPEC) would meet in early September to review the supply situation, and that they had earlier indicated their intention to maintain prices in a range below current levels.

Against this background, and despite the improvement in the global outlook, Directors observed that policymakers continue to face important, if widely varying, challenges. In the advanced countries, it is important to continue efforts to facilitate an orderly rebalancing of growth and demand across the three main currency areas. In some advanced countries, a further tightening of macroeconomic policies may be needed to reduce the risks of overheating, particularly if higher energy prices feed through to underlying inflation. In other advanced countries with margins of slack, macroeconomic policies need to continue to support recovery. More broadly, Directors emphasized that progress with structural reforms needs to continue in almost all developing and most advanced countries in order to strengthen prospects for sustained economic growth.

Directors also expressed concern that, despite the strength of the global recovery, poverty remains unacceptably high, and many poor countries continue to face serious economic problems—compounded in some cases by natural disasters and adverse movements in non-oil commodity prices. Directors agreed that sustained efforts by the poorest countries will be essential, notably in promoting macroeconomic and political stability, good governance, and domestic ownership of the reform agenda. Moreover, stronger support from the international community is also needed, including through debt relief focused on poverty reduction—which requires funding in full the enhanced initiative for Highly Indebted Poor Countries (HIPCs)—a reversal of the declining trend in some advanced countries' official development aid, and reform of protectionist trade policies in advanced economies that particularly affect poor countries. Additional international assistance will also be needed to help address the HIV/AIDS pandemic, which poses a severe human as well as economic threat, especially in sub-Saharan Africa and parts of Asia.

Developments in the Major Currency Areas

In the United States, Directors noted that, following the very rapid expansion in the second half of 1999, some signs of a moderation in the growth of economic activity and demand have emerged in the first half of 2000. Notwithstanding a jump in headline inflation due to higher energy prices, core inflation generally remains contained, aided by the continued strong growth in labor productivity linked to high levels of investment in information technology (IT). Directors expressed concern, however, that the U.S. expansion continues to be accompanied by economic and financial imbalances, including a record external current account deficit and high equity valuations. They also noted that, with labor markets still tight and earlier temporary factors that had held down prices beginning to unwind, inflationary pressures remain a concern. Against this background, Directors generally believed that the Federal Reserve should maintain a cautious stance against inflation, and several Directors considered that some further tightening of monetary policy will likely be needed to restrain inflationary pressures. To avoid adding to demand pressures, Directors stressed that it would be important at least to maintain the current fiscal stance by resisting calls for further tax reductions or additional expenditures, particularly against the background of the upcoming elections. Concerning the longer term, Directors supported plans to preserve prospective fiscal surpluses and pay down the public debt so as to improve national saving and help meet the fiscal requirements associated with an aging population.

Directors welcomed the continuing strength of the expansion in the euro area and the accompanying substantial decline in unemployment. However, they recognized that cyclical positions continue to differ substantially among European countries and that, in some cases, clear signs of overheating have emerged. While core inflation has remained modest, Directors noted that the European Central Bank (ECB) has raised interest rates by a cumulative 2 percentage points since late 1999 to forestall potential inflationary pressures arising from buoyant activity, rising oil prices, and the continued weakness of the euro. Looking forward, they agreed that monetary policy should remain prudent but flexible, responding appropriately to risks arising from both diminishing margins of slack and the potential for a substantial appreciation of the euro.

Directors observed that the central challenge in the euro area is to take advantage of the present cyclical upturn to consolidate fiscal reforms and to decisively accelerate structural reform. They underscored the need to avoid procyclical fiscal policies, particularly in countries that continue to face high debt stocks and substantial future pension liabilities. Directors stressed that the present upturn provides an opportunity to reduce the high tax burden in most of these countries—without weakening the underlying fiscal position—and to accelerate structural reforms in labor and product markets so as to improve longer-term growth and employment prospects. Although progress on this front has been made in many countries in recent years, Directors noted that many structural rigidities remain and that reforms should be deepened and broadened to enhance economic efficiency and expand the effective labor supply.

In Japan, most Directors agreed that a modest recovery is under way, led by strengthening corporate profitability and investment, particularly in IT. They noted, however, that the recovery remains fragile, especially in view of the continued weakness in private consumption, and could be derailed by adverse developments. Directors, therefore, stressed that macroeconomic policies will need to remain supportive until a self-sustaining recovery is clearly under way. In this vein, some Directors expressed concern that the recent ending of the zero interest rate policy could prove premature, especially if the recovery turns out weaker than presently envisaged by the Bank of Japan. While the effective rise in interest rates was small, these Directors underscored that monetary policy should remain accommodative and that ending the zero interest rate policy should not be seen as the first of a series of interest rate increases, which could undermine market sentiment and the still fragile recovery. They also noted the need to build up confidence by sending predictable and consistent signals to markets. Directors noted that, while fiscal consolidation is essential over the medium term, fiscal policy needs to remain supportive of recovery in the near term, and a supplementary budget should be implemented in a timely fashion to cushion the expected withdrawal of fiscal stimulus later this year. They also emphasized that structural reforms remain essential to ensure a durable economic recovery. While important progress has been made, Directors stressed that further efforts are needed in restructuring corporations, credit cooperatives and some regional banks, and strengthening the insurance sector. A few Directors suggested that further opening of the economy would provide an additional impetus to ongoing structural reforms.

Directors welcomed the analysis on the "new economy" and its links to financial markets in the *World Economic Outlook*. They agreed that the recent acceleration in productivity growth in the United States has in part reflected rising investment in new technology, although many considered that the extent to which this reflects a one-time jump in productivity associated with capital deepening, or a sustainable increase in underlying productivity growth, is still unclear. Directors noted that there has been less evidence so far of a link between new technologies and increased productivity growth in many other advanced economies. This could reflect many factors, including the time needed to adapt efficiently to new technology. They added that the benefits of new technology depend on accelerating reforms toward more flexible labor and product markets, and on the availability of capital for start-up companies.

Prospects for Developing and Transition Economies

Directors observed that Latin America continues to recuperate from the crises that affected emerging markets in 1997–98, with growth being fueled by buoyant exports—particularly to the United States—and a recovery in consumer confidence and spending. Inflation has remained in the single digits in most countries, and the current account deficit for the region, relative to GDP, is expected to narrow somewhat in 2000, reflecting healthy exports and some improvement in the terms of trade. Directors acknowledged, however, that these aggregate trends mask important differences across countries. Noting that the region's needs for external funds remain sizable, Directors welcomed the rebound in capital flows to emerging markets in recent months, which has been particularly beneficial to some Latin American countries. They cautioned, however, that these flows are volatile and could reverse if, for instance, global and notably U.S. monetary conditions are tightened further. To foster and sustain more even flows of private capital, Directors encouraged the region's decision makers to take advantage of the economic upswing to continue to strengthen economic fundamentals and reduce vulnerabilities to external shocks, including through further fiscal consolidation and reform, supported by measures to improve the operation of labor and product markets.

Directors observed that the recovery in Asia continues to strengthen, while inflation remains low. They noted that the rapid expansion has been fueled by accommodative macroeconomic policies, as well as the growth of exports—particularly of information technology goods. Rising private domestic demand has also underpinned growth, particularly in those countries most advanced in the recovery where fixed investment is rising rapidly. Directors agreed that in those countries in particular, fiscal positions will need to be consolidated as output gaps shrink. Directors urged countries with less robust recoveries to enhance domestic and foreign confidence through rapid and sustained implementation of sound policies. They cautioned that improved performance in the crisis-affected countries could prove short-lived if the momentum for structural reforms is not maintained, and encouraged those countries to pay particular attention to the financial and corporate sectors, including the underlying institutional and prudential framework. Directors noted that vigorous growth in China and India has buttressed activity in Asia. They underscored, nevertheless, that continued structural reforms are needed to maintain robust growth in these two countries. These include, in China, additional measures to strengthen the banking sector and restructure state-owned enterprises—which have become even more important in light of its prospective entry to the World Trade Organization (WTO)—and, in India, further efforts to consolidate public sector finances and move to a more liberalized economy.

Directors welcomed the better-than-expected recovery in Russia, which has also provided support for other countries in the Commonwealth of Independent States (CIS). They noted that the recovery has benefited from improving external earnings, partly reflecting higher world energy prices and a competitive exchange rate, whose effects have spread to the domestic economy, with rising real wages buoying domestic demand. Directors, however, cautioned that longer-term economic prospects continue to depend upon accelerating structural reform—including tax reform, improvements in the legal framework and competition policy, and measures to reduce barter and arrears, and increase transparency and improve governance. Directors urged the government to seize the opportunity provided by improved short-term prospects and the associated increase in fiscal revenues to further strengthen structural reforms, including by vigorously implementing the 18-month reform plan recently announced by the government.

Directors agreed that economic activity is likely to strengthen in the Central and Eastern European and Baltic countries taking part in the European Union (EU) accession process, bolstered by the upswing in exports to western Europe and by better-than-expected performances in Russia and other countries in the CIS. They emphasized that the stronger outlook is also attributable to generally sound macroeconomic policies and to progress made on structural reforms. Nevertheless, Directors expressed concern about the relatively large, and in some cases growing, external deficits financed in part by sizable capital inflows in most of these countries. They urged these countries to ensure fiscal and monetary discipline and to continue progress on structural reforms so as to reduce external vulnerability, particularly as capital accounts are further liberalized as part of the EU accession process.

Directors observed that economic developments in many Middle Eastern and African countries continue to be shaped significantly by external factors, including changes in commodity prices and growth in export markets. They noted that the rebound in world oil prices has been beneficial to activity and prospects in the oil-producing countries in both of these regions. Directors cautioned, however, that many of the non-oil-producing countries in these regions continue to face substantial terms-of-trade losses as export prices of nonfuel commodities, particularly agricultural products, remain generally depressed, particularly in real terms. Growth in a number of these countries has rebounded in the past year, largely because of appropriate macroeconomic policies and more broad-based reform efforts that allowed these countries to benefit from stronger export market growth. Directors recognized, however, that the necessary adjustments to sustain growth and reduce poverty remain difficult. Directors also stressed the need to continue efforts to liberalize and diversify these economies and to encourage broad-based, private-sector-led growth. In addition, Directors cautioned that, in some countries, fiscal policy needs to be conducted in a less procyclical fashion so as not to exacerbate the boom and bust cycles characteristic in many commodity-dependent countries.

The Transition Process

Directors welcomed the focus on the transition process in the *World Economic Outlook*. They broadly agreed that much has been achieved since the start of transition, and that many of the countries involved now enjoy the benefits of a stable macroeconomic environment. Significant progress has also been made in the difficult task of creating the necessary institutional infrastructure to underpin a market economy. However, Directors noted that progress has differed widely among transition economies, reflecting not only their diversity in historical and cultural backgrounds, geography, and levels of development, but also differences in policy strategies and reform implementation.

Directors considered the difference in output performance between the east Asian and other transition economies particularly striking. They generally concurred that the reform strategy adopted in east Asia has depended on the structure of these economies, where the difficult task of reforming state-owned industrial enterprises could be delayed because these enterprises represent only a small part of the economy: the relatively large agricultural sector rapidly boosted output and provided a pool of labor for new businesses. Directors doubted that such an approach was available to other transition economies outside of east Asia, where large state enterprise sectors needed rapid reform and agricultural sectors were small.

Directors noted that outside of east Asia the transition process has generally been more difficult than anticipated, with output falling rapidly in the early years of transition and currently exceeding the level prevailing at the start of transition in only a handful of economies, and poverty increasing significantly in many countries. Directors also contrasted the generally better output performance of the EU accession candidates of Central and Eastern Europe and the Baltics compared to the CIS countries. They considered that this reflected not only more favorable starting conditions but also stronger structural and institutional reforms in the former group. Directors recognized that in many CIS countries the difficult process of implementing structural and institutional reforms has been slowed by the influence of vested interests, while in the EU accession countries, the external anchor created by the requirements for accession has helped to foster consensus on potentially divisive reforms. Directors agreed that a major challenge for the CIS countries is to foster the necessary internal cohesion to promote needed structural and institutional reforms.

Directors considered that the accession process has provided further momentum to the significant adjustment and reform efforts that the EU accession countries have been pursuing since the start of transition. They believed that EU membership and, at some future point, participation in the Economic and Monetary Union (EMU), should bring substantial long-term benefits to the candidates—leading, for example, to even closer trade and financial integration with western Europe, to reductions in risk premia, and to the provision of a more secure environment for foreign investment. To best achieve these benefits, Directors agreed that the applicants need to retain relatively flexible labor and product market structures to support the economic adjustments that they all still face. Further institutional development is needed, particularly to improve the implementation of laws and regulations. Directors also noted that the applicants need to address a number of fiscal issues, including those associated with further banking sector restructuring and rehabilitation in several cases, as well as expenditure pressures arising from pension, health, and social support systems. In light of these requirements, they urged the candidate countries to reach and maintain a relatively conservative fiscal stance, which would also provide important support for monetary policy. Several Directors also drew attention to the reforms needed within the EU to make it ready for the timely accession of the candidate countries.

STATISTICAL APPENDIX

The statistical appendix presents historical data, as well as projections. It comprises four sections: Assumptions, Data and Conventions, Classification of Countries, and Statistical Tables.

The assumptions underlying the estimates and projections for 2000–2001 and the medium-term scenario for 2002–2005 are summarized in the first section. The second section provides a general description of the data, and the conventions used for calculating country group composites. The classification of countries in the various groups presented in the *World Economic Outlook* is summarized in the third section. Note that the group of advanced economies includes Israel and four newly industrialized Asian economies, which all were added to the industrial country group in the May 1997 issue of the *World Economic Outlook*.

The last, and main, section comprises the statistical tables. Data in these tables have been compiled on the basis of information available through the end of August 2000. The figures for 2000 and beyond are shown with the same degree of precision as the historical figures solely for convenience; since they are projections, the same degree of accuracy is not to be inferred.

Assumptions

Real effective *exchange rates* for the advanced economies are assumed to remain constant at their average levels during the period July 18–August 15. For 2000 and 2001, these assumptions imply average U.S. dollar/SDR conversion rates of 1.327 and 1.322, respectively.

Established *policies* of national authorities are assumed to be maintained. The more specific policy assumptions underlying the projections for selected advanced economies are described in Box A1.

It is assumed that the *price of oil* will average $26.53 a barrel in 2000 and $23.00 a barrel in 2001. In the medium term, the oil price is assumed to remain unchanged in real terms.

With regard to *interest rates*, it is assumed that the London interbank offered rate (LIBOR) on six-month U.S. dollar deposits will average 6.8 percent in 2000 and 7.4 in 2001; that the three-month certificate of deposit rate in Japan will average 0.3 percent in 2000 and 0.5 in 2001; and that the three-month interbank deposit rate for the euro will average 4.6 percent in 2000 and 5.2 percent in 2001.

With respect to *introduction of the euro*, on December 31, 1998 the Council of the European Union decided that, effective January 1, 1999, the irrevocably fixed conversion rates between the euro and currencies of the member states adopting the euro are:

1 euro	= 40.3399	Belgian francs
	= 1.95583	Deutsche mark
	= 166.386	Spanish pesetas
	= 6.55957	French francs
	= 0.787564	Irish pound
	= 1,936.27	Italian lire
	= 40.3399	Luxembourg francs
	= 2.20371	Netherlands guilders
	= 13.7603	Austrian schillings
	= 200.482	Portuguese escudos
	= 5.94573	Finnish markkaa

See Box 5.4 in the October 1998 *World Economic Outlook* for details on how the conversion rates were established.

Data and Conventions

Data and projections for 184 countries form the statistical basis for the *World Economic Outlook* (the World Economic Outlook database). The data are maintained jointly by the IMF's Research Department and area depart-

Box A1. Economic Policy Assumptions Underlying the Projections for Selected Advanced Countries

The short-term fiscal policy assumptions used in the *World Economic Outlook* are based on officially announced budgets, adjusted for differences between the national authorities and the IMF staff regarding macroeconomic assumptions and projected fiscal outturns. The medium-term fiscal projections incorporate policy measures that are judged likely to be implemented. These projections and policy assumptions are generally based on information available through the end of August 2000. In cases where the IMF staff has insufficient information to assess the authorities' budget intentions and prospects for policy implementation, an unchanged structural primary balance is assumed, unless otherwise indicated. Specific assumptions used in some of the advanced economies follow (see also Tables 14–16 in the Statistical Appendix for data on fiscal and structural balances).

United States. The fiscal projections are based on the Clinton Administration's June 2000 Mid-Session Review of the FY2001 Budget. The projections are adjusted for differences between the IMF staff's and the Clinton Administration's macroeconomic assumptions. State and local government fiscal balances are assumed to remain constant as a percent of GDP.

Japan. The projections take account of the FY1999 supplementary budgets and the FY2000 initial budget. The ¥18 trillion stimulus package announced in November 1999 includes additional public investment of ¥6.8 trillion (headline figure) through FY2000, most of which is expected to take place in the first two quarters of FY2000. Local governments are projected to largely offset their share in the stimulus package with cuts in own-account spending elsewhere. A typical supplementary budget of ¥1 trillion is included in the calculations for FY2000, and the initial budget for FY2001 is assumed to be of a similar size as the FY2000 budget. The use of public funds to resolve problems in the banking sector is assumed to decline sharply in FY2001, which is the main factor in the improvement in the fiscal balance in that year.

Germany. The fiscal projections incorporate the government's fiscal consolidation package for 2000 and beyond and the income tax reform package for 2001–2005 that were approved by Parliament in December 1999 and July 2000, respectively. The fiscal projections for 2000 also include the proceeds from the August 2000 sale of mobile phone licenses (UMTS) of DM 99.4 billion (US$47.5 billion), which amounts to 2.5 percent of GDP.

France. The projections are based on the national authorities' targets. For 2000, the projections are adjusted for the better-than-expected 1999 outturn and for the July 2000 announcement of F30 billion expected revenue overperformance. The projections also incorporate the one percentage point reduction in the value-added tax in April as well as other tax cuts included in the 2000 supplementary budget. For 2001, the assumptions in the preliminary budget discussions are adjusted for the expected receipts from the sale of third generation mobile phone licenses, which amount to 1.3 percent of GDP, and for the IMF staff's stronger economic outlook. For the medium term, the projections are broadly consistent with the government's Stability Program, adjusted for the differences between the staff's and the authorities' macroeconomic assumptions.

Italy. The fiscal projections are based on the national authorities' estimates for 1999, on the 2000 budget approved in December 1999 by parliament, and on the medium-term fiscal plan covering the period 2001–2004 released in June 2000. The fiscal measures included in the 2000 budget are assumed to be implemented fully and to have the impact as indicated in the government's fiscal plan. Also, the projections do not include receipts from the sale of Universal Mobile Telecommunications Service (UMTS) licenses. For 2001–2004, the IMF staff's projections build on the authorities' projections at unchanged legislation (*tendenziale*) and factor in differences in the macroeconomic assumptions for the medium term, the effect of changes in legislation needed on the basis of current policies (in particular, expected wage increases and new capital spending), and the announced fiscal targets (*quadro programmatico*). For 2005, the projections assume an unchanged primary structural balance. Details on the measures for 2001 will be unveiled in the Budget Law to be submitted to parliament in September 2000.

United Kingdom. The budget projections are based on the 2000/2001 Budget Report announced by the Chancellor on March 21, 2000. Additionally, the projections incorporate more recent statistical releases from the Office for National Statistics, including the provisional budgetary outturn for FY1999/2000. Projections for 2000 also include the proceeds of the recent mobile phone license auction (about 2.4 percent of GDP) following the Eurostat accounting guidelines. These proceeds are not included in the computation of the structural balance. The projections reflect a slightly different assessment and forecast by the IMF staff of potential and actual output with respect to the Budget Report. For revenues, the medium-term projections incorporate the effect of tax changes introduced in the current and previous budgets.

Canada. The fiscal outlook prepared by the IMF staff assumes tax and spending policies in line with those outlined in the February 2000 budget, adjusted for the staff's economic projections. It is expected that the federal government will continue to target a balanced budget on an ex ante basis, with any unspent portion of the contingency reserve allocated to reducing federal government debt. On this basis, the IMF staff assumes that the federal government budget will be in surplus by Can$3 billion a year (the full amount of the contingency reserve) over the medium term. The consolidated fiscal position for the provinces is assumed to evolve in line with their stated medium-term targets.

Australia. The fiscal projections through FY2004 are based on the 2000/01 budget, which was released in May 2000. For the remainder of the projection period, the IMF staff's projections in-

corporate announced future policy measures that are judged likely to be implemented.

Belgium. The projections for the fiscal deficit are based on the 2000 budget and the 2000–2003 Stability Program adjusted for the difference between the IMF staff's and national authorities' growth projections. It is assumed that revenue windfalls due to higher-than-expected growth will be used for deficit reduction according to rules laid out in the 1999–2002 Stability Program.

Greece. The fiscal projections for 2000 are based on the official budget, adjusted to reflect differences in macroeconomic projections and stronger-than-expected revenue performance to date. Projections beyond 2000 incorporate an unchanged ratio of current primary spending in structural terms and a convergence of domestic interest rates with those in the euro area. The projections do not include potential revenues from the auctioning of third-generation mobile phone licenses, which is anticipated to occur in 2001.

Netherlands. The fiscal projections through 2002 are consistent with the government's rules-based approach to fiscal policy, which comprises medium-term expenditure ceilings (in constant prices) and a baseline path for revenue. Expenditure projections for 2000 are based on the midyear supplementary budget, which allows for spending to be increased up to the ceiling, offsetting substantial growth-related windfalls. For the period after 2002, annual real expenditure growth of 1.2 percent is assumed. On the revenue side, the baseline path includes the effects of planned tax cuts in conjunction with a major tax reform package planned for 2001. This path has been adjusted for the national authorities' most recent projection of tax windfalls and to reflect the staff's growth projection. Beyond 2002, the projections assume a further gradual reduction of the revenue ratio by about 0.3 percent of GDP annually.

Portugal. The fiscal projections for 2000 are based on the IMF staff's estimate of the effects of

Box A1 *(concluded)*

the 2000 budget and changes in fiscal policy since the announcement of the budget, as well as the staff's macroeconomic framework. For 2001, the deficit is based on the government's target in the Stability Program. For 2002–2005, a constant structural primary balance is assumed.

Spain. Fiscal policy projections for 2000 and 2001 are based on the national authorities' revised deficit targets for those years. Projections for subsequent years assume the social security system will continue to accrue a surplus (based on unchanged policies), while the remainder of the public sector moves gradually to structural balance. Marginal improvements in the overall balance of the public sector in 2002 and 2003 are broadly consistent with those envisaged in the authorities' Stability Program.

Sweden. The fiscal projections are based on the authorities' policies as presented in the 2000 Spring budget bill. The authorities have announced nominal expenditure ceilings through 2003 and the objective of achieving a fiscal surplus of 2 percent of GDP on average over the cycle. Recent reports indicate that the authorities may not use the full room above this target for tax cuts in the period ahead, however. The IMF staff has therefore assumed that the authorities will allow the structural surplus to level out at 3 percent of GDP over the medium term.

Switzerland. The projections for 2000 are based on official budget plans. For 2001–2003, projections are in line with the official financial plan

that incorporates announced fiscal measures to balance the Confederation's budget by 2001. Beyond 2003, the general government's structural balance is assumed to remain unchanged.

Monetary policy assumptions are based on the established framework for monetary policy in each country. In most cases, this implies a nonaccommodative stance over the business cycle, so that official interest rates will increase when economic indicators suggest that inflation will rise above its acceptable rate or range, and decrease when indicators suggest that prospective inflation will not exceed the acceptable rate or range, that prospective output growth is below its potential rate, and that the margin of slack in the economy is significant. On this basis, the London interbank offered rate (LIBOR) on six-month U.S. dollar deposits is assumed to average 6.8 percent in 2000 and 7.4 percent in 2001. The projected path for U.S. dollar short-term interest rates reflects the assumption that the U.S. Federal Reserve will raise the target Federal Funds rate by another 50 basis points over the second half of 2000, with no further increases in 2001. The rate on six-month Japanese yen deposits is assumed to average 0.3 percent in 2000, with the current accommodative policy stance being maintained, and 0.5 percent in 2001. The rate on six-month euro deposits is assumed to average 4.6 percent in 2000 and 5.1 percent in 2001. Changes in interest rate assumptions compared with the May 2000 *World Economic Outlook* are summarized in Table 1.1.

ments, with the latter regularly updating country projections based on consistent global assumptions.

Although national statistical agencies are the ultimate providers of historical data and definitions, international organizations are also involved in statistical issues, with the objective of harmonizing methodologies for the national compilation of statistics, including the analytical frameworks, concepts, definitions, classifications,

and valuation procedures used in the production of economic statistics. The World Economic Outlook database reflects information from both national source agencies and international organizations.

The completion in 1993 of the comprehensive revision of the standardized *System of National Accounts 1993* (*SNA*) and the IMF's *Balance of Payments Manual* (*BPM*) represented important improvements in the standards of economic statistics and analysis.[1] The IMF was actively involved in both projects, particularly the new *Balance of Payments Manual*, which reflects the IMF's special interest in countries' external positions. Key changes introduced with the new *Manual* were summarized in Box 13 of the May 1994 *World Economic Outlook*. The process of adapting country balance of payments data to the definitions of the new *BPM* began with the May 1995 *World Economic Outlook*. However, full concordance with the *BPM* is ultimately dependent on the provision by national statistical compilers of revised country data, and hence the *World Economic Outlook* estimates are still only partially adapted to the *BPM*.

The members of the European Union have recently adopted a harmonized system for the compilation of the national accounts, referred to as ESA 1995. All national accounts data from 1995 onwards are now presented on the basis of the new system. Revision by national authorities of data prior to 1995 to conform to the new system has progressed, but has in some cases not been completed. In such cases, historical *World Economic Outlook* data have been carefully adjusted to avoid breaks in the series. Users of EU national accounts data prior to 1995 should nevertheless exercise caution until such time as the revision of historical data by national statistical agencies has been fully completed. See Box 1.2, *Revisions in National Accounts Methodologies*, in the May 2000 *World Economic Outlook*.

Composite data for country groups in the *World Economic Outlook* are either sums or weighted averages of data for individual countries. Arithmetically weighted averages are used for all data except inflation and money growth for the developing and transition country

groups, for which geometric averages are used. The following conventions apply:

- Country group composites for exchange rates, interest rates, and the growth rates of monetary aggregates are weighted by GDP converted to U.S. dollars at market exchange rates (averaged over the preceding three years) as a share of world or group GDP.
- Composites for other data relating to the domestic economy, whether growth rates or ratios, are weighted by GDP valued at purchasing power parities (PPPs) as a share of total world or group GDP.[2]
- Composite unemployment rates and employment growth are weighted by labor force as a share of group labor force.
- Composites relating to the external economy are sums of individual country data after conversion to U.S. dollars at the average market exchange rates in the years indicated for balance of payments data, and at end-of-year market exchange rates for debt denominated in currencies other than U.S. dollars. Composites of changes in foreign trade volumes and prices, however, are arithmetic averages of percentage changes for individual countries weighted by the U.S. dollar value of exports or imports as a share of total world or group exports or imports (in the preceding year).

For central and eastern European countries, external transactions in nonconvertible currencies (through 1990) are converted to U.S. dollars at the implicit U.S. dollar/ruble conversion rates obtained from each country's national currency exchange rate for the U.S. dollar and for the ruble.

Unless otherwise indicated, multiyear averages of growth rates are expressed as compound annual rates of change.

[1]Commission of the European Communities, International Monetary Fund, Organization for Economic Cooperation and Development, United Nations, and World Bank, *System of National Accounts 1993* (Brussels/Luxembourg, New York, Paris, and Washington, 1993); and International Monetary Fund, *Balance of Payments Manual, Fifth Edition* (Washington, 1993).

[2]See Box A1 of the May 2000 *World Economic Outlook* for a summary of the revised PPP-based weights and Annex IV of the May 1993 *World Economic Outlook*. See also Anne Marie Gulde and Marianne Schulze-Ghattas, "Purchasing Power Parity Based Weights for the *World Economic Outlook*," in *Staff Studies for the World Economic Outlook* (International Monetary Fund, December 1993), pp. 106–23.

Classification of Countries

Summary of the Country Classification

The country classification in the *World Economic Outlook* divides the world into three major groups: advanced economies, developing countries, and countries in transition.[3] Rather than being based on strict criteria, economic or otherwise, this classification has evolved over time with the objective of facilitating analysis by providing a reasonably meaningful organization of data. A few countries are presently not included in these groups, either because they are not IMF members, and their economies are not monitored by the IMF, or because databases have not yet been compiled. Cuba and the Democratic People's Republic of Korea are examples of countries that are not IMF members, whereas San Marino, among the advanced economies, is an example of an economy for which a database has not been completed. It should also be noted that, owing to a lack of data, only three of the former republics of the dissolved Socialist Federal Republic of Yugoslavia (Croatia, the former Yugoslav Republic of Macedonia, and Slovenia) are included in the group composites for countries in transition.

Each of the three main country groups is further divided into a number of subgroups. Among the advanced economies, the seven largest in terms of GDP, collectively referred to as the major industrial countries, are distinguished as a subgroup, and so are the 15 current members of the European Union, the 11 members of the euro area, and the four newly industrialized Asian economies. The developing countries are classified by region, as well as into a number of analytical and other groups. A regional breakdown is also used for the classification of the countries in transition. Table A provides an overview of these standard groups in the *World Economic Outlook,* showing the number of countries in each group and the average 1999 shares of groups in aggregate PPP-valued GDP, total exports of goods and services, and population.

A new classification, the euro area, has been added to the Statistical Appendix for some variables. The euro area comprises the countries that formed the European Economic and Monetary Union as of January 1, 1999; namely: Austria, Belgium, Finland, France, Germany, Ireland, Italy, Luxembourg, the Netherlands, Portugal, and Spain. Data shown are aggregates of country data and do not reflect official statistics at this time.

General Features and Compositions of Groups in the *World Economic Outlook* Classification

Advanced Economies

The 28 advanced economies are listed in Table B. The seven largest in terms of GDP—the United States, Japan, Germany, France, Italy, the United Kingdom, and Canada—constitute the subgroup of *major industrial countries,* often referred to as the Group of Seven (G-7) countries. The current members of the *European Union* (15 countries) and the *newly industrialized Asian economies* are also distinguished as subgroups. Composite data shown in the tables under the heading "European Union" cover the current 15 members of the European Union for all years, even though the membership has increased over time.

In 1991 and subsequent years, data for *Germany* refer to west Germany *and* the eastern Länder (i.e., the former German Democratic Republic). Before 1991, economic data are not available on a unified basis or in a consistent manner. Hence, in tables featuring data expressed as annual percent change, these apply to west Germany in years up to and including 1991, but to unified Germany from 1992 onward. In general, data on national accounts and domestic economic and financial activity through 1990 cover west Germany only, whereas data for the central government and balance of payments ap-

---

[3]As used here, the term "country" does not in all cases refer to a territorial entity that is a state as understood by international law and practice. It also covers some territorial entities that are not states, but for which statistical data are maintained on a separate and independent basis.

Table A. Classification by *World Economic Outlook* Groups and Their Shares in Aggregate GDP, Exports of Goods and Services, and Population, 1999[1]

(Percent of total for group or world)

	Number of Countries	GDP		Exports of Goods and Services		Population	
		←		Share of total for			→
		Advanced economies	World	Advanced economies	World	Advanced economies	World
Advanced economies	**28**	**100.0**	**57.4**	**100.0**	**77.6**	**100.0**	**15.5**
Major industrial countries	7	79.8	45.8	63.1	48.9	74.4	11.6
United States		38.2	21.9	18.0	14.0	29.6	4.6
Japan		13.3	7.6	8.6	6.7	13.7	2.1
Germany		8.2	4.7	11.6	9.0	8.9	1.4
France		5.7	3.3	7.1	5.5	6.3	1.0
Italy		5.5	3.2	5.6	4.4	6.1	1.0
United Kingdom		5.6	3.2	6.9	5.4	6.3	1.0
Canada		3.4	2.0	5.1	4.0	3.3	0.5
Other advanced economies	21	20.2	11.6	36.9	28.7	25.6	4.0
Memorandum							
Industrial countries *(former definition)*	23	93.8	53.9	87.1	67.6	90.8	14.1
European Union	15	35.3	20.3	50.6	39.3	40.3	6.3
Euro area	11	27.6	15.8	40.2	31.2	31.3	4.9
Newly industrialized Asian economies	4	5.7	3.3	12.2	9.5	8.6	1.3
		Developing countries	World	Developing countries	World	Developing countries	World
Developing countries	**128**	**100.0**	**36.8**	**100.0**	**18.0**	**100.0**	**77.7**
Regional groups							
Africa	**51**	8.8	3.2	10.2	1.8	15.5	12.0
Sub-Sahara	**48**	6.8	2.5	7.6	1.4	14.0	10.9
Excluding Nigeria and South Africa	**46**	3.9	1.4	4.0	0.7	10.3	8.0
Asia	**27**	57.5	21.2	45.9	8.3	67.1	52.1
China		30.6	11.2	17.1	3.1	27.2	21.1
India		12.4	4.6	4.0	0.7	21.4	16.6
Other Asia	**25**	14.6	5.4	24.8	4.5	18.5	14.4
Middle East and Europe	**17**	10.8	4.0	19.1	3.4	6.5	5.0
Western Hemisphere	**33**	22.9	8.4	24.8	4.5	10.9	8.5
Analytical groups							
By source of export earnings							
Fuel	**18**	9.0	3.3	17.7	3.2	7.0	5.4
Nonfuel	**110**	91.0	33.4	82.3	14.9	93.1	72.3
Manufactures	**9**	64.6	23.7	52.1	9.4	63.4	49.3
Primary products	**42**	6.6	2.4	6.6	1.2	10.8	8.4
Services, income, and private transfers	**35**	3.3	1.2	3.9	0.7	5.1	3.9
Diversified	**24**	16.5	6.1	19.6	3.6	13.8	10.7
By external financing source							
Net creditor countries	**9**	2.9	1.1	11.1	2.0	0.9	0.7
Net debtor countries	**119**	97.2	35.8	89.3	16.2	99.2	77.1
Official financing	**45**	5.7	2.1	5.1	0.9	13.5	10.5
Private financing	**46**	80.9	29.8	72.4	13.1	71.5	55.5
Diversified financing	**28**	7.6	2.8	9.4	1.7	12.5	9.7
Net debtor countries by debt-servicing experience							
Countries with arrears and/or rescheduling during 1994–98	**55**	24.8	9.1	23.2	4.2	28.8	22.4
Other net debtor countries	**61**	72.3	26.6	65.8	11.9	70.3	54.6
Other groups							
Heavily indebted poor countries	**40**	5.1	1.9	4.6	0.8	13.2	10.3
Least developed countries	**46**	4.4	1.6	2.8	0.5	13.6	10.5
Middle East and north Africa	**21**	10.3	3.8	17.6	3.2	7.4	5.8
		Developing countries	World	Developing countries	World	Developing countries	World
Countries in transition	**28**	**100.0**	**5.8**	**100.0**	**4.4**	**100.0**	**6.8**
Central and eastern Europe	18	49.5	2.9	63.2	2.9	44.8	3.1
Excluding Belarus and Ukraine	16	39.9	2.3	57.3	2.5	29.9	2.0
Russia		41.5	2.4	28.8	1.3	36.4	2.5
Transcaucasus and central Asia	9	9.0	0.5	6.0	0.3	18.8	1.3

[1]The GDP shares are based on the purchasing-power-parity (PPP) valuation of country GDPs.

Table B. Advanced Economies by Subgroup

	European Union		Euro Area	Newly Industrialized Asian Economies	Other Countries
Major industrial countries					
	France		France		Canada
	Germany		Germany		Japan
	Italy		Italy		United States
	United Kingdom				
Other advanced economies					
	Austria	Luxembourg	Austria	Hong Kong SAR[1]	Australia
	Belgium	Netherlands	Belgium	Korea	Iceland
	Denmark	Portugal	Finland	Singapore	Israel
	Finland	Spain	Ireland	Taiwan Province	New Zealand
	Greece	Sweden	Luxembourg	of China	Norway
	Ireland		Netherlands		Switzerland
			Portugal		
			Spain		

[1]On July 1, 1997, Hong Kong was returned to the People's Republic of China and became a Special Administrative Region of China.

ply to west Germany through June 1990 and to unified Germany thereafter.

Developing Countries

The group of developing countries (128 countries) includes all countries that are not classified as advanced economies or as countries in transition, together with a few dependent territories for which adequate statistics are available.

The *regional breakdowns* of developing countries in the *World Economic Outlook* conform to the IMF's *International Financial Statistics (IFS)* classification—*Africa, Asia, Europe, Middle East,* and *Western Hemisphere*—with one important exception. Because all of the developing countries in Europe except Cyprus, Malta, and Turkey are included in the group of countries in transition, the *World Economic Outlook* classification places these three countries in a combined *Middle East and Europe* region. In both classifications, Egypt and the Libyan Arab Jamahiriya are included in this region, not in Africa. Three additional regional groupings—two of them constituting part of Africa and one a subgroup of Asia—are included in the *World Economic Outlook* because of their analytical significance. These are *sub-Sahara, sub-Sahara excluding Nigeria and South Africa,* and *Asia excluding China and India.*

The developing countries are also classified according to *analytical criteria* and into *other groups.* The analytical criteria reflect countries' composition of export earnings and other income from abroad, a distinction between net creditor and net debtor countries, and, for the net debtor countries, financial criteria based on external financing source and experience with external debt servicing. Included as "other groups" are currently the heavily indebted poor countries (HIPCs), the least developed countries, and Middle East and north Africa (MENA). The detailed composition of developing countries in the regional, analytical, and other groups is shown in Tables C through E.

The first analytical criterion, by *source of export earnings*, distinguishes among five categories: *fuel* (Standard International Trade Classification—SITC 3); *manufactures* (SITC 5 to 8, less 68); *nonfuel primary products* (SITC 0, 1, 2, 4, and 68); *services, income, and private transfers* (exporters of services and recipients of income from abroad, including workers' remittances); and *diversified export earnings.* Countries whose 1994–98 export earnings in any of the first four of these categories accounted for more than half of total export earnings are allocated to that group, while countries whose export earnings were not dominated by any one of these categories are classi-

Table C. Developing Countries by Region and Main Source of Export Earnings

	Fuel	Manufactures	Primary Products	Services, Income, and Private Transfers	Diversified Source of Export Earnings
Africa					
Sub-Sahara	Angola Congo, Rep. of Equatorial Guinea Gabon Nigeria		Benin Botswana Burkina Faso Burundi Central African Rep. Chad Congo, Democratic Rep. of Côte d'Ivoire Gambia, The Ghana Guinea Guinea-Bissau Liberia Madagascar Malawi Mali Mauritania Namibia Niger Somalia Sudan Swaziland Tanzania Togo Zambia Zimbabwe	Cape Verde Comoros Djibouti Eritrea Ethiopia Lesotho Mozambique, Rep. of Rwanda São Tomé and Príncipe Seychelles Uganda	Cameroon Kenya Mauritius Senegal Sierra Leone South Africa
North Africa	Algeria				Morocco Tunisia
Asia	Brunei Darussalam	Bangladesh China India Malaysia Pakistan Philippines Thailand	Bhutan Cambodia Myanmar Papua New Guinea Solomon Islands Vanuatu Vietnam	Fiji Kiribati Maldives Marshall Islands Micronesia, Federated States of Nepal Samoa Tonga	Afghanistan, Islamic State of Indonesia Lao People's Democratic Rep. Sri Lanka
Middle East and Europe	Bahrain Iran, Islamic Rep. of Iraq Kuwait Libya Oman Qatar Saudi Arabia United Arab Emirates	Turkey		Cyprus Egypt Jordan Lebanon	Malta Syrian Arab Rep. Yemen, Rep. of
Western Hemisphere	Trinidad and Tobago Venezuela	Brazil Mexico	Belize Bolivia Chile Guyana Honduras Nicaragua Paraguay Peru Suriname	Antigua and Barbuda Bahamas, The Barbados Dominican Rep. Grenada Haiti Jamaica Netherlands Antilles Panama St. Kitts and Nevis St. Lucia St. Vincent and the Grenadines	Argentina Colombia Costa Rica Dominica Ecuador El Salvador Guatemala Uruguay

Table D. Developing Countries by Region and Main External Financing Source

Countries	Net Creditor Countries	Net Debtor Countries		
		By main external financing source		
		Official financing	Private financing	Diversified financing
Africa				
Sub-Sahara				
Angola				•
Benin		•		
Botswana	•			
Burkina Faso		•		
Burundi		•		
Cameroon		•		
Cape Verde		•		
Central African Rep.		•		
Chad		•		
Comoros		•		
Congo, Democratic Rep. of		•		
Congo, Rep. of		•		
Côte d'Ivoire				•
Djibouti				•
Equatorial Guinea			•	
Eritrea				•
Ethiopia		•		
Gabon		•		
Gambia, The		•		
Ghana				•
Guinea		•		
Guinea-Bissau		•		
Kenya			•	
Lesotho			•	
Liberia		•		
Madagascar		•		
Malawi		•		
Mali		•		
Mauritania		•		
Mauritius				•
Mozambique, Rep. of		•		
Namibia			•	
Niger		•		
Nigeria				•
Rwanda		•		
São Tomé and Príncipe		•		
Senegal		•		
Seychelles			•	
Sierra Leone			•	
Somalia				•
South Africa			•	
Sudan				•
Swaziland	•			
Tanzania		•		
Togo		•		
Uganda		•		
Zambia		•		
Zimbabwe				•

Table D *(continued)*

Countries	Net Creditor Countries	Net Debtor Countries		
		By main external financing source		
		Official financing	Private financing	Diversified financing
North Africa				
Algeria		•		
Morocco			•	
Tunisia				•
Asia				
Afghanistan, Islamic State of				•
Bangladesh		•		
Bhutan		•		
Brunei Darussalam	•			
Cambodia		•		
China			•	
Fiji			•	
India			•	
Indonesia			•	
Kiribati			•	
Lao People's Democratic Rep.		•		
Malaysia			•	
Maldives			•	
Marshall Islands		•		
Micronesia, Federated States of		•		
Myanmar			•	
Nepal		•		
Pakistan				•
Papua New Guinea				•
Philippines				•
Samoa		•		
Solomon Islands				•
Sri Lanka				•
Thailand			•	
Tonga		•		
Vanuatu			•	
Vietnam		•		
Middle East and Europe				
Bahrain			•	
Cyprus			•	
Egypt			•	
Iran, Islamic Rep. of			•	
Iraq				•
Jordan		•		
Kuwait	•			
Lebanon				•
Libya	•			
Malta			•	
Oman	•			
Qatar	•			
Saudi Arabia	•			
Syrian Arab Rep.				•
Turkey			•	
United Arab Emirates	•			
Yemen, Rep. of				•

Table D *(concluded)*

Countries	Net Creditor Countries	Net Debtor Countries		
		By main external financing source		
		Official financing	Private financing	Diversified financing
Western Hemisphere				
Antigua and Barbuda			•	
Argentina			•	
Bahamas, The			•	
Barbados				•
Belize			•	
Bolivia				•
Brazil			•	
Chile			•	
Colombia			•	
Costa Rica			•	
Dominica				•
Dominican Rep.			•	
Ecuador			•	
El Salvador				•
Grenada				•
Guatemala			•	
Guyana		•		
Haiti		•		
Honduras				•
Jamaica			•	
Mexico			•	
Netherlands Antilles		•		
Nicaragua		•		
Panama			•	
Paraguay			•	
Peru			•	
St. Kitts and Nevis			•	
St. Lucia			•	
St. Vincent and the Grenadines			•	
Suriname			•	
Trinidad and Tobago			•	
Uruguay				•
Venezuela			•	

fied as countries with diversified export earnings (see Table C).

The financial criteria first distinguish between *net creditor* and *net debtor countries*. Net creditor countries are defined as developing countries with positive net external assets at the end of 1998.[4] Countries in the much larger net debtor group are differentiated on the basis of two additional financial criteria: by *main source of external financing* and by *experience with debt servicing*.[5]

Within the classification, *main source of external financing*, three subgroups, based on country es-

[4]If information on the net external asset position is unavailable, the inclusion of countries in this group is based on whether they have cumulated a substantial current account surplus over the past 25 years to 1998.

[5]Within the classification *experience with debt servicing*, a distinction is made between countries with arrears or rescheduling agreements (or both) and other net debtor countries. During the 1994–98 period, 55 countries incurred external payments arrears or entered into official or commercial bank debt-rescheduling agreements. This group of countries is referred to as *countries with arrears and/or rescheduling during 1994–98*.

Table E. Other Developing Country Groups

	Heavily Indebted Poor Countries	Least Developed Countries	Middle East and North Africa		Heavily Indebted Poor Countries	Least Developed Countries	Middle East and North Africa
Africa				**North Africa**			
Sub-Sahara				Algeria			•
Angola	•	•		Morocco			•
Benin	•	•		Tunisia			•
Burkina Faso	•	•		**Asia**			
Burundi	•	•		Afghanistan, Islamic State of		•	
Cameroon	•			Bangladesh		•	
Cape Verde		•		Bhutan		•	
Central African Rep.	•	•		Cambodia		•	
Chad	•	•		Kiribati		•	
Comoros		•		Lao People's Democratic Rep.	•	•	
Congo, Democratic Rep. of	•	•		Maldives		•	
Congo, Rep. of	•			Myanmar	•	•	
Côte d'Ivoire	•			Nepal		•	
Djibouti		•	•	Samoa		•	
Equatorial Guinea		•		Solomon Islands		•	
Ethiopia	•	•		Vanuatu		•	
Gambia, The		•		Vietnam	•		
Ghana	•			**Middle East and Europe**			
Guinea	•	•		Bahrain			•
Guinea-Bissau	•	•		Egypt			•
Kenya	•			Iran, Islamic Rep. of			•
Lesotho		•		Iraq			•
Liberia	•	•		Jordan			•
Madagascar	•	•		Kuwait			•
Malawi	•	•		Lebanon			•
Mali	•	•		Libya			•
Mauritania	•	•	•	Oman			•
Mozambique, Rep. of	•	•		Qatar			•
Niger	•	•		Saudi Arabia			•
Rwanda	•	•		Syrian Arab Rep.			•
São Tomé and Príncipe	•	•		United Arab Emirates			•
Senegal	•			Yemen, Rep. of	•	•	•
Sierra Leone	•	•		**Western Hemisphere**			
Somalia	•	•	•	Bolivia	•		
Sudan	•	•	•	Guyana	•		
Tanzania	•	•		Haiti		•	
Togo	•	•		Honduras	•		
Uganda	•	•		Nicaragua	•		
Zambia	•	•					

timates of the composition of external financing, are identified: *countries relying largely on official financing, countries relying largely on private financing,* and *countries with diversified financing source.* Net debtor countries are allocated to the first two of these subgroups according to whether their official financing, including official grants, or their private financing, including direct and portfolio investment, accounted for more than two-thirds of their total 1994–98 external financing. Countries that do not meet either of these two criteria are classified as

Table F. Countries in Transition by Region

Central and Eastern Europe		Russia	Transcaucasus and Central Asia
Albania	Lithuania	Russia	Armenia
Belarus	Macedonia, former Yugoslav Rep. of		Azerbaijan
Bosnia and Herzegovina	Moldova		Georgia
Bulgaria	Poland		Kazakhstan
Croatia	Romania		Kyrgyz Rep.
Czech Rep.	Slovak Rep.		Mongolia
Estonia	Slovenia		Tajikistan
Hungary	Ukraine		Turkmenistan
Latvia	Yugoslavia, Federal Rep. of (Serbia/Montenegro)		Uzbekistan

countries with diversified financing source (see Table D).

The *other groups* of developing countries (see Table E) constitute the HIPCs, the *least developed countries,* and MENA countries. The first group comprises 40 of the countries (all except Nigeria) considered by the IMF and the World Bank for their debt initiative, known as the HIPC Initiative.[6] The group of least developed countries comprises 46 of the 47 developing countries classified as "least developed" by the United Nations (Tuvalu, not being an IMF member, is excluded). Finally, Middle East and north Africa, also referred to as the MENA countries, is a new *World Economic Outlook* group, whose composition straddles the Africa and Middle East and Europe regions. It is defined as the Arab League countries plus the Islamic Republic of Iran.

Countries in Transition

The group of countries in transition (28 countries) comprises central and eastern European countries (including the Baltic countries),

Russia, the other states of the former Soviet Union, and Mongolia. The transition country group is divided into three regional subgroups: *central and eastern Europe, Russia,* and *Transcaucasus and central Asia.* The detailed country composition is shown in Table F.

One common characteristic of these countries is the transitional state of their economies from a centrally administered system to one based on market principles. Another is that this transition involves the transformation of sizable industrial sectors whose capital stocks have proven largely obsolete. Although several other countries are also "in transition" from partially command-based economic systems toward market-based systems (including China, Cambodia, the Lao People's Democratic Republic, Vietnam, and a number of African countries), most of these are largely rural, low-income economies for whom the principal challenge is one of economic development. These countries are therefore classified in the developing country group rather than in the group of countries in transition.

[6]See David Andrews, Anthony R. Boote, Syed S. Rizavi, and Sukwinder Singh, *Debt Relief for Low-Income Countries: The Enhanced HIPC Initiative,* Pamphlet Series, No. 51 (Washington: International Monetary Fund, November 1999)

List of Tables

Table 1. Summary of World Output[1]
(Annual percent change)

	Ten-Year Averages		1992	1993	1994	1995	1996	1997	1998	1999	2000	2001
	1982–91	1992–2001										
World	**3.3**	**3.5**	**2.0**	**2.3**	**3.7**	**3.6**	**4.1**	**4.1**	**2.6**	**3.4**	**4.7**	**4.2**
Advanced economies	**3.1**	**2.9**	**2.1**	**1.4**	**3.3**	**2.7**	**3.2**	**3.4**	**2.4**	**3.2**	**4.2**	**3.2**
United States	2.9	3.7	3.1	2.7	4.0	2.7	3.6	4.4	4.4	4.2	5.2	3.2
European Union	2.6	2.2	1.2	−0.4	2.8	2.4	1.7	2.6	2.7	2.4	3.4	3.3
Japan	4.1	1.1	1.0	0.3	0.6	1.5	5.0	1.6	−2.5	0.2	1.4	1.8
Other advanced economies	4.3	4.4	3.4	4.1	5.8	5.0	4.1	4.7	1.0	5.5	5.8	4.4
Developing countries	**4.3**	**5.6**	**6.3**	**6.4**	**6.7**	**6.1**	**6.5**	**5.7**	**3.5**	**3.8**	**5.6**	**5.7**
Regional groups												
Africa	2.3	2.6	−0.7	0.2	2.3	3.1	5.7	2.8	3.1	2.2	3.4	4.4
Asia	6.9	7.5	9.4	9.3	9.6	9.0	8.3	6.5	4.1	5.9	6.7	6.6
Middle East and Europe	3.3	3.7	5.7	3.8	0.6	4.3	4.5	5.1	3.1	0.8	4.7	4.1
Western Hemisphere	1.8	3.4	3.6	4.1	5.0	1.7	3.6	5.4	2.2	0.3	4.3	4.5
Analytical groups												
By source of export earnings												
Fuel	2.3	2.8	6.0	1.1	0.3	2.8	3.3	4.1	2.3	1.0	4.4	3.5
Nonfuel	4.6	5.9	6.4	7.0	7.4	6.5	6.8	5.9	3.6	4.0	5.8	5.9
By external financing source												
Net creditor countries	1.4	2.8	6.1	2.2	1.8	2.7	2.1	4.1	1.2	0.4	4.4	3.4
Net debtor countries	4.4	5.7	6.3	6.5	6.8	6.2	6.6	5.8	3.5	3.9	5.7	5.7
Official financing	2.7	3.7	1.8	1.7	2.5	5.2	5.4	4.0	3.8	3.4	4.3	5.0
Private financing	4.8	6.1	6.9	7.5	7.7	6.6	6.9	6.1	3.6	4.0	5.9	6.0
Diversified financing	2.6	4.0	4.8	2.4	3.5	4.4	5.2	4.2	3.0	3.2	4.9	4.2
Net debtor countries by debt-servicing experience												
Countries with arrears and/or rescheduling during 1994–98	2.7	3.5	2.8	3.7	4.6	5.1	5.0	4.2	−0.8	2.1	4.2	4.6
Other net debtor countries	5.3	6.5	7.8	7.7	7.7	6.7	7.3	6.4	5.1	4.5	6.2	6.1
Countries in transition	**1.4**	**−2.1**	**−14.4**	**−7.6**	**−7.6**	**−1.5**	**−0.5**	**1.6**	**−0.8**	**2.4**	**4.9**	**4.1**
Central and eastern Europe	...	—	−8.8	−3.9	−3.0	1.6	1.7	2.1	2.0	1.3	3.1	4.2
Excluding Belarus and Ukraine	...	2.2	−5.3	0.1	3.1	5.5	3.9	2.5	2.0	1.8	3.8	4.6
Russia	...	−4.2	−19.4	−10.4	−11.6	−4.2	−3.4	0.9	−4.9	3.2	7.0	4.0
Transcaucasus and central Asia	...	−2.4	−14.1	−11.0	−11.5	−5.0	1.3	2.6	2.5	4.6	5.3	4.5
Memorandum												
Median growth rate												
Advanced economies	3.1	3.0	1.5	0.7	4.1	2.9	3.1	3.7	2.9	3.5	4.0	3.4
Developing countries	3.2	3.9	3.8	3.0	3.8	4.3	4.6	4.4	3.5	3.3	4.1	4.5
Countries in transition	1.3	0.1	−11.4	−7.8	−1.9	1.9	3.1	3.7	3.9	3.0	4.0	4.4
Output per capita												
Advanced economies	2.5	2.3	1.4	0.8	2.6	2.1	2.5	2.8	1.8	2.7	3.6	2.7
Developing countries	2.0	3.9	3.8	4.4	4.8	4.3	4.9	4.2	1.9	2.2	4.1	4.2
Countries in transition	0.8	−2.1	−14.6	−7.7	−7.6	−1.4	−0.3	1.7	−0.6	2.5	5.0	4.3
World growth based on market exchange rates	**3.0**	**2.7**	**0.8**	**1.1**	**3.0**	**2.8**	**3.5**	**3.4**	**2.0**	**2.9**	**4.2**	**3.5**
Value of world output in billions of U.S. dollars												
At market exchange rates	16,855	28,935	24,049	24,929	26,455	29,028	29,823	29,719	29,513	30,614	31,779	33,439
At purchasing power parities	21,436	37,102	29,089	30,467	32,170	33,996	36,032	38,123	39,489	41,344	43,802	46,507

[1]Real GDP.

Table 2. Advanced Economies: Real GDP and Total Domestic Demand
(Annual percent change)

| | Ten-Year Averages | | 1992 | 1993 | 1994 | 1995 | 1996 | 1997 | 1998 | 1999 | 2000 | 2001 | Fourth Quarter[1] | | |
	1982–91	1992–2001											1999	2000	2001
Real GDP															
Advanced economies	**3.1**	**2.9**	**2.1**	**1.4**	**3.3**	**2.7**	**3.2**	**3.4**	**2.4**	**3.2**	**4.2**	**3.2**	...	...	...
Major industrial countries	3.0	2.7	2.0	1.3	3.0	2.3	3.0	3.2	2.5	2.9	3.9	2.9	3.4	3.7	2.9
United States	2.9	3.7	3.1	2.7	4.0	2.7	3.6	4.4	4.4	4.2	5.2	3.2	5.0	4.1	3.0
Japan	4.1	1.1	1.0	0.3	0.6	1.5	5.0	1.6	−2.5	0.2	1.4	1.8	−0.2	3.2	2.3
Germany	2.7	1.7	2.2	−1.1	2.3	1.7	0.8	1.4	2.1	1.6	2.9	3.3	2.4	3.2	3.7
France	2.4	2.1	1.5	−0.9	2.1	1.8	1.1	2.0	3.2	2.9	3.5	3.5	3.2	3.6	3.5
Italy	2.3	1.7	0.8	−0.9	2.2	2.9	1.1	1.8	1.5	1.4	3.1	3.0	2.3	3.2	3.0
United Kingdom[2]	2.7	2.6	0.1	2.3	4.4	2.8	2.6	3.5	2.6	2.1	3.1	2.8	2.8	3.1	2.4
Canada	2.3	3.2	0.9	2.3	4.7	2.8	1.5	4.4	3.3	4.5	4.7	2.8	4.9	3.9	2.5
Other advanced economies	3.7	3.7	2.4	1.9	4.6	4.3	3.7	4.2	2.0	4.7	5.1	4.2	...	...	...
Spain	3.2	2.6	0.7	−1.2	2.3	2.7	2.4	3.8	4.0	3.7	4.1	3.5	3.9	3.7	3.7
Netherlands	2.5	3.0	2.0	0.8	3.2	2.3	3.0	3.8	3.7	3.6	3.9	3.5	...	...	...
Belgium	2.2	2.2	1.6	−1.5	3.0	2.5	1.0	3.5	2.7	2.5	3.9	3.0	...	...	...
Sweden	1.9	2.2	−1.4	−2.2	4.1	3.7	1.1	2.0	3.0	3.8	4.4	3.4	...	...	...
Austria	2.7	2.1	1.3	0.5	2.4	1.7	2.0	1.2	2.9	2.2	3.5	2.9	...	...	...
Denmark	2.1	2.3	0.6	—	5.5	2.8	2.5	3.1	2.5	1.7	2.1	2.1	2.4	1.2	1.6
Finland	2.2	3.2	−3.3	−1.1	4.0	3.8	4.0	6.3	5.5	4.0	5.0	4.0	3.5	3.4	6.4
Greece[3]	1.9	2.3	0.7	−1.6	2.0	2.1	2.4	3.4	3.7	3.5	3.5	3.9	...	...	...
Portugal	3.0	2.7	1.9	−1.4	2.4	2.9	3.4	3.7	4.2	3.0	3.4	3.5	...	...	...
Ireland	3.5	7.4	3.3	2.6	5.8	9.5	7.7	10.7	8.9	9.9	8.7	6.9	...	...	...
Luxembourg	5.0	5.2	5.8	8.5	4.1	3.5	2.9	7.3	5.0	5.2	5.1	5.0	...	...	...
Switzerland	1.8	1.2	−0.1	−0.5	0.5	0.5	0.3	1.7	2.1	1.7	3.0	2.6	2.7	2.6	2.5
Norway	2.6	3.3	3.3	2.7	5.5	3.8	4.9	4.7	2.0	0.9	3.0	2.4	...	...	...
Israel	3.6	4.5	6.8	3.4	8.0	6.8	4.6	2.9	2.2	2.2	4.0	4.0	...	...	...
Iceland	2.4	2.7	−4.1	0.6	3.7	0.9	5.6	5.3	4.7	4.5	4.0	2.1	...	...	...
Korea	8.9	5.8	5.4	5.5	8.3	8.9	6.8	5.0	−6.7	10.7	8.8	6.5	13.0	6.1	6.3
Australia	2.9	4.1	2.6	3.8	5.0	4.4	4.0	3.9	5.2	4.4	4.0	3.4	4.0	3.9	3.0
Taiwan Province of China	8.1	6.1	6.8	6.3	6.5	6.0	5.7	6.8	4.7	5.7	6.5	6.0	6.8	5.9	6.0
Hong Kong SAR	6.1	4.1	6.3	6.1	5.4	3.9	4.5	5.0	−5.1	2.9	8.0	4.8	9.1	3.3	6.5
Singapore	7.1	7.4	6.5	12.7	11.4	8.0	7.5	8.4	0.4	5.4	7.9	5.9	7.1	6.5	7.3
New Zealand	1.2	3.1	0.9	5.1	5.9	4.0	3.2	2.1	−0.2	3.4	4.0	3.2	5.7	1.5	3.8
Memorandum															
Industrial countries	2.9	2.7	1.9	1.1	3.1	2.4	3.0	3.2	2.7	3.0	3.9	3.0	...	...	...
European Union	2.6	2.2	1.2	−0.4	2.8	2.4	1.7	2.6	2.7	2.4	3.4	3.3	...	...	...
Euro area	2.6	2.1	1.5	−0.8	2.4	2.3	1.5	2.3	2.7	2.4	3.5	3.4	...	...	...
Newly industrialized Asian economies	8.1	5.8	6.0	6.3	7.6	7.3	6.2	5.8	−2.3	7.8	7.9	6.1	10.5	6.1	6.6
Real total domestic demand															
Advanced economies	**3.2**	**3.0**	**2.0**	**1.0**	**3.4**	**2.7**	**3.2**	**3.1**	**2.7**	**3.9**	**4.3**	**3.3**	...	...	...
Major industrial countries	3.0	2.9	2.0	1.1	3.1	2.2	3.1	3.0	3.2	3.6	4.1	3.1	4.0	3.9	3.0
United States	3.0	4.2	3.1	3.3	4.4	2.5	3.7	4.7	5.5	5.2	6.0	3.5	5.9	4.9	3.1
Japan	4.1	1.0	0.4	0.1	1.0	2.3	5.7	0.2	−3.1	0.5	0.9	2.0	0.3	2.5	2.8
Germany	2.5	1.7	2.8	−1.0	2.2	1.7	0.3	0.6	2.4	2.4	2.2	3.3	2.2	2.8	3.5
France	2.4	1.8	0.8	−1.6	2.1	1.7	0.7	0.8	3.8	2.9	3.6	3.4	2.7	3.8	3.2
Italy	2.6	1.3	0.9	−5.1	1.7	2.0	0.9	2.5	2.9	2.5	2.2	2.7	1.8	2.5	2.5
United Kingdom	2.8	3.0	0.8	2.2	3.4	1.8	3.1	3.7	4.6	3.7	3.5	3.4	4.0	3.1	2.9
Canada	2.4	2.9	0.9	1.4	3.2	1.7	1.4	6.2	2.2	4.2	5.4	2.9	6.3	4.0	2.3
Other advanced economies	3.9	3.4	2.3	0.9	4.6	4.5	3.6	3.6	0.8	4.9	5.0	4.1	...	...	...
Memorandum															
Industrial countries	3.0	2.8	1.8	0.8	3.1	2.4	3.0	3.1	3.4	3.6	4.1	3.2	...	...	...
European Union	2.7	2.1	1.3	−1.7	2.4	2.1	1.4	2.2	3.7	3.1	3.1	3.3	...	...	...
Euro area	2.7	1.9	1.5	−2.3	2.1	2.1	1.0	1.9	3.5	3.0	3.0	3.3	...	...	...
Newly industrialized Asian economies	8.3	5.1	6.3	5.9	8.3	7.6	6.5	4.1	−9.0	7.9	8.2	6.1	...	...	...

[1]From fourth quarter of preceding year.
[2]Average of expenditure, income, and output estimates of GDP at market prices.
[3]Based on revised national accounts for 1988 onward.

Table 3. Advanced Economies: Components of Real GDP
(Annual percent change)

	Ten-Year Averages		1992	1993	1994	1995	1996	1997	1998	1999	2000	2001
	1982–91	1992–2001										
Private consumer expenditure												
Advanced economies	**3.3**	**2.9**	**2.4**	**1.7**	**3.0**	**2.7**	**2.9**	**2.7**	**2.8**	**3.9**	**3.7**	**2.8**
Major industrial countries	3.1	2.7	2.3	1.7	2.7	2.4	2.6	2.5	3.2	3.7	3.5	2.5
United States	3.3	3.7	2.9	3.4	3.8	3.0	3.2	3.6	4.7	5.3	5.1	2.7
Japan	3.8	1.3	2.1	1.2	1.9	2.1	2.9	0.5	−0.5	1.2	0.6	1.0
Germany	2.7	1.8	2.8	0.2	1.0	2.2	1.0	0.7	2.0	2.6	2.2	3.2
France	2.1	1.6	0.9	−0.4	1.2	1.2	1.3	0.2	3.4	2.3	3.1	3.1
Italy	2.7	1.5	1.9	−3.7	1.5	1.7	1.2	3.0	2.3	1.7	2.4	2.6
United Kingdom	3.1	3.0	0.5	2.9	2.9	1.7	3.6	3.9	4.0	4.3	3.2	2.6
Canada	2.6	2.8	1.8	1.8	3.1	2.1	2.5	4.4	2.9	3.5	3.6	2.3
Other advanced economies	3.7	3.5	3.1	1.7	4.0	3.8	3.9	3.5	1.5	4.8	4.6	4.2
Memorandum												
Industrial countries	3.1	2.7	2.2	1.4	2.7	2.4	2.6	2.5	3.2	3.7	3.5	2.6
European Union	2.6	2.1	1.7	−0.4	1.7	1.8	1.9	2.0	3.1	3.0	3.0	3.1
Euro area	2.6	1.9	2.0	−1.0	1.4	1.8	1.6	1.6	3.0	2.8	2.9	3.2
Newly industrialized Asian economies	8.1	5.7	6.8	7.1	8.1	6.9	6.5	5.3	−4.2	7.5	7.3	6.1
Public consumption												
Advanced economies	**2.6**	**1.5**	**1.8**	**0.8**	**0.9**	**0.9**	**1.5**	**1.3**	**1.5**	**1.7**	**2.1**	**2.1**
Major industrial countries	2.3	1.3	1.5	0.6	0.8	0.7	1.1	1.0	1.3	1.7	2.2	2.2
United States	2.7	1.1	0.4	−0.4	0.2	—	0.5	1.8	1.5	2.1	2.7	2.2
Japan	2.3	1.9	2.0	2.4	2.4	3.3	1.9	1.5	1.5	1.3	1.2	1.8
Germany	1.1	1.2	5.0	0.1	2.4	1.5	1.8	−0.9	0.5	−0.1	0.8	1.3
France	2.7	1.9	3.8	4.6	0.7	—	2.3	1.7	0.7	2.5	1.2	1.2
Italy	2.4	0.4	0.6	−0.2	−0.8	−2.1	1.1	0.9	0.7	0.8	1.7	1.4
United Kingdom	1.2	1.9	0.5	−0.8	1.4	1.6	1.7	−1.4	1.1	3.0	4.7	7.4
Canada	2.6	0.2	1.0	0.1	−1.2	−0.5	−1.4	−1.2	1.6	1.3	1.6	0.9
Other advanced economies	3.6	2.1	3.0	2.0	1.3	1.8	3.4	2.3	2.5	1.7	1.8	1.4
Memorandum												
Industrial countries	2.4	1.4	1.6	0.7	0.9	0.8	1.1	1.2	1.4	1.8	2.1	2.1
European Union	2.1	1.4	2.6	1.1	1.0	0.8	1.6	0.5	1.2	1.6	1.8	2.3
Euro area	2.4	1.4	3.2	1.4	1.0	0.5	1.6	0.9	1.2	1.3	1.4	1.3
Newly industrialized Asian economies	6.2	2.9	6.2	3.7	1.0	2.0	7.5	3.3	2.5	−0.4	1.6	1.8
Gross fixed capital formation												
Advanced economies	**3.6**	**4.6**	**1.8**	**0.1**	**4.7**	**4.2**	**6.3**	**5.4**	**5.0**	**5.8**	**7.1**	**5.3**
Major industrial countries	3.3	4.6	2.2	0.4	4.3	3.4	6.6	5.3	5.7	6.2	7.1	5.2
United States	2.6	7.7	5.2	5.7	7.3	5.4	8.4	8.8	10.7	9.1	10.7	6.3
Japan	5.3	0.3	−1.5	−2.0	−0.8	1.7	11.1	−0.8	−7.4	−1.2	1.1	3.4
Germany	2.7	1.6	4.5	−4.5	4.0	−0.7	−0.8	0.6	3.0	3.3	2.7	4.0
France	2.9	2.2	−1.4	−6.4	1.6	2.2	—	0.5	6.1	7.3	6.6	6.7
Italy	2.1	1.5	−1.4	−10.9	0.1	6.0	3.6	1.2	4.1	4.4	5.7	3.8
United Kingdom	4.3	3.9	−0.7	0.8	3.6	2.9	4.9	7.5	10.1	6.1	1.3	3.1
Canada	2.4	5.2	−1.3	−2.7	7.4	−1.9	5.8	15.4	3.4	10.1	11.7	5.9
Other advanced economies	4.7	4.3	—	−1.3	6.4	7.5	5.2	6.0	2.4	4.2	7.1	5.9
Memorandum												
Industrial countries	3.3	4.5	1.6	−0.3	4.4	3.9	6.2	5.5	5.9	6.1	6.8	5.1
European Union	3.2	2.6	−0.3	−5.7	2.6	3.7	2.3	3.4	6.2	5.5	4.5	4.7
Euro area	3.0	2.3	0.2	−6.8	2.3	3.4	1.6	2.4	5.3	5.3	5.1	4.9
Newly industrialized Asian economies	9.8	5.3	5.9	6.9	9.8	9.8	7.4	4.3	−9.3	0.4	11.1	8.8

Table 3 *(concluded)*

	Ten-Year Averages		1992	1993	1994	1995	1996	1997	1998	1999	2000	2001
	1982–91	1992–2001										
Final domestic demand												
Advanced economies	**3.2**	**2.9**	**2.1**	**1.1**	**2.9**	**2.6**	**3.4**	**2.9**	**2.8**	**3.9**	**4.2**	**3.3**
Major industrial countries	3.1	2.8	2.0	1.1	2.6	2.2	3.3	2.7	3.2	3.9	4.1	3.0
United States	3.1	4.1	2.8	3.1	3.8	2.9	3.7	4.3	5.4	5.6	5.9	3.4
Japan	4.1	1.0	0.9	0.3	1.1	2.1	5.3	0.1	−2.5	0.5	0.8	1.8
Germany	2.4	1.6	3.6	−0.9	2.0	1.4	0.7	0.3	1.9	2.2	2.0	3.1
France	2.4	1.8	1.1	−0.4	1.1	1.1	1.3	0.6	3.2	3.3	3.4	3.4
Italy	2.5	1.3	1.0	−4.5	0.8	1.7	1.7	2.2	2.4	2.0	3.0	2.7
United Kingdom	2.8	2.9	0.3	1.8	2.7	1.9	3.4	3.5	4.5	4.4	3.1	3.6
Canada	2.5	2.7	1.0	0.6	2.8	0.8	2.2	5.2	2.8	4.4	5.0	2.8
Other advanced economies	3.9	3.4	2.3	1.2	4.1	4.3	4.1	3.8	1.5	4.0	4.9	4.3
Memorandum												
Industrial countries	3.0	2.8	1.9	0.8	2.6	2.3	3.2	2.8	3.3	3.9	4.0	3.1
European Union	2.6	2.1	1.5	−1.2	1.7	1.9	1.9	2.0	3.3	3.3	3.1	3.3
Euro area	2.6	1.9	1.9	−1.7	1.5	1.8	1.6	1.7	3.1	3.0	3.1	3.2
Newly industrialized Asian economies	8.3	5.2	6.1	6.5	7.7	7.4	7.1	4.6	−5.4	4.2	7.8	6.5
Stock building[1]												
Advanced economies	**—**	**—**	**—**	**−0.1**	**0.5**	**—**	**−0.2**	**0.2**	**−0.1**	**—**	**0.1**	**0.1**
Major industrial countries	—	0.1	—	−0.1	0.5	−0.1	−0.1	0.3	0.1	−0.2	0.1	0.1
United States	−0.1	0.1	0.3	—	0.7	−0.5	—	0.4	0.2	−0.4	0.1	0.1
Japan	0.1	—	−0.5	−0.1	−0.2	0.2	0.4	0.1	−0.6	0.1	0.1	0.3
Germany	0.1	—	−0.7	−0.1	0.3	0.3	−0.5	0.2	0.4	0.2	0.2	0.2
France	0.1	—	−0.3	−1.1	0.9	0.6	−0.6	0.2	0.5	−0.4	0.3	—
Italy	0.1	—	−0.1	−0.7	0.8	0.2	−0.7	0.3	0.6	0.4	−0.7	—
United Kingdom	—	0.1	0.5	0.4	0.7	—	−0.4	0.3	0.1	−0.7	0.4	−0.1
Canada	−0.1	0.2	−0.1	0.8	0.3	0.9	−0.8	1.0	−0.5	−0.2	0.4	0.1
Other advanced economies	0.1	—	—	−0.3	0.5	0.3	−0.4	−0.2	−0.7	0.7	0.1	−0.1
Memorandum												
Industrial countries	—	0.1	−0.1	−0.1	0.5	—	−0.2	0.3	0.1	−0.2	0.1	0.1
European Union	0.1	—	−0.2	−0.4	0.6	0.3	−0.5	0.2	0.3	−0.2	—	—
Euro area	0.1	—	−0.3	−0.6	0.6	0.3	−0.5	0.2	0.4	—	—	0.1
Newly industrialized Asian economies	—	−0.1	0.2	−0.5	0.6	0.3	−0.5	−0.6	−3.5	2.9	0.3	−0.4
Foreign balance[1]												
Advanced economies	**−0.1**	**−0.1**	**—**	**0.3**	**−0.1**	**0.1**	**—**	**0.3**	**−0.4**	**−0.6**	**−0.2**	**−0.1**
Major industrial countries	−0.1	−0.2	—	0.2	—	0.1	−0.1	0.1	−0.8	−0.9	−0.3	−0.2
United States	−0.1	−0.5	−0.1	−0.6	−0.4	0.1	−0.1	−0.3	−1.3	−1.2	−1.0	−0.3
Japan	—	0.1	0.6	0.2	−0.3	−0.8	−0.5	1.4	0.5	−0.3	0.6	−0.2
Germany	0.1	0.1	−0.6	−0.1	0.1	—	0.5	0.8	−0.3	−0.8	0.8	0.1
France	—	0.3	0.7	0.7	—	—	0.4	1.2	−0.5	0.1	—	0.2
Italy	−0.2	0.4	−0.1	4.3	0.6	1.0	0.2	−0.6	−1.3	−1.0	1.0	0.3
United Kingdom	−0.4	−0.5	−0.8	0.1	0.9	1.0	−0.5	−0.3	−2.0	−1.6	−0.6	−0.8
Canada	−0.1	0.3	0.4	0.9	1.5	1.0	0.2	−1.8	1.1	0.4	−0.5	−0.1
Other advanced economies	—	0.4	0.1	1.0	−0.1	−0.1	0.1	0.8	1.2	0.2	0.4	0.2
Memorandum												
Industrial countries	−0.1	−0.1	0.1	0.3	—	0.1	—	0.2	−0.8	−0.8	−0.2	−0.1
European Union	−0.1	0.1	−0.1	1.2	0.4	0.3	0.2	0.4	−0.8	−0.6	0.3	—
Euro area	−0.1	0.2	—	1.5	0.3	0.3	0.4	0.5	−0.6	−0.5	0.5	0.2
Newly industrialized Asian economies	0.4	1.0	−0.6	0.6	−0.7	0.2	−0.1	1.9	6.5	1.4	0.7	0.5

[1]Changes expressed as percent of GDP in the preceding period.

Table 4. Advanced Economies: Unemployment, Employment, and Real Per Capita GDP
(Percent)

	Ten-Year Averages[1]		1992	1993	1994	1995	1996	1997	1998	1999	2000	2001
	1982–91	1992–2001										
Unemployment rate												
Advanced economies	**7.0**	**6.7**	**7.1**	**7.5**	**7.4**	**7.0**	**7.0**	**6.8**	**6.7**	**6.3**	**5.9**	**5.7**
Major industrial countries	6.9	6.5	7.1	7.2	7.0	6.6	6.7	6.4	6.2	6.0	5.7	5.8
United States[2]	7.0	5.4	7.5	6.9	6.1	5.6	5.4	4.9	4.5	4.2	4.1	4.4
Japan	2.5	3.7	2.2	2.5	2.9	3.1	3.3	3.4	4.1	4.7	5.0	5.3
Germany	7.3	8.1	6.3	7.6	8.2	7.9	8.6	9.5	9.0	8.3	7.9	7.6
France	9.5	11.2	10.3	11.6	12.3	11.7	12.4	12.5	11.7	11.3	9.8	8.8
Italy[3]	10.5	11.1	10.7	10.1	11.1	11.6	11.6	11.7	11.8	11.4	10.7	10.1
United Kingdom[4]	9.0	6.6	9.6	10.2	9.2	8.0	7.3	5.5	4.7	4.3	3.9	4.0
Canada	9.7	9.0	11.2	11.4	10.4	9.4	9.6	9.1	8.3	7.6	6.6	6.5
Other advanced economies	7.2	7.6	7.4	8.7	8.8	8.2	8.1	7.8	8.1	7.3	6.2	5.7
Spain	18.6	19.2	18.4	22.7	24.2	22.9	22.2	20.8	18.8	15.9	14.0	12.6
Netherlands	8.2	5.0	5.4	6.5	7.6	7.1	6.6	5.5	4.1	3.2	2.3	2.0
Belgium	9.4	8.9	7.3	8.8	10.0	9.9	9.7	9.4	9.5	9.0	8.3	7.7
Sweden	2.5	6.6	5.3	8.2	8.0	7.7	8.1	8.0	6.5	5.6	4.6	4.0
Austria	3.4	4.0	3.4	4.0	3.8	3.9	4.3	4.4	4.7	4.4	3.5	3.5
Denmark	9.2	8.4	10.9	12.0	11.9	10.1	8.6	7.8	6.4	5.6	5.4	5.5
Finland	4.9	12.6	11.7	16.4	16.6	15.4	14.6	12.6	11.4	10.3	9.0	8.2
Greece	7.6	10.2	8.7	9.7	9.6	9.1	9.8	9.7	10.8	11.7	11.5	11.3
Portugal	7.0	5.5	4.1	5.5	6.8	7.2	7.3	6.7	5.0	4.4	4.1	4.0
Ireland	15.1	9.9	15.2	15.5	14.1	12.1	11.5	9.8	7.4	5.6	4.5	4.0
Luxembourg	1.5	2.7	1.6	2.1	2.7	3.0	3.3	3.3	3.3	2.9	2.7	2.3
Switzerland	0.7	3.6	2.6	4.5	4.7	4.2	4.7	5.2	3.9	2.7	2.0	1.9
Norway	3.4	4.2	5.9	5.9	5.4	4.7	4.1	3.3	2.4	3.2	3.6	3.6
Israel	7.1	8.4	11.2	10.0	7.8	6.9	6.7	7.7	8.5	8.9	8.4	8.2
Iceland	1.1	3.3	3.0	4.4	4.8	5.0	4.3	2.8	2.9	1.9	1.8	1.8
Korea	3.3	3.5	2.4	2.8	2.4	2.0	2.0	2.6	6.8	6.3	4.2	3.5
Australia	8.1	8.6	10.8	10.9	9.8	8.5	8.6	8.6	8.0	7.2	6.7	6.6
Taiwan Province of China	2.1	2.2	1.5	1.5	1.6	1.8	2.6	2.7	2.7	2.9	2.5	2.3
Hong Kong SAR	2.5	3.2	2.0	2.0	1.9	3.2	2.8	2.2	4.7	6.1	4.0	3.1
Singapore	3.3	2.7	2.7	2.7	2.6	2.7	2.0	1.8	3.2	3.5	2.9	2.5
New Zealand	6.0	7.4	10.3	9.5	8.2	6.3	6.1	6.7	7.5	6.8	6.4	6.4
Memorandum												
Industrial countries	7.3	7.1	7.5	8.0	7.9	7.4	7.4	7.1	6.8	6.4	6.0	6.0
European Union	9.3	9.6	9.3	10.6	11.0	10.5	10.6	10.3	9.5	8.8	8.0	7.5
Euro area	9.7	10.4	9.4	10.8	11.6	11.2	11.5	11.5	10.8	9.9	9.0	8.3
Newly industrialized Asian economies	2.9	3.1	2.1	2.4	2.2	2.1	2.2	2.6	5.4	5.2	3.7	3.1
Growth in employment												
Advanced economies	**1.2**	**0.9**	**—**	**—**	**1.1**	**1.1**	**1.0**	**1.5**	**1.1**	**1.3**	**1.3**	**0.9**
Major industrial countries	1.2	0.8	0.1	0.1	1.0	0.8	0.8	1.5	1.0	1.0	1.0	0.7
United States	1.6	1.5	0.7	1.5	2.3	1.5	1.4	2.2	1.5	1.5	1.2	0.6
Japan	1.3	0.1	1.1	0.2	0.1	0.1	0.5	1.1	–0.6	–0.8	–0.2	0.2
Germany	0.7	0.2	0.2	–1.4	–0.2	0.1	–0.3	–0.2	0.9	1.1	1.0	0.7
France	0.3	0.9	–1.1	–1.0	0.9	0.7	—	1.0	1.8	1.8	2.6	1.9
Italy	0.5	–0.2	–1.1	–4.1	–1.6	–0.6	0.5	0.4	1.1	1.3	1.3	1.0
United Kingdom	0.7	0.3	–2.8	–0.7	0.8	0.9	1.0	1.9	1.5	0.7	0.2	—
Canada	1.3	1.8	–0.7	0.8	2.0	1.9	0.8	2.3	2.6	2.8	2.9	2.5
Other advanced economies	1.5	1.3	–0.2	–0.4	1.3	2.2	1.5	1.6	1.2	2.1	2.0	1.6
Memorandum												
Industrial countries	1.1	0.9	–0.2	–0.2	0.9	1.0	0.9	1.5	1.4	1.2	1.2	0.8
European Union	0.7	0.5	–1.2	–1.8	–0.1	0.7	0.6	1.0	2.0	1.6	1.6	1.1
Euro area	0.7	0.6	–0.8	–2.1	–0.3	0.6	0.5	0.9	2.0	1.9	1.9	1.4
Newly industrialized Asian economies	2.6	1.4	1.9	1.5	2.8	2.3	1.7	1.7	–2.1	1.5	1.6	1.5

Table 4 *(concluded)*

| | Ten-Year Averages[1] | | 1992 | 1993 | 1994 | 1995 | 1996 | 1997 | 1998 | 1999 | 2000 | 2001 |
	1982–91	1992–2001										
Growth in real per capita GDP												
Advanced economies	**2.5**	**2.3**	**1.4**	**0.8**	**2.6**	**2.1**	**2.5**	**2.8**	**1.8**	**2.7**	**3.6**	**2.7**
Major industrial countries	2.3	2.1	1.3	0.6	2.4	1.7	2.4	2.6	1.9	2.4	3.4	2.5
United States	1.9	2.8	1.9	1.5	3.1	1.8	2.6	3.4	3.3	3.4	4.4	2.4
Japan	3.5	0.9	0.7	—	0.4	1.2	4.8	1.3	–2.8	—	1.3	1.6
Germany	2.4	1.4	1.5	–1.8	2.1	1.4	0.5	1.2	2.1	1.5	2.9	3.2
France	2.0	1.7	1.1	–1.3	1.6	1.4	0.7	1.6	2.8	2.5	3.2	3.2
Italy	2.1	1.8	1.1	0.5	1.9	2.7	1.0	1.6	1.5	1.5	3.2	3.1
United Kingdom	2.4	2.5	–0.3	2.1	4.0	2.4	2.2	4.6	2.5	1.9	2.9	2.7
Canada	1.1	2.1	–0.2	1.2	3.5	1.7	–0.6	3.3	3.3	3.5	3.7	1.9
Other advanced economies	3.1	3.0	1.7	1.3	3.8	3.4	3.0	3.5	1.3	4.0	4.5	3.6
Memorandum												
Industrial countries	2.3	2.2	1.2	0.5	2.4	1.8	2.3	2.7	2.2	2.5	3.4	2.5
European Union	2.3	2.0	0.8	–0.4	2.5	2.1	1.4	2.5	2.6	2.3	3.3	3.2
Euro area	2.3	1.9	1.1	–0.8	2.1	2.0	1.2	2.1	2.6	2.3	3.3	3.3
Newly industrialized Asian economies	6.9	4.6	5.0	5.3	6.2	5.8	5.0	4.3	–3.6	6.6	6.8	5.0

[1]Compound annual rate of change for employment and per capita GDP; arithmetic average for unemployment rate.
[2]The projections for unemployment have been adjusted to reflect the new survey techniques adopted by the U.S. Bureau of Labor Statistics in January 1994.
[3]New series starting in 1993, reflecting revisions in the labor force surveys and the definition of unemployment to bring data in line with those of other advanced economies.
[4]Unemployment rate is on a claimant count basis.

Table 5. Developing Countries: Real GDP

(Annual percent change)

| | Ten-Year Averages | | 1992 | 1993 | 1994 | 1995 | 1996 | 1997 | 1998 | 1999 | 2000 | 2001 |
	1982–91	1992–2001										
Developing countries	**4.3**	**5.6**	**6.3**	**6.4**	**6.7**	**6.1**	**6.5**	**5.7**	**3.5**	**3.8**	**5.6**	**5.7**
Regional groups												
Africa	2.3	2.6	−0.7	0.2	2.3	3.1	5.7	2.8	3.1	2.2	3.4	4.4
Sub-Sahara	2.0	2.6	−1.1	0.6	1.8	3.9	5.2	3.4	2.4	2.1	3.3	4.3
Excluding Nigeria and South Africa	2.3	2.9	−1.2	−0.1	1.5	4.7	5.5	4.0	3.5	2.8	3.5	4.6
Asia	6.9	7.5	9.4	9.3	9.6	9.0	8.3	6.5	4.1	5.9	6.7	6.6
Excluding China and India	5.0	4.5	6.5	6.2	6.9	7.5	6.9	3.7	−5.0	3.1	4.8	5.1
Middle East and Europe	3.3	3.7	5.7	3.8	0.6	4.3	4.5	5.1	3.1	0.8	4.7	4.1
Western Hemisphere	1.8	3.4	3.6	4.1	5.0	1.7	3.6	5.4	2.2	0.3	4.3	4.5
Analytical groups												
By source of export earnings												
Fuel	2.3	2.8	6.0	1.1	0.3	2.8	3.3	4.1	2.3	1.0	4.4	3.5
Manufactures	5.5	6.7	7.5	8.2	8.3	7.2	7.3	6.4	4.8	5.1	6.5	6.3
Nonfuel primary products	2.2	4.6	3.6	3.9	5.2	6.7	5.7	5.4	3.1	2.3	4.5	5.5
Services, income, and private transfers	3.9	4.3	0.1	4.0	3.8	4.9	5.2	5.2	4.7	5.3	4.7	4.8
Diversified	2.9	3.5	4.8	4.7	5.8	4.0	5.7	4.4	−1.6	−0.4	3.2	4.3
By external financing source												
Net creditor countries	1.4	2.8	6.1	2.2	1.8	2.7	2.1	4.1	1.2	0.4	4.4	3.4
Net debtor countries	4.4	5.7	6.3	6.5	6.8	6.2	6.6	5.8	3.5	3.9	5.7	5.7
Official financing	2.7	3.7	1.8	1.7	2.5	5.2	5.4	4.0	3.8	3.4	4.3	5.0
Private financing	4.8	6.1	6.9	7.5	7.7	6.6	6.9	6.1	3.6	4.0	5.9	6.0
Diversified financing	2.6	4.0	4.8	2.4	3.5	4.4	5.2	4.2	3.0	3.2	4.9	4.2
Net debtor countries by debt-servicing experience												
Countries with arrears and/or rescheduling during 1994–98	2.7	3.5	2.8	3.7	4.6	5.1	5.0	4.2	−0.8	2.1	4.2	4.6
Other net debtor countries	5.3	6.5	7.8	7.7	7.7	6.7	7.3	6.4	5.1	4.5	6.2	6.1
Other groups												
Heavily indebted poor countries	2.3	4.0	1.4	1.7	2.8	6.1	6.2	4.9	3.7	3.4	4.3	5.2
Least developed countries	2.2	3.9	1.0	1.3	2.3	6.2	5.6	4.4	4.0	4.0	4.8	5.3
Middle East and north Africa	2.9	3.5	4.7	1.9	2.5	2.6	4.6	3.6	3.7	2.8	4.6	3.9
Memorandum												
Real per capita GDP												
Developing countries	2.0	3.9	3.8	4.4	4.8	4.3	4.9	4.2	1.9	2.2	4.1	4.2
Regional groups												
Africa	−0.5	0.2	−3.1	−2.3	−0.2	1.1	3.1	0.4	0.7	−0.2	1.0	2.0
Asia	5.0	6.1	7.6	7.6	8.0	7.4	6.7	5.1	3.0	4.6	5.4	5.4
Middle East and Europe	0.1	1.1	−0.7	1.5	−2.0	−1.1	5.5	3.2	1.0	−1.4	2.6	2.2
Western Hemisphere	−0.3	1.7	1.5	2.2	3.2	1.1	1.0	4.2	−0.1	−1.2	2.7	3.0

Table 6. Developing Countries—by Country: Real GDP[1]

(Annual percent change)

	Average 1982–91	1992	1993	1994	1995	1996	1997	1998	1999
Africa	**2.3**	**−0.7**	**0.2**	**2.3**	**3.1**	**5.7**	**2.8**	**3.1**	**2.2**
Algeria	2.2	1.6	−2.1	−0.9	3.8	3.8	1.1	5.1	3.3
Angola	2.7	−5.8	−24.0	1.3	7.1	7.9	6.2	3.1	2.7
Benin	1.3	4.0	3.5	4.4	4.6	5.5	5.7	4.5	4.9
Botswana	10.8	3.0	2.0	3.4	4.7	6.8	7.6	6.2	7.3
Burkina Faso	3.5	2.5	−0.8	1.2	4.0	6.0	4.8	6.2	5.8
Burundi	3.8	0.7	−5.9	−3.7	−7.3	−8.4	0.4	4.5	−0.8
Cameroon	1.3	−3.1	−3.2	−2.5	3.3	5.0	5.1	5.0	4.4
Cape Verde	2.0	−6.3	12.7	11.5	3.8	3.8	4.7	7.6	7.9
Central African Republic	0.7	−6.2	0.1	5.0	7.6	−4.6	5.7	4.8	3.4
Chad	6.6	2.4	−2.1	5.7	1.3	2.4	4.5	6.0	−0.7
Comoros	1.3	8.5	3.0	−5.3	−3.9	−0.4	—	—	1.0
Congo, Dem. Rep. of	−0.3	−10.5	−13.5	−3.9	0.7	0.9	−8.2	−3.5	−14.0
Congo, Rep. of	5.8	2.6	−1.0	−5.5	4.0	4.3	−0.6	3.7	−3.0
Côte d'Ivoire	0.6	−0.2	−0.2	2.0	7.1	6.8	6.8	4.5	2.8
Djibouti	0.1	−0.2	−3.9	−2.9	−3.6	−3.7	0.7	0.8	1.3
Equatorial Guinea	1.6	10.7	6.3	5.1	14.3	29.1	71.2	22.0	15.1
Eritrea	...	...	−2.5	9.8	2.9	6.8	7.9	3.9	3.0
Ethiopia	1.3	−3.7	12.0	1.6	6.2	10.6	5.2	−0.5	6.3
Gabon	2.7	−3.3	2.4	3.4	7.0	5.1	4.3	3.7	−9.6
Gambia, The	4.7	4.4	6.1	3.8	−3.4	5.3	5.4	4.1	5.3
Ghana	2.9	3.9	5.0	3.2	4.0	4.6	4.2	4.7	4.4
Guinea	3.6	4.6	4.3	4.4	4.6	4.8	4.5	3.2	4.5
Guinea-Bissau	2.9	1.1	2.1	3.2	4.4	4.6	5.4	−28.1	8.7
Kenya	4.0	−0.8	0.4	2.6	4.4	4.1	2.1	2.1	1.5
Lesotho	4.9	4.6	3.7	3.7	5.9	9.4	4.6	−3.8	0.5
Liberia	...	...	...	...	...	...	...	...	...
Madagascar	0.9	1.2	2.1	—	1.7	2.1	3.7	3.9	4.7
Malawi	3.6	−7.3	9.7	−10.3	16.7	7.3	3.8	3.3	4.5
Mali	2.1	8.4	−2.4	2.2	6.4	2.1	6.8	3.4	1.1
Mauritania	4.4	1.7	5.5	4.6	4.5	4.7	4.8	3.5	4.1
Mauritius	6.4	4.8	6.7	4.3	3.5	5.1	5.5	5.6	5.4
Morocco	4.8	−4.0	−1.0	10.4	−6.6	12.2	−2.2	6.8	−0.7
Mozambique, Rep. of	0.1	−8.1	8.7	7.5	4.3	7.1	11.1	12.0	8.8
Namibia	0.8	7.2	−1.6	6.2	3.2	2.1	2.6	3.0	2.9
Niger	0.2	−6.5	1.4	4.0	2.6	3.4	3.3	8.3	2.5
Nigeria	3.5	2.6	2.2	−0.6	2.6	6.4	3.1	1.9	1.1
Rwanda	1.5	6.6	−8.3	−49.5	32.8	15.8	12.8	9.5	5.9
São Tomé and Príncipe	−0.3	0.7	1.1	2.2	2.0	1.5	1.0	2.5	2.5
Senegal	2.7	2.2	−2.2	2.9	5.2	5.1	5.0	5.7	5.1
Seychelles	4.3	6.9	6.5	−0.8	−0.6	4.7	4.3	2.3	2.0
Sierra Leone	−0.2	−9.6	0.1	3.5	−10.0	5.0	−17.6	−0.8	−8.1
Somalia	...	...	...	...	...	...	...	...	...
South Africa	0.9	−2.1	1.2	3.2	3.1	4.2	2.5	0.6	1.2
Sudan	2.6	3.0	3.8	1.8	8.9	8.2	6.6	5.1	5.9
Swaziland	6.5	1.3	3.3	3.5	3.0	3.6	4.0	2.7	3.1
Tanzania	3.4	0.6	1.2	1.6	3.6	4.5	3.5	3.3	4.6
Togo	1.4	−4.0	−15.1	15.0	7.8	9.6	4.2	−2.2	2.4
Tunisia	3.4	7.8	2.2	3.3	2.4	7.0	5.4	5.0	6.2
Uganda	3.4	3.2	8.6	5.6	10.9	7.7	4.8	5.5	7.8
Zambia	0.2	2.0	−0.1	−13.3	−2.3	6.5	3.5	−2.2	2.4
Zimbabwe	3.7	−9.0	1.1	7.1	−0.6	8.7	3.7	2.5	−0.1

Table 6 *(continued)*

	Average 1982–91	1992	1993	1994	1995	1996	1997	1998	1999
Asia	**6.9**	**9.4**	**9.3**	**9.6**	**9.0**	**8.3**	**6.5**	**4.1**	**5.9**
Afghanistan, Islamic State of	...	...	...	...	...	...	...	...	...
Bangladesh	4.4	4.8	4.3	4.5	4.8	5.0	5.3	5.0	5.2
Bhutan	7.0	4.4	5.0	5.1	6.9	6.0	5.7	4.6	6.5
Brunei Darussalam	...	−1.1	0.5	1.8	3.0	3.6	4.1	1.0	2.5
Cambodia	...	4.8	7.5	7.0	7.7	7.0	1.0	1.0	4.0
China	9.5	14.2	13.5	12.6	10.5	9.6	8.8	7.8	7.1
Fiji	2.0	4.8	3.5	4.2	2.4	3.3	3.6	4.0	4.5
India	5.4	4.2	5.0	6.7	7.6	7.1	4.7	6.3	6.4
Indonesia	5.5	7.2	7.3	7.5	8.2	8.0	4.5	−13.0	0.3
Kiribati	1.0	−1.6	0.8	7.2	6.5	2.6	3.3	6.1	2.5
Lao P.D. Republic	4.5	7.0	5.9	8.1	7.1	6.9	6.5	5.0	6.5
Malaysia	6.3	8.9	9.9	9.2	9.8	10.0	7.3	−7.4	5.6
Maldives	10.2	6.3	6.2	6.6	7.2	6.5	6.2	6.0	6.0
Marshall Islands	...	0.1	5.4	2.7	−1.9	−13.1	−5.3	−4.3	−1.8
Micronesia, Fed. States of	...	−1.2	5.7	−0.9	1.3	−0.5	−3.8	−2.8	−2.0
Myanmar	0.6	9.7	5.9	6.8	7.2	7.0	7.0	7.0	7.0
Nepal	4.6	4.1	3.8	8.2	3.5	5.3	5.0	3.0	3.9
Pakistan	6.0	7.8	1.9	3.9	4.1	4.9	1.0	2.6	2.7
Papua New Guinea	2.3	11.8	16.6	1.9	−2.6	2.9	−2.4	1.4	3.8
Philippines	1.3	0.3	2.1	4.4	4.8	5.8	5.2	−0.6	3.3
Samoa	13.7	4.1	1.7	−0.1	6.8	6.1	1.6	1.3	2.5
Solomon Islands	1.7	9.5	2.0	5.4	10.5	3.5	−2.3	0.5	−0.5
Sri Lanka	4.2	4.3	6.9	5.6	5.5	3.8	6.4	4.7	4.3
Thailand	8.1	8.1	8.4	9.0	8.9	5.9	−1.7	−10.2	4.2
Tonga	2.3	0.3	3.7	5.0	4.8	−1.4	−4.4	−1.5	—
Vanuatu	3.1	−0.7	4.5	1.3	2.3	0.4	0.6	6.0	−2.5
Vietnam	5.9	8.6	8.1	8.8	9.5	9.3	8.2	3.5	4.2
Middle East and Europe	**3.3**	**5.7**	**3.8**	**0.6**	**4.3**	**4.5**	**5.1**	**3.1**	**0.8**
Bahrain	3.5	6.7	12.9	−0.2	3.9	4.1	3.1	4.8	2.9
Cyprus	6.0	9.7	0.7	5.9	6.1	1.9	2.4	5.0	4.5
Egypt	5.4	−4.2	2.9	4.2	4.5	4.9	5.5	5.6	6.0
Iran, Islamic Republic of	3.4	6.1	2.1	0.9	2.9	5.5	3.4	2.2	2.5
Iraq	...	...	...	...	...	...	...	...	...
Jordan	2.0	17.0	5.8	7.6	3.9	1.0	1.3	1.7	1.6
Kuwait	−5.7	77.4	34.2	8.4	1.2	1.2	2.3	2.0	−2.4
Lebanon	−2.8	4.5	7.0	8.0	6.5	4.0	4.0	3.0	−1.0
Libya	0.6	−4.2	−4.6	−2.2	−1.6	1.2	1.3	−3.0	2.0
Malta	4.1	6.7	4.0	5.0	7.3	3.2	3.7	3.1	3.5
Oman	7.5	8.5	6.1	3.8	4.8	2.9	6.2	2.9	2.5
Qatar	−1.5	9.7	−0.6	2.3	2.9	4.8	24.0	12.3	7.6
Saudi Arabia	1.2	2.8	−0.6	0.5	0.5	1.4	2.7	1.6	−1.0
Syrian Arab Republic	1.9	10.6	5.0	7.7	5.8	4.4	1.8	7.6	−1.2
Turkey	4.8	5.0	7.7	−4.7	8.1	6.9	7.6	3.1	−5.0
United Arab Emirates	−0.1	3.8	5.1	8.4	19.0	4.8	8.1	0.2	0.5
Yemen, Republic of	...	4.9	2.9	−0.5	8.6	5.6	5.2	2.5	3.3

Table 6 *(concluded)*

	Average 1982–91	1992	1993	1994	1995	1996	1997	1998	1999
Western Hemisphere	**1.8**	**3.6**	**4.1**	**5.0**	**1.7**	**3.6**	**5.4**	**2.2**	**0.3**
Antigua and Barbuda	6.7	0.8	5.1	6.2	−5.0	6.1	5.6	3.9	3.2
Argentina	0.4	10.3	6.3	5.8	−2.8	5.5	8.1	3.9	−3.1
Bahamas, The	2.9	−2.0	1.7	0.9	0.3	4.2	3.3	3.0	6.0
Barbados	0.7	−5.7	0.8	4.0	2.9	4.1	2.6	4.8	2.9
Belize	5.1	10.2	3.3	1.8	3.3	2.0	3.6	4.5	4.5
Bolivia	0.6	1.6	4.3	4.7	4.7	4.4	4.4	4.7	2.5
Brazil	2.1	−0.5	4.9	5.9	4.2	2.7	3.6	−0.1	1.0
Chile	3.2	12.3	7.0	5.7	10.6	7.4	7.4	3.4	−1.1
Colombia	3.4	4.0	5.4	5.8	5.2	2.1	3.4	0.5	−4.5
Costa Rica	2.7	9.0	6.3	4.9	4.0	0.3	5.8	8.0	8.4
Dominica	4.3	2.1	1.7	1.4	2.3	2.1	0.6	4.8	3.5
Dominican Republic	2.0	8.0	3.0	4.3	4.8	7.3	8.2	7.3	8.3
Ecuador	2.2	3.6	2.0	4.4	2.3	2.0	3.4	0.4	−7.3
El Salvador	1.4	7.4	7.4	6.0	6.4	1.8	4.3	3.2	2.0
Grenada	5.8	1.1	−1.2	3.3	3.1	2.9	4.2	5.8	6.2
Guatemala	1.2	4.8	3.9	4.0	4.9	3.0	4.1	5.1	3.5
Guyana	−1.9	7.8	8.2	8.5	5.0	7.9	6.2	−1.7	3.0
Haiti	0.3	−13.2	−2.4	−8.3	4.4	2.7	1.1	3.0	2.0
Honduras	2.5	5.6	6.2	−1.3	4.1	3.6	5.1	2.9	−1.9
Jamaica	2.8	1.6	1.5	1.0	0.2	−1.5	−1.7	−0.5	—
Mexico	1.4	3.6	2.0	4.4	−6.2	5.2	6.8	4.9	3.5
Netherlands Antilles	0.1	3.7	0.3	2.4	—	−2.4	3.0	3.0	3.0
Nicaragua	−1.9	0.4	−0.2	3.3	4.2	5.0	4.9	4.2	6.7
Panama	1.4	8.2	5.5	2.9	1.8	2.8	4.5	4.1	3.2
Paraguay	2.8	1.8	4.1	3.1	4.7	1.3	3.5	3.5	4.0
Peru	−1.0	−1.6	6.4	13.1	7.3	2.5	6.8	0.3	3.8
St. Kitts and Nevis	5.6	3.5	5.0	5.5	3.7	6.1	6.6	3.6	2.0
St. Lucia	6.6	7.1	2.0	2.1	4.1	1.4	2.1	2.9	3.1
St. Vincent and the Grenadines	6.2	5.9	2.3	−2.0	8.3	1.2	3.1	5.7	4.0
Suriname	−0.8	4.0	−9.5	−5.4	7.1	6.7	5.6	1.9	5.0
Trinidad and Tobago	−2.6	−1.7	−1.4	3.6	4.0	3.8	3.1	4.8	6.8
Uruguay	0.6	7.9	2.7	7.3	−1.5	5.4	4.9	4.6	−3.2
Venezuela	1.9	6.1	0.3	−2.4	4.0	−0.2	6.4	−0.1	−7.2

[1]For many countries, figures for recent years are IMF staff estimates. Data for some countries are for fiscal years.

Table 7. Countries in Transition: Real GDP[1]
(Annual percent change)

	Average 1982–91	1992	1993	1994	1995	1996	1997	1998	1999
Central and eastern Europe	...	**−8.8**	**−3.9**	**−3.0**	**1.6**	**1.7**	**2.1**	**2.0**	**1.3**
Albania	−2.6	−7.2	9.6	9.4	8.9	9.1	−7.0	7.9	7.2
Belarus	...	−9.7	−7.0	−12.6	−10.4	2.8	10.5	11.6	−2.4
Bosnia and Herzegovina	...	...	...	...	32.4	85.8	39.9	12.8	8.6
Bulgaria	0.3	−7.3	−1.5	1.7	2.2	−10.9	−6.9	3.5	2.4
Croatia	...	...	−8.0	5.9	5.7	5.9	6.8	2.5	−0.3
Czech Republic	...	...	0.1	2.2	5.9	4.8	−1.0	−2.2	−0.2
Czechoslovakia, former	0.3	−8.5	...	...	...	...	...	...	...
Estonia	...	−21.6	−8.2	−2.0	4.3	3.9	10.6	4.7	−1.1
Hungary	−0.4	−3.1	−0.6	2.9	1.5	1.3	4.6	4.9	4.5
Latvia	...	−35.2	−16.1	0.6	−0.8	3.3	8.6	3.9	0.1
Lithuania	...	−21.3	−16.2	−9.8	3.3	4.7	7.3	5.1	−4.1
Macedonia, former Yugoslav Rep. of	...	...	−7.5	−1.8	−1.1	1.2	1.4	2.9	2.7
Moldova	...	−29.7	−1.2	−31.2	−1.4	−7.8	1.3	−6.5	−4.4
Poland	0.2	2.6	3.8	5.2	7.0	6.0	6.8	4.8	4.1
Romania	−0.8	−8.8	1.5	3.9	7.1	3.9	−6.1	−5.4	−3.2
Slovak Republic	...	...	−3.7	4.9	6.9	6.6	6.5	4.4	1.9
Slovenia	...	...	2.8	5.3	4.1	3.5	4.6	3.9	4.9
Ukraine	...	−17.0	−14.2	−22.9	−12.2	−10.0	−3.0	−1.9	−0.4
Yugoslavia, former	−2.3	−34.0	...	...	...	...	...	...	...
Russia	...	**−19.4**	**−10.4**	**−11.6**	**−4.2**	**−3.4**	**0.9**	**−4.9**	**3.2**
Transcaucasus and central Asia	...	**−14.1**	**−11.0**	**−11.5**	**−5.0**	**1.3**	**2.6**	**2.5**	**4.6**
Armenia	...	−52.6	−14.1	5.4	6.9	5.9	3.3	7.2	3.3
Azerbaijan	...	−22.7	−23.1	−19.7	−11.8	1.3	5.8	10.0	7.4
Georgia	...	−44.9	−29.3	−10.4	2.6	10.5	10.7	2.9	3.3
Kazakhstan	...	−5.3	−9.2	−12.6	−8.2	0.5	1.7	−1.9	1.7
Kyrgyz Republic	...	−13.9	−15.5	−19.8	−5.8	7.1	9.9	2.1	3.6
Mongolia	3.5	−9.5	−3.0	2.3	6.3	2.4	4.0	3.5	3.3
Tajikistan	...	−28.9	−11.1	−21.4	−12.5	−4.4	1.7	5.3	3.7
Turkmenistan	...	−5.3	−10.0	−17.3	−7.2	−6.7	−11.3	5.0	16.0
Uzbekistan	...	−11.1	−2.3	−4.2	−0.9	1.6	2.5	4.3	4.4

[1]Data for some countries refer to real net material product (NMP) or are estimates based on NMP. For many countries, figures for recent years are IMF staff estimates. The figures should be interpreted only as indicative of broad orders of magnitude because reliable, comparable data are not generally available. In particular, the growth of output of new private enterprises of the informal economy is not fully reflected in the recent figures.

Table 8. Summary of Inflation
(Percent)

	Ten-Year Averages 1982–91	Ten-Year Averages 1992–2001	1992	1993	1994	1995	1996	1997	1998	1999	2000	2001
GDP deflators												
Advanced economies	**4.9**	**2.0**	**3.2**	**2.7**	**2.2**	**2.3**	**1.8**	**1.7**	**1.4**	**1.0**	**1.5**	**1.8**
United States	3.7	2.0	2.4	2.4	2.1	2.2	1.9	1.9	1.3	1.5	2.2	2.3
European Union	6.1	2.5	4.4	3.5	2.7	3.1	2.5	1.9	2.0	1.5	1.6	1.8
Japan	1.8	–0.1	1.7	0.6	0.2	–0.6	–1.4	0.3	0.3	–0.9	–1.1	0.4
Other advanced economies	8.7	2.5	3.8	3.8	3.3	3.4	2.9	2.2	1.5	0.3	2.2	1.6
Consumer prices												
Advanced economies	**4.9**	**2.3**	**3.5**	**3.1**	**2.6**	**2.6**	**2.4**	**2.1**	**1.5**	**1.4**	**2.3**	**2.1**
United States	4.1	2.6	3.0	3.0	2.6	2.8	2.9	2.3	1.6	2.2	3.2	2.6
European Union	5.7	2.5	4.6	3.8	3.0	2.9	2.5	1.8	1.4	1.4	2.1	1.9
Japan	1.9	0.6	1.7	1.2	0.7	–0.1	0.1	1.7	0.6	–0.3	–0.2	0.5
Other advanced economies	8.8	2.8	3.8	3.4	3.3	3.8	3.2	2.4	2.6	1.0	2.3	2.5
Developing countries	**45.1**	**21.0**	**42.8**	**48.7**	**54.7**	**23.2**	**15.3**	**9.7**	**10.1**	**6.6**	**6.2**	**5.2**
Regional groups												
Africa	19.5	25.2	47.1	39.0	54.8	35.2	30.2	13.6	9.1	11.8	12.7	8.6
Asia	9.7	7.6	8.6	10.8	16.0	13.2	8.3	4.7	7.5	2.4	2.4	3.3
Middle East and Europe	21.2	24.8	26.5	26.6	33.2	39.2	26.9	25.4	25.3	20.4	17.4	9.5
Western Hemisphere	163.0	50.2	150.3	194.6	200.3	36.0	21.6	13.4	10.2	9.3	8.9	7.0
Analytical groups												
By source of export earnings												
Fuel	13.6	21.4	22.1	26.2	31.8	42.9	32.0	16.2	14.7	12.3	10.9	9.4
Nonfuel	50.5	21.0	45.7	51.8	57.6	21.3	13.6	9.0	9.7	6.1	5.8	4.8
By external financing source												
Net creditor countries	2.7	3.5	4.2	5.5	3.9	5.7	3.8	1.8	1.7	1.2	3.1	4.2
Net debtor countries	47.1	21.6	44.5	50.5	56.8	23.9	15.6	9.9	10.4	6.8	6.3	5.2
Official financing	33.7	24.7	59.2	37.4	64.1	30.2	22.8	11.3	8.1	11.1	10.5	7.1
Private financing	53.7	21.7	46.8	55.7	61.0	21.8	13.8	9.2	10.0	5.7	5.3	4.4
Diversified financing	22.5	20.0	24.5	28.3	25.8	33.4	28.2	15.0	13.6	11.5	11.5	10.6
Net debtor countries by debt-servicing experience												
Countries with arrears and/or rescheduling during 1994–98	97.3	52.8	152.3	196.9	217.6	40.1	20.3	10.9	16.7	12.4	10.3	7.7
Other net debtor countries	27.4	11.0	14.1	14.1	18.6	18.1	13.9	9.5	8.3	4.9	5.0	4.4
Countries in transition	**15.5**	**117.9**	**788.9**	**634.4**	**274.1**	**133.5**	**42.4**	**27.3**	**21.8**	**43.8**	**18.3**	**12.5**
Central and eastern Europe	...	74.7	278.4	366.9	151.7	72.2	32.1	38.4	18.7	20.6	18.8	11.5
Excluding Belarus and Ukraine	...	34.2	104.8	85.2	47.5	24.8	23.3	41.4	17.0	11.0	11.8	7.5
Russia	...	155.3	1,734.7	874.7	307.4	197.4	47.6	14.7	27.7	85.9	18.6	13.8
Transcaucasus and central Asia	...	192.0	949.2	1,428.7	1,800.7	265.5	80.9	32.9	13.0	15.4	14.4	12.8
Memorandum												
Median inflation rate												
Advanced economies	5.4	2.2	3.2	3.0	2.4	2.4	2.1	1.7	1.6	1.4	2.2	2.4
Developing countries	9.4	7.2	10.0	9.5	10.6	10.1	7.4	6.7	5.7	3.9	3.7	4.0
Countries in transition	11.9	155.5	839.1	472.3	132.1	39.3	24.1	14.8	9.8	8.0	8.9	6.9

Table 9. Advanced Economies: GDP Deflators and Consumer Prices

(Annual percent change)

	Ten-Year Averages		1992	1993	1994	1995	1996	1997	1998	1999	2000	2001	Fourth Quarter[1]		
	1982–91	1992–2001											1999	2000	2001
GDP deflators															
Advanced economies	**4.9**	**2.0**	**3.2**	**2.7**	**2.2**	**2.3**	**1.8**	**1.7**	**1.4**	**1.0**	**1.5**	**1.8**	...	...	...
Major industrial countries	4.0	1.7	2.8	2.3	1.8	1.9	1.5	1.6	1.2	1.0	1.4	1.8	0.9	1.8	1.8
United States	3.7	2.0	2.4	2.4	2.1	2.2	1.9	1.9	1.3	1.5	2.2	2.3	1.5	2.6	2.3
Japan	1.8	−0.1	1.7	0.6	0.2	−0.6	−1.4	0.3	0.3	−0.9	−1.1	0.4	−1.4	−0.5	0.7
Germany	2.8	1.9	5.0	3.7	2.5	2.0	1.0	0.8	1.1	0.9	0.4	1.5	0.4	1.6	1.1
France	5.3	1.3	2.0	2.3	1.7	1.6	1.4	1.4	0.9	0.3	0.6	0.8	0.3	0.8	0.8
Italy	9.5	3.2	4.5	3.9	3.5	5.0	5.3	2.4	2.7	1.5	1.7	1.7	1.4	1.7	1.6
United Kingdom	5.9	2.7	4.0	2.7	1.5	2.5	3.3	2.9	3.0	2.5	2.0	2.3	2.3	1.8	2.5
Canada	4.2	1.5	1.3	1.5	1.1	2.3	1.7	1.0	−0.6	1.6	3.2	2.0	3.1	3.0	1.9
Other advanced economies	8.8	3.0	5.0	4.4	3.8	3.9	2.9	2.4	2.3	1.0	2.3	1.9	...	...	...
Spain	8.9	3.7	6.9	4.3	3.8	5.0	3.2	2.1	2.3	3.1	3.4	2.5	...	...	...
Netherlands	1.7	2.1	2.3	1.9	2.3	1.8	1.2	2.0	1.9	1.3	3.1	3.1	...	...	...
Belgium	4.1	1.8	3.6	3.7	1.8	1.8	1.2	1.3	1.6	0.9	0.9	1.3	...	...	...
Sweden	7.9	1.7	1.0	2.6	2.4	3.5	1.4	1.2	1.3	0.5	1.7	1.8	...	...	...
Austria	3.3	2.0	4.3	2.8	2.8	2.3	1.3	1.6	0.6	0.6	1.5	1.7	...	...	...
Denmark	5.2	2.2	2.9	1.4	1.7	1.8	2.5	1.6	2.1	2.7	3.1	1.9	...	...	...
Finland	6.1	1.8	0.9	2.3	2.0	4.1	−0.2	2.1	3.1	0.7	1.6	1.4	...	...	...
Greece	18.4	7.8	14.8	14.5	11.2	11.2	7.3	6.7	4.9	2.9	3.1	2.5	...	...	...
Portugal	16.9	5.0	10.6	7.0	6.1	7.4	3.5	3.2	4.3	3.2	2.2	3.0	...	...	...
Ireland	5.6	4.0	2.8	5.2	1.7	2.7	2.3	3.5	5.6	6.2	5.5	4.7	...	...	...
Luxembourg	3.2	2.2	1.3	0.8	4.9	4.3	1.7	3.3	1.5	1.1	1.3	1.4	...	...	...
Switzerland	3.7	1.2	2.7	2.7	1.6	1.1	0.4	−0.1	0.2	0.7	1.4	1.4	...	...	...
Norway	5.2	2.9	−0.4	2.1	−0.2	3.1	4.3	3.0	−0.8	6.6	12.6	−0.2	...	...	...
Israel	80.8	8.5	12.3	11.6	12.2	9.4	11.4	8.8	6.7	6.4	2.5	3.8	...	...	...
Iceland	28.6	3.5	4.4	2.8	2.0	2.9	2.0	3.5	5.8	4.0	4.3	3.5	...	...	...
Korea	6.9	4.1	7.6	7.1	7.7	7.1	3.9	3.1	5.1	−1.6	1.7	0.1	...	...	...
Australia	6.8	1.4	1.4	1.5	1.0	1.5	2.0	1.4	0.4	1.1	2.2	1.6	...	...	...
Taiwan Province of China	2.3	2.1	3.9	3.5	1.9	1.9	2.7	1.9	2.1	−0.7	1.2	2.7	...	...	...
Hong Kong SAR	8.0	3.1	9.7	8.5	6.9	2.6	5.9	5.8	0.9	−5.6	−4.7	2.0	...	...	...
Singapore	2.5	1.2	1.5	3.3	2.9	2.6	1.3	0.7	−1.8	−1.3	1.4	2.1	...	...	...
New Zealand	8.9	1.9	1.7	2.6	1.5	2.8	1.9	—	1.4	0.1	2.8	3.9	...	...	...
Memorandum															
Industrial countries	4.5	1.9	3.0	2.5	1.9	2.1	1.6	1.6	1.3	1.2	1.6	1.8	...	...	...
European Union	6.1	2.5	4.4	3.5	2.7	3.1	2.5	1.9	2.0	1.5	1.6	1.8	...	...	...
Euro area	5.8	2.3	4.3	3.5	2.7	3.0	2.3	1.6	1.7	1.3	1.4	1.7	...	...	...
Newly industrialized Asian economies	5.4	3.2	6.4	5.9	5.5	4.7	3.6	2.9	3.1	−1.8	0.8	1.3	...	...	...
Consumer prices															
Advanced economies	**4.9**	**2.3**	**3.5**	**3.1**	**2.6**	**2.6**	**2.4**	**2.1**	**1.5**	**1.4**	**2.3**	**2.1**	...	...	...
Major industrial countries	4.2	2.2	3.2	2.8	2.2	2.3	2.2	2.0	1.3	1.4	2.2	1.9	1.5	2.2	1.9
United States	4.1	2.6	3.0	3.0	2.6	2.8	2.9	2.3	1.6	2.2	3.2	2.6	2.6	3.1	2.5
Japan	1.9	0.6	1.7	1.2	0.7	−0.1	0.1	1.7	0.6	−0.3	−0.2	0.5	−1.0	0.3	0.4
Germany[2]	2.3	2.1	5.0	4.5	2.7	1.7	1.2	1.5	0.6	0.7	1.7	1.5	1.1	1.5	1.5
France	5.3	1.5	2.4	2.1	1.7	1.8	2.1	1.3	0.7	0.6	1.5	1.1	−1.0	1.3	1.2
Italy	8.5	3.2	5.3	4.6	4.1	5.2	3.9	1.7	1.7	1.7	2.5	1.6	2.0	2.2	1.6
United Kingdom[3]	5.6	2.8	4.7	3.0	2.4	2.8	3.0	2.8	2.7	2.3	2.0	2.4	2.2	2.2	2.5
Canada	5.3	1.6	1.5	1.8	0.2	1.9	1.6	1.6	1.0	1.7	2.3	2.1	2.4	2.3	2.0
Other advanced economies	8.4	3.1	4.8	4.2	4.1	3.8	3.2	2.3	2.4	1.3	2.4	2.6	...	...	...
Memorandum															
Industrial countries	4.6	2.2	3.4	3.0	2.4	2.4	2.2	2.0	1.3	1.5	2.3	2.0	...	...	...
European Union	5.7	2.5	4.6	3.8	3.0	2.9	2.5	1.8	1.4	1.4	2.1	1.9	...	...	...
Euro area	5.4	2.4	4.4	3.8	3.0	2.8	2.3	1.6	1.1	1.2	2.1	1.7	...	...	...
Newly industrialized Asian economies	4.2	3.7	5.9	4.6	5.7	4.6	4.3	3.4	4.5	—	1.4	2.6	...	...	...

[1]From fourth quarter of preceding year.
[2]Based on the revised consumer price index for united Germany introduced in September 1995.
[3]Retail price index excluding mortgage interest.

Table 10. Advanced Economies: Hourly Earnings, Productivity, and Unit Labor Costs in Manufacturing

(Annual percent change)

	Ten-Year Averages		1992	1993	1994	1995	1996	1997	1998	1999	2000	2001
	1982–91	1992–2001										
Hourly earnings												
Advanced economies	**6.6**	**3.7**	**5.9**	**4.0**	**3.4**	**3.1**	**3.0**	**3.4**	**3.4**	**3.5**	**3.4**	**3.5**
Major industrial countries	5.6	3.4	5.4	3.6	2.9	2.7	2.4	3.3	3.6	3.2	3.5	3.3
United States	4.6	3.6	4.6	2.8	2.8	2.1	1.3	3.7	5.8	4.9	4.3	4.0
Japan	4.0	2.0	4.6	2.8	2.4	2.4	1.7	3.1	1.0	−0.5	1.3	1.7
Germany	4.9	3.8	9.5	6.8	2.1	4.0	4.3	1.1	1.7	2.4	2.7	3.1
France	6.8	3.0	4.8	3.9	3.7	1.6	2.6	3.2	2.6	2.6	3.2	2.3
Italy	11.2	3.5	6.7	5.4	3.1	4.7	5.8	4.6	−2.0	2.4	2.5	2.5
United Kingdom	9.9	4.7	6.6	4.7	5.0	4.4	4.3	4.2	4.6	4.0	4.8	4.1
Canada	5.0	2.3	3.5	2.1	1.6	1.4	3.1	0.9	2.2	0.1	4.5	3.4
Other advanced economies	10.8	5.0	8.1	5.9	5.9	5.2	5.4	4.0	2.9	4.6	3.3	4.3
Memorandum												
Industrial countries	6.0	3.5	5.5	3.7	3.0	2.9	2.6	3.3	3.5	3.2	3.5	3.4
European Union	7.9	3.9	7.2	5.4	3.6	3.9	4.1	3.2	2.2	3.0	3.4	3.3
Euro area	7.4	3.7	7.3	5.5	3.1	3.6	3.9	2.8	1.6	2.7	3.1	3.1
Newly industrialized Asian economies	13.2	7.4	14.1	9.2	11.4	7.8	10.1	5.5	1.0	8.0	2.0	5.3
Productivity												
Advanced economies	**3.4**	**3.7**	**3.2**	**2.1**	**4.9**	**3.8**	**3.4**	**4.4**	**2.3**	**4.7**	**4.7**	**3.1**
Major industrial countries	3.3	3.6	3.3	1.8	4.6	3.6	3.5	4.6	2.3	4.6	4.8	3.1
United States	3.0	4.5	5.1	2.2	3.1	3.9	4.0	5.0	5.3	6.4	6.2	4.0
Japan	3.2	1.7	−3.7	−1.0	3.3	4.7	3.8	4.8	−4.2	3.5	4.4	2.1
Germany	3.7	4.5	4.2	2.9	8.7	4.5	5.4	7.0	4.5	2.5	2.4	2.8
France	3.8	4.1	4.4	0.4	9.0	3.9	2.9	6.4	4.0	3.3	3.5	3.3
Italy	3.1	2.7	4.4	0.6	6.0	3.6	3.7	2.7	−1.9	1.1	4.5	2.2
United Kingdom	5.7	2.2	6.4	4.9	4.5	−0.5	−1.0	0.5	−0.3	3.6	2.3	1.4
Canada	2.3	2.0	4.1	6.3	4.9	1.1	0.8	−0.3	−3.4	1.9	3.7	1.3
Other advanced economies	3.4	3.8	2.7	3.4	6.3	4.3	3.0	3.7	2.5	5.0	4.3	2.9
Memorandum												
Industrial countries	3.2	3.5	3.2	2.0	4.8	3.5	3.3	4.3	2.3	4.2	4.4	2.9
European Union	3.8	3.4	4.1	2.7	7.5	3.3	2.8	4.1	2.2	2.4	2.9	2.4
Euro area	3.5	3.7	3.7	2.3	8.0	4.0	3.8	4.8	2.6	2.2	3.0	2.5
Newly industrialized Asian economies	7.8	6.7	4.2	3.5	6.4	8.0	6.5	5.9	2.3	14.3	10.5	5.9
Unit labor costs												
Advanced economies	**3.2**	**—**	**2.7**	**1.9**	**−1.4**	**−0.6**	**−0.4**	**−0.9**	**1.2**	**−1.1**	**−1.2**	**0.4**
Major industrial countries	2.2	−0.2	2.1	1.8	−1.6	−0.9	−1.1	−1.2	1.4	−1.3	−1.3	0.2
United States	1.6	−0.8	−0.5	0.6	−0.2	−1.7	−2.6	−1.3	0.5	−1.4	−1.8	—
Japan	0.8	0.3	8.6	3.8	−0.9	−2.2	−2.0	−1.6	5.4	−3.9	−3.0	−0.3
Germany	1.1	−0.7	5.1	3.8	−6.1	−0.4	−1.1	−5.5	−2.7	−0.1	0.3	0.3
France	2.9	−1.0	0.3	3.6	−4.9	−2.3	−0.3	−3.0	−1.3	−0.7	−0.3	−1.0
Italy	7.8	0.8	2.2	4.8	−2.7	1.1	2.0	1.8	−0.2	1.3	−1.9	0.3
United Kingdom	3.9	2.5	0.2	−0.2	0.6	4.9	5.3	3.7	4.9	0.4	2.5	2.6
Canada	2.6	0.3	−0.5	−3.9	−3.2	0.3	2.4	1.3	5.7	−1.8	0.7	2.0
Other advanced economies	7.3	1.0	4.9	2.3	−0.5	0.7	2.1	0.2	0.5	−0.1	−0.9	1.4
Memorandum												
Industrial countries	2.7	—	2.4	1.7	−1.7	−0.6	−0.6	−1.0	1.3	−0.9	−0.8	0.5
European Union	4.1	0.5	3.0	2.7	−3.5	0.6	1.3	−0.8	0.1	0.6	0.5	0.9
Euro area	3.8	—	3.5	3.2	−4.5	−0.4	0.1	−1.9	−1.0	0.6	0.1	0.5
Newly industrialized Asian economies	4.3	0.2	7.3	4.6	3.2	−1.1	2.3	−0.7	−0.8	−4.6	−7.0	−0.4

Table 11. Developing Countries: Consumer Prices
(Annual percent change)

| | Ten-Year Averages | | 1992 | 1993 | 1994 | 1995 | 1996 | 1997 | 1998 | 1999 | 2000 | 2001 |
	1982–91	1992–2001										
Developing countries	**45.1**	**21.0**	**42.8**	**48.7**	**54.7**	**23.2**	**15.3**	**9.7**	**10.1**	**6.6**	**6.2**	**5.2**
Regional groups												
Africa	19.5	25.2	47.1	39.0	54.8	35.2	30.2	13.6	9.1	11.8	12.7	8.6
Sub-Sahara	22.7	30.5	56.9	47.9	68.7	40.7	36.6	16.6	10.7	14.9	16.1	10.6
Excluding Nigeria and South Africa	28.5	46.2	91.6	73.7	121.7	57.3	58.8	23.3	13.0	22.3	25.1	13.8
Asia	9.7	7.6	8.6	10.8	16.0	13.2	8.3	4.7	7.5	2.4	2.4	3.3
Excluding China and India	13.2	8.7	9.5	8.3	8.0	9.1	7.7	6.4	21.2	9.0	3.7	5.1
Middle East and Europe	21.2	24.8	26.5	26.6	33.2	39.2	26.9	25.4	25.3	20.4	17.4	9.5
Western Hemisphere	163.0	50.2	150.3	194.6	200.3	36.0	21.6	13.4	10.2	9.3	8.9	7.0
Analytical groups												
By source of export earnings												
Fuel	13.6	21.4	22.1	26.2	31.8	42.9	32.0	16.2	14.7	12.3	10.9	9.4
Manufactures	49.5	23.9	54.2	67.6	75.6	23.8	13.6	8.7	7.4	4.6	5.0	4.1
Nonfuel primary products	70.9	28.9	67.8	46.7	62.7	29.8	28.7	16.5	11.5	14.6	14.6	10.8
Services, income, and private transfers	22.4	8.3	21.7	11.7	9.9	10.5	7.6	5.5	4.6	3.8	4.3	4.3
Diversified	52.0	11.0	16.7	13.8	11.2	10.7	9.0	7.9	20.4	9.7	5.9	5.4
By external financing source												
Net creditor countries	2.7	3.5	4.2	5.5	3.9	5.7	3.8	1.8	1.7	1.2	3.1	4.2
Net debtor countries	47.1	21.6	44.5	50.5	56.8	23.9	15.6	9.9	10.4	6.8	6.3	5.2
Official financing	33.7	24.7	59.2	37.4	64.1	30.2	22.8	11.3	8.1	11.1	10.5	7.1
Private financing	53.7	21.7	46.8	55.7	61.0	21.8	13.8	9.2	10.0	5.7	5.3	4.4
Diversified financing	22.5	20.0	24.5	28.3	25.8	33.4	28.2	15.0	13.6	11.5	11.5	10.6
Net debtor countries by debt-servicing experience												
Countries with arrears and/or rescheduling during 1994–98	97.3	52.8	152.3	196.9	217.6	40.1	20.3	10.9	16.7	12.4	10.3	7.7
Other net debtor countries	27.4	11.0	14.1	14.1	18.6	18.1	13.9	9.5	8.3	4.9	5.0	4.4
Other groups												
Heavily indebted poor countries	46.4	39.3	79.8	60.4	92.4	49.5	49.2	20.7	14.1	19.2	19.8	12.5
Least developed countries	29.0	41.5	87.5	68.9	102.5	50.5	51.5	20.0	13.2	20.1	20.7	11.7
Middle East and north Africa	14.5	12.8	18.0	16.9	18.3	24.5	14.4	9.1	8.5	7.0	6.5	6.1
Memorandum												
Median												
Developing countries	9.4	7.2	10.0	9.5	10.6	10.1	7.4	6.7	5.7	3.9	3.7	4.0
Regional groups												
Africa	9.8	9.1	11.1	9.7	24.7	12.3	7.7	7.4	5.8	3.6	4.3	3.8
Asia	8.2	6.8	9.1	6.7	8.2	8.4	7.5	6.7	8.1	5.2	3.5	4.8
Middle East and Europe	6.1	4.1	6.2	5.0	4.1	5.1	7.0	3.6	2.9	2.0	2.5	3.1
Western Hemisphere	14.3	7.5	12.1	10.7	8.3	10.2	7.4	7.2	5.1	4.9	5.2	4.5

Table 12. Developing Countries—by Country: Consumer Prices[1]
(Annual percent change)

	Average 1982–91	1992	1993	1994	1995	1996	1997	1998	1999
Africa	**19.5**	**47.1**	**39.0**	**54.8**	**35.2**	**30.2**	**13.6**	**9.1**	**11.8**
Algeria	10.7	31.7	20.5	29.0	29.8	18.7	5.7	4.9	2.6
Angola	8.1	299.1	1,379.5	949.8	2,672.2	4,146.0	111.2	107.4	248.2
Benin	1.4	5.9	0.4	38.5	14.5	4.9	3.8	5.8	0.3
Botswana	11.8	16.2	14.3	10.5	10.5	10.1	8.8	6.5	7.2
Burkina Faso	1.6	−2.0	0.6	24.7	7.8	6.1	2.3	5.0	−1.1
Burundi	7.2	4.5	9.7	14.7	19.4	26.4	31.1	12.5	3.6
Cameroon	6.1	1.9	−3.7	12.7	25.8	6.6	5.2	—	2.9
Cape Verde	10.8	13.4	5.8	3.3	8.4	6.0	8.6	4.4	4.4
Central African Republic	2.8	−0.8	−2.9	24.5	19.2	3.7	1.6	−1.9	−1.5
Chad	3.5	−3.8	31.4	41.3	9.1	11.8	5.9	4.4	−8.3
Comoros	2.7	−1.4	2.0	25.3	7.1	1.4	1.0	1.0	3.0
Congo, Dem. Rep. of	113.2	4,129.2	1,893.1	23,760.5	541.8	616.8	198.5	29.1	284.9
Congo, Rep. of	−0.5	−3.9	5.0	42.9	8.6	10.2	13.2	1.8	3.1
Côte d'Ivoire	4.2	4.2	2.1	26.0	14.3	2.7	5.6	4.5	0.7
Djibouti	4.7	3.4	4.4	6.5	4.5	2.6	2.4	2.0	2.0
Equatorial Guinea	16.6	1.0	1.6	38.9	11.4	6.0	3.0	3.0	3.0
Eritrea	...	...	4.6	11.6	10.7	9.3	1.3	16.6	8.3
Ethiopia	6.1	21.0	10.0	1.2	13.4	0.9	−6.4	3.7	4.2
Gabon	5.0	−10.8	0.6	36.1	10.0	4.5	4.1	2.3	−0.7
Gambia, The	17.3	12.0	5.9	4.0	4.0	4.8	3.1	1.1	2.5
Ghana	34.5	10.1	24.9	24.9	59.5	46.6	27.9	19.3	12.4
Guinea	29.6	16.6	7.2	4.2	5.6	3.0	1.9	5.1	4.5
Guinea-Bissau	55.9	69.4	48.2	15.2	45.4	50.7	49.1	8.0	−0.9
Kenya	12.3	27.3	45.9	28.8	1.5	9.0	11.2	6.6	3.5
Lesotho	14.5	17.0	13.8	7.2	9.9	9.1	8.5	7.8	6.0
Liberia	...	...	...	...	...	...	...	...	...
Madagascar	15.5	15.3	9.3	39.0	49.0	19.8	4.5	6.2	9.9
Malawi	15.7	23.2	22.8	34.7	83.1	37.7	9.1	29.8	44.8
Mali	1.8	−5.9	−0.6	24.8	12.4	6.5	−0.7	4.1	−1.2
Mauritania	8.3	10.1	9.3	4.1	6.5	4.7	4.5	8.0	4.0
Mauritius	8.0	2.9	8.9	9.4	6.1	5.8	7.9	5.3	5.6
Morocco	6.8	5.7	5.2	5.1	6.1	3.0	1.0	2.7	0.7
Mozambique, Rep. of	45.0	45.1	42.3	63.1	54.4	44.6	6.4	0.6	3.1
Namibia	12.6	17.7	8.5	10.8	10.0	8.0	8.8	6.2	8.6
Niger	−0.2	−4.6	−0.3	35.5	10.9	5.3	3.0	4.6	2.9
Nigeria	18.7	44.6	57.2	57.0	72.8	29.3	8.5	10.0	6.6
Rwanda	5.6	9.5	12.5	64.0	22.0	8.9	11.7	6.8	−2.4
São Tomé and Príncipe	21.1	33.7	25.5	51.2	36.8	42.0	69.0	42.1	16.3
Senegal	5.1	−0.1	−0.6	32.0	8.1	2.8	1.7	2.4	0.8
Seychelles	2.2	3.2	1.3	1.8	−0.3	−1.1	0.6	1.0	1.5
Sierra Leone	76.5	65.5	22.2	24.2	26.0	23.1	14.9	35.5	29.6
Somalia	...	...	...	...	...	...	...	...	...
South Africa	14.7	13.9	9.7	9.0	8.6	7.4	8.6	6.9	5.2
Sudan	51.8	117.6	101.3	115.5	68.4	132.8	46.7	17.1	16.0
Swaziland	13.3	7.6	12.0	13.8	12.3	6.4	7.1	8.1	6.1
Tanzania	30.3	21.9	23.6	37.1	26.5	21.0	16.1	12.6	7.9
Togo	3.5	1.6	−0.1	35.3	15.8	4.6	7.1	1.0	−0.9
Tunisia	8.3	5.8	4.0	4.6	6.3	3.8	3.7	3.1	2.7
Uganda	98.9	42.2	30.0	6.5	6.1	7.5	7.8	5.8	−0.2
Zambia	53.7	165.7	183.3	54.6	34.9	43.1	24.4	24.5	26.8
Zimbabwe	14.9	42.1	27.6	22.2	22.6	21.4	18.8	32.3	58.2

Table 12 *(continued)*

	Average 1982–91	1992	1993	1994	1995	1996	1997	1998	1999
Asia	**9.7**	**8.6**	**10.8**	**16.0**	**13.2**	**8.3**	**4.7**	**7.5**	**2.4**
Afghanistan, Islamic State of	...	...	...	...	...	...	...	...	...
Bangladesh	9.5	3.5	3.1	6.3	7.7	4.5	4.8	8.0	6.2
Bhutan	9.8	16.0	8.9	8.1	10.7	7.0	7.0	7.0	7.0
Brunei Darussalam	...	1.3	4.3	2.4	6.0	2.0	1.7	—	1.0
Cambodia	...	75.0	114.3	−0.5	7.7	6.8	8.0	14.8	7.9
China	7.1	6.4	14.7	24.1	17.1	8.3	2.8	−0.8	−1.4
Fiji	6.6	8.2	6.5	4.9	5.2	0.6	—	2.2	2.2
India	8.9	11.8	6.4	10.2	10.2	9.0	7.2	13.2	4.7
Indonesia	8.3	7.5	9.7	8.5	9.4	7.9	6.6	58.0	20.8
Kiribati	2.8	4.2	6.1	5.3	4.1	−1.5	2.2	4.7	2.0
Lao P.D. Republic	40.8	9.8	6.3	6.8	19.4	13.0	19.3	81.0	36.0
Malaysia	2.7	4.7	3.5	3.7	3.4	3.5	2.7	5.3	2.8
Maldives	5.2	16.8	20.1	3.4	5.5	6.2	7.2	5.0	2.3
Marshall Islands	...	10.3	5.0	5.6	8.3	9.6	4.8	4.0	3.0
Micronesia, Fed. States of	...	5.0	6.0	4.0	4.0	4.0	3.0	3.0	3.0
Myanmar	15.1	22.3	33.6	22.4	28.9	20.0	10.0	10.0	10.0
Nepal	7.8	19.3	5.9	9.1	8.7	9.2	8.1	8.4	11.4
Pakistan	7.0	9.4	9.8	11.3	13.0	10.8	11.8	7.8	5.7
Papua New Guinea	5.7	4.3	5.0	2.9	17.3	11.6	3.9	13.6	14.9
Philippines	13.6	8.6	6.9	8.4	8.0	9.0	5.9	9.7	6.7
Samoa	4.2	9.0	1.7	12.1	−2.9	5.4	6.9	2.2	3.0
Solomon Islands	11.6	9.2	9.2	13.3	9.6	11.8	8.1	12.4	8.3
Sri Lanka	11.7	11.4	11.7	8.4	7.7	15.9	9.6	9.4	4.7
Thailand	3.8	4.1	3.4	5.1	5.8	5.9	5.6	8.1	0.3
Tonga	10.3	8.7	3.1	2.4	0.3	2.8	1.8	2.9	3.0
Vanuatu	6.8	4.1	3.6	2.3	2.2	0.9	2.9	3.2	2.0
Vietnam	132.6	37.8	8.4	9.5	16.9	5.6	3.1	7.8	4.2
Middle East and Europe	**21.2**	**26.5**	**26.6**	**33.2**	**39.2**	**26.9**	**25.4**	**25.3**	**20.4**
Bahrain	0.7	−0.3	2.6	0.4	3.1	−0.1	4.5	−0.4	−1.3
Cyprus	4.3	6.5	4.9	4.7	2.6	3.0	3.6	2.2	1.8
Egypt	18.4	21.1	11.2	9.0	9.4	7.0	6.2	4.7	3.8
Iran, Islamic Republic of	18.0	24.4	22.9	35.2	49.4	23.2	17.3	20.0	20.4
Iraq	...	...	...	...	...	...	...	...	...
Jordan	5.4	4.0	3.3	3.6	2.3	6.5	3.0	3.1	0.6
Kuwait	4.0	−0.5	0.4	2.5	2.7	3.6	0.7	0.5	1.9
Lebanon	80.2	99.8	24.7	8.0	10.6	8.9	7.7	4.5	0.2
Libya	7.7	18.0	23.0	14.5	11.0	13.0	8.0	7.0	6.0
Malta	1.4	1.8	4.0	4.1	4.0	2.4	3.1	2.4	2.5
Oman	1.6	1.0	1.1	−0.7	−1.1	0.3	−0.2	−0.9	0.8
Qatar	3.3	3.0	−0.9	1.4	3.0	7.1	2.7	2.9	2.0
Saudi Arabia	—	−0.4	0.8	0.6	5.0	0.9	−0.4	−0.2	−1.2
Syrian Arab Republic	21.8	3.4	23.6	3.9	7.7	8.9	1.9	−0.4	−2.1
Turkey	48.5	70.1	66.1	106.3	93.7	82.3	85.7	84.6	64.9
United Arab Emirates	4.0	6.2	5.0	4.0	5.1	2.6	2.1	2.0	2.0
Yemen, Republic of	...	50.6	62.3	71.8	62.5	41.8	4.3	11.2	7.0

Table 12 *(concluded)*

	Average 1982–91	1992	1993	1994	1995	1996	1997	1998	1999
Western Hemisphere	**163.0**	**150.3**	**194.6**	**200.3**	**36.0**	**21.6**	**13.4**	**10.2**	**9.3**
Antigua and Barbuda	3.8	3.0	3.1	6.5	2.7	3.0	0.3	3.3	1.6
Argentina	452.7	24.9	10.6	4.2	3.4	0.2	0.8	0.9	−1.2
Bahamas, The	5.1	5.7	2.7	1.3	2.1	1.4	0.5	1.3	1.5
Barbados	4.9	6.0	1.2	−0.1	2.4	1.8	3.6	1.7	0.5
Belize	3.4	2.4	1.4	2.5	2.9	6.3	1.1	−0.9	−1.0
Bolivia	220.0	12.1	8.5	7.9	10.2	89.1	91.5	91.9	93.8
Brazil	384.7	1,022.5	1,927.4	2,075.8	66.0	15.8	6.9	3.2	4.9
Chile	20.5	15.4	12.7	11.4	8.2	7.4	6.1	5.1	3.3
Colombia	23.9	27.1	22.5	22.8	20.9	20.8	18.5	18.7	10.9
Costa Rica	24.8	21.8	9.8	13.5	23.2	17.6	13.3	11.7	10.1
Dominica	3.9	5.3	1.6	—	1.3	1.7	2.4	0.9	1.6
Dominican Republic	28.8	4.3	5.3	8.3	12.5	5.4	8.3	4.8	6.5
Ecuador	39.7	54.6	45.0	27.3	22.9	24.4	30.6	36.1	52.2
El Salvador	19.0	11.2	18.5	10.6	10.1	9.8	4.5	2.5	0.6
Grenada	3.6	3.8	2.8	2.6	2.2	2.8	1.3	1.4	0.5
Guatemala	14.9	10.2	13.4	12.5	8.4	11.0	9.2	6.6	5.3
Guyana	37.6	28.2	12.0	12.4	12.2	7.1	3.6	4.6	7.5
Haiti	8.8	21.3	18.8	37.4	30.2	21.9	16.2	10.0	10.0
Honduras	10.2	8.8	10.7	18.2	29.5	23.8	20.2	13.7	11.6
Jamaica	22.7	57.5	24.3	33.2	21.7	21.5	9.1	8.1	6.3
Mexico	64.4	15.5	9.8	7.0	35.0	34.4	20.6	15.9	16.6
Netherlands Antilles	2.9	1.5	1.9	1.9	2.7	3.5	3.5	3.5	3.5
Nicaragua	898.4	40.5	20.4	7.7	11.2	11.6	9.2	13.0	11.2
Panama	1.2	1.8	0.5	1.3	0.9	1.3	1.3	0.6	1.3
Paraguay	22.8	15.2	18.2	20.5	13.4	9.8	8.3	7.0	6.0
Peru	381.1	73.5	48.6	23.7	11.1	11.5	8.5	7.3	3.5
St. Kitts and Nevis	2.8	2.9	1.8	1.4	3.0	2.0	8.9	3.6	4.1
St. Lucia	3.1	4.6	0.8	2.7	5.9	0.9	—	2.8	1.0
St. Vincent and the Grenadines	3.8	3.5	4.3	1.0	1.7	4.4	0.4	2.1	1.0
Suriname	14.5	43.7	143.4	368.5	235.5	−0.8	7.2	20.8	28.7
Trinidad and Tobago	10.1	6.5	13.2	3.7	5.3	−2.7	3.6	5.7	3.4
Uruguay	67.3	68.5	54.2	44.7	42.2	28.3	19.8	10.8	5.7
Venezuela	25.1	31.4	38.1	60.8	59.9	99.9	50.0	35.8	23.6

[1]For many countries, figures for recent years are IMF staff estimates. Data for some countries are for fiscal years.

Table 13. Countries in Transition: Consumer Prices[1]

(Annual percent change)

	Average 1982–91	1992	1993	1994	1995	1996	1997	1998	1999
Central and eastern Europe	...	**278.4**	**366.9**	**151.7**	**72.2**	**32.1**	**38.4**	**18.7**	**20.6**
Albania	3.1	226.0	85.0	22.6	7.8	12.7	33.2	20.6	0.4
Belarus	...	969.0	1,190.2	2,434.1	709.3	52.7	63.8	73.0	293.7
Bosnia and Herzegovina	...	...	...	...	−4.0	−25.0	14.0	10.8	5.0
Bulgaria	21.3	82.0	72.8	96.0	62.1	123.0	1,082.2	22.3	2.1
Croatia	...	...	1,516.6	97.5	2.0	3.5	3.6	5.7	4.2
Czech Republic	...	...	20.8	10.0	9.1	8.8	8.5	10.6	2.1
Czechoslovakia, former	7.0	11.0	...	...	...	...	...	...	...
Estonia	...	1,069.0	89.8	47.7	29.0	23.1	11.2	8.2	3.3
Hungary	13.5	22.8	22.4	18.8	28.3	23.5	18.3	14.3	10.0
Latvia	...	951.3	109.1	35.8	25.1	17.6	8.0	4.7	2.4
Lithuania	...	1,021.0	410.4	72.1	39.5	24.7	8.8	5.1	0.8
Macedonia, former Yugoslav Rep. of	...	...	338.7	127.5	15.7	2.3	2.6	−0.1	−0.7
Moldova	...	1,276.0	788.5	329.6	30.2	23.5	11.8	7.7	39.3
Poland	77.7	43.0	35.3	32.2	27.9	19.9	14.9	11.8	7.3
Romania	22.5	210.4	256.1	136.7	32.3	38.8	154.8	59.1	45.8
Slovak Republic	...	...	23.0	13.4	9.9	5.8	6.1	6.7	10.7
Slovenia	...	...	32.9	21.0	13.5	9.9	8.4	8.0	6.1
Ukraine	...	1,210.0	4,734.9	891.2	376.4	80.2	15.9	10.6	22.7
Yugoslavia, former	155.9	6,146.6	...	...	...	...	...	...	...
Russia	...	**1,734.7**	**874.7**	**307.4**	**197.4**	**47.6**	**14.7**	**27.7**	**85.9**
Transcaucasus and central Asia	...	**949.2**	**1,428.7**	**1,800.7**	**265.5**	**80.9**	**32.9**	**13.0**	**15.4**
Armenia	...	824.5	3,731.8	5,273.4	176.7	18.7	14.0	8.7	0.7
Azerbaijan	...	912.6	1,129.7	1,664.0	412.0	19.7	3.5	−0.8	−8.3
Georgia	...	887.4	3,125.4	15,606.5	162.7	39.4	7.1	3.6	19.1
Kazakhstan	...	1,515.7	1,662.3	1,879.9	176.3	39.1	17.4	7.3	8.4
Kyrgyz Republic	...	853.8	772.4	190.1	39.1	31.9	23.4	10.3	35.7
Mongolia	2.1	202.6	268.4	87.6	56.8	46.8	36.6	9.4	7.6
Tajikistan	...	1,156.7	2,194.9	350.4	610.0	418.2	88.0	43.2	27.6
Turkmenistan	...	492.9	3,102.4	1,748.3	1,005.2	992.4	83.7	16.8	23.5
Uzbekistan	...	645.2	534.2	1,568.3	304.6	54.0	70.9	29.0	29.1

[1]For many countries, inflation for the earlier years is measured on the basis of a retail price index. Consumer price indices with a broader and more up-to-date coverage are typically used for more recent years.

Table 14. Summary Financial Indicators
(Percent)

	1992	1993	1994	1995	1996	1997	1998	1999	2000	2001
Advanced economies										
Central government fiscal balance[1]										
Advanced economies	−4.1	−4.4	−3.7	−3.3	−2.7	−1.5	−1.7	−1.4	−0.6	−0.6
United States	−4.9	−4.2	−3.0	−2.6	−1.8	−0.6	0.6	1.3	2.0	2.0
European Union	−5.0	−6.0	−5.2	−4.6	−3.9	−2.4	−1.7	−0.9	0.3	−0.4
Euro area	−4.3	−5.2	−4.6	−4.2	−3.8	−2.4	−2.2	−1.5	−0.4	−0.7
Japan	−1.7	−2.7	−3.5	−4.0	−4.3	−4.0	−9.2	−11.4	−11.4	−10.4
Other advanced economies	−2.5	−2.1	−1.5	−1.0	−0.2	0.6	−0.2	−0.2	0.2	0.6
General government fiscal balance[1]										
Advanced economies	−4.3	−4.7	−4.0	−3.8	−3.1	−1.7	−1.3	−0.9	−0.2	−0.1
United States	−6.0	−5.1	−3.8	−3.3	−2.4	−1.3	—	0.7	1.4	1.5
European Union	−5.2	−6.3	−5.6	−5.4	−4.3	−2.4	−1.7	−0.7	0.7	—
Euro area	−4.7	−5.7	−5.2	−5.2	−4.4	−2.6	−2.2	−1.3	0.1	−0.4
Japan	1.5	−1.6	−2.3	−3.6	−4.2	−3.3	−4.7	−7.4	−8.2	−6.3
Other advanced economies	−3.3	−2.6	−1.9	−1.1	−0.2	0.7	−0.4	0.2	0.8	1.0
General government structural balance[2]										
Advanced economies	−3.9	−3.6	−3.2	−3.1	−2.4	−1.2	−0.6	−0.4	−0.5	−0.4
Growth of broad money										
Advanced economies	3.0	3.7	2.5	4.3	4.9	5.0	6.8	. . .	. . .	. . .
United States	1.8	1.4	0.6	3.9	4.5	5.7	8.5	6.1	. . .	. . .
Euro area	7.1	6.3	2.3	5.7	4.0	4.4	4.6	7.2	. . .	. . .
Japan	−0.4	1.4	2.9	3.2	2.9	3.8	4.4	2.6	. . .	. . .
Other advanced economies	8.1	7.7	9.4	8.3	8.5	6.3	10.3	. . .	. . .	. . .
Short-term interest rates[3]										
United States	3.5	3.1	4.4	5.7	5.1	5.2	4.9	4.8	6.1	6.7
Japan	4.0	2.4	1.9	0.8	0.3	0.3	0.2	—	0.2	0.5
Euro area	11.1	8.6	6.3	6.1	4.6	4.1	3.9	2.9	4.4	5.1
LIBOR	3.9	3.4	5.1	6.1	5.6	5.9	5.6	5.5	6.8	7.4
Developing countries										
Central government fiscal balance[1]										
Weighted average	−3.0	−3.2	−2.7	−2.6	−2.3	−2.6	−4.0	−4.5	−3.5	−3.1
Median	−3.7	−4.0	−3.7	−3.3	−2.8	−2.6	−3.0	−3.1	−2.6	−1.8
General government fiscal balance[1]										
Weighted average	−3.6	−3.7	−3.8	−3.4	−2.9	−3.2	−4.7	−5.2	−3.9	−3.5
Median	−3.7	−3.9	−3.7	−3.3	−2.8	−2.5	−3.2	−3.2	−2.3	−1.7
Growth of broad money										
Weighted average	108.0	115.7	94.3	25.2	23.2	20.6	16.5	14.7	13.4	11.8
Median	17.9	16.2	18.8	16.3	14.4	15.1	9.7	11.1	10.0	9.3
Countries in transition										
Central government fiscal balance[1]	−9.7	−6.2	−7.4	−4.6	−4.6	−4.6	−3.6	−2.2	0.2	−1.5
General government fiscal balance[1]	−14.2	−6.8	−7.3	−4.6	−5.8	−5.3	−5.0	−2.4	0.3	−2.1
Growth of broad money	429.0	424.4	192.9	75.0	32.1	32.5	20.1	38.3	25.6	19.4

[1]Percent of GDP.
[2]Percent of potential GDP.
[3]For the United States, three-month treasury bills; for Japan, three-month certificates of deposit; for LIBOR, London interbank offered rate on six-month U.S. dollar deposits.

Table 15. Advanced Economies: General and Central Government Fiscal Balances and Balances Excluding Social Security Transactions[1]

(Percent of GDP)

	1992	1993	1994	1995	1996	1997	1998	1999	2000	2001
General government fiscal balance										
Advanced economies	**−4.3**	**−4.7**	**−4.0**	**−3.8**	**−3.1**	**−1.7**	**−1.3**	**−0.9**	**−0.2**	**−0.1**
Major industrial countries	−4.5	−5.0	−4.2	−4.1	−3.5	−2.0	−1.4	−1.1	−0.3	−0.3
United States	−6.0	−5.1	−3.8	−3.3	−2.4	−1.3	—	0.7	1.4	1.5
Japan	1.5	−1.6	−2.3	−3.6	−4.2	−3.3	−4.7	−7.4	−8.2	−6.3
Germany[2]	−2.5	−3.2	−2.5	−3.4	−3.5	−2.7	−2.1	−1.5	1.6	−1.2
France[2,3]	−4.1	−5.9	−5.5	−5.5	−4.2	−3.0	−2.7	−1.8	−1.2	0.3
Italy	−9.5	−9.4	−9.1	−7.6	−7.1	−2.7	−2.8	−1.9	−1.3	−0.9
United Kingdom[2,4]	−6.5	−8.0	−6.8	−5.8	−4.1	−1.6	0.2	1.6	3.6	0.8
Canada	−9.2	−8.7	−6.7	−5.4	−2.8	0.2	0.2	2.2	3.0	2.9
Other advanced economies	−3.2	−3.6	−3.0	−2.7	−1.5	−0.6	−0.8	−0.3	0.4	0.5
Spain	−4.0	−6.7	−6.1	−7.0	−5.0	−3.2	−2.6	−1.1	−0.4	—
Netherlands	−3.8	−3.1	−3.6	−4.2	−1.8	−1.2	−0.8	0.5	1.6	0.4
Belgium	−8.0	−7.3	−5.0	−4.3	−3.8	−1.9	−0.9	−0.7	−0.1	0.5
Sweden	−7.5	−11.8	−10.8	−7.7	−3.5	−1.7	1.9	1.9	3.4	3.1
Austria	−1.9	−4.2	−4.8	−5.1	−3.7	−1.6	−2.5	−2.0	−1.7	−1.5
Denmark	−2.2	−2.8	−2.4	−2.3	−1.0	0.1	1.2	3.0	2.4	2.4
Finland	−5.6	−7.3	−5.7	−3.7	−3.2	−1.5	1.3	1.9	4.8	4.7
Greece	−12.8	−13.8	−10.0	−10.2	−7.4	−3.9	−2.5	−1.8	−1.0	−0.6
Portugal	−2.9	−6.1	−6.0	−4.6	−3.8	−2.5	−2.1	−2.0	−1.2	−1.1
Ireland	−2.8	−2.5	−2.1	−2.6	−0.6	0.8	2.1	3.7	3.7	3.1
Luxembourg	2.3	5.2	4.2	2.2	2.7	3.6	3.3	2.4	2.5	3.0
Switzerland	−3.4	−3.6	−2.9	−1.9	−2.2	−2.4	−1.1	−1.4	−1.2	−1.4
Norway	−1.7	−1.4	0.4	3.5	6.6	7.9	3.6	4.8	11.2	9.5
Israel	−3.3	−2.7	−3.3	−4.4	−5.6	−4.0	−3.6	−4.8	−3.3	−3.1
Iceland	−2.8	−4.5	−4.7	−3.0	−1.6	—	0.8	1.2	1.3	1.5
Korea[5]	0.1	1.3	1.0	1.3	1.0	−0.9	−3.8	−2.7	−1.6	−0.5
Australia[6]	−4.7	−4.4	−3.4	−2.1	−0.9	—	0.2	0.7	0.8	0.5
Taiwan Province of China	0.3	0.6	0.2	0.4	0.3	0.6	2.2	0.1	−0.5	−0.4
Hong Kong SAR	2.5	2.3	1.3	−0.3	2.2	6.6	−1.8	−0.2	−0.2	1.0
Singapore	11.3	14.4	13.9	12.2	9.3	9.2	3.6	3.3	2.4	3.1
New Zealand[7]	−4.1	−0.1	2.0	3.3	2.8	2.3	2.2	1.3	0.8	1.4
Memorandum										
Industrial countries	−4.5	−5.1	−4.3	−4.2	−3.3	−1.9	−1.3	−0.9	−0.1	−0.1
European Union	−5.2	−6.3	−5.6	−5.4	−4.3	−2.4	−1.7	−0.7	0.7	—
Euro area	−4.7	−5.7	−5.2	−5.2	−4.4	−2.6	−2.2	−1.3	0.1	−0.4
Newly industrialized Asian economies	1.2	2.1	1.7	1.6	1.6	1.2	−1.1	−1.1	−0.8	—
Fiscal balance excluding social security transactions										
United States	−6.2	−5.3	−4.2	−3.7	−2.7	−1.7	−0.7	−0.3	—	—
Japan	−2.0	−4.8	−5.1	−6.5	−6.8	−5.9	−6.8	−9.2	−9.5	−7.3
Germany	−2.4	−3.4	−2.6	−3.0	−3.1	−2.8	−2.3	−1.9	1.4	−1.3
France	−3.5	−4.6	−4.7	−4.8	−3.6	−2.5	−2.6	−1.9	−1.3	−0.2
Italy	−5.2	−5.4	−4.5	−5.6	−5.3	−0.7	1.3	2.8	3.2	3.6
Canada	−7.1	−6.5	−4.5	−3.3	−0.6	2.4	2.2	3.9	4.4	3.8

Table 15 *(concluded)*

	1992	1993	1994	1995	1996	1997	1998	1999	2000	2001
Central government fiscal balance										
Advanced economies	**−4.1**	**−4.4**	**−3.7**	**−3.3**	**−2.7**	**−1.5**	**−1.7**	**−1.4**	**−0.6**	**−0.6**
Major industrial countries	−4.4	−4.5	−3.8	−3.4	−2.9	−1.7	−1.8	−1.5	−0.7	−0.8
United States[8]	−4.9	−4.2	−3.0	−2.6	−1.8	−0.6	0.6	1.3	2.0	2.0
Japan[9]	−1.7	−2.7	−3.5	−4.0	−4.3	−4.0	−9.2	−11.4	−11.4	−10.4
Germany[10]	−1.2	−2.1	−1.5	−1.4	−2.2	−1.7	−1.5	−1.3	1.4	−1.0
France[10]	−3.3	−4.8	−4.8	−4.2	−3.7	−3.5	−3.0	−2.3	−2.3	−0.6
Italy	−10.3	−9.9	−9.1	−7.1	−6.8	−2.6	−2.8	−1.5	−0.9	−0.6
United Kingdom	−7.3	−8.2	−6.7	−5.5	−4.2	−1.6	0.2	1.7	3.6	0.9
Canada	−5.1	−5.5	−4.6	−3.9	−2.0	0.5	0.5	0.6	0.9	1.1
Other advanced economies	−3.3	−3.9	−3.1	−2.8	−1.7	−0.9	−1.0	−0.7	−0.2	—
Memorandum										
Industrial countries	−4.3	−4.7	−4.0	−3.5	−2.9	−1.7	−1.7	−1.4	−0.6	−0.6
European Union	−5.0	−6.0	−5.2	−4.6	−3.9	−2.4	−1.7	−0.9	0.3	−0.4
Euro area	−4.3	−5.2	−4.6	−4.2	−3.8	−2.4	−2.2	−1.5	−0.4	−0.7
Newly industrialized Asian economies	−0.3	0.8	1.0	1.0	1.0	0.9	−1.3	−1.4	−1.2	−0.5

[1]On a national income accounts basis except as indicated in footnotes. See Box A.1 for a summary of the policy assumptions underlying the projections.

[2]Includes mobile telephone license receipts equivalent to 2.5 percent of GDP in 2000 for Germany, 1.3 percent of GDP in 2001 for France, and 2.4 percent of GDP in 2000 for the United Kingdom.

[3]Adjusted for valuation changes of the foreign exchange stabilization fund.

[4]Excludes asset sales.

[5]Data include social security transactions (that is, the operations of the public pension plan).

[6]Data exclude net advances (primarily privatization receipts and net policy-related lending).

[7]Data from 1992 onward are on an accrual basis and are not strictly comparable with previous cash-based data.

[8]Data are on a budget basis.

[9]Data are on a national income basis and exclude social security transactions.

[10]Data are on an administrative basis and exclude social security transactions.

Table 16. Advanced Economies: General Government Structural Balances[1]

(Percent of potential GDP)

	1992	1993	1994	1995	1996	1997	1998	1999	2000	2001
Structural balance[2]										
Advanced economies	**-3.9**	**-3.6**	**-3.2**	**-3.1**	**-2.4**	**-1.2**	**-0.6**	**-0.4**	**-0.5**	**-0.4**
Major industrial countries	-3.8	-3.6	-3.1	-3.1	-2.5	-1.3	-0.7	-0.5	-0.6	-0.5
United States	-4.7	-3.7	-2.7	-2.1	-1.4	-0.6	0.3	0.6	0.8	0.9
Japan	0.9	-1.4	-1.7	-2.9	-4.5	-3.5	-3.3	-5.5	-6.5	-4.9
Germany[3,4]	-4.0	-3.1	-2.5	-3.4	-2.7	-1.6	-1.2	-0.6	-0.4	-1.2
France[4]	-3.8	-3.8	-3.9	-4.0	-2.4	-1.4	-1.6	-0.7	-0.8	-1.3
Italy	-9.4	-8.2	-7.9	-7.0	-6.0	-1.5	-1.5	-0.3	-0.3	-0.3
United Kingdom[4]	-3.5	-4.5	-4.2	-4.2	-2.9	-0.9	0.3	1.5	0.9	0.2
Canada	-4.9	-4.4	-3.9	-2.9	—	2.1	1.7	2.6	2.4	2.2
Other advanced economies	-4.3	-3.7	-3.5	-3.1	-1.6	-0.6	-0.3	0.2	0.3	0.2
Spain	-5.2	-5.0	-5.2	-5.1	-3.3	-2.0	-1.9	-1.0	-0.8	-0.4
Netherlands	-3.7	-1.9	-2.7	-3.0	-0.9	-0.8	-0.9	-0.1	-0.3	-1.2
Belgium	-8.0	-5.0	-3.0	-2.6	-1.5	-0.5	0.1	0.1	-0.4	-0.3
Sweden	-5.7	-5.9	-6.7	-5.2	0.2	1.7	5.1	4.1	3.8	3.0
Austria	-2.6	-3.7	-4.6	-4.9	-3.4	-0.8	-1.8	-1.2	-1.3	-1.4
Denmark	-1.1	-1.1	-1.2	-1.7	-0.7	—	0.7	2.4	1.9	2.0
Finland	-1.1	-0.7	-0.5	0.4	0.5	0.3	1.9	2.3	4.5	4.2
Greece	-7.1	-5.9	-3.9	-3.5	-2.4	-1.2	-0.8	-0.6	-0.4	-0.3
Portugal	-4.4	-5.4	-5.0	-3.6	-2.9	-2.0	-2.1	-2.0	-1.8	-1.5
Ireland	-2.1	-0.4	0.3	-1.5	0.2	0.3	1.1	2.0	1.6	0.9
Norway[5]	-2.8	-2.0	-0.9	0.6	-1.8	-1.8	-2.3	0.1	0.7	0.9
Australia[6]	-2.9	-2.7	-2.2	-1.3	-0.3	0.5	0.5	0.8	0.9	0.5
New Zealand[7]	-3.3	-0.4	0.4	1.7	1.4	1.3	1.2	0.7	0.8	1.2
Memorandum										
European Union[8]	-5.0	-4.5	-4.2	-4.3	-3.0	-1.2	-0.9	—	-0.1	-0.5
Euro area[8]	-5.3	-4.5	-4.2	-4.3	-3.2	-1.4	-1.3	-0.5	-0.4	-0.8

[1]On a national income accounts basis.

[2]The structural budget position is defined as the actual budget deficit (or surplus) less the effects of cyclical deviations of output from potential output. Because of the margin of uncertainty that attaches to estimates of cyclical gaps and to tax and expenditure elasticities with respect to national income, indicators of structural budget positions should be interpreted as broad orders of magnitude. Moreover, it is important to note that changes in structural budget balances are not necessarily attributable to policy changes but may reflect the built-in momentum of existing expenditure programs. In the period beyond that for which specific consolidation programs exist, it is assumed that the structural deficit remains unchanged.

[3]The estimate of the fiscal impulse for 1995 is affected by the assumption by the federal government of the debt of the Treuhandanstalt and various other agencies, which were formerly held outside the general government sector. At the public sector level, there would be an estimated withdrawal of fiscal impulse amounting to just over 1 percent of GDP.

[4]Excludes mobile telephone license receipts.

[5]Excludes oil.

[6]Excludes commonwealth government privatization receipts.

[7]Excludes privatization proceeds.

[8]Excludes Luxembourg.

Table 17. Advanced Economies: Monetary Aggregates

(Annual percent change)[1]

	1992	1993	1994	1995	1996	1997	1998	1999
Narrow money[2]								
Advanced economies	**7.8**	**8.1**	**4.4**	**5.3**	**4.2**	**4.2**	**5.4**	...
Major industrial countries	7.9	7.6	3.9	4.7	3.6	3.7	5.1	...
United States	14.4	10.6	2.5	−1.5	−4.5	−1.2	2.2	1.8
Japan	1.9	3.4	4.9	12.8	10.0	8.9	6.1	11.8
Euro area	3.9	6.0	4.4	6.4	7.5	6.9	9.5	10.2
Germany	10.8	8.5	5.2	6.8	12.4	2.3	11.1	...
France	−0.2	1.4	2.8	7.7	0.8	6.5	3.1	...
Italy	0.7	7.6	3.4	1.4	3.9	7.7	9.0	...
United Kingdom	2.8	6.0	6.8	5.6	6.7	6.4	5.3	11.8
Canada	6.1	14.4	7.5	6.6	17.0	9.9	8.0	10.3
Other advanced economies	7.2	10.8	6.8	8.7	7.9	6.5	6.9	...
Memorandum								
Newly industrialized Asian economies	12.8	17.6	11.2	11.9	4.3	−3.8	2.0	20.9
Broad money[3]								
Advanced economies	**3.0**	**3.7**	**2.5**	**4.3**	**4.9**	**5.0**	**6.8**	...
Major industrial countries	2.2	2.6	1.7	3.7	4.2	4.6	6.5	...
United States	1.8	1.4	0.6	3.9	4.5	5.7	8.5	6.1
Japan	−0.4	1.4	2.9	3.2	2.9	3.8	4.4	2.6
Euro area	7.1	6.3	2.3	5.7	4.0	4.4	4.6	7.2
Germany	7.6	10.9	1.6	3.6	8.7	3.6	7.3	...
France	5.1	−2.9	1.8	4.6	−3.3	2.0	2.7	...
Italy	0.1	3.8	1.0	−1.9	3.8	9.0	5.6	...
United Kingdom	2.8	4.9	4.2	9.9	9.6	5.6	8.3	3.8
Canada	3.1	2.8	2.7	4.0	2.0	−1.5	1.2	5.5
Other advanced economies	7.1	9.1	6.5	7.4	8.6	6.9	8.3	...
Memorandum								
Newly industrialized Asian economies	16.1	15.5	17.1	12.8	11.5	11.8	21.5	18.8

[1]Based on end-of-period data except for Japan, which is based on monthly averages.

[2]M1 except for the United Kingdom, where M0 is used here as a measure of narrow money; it comprises notes in circulation plus bankers' operational deposits. M1 is generally currency in circulation plus private demand deposits. In addition, the United States includes traveler's checks of nonbank issues and other checkable deposits and excludes private sector float and demand deposits of banks. Japan includes government demand deposits and excludes float. Germany includes demand deposits at fixed interest rates. Canada excludes private sector float.

[3]M2, defined as M1 plus quasi-money, except for Japan, Germany, and the United Kingdom, for which the data are based on M2 plus certificates of deposit (CDs), M3, and M4, respectively. Quasi-money is essentially private term deposits and other notice deposits. The United States also includes money market mutual fund balances, money market deposit accounts, overnight repurchase agreements, and overnight Eurodollars issued to U.S. residents by foreign branches of U.S. banks. For Japan, M2 plus CDs is currency in circulation plus total private and public sector deposits and installments of Sogo Banks plus CDs. For Germany M3 is M1 plus private time deposits with maturities of less than four years plus savings deposits at statutory notice. For Italy, M2 comprises M1 plus term deposits, passbooks from the Postal Office, and CDs with maturities of less than 18 months. For the United Kingdom, M4 is composed of non-interest-bearing M1, private sector interest-bearing sterling sight bank deposits, private sector sterling time banks deposits, private sector holdings of sterling bank CDs, private sector holdings of building society shares and deposits, and sterling CDs less building society holdings of banks deposits and bank CDs and notes and coins.

Table 18. Advanced Economies: Interest Rates

(Percent a year)

	1992	1993	1994	1995	1996	1997	1998	1999	August 2000
Policy-related interest rate[1]									
Major industrial countries	**6.3**	**4.7**	**4.5**	**5.4**	**4.4**	**4.2**	**4.3**	...	...
United States	3.6	3.0	4.2	5.9	5.3	5.5	5.4	5.0	6.5
Japan	4.6	3.0	2.1	1.2	0.4	0.4	0.4	0.0	0.0
Euro area	...	...	...	...	...	...	3.3	2.7	4.3
Germany	9.4	7.4	5.3	4.4	3.2	3.1	3.3	...	...
France	10.7	8.6	5.6	6.3	3.7	3.3	3.4	...	...
Italy	14.5	10.5	8.8	10.7	8.6	6.6	4.8	...	...
United Kingdom	9.4	5.9	5.5	6.7	6.0	6.6	7.2	5.3	6.0
Canada	6.6	4.6	5.1	6.9	4.3	3.3	4.9	4.7	5.8
Short-term interest rate[2]									
Advanced economies	**6.9**	**5.3**	**4.9**	**5.1**	**4.1**	**4.1**	**4.0**	**3.5**	...
Major industrial countries	6.1	4.6	4.4	4.7	3.7	3.7	3.7	3.3	...
United States	3.5	3.1	4.4	5.7	5.1	5.2	4.9	4.8	6.6
Japan	4.0	2.4	1.9	0.8	0.3	0.3	0.2	0.0	0.2
Euro area	11.1	8.6	6.3	6.1	4.6	4.1	3.9	2.9	4.8
Germany	9.5	7.2	5.3	4.5	3.3	3.3	3.5	...	...
France	9.5	7.2	5.3	4.5	3.3	3.3	3.7	...	...
Italy	14.5	10.5	8.8	10.7	8.6	6.6	4.8	...	...
United Kingdom	9.5	5.9	5.5	6.7	6.0	6.9	7.4	5.3	6.2
Canada	6.6	4.8	5.5	7.1	4.2	3.2	4.7	4.7	5.9
Other advanced economies	10.6	8.7	7.4	7.3	6.1	5.7	5.8	4.4	...
Memorandum									
Newly industrialized Asian economies	9.8	8.5	9.0	9.2	8.8	9.7	10.4	6.3	...
Long-term interest rate[3]									
Advanced economies	**8.0**	**6.6**	**7.2**	**6.8**	**6.1**	**5.5**	**4.5**	**4.7**	...
Major industrial countries	7.5	6.2	6.8	6.4	5.8	5.2	4.2	4.5	...
United States	7.0	5.9	7.1	6.6	6.4	6.4	5.3	5.6	5.8
Japan	5.1	4.0	4.2	3.3	3.0	2.1	1.3	1.7	1.8
Euro area	9.8	8.1	8.2	8.5	7.1	5.9	4.7	4.6	...
Germany	7.9	6.4	7.1	6.9	6.2	5.6	4.6	...	...
France	8.6	6.9	7.4	7.6	6.4	5.6	4.8	...	...
Italy	13.3	11.3	10.6	12.2	9.4	6.9	4.9	...	...
United Kingdom	9.1	7.5	8.2	8.2	7.8	7.0	5.5	5.4	5.4
Canada	8.1	7.2	8.4	8.1	7.2	6.1	5.3	5.6	5.8
Other advanced economies	10.5	8.7	9.3	9.1	7.8	6.8	5.9	5.5	...
Memorandum									
Newly industrialized Asian economies	13.7	10.9	11.2	11.0	9.7	10.5	11.4	7.9	...

[1]For the United States, federal funds rate; for Japan, overnight call rate; for Germany, repurchase rate; for France, day-to-day money rate; for Italy, three-month treasury bill gross rate; for the United Kingdom, base lending rate; for Canada, overnight money market financing rate; for the euro area, repurchase rate.

[2]For the United States, three-month certificates of deposit (CDs) in secondary markets; for Japan three-month CDs; for Germany, France, and the United Kingdom, three-month interbank deposits; for Italy, three-month treasury bills gross rate; and for Canada, three-month prime corporate paper.

[3]For the United States, yield on ten-year treasury bonds; for Japan, over-the-counter sales yield on ten-year government bonds with longest residual maturity; for Germany, yield on government bonds with maturities of nine to ten years; for France, long-term (seven- to ten-year) government bond yield (Emprunts d'Etat à long terme TME); for Italy, secondary market yield on fixed-coupon (BTP) government bonds with two to four years' residual maturity; for the United Kingdom, yield on medium-dated (ten-year) government stock; and for Canada, average yield on government bonds with residual maturities of over ten years.

Table 19. Advanced Economies: Exchange Rates

	1992	1993	1994	1995	1996	1997	1998	1999	Exchange Rate Assumption[1] 2000
						National currency units per U.S. dollar			
U.S. dollar nominal exchange rates									
Japanese yen	126.7	111.2	102.2	94.1	108.8	121.0	130.9	113.9	107.9
Euro[2]	...	...	...	...	...	...	...	1.07	0.92
Deutsche mark	1.56	1.65	1.62	1.43	1.50	1.73	1.76	1.84	2.13
French franc	5.29	5.66	5.55	4.99	5.12	5.84	5.90	6.16	7.15
Italian lira	1,232	1,574	1,612	1,629	1,543	1,703	1,736	1,817	2,111
Pound sterling[2]	1.76	1.50	1.53	1.58	1.56	1.64	1.66	1.62	1.50
Canadian dollar	1.21	1.29	1.37	1.37	1.36	1.38	1.48	1.49	1.49
Spanish peseta	102.4	127.3	134.0	124.7	126.7	146.4	149.4	156.2	181.4
Netherlands guilder	1.76	1.86	1.82	1.61	1.69	1.95	1.98	2.07	2.40
Belgian franc	32.1	34.6	33.5	29.5	31.0	35.8	36.3	37.9	44.0
Swedish krona	5.82	7.78	7.72	7.13	6.71	7.63	7.95	8.26	9.05
Austrian schilling	11.0	11.6	11.4	10.1	10.6	12.2	12.4	12.9	15.0
Danish krone	6.04	6.48	6.36	5.60	5.80	6.60	6.70	6.98	8.13
Finnish markka	4.48	5.71	5.22	4.37	4.59	5.19	5.34	5.58	6.48
Greek drachma	190.6	229.2	242.6	231.7	240.7	273.1	295.5	305.6	357.0
Portuguese escudo	135.0	160.8	166.0	151.1	154.2	175.3	180.1	188.2	218.5
Irish pound	0.59	0.68	0.67	0.62	0.63	0.66	0.70	0.74	0.86
Swiss franc	1.41	1.48	1.37	1.18	1.24	1.45	1.45	1.50	1.70
Norwegian krone	6.21	7.09	7.06	6.34	6.45	7.07	7.55	7.80	8.99
Israeli new sheqel	2.46	2.83	3.01	3.01	3.19	3.45	3.80	4.14	4.16
Icelandic krona	57.55	67.60	69.94	64.69	66.50	70.90	70.96	72.34	76.29
Korean won	780.7	802.7	803.4	771.3	804.5	951.3	1,401.4	1,188.8	1,090.2
Australian dollar	1.36	1.47	1.37	1.35	1.28	1.35	1.59	1.55	1.74
New Taiwan dollar	25.16	26.39	26.46	26.49	27.46	28.70	33.46	32.27	30.79
Hong Kong dollar	7.74	7.74	7.73	7.74	7.73	7.74	7.75	7.76	7.74
Singapore dollar	1.63	1.62	1.53	1.42	1.41	1.48	1.67	1.69	1.68
									Percent change from previous assumption[3]
					Index, 1980–89 = 100				
Real effective exchange rates[4]									
United States	72.6	74.7	73.9	69.2	73.3	79.8	85.2	86.1	—
Japan	119.7	145.4	154.7	161.1	136.6	126.9	115.7	129.3	−0.6
Euro[5]	111.8	109.4	107.1	112.0	112.1	99.7	95.8	89.8	—
Germany	116.3	124.2	128.2	137.7	135.9	126.8	123.3	118.8	—
France	91.7	92.5	91.4	92.4	89.5	85.2	83.9	81.4	—
United Kingdom	98.6	90.6	91.2	86.7	88.8	108.0	119.0	123.5	0.3
Italy	107.3	90.5	84.9	78.6	88.0	90.4	90.9	89.7	—
Canada	112.0	102.2	94.3	93.8	93.6	94.7	90.1	86.5	0.4
Spain	121.8	113.1	106.2	104.7	108.3	106.6	110.2	112.6	—
Netherlands	91.9	93.3	93.1	94.0	90.6	85.4	83.0	81.1	—
Belgium	97.7	99.6	99.3	102.9	100.1	95.8	94.8	93.9	—
Sweden	106.9	81.4	79.1	77.7	86.1	81.5	79.0	76.4	−0.5
Austria	89.8	90.4	88.5	85.4	81.5	77.2	75.7	73.8	—
Denmark	108.7	112.8	111.4	114.2	111.6	109.2	109.6	111.9	0.1
Finland	77.6	65.9	69.4	77.4	72.6	69.0	69.0	67.1	—
Greece	102.1	101.9	104.2	111.0	115.0	119.1	115.0	116.7	—
Portugal	138.5	135.9	132.1	136.2	134.9	131.9	132.1	132.1	—
Ireland	76.4	70.5	67.2	64.6	64.1	62.1	57.7	55.7	−0.1
Switzerland	112.7	114.1	124.1	131.6	131.2	125.6	131.2	129.3	0.5
Norway	100.0	99.1	100.2	107.3	111.4	116.1	115.1	118.8	0.7
Australia	96.3	89.0	93.7	93.2	109.2	113.0	101.7	103.0	0.7
New Zealand	98.5	99.4	105.5	111.9	124.6	128.2	111.2	108.5	−0.7

[1]Average exchange rates for the period July 18–August 15, 2000. See "Assumptions" in the Introduction to the Statistical Appendix.
[2]Expressed in U.S. dollars per currency unit.
[3]In nominal effective terms. Average July 18–August 15, 2000 rates compared with May 11–June 8, 2000 rates.
[4]Defined as the ratio, in common currency, of the normalized unit labor costs in the manufacturing sector to the weighted average of those of its industrial country trading partners, using 1989–91 trade weights.
[5]An effective euro is used prior to January 1, 1999. See Box 5.5 in the *World Economic Outlook*, October 1998.

Table 20. Developing Countries: Central Government Fiscal Balances

(Percent of GDP)

	1992	1993	1994	1995	1996	1997	1998	1999	2000	2001
Developing countries	**−3.0**	**−3.2**	**−2.7**	**−2.6**	**−2.3**	**−2.6**	**−4.0**	**−4.5**	**−3.5**	**−3.1**
Regional groups										
Africa	−6.7	−7.4	−5.3	−3.9	−3.0	−2.9	−3.9	−3.8	−1.3	−1.6
Sub-Sahara	−8.0	−8.0	−5.9	−4.1	−3.6	−3.5	−4.1	−4.2	−1.9	−2.2
Excluding Nigeria and South Africa	−9.6	−7.8	−6.5	−5.0	−4.2	−3.8	−4.1	−4.6	−3.4	−2.7
Asia	−3.0	−3.0	−2.5	−2.4	−2.1	−2.6	−3.8	−4.6	−4.4	−4.1
Excluding China and India	−1.9	−1.9	−1.2	−0.8	−0.9	−1.8	−3.1	−3.4	−4.0	−3.3
Middle East and Europe	−5.5	−7.5	−5.8	−4.4	−4.5	−3.8	−6.9	−5.4	−1.5	−1.2
Western Hemisphere	−0.4	−0.2	−0.9	−1.8	−1.5	−1.8	−3.2	−4.1	−2.7	−1.9
Analytical groups										
By source of export earnings										
Fuel	−5.1	−7.5	−6.8	−4.1	−1.4	−1.1	−6.4	−3.0	4.1	1.1
Manufactures	−2.3	−2.5	−2.2	−2.6	−2.5	−3.0	−4.2	−5.2	−4.5	−3.7
Nonfuel primary products	−5.2	−5.2	−3.6	−2.4	−1.8	−1.9	−2.4	−3.4	−3.4	−2.6
Services, income, and private transfers	−3.7	−3.5	−3.6	−2.8	−3.5	−3.1	−3.1	−3.0	−3.3	−2.9
Diversified	−2.7	−2.5	−1.9	−2.0	−2.1	−2.0	−2.6	−2.9	−3.4	−3.0
By external financing source										
Net creditor countries	−8.7	−9.0	−8.0	−5.5	−3.2	−1.0	−8.0	−5.6	3.6	1.6
Net debtor countries	−2.7	−3.0	−2.6	−2.5	−2.3	−2.6	−3.9	−4.4	−3.7	−3.2
Official financing	−5.9	−6.8	−5.2	−3.4	−2.3	−2.4	−3.6	−3.3	−2.6	−2.3
Private financing	−2.2	−2.2	−2.0	−2.3	−2.1	−2.5	−3.7	−4.6	−4.1	−3.4
Diversified financing	−5.9	−6.3	−5.7	−4.3	−4.0	−4.1	−5.2	−5.2	−3.0	−2.9
Net debtor countries by debt-servicing experience										
Countries with arrears and/or rescheduling during 1994–98	−2.7	−3.2	−2.2	−2.0	−1.3	−1.8	−4.1	−3.6	−1.1	−1.5
Other net debtor countries	−2.8	−2.9	−2.7	−2.8	−2.6	−2.9	−3.8	−4.7	−4.5	−3.8
Other groups										
Heavily indebted poor countries	−9.3	−8.0	−6.1	−4.3	−3.7	−3.7	−3.5	−3.7	−3.6	−3.1
Least developed countries	−9.1	−7.3	−6.4	−5.4	−4.6	−4.0	−4.3	−4.7	−4.1	−3.9
Middle East and north Africa	−5.4	−7.4	−5.8	−4.3	−2.6	−1.9	−5.3	−2.4	2.2	0.1
Memorandum										
Median										
Developing countries	−3.7	−4.0	−3.7	−3.3	−2.8	−2.6	−3.0	−3.1	−2.6	−1.8
Regional groups										
Africa	−5.7	−6.0	−5.2	−3.8	−4.7	−2.5	−2.9	−3.3	−2.5	−2.4
Asia	−4.7	−4.0	−2.8	−3.4	−2.7	−2.3	−3.0	−3.4	−3.4	−3.0
Middle East and Europe	−3.6	−7.2	−5.0	−4.1	−3.2	−3.3	−6.6	−3.0	0.5	−1.3
Western Hemisphere	−1.7	−1.3	−1.0	−1.8	−1.7	−2.4	−2.3	−2.8	−2.2	−1.5

Table 21. Developing Countries: Broad Money Aggregates

(Annual percent change)

	1992	1993	1994	1995	1996	1997	1998	1999	2000	2001
Developing countries	**108.0**	**115.7**	**94.3**	**25.2**	**23.2**	**20.6**	**16.5**	**14.7**	**13.4**	**11.8**
Regional groups										
Africa	32.1	27.6	39.0	23.8	21.2	18.8	16.3	20.2	14.6	11.0
Sub-Sahara	36.9	31.6	48.2	28.9	24.5	20.1	17.7	22.8	15.6	12.2
Asia	22.9	27.9	24.4	23.1	21.0	18.3	18.2	13.8	13.7	13.8
Excluding China and India	20.6	22.6	17.5	21.9	19.4	17.7	20.8	11.4	12.1	13.1
Middle East and Europe	27.3	26.7	40.2	33.3	34.3	30.4	21.7	26.7	16.5	12.4
Western Hemisphere	367.8	400.8	246.4	24.6	22.1	19.9	12.8	10.3	11.7	9.3
Analytical groups										
By source of export earnings										
Fuel	19.3	21.3	24.5	20.1	21.5	22.8	6.5	17.6	13.5	11.1
Manufactures	191.5	215.8	161.8	30.7	24.6	19.4	17.6	15.4	14.2	12.2
Nonfuel primary products	55.7	46.4	50.3	30.6	28.5	23.7	15.0	18.9	16.2	15.0
Services, income, and private transfers	22.0	18.3	14.9	14.2	12.0	15.1	11.0	11.9	9.0	9.0
Diversified	28.6	27.6	19.7	11.9	20.1	22.5	21.3	9.1	10.3	9.4
By external financing source										
Net creditor countries	4.7	3.4	5.0	5.5	6.3	7.5	3.6	7.0	3.9	6.0
Net debtor countries	117.4	126.4	101.8	26.5	24.3	21.4	17.3	15.1	14.0	12.1
Official financing	38.0	31.8	41.2	20.3	18.9	16.3	16.7	18.0	13.9	10.3
Private financing	143.7	154.1	117.7	26.4	24.5	21.3	18.3	14.5	13.7	12.1
Diversified financing	34.5	36.0	36.7	30.2	23.2	19.6	15.1	20.2	16.6	12.6
Net debtor countries by debt-servicing experience										
Countries with arrears and/or rescheduling during 1994–98	381.5	500.1	325.9	29.5	19.7	18.2	16.3	14.4	13.7	11.5
Other net debtor countries	28.2	27.2	29.6	24.7	27.2	23.2	17.9	15.5	14.1	12.4
Other groups										
Heavily indebted poor countries	60.5	50.4	67.1	40.5	34.7	25.5	19.2	22.8	18.4	16.0
Least developed countries	65.9	56.4	62.9	40.7	33.6	23.0	19.4	23.8	18.7	16.7
Middle East and north Africa	15.9	16.2	13.2	14.0	13.2	15.8	4.8	11.2	9.2	8.9
Memorandum										
Median										
Developing countries	17.9	16.2	18.8	16.3	14.4	15.1	9.7	11.1	10.0	9.3
Regional groups										
Africa	13.3	13.6	32.6	16.2	14.4	15.4	8.1	11.7	9.9	9.1
Asia	18.0	18.8	18.4	16.7	15.7	16.6	12.6	13.5	13.3	11.7
Middle East and Europe	14.3	10.3	10.0	9.4	8.6	9.9	8.0	11.1	8.8	8.6
Western Hemisphere	25.1	17.0	17.2	19.9	16.7	15.5	10.3	9.8	9.5	8.7

Table 22. Summary of World Trade Volumes and Prices
(Annual percent change)

| | Ten-Year Averages | | 1992 | 1993 | 1994 | 1995 | 1996 | 1997 | 1998 | 1999 | 2000 | 2001 |
	1982–91	1992–2001										
Trade in goods and services												
World trade[1]												
Volume	5.0	7.0	4.5	3.8	9.0	8.9	6.7	9.8	4.3	5.1	10.0	7.8
Price deflator												
In U.S. dollars	1.5	−0.4	2.7	−4.1	2.5	9.0	−1.0	−4.9	−5.6	−1.2	−0.9	0.4
In SDRs	—	—	−0.2	−3.3	—	2.9	3.4	0.3	−4.2	−2.0	2.1	0.8
Volume of trade												
Exports												
Advanced economies	5.5	6.8	5.1	3.3	8.9	8.8	6.0	10.4	3.9	4.8	9.9	7.6
Developing countries	4.6	8.1	10.8	7.9	12.5	7.0	9.4	10.7	3.7	3.5	8.8	7.1
Imports												
Advanced economies	6.1	7.1	4.7	1.5	9.6	8.9	6.3	9.2	5.7	7.6	10.3	7.9
Developing countries	2.5	7.6	10.6	11.2	7.2	9.6	8.9	10.4	0.3	—	10.0	9.0
Terms of trade												
Advanced economies	0.9	0.1	0.8	0.5	—	−0.1	−0.3	−0.6	1.3	−0.1	−1.0	0.7
Developing countries	−3.4	0.6	−2.2	0.6	0.7	3.4	1.6	0.6	−4.6	2.7	4.6	−1.4
Trade in goods												
World trade[1]												
Volume	5.0	7.1	4.6	3.5	10.0	9.8	5.8	10.0	4.1	5.2	10.4	7.7
Price deflator												
In U.S. dollars	1.5	−0.5	2.1	−4.1	2.5	9.2	−0.8	−6.0	−5.8	−1.2	−0.5	0.5
In SDRs	—	−0.1	−0.8	−3.3	—	3.0	3.7	−0.8	−4.4	−1.9	2.5	0.9
World trade prices in U.S. dollars[2]												
Manufactures	3.7	−0.8	3.5	−5.8	3.1	10.2	−3.1	−7.8	−1.2	−1.2	−5.3	1.1
Oil	−5.8	1.7	−1.7	−11.8	−5.0	7.9	18.4	−5.4	−32.1	37.5	47.5	−13.3
Nonfuel primary commodities	−0.2	0.2	0.1	1.8	13.4	8.4	−1.2	−3.2	−14.7	−7.1	3.2	4.5
World trade prices in SDRs[2]												
Manufactures	2.2	−0.4	0.6	−4.9	0.5	4.0	1.2	−2.7	0.2	−2.0	−2.4	1.4
Oil	−7.2	2.1	−4.5	−11.1	−7.3	1.8	23.7	−0.2	−31.2	36.5	52.0	−13.0
Nonfuel primary commodities	−1.7	0.6	−2.8	2.7	10.6	2.3	3.3	2.2	−13.5	−7.8	6.4	4.8
World trade prices in euros[2]												
Manufactures	2.6	2.3	−1.2	4.7	2.0	0.1	−0.6	5.2	0.4	3.1	7.7	2.2
Oil	−6.8	4.9	−6.2	−2.0	−6.0	−2.0	21.6	7.9	−31.0	43.6	67.7	−12.3
Nonfuel primary commodities	−1.3	3.4	−4.5	13.1	12.2	−1.6	1.5	10.5	−13.3	−2.9	17.4	5.7

Table 22 *(concluded)*

	Ten-Year Averages		1992	1993	1994	1995	1996	1997	1998	1999	2000	2001
	1982–91	1992–2001										
Trade in goods												
Volume of trade												
Exports												
Advanced economies	5.5	6.8	4.6	2.7	9.5	9.1	5.4	10.9	3.9	4.3	10.2	7.3
Developing countries	4.3	8.5	9.8	7.0	12.7	10.6	8.7	10.9	3.5	5.3	10.3	7.0
Fuel exporters	2.3	3.8	9.9	1.6	4.2	2.4	6.9	3.9	–0.4	1.1	8.1	1.4
Nonfuel exporters	6.1	10.0	9.8	9.2	15.7	13.1	9.2	13.1	4.6	6.1	10.8	8.6
Imports												
Advanced economies	6.1	7.2	4.8	1.9	11.0	9.5	5.2	9.5	5.4	7.6	10.4	7.7
Developing countries	1.9	8.2	14.6	10.3	8.2	11.7	7.8	8.8	0.2	0.5	11.2	9.9
Fuel exporters	–2.7	2.2	26.4	–6.1	–15.6	2.2	–1.6	12.5	7.3	–6.3	3.2	5.7
Nonfuel exporters	3.7	9.3	11.2	14.9	13.7	13.4	9.3	8.2	–0.9	1.6	12.6	10.6
Price deflators in SDRs												
Exports												
Advanced economies	0.8	–0.6	–0.5	–3.2	0.1	3.4	2.2	–2.3	–3.1	–2.8	–0.5	1.1
Developing countries	–3.1	1.5	–3.3	–1.5	—	2.9	8.1	3.2	–9.2	4.5	12.6	–0.5
Fuel exporters	–6.9	3.0	–7.0	–4.7	–3.5	4.4	19.3	3.0	–23.9	26.7	38.2	–8.3
Nonfuel exporters	–0.6	1.2	–1.8	–0.3	1.2	2.4	4.9	3.2	–5.1	–0.3	6.2	1.7
Imports												
Advanced economies	–0.2	–0.8	–1.8	–5.1	–0.3	2.9	3.1	–1.5	–4.8	–2.8	1.8	0.7
Developing countries	0.5	1.3	–2.2	0.2	–0.6	0.5	6.5	3.7	–3.6	1.8	6.5	0.8
Fuel exporters	0.6	3.4	–9.5	1.5	2.5	6.6	8.2	3.5	–1.3	8.0	15.1	0.9
Nonfuel exporters	0.5	1.0	–0.1	–0.2	–1.4	–0.6	6.2	3.7	–4.0	0.7	5.1	0.8
Terms of trade												
Advanced economies	1.1	0.2	1.4	2.0	0.4	0.4	–0.8	–0.8	1.7	—	–2.3	0.5
Developing countries	–3.5	0.2	–1.2	–1.8	0.6	2.4	1.4	–0.5	–5.8	2.6	5.7	–1.3
Fuel exporters	–7.5	–0.4	2.8	–6.2	–5.9	–2.1	10.2	–0.4	–22.9	17.3	20.1	–9.2
Nonfuel exporters	–1.1	0.2	–1.6	–0.1	2.6	3.1	–1.2	–0.5	–1.1	–1.0	1.1	0.9
Memorandum												
World exports in billions of U.S. dollars												
Goods and services	3,064	6,337	4,699	4,698	5,256	6,224	6,546	6,800	6,674	6,889	7,497	8,084
Goods	2,452	5,063	3,708	3,699	4,179	5,004	5,244	5,443	5,314	5,494	6,036	6,511

[1] Average of annual percent change for world exports and imports. The estimates of world trade comprise, in addition to trade of advanced economies and developing countries (which is summarized in the table), trade of countries in transition.

[2] As represented, respectively, by the export unit value index for the manufactures of the advanced economies; the average of U.K. Brent, Dubai, and West Texas Intermediate crude oil spot prices; and the average of world market prices for nonfuel primary commodities weighted by their 1987–89 shares in world commodity exports.

Table 23. Nonfuel Commodity Prices[1]
(Annual percent change; U.S. dollar terms)

	Ten-Year Averages		1992	1993	1994	1995	1996	1997	1998	1999	2000	2001
	1982–91	1992–2001										
Nonfuel primary commodities	**−0.2**	**0.2**	**0.1**	**1.8**	**13.4**	**8.4**	**−1.2**	**−3.2**	**−14.7**	**−7.1**	**3.2**	**4.5**
Food	−2.0	−1.0	2.3	−1.3	5.2	8.1	12.2	−10.6	−12.6	−15.6	−0.5	7.4
Beverages	−4.5	1.1	−13.9	6.3	74.9	0.9	−17.4	32.6	−15.2	−21.3	−8.4	2.6
Agricultural raw materials	2.6	1.3	2.7	16.2	9.5	4.3	−2.7	−6.8	−16.4	2.2	3.2	4.3
Metals	1.0	0.1	−2.3	−14.2	16.6	19.5	−11.9	3.7	−16.2	−1.5	13.3	1.7
Fertilizers	−1.7	0.7	−5.0	−15.4	8.0	10.6	13.7	1.1	2.8	−4.0	−4.9	3.8
Advanced economies	**0.3**	**0.6**	**2.0**	**3.1**	**8.4**	**6.8**	**2.8**	**−6.2**	**−14.2**	**−3.2**	**5.5**	**3.0**
Developing countries	**−0.9**	**—**	**−2.8**	**3.0**	**18.7**	**7.9**	**−4.7**	**2.9**	**−16.2**	**−10.9**	**3.0**	**2.9**
Regional groups												
Africa	−1.1	−0.2	−6.5	2.8	21.6	6.3	−6.3	8.8	−14.7	−12.7	1.7	2.4
Sub-Sahara	−1.1	−0.2	−6.7	4.6	22.6	5.9	−7.8	9.7	−16.1	−13.6	2.2	2.8
Asia	−0.8	0.6	3.2	10.3	13.8	8.7	−4.7	−6.9	−15.0	−6.7	3.3	3.2
Excluding China and India	−0.7	0.8	4.5	11.9	14.5	8.8	−5.9	−7.6	−14.9	−6.2	3.5	3.1
Middle East and Europe	0.2	−0.4	−5.6	−11.2	14.6	13.1	−2.7	3.2	−10.6	−6.2	3.1	2.0
Western Hemisphere	−0.9	−0.5	−6.2	−3.4	23.1	7.6	−4.0	10.4	−18.2	−14.2	3.4	2.9
Analytical groups												
By source of export earnings												
Fuel	−0.1	1.5	−1.1	16.7	11.3	6.6	−9.5	3.4	−16.9	−4.1	10.4	2.8
Manufactures	−1.5	−0.2	−1.0	7.6	12.0	7.9	−1.9	−1.9	−15.2	−11.9	2.1	3.8
Primary products	−0.2	−0.5	−5.1	−3.7	23.6	11.6	−10.4	7.8	−16.2	−14.3	4.9	3.2
Services, income, and private transfers	−0.8	−0.7	−8.1	−0.4	18.0	9.6	−5.9	2.7	−13.0	−10.7	1.8	3.0
Diversified	−0.7	0.4	−2.6	1.5	24.4	5.5	−3.4	5.4	−17.4	−8.1	2.3	1.8
By external financing source												
Net creditor countries	0.1	1.9	−2.9	−6.3	25.2	18.8	−13.6	4.2	−14.7	−0.5	15.1	1.7
Net debtor countries	−0.9	—	−2.8	3.0	18.7	7.9	−4.7	2.9	−16.2	−10.9	3.0	2.9
Official financing	−0.9	−0.6	−8.7	0.4	24.0	7.5	−8.1	9.0	−15.3	−11.9	0.7	2.7
Private financing	−1.0	−0.3	−2.6	2.7	16.6	8.4	−3.3	2.4	−16.7	−12.6	3.4	3.3
Diversified financing	−0.4	0.9	1.1	5.4	21.1	6.8	−6.0	0.5	−15.2	−5.7	3.4	1.9
Net debtor countries by debt-servicing experience												
Countries with arrears and/or rescheduling during 1994–98	−1.0	−0.3	−5.2	−0.6	19.8	6.2	−2.5	8.6	−16.7	−12.6	2.4	2.5
Other net debtor countries	−0.7	0.2	−0.8	5.8	17.9	9.1	−6.2	−1.3	−15.8	−9.6	3.4	3.2
Other groups												
Heavily indebted poor countries	−1.5	—	−8.1	6.5	28.7	5.4	−10.2	12.6	−16.0	−15.1	1.1	3.3
Least developed countries	−0.1	−0.6	−9.3	−1.6	29.7	10.5	−13.1	13.2	−19.9	−11.9	4.0	2.4
Middle East and north Africa	−0.9	−0.2	−7.8	−11.7	14.4	14.4	—	0.8	−4.8	−5.8	0.7	1.1
Memorandum												
Average oil spot price[2]	15.2	−1.7	−1.7	−11.8	−5.0	7.9	18.4	−5.4	−32.1	37.5	47.5	−13.3
In U.S. dollars a barrel	22.5	18.9	19.04	16.79	15.95	17.20	20.37	19.27	13.07	17.98	26.53	23.00
Export unit value of manufactures[3]	3.7	−0.8	3.5	−5.8	3.1	10.2	−3.1	−7.8	−1.2	−1.2	−5.3	1.1

[1]Averages of world market prices for individual commodities weighted by 1987–89 exports as a share of world commodity exports and total commodity exports for the indicated country group, respectively.
[2]Average of U.K. Brent, Dubai, and West Texas Intermediate crude oil spot prices.
[3]For the manufactures exported by the advanced economies.

Table 24. Advanced Economies: Export Volumes, Import Volumes, and Terms of Trade in Goods and Services

(Annual percent change)

| | Ten-Year Averages | | 1992 | 1993 | 1994 | 1995 | 1996 | 1997 | 1998 | 1999 | 2000 | 2001 |
	1982–91	1992–2001										
Export volume												
Advanced economies	**5.5**	**6.8**	**5.1**	**3.3**	**8.9**	**8.8**	**6.0**	**10.4**	**3.9**	**4.8**	**9.9**	**7.6**
Major industrial countries	5.1	6.3	4.5	1.9	8.2	8.3	5.8	10.6	3.8	3.5	9.5	6.8
United States	6.1	7.1	6.2	3.3	8.9	10.3	8.2	12.3	2.3	2.9	8.8	8.2
Japan	4.6	4.6	4.9	1.3	4.6	5.4	6.3	11.6	−2.5	1.9	9.7	4.0
Germany	5.7	5.3	−0.8	−5.5	7.6	5.7	5.1	11.3	7.0	5.1	11.4	7.3
France	4.5	6.2	5.4	—	7.7	7.4	3.5	10.7	8.8	3.8	8.6	7.0
Italy	4.5	6.4	7.3	9.0	9.8	12.6	0.6	6.5	3.3	−0.4	9.3	7.1
United Kingdom	3.5	6.2	4.1	3.9	9.2	9.5	7.5	8.6	2.6	3.3	7.5	5.7
Canada	5.4	9.2	7.9	10.9	13.1	9.0	5.9	8.8	8.9	10.0	11.1	7.0
Other advanced economies	6.3	7.9	6.4	5.8	10.1	9.7	6.3	10.2	4.3	6.9	10.6	8.8
Memorandum												
Industrial countries	5.0	6.4	4.4	2.2	8.4	7.9	5.7	10.4	4.4	4.2	9.4	7.1
European Union	4.8	6.3	3.4	1.2	8.8	8.0	4.7	9.9	6.2	4.5	9.5	7.3
Euro area	5.0	6.4	3.4	0.6	8.6	7.9	4.3	10.2	7.0	4.6	9.9	7.7
Newly industrialized Asian economies	10.9	10.3	11.7	12.1	12.4	15.2	7.9	10.8	0.9	8.9	13.0	10.6
Import volume												
Advanced economies	**6.1**	**7.1**	**4.7**	**1.5**	**9.6**	**8.9**	**6.3**	**9.2**	**5.7**	**7.6**	**10.3**	**7.9**
Major industrial countries	5.8	7.0	4.1	0.6	9.0	8.2	6.4	9.3	7.7	7.9	10.2	7.3
United States	6.6	10.2	6.6	9.1	12.0	8.2	8.6	13.7	11.9	10.7	13.0	8.0
Japan	5.6	4.3	−0.7	−0.3	8.9	14.2	11.9	0.5	−7.6	5.3	6.8	6.3
Germany	5.3	5.3	1.5	−5.4	7.3	5.9	3.1	8.4	8.6	8.1	9.1	7.4
France	4.5	5.3	1.8	−3.7	8.2	7.7	1.6	6.2	12.1	3.7	9.6	6.8
Italy	5.9	4.7	7.4	−10.9	8.1	9.7	−0.3	10.2	9.1	3.4	6.2	6.5
United Kingdom	5.3	7.1	6.8	3.2	5.4	5.5	9.1	9.2	8.8	7.6	8.2	6.9
Canada	5.8	8.5	6.2	7.4	8.3	6.2	5.8	15.1	6.1	9.4	13.2	7.5
Other advanced economies	6.6	7.3	5.8	3.0	10.7	10.2	6.2	9.0	2.3	7.1	10.5	9.1
Memorandum												
Industrial countries	5.6	6.9	3.8	0.2	9.0	8.0	6.0	9.4	8.0	7.4	9.8	7.4
European Union	5.3	5.9	3.6	−3.3	7.8	7.2	3.9	8.9	9.3	6.4	8.7	7.5
Euro area	5.5	5.8	3.4	−4.5	8.1	7.5	3.0	8.8	9.6	6.3	8.9	7.6
Newly industrialized Asian economies	11.4	9.2	12.6	11.2	13.9	15.1	8.2	8.2	−8.9	8.3	14.1	11.9
Terms of trade												
Advanced economies	**0.9**	**0.1**	**0.8**	**0.5**	**—**	**−0.1**	**−0.3**	**−0.6**	**1.3**	**−0.1**	**−1.0**	**0.7**
Major industrial countries	0.8	0.2	0.9	0.5	—	—	−0.5	−0.6	2.1	0.2	−1.5	1.1
United States	0.5	0.6	−0.4	0.9	—	−0.4	0.5	1.9	3.3	−0.7	−0.8	2.1
Japan	2.3	−0.5	1.6	1.8	1.3	—	−6.4	−4.5	2.6	1.0	−3.7	1.9
Germany	−0.8	0.4	2.4	2.5	0.1	1.2	−0.7	−1.8	1.8	0.9	−2.6	0.4
France	0.3	0.2	1.1	−1.7	0.2	0.1	−1.2	0.3	1.6	−0.5	0.1	2.0
Italy	2.2	−0.7	0.2	−4.4	−0.9	−2.3	4.3	−1.5	2.4	−1.7	−2.7	—
United Kingdom	0.2	0.5	1.5	0.3	−2.0	−2.5	1.0	2.7	2.6	1.2	0.4	0.2
Canada	−0.2	0.2	−0.6	−1.9	−0.7	2.8	2.2	−1.1	−3.5	3.1	3.7	−1.3
Other advanced economies	1.0	—	0.4	0.5	−0.1	−0.2	0.1	−0.6	0.1	−0.6	0.1	−0.1
Memorandum												
Industrial countries	0.8	0.2	0.8	0.5	—	0.2	−0.2	−0.5	1.5	0.1	−0.9	0.8
European Union	0.6	0.1	1.5	0.1	−0.5	−0.3	0.3	−0.4	1.6	−0.2	−0.9	0.4
Euro area	0.6	0.1	1.6	0.2	−0.2	0.1	0.1	−0.8	1.4	−0.4	−1.2	0.5
Newly industrialized Asian economies	1.1	−0.7	0.5	0.6	−0.3	−1.7	−0.5	−1.1	−0.2	−2.0	−2.1	—
Memorandum												
Trade in goods												
Advanced economies												
Export volume	5.5	6.8	4.6	2.7	9.5	9.1	5.4	10.9	3.9	4.3	10.2	7.3
Import volume	6.1	7.2	4.8	1.9	11.0	9.5	5.2	9.5	5.4	7.6	10.4	7.7
Terms of trade	1.1	0.2	1.4	2.0	0.4	0.4	−0.8	−0.8	1.7	—	−2.3	0.5

Table 25. Developing Countries—by Region: Total Trade in Goods
(Annual percent change)

	Ten-Year Averages		1992	1993	1994	1995	1996	1997	1998	1999	2000	2001
	1982–91	1992–2001										
Developing countries												
Value in U.S. dollars												
Exports	1.2	9.4	7.8	4.5	15.3	20.4	12.1	8.2	−7.7	9.5	20.4	5.9
Imports	2.6	8.8	13.2	9.4	9.5	19.1	9.4	6.6	−4.6	1.5	15.1	10.3
Volume												
Exports	4.3	8.5	9.8	7.0	12.7	10.6	8.7	10.9	3.5	5.3	10.3	7.0
Imports	1.9	8.2	14.6	10.3	8.2	11.7	7.8	8.8	0.2	0.5	11.2	9.9
Unit value in U.S. dollars												
Exports	−1.6	1.1	−0.5	−2.4	2.5	9.0	3.4	−2.2	−10.5	5.3	9.2	−0.9
Imports	2.0	1.0	0.7	−0.6	1.9	6.4	1.9	−1.7	−5.0	2.6	3.4	0.5
Terms of trade	−3.5	0.2	−1.2	−1.8	0.6	2.4	1.4	−0.5	−5.8	2.6	5.7	−1.3
Memorandum												
Real GDP growth in developing country trading partners	3.8	3.4	3.2	3.0	4.2	3.6	4.1	3.9	1.2	3.1	4.0	3.5
Market prices of nonfuel commodities exported by developing countries	−0.9	—	−2.8	3.0	18.7	7.9	−4.7	2.9	−16.2	−10.9	3.0	2.9
Regional groups												
Africa												
Value in U.S. dollars												
Exports	0.6	4.5	−0.8	−5.3	3.7	18.5	11.6	1.8	−13.7	7.2	25.6	1.7
Imports	−0.9	4.9	7.0	−3.9	5.1	20.4	1.4	3.9	−0.8	0.7	9.0	7.8
Volume												
Exports	2.7	2.9	−0.3	0.2	−0.5	5.9	6.7	3.2	0.3	1.3	6.6	5.5
Imports	0.7	3.9	2.2	−0.7	0.8	8.6	3.2	6.5	4.0	2.1	6.2	6.7
Unit value in U.S. dollars												
Exports	−0.1	2.1	−0.3	−5.5	6.4	13.1	5.1	−1.3	−13.9	6.2	18.9	−3.4
Imports	1.0	1.4	4.9	−2.7	5.0	12.3	−0.8	−2.1	−4.5	−0.9	2.7	1.4
Terms of trade	−1.1	0.7	−4.9	−2.8	1.3	0.7	6.0	0.8	−9.8	7.1	15.8	−4.7
Sub-Sahara												
Value in U.S. dollars												
Exports	0.5	4.2	—	−4.8	4.8	18.5	11.0	1.5	−13.9	5.6	22.8	1.8
Imports	−1.6	4.9	5.2	−3.3	2.7	21.8	3.9	6.5	−2.8	−0.7	9.2	8.2
Volume												
Exports	2.2	4.4	1.2	1.5	3.6	8.9	9.5	4.7	−0.3	1.4	8.5	6.0
Imports	0.3	5.4	2.9	0.5	2.4	13.2	7.4	9.5	3.8	0.7	7.2	7.2
Unit value in U.S. dollars												
Exports	−0.4	—	−1.1	−6.1	1.9	9.1	1.6	−3.1	−13.5	4.5	13.4	−3.6
Imports	−0.1	−0.4	2.3	−3.8	0.8	7.6	−3.1	−2.5	−6.2	−1.3	2.0	1.3
Terms of trade	−0.4	0.4	−3.3	−2.4	1.1	1.3	4.9	−0.6	−7.8	5.8	11.2	−4.9

Table 25 (concluded)

	Ten-Year Averages		1992	1993	1994	1995	1996	1997	1998	1999	2000	2001
	1982–91	1992–2001										
Asia												
Value in U.S. dollars												
Exports	8.5	12.4	14.9	11.6	23.7	23.2	10.2	12.1	−2.0	8.1	14.0	10.0
Imports	7.9	10.6	12.9	19.4	17.2	23.8	10.8	1.2	−13.5	9.1	17.3	12.8
Volume												
Exports	8.4	10.8	9.8	10.7	19.7	13.5	8.3	17.0	4.0	6.0	10.9	8.7
Imports	6.6	9.8	11.0	19.1	15.3	15.4	9.7	4.5	−7.4	6.5	13.2	13.1
Unit value in U.S. dollars												
Exports	0.5	1.8	4.9	0.9	3.3	8.5	1.8	−3.8	−5.4	3.8	3.0	1.3
Imports	1.4	1.2	2.7	0.3	1.9	6.8	1.5	−3.0	−6.7	5.9	3.0	−0.2
Terms of trade	−0.8	0.6	2.2	0.7	1.4	1.6	0.3	−0.9	1.3	−2.0	—	1.5
Excluding China and India												
Value in U.S. dollars												
Exports	7.7	10.9	15.5	12.5	18.5	22.4	6.0	7.3	−3.5	9.3	13.6	9.8
Imports	8.2	8.4	9.9	14.1	19.3	27.0	6.3	−0.6	−22.8	6.5	17.5	15.5
Volume												
Exports	8.8	8.4	8.2	10.0	15.6	10.5	3.8	8.6	6.3	4.9	8.9	8.2
Imports	7.9	7.0	6.9	13.2	17.5	16.5	4.9	−0.2	−15.3	1.6	13.2	16.2
Unit value in U.S. dollars												
Exports	−0.5	2.8	7.0	2.3	2.6	10.8	2.1	−1.0	−8.6	7.9	4.6	1.6
Imports	0.5	1.9	3.3	0.8	1.7	9.0	1.5	−0.3	−8.6	10.0	4.0	−0.5
Terms of trade	−1.0	0.8	3.6	1.5	0.9	1.7	0.6	−0.6	—	−1.9	0.6	2.2
Middle East and Europe												
Value in U.S. dollars												
Exports	−4.5	6.6	5.7	−1.9	7.2	13.8	17.6	1.6	−21.7	21.6	36.9	−3.9
Imports	0.4	5.2	9.9	2.2	−10.5	18.5	9.3	7.3	1.1	−2.7	15.3	5.4
Volume												
Exports	2.0	5.3	13.6	2.3	8.2	4.0	8.9	3.4	−0.6	2.5	10.0	1.7
Imports	−1.3	4.8	22.7	2.4	−11.2	9.5	5.9	10.3	5.5	−4.0	4.8	5.5
Unit value in U.S. dollars												
Exports	−5.3	1.5	−4.7	−4.1	−1.3	9.2	8.8	−1.7	−19.6	18.8	22.8	−6.1
Imports	2.5	1.3	−5.7	0.3	2.1	8.6	3.5	−2.2	−3.9	2.2	9.7	−0.1
Terms of trade	−7.6	0.2	1.1	−4.3	−3.4	0.6	5.1	0.5	−16.3	16.2	12.0	−6.0
Western Hemisphere												
Value in U.S. dollars												
Exports	2.3	9.6	5.3	6.0	15.5	22.3	11.2	10.2	−4.1	5.1	17.9	8.9
Imports	1.1	10.8	21.6	8.2	17.4	10.8	10.7	18.2	4.9	−6.0	13.9	10.8
Volume												
Exports	4.9	10.5	12.8	10.5	12.5	13.9	10.2	10.3	7.5	7.4	10.8	8.7
Imports	0.2	10.4	19.6	10.3	17.6	8.2	7.5	17.1	8.2	−5.7	14.4	9.0
Unit value in U.S. dollars												
Exports	−0.3	−0.4	−4.2	−4.0	2.9	7.7	0.9	−0.1	−10.8	−1.9	6.9	0.4
Imports	2.9	0.3	1.7	−1.9	0.1	1.5	3.1	1.4	−3.1	−0.4	−0.2	1.6
Terms of trade	−3.1	−0.7	−5.7	−2.2	2.8	6.2	−2.1	−1.4	−7.9	−1.4	7.1	−1.2

Table 26. Developing Countries—by Source of Export Earnings: Total Trade in Goods
(Annual percent change)

	Ten-Year Averages		1992	1993	1994	1995	1996	1997	1998	1999	2000	2001
	1982–91	1992–2001										
Fuel												
Value in U.S. dollars												
Exports	−4.9	6.0	3.1	−4.1	1.7	13.0	21.4	1.3	−26.9	29.0	46.2	−6.7
Imports	−1.9	4.4	11.9	−5.9	−11.3	14.2	1.3	9.5	4.3	1.1	15.8	6.2
Volume												
Exports	2.3	3.8	9.9	1.6	4.2	2.4	6.9	3.9	−0.4	1.1	8.1	1.4
Imports	−2.7	2.2	26.4	−6.1	−15.6	2.2	−1.6	12.5	7.3	−6.3	3.2	5.7
Unit value in U.S. dollars												
Exports	−5.5	2.6	−4.2	−5.5	−1.1	10.7	14.2	−2.3	−25.0	27.8	34.1	−8.6
Imports	2.1	3.0	−6.8	0.7	5.1	13.0	3.6	−1.9	−2.7	8.9	11.6	0.6
Terms of trade	−7.5	−0.4	2.8	−6.2	−5.9	−2.1	10.2	−0.4	−22.9	17.3	20.1	−9.2
Nonfuel												
Value in U.S. dollars												
Exports	5.6	10.5	9.8	7.8	20.0	22.6	9.6	10.3	−2.5	5.5	14.0	10.0
Imports	4.4	9.8	13.6	13.6	14.3	20.0	10.8	6.2	−6.0	1.6	15.0	11.1
Volume												
Exports	6.1	10.0	9.8	9.2	15.7	13.1	9.2	13.1	4.6	6.1	10.8	8.6
Imports	3.7	9.3	11.2	14.9	13.7	13.4	9.3	8.2	−0.9	1.6	12.6	10.6
Unit value in U.S. dollars												
Exports	0.9	0.8	1.1	−1.1	3.8	8.5	0.4	−2.1	−6.4	0.5	3.0	1.4
Imports	2.0	0.6	2.8	−1.0	1.1	5.3	1.7	−1.7	−5.4	1.5	1.9	0.5
Terms of trade	−1.1	0.2	−1.6	−0.1	2.6	3.1	−1.2	−0.5	−1.1	−1.0	1.1	0.9
Manufactures												
Value in U.S. dollars												
Exports	8.2	12.3	12.6	10.8	23.5	23.4	12.0	11.2	−1.4	7.5	14.4	11.4
Imports	7.0	11.2	13.7	18.4	14.9	21.5	13.1	5.4	−7.7	6.2	17.3	12.5
Volume												
Exports	8.2	11.7	10.0	11.3	19.2	14.6	10.4	15.4	3.6	9.9	12.6	10.3
Imports	5.5	11.0	12.6	20.5	13.0	14.9	10.5	8.3	−3.3	7.3	15.3	12.2
Unit value in U.S. dollars												
Exports	0.2	0.7	2.6	−0.4	3.7	7.7	1.5	−3.4	−4.7	−2.2	1.6	1.0
Imports	1.9	0.3	1.8	−1.7	2.1	4.9	2.6	−2.6	−4.7	−0.3	1.4	0.3
Terms of trade	−1.7	0.3	0.7	1.3	1.6	2.7	−1.1	−0.9	0.1	−1.9	0.3	0.7
Nonfuel primary products												
Value in U.S. dollars												
Exports	3.1	7.8	4.6	0.3	17.6	25.2	6.2	7.7	−5.3	4.9	10.9	8.6
Imports	1.0	8.1	11.4	4.3	10.5	25.8	10.1	8.1	−1.2	−5.6	10.4	10.3
Volume												
Exports	2.1	7.6	5.9	5.5	8.4	9.0	11.6	9.9	4.5	7.8	7.6	6.4
Imports	−0.3	7.4	9.0	5.0	9.0	17.7	7.6	10.4	4.8	−4.8	7.8	8.8
Unit value in U.S. dollars												
Exports	2.0	0.4	−1.4	−4.5	9.5	15.4	−4.7	−2.0	−9.1	−2.9	3.4	2.3
Imports	2.4	0.8	2.1	−0.8	2.1	6.9	2.4	−1.7	−5.5	−1.3	2.7	1.9
Terms of trade	−0.4	−0.5	−3.4	−3.7	7.2	7.9	−6.9	−0.3	−3.8	−1.7	0.7	0.4

Table 26 *(concluded)*

	Ten-Year Averages		1992	1993	1994	1995	1996	1997	1998	1999	2000	2001
	1982–91	1992–2001										
Services, income, and private transfers												
Value in U.S. dollars												
Exports	0.2	6.0	−2.1	2.0	6.2	38.1	−2.9	11.2	−4.8	−1.4	11.0	8.7
Imports	2.4	5.7	2.3	6.7	4.6	16.2	8.7	5.7	3.9	0.5	4.7	4.1
Volume												
Exports	1.1	4.9	6.8	−0.1	2.8	12.6	−0.7	10.6	−0.1	4.6	8.1	5.6
Imports	−0.1	4.8	−5.0	2.3	11.7	12.8	2.9	6.9	8.8	3.5	2.3	2.6
Unit value in U.S. dollars												
Exports	1.8	1.7	−6.9	3.0	3.2	23.6	−2.3	3.4	−3.7	−5.4	3.0	2.5
Imports	4.6	1.3	8.6	4.8	−5.0	3.6	6.0	−0.6	−4.4	−2.8	2.5	1.2
Terms of trade	−2.6	0.4	−14.2	−1.7	8.7	19.3	−7.9	4.0	0.8	−2.6	0.4	1.3
Diversified												
Value in U.S. dollars												
Exports	2.8	6.9	6.6	4.1	13.3	17.8	5.4	8.5	−4.6	0.1	13.8	5.8
Imports	1.4	7.4	18.2	7.3	17.0	15.1	5.1	8.0	−6.0	−8.7	12.7	8.4
Volume												
Exports	4.7	6.2	11.1	6.4	10.7	10.3	6.0	7.4	8.3	−6.5	6.0	3.8
Imports	3.1	6.7	14.5	8.4	18.0	8.1	8.2	7.5	1.2	−13.1	9.1	8.8
Unit value in U.S. dollars												
Exports	1.5	1.5	−0.4	−2.1	2.2	7.0	−0.4	1.2	−11.2	11.2	7.6	2.1
Imports	0.8	1.1	3.5	−1.1	0.1	6.3	−2.9	0.8	−7.5	9.8	3.4	—
Terms of trade	0.6	0.4	−3.8	−0.9	2.1	0.7	2.5	0.4	−4.0	1.3	4.1	2.1

Table 27. Summary of Payments Balances on Current Account
(Billions of U.S. dollars)

	1992	1993	1994	1995	1996	1997	1998	1999	2000	2001
Advanced economies	**−9.1**	**69.4**	**34.5**	**57.5**	**43.8**	**91.9**	**51.3**	**−134.2**	**−175.9**	**−187.8**
United States	−47.7	−82.7	−118.6	−109.5	−123.3	−140.5	−217.1	−331.5	−418.5	−438.4
European Union	−75.9	11.5	20.6	55.6	90.8	124.9	90.6	25.1	38.7	54.7
Euro area[1]	−52.7	26.1	17.9	55.3	86.1	110.3	87.2	39.9	55.6	78.4
Japan	112.3	132.0	130.6	111.4	65.8	94.1	121.0	106.8	121.2	122.4
Other advanced economies	2.2	8.6	2.0	−0.1	10.5	13.4	56.7	65.4	82.7	73.5
Memorandum										
Industrial countries	−25.5	51.2	21.8	56.7	48.9	85.8	−15.8	−194.1	−224.7	−230.0
Newly industrialized Asian economies	16.3	20.8	16.1	5.9	0.3	9.7	67.9	62.5	51.1	45.3
Developing countries	**−84.8**	**−121.1**	**−87.1**	**−98.1**	**−74.3**	**−57.7**	**−93.6**	**−24.1**	**21.1**	**−30.3**
Regional groups										
Africa	−10.6	−11.6	−11.9	−16.8	−6.7	−7.9	−20.4	−16.8	−3.6	−9.1
Asia	−12.6	−33.9	−18.4	−42.6	−38.6	9.0	46.1	45.2	39.4	23.8
Middle East and Europe	−26.9	−29.4	−4.6	−1.6	9.9	6.4	−29.9	3.8	43.9	21.5
Western Hemisphere	−34.8	−46.1	−52.2	−37.1	−38.9	−65.1	−89.5	−56.3	−58.7	−66.5
Analytical groups										
By source of export earnings										
Fuel	−30.0	−24.3	−5.0	1.2	30.8	22.0	−34.9	8.8	72.3	41.6
Nonfuel	−54.8	−96.8	−82.2	−99.4	−105.4	−79.8	−59.1	−32.8	−51.0	−71.7
By external financing source										
Net creditor countries	−15.2	−13.0	−6.4	1.9	13.3	12.0	−21.0	3.2	44.8	29.5
Net debtor countries	−69.5	−107.7	−80.4	−99.7	−87.2	−69.0	−72.5	−26.8	−22.9	−58.7
Official financing	−6.1	−8.3	−10.1	−12.0	−8.9	−5.1	−10.7	−7.4	−0.9	−3.1
Private financing	−39.7	−73.2	−58.1	−73.0	−68.3	−49.1	−43.5	−17.2	−28.8	−48.5
Diversified financing	−15.4	−21.2	−16.8	−17.5	−15.1	−17.2	−15.7	−7.0	0.4	−9.4
Net debtor countries by debt-servicing experience										
Countries with arrears and/or rescheduling during 1994–98	−22.5	−30.7	−21.3	−48.1	−41.4	−49.1	−58.5	−24.0	−8.9	−29.1
Other net debtor countries	−47.1	−77.3	−59.3	−51.8	−46.1	−20.6	−14.3	−3.4	−14.9	−30.8
Countries in transition	**−5.1**	**−8.1**	**2.2**	**−1.4**	**−16.8**	**−20.4**	**−26.4**	**−3.8**	**6.9**	**−3.4**
Central and eastern Europe	−2.3	−9.8	−5.2	−4.8	−16.9	−19.3	−22.6	−22.7	−23.8	−24.2
Excluding Belarus and Ukraine	−1.9	−8.5	−3.4	−2.8	−15.2	−17.1	−20.4	−22.4	−22.7	−23.1
Russia	−1.2	2.6	8.2	4.9	3.8	2.8	1.0	20.8	31.6	23.1
Transcaucasus and central Asia	−1.6	−0.9	−0.7	−1.5	−3.7	−3.9	−4.8	−1.9	−1.0	−2.3
Total[2]	**−99.0**	**−59.7**	**−50.3**	**−42.0**	**−47.3**	**13.8**	**−68.8**	**−162.1**	**−148.0**	**−221.5**
In percent of total world current account transactions	−1.0	−0.6	−0.5	−0.3	−0.4	0.1	−0.5	−1.2	−1.0	−1.4
In percent of world GDP	−0.4	−0.2	−0.2	−0.1	−0.2	—	−0.2	−0.5	−0.5	−0.7
Memorandum										
Emerging market countries, excluding Asian countries in surplus[3]	−87.2	−105.0	−76.1	−76.0	−75.6	−101.7	−174.6	−74.5	−16.4	−67.8

[1]Calculated as the sum of the balances of individual euro area countries.
[2]Reflects errors, omissions, and asymmetries in balance of payments statistics on current account, as well as the exclusion of data for international organizations and a limited number of countries. See "Classification of Countries" in the introduction to this Statistical Appendix.
[3]All developing and transition countries excluding China, Hong Kong SAR, Korea, Malaysia, the Philippines, Singapore, Taiwan Province of China, and Thailand.

Table 28. Advanced Economies: Balance of Payments on Current Account

	1992	1993	1994	1995	1996	1997	1998	1999	2000	2001
					Billions of U.S. dollars					
Advanced economies	**−9.1**	**69.4**	**34.5**	**57.5**	**43.8**	**91.9**	**51.3**	**−134.2**	**−175.9**	**−187.8**
Major industrial countries	−14.2	18.8	−6.6	6.9	−2.5	23.4	−52.4	−217.6	−265.5	−275.9
United States	−47.7	−82.7	−118.6	−109.5	−123.3	−140.5	−217.1	−331.5	−418.5	−438.4
Japan	112.3	132.0	130.6	111.4	65.8	94.1	121.0	106.8	121.2	122.4
Germany	−14.7	−9.8	−23.9	−20.7	−7.9	−2.8	−4.6	−19.8	−3.7	—
France	3.8	9.2	7.4	10.9	20.5	39.4	39.4	38.8	35.7	46.8
Italy	−29.2	7.8	13.2	25.1	40.0	32.4	20.0	8.2	11.1	14.7
United Kingdom	−17.8	−15.9	−2.2	−5.9	−0.9	10.8	−0.1	−17.8	−20.9	−28.8
Canada	−21.0	−21.8	−13.0	−4.4	3.4	−10.1	−11.0	−2.3	9.6	7.3
Other advanced economies	5.1	50.7	41.1	50.6	46.3	68.5	103.7	83.4	89.6	88.1
Spain	−21.3	−5.8	−6.6	0.2	0.2	2.3	−1.4	−12.8	−12.6	−11.1
Netherlands	7.4	13.7	17.8	24.1	21.7	27.6	25.3	22.5	22.9	25.4
Belgium-Luxembourg	6.6	11.2	12.6	14.2	13.8	13.9	12.2	11.7	10.9	12.1
Sweden	−7.4	−2.6	2.4	7.2	7.2	7.5	7.0	6.1	6.2	6.2
Austria	−0.6	−1.2	−2.9	−5.4	−4.8	−5.3	−4.8	−5.8	−3.8	−3.6
Denmark	4.1	4.7	2.7	1.9	3.1	1.1	0.3	2.0	3.4	4.6
Finland	−5.1	−1.1	1.1	5.3	5.1	6.8	7.3	6.8	6.8	6.7
Greece	−2.1	−0.7	−0.1	−2.9	−4.6	−4.8	−3.6	−5.1	−5.7	−5.8
Portugal	−0.2	0.2	−2.2	−0.1	−4.5	−6.1	−7.9	−10.0	−11.0	−11.7
Ireland	0.5	1.8	1.5	1.7	2.0	1.9	1.7	0.3	−0.6	−0.9
Switzerland	15.1	19.5	17.5	21.4	22.0	25.8	23.9	29.3	24.2	26.0
Norway	4.5	3.5	3.7	4.9	10.2	8.7	−1.9	6.0	22.6	20.7
Israel	0.1	−2.6	−3.4	−5.2	−5.4	−3.5	−0.8	−2.6	−2.3	−3.2
Iceland	−0.2	—	0.1	0.1	−0.1	−0.1	−0.6	−0.6	−0.7	−0.7
Korea	−3.9	1.0	−3.9	−8.5	−23.0	−8.2	40.6	25.0	11.1	1.9
Australia	−11.2	−9.8	−17.2	−19.6	−15.8	−12.7	−18.2	−22.5	−18.6	−19.1
Taiwan Province of China	8.5	7.0	6.5	5.5	11.0	7.7	3.5	7.0	6.6	7.9
Hong Kong SAR	5.8	8.6	2.1	−5.5	−1.6	−6.8	2.9	9.3	11.2	11.8
Singapore	5.9	4.2	11.4	14.4	13.9	16.9	21.0	21.3	22.1	23.7
New Zealand	−1.4	−1.0	−1.9	−3.1	−4.0	−4.3	−2.7	−4.4	−3.2	−2.9
Memorandum										
Industrial countries	−25.5	51.2	21.8	56.7	48.9	85.8	−15.8	−194.1	−224.7	−230.0
European Union	−75.9	11.5	20.6	55.6	90.8	124.9	90.6	25.1	38.7	54.7
Euro area[1]	−52.7	26.1	17.9	55.3	86.1	110.3	87.2	39.9	55.6	78.4
Newly industrialized Asian economies	16.3	20.8	16.1	5.9	0.3	9.7	67.9	62.5	51.1	45.3
					Percent of GDP					
United States	−0.8	−1.2	−1.7	−1.5	−1.6	−1.7	−2.5	−3.6	−4.2	−4.2
Japan	3.0	3.1	2.8	2.2	1.4	2.2	3.2	2.5	2.6	2.6
Germany	−0.7	−0.5	−1.1	−0.8	−0.3	−0.1	−0.2	−0.9	−0.2	—
France	0.3	0.7	0.5	0.7	1.3	2.8	2.7	2.7	2.7	3.4
Italy	−2.4	0.8	1.3	2.3	3.2	2.8	1.7	0.7	1.0	1.3
United Kingdom	−1.7	−1.7	−0.2	−0.5	−0.1	0.8	—	−1.2	−1.5	−2.0
Canada	−3.6	−3.9	−2.3	−0.8	0.6	−1.6	−1.8	−0.4	1.4	1.0
Spain	−3.5	−1.2	−1.3	—	—	0.4	−0.2	−2.2	−2.2	−1.9
Netherlands	2.2	4.2	5.1	5.8	5.3	7.3	6.5	5.7	6.2	6.5
Belgium-Luxembourg	2.8	4.9	5.1	4.8	4.8	5.3	4.5	4.4	4.4	4.7
Sweden	−2.9	−1.3	1.1	3.0	2.7	3.2	2.9	2.6	2.6	2.5
Austria	−0.3	−0.6	−1.4	−2.3	−2.1	−2.5	−2.3	−2.8	−2.0	−1.8
Denmark	2.8	3.4	1.8	1.1	1.7	0.7	0.1	1.1	2.1	2.8
Finland	−4.7	−1.3	1.1	4.1	4.0	5.6	5.7	5.2	5.6	5.3
Greece	−2.2	−0.8	−0.1	−2.4	−3.7	−4.0	−3.0	−4.1	−4.9	−4.9
Portugal	−0.2	0.3	−2.5	−0.1	−4.0	−5.7	−7.0	−8.8	−10.4	−10.5
Ireland	1.0	3.6	2.7	2.6	2.8	2.5	2.0	0.3	−0.6	−0.9
Switzerland	6.2	8.2	6.7	7.0	7.4	10.1	9.1	11.3	10.0	10.3
Norway	3.5	3.0	3.0	3.3	6.5	5.6	−1.3	3.9	14.3	13.3
Israel	0.2	−3.9	−4.5	−5.9	−5.6	−3.5	−0.9	−2.6	−2.2	−2.9
Iceland	−2.4	0.8	2.0	0.8	−1.8	−1.5	−6.8	−6.7	−7.7	−7.6
Korea	−1.3	0.3	−1.0	−1.7	−4.4	−1.7	12.8	6.1	2.3	0.4
Australia	−3.7	−3.3	−5.1	−5.4	−3.9	−3.1	−5.0	−5.7	−4.8	−4.9
Taiwan Province of China	4.0	3.2	2.7	2.1	4.0	2.7	1.3	2.5	2.1	2.2
Hong Kong SAR	5.7	7.4	1.6	−3.9	−1.0	−4.0	1.8	5.9	6.9	6.8
Singapore	12.0	7.3	16.3	17.3	15.2	17.9	25.4	25.0	23.6	22.8
New Zealand	−3.5	−2.4	−3.8	−5.2	−6.1	−6.7	−5.1	−8.1	−6.2	5.3

[1]Calculated as the sum of the balances of individual euro area countries.

Table 29. Advanced Economies: Current Account Transactions
(Billions of U.S. dollars)

	1992	1993	1994	1995	1996	1997	1998	1999	2000	2001
Exports	2,984.8	2,934.0	3,304.0	3,938.0	4,059.1	4,168.6	4,125.7	4,216.3	4,508.1	4,890.3
Imports	2,958.7	2,843.6	3,230.0	3,849.1	4,001.1	4,098.2	4,061.1	4,293.0	4,695.2	5,085.3
Trade balance	26.1	90.4	74.0	89.0	58.0	70.4	64.6	−76.7	−187.2	−195.0
Services, credits	832.6	833.2	889.6	1,006.0	1,062.9	1,093.4	1,105.6	1,142.0	1,184.1	1,271.2
Services, debits	781.6	773.2	823.4	938.3	985.8	1,000.8	1,033.3	1,071.9	1,085.9	1,155.3
Balance on services	51.1	60.0	66.2	67.7	77.1	92.6	72.3	70.2	98.2	115.9
Balance on goods and services	77.2	150.4	140.2	156.7	135.1	163.0	136.9	−6.6	−88.9	−79.1
Income, net	−16.3	−4.7	−16.2	−17.1	2.3	15.8	5.4	−28.3	−2.2	−18.4
Current transfers, net	−70.0	−76.2	−89.5	−82.2	−93.5	−86.8	−91.0	−99.3	−84.8	−90.3
Current account balance	**−9.1**	**69.4**	**34.5**	**57.5**	**43.8**	**91.9**	**51.3**	**−134.2**	**−175.9**	**−187.8**
Balance on goods and services										
Advanced economies	**77.2**	**150.4**	**140.2**	**156.7**	**135.1**	**163.0**	**136.9**	**−6.6**	**−88.9**	**−79.1**
Major industrial countries	47.6	81.2	70.7	85.0	55.6	75.0	18.8	−115.1	−205.0	−193.6
United States	−35.7	−69.0	−97.0	−96.0	−102.1	−105.9	−166.9	−265.0	−359.1	−358.9
Japan	80.7	96.5	96.4	74.7	21.2	47.3	73.2	69.1	73.0	76.1
Germany	−3.6	7.4	10.0	18.0	25.2	29.0	32.3	20.3	17.4	20.6
France	21.5	24.5	25.0	28.9	31.2	45.7	43.7	41.6	37.9	48.7
Italy	0.2	32.2	37.0	45.3	62.2	47.6	39.8	23.2	24.0	27.1
United Kingdom	−13.0	−10.1	−7.0	−4.4	−6.5	0.8	−11.5	−23.1	−24.5	−29.8
Canada	−2.6	−0.4	6.3	18.4	24.4	10.4	8.2	18.7	26.4	22.6
Other advanced economies	29.6	69.2	69.5	71.7	79.5	87.9	118.1	108.6	116.0	114.5
Memorandum										
Industrial countries	73.2	139.7	135.0	160.6	144.6	162.8	78.8	−57.6	−125.5	−110.0
European Union	12.5	92.0	111.6	145.0	174.6	185.1	158.6	107.8	103.0	119.3
Euro area	17.5	90.9	106.2	136.0	165.5	172.5	162.5	121.3	116.7	137.7
Newly industrialized Asian economies	9.6	16.9	11.9	4.3	−1.1	6.3	62.1	56.2	41.2	36.3
Income, net										
Advanced economies	**−16.3**	**−4.7**	**−16.2**	**−17.1**	**2.3**	**15.8**	**5.4**	**−28.3**	**−2.2**	**−18.4**
Major industrial countries	18.8	21.2	15.1	5.3	32.7	32.5	18.2	−8.0	19.1	1.7
United States	23.0	23.9	16.7	20.5	18.9	6.2	−6.2	−18.5	−17.4	−37.4
Japan	35.4	40.6	40.3	44.4	53.6	55.6	56.6	49.7	57.2	59.4
Germany	21.7	16.6	3.0	0.1	0.9	−1.4	−6.6	−12.7	2.3	2.5
France	−8.7	−9.1	−6.8	−9.0	−2.7	2.6	5.6	7.0	6.8	7.4
Italy	−21.9	−17.2	−16.7	−15.6	−15.0	−11.2	−12.3	−10.5	−8.8	−8.1
United Kingdom	−13.3	−12.8	−2.4	−12.4	−1.5	1.7	0.7	−1.3	−3.2	−5.9
Canada	−17.5	−20.8	−19.0	−22.7	−21.6	−21.0	−19.7	−21.7	−17.9	−16.2
Other advanced economies	−35.1	−25.9	−31.3	−22.4	−30.5	−16.8	−12.8	−20.4	−21.2	−20.1
Memorandum										
Industrial countries	−21.2	−6.7	−18.5	−18.8	1.4	12.6	2.3	−32.4	−10.9	−28.7
European Union	−55.1	−46.2	−46.2	−52.4	−40.3	−24.3	−28.5	−42.9	−31.3	−33.0
Euro area	−24.1	−18.8	−31.7	−28.9	−25.2	−15.0	−22.3	−33.7	−20.0	−19.2
Newly industrialized Asian economies	6.0	4.0	4.6	4.5	4.2	6.8	6.1	7.9	12.8	14.5

Table 30. Developing Countries: Payments Balances on Current Account

	1992	1993	1994	1995	1996	1997	1998	1999	2000	2001
					Billions of U.S. dollars					
Developing countries	**−84.8**	**−121.1**	**−87.1**	**−98.1**	**−74.3**	**−57.7**	**−93.6**	**−24.1**	**21.1**	**−30.3**
Regional groups										
Africa	−10.6	−11.6	−11.9	−16.8	−6.7	−7.9	−20.4	−16.8	−3.6	−9.1
Sub-Sahara	−10.1	−10.6	−8.7	−12.6	−7.4	−10.7	−18.7	−16.1	−9.1	−13.6
Excluding Nigeria and South Africa	−10.7	−9.9	−7.2	−9.1	−8.4	−10.7	−13.7	−11.8	−9.2	−10.7
Asia	−12.6	−33.9	−18.4	−42.6	−38.6	9.0	46.1	45.2	39.4	23.8
Excluding China and India	−15.6	−20.4	−24.3	−38.7	−39.9	−24.8	23.7	32.3	28.0	15.1
Middle East and Europe	−26.9	−29.4	−4.6	−1.6	9.9	6.4	−29.9	3.8	43.9	21.5
Western Hemisphere	−34.8	−46.1	−52.2	−37.1	−38.9	−65.1	−89.5	−56.3	−58.7	−66.5
Analytical groups										
By source of export earnings										
Fuel	−30.0	−24.3	−5.0	1.2	30.8	22.0	−34.9	8.8	72.3	41.6
Manufactures	−27.3	−60.0	−40.0	−53.0	−54.9	−24.3	−2.3	0.4	−14.3	−26.2
Nonfuel primary products	−11.6	−13.0	−11.7	−14.6	−16.6	−17.9	−18.2	−10.2	−12.6	−15.3
Services, income, and private transfers	−3.1	−5.1	−6.4	−7.0	−8.6	−8.3	−12.2	−10.0	−10.1	−9.5
Diversified	−12.8	−18.8	−24.0	−24.8	−25.1	−29.2	−26.0	−13.1	−14.2	−20.9
By external financing source										
Net creditor countries	−15.2	−13.0	−6.4	1.9	13.3	12.0	−21.0	3.2	44.8	29.5
Net debtor countries	−69.5	−107.7	−80.4	−99.7	−87.2	−69.0	−72.5	−26.8	−22.9	−58.7
Official financing	−6.1	−8.3	−10.1	−12.0	−8.9	−5.1	−10.7	−7.4	−0.9	−3.1
Private financing	−39.7	−73.2	−58.1	−73.0	−68.3	−49.1	−43.5	−17.2	−28.8	−48.5
Diversified financing	−15.4	−21.2	−16.8	−17.5	−15.1	−17.2	−15.7	−7.0	0.4	−9.4
Net debtor countries by debt-servicing experience										
Countries with arrears and/or rescheduling during 1994–98	−22.5	−30.7	−21.3	−48.1	−41.4	−49.1	−58.5	−24.0	−8.9	−29.1
Other net debtor countries	−47.1	−77.3	−59.3	−51.8	−46.1	−20.6	−14.3	−3.4	−14.9	−30.8
Other groups										
Heavily indebted poor countries	−12.0	−14.0	−10.2	−12.6	−12.8	−13.9	−15.3	−13.6	−12.6	−15.2
Least developed countries	−9.2	−9.0	−6.9	−8.9	−9.7	−9.9	−13.1	−13.3	−12.0	−14.4
Middle East and north Africa	−27.6	−25.6	−13.3	−6.2	12.1	10.5	−35.1	3.1	54.5	29.9

Table 30 *(concluded)*

	Ten-Year Averages		1992	1993	1994	1995	1996	1997	1998	1999	2000	2001
	1982–91	1992–2001										
					Percent of exports of goods and services							
Developing countries	**−14.9**	**−1.9**	**−11.8**	**−16.1**	**−10.1**	**−9.6**	**−6.5**	**−4.6**	**−8.1**	**−1.9**	**1.4**	**−1.9**
Regional groups												
Africa	−7.6	−5.7	−10.3	−11.8	−11.7	−14.0	−5.0	−5.8	−16.9	−13.1	−2.3	−5.7
Sub-Sahara	−11.5	−11.6	−13.0	−14.3	−11.2	−13.6	−7.3	−10.3	−20.5	−16.9	−8.0	−11.6
Excluding Nigeria and South Africa	−28.4	−18.1	−28.4	−27.3	−19.0	−20.2	−17.0	−21.2	−29.9	−23.9	−16.0	−18.1
Asia	−4.9	3.3	−4.7	−11.4	−5.0	−9.4	−7.7	1.6	8.6	7.8	6.0	3.3
Excluding China and India	−14.4	3.9	−9.6	−11.1	−11.1	−14.5	−13.8	−8.0	8.3	10.4	8.0	3.9
Middle East and Europe	−38.2	6.9	−15.2	−16.7	−2.5	−0.8	4.1	2.5	−14.1	1.6	13.7	6.9
Western Hemisphere	−10.2	−17.8	−20.0	−25.8	−25.7	−15.4	−14.5	−22.2	−31.4	−19.0	−17.1	−17.8
Analytical groups												
By source of export earnings												
Fuel	−34.6	13.6	−16.9	−14.1	−2.8	0.6	13.3	9.2	−19.6	3.9	22.3	13.6
Manufactures	−7.3	−3.0	−8.4	−17.0	−9.3	−10.1	−9.3	−3.7	−0.4	0.1	−1.8	−3.0
Nonfuel primary products	−21.8	−15.5	−23.8	−26.3	−20.3	−20.4	−21.7	−21.8	−22.9	−12.3	−13.9	−15.5
Services, income, and private transfers	−17.4	−16.7	−9.7	−15.0	−17.2	−15.9	−18.7	−16.9	−25.7	−20.2	−19.1	−16.7
Diversified	−2.5	−8.6	−9.4	−13.2	−15.0	−13.3	−12.8	−13.7	−12.8	−6.4	−6.2	−8.6
By external financing source												
Net creditor countries	−47.9	16.7	−13.9	−12.0	−5.8	1.6	9.5	8.3	−19.4	2.4	23.8	16.7
Net debtor countries	−8.9	−4.2	−11.3	−16.7	−10.7	−11.0	−8.7	−6.3	−6.9	−2.4	−1.8	−4.2
Official financing	−12.0	−3.9	−14.7	−20.1	−23.5	−23.0	−14.9	−7.9	−18.1	−11.6	−1.1	−3.9
Private financing	−4.9	−4.3	−8.3	−14.4	−9.6	−10.0	−8.4	−5.5	−5.1	−1.9	−2.8	−4.3
Diversified financing	−19.7	−5.8	−23.1	−31.6	−22.8	−19.8	−14.5	−14.8	−14.5	−5.7	0.2	−5.8
Net debtor countries by debt-servicing experience												
Countries with arrears and/or rescheduling during 1994–98	−18.3	−7.6	−11.8	−15.9	−10.0	−19.8	−15.2	−16.4	−21.6	−8.1	−2.4	−7.6
Other net debtor countries	−4.7	−3.0	−11.2	−17.2	−11.0	−7.9	−6.3	−2.6	−1.8	−0.4	−1.6	−3.0
Other groups												
Heavily indebted poor countries	−36.2	−22.0	−35.0	−41.4	−27.0	−27.1	−24.0	−25.0	−28.4	−23.4	−19.2	−22.0
Least developed countries	−46.7	−31.7	−41.7	−40.3	−27.9	−29.8	−29.5	−28.4	−39.7	−36.3	−27.8	−31.7
Middle East and north Africa	−39.2	10.1	−15.9	−15.0	−7.6	−3.2	5.4	4.6	−19.2	1.4	17.8	10.1
Memorandum												
Median												
Developing countries	−15.3	−10.8	−17.7	−20.3	−14.4	−13.3	−14.3	−11.7	−17.3	−12.3	−10.5	−10.8

Table 31. Developing Countries—by Region: Current Account Transactions
(Billions of U.S. dollars)

	1992	1993	1994	1995	1996	1997	1998	1999	2000	2001
Developing countries										
Exports	586.7	613.1	706.9	851.2	954.3	1,032.8	953.0	1,043.9	1,256.9	1,330.9
Imports	605.3	662.3	725.1	863.9	945.4	1,007.9	961.2	975.9	1,123.5	1,239.7
Trade balance	−18.6	−49.2	−18.2	−12.7	8.9	24.9	−8.2	68.0	133.4	91.2
Services, net	−55.5	−47.7	−40.9	−55.1	−60.2	−66.8	−54.2	−57.9	−70.3	−75.4
Balance on goods and services	−74.1	−96.9	−59.1	−67.8	−51.3	−41.9	−62.3	10.1	63.0	15.8
Income, net	−39.5	−51.2	−56.0	−62.8	−59.7	−60.2	−72.3	−79.5	−90.1	−97.9
Current transfers, net	28.8	27.1	28.1	32.5	36.6	44.4	41.0	45.3	48.2	51.8
Current account balance	**−84.8**	**−121.1**	**−87.1**	**−98.1**	**−74.3**	**−57.7**	**−93.6**	**−24.1**	**21.1**	**−30.3**
Memorandum										
Exports of goods and services	718.9	750.0	860.3	1,021.0	1,143.4	1,242.4	1,155.3	1,249.1	1,482.2	1,575.7
Interest payments	79.7	82.5	87.8	101.8	106.1	107.8	114.6	116.1	129.3	138.9
Oil trade balance	134.3	116.4	114.7	130.1	164.4	159.5	103.6	147.6	226.7	200.3
Regional groups										
Africa										
Exports	86.7	82.1	85.1	100.8	112.4	114.5	98.8	105.9	133.0	135.3
Imports	81.7	78.5	82.5	99.3	100.6	104.6	103.7	104.4	113.8	122.7
Trade balance	5.0	3.6	2.6	1.5	11.8	9.9	−5.0	1.4	19.2	12.5
Services, net	−9.2	−8.6	−9.1	−11.0	−10.2	−9.9	−9.3	−9.7	−11.4	−11.5
Balance on goods and services	−4.2	−5.0	−6.5	−9.5	1.6	—	−14.3	−8.3	7.8	1.0
Income, net	−17.8	−16.7	−15.9	−17.4	−18.9	−18.9	−17.7	−19.7	−23.2	−22.2
Current transfers, net	11.4	10.1	10.5	10.0	10.6	11.0	11.6	11.1	11.9	12.1
Current account balance	**−10.6**	**−11.6**	**−11.9**	**−16.8**	**−6.7**	**−7.9**	**−20.4**	**−16.8**	**−3.6**	**−9.1**
Memorandum										
Exports of goods and services	103.0	98.3	102.1	120.0	133.5	136.3	120.5	128.2	156.2	160.3
Interest payments	14.6	13.6	13.9	15.9	16.1	15.8	15.7	15.2	15.7	16.0
Oil trade balance	24.1	20.2	18.7	22.0	31.2	29.9	19.6	26.0	45.8	40.9
Asia										
Exports	222.2	248.0	306.8	378.0	416.6	467.1	457.7	494.7	563.7	620.2
Imports	233.2	278.5	326.4	403.9	447.6	452.9	391.9	427.6	501.6	565.6
Trade balance	−11.0	−30.5	−19.6	−25.9	−31.0	14.2	65.8	67.1	62.1	54.7
Services, net	−6.2	−9.6	−10.1	−18.7	−16.4	−22.4	−21.1	−22.8	−24.7	−30.8
Balance on goods and services	−17.2	−40.1	−29.7	−44.6	−47.4	−8.1	44.6	44.3	37.5	23.9
Income, net	−8.7	−9.6	−7.9	−17.9	−14.8	−12.5	−21.6	−24.4	−25.4	−29.6
Current transfers, net	13.3	15.7	19.2	19.8	23.6	29.6	23.1	25.4	27.3	29.6
Current account balance	**−12.6**	**−33.9**	**−18.4**	**−42.6**	**−38.6**	**9.0**	**46.1**	**45.2**	**39.4**	**23.8**
Memorandum										
Exports of goods and services	265.0	296.9	369.3	452.8	502.3	561.7	538.1	582.2	662.4	728.3
Interest payments	20.7	22.2	24.9	26.8	29.6	27.1	30.4	35.1	36.4	40.9
Oil trade balance	−4.2	−5.8	−6.2	−7.7	−12.6	−12.6	−6.6	−10.6	−18.5	−19.5

Table 31 *(concluded)*

	1992	1993	1994	1995	1996	1997	1998	1999	2000	2001
Middle East and Europe										
Exports	144.7	141.9	152.1	173.0	203.4	206.7	161.9	196.8	269.4	258.8
Imports	147.4	150.6	134.7	159.6	174.4	187.1	189.2	184.1	212.2	223.6
Trade balance	−2.7	−8.6	17.4	13.5	29.0	19.6	−27.3	12.8	57.2	35.2
Services, net	−29.3	−21.6	−13.5	−17.6	−25.3	−22.6	−11.7	−16.9	−22.5	−20.9
Balance on goods and services	−32.0	−30.2	3.9	−4.2	3.7	−3.0	−39.0	−4.1	34.7	14.3
Income, net	13.9	11.4	6.7	15.8	19.3	21.4	20.3	18.3	19.6	17.8
Current transfers, net	−8.7	−10.6	−15.2	−13.2	−13.1	−12.0	−11.2	−10.4	−10.4	−10.7
Current account balance	**−26.9**	**−29.4**	**−4.6**	**−1.6**	**9.9**	**6.4**	**−29.9**	**3.8**	**43.9**	**21.5**
Memorandum										
Exports of goods and services	176.6	176.1	185.5	206.9	240.1	251.8	211.5	242.3	319.7	312.7
Interest payments	10.8	11.7	12.1	14.7	14.3	15.4	16.0	12.7	14.5	17.3
Oil trade balance	99.3	88.1	87.2	97.9	119.9	117.4	74.9	107.3	165.5	147.6
Western Hemisphere										
Exports	133.2	141.1	163.0	199.4	221.9	244.6	234.6	246.5	290.7	316.6
Imports	143.0	154.7	181.6	201.2	222.8	263.4	276.4	259.7	295.9	327.7
Trade balance	−9.8	−13.6	−18.6	−1.8	−0.9	−18.8	−41.7	−13.2	−5.2	−11.1
Services, net	−10.8	−8.0	−8.3	−7.8	−8.2	−11.9	−12.0	−8.6	−11.7	−12.3
Balance on goods and services	−20.7	−21.6	−26.9	−9.5	−9.1	−30.7	−53.7	−21.8	−16.9	−23.4
Income, net	−26.9	−36.3	−38.9	−43.3	−45.3	−50.2	−53.3	−53.7	−61.1	−63.8
Current transfers, net	12.8	11.8	13.6	15.8	15.6	15.9	17.5	19.2	19.3	20.8
Current account balance	**−34.8**	**−46.1**	**−52.2**	**−37.1**	**−38.9**	**−65.1**	**−89.5**	**−56.3**	**−58.7**	**−66.5**
Memorandum										
Exports of goods and services	174.3	178.8	203.4	241.3	267.4	292.6	285.1	296.4	343.9	374.5
Interest payments	33.6	35.0	36.7	44.4	46.1	49.5	52.6	53.1	62.7	64.7
Oil trade balance	15.1	13.9	15.1	17.9	26.0	24.8	15.6	24.9	33.9	31.2

Table 32. Developing Countries—by Analytical Criteria: Current Account Transactions
(Billions of U.S. dollars)

	1992	1993	1994	1995	1996	1997	1998	1999	2000	2001
By source of export earnings										
Fuel										
Exports	164.1	157.4	160.1	181.0	219.7	222.6	162.8	210.0	307.1	286.4
Imports	131.4	123.7	109.8	125.4	126.9	139.0	144.9	146.5	169.7	180.1
Trade balance	32.6	33.7	50.3	55.6	92.7	83.7	17.8	63.5	137.5	106.3
Services, net	−48.7	−40.4	−32.8	−39.1	−49.1	−49.9	−39.8	−41.3	−51.2	−51.3
Balance on goods and services	−16.1	−6.7	17.5	16.5	43.6	33.7	−22.0	22.3	86.3	55.0
Income, net	6.1	3.7	0.7	7.6	9.2	9.8	9.3	7.8	7.7	8.6
Current transfers, net	−20.1	−21.3	−23.2	−22.8	−22.0	−21.6	−22.2	−21.3	−21.7	−22.0
Current account balance	**−30.0**	**−24.3**	**−5.0**	**1.2**	**30.8**	**22.0**	**−34.9**	**8.8**	**72.3**	**41.6**
Memorandum										
Exports of goods and services	178.1	171.6	174.8	192.7	232.0	237.7	178.2	226.0	324.6	304.6
Interest payments	14.5	14.6	15.0	18.3	17.3	18.3	18.6	11.6	15.4	16.3
Oil trade balance	140.6	125.0	122.9	139.8	178.0	175.4	115.9	159.1	246.1	221.4
Nonfuel exports										
Exports	422.7	455.7	546.9	670.4	734.8	810.7	790.7	834.6	951.1	1,045.8
Imports	473.9	538.6	615.4	738.7	818.7	869.3	816.7	829.7	954.1	1,059.8
Trade balance	−51.2	−82.9	−68.5	−68.3	−83.9	−58.6	−26.0	4.9	−3.1	−14.1
Services, net	−6.8	−7.4	−8.2	−16.0	−11.3	−17.1	−14.7	−17.0	−19.5	−24.3
Balance on goods and services	−58.1	−90.2	−76.7	−84.3	−95.1	−75.7	−40.6	−12.0	−22.5	−38.4
Income, net	−45.7	−54.9	−56.7	−70.4	−68.9	−70.1	−81.6	−87.5	−98.4	−107.0
Current transfers, net	48.9	48.4	51.3	55.3	58.6	66.0	63.2	66.6	69.9	73.8
Current account balance	**−54.8**	**−96.8**	**−82.2**	**−99.4**	**−105.4**	**−79.8**	**−59.1**	**−32.8**	**−51.0**	**−71.7**
Memorandum										
Exports of goods and services	540.9	578.4	685.5	828.3	911.6	1,005.2	977.5	1,023.8	1,159.0	1,272.5
Interest payments	65.2	68.0	72.8	83.5	88.8	89.6	96.1	104.5	114.0	122.7
Oil trade balance	−6.3	−8.6	−8.2	−9.6	−13.4	−15.5	−11.9	−10.8	−18.2	−20.0
Manufactures										
Exports	261.8	290.0	358.2	442.1	495.0	550.3	542.8	583.5	667.2	743.1
Imports	283.5	335.8	385.8	468.5	529.8	558.2	515.3	547.1	641.9	722.3
Trade balance	−21.7	−45.8	−27.6	−26.4	−34.8	−7.9	27.5	36.4	25.3	20.8
Services, net	−7.8	−5.4	−8.2	−14.7	−10.0	−12.6	−8.0	−12.1	−13.1	−18.3
Balance on goods and services	−29.5	−51.2	−35.8	−41.2	−44.8	−20.5	19.5	24.3	12.2	2.5
Income, net	−19.0	−31.3	−30.1	−40.6	−42.0	−42.5	−55.2	−59.5	−65.1	−71.0
Current transfers, net	21.2	22.5	25.9	28.8	31.9	38.7	33.4	35.6	38.5	42.3
Current account balance	**−27.3**	**−60.0**	**−40.0**	**−53.0**	**−54.9**	**−24.3**	**−2.3**	**0.4**	**−14.3**	**−26.2**
Memorandum										
Exports of goods and services	324.4	352.8	431.4	526.8	592.6	661.6	647.6	688.0	786.3	873.8
Interest payments	37.3	40.7	42.9	48.6	52.6	50.4	53.4	60.3	66.4	71.4
Oil trade balance	−6.0	−7.7	−7.8	−9.7	−13.2	−12.9	−10.7	−9.6	−18.0	−18.3

Table 32 *(continued)*

	1992	1993	1994	1995	1996	1997	1998	1999	2000	2001
Nonfuel primary products										
Exports	39.1	39.3	46.2	57.8	61.4	66.1	62.6	65.7	72.8	79.0
Imports	43.9	45.8	50.6	63.7	70.1	75.8	74.9	70.7	78.0	86.1
Trade balance	−4.7	−6.5	−4.4	−5.9	−8.8	−9.7	−12.3	−5.0	−5.2	−7.0
Services, net	−4.8	−4.8	−4.3	−5.2	−5.3	−5.6	−5.0	−4.5	−5.0	−5.2
Balance on goods and services	−9.5	−11.3	−8.7	−11.1	−14.0	−15.3	−17.3	−9.5	−10.3	−12.2
Income, net	−9.1	−8.3	−9.6	−10.0	−10.2	−10.2	−9.2	−9.4	−11.3	−11.9
Current transfers, net	7.0	6.6	6.7	6.4	7.7	7.5	8.3	8.7	9.0	8.8
Current account balance	**−11.6**	**−13.0**	**−11.7**	**−14.6**	**−16.6**	**−17.9**	**−18.2**	**−10.2**	**−12.6**	**−15.3**
Memorandum										
Exports of goods and services	48.7	49.3	57.3	71.6	76.4	82.1	79.3	82.9	90.7	98.6
Interest payments	8.3	7.8	8.1	9.2	9.0	9.1	9.5	9.4	10.1	10.6
Oil trade balance	−3.6	−2.8	−2.6	−3.1	−3.8	−4.3	−3.4	−3.6	−3.7	−3.8
Services, income, and private transfers										
Exports	11.5	11.8	12.5	17.3	16.8	18.7	17.8	17.5	19.4	21.1
Imports	35.4	37.8	39.6	46.0	50.0	52.9	54.9	55.2	57.8	60.2
Trade balance	−23.9	−26.0	−27.1	−28.7	−33.2	−34.2	−37.1	−37.7	−38.4	−39.0
Services, net	10.2	10.4	12.2	12.5	14.6	14.7	12.8	15.3	15.9	17.3
Balance on goods and services	−13.7	−15.7	−14.9	−16.2	−18.6	−19.5	−24.4	−22.4	−22.5	−21.8
Income, net	−0.8	−0.9	−0.8	−0.9	0.5	0.7	0.4	—	−0.3	−0.6
Current transfers, net	11.3	11.5	9.3	10.2	9.5	10.5	11.8	12.4	12.7	12.9
Current account balance	**−3.1**	**−5.1**	**−6.4**	**−7.0**	**−8.6**	**−8.3**	**−12.2**	**−10.0**	**−10.1**	**−9.5**
Memorandum										
Exports of goods and services	31.9	33.9	37.1	43.8	45.7	48.8	47.6	49.4	53.0	56.9
Interest payments	3.3	3.3	3.0	3.1	3.0	2.9	2.8	2.8	3.1	3.3
Oil trade balance	−1.4	−1.5	−2.0	−2.0	−2.6	−2.7	−3.1	−4.0	−5.3	−5.1
Diversified										
Exports	110.2	114.7	129.9	153.1	161.4	175.1	167.1	167.2	190.2	201.2
Imports	111.0	119.1	139.4	160.4	168.5	182.0	171.2	156.3	176.1	191.0
Trade balance	−0.9	−4.5	−9.5	−7.3	−7.1	−6.9	−4.0	10.9	14.1	10.2
Services, net	−4.5	−7.5	−7.8	−8.5	−10.4	−13.4	−14.1	−15.4	−16.9	−17.9
Balance on goods and services	−5.3	−12.0	−17.3	−15.8	−17.5	−20.3	−18.1	−4.5	−2.8	−7.6
Income, net	−16.8	−14.4	−16.2	−18.9	−17.2	−18.0	−17.5	−18.4	−21.2	−23.0
Current transfers, net	9.4	7.7	9.5	9.9	9.5	9.1	9.7	9.9	9.7	9.7
Current account balance	**−12.8**	**−18.8**	**−24.0**	**−24.8**	**−25.1**	**−29.2**	**−26.0**	**−13.1**	**−14.2**	**−20.9**
Memorandum										
Exports of goods and services	135.8	142.4	159.6	186.1	196.6	212.3	202.6	202.9	227.6	241.8
Interest payments	16.3	16.1	18.9	22.5	24.2	27.1	30.3	32.0	34.4	37.3
Oil trade balance	4.7	3.4	4.2	5.1	6.2	3.9	5.0	5.6	7.6	6.0

Table 32 *(continued)*

	1992	1993	1994	1995	1996	1997	1998	1999	2000	2001
By external financing source										
Net debtor countries										
Exports	490.0	517.3	609.5	740.8	823.7	899.5	856.6	924.2	1,082.7	1,169.2
Imports	536.3	593.9	660.2	791.4	872.0	928.8	878.6	893.6	1,035.6	1,148.7
Trade balance	−46.2	−76.6	−50.8	−50.7	−48.2	−29.3	−22.0	30.6	47.1	20.5
Services, net	−21.8	−20.8	−20.4	−28.2	−24.4	−30.0	−26.3	−28.5	−33.2	−38.3
Balance on goods and services	−68.0	−97.4	−71.2	−78.8	−72.6	−59.3	−48.3	2.1	13.9	−17.8
Income, net	−53.0	−61.5	−63.5	−77.9	−75.1	−77.1	−88.4	−96.2	−107.4	−115.4
Current transfers, net	51.5	51.2	54.2	57.0	60.6	67.5	64.2	67.4	70.7	74.5
Current account balance	**−69.5**	**−107.7**	**−80.4**	**−99.7**	**−87.2**	**−69.0**	**−72.5**	**−26.8**	**−22.9**	**−58.7**
Memorandum										
Exports of goods and services	612.7	644.8	753.2	904.5	1,007.2	1,101.3	1,050.6	1,120.1	1,298.2	1,403.9
Interest payments	77.7	80.7	85.8	98.8	102.8	103.9	110.4	111.6	124.9	133.3
Oil trade balance	51.4	42.1	41.0	46.8	62.6	59.8	40.8	65.2	98.1	87.3
Official financing										
Exports	32.6	32.0	32.8	40.3	46.8	51.0	45.7	49.9	62.3	64.1
Imports	37.1	38.8	42.9	51.1	54.4	54.5	55.8	56.8	61.1	65.9
Trade balance	−4.5	−6.8	−10.0	−10.8	−7.5	−3.4	−10.0	−6.9	1.2	−1.8
Services, net	−3.5	−3.4	−3.6	−4.0	−4.1	−4.1	−4.9	−4.4	−5.0	−4.7
Balance on goods and services	−8.0	−10.2	−13.6	−14.8	−11.6	−7.5	−15.0	−11.3	−3.7	−6.5
Income, net	−6.9	−6.2	−5.4	−6.1	−6.6	−6.6	−5.7	−6.4	−7.9	−7.3
Current transfers, net	8.8	8.2	9.0	9.0	9.3	9.1	10.0	10.3	10.8	10.8
Current account balance	**−6.1**	**−8.3**	**−10.1**	**−12.0**	**−8.9**	**−5.1**	**−10.7**	**−7.4**	**−0.9**	**−3.1**
Memorandum										
Exports of goods and services	41.3	41.2	42.8	52.0	59.6	64.2	58.9	64.0	77.0	79.8
Interest payments	7.5	6.9	6.6	7.3	7.3	7.4	7.3	6.8	7.1	7.0
Oil trade balance	11.8	10.4	8.7	10.0	13.6	14.3	9.7	12.8	21.4	19.7
Private financing										
Exports	377.0	406.6	490.7	602.2	662.0	728.1	698.8	740.4	851.8	930.4
Imports	402.4	457.3	521.8	629.1	692.7	739.1	695.0	704.6	818.6	907.2
Trade balance	−25.4	−50.7	−31.2	−26.8	−30.7	−10.9	3.8	35.8	33.2	23.2
Services, net	−8.3	−7.0	−9.3	−16.0	−11.1	−14.4	−11.6	−17.3	−20.4	−25.8
Balance on goods and services	−33.7	−57.7	−40.4	−42.8	−41.8	−25.4	−7.8	18.4	12.8	−2.6
Income, net	−36.9	−47.2	−50.0	−66.3	−65.5	−68.9	−77.1	−80.9	−88.9	−97.1
Current transfers, net	30.9	31.7	32.4	36.1	39.0	45.1	41.4	45.2	47.3	51.2
Current account balance	**−39.7**	**−73.2**	**−58.1**	**−73.0**	**−68.3**	**−49.1**	**−43.5**	**−17.2**	**−28.8**	**−48.5**
Memorandum										
Exports of goods and services	475.7	509.2	606.9	733.4	807.9	889.2	856.2	898.4	1,027.7	1,122.1
Interest payments	60.2	62.7	68.3	79.3	83.1	84.2	90.7	92.6	104.1	111.9
Oil trade balance	11.0	7.9	8.4	9.6	12.7	11.1	7.5	12.7	15.5	11.8

Table 32 *(continued)*

	1992	1993	1994	1995	1996	1997	1998	1999	2000	2001
Diversified financing										
Exports	54.2	54.5	59.2	71.4	83.9	92.6	90.2	104.4	133.4	140.4
Imports	65.1	70.5	74.5	88.4	100.1	110.6	102.6	107.3	126.7	142.9
Trade balance	−11.0	−16.0	−15.3	−17.0	−16.2	−18.0	−12.5	−2.8	6.8	−2.5
Services, net	−5.5	−6.6	−5.7	−7.1	−7.8	−10.2	−9.5	−6.4	−7.8	−8.0
Balance on goods and services	−16.5	−22.7	−21.1	−24.0	−24.0	−28.3	−22.0	−9.3	−1.0	−10.5
Income, net	−8.7	−7.5	−6.5	−4.5	−1.6	−0.8	−4.9	−8.1	−9.6	−9.9
Current transfers, net	9.8	9.0	10.7	11.1	10.5	11.9	11.2	10.4	11.0	11.0
Current account balance	**−15.4**	**−21.2**	**−16.8**	**−17.5**	**−15.1**	**−17.2**	**−15.7**	**−7.0**	**0.4**	**−9.4**
Memorandum										
Exports of goods and services	66.6	66.9	73.8	88.4	104.5	115.6	108.5	123.4	152.6	161.4
Interest payments	8.9	9.1	9.6	10.3	10.1	10.3	10.7	10.5	12.0	12.6
Oil trade balance	12.5	10.0	9.8	12.5	17.5	19.6	14.2	24.0	41.4	38.1
Net debtor countries by debt-servicing experience										
Countries with arrears and/or rescheduling during 1994–98										
Exports	162.1	163.2	179.8	205.9	230.6	251.3	230.0	254.9	317.5	334.5
Imports	153.7	160.4	173.9	218.6	238.1	257.4	239.0	230.7	269.7	303.4
Trade balance	8.4	2.8	5.9	−12.7	−7.5	−6.1	−9.0	24.1	47.8	31.0
Services, net	−17.0	−18.9	−18.0	−24.0	−28.6	−34.1	−35.5	−30.8	−34.2	−36.0
Balance on goods and services	−8.6	−16.2	−12.1	−36.6	−36.1	−40.3	−44.5	−6.7	13.6	−5.0
Income, net	−29.1	−28.7	−25.9	−28.4	−22.3	−25.6	−31.4	−35.5	−41.3	−43.0
Current transfers, net	15.1	14.2	16.7	16.9	17.0	16.8	17.4	18.2	18.8	18.9
Current account balance	**−22.5**	**−30.7**	**−21.3**	**−48.1**	**−41.4**	**−49.1**	**−58.5**	**−24.0**	**−8.9**	**−29.1**
Memorandum										
Exports of goods and services	190.2	192.9	212.8	243.1	272.6	299.3	271.3	296.4	362.6	384.0
Interest payments	29.6	30.9	29.9	35.8	37.5	39.7	43.4	45.0	48.4	49.5
Oil trade balance	42.1	34.1	33.3	37.0	48.2	48.0	36.1	53.2	85.8	80.3
Other net debtor countries										
Exports	325.4	351.4	426.6	531.5	589.7	644.1	623.2	665.4	760.6	829.8
Imports	380.4	431.2	484.0	570.1	631.3	668.3	636.6	659.7	762.5	841.7
Trade balance	−55.0	−79.7	−57.4	−38.6	−41.5	−24.2	−13.4	5.6	−1.9	−11.9
Services, net	−4.4	−1.4	−2.0	−3.8	4.7	4.6	9.7	2.8	1.4	−1.9
Balance on goods and services	−59.4	−81.1	−59.4	−42.3	−36.8	−19.6	−3.6	8.4	−0.5	−13.8
Income, net	−24.1	−33.1	−37.2	−49.5	−52.7	−51.5	−57.2	−60.7	−66.0	−72.2
Current transfers, net	36.4	36.9	37.3	40.0	43.3	50.5	46.5	48.9	51.5	55.2
Current account balance	**−47.1**	**−77.3**	**−59.3**	**−51.8**	**−46.1**	**−20.6**	**−14.3**	**−3.4**	**−14.9**	**−30.8**
Memorandum										
Exports of goods and services	419.7	448.9	537.1	657.7	730.9	797.6	775.6	819.3	930.4	1,014.4
Interest payments	47.7	49.5	55.5	62.4	64.4	63.4	66.5	65.9	75.6	82.9
Oil trade balance	9.9	8.4	7.9	9.9	14.6	12.1	4.9	12.2	12.5	7.3

Table 32 *(concluded)*

	1992	1993	1994	1995	1996	1997	1998	1999	2000	2001
Other groups										
Heavily indebted poor countries										
Exports	26.9	26.1	29.8	36.9	42.8	45.0	42.7	45.8	52.9	55.2
Imports	31.8	33.2	34.9	42.2	47.7	50.5	51.4	53.2	57.5	62.4
Trade balance	−5.0	−7.0	−5.2	−5.2	−5.0	−5.6	−8.7	−7.4	−4.6	−7.2
Services, net	−5.3	−5.2	−4.8	−5.9	−6.5	−7.0	−6.7	−5.9	−6.3	−6.3
Balance on goods and services	−10.3	−12.2	−10.0	−11.2	−11.5	−12.6	−15.5	−13.3	−10.9	−13.6
Income, net	−8.5	−8.2	−8.2	−9.0	−9.8	−9.5	−9.3	−10.1	−11.9	−11.7
Current transfers, net	6.7	6.4	7.9	7.6	8.5	8.2	9.4	9.9	10.2	10.1
Current account balance	**−12.0**	**−14.0**	**−10.2**	**−12.6**	**−12.8**	**−13.9**	**−15.3**	**−13.6**	**−12.6**	**−15.2**
Memorandum										
Exports of goods and services	34.4	33.8	37.9	46.6	53.4	55.7	53.9	58.0	65.8	69.1
Interest payments	6.8	6.7	6.7	7.0	7.2	6.8	7.3	6.8	7.0	7.1
Oil trade balance	2.9	2.1	1.8	2.6	4.2	4.2	2.4	4.8	8.4	7.0
Least developed countries										
Exports	17.4	17.3	19.7	24.3	26.7	28.8	26.6	29.5	35.7	37.4
Imports	26.3	26.7	27.7	32.9	35.7	37.7	38.7	40.9	43.9	47.7
Trade balance	−8.9	−9.4	−8.0	−8.6	−9.0	−8.9	−12.1	−11.4	−8.2	−10.3
Services, net	−4.0	−3.6	−3.6	−4.6	−4.7	−4.7	−4.6	−4.5	−4.8	−5.0
Balance on goods and services	−12.8	−13.0	−11.6	−13.2	−13.7	−13.6	−16.7	−15.9	−13.0	−15.3
Income, net	−4.0	−3.7	−4.7	−5.1	−5.5	−5.5	−6.0	−6.8	−8.6	−8.7
Current transfers, net	7.6	7.7	9.4	9.4	9.6	9.1	9.5	9.4	9.6	9.6
Current account balance	**−9.2**	**−9.0**	**−6.9**	**−8.9**	**−9.7**	**−9.9**	**−13.1**	**−13.3**	**−12.0**	**−14.4**
Memorandum										
Exports of goods and services	22.2	22.3	24.8	29.8	32.7	34.9	33.0	36.5	43.1	45.4
Interest payments	3.9	3.8	3.9	4.1	4.3	4.0	4.6	4.1	4.4	4.5
Oil trade balance	1.5	0.7	0.8	1.3	2.3	2.3	0.7	3.0	6.2	5.0
Middle East and north Africa										
Exports	148.6	144.2	148.0	167.2	194.8	198.9	152.1	191.7	272.0	258.3
Imports	142.8	139.2	132.2	147.5	153.2	160.5	166.7	168.0	190.2	200.6
Trade balance	5.8	5.1	15.8	19.7	41.6	38.3	−14.7	23.7	81.8	57.8
Services, net	−35.8	−28.8	−19.2	−24.5	−31.3	−32.2	−24.3	−24.8	−32.7	−32.0
Balance on goods and services	−30.0	−23.7	−3.4	−4.8	10.3	6.1	−38.9	−1.1	49.0	25.8
Income, net	10.3	8.0	3.8	11.6	14.3	16.4	15.7	15.1	16.7	15.8
Current transfers, net	−8.0	−9.9	−13.6	−13.0	−12.5	−12.1	−11.8	−10.9	−11.2	−11.6
Current account balance	**−27.6**	**−25.6**	**−13.3**	**−6.2**	**12.1**	**10.5**	**−35.1**	**3.1**	**54.5**	**29.9**
Memorandum										
Exports of goods and services	173.6	170.5	175.5	192.8	222.6	229.2	183.0	224.2	306.8	295.1
Interest payments	−11.9	−12.4	−12.5	−15.3	−15.1	−15.7	−15.7	−11.8	−11.7	−13.0
Oil trade balance	112.9	101.0	98.7	110.8	136.3	134.3	88.6	122.5	190.3	171.9

Table 33. Summary of Balance of Payments and External Financing
(Billions of U.S. dollars)

	1992	1993	1994	1995	1996	1997	1998	1999	2000	2001
Developing countries										
Balance of payments[1]										
Balance on current account	−84.8	−121.1	−87.1	−98.1	−74.3	−57.7	−93.6	−24.1	21.1	−30.3
Balance on goods and services	−74.1	−96.9	−59.1	−67.8	−51.3	−41.9	−62.3	10.1	63.0	15.8
Income, net	−39.5	−51.2	−56.0	−62.8	−59.7	−60.2	−72.3	−79.5	−90.1	−97.9
Current transfers, net	28.8	27.1	28.1	32.5	36.6	44.4	41.0	45.3	48.2	51.8
Balance on capital and financial account	91.8	135.6	108.9	121.6	110.6	107.8	123.5	59.9	9.9	52.3
Balance on capital account[2]	14.3	16.5	7.3	14.5	18.4	10.4	6.6	3.2	10.7	8.7
Balance on financial account	77.5	119.0	101.6	107.1	92.1	97.4	116.9	56.7	−0.8	43.5
Direct investment, net	32.3	52.1	74.9	84.5	108.7	128.7	126.4	126.6	116.2	115.6
Portfolio investment, net	55.5	95.5	95.2	22.5	69.9	37.5	16.7	20.2	18.1	39.2
Other investment, net	36.1	9.7	−20.1	67.2	9.1	−11.7	−44.1	−63.3	−70.4	−29.6
Reserve assets	−46.4	−38.2	−48.5	−67.0	−95.6	−57.1	17.9	−26.8	−64.7	−81.6
Errors and omissions, net	−7.0	−14.5	−21.9	−23.5	−36.2	−50.1	−29.8	−35.8	−31.0	−22.0
Capital flows										
Total capital flows, net[3]	123.9	157.2	150.1	174.1	187.7	154.5	99.0	83.5	64.0	125.1
Net official flows	21.9	49.2	25.3	31.4	8.4	22.5	43.1	30.6	31.0	27.0
Net private flows[4]	102.0	108.0	124.7	142.7	179.4	132.0	55.9	52.9	32.9	98.1
Direct investment, net	32.3	52.1	74.9	84.5	108.7	128.7	126.4	126.6	116.2	115.6
Private portfolio investment, net	55.5	66.9	89.2	17.8	57.3	30.2	3.0	7.9	7.0	29.7
Other private flows, net	14.2	−11.0	−39.4	40.4	13.4	−26.9	−73.5	−81.7	−90.3	−47.1
External financing[5]										
Net external financing[6]	174.8	188.8	170.2	209.5	236.2	240.8	183.7	152.6	173.4	220.6
Nondebt-creating flows	58.9	94.6	98.3	109.7	142.6	154.6	135.2	136.8	144.8	146.1
Capital transfers[7]	14.3	16.5	7.3	14.5	18.4	10.4	6.6	3.2	10.7	8.7
Foreign direct investment and equity security liabilities[8]	44.6	78.0	91.0	95.2	124.1	144.1	128.6	133.7	134.2	137.3
Net external borrowing[9]	115.9	94.2	71.9	99.8	93.6	86.3	48.5	15.8	28.5	74.6
Borrowing from official creditors[10]	20.9	50.0	25.7	30.9	11.3	12.7	33.8	26.7	28.9	25.7
Of which,										
Credit and loans from IMF[11]	−0.4	−0.1	−0.8	12.6	−2.9	0.8	8.5	1.2	. . .	. . .
Borrowing from banks[12]	15.6	17.8	−28.0	24.5	22.5	28.5	29.6	−7.3	2.1	10.5
Borrowing from other private creditors	79.4	26.4	74.2	44.5	59.8	45.1	−14.9	−3.7	−2.5	38.3
Memorandum										
Balance on goods and services in percent of GDP[13]	−1.9	−2.2	−1.4	−1.5	−1.0	−0.8	−1.2	0.2	1.1	0.3
Scheduled amortization of external debt	111.9	122.1	125.2	153.5	200.4	223.7	223.6	254.8	237.9	219.5
Gross external financing[14]	286.7	310.9	295.4	363.1	436.6	464.5	407.3	407.5	411.3	440.1
Gross external borrowing[15]	227.8	216.4	197.1	253.4	294.0	310.0	272.1	270.6	266.4	294.1
Exceptional external financing, net	31.1	35.2	28.0	23.8	24.9	7.1	18.1	25.1	20.3	14.8
Of which,										
Arrears on debt service	7.5	11.8	−6.1	−3.9	−3.9	−4.5	0.5	0.1	. . .	. . .
Debt forgiveness	0.3	1.8	0.9	2.7	9.1	2.7	1.8	1.7	. . .	. . .
Rescheduling of debt service	16.2	23.1	26.1	19.7	23.6	14.2	4.6	7.7	. . .	. . .
Countries in transition										
Balance of payments[1]										
Balance on current account	−5.1	−8.1	2.2	−1.4	−16.8	−20.4	−26.4	−3.8	6.9	−3.4
Balance on goods and services	−1.0	−8.6	3.0	−4.9	−18.5	−18.8	−22.1	3.1	15.7	4.3
Income, net	−11.3	−6.1	−5.2	−2.2	−5.1	−8.5	−12.1	−14.8	−16.5	−16.2
Current transfers, net	7.1	6.6	4.4	5.7	6.7	6.8	7.8	7.9	7.7	8.6
Balance on capital and financial account	8.9	12.9	−0.7	5.8	23.2	33.9	33.7	8.0	−4.6	3.7
Balance on capital account[2]	3.0	2.8	9.7	−1.6	1.4	11.0	−0.1	1.8	0.6	0.5
Balance on financial account	5.9	10.1	−10.4	7.4	21.7	22.9	33.8	6.1	−5.1	3.2
Direct investment, net	4.2	6.0	5.3	13.0	12.8	17.2	20.3	20.7	21.7	23.5
Portfolio investment, net	0.1	8.7	17.3	14.6	14.7	10.6	5.9	−7.1	8.3	9.5
Other investment, net	3.3	6.4	−27.7	17.4	−3.5	4.6	8.6	−0.4	−14.5	−15.4
Reserve assets	−1.7	−11.0	−5.3	−37.7	−2.2	−9.5	−1.1	−7.1	−20.7	−14.4
Errors and omissions, net	−3.8	−4.8	−1.5	−4.4	−6.4	−13.5	−7.3	−4.2	−2.3	−0.4

Table 33 (concluded)

	1992	1993	1994	1995	1996	1997	1998	1999	2000	2001
Capital flows										
Total capital flows, net[3]	7.6	21.1	−5.1	45.1	23.9	32.4	34.9	13.2	15.5	17.6
Net official flows	3.0	−0.8	−13.7	−5.9	4.6	26.2	6.5	−0.2	−0.5	−0.6
Net private flows[4]	4.6	21.9	8.6	51.1	19.3	6.2	28.4	13.4	16.0	18.2
Direct investment, net	4.2	6.0	5.3	13.0	12.8	17.2	20.3	20.7	21.7	23.5
Private portfolio investment, net	0.1	8.7	17.3	14.6	14.7	10.6	6.0	−7.1	8.3	9.2
Other private flows, net	0.3	7.3	−14.0	23.4	−8.1	−21.6	2.0	−0.3	−14.0	−14.6
External financing[5]										
Net external financing[6]	12.4	18.3	11.1	29.7	32.9	71.5	52.9	47.4	36.0	38.3
Nondebt-creating flows	6.2	8.8	15.3	11.7	14.7	30.9	21.8	23.1	23.9	27.3
Capital transfers[7]	3.0	2.8	9.7	−1.6	1.4	11.0	−0.1	1.8	0.6	0.5
Foreign direct investment anf equity security liabilities[8]	3.2	6.1	5.6	13.4	13.3	19.9	22.0	21.3	23.3	26.8
Net external borrowing[9]	6.1	9.5	−4.2	17.9	18.1	40.6	31.1	24.3	12.1	11.0
Borrowing from official creditors[10]	2.9	−0.8	−10.7	−4.7	4.9	19.0	8.2	−0.2	−0.5	−0.6
Of which,										
Credit and loans from IMF[11]	1.6	3.7	2.4	4.7	3.7	2.5	5.5	−3.6	. . .	. . .
Borrowing from banks[12]	−1.2	7.4	4.2	−1.7	2.3	4.1	2.9	−0.4	1.2	1.3
Borrowing from other private creditors	4.5	2.8	2.3	24.4	10.9	17.5	20.0	24.8	11.4	10.3
Memorandum										
Balance on goods and services in percent of GDP[13]	−0.3	−1.8	0.5	−0.6	−2.1	−2.0	−2.8	0.5	2.1	0.5
Scheduled amortization of external debt	30.9	26.2	26.0	28.3	26.9	20.5	24.5	32.1	33.9	33.2
Gross external financing[14]	43.3	44.5	37.1	57.9	59.8	92.0	77.4	79.6	69.8	71.5
Gross external borrowing[15]	37.1	35.7	21.9	46.2	45.0	61.1	55.6	56.4	45.9	44.2
Exceptional external financing, net	19.4	21.5	19.3	16.8	13.6	7.0	7.8	9.2	0.5	0.5
Of which,										
Arrears on debt service	7.3	2.1	3.8	−0.5	1.0	2.5	3.1	8.1	. . .	. . .
Debt forgiveness	2.4	2.1	—	0.5	0.9	—	—	—	. . .	. . .
Rescheduling of debt service	9.5	16.7	13.2	13.9	9.9	3.3	2.8	0.2	. . .	. . .

[1]Standard presentation in accordance with the 5th edition of the International Monetary Fund's *Balance of Payments Manual* (1993).

[2]Comprises capital transfers—including debt forgiveness—and acquisition/disposal of nonproduced, nonfinancial assets.

[3]Comprise net direct investment, net portfolio investment, and other long- and short-term net investment flows, including official and private borrowing. In the standard balance of payments presentation above, total net capital flows are equal to the balance on financial account minus the change in reserve assets.

[4]Because of limitations on the data coverage for net official flows, the residually derived data for net private flows may include some official flows.

[5]As defined in the *World Economic Outlook* (see footnote 6). It should be noted that there is no generally accepted standard definition of external financing.

[6]Defined as the sum of—with opposite sign—the goods and services balance, net income and current transfers, direct investment abroad, the change in reserve assets, the net acquisition of other assets (such as recorded private portfolio assets, export credit, and the collateral for debt-reduction operations), and the net errors and omissions. Thus, net external financing, according to the definition adopted in the *World Economic Outlook*, measures the total amount required to finance the current account, direct investment outflows, net reserve transactions (often at the discretion of the monetary authorities), the net acquisition of nonreserve external assets, and the net transactions underlying the errors and omissions (not infrequently reflecting capital flight).

[7]Including other transactions on capital account.

[8]Debt-creating foreign direct investment liabilities are not included.

[9]Net disbursement of long- and short-term credits, including exceptional financing, by both official and private creditors.

[10]Net disbursement by official creditors, based on directly reported flows and flows derived from information on external debt.

[11]Comprise use of International Monetary Fund resources under the General Resources Account, Trust Fund, and Poverty Reduction and Growth Facility (PRGF). For further detail, see Table 37.

[12]Net disbursement by commercial banks, based on directly reported flows and cross-border claims and liabilities reported in the International Banking section of the International Monetary Fund's *International Financial Statistics*.

[13]This is often referred to as the "resource balance" and, with opposite sign, the "net resource transfer."

[14]Net external financing plus amortization due on external debt.

[15]Net external borrowing plus amortization due on external debt.

Table 34. Developing Countries—by Region: Balance of Payments and External Financing[1]

(Billions of U.S. dollars)

	1992	1993	1994	1995	1996	1997	1998	1999	2000	2001
Africa										
Balance of payments										
Balance on current account	−10.6	−11.6	−11.9	−16.8	−6.7	−7.9	−20.4	−16.8	−3.6	−9.1
Balance on capital account	2.8	3.5	3.1	3.4	6.8	5.0	3.9	5.2	8.1	3.7
Balance on financial account	8.2	10.1	9.4	13.8	1.8	3.7	14.0	11.2	−4.5	4.5
Change in reserves (− = increase)	0.9	2.9	−6.0	−3.1	−9.2	−10.6	1.3	−2.9	−14.3	−7.9
Other official flows, net	9.0	6.1	7.8	8.9	3.2	2.1	6.0	3.8	0.9	4.4
Private flows, net	−1.7	1.1	7.5	7.9	7.8	12.1	6.8	10.3	9.0	7.9
External financing										
Net external financing	13.4	11.3	20.3	25.9	21.8	28.1	25.9	28.1	25.3	23.5
Nondebt-creating inflows	5.9	7.4	7.8	11.7	15.6	22.1	21.2	24.4	23.6	20.6
Net external borrowing	7.5	3.8	12.6	14.2	6.2	6.0	4.7	3.7	1.7	2.9
From official creditors	8.9	5.9	7.6	8.6	3.0	1.8	5.8	3.5	0.7	4.2
Of which,										
Credit and loans from IMF	−0.2	0.2	0.9	0.8	0.6	−0.5	−0.4	−0.2	. . .	. . .
From banks	−3.1	—	2.5	2.0	−0.2	−0.8	−0.3	0.3	0.3	1.8
From other private creditors	1.6	−2.2	2.5	3.6	3.4	5.0	−0.7	−0.1	0.8	−3.1
Memorandum										
Exceptional financing	15.6	11.6	15.8	15.3	19.2	14.2	4.1	9.6	4.7	3.7
Sub-Sahara										
Balance of payments										
Balance on current account	−10.1	−10.6	−8.7	−12.6	−7.4	−10.7	−18.7	−16.1	−9.1	−13.6
Balance on capital account	2.7	3.4	3.0	3.4	6.7	4.9	3.7	4.8	7.9	3.6
Balance on financial account	7.3	9.1	6.5	10.0	2.9	6.5	12.7	10.2	1.5	9.2
Change in reserves (− = increase)	1.6	3.1	−3.6	−4.2	−6.5	−5.9	0.5	−3.8	−7.1	−5.7
Other official flows, net	8.6	5.6	5.6	5.5	3.5	3.0	6.2	3.8	−0.4	3.9
Private flows, net	−2.9	0.4	4.6	8.7	6.0	9.4	6.0	10.2	9.0	11.1
External financing										
Net external financing	11.8	10.0	15.0	23.2	20.0	26.0	25.2	27.6	23.9	25.9
Nondebt-creating inflows	4.9	6.3	6.5	11.0	14.4	20.3	19.6	22.5	21.1	18.5
Net external borrowing	6.9	3.7	8.5	12.2	5.6	5.8	5.6	5.1	2.8	7.4
From official creditors	8.6	5.4	5.3	5.2	3.3	2.6	6.0	3.5	−0.7	3.6
Of which,										
Credit and loans from IMF	—	0.7	0.5	0.6	0.1	−0.5	−0.3	−0.1	. . .	. . .
From banks	−3.0	−0.1	1.9	1.4	−0.4	−1.3	−0.5	—	−0.2	1.4
From other private creditors	1.3	−1.7	1.3	5.6	2.8	4.5	0.1	1.6	3.7	2.4
Memorandum										
Exceptional financing	15.0	11.6	10.1	9.2	14.7	10.6	3.1	8.9	4.6	3.7
Asia										
Balance of payments										
Balance on current account	−12.6	−33.9	−18.4	−42.6	−38.6	9.0	46.1	45.2	39.4	23.8
Balance on capital account	9.9	12.8	3.1	8.9	10.6	3.3	−1.0	−5.4	0.5	3.6
Balance on financial account	8.4	32.0	28.0	51.7	57.5	22.1	−25.2	−16.0	−20.9	−13.7
Change in reserves (− = increase)	−14.6	−23.5	−43.8	−33.0	−39.3	−20.5	−16.7	−30.8	−23.8	−49.2
Other official flows, net	11.5	11.3	11.5	7.6	−1.0	4.6	13.7	11.6	8.5	11.3
Private flows, net	11.6	44.1	60.2	77.2	97.9	37.9	−22.2	3.2	−5.6	24.3
External financing										
Net external financing	44.8	72.8	73.4	89.7	104.5	88.3	30.6	42.1	61.2	91.4
Nondebt-creating inflows	28.7	48.2	46.2	58.7	68.6	61.5	53.6	37.5	50.2	58.7
Net external borrowing	16.1	24.5	27.2	31.0	35.9	26.8	−23.0	4.6	11.0	32.7
From official creditors	11.5	10.7	10.9	6.5	−1.9	3.5	13.3	11.7	8.5	11.2
Of which,										
Credit and loans from IMF	1.3	0.6	−0.8	−1.5	−1.7	5.0	6.6	1.7	. . .	. . .
From banks	7.3	10.5	10.3	16.8	24.6	23.0	1.6	−15.0	−3.6	6.2
From other private creditors	−2.7	3.3	5.9	7.7	13.2	0.3	−38.0	7.9	6.1	15.2
Memorandum										
Exceptional financing	2.2	0.8	1.2	0.5	0.8	−8.1	12.0	15.3	16.4	10.4

Table 34 *(concluded)*

	1992	1993	1994	1995	1996	1997	1998	1999	2000	2001
Asia, excluding China and India										
Balance of payments										
Balance on current account	−15.6	−20.4	−24.3	−38.7	−39.9	−24.8	23.7	32.3	28.0	15.1
Balance on capital account	9.9	12.8	3.1	8.9	10.6	3.3	−1.0	−5.3	0.5	3.6
Balance on financial account	3.6	7.6	25.8	30.8	41.3	32.5	−18.1	−17.9	−23.4	−15.9
Change in reserves (− = increase)	−14.8	−17.2	−3.9	−12.7	−5.0	20.0	−7.6	−16.3	−13.7	−26.7
Other official flows, net	5.1	5.4	2.8	3.7	−3.3	3.1	8.1	4.6	3.5	3.4
Private flows, net	13.2	19.4	26.9	39.8	49.5	9.5	−18.6	−6.2	−13.2	7.4
External financing										
Net external financing	32.0	33.0	25.0	46.1	49.6	15.1	−12.8	−11.2	1.7	19.6
Nondebt-creating inflows	17.0	18.8	7.0	20.8	24.1	9.9	10.7	−2.8	6.5	12.6
Net external borrowing	15.0	14.2	18.0	25.2	25.5	5.2	−23.5	−8.3	−4.8	7.1
From official creditors	5.1	4.8	2.2	2.6	−4.2	1.9	7.7	4.7	3.5	3.3
Of which,										
Credit and loans from IMF	0.1	0.1	0.4	−0.3	−0.4	5.7	7.0	2.1	. . .	. . .
From banks	3.2	3.4	6.6	11.1	20.7	15.7	−1.3	−13.2	−8.4	−2.1
From other private creditors	6.7	6.0	9.2	11.5	9.0	−12.3	−29.9	0.2	0.1	5.8
Memorandum										
Exceptional financing	2.2	0.8	1.2	0.5	0.8	−8.1	12.0	15.3	16.4	10.4
Middle East and Europe										
Balance of payments										
Balance on current account	−26.9	−29.4	−4.6	−1.6	9.9	6.4	−29.9	3.8	43.9	21.5
Balance on capital account	1.0	−0.3	1.1	1.7	—	1.1	2.7	2.0	0.8	0.2
Balance on financial account	27.0	32.3	12.7	5.7	−7.2	2.7	31.5	0.2	−32.8	−13.5
Change in reserves (− = increase)	−9.8	3.1	−3.0	−7.6	−17.7	−12.0	14.3	−3.4	−17.0	−15.0
Other official flows, net	−2.0	1.9	−1.3	1.6	0.9	0.3	7.5	4.6	2.1	0.7
Private flows, net	38.7	27.3	17.1	11.6	9.6	14.4	9.6	−1.0	−17.9	0.8
External financing										
Net external financing	48.5	23.1	11.9	9.6	17.7	23.6	30.3	7.0	−1.3	11.6
Nondebt-creating inflows	4.6	4.5	6.2	7.3	7.4	5.9	7.3	6.3	8.2	10.2
Net external borrowing	43.8	18.7	5.7	2.3	10.3	17.8	23.1	0.8	−9.5	1.4
From official creditors	−2.0	2.0	−1.3	−1.0	−0.8	−1.0	−1.1	−1.7	1.0	−0.4
Of which,										
Credit and loans from IMF	0.1	—	0.4	0.4	0.1	0.2	−0.1	0.6	. . .	. . .
From banks	11.5	1.6	−9.7	0.2	−3.6	2.6	12.5	5.2	−1.0	−1.5
From other private creditors	34.3	15.1	16.7	3.0	14.7	16.2	11.6	−2.7	−9.5	3.3
Memorandum										
Exceptional financing	3.3	13.9	4.8	3.8	−0.3	0.7	0.8	0.6	0.3	0.4
Western Hemisphere										
Balance of payments										
Balance on current account	−34.8	−46.1	−52.2	−37.1	−38.9	−65.1	−89.5	−56.3	−58.7	−66.5
Balance on capital account	0.5	0.6	—	0.4	1.0	1.1	1.0	1.4	1.3	1.2
Balance on financial account	33.8	44.6	51.5	35.9	40.0	69.0	96.6	61.3	57.4	66.2
Change in reserves (− = increase)	−22.9	−20.7	4.3	−23.4	−29.4	−14.1	18.9	10.3	−9.6	−9.5
Other official flows, net	3.4	29.9	7.3	13.3	5.3	15.5	16.0	10.6	19.5	10.6
Private flows, net	53.4	35.5	39.9	46.0	64.0	67.6	61.7	40.4	47.5	65.1
External financing										
Net external financing	68.1	81.7	64.6	84.3	92.2	100.8	96.9	75.4	88.1	94.2
Nondebt-creating inflows	19.6	34.4	38.2	32.0	51.1	65.1	53.1	68.7	62.8	56.6
Net external borrowing	48.4	47.2	26.4	52.3	41.1	35.7	43.8	6.7	25.3	37.6
From official creditors	2.4	31.5	8.4	16.7	11.0	8.5	15.9	13.3	18.7	10.8
Of which,										
Credit and loans from IMF	−1.6	−0.9	−1.3	12.9	−2.0	−4.0	2.5	−0.9	. . .	. . .
From banks	−0.1	5.6	−31.0	5.5	1.7	3.7	15.7	2.2	6.4	4.0
From other private creditors	46.1	10.1	49.0	30.1	28.5	23.6	12.2	−8.8	0.1	22.9
Memorandum										
Exceptional financing	9.9	8.9	6.2	4.1	5.2	0.2	1.1	−0.4	−1.0	0.3

[1]For definitions, see footnotes to Table 33.

Table 35. Developing Countries—by Analytical Criteria: Balance of Payments and External Financing[1]

(Billions of U.S. dollars)

	1992	1993	1994	1995	1996	1997	1998	1999	2000	2001
By source of export earnings										
Fuel										
Balance of payments										
Balance on current account	−30.0	−24.3	−5.0	1.2	30.8	22.0	−34.9	8.8	72.3	41.6
Balance on capital account	1.0	0.1	1.6	1.6	3.6	1.0	2.7	2.4	0.3	−0.1
Balance on financial account	34.2	30.2	17.9	7.7	−27.7	−11.4	33.5	−1.0	−58.3	−31.3
Change in reserves (− = increase)	0.3	11.4	1.8	1.7	−22.4	−14.6	19.0	5.1	−25.3	−13.9
Other official flows, net	9.9	4.0	5.8	7.5	6.2	6.0	12.6	7.1	1.1	0.4
Private flows, net	24.1	14.8	10.3	−1.5	−11.5	−2.8	1.9	−13.3	−34.1	−17.8
External financing										
Net external financing	41.3	11.0	19.4	3.2	7.9	15.6	32.4	0.3	−20.1	−6.1
Nondebt-creating inflows	3.9	1.8	4.6	4.1	11.0	7.6	10.9	8.4	7.5	11.4
Net external borrowing	37.4	9.2	14.9	−1.0	−3.1	8.0	21.6	−8.1	−27.7	−17.5
From official creditors	8.9	4.9	6.3	4.3	6.3	3.4	3.3	1.2	0.6	−0.5
Of which,										
Credit and loans from IMF	−0.5	−0.8	0.4	−0.2	0.7	−0.3	−0.6	−0.5	. . .	. . .
From banks	5.5	2.7	−2.1	−1.8	−7.9	−0.2	9.0	2.5	−2.0	−0.9
From other private creditors	23.0	1.7	10.7	−3.5	−1.5	4.8	9.3	−11.8	−26.3	−16.1
Memorandum										
Exceptional financing	10.3	17.4	13.6	12.9	14.1	8.1	5.9	4.4	0.1	0.4
Nonfuel										
Balance of payments										
Balance on current account	−54.8	−96.8	−82.2	−99.4	−105.4	−79.8	−59.1	−32.8	−51.0	−71.7
Balance on capital account	13.4	16.4	5.7	12.9	14.9	9.4	3.9	0.8	10.3	8.8
Balance on financial account	43.3	88.9	83.8	99.5	120.1	109.0	83.8	57.6	57.4	74.7
Change in reserves (− = increase)	−46.6	−49.6	−50.3	−68.8	−73.2	−42.5	−1.1	−32.0	−39.6	−67.9
Other official flows, net	12.0	45.3	19.6	24.0	2.2	16.5	30.6	23.5	30.0	26.6
Private flows, net	77.9	93.1	114.6	144.3	191.1	135.0	54.3	66.1	67.0	115.9
External financing										
Net external financing	133.4	177.9	150.9	206.5	228.6	225.4	151.7	152.3	193.4	226.7
Nondebt-creating inflows	55.0	92.8	93.9	105.7	131.9	147.2	124.7	128.4	137.4	134.9
Net external borrowing	78.5	85.0	57.0	100.8	96.7	78.3	27.0	23.8	56.0	91.9
From official creditors	12.0	45.2	19.4	26.6	5.0	9.4	30.6	25.5	28.3	26.3
Of which,										
Credit and loans from IMF	—	0.6	−1.2	12.8	−3.6	1.2	9.1	1.8	. . .	. . .
From banks	10.1	15.2	−25.8	26.2	30.4	28.6	20.5	−9.8	4.1	11.4
From other private creditors	56.4	24.7	63.5	47.9	61.3	40.3	−24.1	8.1	23.6	54.2
Memorandum										
Exceptional financing	20.8	17.8	14.4	10.9	10.8	−1.0	12.2	20.6	20.2	14.4
By external financing source										
Net creditor countries										
Balance of payments										
Balance on current account	−15.2	−13.0	−6.4	1.9	13.3	12.0	−21.0	3.2	44.8	29.5
Balance on capital account	0.7	−0.4	0.7	0.2	−0.2	0.6	2.3	1.7	0.4	−0.1
Balance on financial account	19.9	18.6	13.3	8.5	−6.0	−5.5	21.7	4.4	−32.0	−19.4
Change in reserves (− = increase)	−4.4	7.6	1.5	0.5	−10.0	−9.6	11.3	3.3	−10.7	−8.9
Other official flows, net	0.2	0.5	0.2	2.7	2.2	1.1	8.3	5.5	0.1	0.5
Private flows, net	24.1	10.5	11.5	5.2	1.9	2.9	2.0	−4.4	−21.4	−11.0
External financing										
Net external financing	15.0	11.0	6.1	2.1	6.9	4.1	6.6	0.1	−11.5	−3.3
Nondebt-creating inflows	0.8	−0.6	0.8	0.3	0.3	0.7	2.5	1.9	1.6	4.2
Net external borrowing	14.2	11.6	5.3	1.8	6.7	3.4	4.1	−1.8	−13.1	−7.5
From official creditors	0.2	0.5	0.2	0.1	0.6	−0.2	−0.3	−0.9	−1.0	−0.6
Of which,										
Credit and loans from IMF	—	—	—	—	—	—	—	—	. . .	. . .
From banks	6.7	3.4	−1.0	1.7	−1.5	3.7	8.2	3.0	−0.8	−1.1
From other private creditors	7.2	7.6	6.1	−0.1	7.6	—	−3.9	−3.9	−11.3	−5.8
Memorandum										
Exceptional financing	—	—	—	—	—	—	—	—	—	—

Table 35 *(continued)*

	1992	1993	1994	1995	1996	1997	1998	1999	2000	2001
Net debtor countries										
Balance of payments										
Balance on current account	−69.5	−107.7	−80.4	−99.7	−87.2	−69.0	−72.5	−26.8	−22.9	−58.7
Balance on capital account	13.7	17.0	6.6	14.3	18.6	9.8	4.3	1.5	10.3	8.8
Balance on financial account	57.6	99.7	87.7	98.1	96.4	102.2	93.9	51.8	30.3	61.8
Change in reserves (− = increase)	−42.2	−46.7	−50.5	−68.0	−87.3	−48.2	5.5	−30.6	−54.7	−73.6
Other official flows, net	21.9	48.9	25.2	28.7	6.1	21.3	34.7	25.0	30.7	26.3
Private flows, net	77.9	97.4	113.1	137.4	177.6	129.1	53.7	57.3	54.4	109.1
External financing										
Net external financing	160.1	178.2	164.2	207.6	229.5	236.9	177.2	152.9	185.1	224.2
Nondebt-creating inflows	58.2	95.1	97.6	109.6	142.4	154.0	132.9	135.1	143.5	142.1
Net external borrowing	101.9	83.2	66.6	98.0	87.1	82.9	44.4	17.7	41.7	82.0
From official creditors	21.0	49.7	25.5	30.7	10.7	12.9	34.0	27.5	29.7	26.2
Of which,										
Credit and loans from IMF	−0.4	−0.1	−0.8	12.6	−2.9	0.8	8.5	1.2	. . .	. . .
From banks	8.9	14.5	−27.0	22.8	24.0	24.8	21.3	−10.3	3.0	11.7
From other private creditors	72.0	19.0	68.0	44.6	52.4	45.3	−11.0	0.5	9.1	44.2
Memorandum										
Exceptional financing	31.1	35.2	28.0	23.8	24.9	7.1	18.1	25.1	20.3	14.8
Official financing										
Balance of payments										
Balance on current account	−6.1	−8.3	−10.1	−12.0	−8.9	−5.1	−10.7	−7.4	−0.9	−3.1
Balance on capital account	3.3	4.3	4.1	4.1	4.2	6.9	5.9	6.5	10.1	5.3
Balance on financial account	2.5	2.6	5.6	8.1	4.5	−1.5	5.5	1.8	−8.8	−1.8
Change in reserves (− = increase)	−0.4	0.5	−2.7	−1.4	−4.2	−6.3	1.2	−1.1	−9.3	−5.0
Other official flows, net	5.5	4.0	5.3	5.8	2.4	4.8	4.2	1.9	−4.0	3.4
Private flows, net	−2.5	−1.9	3.0	3.6	6.3	—	0.1	0.9	4.5	−0.2
External financing										
Net external financing	6.8	5.3	10.4	12.5	10.4	8.6	10.6	9.4	9.7	7.7
Nondebt-creating inflows	2.5	3.8	5.2	5.1	6.3	9.2	8.9	9.2	13.2	8.5
Net external borrowing	4.3	1.5	5.2	7.4	4.0	−0.6	1.7	0.2	−3.6	−0.8
From official creditors	5.4	3.9	5.2	5.7	2.3	4.7	4.1	1.7	−4.2	3.2
Of which,										
Credit and loans from IMF	−0.1	−0.5	1.1	1.1	0.9	0.2	—	—	. . .	. . .
From banks	0.2	−0.8	−0.5	0.4	0.1	−0.6	—	−0.2	−0.5	0.2
From other private creditors	−1.2	−1.7	0.5	1.3	1.7	−4.6	−2.4	−1.4	1.1	−4.3
Memorandum										
Exceptional financing	7.2	5.9	12.4	12.7	13.1	0.6	5.3	4.5	3.4	2.5
Private financing										
Balance of payments										
Balance on current account	−39.7	−73.2	−58.1	−73.0	−68.3	−49.1	−43.5	−17.2	−28.8	−48.5
Balance on capital account	9.4	11.1	1.6	8.2	9.9	2.5	−2.1	−5.8	—	2.9
Balance on financial account	39.2	76.5	68.9	80.4	90.8	83.4	76.0	43.0	43.5	56.6
Change in reserves (− = increase)	−41.8	−45.8	−39.9	−60.8	−67.6	−45.0	6.0	−21.4	−34.2	−59.1
Other official flows, net	6.5	40.3	16.7	21.2	−0.3	13.9	24.2	18.8	29.6	18.2
Private flows, net	74.5	82.0	92.1	120.1	158.7	114.6	45.8	45.6	48.1	97.4
External financing										
Net external financing	136.9	149.6	131.8	174.0	195.6	208.1	150.9	126.4	166.7	197.1
Nondebt-creating inflows	50.3	81.8	83.4	91.0	119.8	134.2	112.3	113.8	120.1	119.8
Net external borrowing	86.6	67.8	48.4	83.0	75.8	73.9	38.6	12.5	46.5	77.2
From official creditors	5.9	41.3	17.2	23.5	4.5	5.6	23.7	21.4	28.7	18.3
Of which,										
Credit and loans from IMF	−0.9	0.3	−2.2	11.9	−3.3	0.4	7.6	0.7	. . .	. . .
From banks	10.8	15.5	−27.5	23.7	29.1	28.2	20.0	−10.1	3.2	10.2
From other private creditors	70.0	11.1	58.6	35.9	42.1	40.1	−5.1	1.3	14.6	48.7
Memorandum										
Exceptional financing	8.8	7.6	4.9	2.3	1.7	0.4	13.1	11.2	11.0	8.6

Table 35 *(continued)*

	1992	1993	1994	1995	1996	1997	1998	1999	2000	2001
Diversified financing										
Balance of payments										
Balance on current account	−15.4	−21.2	−16.8	−17.5	−15.1	−17.2	−15.7	−7.0	0.4	−9.4
Balance on capital account	0.8	1.4	0.8	0.8	4.4	0.4	0.5	0.6	0.1	0.4
Balance on financial account	8.1	17.0	15.1	13.6	11.7	19.3	11.4	11.8	2.2	9.6
Change in reserves (− = increase)	0.3	−0.3	−6.0	−2.7	−10.7	−0.2	−2.2	−5.4	−5.2	−6.3
Other official flows, net	7.9	5.2	3.4	1.8	3.8	2.9	6.7	4.8	5.6	5.2
Private flows, net	−0.2	12.2	17.7	14.5	18.7	16.6	6.9	12.4	1.8	10.7
External financing										
Net external financing	8.4	18.6	21.8	20.7	29.1	22.2	15.1	19.1	9.3	18.7
Nondebt-creating inflows	4.7	8.9	8.4	11.8	15.8	10.0	10.7	11.4	9.3	13.0
Net external borrowing	3.7	9.7	13.5	8.8	13.3	12.2	4.4	7.7	—	5.7
From official creditors	7.7	5.1	3.3	1.7	3.7	2.9	6.6	4.8	5.6	5.1
Of which,										
Credit and loans from IMF	0.5	0.1	0.3	−0.3	−0.5	0.2	1.0	0.6	...	...
From banks	−3.5	0.6	3.5	1.6	0.1	−0.3	−0.3	−0.4	0.3	1.0
From other private creditors	−0.5	4.0	6.7	5.5	9.5	9.5	−2.0	3.3	−5.9	−0.4
Memorandum										
Exceptional financing	12.9	9.8	7.9	6.7	10.1	6.3	−0.3	9.6	5.9	3.6
Net debtor countries by debt-servicing experience										
Countries with arrears and/or rescheduling during 1994–98										
Balance of payments										
Balance on current account	−22.5	−30.7	−21.3	−48.1	−41.4	−49.1	−58.5	−24.0	−8.9	−29.1
Balance on capital account	2.7	3.2	2.9	4.5	7.7	6.2	5.0	5.5	9.2	4.3
Balance on financial account	17.5	26.1	24.5	40.2	39.1	55.3	57.5	25.7	4.7	27.5
Change in reserves (− = increase)	−16.4	−9.4	−14.8	−22.4	−23.6	−4.1	17.4	3.4	−28.2	−16.8
Other official flows, net	7.6	4.7	3.8	3.1	−4.1	3.9	13.5	10.2	8.0	5.7
Private flows, net	26.3	30.7	35.5	59.5	66.8	55.5	26.5	12.0	24.9	38.6
External financing										
Net external financing	36.6	41.8	42.0	69.8	68.7	66.2	51.5	26.8	50.6	53.6
Nondebt-creating inflows	11.4	18.2	25.2	26.8	42.7	37.7	39.7	39.7	50.4	41.6
Net external borrowing	25.3	23.6	16.8	43.0	26.0	28.5	11.9	−12.9	0.2	12.0
From official creditors	7.6	4.6	3.7	2.9	−4.3	3.7	13.4	10.1	7.8	5.5
Of which,										
Credit and loans from IMF	−1.0	−0.8	1.0	0.5	0.7	3.9	10.9	5.6	...	...
From banks	0.2	−2.8	−36.7	4.7	7.3	12.1	7.4	−7.2	−3.1	4.0
From other private creditors	17.6	21.8	49.7	35.4	23.0	12.6	−8.9	−15.7	−4.6	2.6
Memorandum										
Exceptional financing	28.8	32.9	26.8	23.3	24.5	6.4	17.7	20.5	15.8	12.8
Other net debtor countries										
Balance of payments										
Balance on current account	−47.1	−77.3	−59.3	−51.8	−46.1	−20.6	−14.3	−3.4	−14.9	−30.8
Balance on capital account	10.9	13.7	3.7	9.7	10.9	3.6	−0.7	−4.0	1.1	4.5
Balance on financial account	40.0	74.3	63.7	58.3	59.0	47.7	37.9	26.6	26.5	35.5
Change in reserves (− = increase)	−25.6	−36.4	−35.2	−45.3	−62.0	−43.5	−10.8	−33.5	−25.9	−55.9
Other official flows, net	13.9	43.9	21.2	25.6	10.2	17.5	21.3	14.9	22.9	20.8
Private flows, net	51.7	66.8	77.7	77.9	110.8	73.7	27.4	45.3	29.5	70.6
External financing										
Net external financing	123.1	136.0	122.1	137.6	160.5	170.6	125.6	125.8	134.4	170.4
Nondebt-creating inflows	46.7	77.0	72.4	82.6	99.6	116.2	93.0	95.3	92.8	100.4
Net external borrowing	76.4	59.0	49.7	55.0	60.9	54.4	32.6	30.5	41.5	70.0
From official creditors	13.1	44.8	21.7	27.8	15.0	9.2	20.8	17.5	22.0	20.8
Of which,										
Credit and loans from IMF	0.6	0.6	−1.8	12.1	−3.6	−3.1	−2.4	−4.4	...	...
From banks	8.7	17.3	9.7	18.1	16.7	12.7	13.9	−3.0	6.1	7.7
From other private creditors	54.6	−3.1	18.3	9.1	29.3	32.6	−2.1	16.1	13.5	41.6
Memorandum										
Exceptional financing	2.2	2.3	1.2	0.5	0.3	0.7	0.4	4.5	4.5	2.0

Table 35 *(concluded)*

	1992	1993	1994	1995	1996	1997	1998	1999	2000	2001
Other groups										
Heavily indebted poor countries										
Balance of payments										
Balance on current account	−12.0	−14.0	−10.2	−12.6	−12.8	−13.9	−15.3	−13.6	−12.6	−15.2
Balance on capital account	2.3	3.4	2.9	3.5	8.0	6.1	4.6	5.5	9.3	4.8
Balance on financial account	7.2	8.3	7.0	7.7	3.2	6.1	9.3	7.6	2.3	9.8
Change in reserves (− = increase)	0.2	1.6	−2.4	−1.4	−4.1	−0.9	0.6	−2.5	−2.0	−2.3
Other official flows, net	4.6	3.3	3.4	3.9	2.7	3.1	5.1	2.7	−1.5	4.5
Private flows, net	2.4	3.4	5.9	5.2	4.6	4.0	3.6	7.4	5.8	7.6
External financing										
Net external financing	10.0	9.1	10.7	12.2	13.1	11.0	14.0	16.2	13.2	16.8
Nondebt-creating inflows	3.3	5.3	5.4	6.3	11.9	10.6	9.6	11.4	14.0	10.1
Net external borrowing	6.7	3.8	5.2	5.9	1.2	0.5	4.5	4.8	−0.8	6.7
From official creditors	4.5	3.2	3.3	3.7	2.5	3.0	5.0	2.6	−1.6	4.4
Of which,										
Credit and loans from IMF	−0.1	−0.2	0.5	0.6	0.3	—	0.2	0.2	. . .	. . .
From banks	0.3	0.1	0.7	1.1	0.4	−1.3	−0.7	−0.3	−0.8	0.2
From other private creditors	1.9	0.6	1.2	1.0	−1.7	−1.2	0.1	2.5	1.6	2.2
Memorandum										
Exceptional financing	12.2	10.2	9.8	9.6	15.1	−0.2	0.6	6.9	5.0	4.6
Least developed countries										
Balance of payments										
Balance on current account	−9.2	−9.0	−6.9	−8.9	−9.7	−9.9	−13.1	−13.3	−12.0	−14.4
Balance on capital account	2.7	3.4	2.5	3.0	7.0	5.1	3.9	4.8	9.1	4.4
Balance on financial account	5.5	4.8	4.3	5.1	1.5	4.1	8.4	8.2	2.1	9.6
Change in reserves (- = increase)	0.3	0.6	−1.4	−0.7	−3.0	−0.4	0.8	−1.2	−1.3	−1.3
Other official flows, net	2.2	3.2	5.3	4.1	3.8	7.1	5.0	3.4	−2.4	3.9
Private flows, net	3.0	0.9	0.4	1.8	0.7	−2.6	2.6	6.0	5.8	7.0
External financing										
Net external financing	8.0	8.4	8.6	10.6	11.9	10.7	11.7	14.6	12.6	15.7
Nondebt-creating inflows	5.0	6.0	4.8	5.6	10.2	8.9	8.7	10.7	13.9	10.0
Net external borrowing	3.0	2.4	3.9	5.0	1.7	1.8	3.0	3.9	−1.3	5.7
From official creditors	2.1	3.1	5.2	3.9	3.6	7.1	4.9	3.2	−2.5	3.8
Of which,										
Credit and loans from IMF	0.2	−0.1	0.2	0.5	0.1	0.1	0.1	—	. . .	. . .
From banks	0.3	0.2	−0.3	0.2	—	−0.5	−0.4	−0.1	−0.2	—
From other private creditors	0.6	−1.0	−1.0	0.9	−1.9	−4.7	−1.5	0.8	1.3	1.8
Memorandum										
Exceptional financing	7.6	6.9	6.7	5.0	9.3	6.1	5.9	5.2	3.3	3.5
Middle East and north Africa										
Balance of payments										
Balance on current account	−27.6	−25.6	−13.3	−6.2	12.1	10.5	−35.1	3.1	54.5	29.9
Balance on capital account	1.2	−0.2	1.2	1.8	0.2	1.2	2.9	2.4	1.0	0.3
Balance on financial account	26.1	26.0	21.3	11.0	−11.8	−4.3	34.3	2.8	−44.2	−22.4
Change in reserves (- = increase)	−9.1	3.6	−4.3	−2.0	−16.5	−13.4	15.2	3.1	−20.4	−13.5
Other official flows, net	−1.0	—	2.3	5.5	2.2	1.0	9.4	7.0	2.5	2.4
Private flows, net	36.2	22.5	23.3	7.6	2.5	8.1	9.7	−7.2	−26.3	−11.4
External financing										
Net external financing	43.5	12.4	24.8	7.9	11.0	15.4	29.0	−0.2	−11.7	−0.8
Nondebt-creating inflows	4.4	4.0	5.8	6.7	6.9	6.6	8.3	7.3	8.1	10.3
Net external borrowing	39.0	8.3	18.9	1.2	4.1	8.8	20.7	−7.5	−19.8	−11.1
From official creditors	−1.0	—	2.3	2.9	0.6	−0.3	0.8	0.6	1.4	1.3
Of which,										
Credit and loans from IMF	−0.1	−0.5	0.5	0.2	0.6	0.3	−0.1	—	. . .	. . .
From banks	9.4	−0.7	−2.1	−1.2	−6.4	0.9	9.5	2.8	−1.6	−1.7
From other private creditors	30.6	9.1	18.7	−0.4	10.0	8.3	10.3	−10.9	−19.6	−10.8
Memorandum										
Exceptional financing	5.5	15.4	11.9	11.5	5.6	5.8	3.4	2.7	1.8	1.9

[1]For definitions, see footnotes to Table 33.

Table 36. Developing Countries: Reserves[1]

	1992	1993	1994	1995	1996	1997	1998	1999	2000	2001
	Billions of U.S. dollars									
Developing countries	**261.0**	**307.1**	**362.3**	**428.9**	**522.6**	**573.1**	**586.1**	**622.3**	**686.5**	**767.9**
Regional groups										
Africa	18.5	19.8	24.8	26.6	31.7	43.2	41.6	41.9	55.9	63.5
Sub-Sahara	12.3	13.5	15.9	19.1	21.5	28.9	28.1	29.1	35.8	41.3
Asia	86.7	109.4	157.9	184.5	230.2	248.7	273.6	306.6	330.3	379.4
Excluding China and India	59.1	75.7	84.1	89.8	101.7	80.0	95.8	115.1	128.7	155.3
Middle East and Europe	66.8	68.6	74.5	87.7	104.3	111.5	110.2	120.2	137.3	152.3
Western Hemisphere	89.1	109.2	105.1	130.0	156.3	169.7	160.8	153.5	163.1	172.6
Analytical groups										
By source of export earnings										
Fuel	51.6	49.0	50.5	51.9	70.9	83.2	77.0	80.5	105.4	119.1
Manufactures	120.6	156.6	192.1	244.8	300.8	324.8	339.2	363.4	392.3	443.9
Nonfuel primary products	23.1	23.8	32.6	37.5	42.0	45.8	42.8	43.2	46.2	51.1
Services, income, and private transfers	18.8	23.4	26.5	30.6	34.0	35.9	35.9	35.0	33.7	35.8
Diversified	47.0	54.2	60.6	64.1	74.9	83.3	91.2	100.2	108.9	118.0
By external financing source										
Net creditor countries	30.4	29.1	30.3	34.6	42.7	45.5	43.4	49.8	60.5	69.5
Net debtor countries	234.8	282.4	336.8	399.3	485.3	533.6	549.0	579.1	633.4	706.8
Official financing	10.6	11.5	14.3	14.5	17.4	22.2	20.7	21.2	30.4	35.3
Private financing	189.6	233.5	276.8	336.3	409.3	449.7	463.0	486.4	520.6	579.7
Diversified financing	26.8	29.2	35.3	37.1	46.0	47.7	50.7	55.7	60.5	66.6
Net debtor countries by debt-servicing experience										
Countries with arrears and/or rescheduling during 1994–98	63.9	74.5	90.7	107.8	134.7	132.9	129.2	127.1	154.9	171.5
Other net debtor countries	166.7	203.5	241.4	286.6	345.3	394.8	413.5	445.4	471.2	527.1
Other groups										
Heavily indebted poor countries	6.5	6.0	7.8	10.3	12.4	13.7	13.4	15.5	17.1	19.2
Least developed countries	7.4	8.1	9.7	10.4	10.8	11.1	11.3	11.4	12.1	13.2
Middle East and north Africa	64.5	66.1	72.8	80.2	95.1	104.3	101.1	106.3	126.7	140.2
	Ratio of reserve to imports of goods and services[2]									
Developing countries	**32.9**	**36.3**	**39.4**	**39.4**	**43.7**	**44.6**	**48.1**	**50.2**	**48.4**	**49.2**
Regional groups										
Africa	17.2	19.1	22.8	20.6	24.1	31.7	30.8	30.7	37.6	39.9
Sub-Sahara	15.1	17.2	19.7	19.6	21.2	27.1	27.2	28.1	31.7	34.1
Asia	30.7	32.5	39.6	37.1	41.9	43.6	55.4	57.0	52.9	53.9
Excluding China and India	32.6	36.3	33.7	28.7	29.9	23.1	35.7	40.4	39.0	41.2
Middle East and Europe	32.0	33.3	41.0	41.6	44.1	43.7	44.0	48.8	48.2	51.0
Western Hemisphere	45.7	54.5	45.7	51.8	56.5	52.5	47.5	48.2	45.2	43.4
Analytical groups										
By source of export earnings										
Fuel	26.6	27.5	32.1	29.4	37.6	40.8	38.5	39.5	44.2	47.7
Manufactures	34.1	38.8	41.1	43.1	47.2	47.6	54.0	54.7	50.7	50.9
Nonfuel primary products	39.7	39.3	49.4	45.4	46.4	47.1	44.3	46.8	45.7	46.1
Services, income, and private transfers	41.2	47.3	51.0	51.0	52.8	52.6	49.9	48.8	44.7	45.5
Diversified	33.3	35.1	34.2	31.7	35.0	35.8	41.3	48.3	47.3	47.3

253

Table 36 *(concluded)*

	1992	1993	1994	1995	1996	1997	1998	1999	2000	2001
By external financing source										
Net creditor countries	26.4	27.0	30.9	31.9	36.2	35.7	35.5	39.9	43.5	48.8
Net debtor countries	34.5	38.1	40.9	40.6	44.9	46.0	50.0	51.8	49.3	49.7
Official financing	21.4	22.5	25.4	21.7	24.4	30.9	28.0	28.1	37.6	40.9
Private financing	37.2	41.2	42.8	43.3	48.2	49.2	53.6	55.3	51.3	51.5
Diversified financing	32.3	32.6	37.2	33.0	35.8	33.2	38.8	42.0	39.4	38.8
Net debtor countries by debt-servicing experience										
Countries with arrears and/or rescheduling during 1994–98	32.2	35.6	40.3	38.5	43.6	39.2	40.9	41.9	44.4	44.1
Other net debtor countries	34.8	38.4	40.5	40.9	45.0	48.3	53.1	54.9	50.6	51.3
Other groups										
Heavily indebted poor countries	14.5	13.1	16.3	17.8	19.1	20.1	19.3	21.8	22.3	23.2
Least developed countries	21.0	23.0	26.6	24.2	23.2	22.8	22.9	21.7	21.6	21.7
Middle East and north Africa	31.7	34.1	40.7	40.6	44.8	46.7	45.6	47.2	49.2	52.0

[1]In this table, official holdings of gold are valued at SDR 35 an ounce. This convention results in a marked underestimate of reserves for countries that have substantial gold holdings.
[2]Reserves at year-end in percent of imports of goods and services for the year indicated.

Table 37. Net Credit and Loans from IMF[1]

(Billions of U.S. dollars)

	1991	1992	1993	1994	1995	1996	1997	1998	1999
Advanced economies	—	**0.3**	—	—	**−0.1**	**−0.1**	**11.3**	**5.2**	**−10.3**
Newly industrialized Asian economies	—	—	—	—	—	—	11.3	5.2	−10.3
Developing countries	**1.1**	**−0.4**	**−0.1**	**−0.8**	**12.6**	**−2.9**	**0.8**	**8.5**	**1.3**
Regional groups									
Africa	0.2	−0.2	0.2	0.9	0.8	0.6	−0.5	−0.4	−0.2
Sub-Sahara	—	—	0.7	0.5	0.6	0.1	−0.5	−0.3	−0.1
Asia	1.9	1.3	0.6	−0.8	−1.5	−1.7	5.0	6.6	1.7
Excluding China and India	0.2	0.1	0.1	0.4	−0.3	−0.4	5.7	7.0	2.1
Middle East and Europe	—	0.1	—	0.4	0.4	0.1	0.2	−0.1	0.6
Western Hemisphere	−1.0	−1.6	−0.9	−1.3	12.9	−2.0	−4.0	2.5	−0.9
Analytical groups									
By source of export earnings									
Fuel	0.6	−0.5	−0.8	0.4	−0.2	0.7	−0.3	−0.6	−0.5
Manufactures	1.9	0.4	−1.2	−2.0	10.8	−4.0	−1.4	4.3	1.4
Nonfuel primary products	−0.3	—	−0.1	0.2	0.4	0.1	—	—	—
Services, income, and private transfers	0.1	0.2	0.1	—	−0.1	−0.1		0.1	—
Diversified	−1.1	−0.5	1.8	0.6	1.7	0.3	2.5	4.7	0.4
By external financing source									
Net creditor countries	—	—	—	—	—	—	—	—	—
Net debtor countries	1.1	−0.4	−0.1	−0.8	12.6	−2.9	0.8	8.5	1.3
Official financing	0.4	−0.1	−0.5	1.1	1.1	0.9	0.2	—	—
Private financing	0.3	−0.9	0.3	−2.2	11.9	−3.3	0.4	7.6	0.7
Diversified financing	0.3	0.5	0.1	0.3	−0.3	−0.5	0.2	1.0	0.6
Net debtor countries by debt-servicing experience									
Countries with arrears and/or rescheduling during 1994–98	−0.6	−1.0	−0.8	1.0	0.5	0.7	3.9	10.9	5.6
Other net debtor countries	1.7	0.6	0.6	−1.8	12.1	−3.6	−3.1	−2.4	−4.3
Other groups									
Heavily indebted poor countries	0.1	−0.1	−0.2	0.5	0.6	0.3	—	0.2	0.2
Least developed countries	0.1	0.2	−0.1	0.2	0.5	0.1	0.1	0.1	—
Middle East and north Africa	0.2	−0.1	−0.5	0.5	0.2	0.6	0.3	−0.1	—
Countries in transition	**2.4**	**1.6**	**3.7**	**2.4**	**4.7**	**3.7**	**2.5**	**5.5**	**−3.6**
Central and eastern Europe	2.4	0.5	2.0	0.5	−1.3	—	0.7	−0.1	—
Excluding Belarus and Ukraine	2.4	0.5	2.0	0.2	−2.7	−0.8	0.4	−0.4	—
Russia	—	1.0	1.5	1.5	5.5	3.2	1.5	5.3	−3.6
Transcaucasus and central Asia	—	—	0.2	0.3	0.6	0.5	0.2	0.3	—
Memorandum									
Total									
Net credit provided under:									
General Resources Account	2.520	0.644	3.374	0.594	15.633	0.291	14.355	18.811	−12.856
Trust Fund	−0.069	—	−0.060	−0.014	−0.015	—	−0.007	−0.001	−0.001
PRGF	1.070	0.733	0.253	0.998	1.619	0.325	0.179	0.374	0.193
Disbursements at year-end under:[2]									
General Resources Account	31.821	31.217	34.503	37.276	53.275	51.824	62.703	84.961	69.913
Trust Fund	0.226	0.217	0.157	0.153	0.141	0.137	0.121	0.126	0.122
PRGF	4.499	5.041	5.285	6.634	8.342	8.392	8.049	8.788	8.760

[1]Includes net disbursements from programs under the General Resources Account, Trust Fund and Poverty Reduction and Growth Facility (formerly ESAF-Enhanced Structural Adjustment Facility). The data are on a transactions basis, with conversion to U.S. dollar values at annual average exchange rates.
[2]Converted to U.S. dollar values at end-of-period exchange rates.

Table 38. Summary of External Debt and Debt Service

	1992	1993	1994	1995	1996	1997	1998	1999	2000	2001
					Billions of U.S. dollars					
External debt										
Developing countries	**1,336.4**	**1,460.4**	**1,582.1**	**1,707.0**	**1,786.8**	**1,866.6**	**1,994.6**	**2,041.8**	**2,068.1**	**2,137.2**
Regional groups										
Africa	256.3	268.0	287.5	308.0	305.5	300.1	299.7	303.8	301.3	304.3
Asia	403.3	456.1	509.5	560.8	595.8	641.6	661.6	676.4	690.5	717.7
Middle East and Europe	197.7	212.5	221.6	221.4	241.0	255.4	284.7	297.0	301.5	311.8
Western Hemisphere	479.0	523.7	563.6	616.8	644.5	669.4	748.6	764.5	774.8	803.4
Analytical groups										
By external financing source										
Net creditor countries	36.9	39.0	38.0	28.5	46.5	57.7	72.0	78.1	75.7	76.8
Net debtor countries	1,300.3	1,422.2	1,545.0	1,679.4	1,741.0	1,809.6	1,923.4	1,964.4	1,993.2	2,061.1
Official financing	150.1	159.5	179.3	184.2	183.4	180.0	183.7	184.7	179.5	179.6
Private financing	914.1	1,000.2	1,084.5	1,200.3	1,263.9	1,337.2	1,439.4	1,466.6	1,493.0	1,549.2
Diversified financing	213.3	230.3	248.1	261.4	265.2	266.6	275.3	290.6	299.3	310.8
Net debtor countries by debt-servicing experience										
Countries with arrears and/or rescheduling during 1994–98	577.8	618.4	663.7	702.9	725.5	749.8	803.1	817.7	812.3	824.2
Other net debtor countries	719.8	801.1	878.5	973.7	1,012.9	1,057.3	1,117.7	1,144.3	1,178.5	1,234.6
Countries in transition	**213.9**	**235.8**	**258.7**	**276.4**	**300.4**	**312.0**	**347.3**	**348.5**	**361.3**	**372.1**
Central and eastern Europe	106.7	118.2	123.9	138.7	151.2	160.7	175.7	180.4	189.2	197.5
Excluding Belarus and Ukraine	102.5	112.5	114.1	127.5	139.8	146.5	161.4	165.9	175.4	183.3
Russia	105.4	112.7	127.5	128.0	136.1	134.6	152.4	147.6	149.8	150.4
Transcaucasus and central Asia	1.8	4.9	7.4	9.7	13.0	16.7	19.2	20.5	22.2	24.2
Debt-service payments[1]										
Developing countries	**166.6**	**176.1**	**192.0**	**241.2**	**284.5**	**307.4**	**309.6**	**355.2**	**342.6**	**347.4**
Regional groups										
Africa	20.4	27.4	27.9	32.3	33.3	28.5	26.3	26.5	27.4	36.1
Asia	49.7	51.8	61.6	78.5	78.2	82.9	97.5	110.5	97.6	103.4
Middle East and Europe	23.0	25.1	26.5	33.4	45.9	39.0	39.5	41.3	43.9	42.4
Western Hemisphere	73.6	71.7	76.0	96.9	127.1	156.9	146.2	176.9	173.8	165.5
Analytical groups										
By external financing source										
Net creditor countries	2.4	3.4	7.4	7.8	13.3	8.5	8.3	8.9	8.1	10.6
Net debtor countries	164.4	172.9	184.8	233.5	271.4	299.0	301.4	346.4	334.6	336.9
Official financing	6.9	15.3	15.5	22.1	14.8	13.7	12.1	12.2	12.2	16.6
Private financing	134.7	136.1	147.0	179.5	213.7	248.3	255.2	301.2	291.2	282.0
Diversified financing	19.7	16.4	17.9	21.4	26.6	23.0	22.9	22.1	22.2	30.9
Net debtor countries by debt-servicing experience										
Countries with arrears and/or rescheduling during 1994–98	52.4	62.6	62.7	86.3	97.4	117.7	125.4	159.7	137.6	129.9
Other net debtor countries	111.7	110.1	121.9	147.0	173.8	181.1	175.8	186.5	196.8	206.7
Countries in transition	**24.9**	**18.4**	**21.0**	**30.1**	**31.7**	**30.5**	**50.3**	**50.5**	**51.3**	**51.9**
Central and eastern Europe	12.2	11.9	16.1	22.0	23.2	22.8	30.4	35.5	35.3	36.2
Excluding Belarus and Ukraine	12.2	11.6	14.2	20.3	21.9	21.2	28.1	32.3	33.0	33.8
Russia	12.6	6.2	4.3	6.4	6.9	5.9	16.3	12.9	12.9	12.9
Transcaucasus and central Asia	0.1	0.3	0.6	1.7	1.5	1.8	3.7	2.1	3.1	2.9

Table 38 (concluded)

	1992	1993	1994	1995	1996	1997	1998	1999	2000	2001
					Percent of exports of goods and services					
External debt[2]										
Developing countries	**185.9**	**194.7**	**183.9**	**167.2**	**156.3**	**150.2**	**172.7**	**163.5**	**139.5**	**135.6**
Regional groups										
Africa	248.8	272.6	281.6	256.7	228.8	220.2	248.6	237.0	192.9	189.8
Asia	152.2	153.7	138.0	123.9	118.6	114.2	122.9	116.2	104.2	98.6
Middle East and Europe	112.0	120.7	119.4	107.0	100.3	101.4	134.6	122.5	94.3	99.7
Western Hemisphere	274.9	292.9	277.1	255.6	241.1	228.8	262.6	257.9	225.3	214.5
Analytical groups										
By external financing source										
Net creditor countries	33.9	36.2	34.5	23.7	33.3	39.8	66.6	58.7	40.1	43.4
Net debtor countries	212.2	220.6	205.1	185.7	172.9	164.3	183.1	175.4	153.5	146.8
Official financing	363.0	387.5	418.8	353.9	307.9	280.3	312.0	288.4	233.0	225.0
Private financing	192.1	196.4	178.7	163.7	156.4	150.4	168.1	163.2	145.3	138.1
Diversified financing	320.4	344.1	336.4	295.7	253.7	230.6	253.6	235.4	196.1	192.6
Net debtor countries by debt-servicing experience										
Countries with arrears and/or rescheduling during 1994–98	303.7	320.6	312.0	289.2	266.2	250.5	296.1	275.8	224.0	214.6
Other net debtor countries	171.5	178.4	163.6	148.0	138.6	132.5	144.1	139.7	126.7	121.7
Countries in transition	**131.3**	**130.0**	**127.8**	**106.8**	**106.9**	**105.5**	**121.0**	**123.8**	**112.1**	**107.2**
Central and eastern Europe	112.6	116.1	109.1	94.0	93.5	91.7	95.2	99.6	95.5	89.7
Excluding Belarus and Ukraine	129.0	134.3	118.8	101.3	103.8	99.9	101.5	104.9	101.4	94.6
Russia	183.4	171.1	166.1	134.2	132.4	130.5	174.6	175.0	144.5	142.3
Transcaucasus and central Asia	17.1	36.0	60.8	61.5	78.5	96.7	127.9	127.8	108.0	114.6
Debt-service payments										
Developing countries	**23.2**	**23.5**	**22.3**	**23.6**	**24.9**	**24.7**	**26.8**	**28.4**	**23.1**	**22.0**
Regional groups										
Africa	19.8	27.9	27.3	26.9	24.9	20.9	21.8	20.7	17.5	22.5
Asia	18.8	17.5	16.7	17.3	15.6	14.8	18.1	19.0	14.7	14.2
Middle East and Europe	13.0	14.3	14.3	16.2	19.1	15.5	18.7	17.1	13.7	13.5
Western Hemisphere	42.2	40.1	37.3	40.1	47.5	53.6	51.3	59.7	50.5	44.2
Analytical groups										
By external financing source										
Net creditor countries	2.2	3.1	6.7	6.5	9.5	5.8	7.7	6.7	4.3	6.0
Net debtor countries	26.8	26.8	24.5	25.8	26.9	27.2	28.7	30.9	25.8	24.0
Official financing	16.8	37.2	36.2	42.5	24.8	21.4	20.5	19.0	15.8	20.8
Private financing	28.3	26.7	24.2	24.5	26.4	27.9	29.8	33.5	28.3	25.1
Diversified financing	29.5	24.5	24.2	24.2	25.4	19.9	21.1	17.9	14.6	19.2
Net debtor countries by debt-servicing experience										
Countries with arrears and/or rescheduling during 1994–98	27.6	32.4	29.5	35.5	35.7	39.3	46.2	53.9	37.9	33.8
Other net debtor countries	26.6	24.5	22.7	22.3	23.8	22.7	22.7	22.8	21.1	20.4
Countries in transition	**15.3**	**10.1**	**10.4**	**11.6**	**11.3**	**10.3**	**17.5**	**17.9**	**15.9**	**15.0**
Central and eastern Europe	12.9	11.6	14.2	14.9	14.4	13.0	16.4	19.6	17.8	16.4
Excluding Belarus and Ukraine	15.4	13.9	14.8	16.2	16.3	14.5	17.7	20.4	19.1	17.5
Russia	21.9	9.4	5.6	6.7	6.7	5.7	18.7	15.3	12.4	12.2
Transcaucasus and central Asia	1.0	2.3	4.8	10.6	9.1	10.4	24.3	13.3	14.8	13.5

[1]Debt-service payments refer to actual payments of interest on total debt plus actual amortization payments on long-term debt. The projections incorporate the impact of exceptional financing items.
[2]Total debt at year-end in percent of exports of goods and services in year indicated.

Table 39. Developing Countries—by Region: External Debt, by Maturity and Type of Creditor
(Billions of U.S. dollars)

	1992	1993	1994	1995	1996	1997	1998	1999	2000	2001
Developing countries										
Total debt	**1,336.4**	**1,460.4**	**1,582.1**	**1,707.0**	**1,786.8**	**1,866.6**	**1,994.6**	**2,041.8**	**2,068.1**	**2,137.2**
By maturity										
Short-term	209.7	243.2	245.1	281.5	305.5	377.8	376.2	299.0	270.2	277.3
Long-term	1,126.7	1,217.1	1,337.0	1,425.6	1,481.3	1,488.8	1,618.4	1,742.8	1,798.0	1,859.9
By type of creditor										
Official	629.1	674.4	731.9	773.5	826.4	785.3	832.0	856.3	856.8	867.4
Banks	343.0	356.4	353.7	431.4	481.0	545.8	572.9	559.3	562.0	578.5
Other private	365.5	429.9	496.7	502.3	479.6	535.6	589.9	626.3	649.5	691.5
Regional groups										
Africa										
Total debt	**256.3**	**268.0**	**287.5**	**308.0**	**305.5**	**300.1**	**299.7**	**303.8**	**301.3**	**304.3**
By maturity										
Short-term	21.8	29.0	33.6	37.1	38.8	55.2	53.7	57.3	35.1	37.2
Long-term	234.5	239.0	253.9	270.9	266.7	244.9	246.0	246.5	266.2	267.1
By type of creditor										
Official	175.3	184.0	200.0	212.1	211.7	204.7	208.8	211.1	203.6	200.8
Banks	44.6	42.7	43.8	43.1	42.3	38.7	35.1	35.0	36.3	37.4
Other private	36.4	41.4	43.7	52.7	51.5	56.8	55.8	57.7	61.4	66.0
Sub-Sahara										
Total debt	**201.7**	**212.5**	**226.0**	**241.6**	**239.3**	**238.8**	**238.2**	**245.9**	**244.5**	**251.7**
By maturity										
Short-term	19.7	26.9	31.6	35.3	36.5	43.8	42.1	45.4	23.1	24.9
Long-term	182.0	185.6	194.4	206.3	202.8	195.0	196.2	200.5	221.4	226.8
By type of creditor										
Official	145.5	154.2	164.6	171.3	169.8	165.3	169.5	174.7	168.4	169.9
Banks	19.2	18.4	19.1	19.6	20.4	19.2	15.5	15.8	17.3	18.5
Other private	37.1	39.9	42.3	50.7	49.0	54.2	53.3	55.3	58.8	63.3
Asia										
Total debt	**403.3**	**456.1**	**509.5**	**560.8**	**595.8**	**641.6**	**661.6**	**676.4**	**690.5**	**717.7**
By maturity										
Short-term	60.4	69.0	77.1	101.0	107.6	152.4	148.4	69.5	60.6	61.4
Long-term	342.9	387.2	432.4	459.8	488.2	489.2	513.2	607.0	629.9	656.3
By type of creditor										
Official	205.1	226.7	254.6	255.1	266.5	267.2	289.3	306.7	316.6	325.0
Banks	108.3	108.1	122.4	160.5	192.1	218.1	213.3	194.5	190.5	198.5
Other private	89.8	121.3	132.5	145.1	137.2	156.3	159.0	175.3	183.5	194.2
Middle East and Europe										
Total debt	**197.7**	**212.5**	**221.6**	**221.4**	**241.0**	**255.4**	**284.7**	**297.0**	**301.5**	**311.8**
By maturity										
Short-term	58.3	72.3	57.9	60.2	68.1	74.7	85.8	87.3	89.3	91.3
Long-term	139.4	140.2	163.6	161.2	172.8	180.8	198.9	209.8	212.2	220.5
By type of creditor										
Official	91.0	100.1	106.7	119.3	115.1	108.0	112.1	113.1	114.9	117.8
Banks	63.8	61.8	66.5	67.9	87.2	124.6	145.5	154.6	157.1	161.7
Other private	44.1	50.9	48.5	34.3	38.9	22.9	27.2	29.5	29.6	32.4
Western Hemisphere										
Total debt	**479.0**	**523.7**	**563.6**	**616.8**	**644.5**	**669.4**	**748.6**	**764.5**	**774.8**	**803.4**
By maturity										
Short-term	69.1	73.0	76.5	83.2	90.9	95.6	88.3	85.0	85.0	87.5
Long-term	410.0	450.7	487.1	533.7	553.6	573.9	660.3	679.6	689.7	716.0
By type of creditor										
Official	157.6	163.6	170.7	186.9	233.2	205.4	221.8	225.4	221.7	223.8
Banks	126.2	143.7	121.0	159.8	159.3	164.4	179.0	175.2	178.1	180.8
Other private	195.2	216.3	272.0	270.2	252.0	299.6	347.9	363.8	375.0	398.8

Table 40. Developing Countries—by Analytical Criteria: External Debt, by Maturity and Type of Creditor
(Billions of U.S. dollars)

	1992	1993	1994	1995	1996	1997	1998	1999	2000	2001
By source of export earnings										
Fuel										
Total debt	**202.9**	**213.7**	**222.2**	**215.0**	**222.7**	**222.9**	**240.0**	**245.1**	**237.5**	**233.3**
By maturity										
Short-term	44.4	55.6	53.8	52.9	57.4	65.3	74.5	75.6	53.3	54.4
Long-term	158.5	158.1	168.4	162.1	165.3	157.6	165.5	169.5	184.2	178.9
By type of creditor										
Official	78.3	89.8	99.1	111.0	104.7	97.7	98.2	98.4	94.3	89.9
Banks	65.0	62.9	63.7	59.8	75.2	82.6	94.7	96.8	94.1	93.8
Other private	59.6	61.0	59.5	44.2	42.7	42.6	47.2	49.9	49.0	49.6
Nonfuel										
Total debt	**1,133.7**	**1,246.9**	**1,360.2**	**1,492.3**	**1,564.3**	**1,643.9**	**1,754.9**	**1,796.9**	**1,830.8**	**1,904.1**
By maturity										
Short-term	165.3	187.6	191.4	228.6	248.1	312.6	301.7	223.5	216.9	222.9
Long-term	968.4	1,059.3	1,168.8	1,263.6	1,316.2	1,331.4	1,453.1	1,573.5	1,614.0	1,681.2
By type of creditor										
Official	551.0	584.9	633.1	662.7	721.9	687.8	734.1	758.1	762.6	777.7
Banks	278.0	293.4	290.1	371.6	405.8	463.2	478.2	462.5	467.9	484.6
Other private	305.9	368.9	437.2	458.1	436.8	493.0	542.7	576.4	600.5	641.9
Manufactures										
Total debt	**599.6**	**676.9**	**727.0**	**807.7**	**858.6**	**904.2**	**981.1**	**997.7**	**1,008.2**	**1,053.8**
By maturity										
Short-term	105.2	118.0	115.0	139.5	160.3	163.1	140.6	127.7	117.9	119.3
Long-term	494.3	558.9	612.1	668.2	698.3	741.1	840.5	869.9	890.2	934.6
By type of creditor										
Official	237.2	254.2	277.9	289.7	341.2	326.3	362.3	380.2	386.2	398.4
Banks	177.7	193.6	178.9	250.5	254.6	292.5	302.7	291.8	298.1	313.2
Other private	184.7	229.1	270.2	267.5	262.8	285.4	316.1	325.6	323.9	342.3
Nonfuel primary products										
Total debt	**175.8**	**183.6**	**196.2**	**208.1**	**207.9**	**205.4**	**213.3**	**220.5**	**228.2**	**236.1**
By maturity										
Short-term	17.3	18.8	19.4	21.4	21.0	19.6	16.5	15.0	17.2	18.4
Long-term	158.5	164.8	176.8	186.7	186.9	185.9	196.8	205.6	211.0	217.8
By type of creditor										
Official	116.1	122.8	132.2	137.1	133.0	129.7	131.9	135.4	136.6	139.2
Banks	28.3	29.1	31.9	34.3	36.6	35.7	35.0	34.8	36.8	37.2
Other private	31.5	31.7	32.0	36.7	38.3	40.1	46.4	50.3	54.9	59.8
Services, income, and private transfers										
Total debt	**77.4**	**74.2**	**84.6**	**87.0**	**85.2**	**84.1**	**86.2**	**87.4**	**84.3**	**87.2**
By maturity										
Short-term	9.3	8.1	7.8	6.6	4.4	4.9	5.4	5.7	5.5	5.7
Long-term	68.0	66.2	76.8	80.4	80.7	79.2	80.7	81.8	78.9	81.6
By type of creditor										
Official	61.1	61.2	64.1	71.6	69.6	67.2	68.5	67.7	62.7	63.7
Banks	12.6	7.6	7.0	7.7	7.1	7.1	7.3	8.4	8.9	8.7
Other private	4.8	5.7	13.6	7.9	8.6	9.9	10.5	11.5	13.0	15.0
Diversified										
Total debt	**280.8**	**311.9**	**352.2**	**389.3**	**412.5**	**449.9**	**474.1**	**491.1**	**509.9**	**526.7**
By maturity										
Short-term	33.4	42.7	49.1	61.1	62.4	125.0	139.1	75.0	76.2	79.6
Long-term	247.3	269.2	303.0	328.1	350.1	324.9	335.0	416.0	433.7	447.1
By type of creditor										
Official	136.5	146.4	158.6	164.1	177.9	164.4	171.1	174.6	177.0	176.3
Banks	59.4	63.1	72.2	79.0	107.5	127.9	133.2	127.5	124.2	125.6
Other private	84.9	102.4	121.4	146.1	127.1	157.6	169.7	189.0	208.7	224.8

Table 40 *(continued)*

	1992	1993	1994	1995	1996	1997	1998	1999	2000	2001
By external financing source										
Net creditor countries										
Total debt	**36.9**	**39.0**	**38.0**	**28.5**	**46.5**	**57.7**	**72.0**	**78.1**	75.7	76.8
By maturity										
Short-term	18.0	22.4	24.7	22.1	26.5	30.8	36.8	36.9	36.7	37.6
Long-term	19.0	16.7	13.3	6.4	20.0	26.9	35.1	41.2	38.9	39.2
By type of creditor										
Official	3.4	3.8	4.1	4.4	5.2	5.4	6.1	5.7	5.1	4.5
Banks	16.0	16.1	19.9	21.3	40.0	50.7	62.4	66.5	64.3	64.9
Other private	17.5	19.1	14.0	2.8	1.3	1.6	3.5	5.8	6.3	7.4
Net debtor countries										
Total debt	**1,300.3**	**1,422.2**	**1,545.0**	**1,679.4**	**1,741.0**	**1,809.6**	**1,923.4**	**1,964.4**	1,993.2	2,061.1
By maturity										
Short-term	191.9	221.1	220.7	259.6	279.1	347.2	339.6	262.3	233.7	240.0
Long-term	1,108.4	1,201.1	1,324.3	1,419.8	1,461.9	1,462.4	1,583.8	1,702.2	1,759.6	1,821.2
By type of creditor										
Official	626.5	671.4	728.6	769.9	821.9	780.6	826.6	851.4	852.5	863.6
Banks	327.0	340.2	333.9	410.1	441.0	495.1	510.6	492.7	497.7	513.6
Other private	348.0	410.8	482.7	499.6	478.3	534.0	586.4	620.5	643.2	684.0
Official financing										
Total debt	**150.1**	**159.5**	**179.3**	**184.2**	**183.4**	**180.0**	**183.7**	**184.7**	179.5	179.6
By maturity										
Short-term	9.2	9.4	8.5	8.4	6.1	5.5	4.7	4.7	4.8	5.1
Long-term	140.9	150.1	170.8	175.8	177.2	174.4	179.0	180.0	174.7	174.5
By type of creditor										
Official	117.9	125.6	138.9	151.2	150.9	148.9	152.5	152.9	147.2	145.9
Banks	28.2	26.3	26.2	23.7	22.7	20.4	19.7	18.8	16.9	15.8
Other private	5.1	7.9	14.3	9.5	9.9	10.8	11.6	13.1	15.5	18.1
Private financing										
Total debt	**914.1**	**1,000.2**	**1,084.5**	**1,200.3**	**1,263.9**	**1,337.2**	**1,439.4**	**1,466.6**	1,493.0	1,549.2
By maturity										
Short-term	142.9	160.7	163.5	195.2	211.0	266.0	258.9	182.0	179.7	186.3
Long-term	771.3	839.5	921.0	1,005.1	1,052.8	1,071.2	1,180.4	1,284.5	1,313.4	1,362.8
By type of creditor										
Official	348.9	368.4	399.4	418.8	481.0	453.6	490.1	508.5	513.7	521.4
Banks	251.5	269.8	263.5	341.3	368.9	422.9	441.3	423.5	426.9	442.2
Other private	313.7	362.0	421.6	440.1	413.9	460.7	508.0	534.6	552.4	585.6
Diversified financing										
Total debt	**213.3**	**230.3**	**248.1**	**261.4**	**265.2**	**266.6**	**275.3**	**290.6**	299.3	310.8
By maturity										
Short-term	26.9	32.3	40.8	48.2	55.6	59.8	60.1	60.3	33.8	33.1
Long-term	186.3	198.0	207.3	213.2	209.6	206.8	215.2	230.3	265.5	277.7
By type of creditor										
Official	148.2	157.5	170.1	174.7	170.4	162.1	170.9	179.1	181.7	186.7
Banks	35.6	33.7	35.9	39.0	43.5	44.9	41.5	42.3	44.6	45.6
Other private	29.5	39.1	42.0	47.8	51.3	59.6	62.8	69.2	72.9	78.5

Table 40 (concluded)

	1992	1993	1994	1995	1996	1997	1998	1999	2000	2001
Net debtor countries by debt-servicing experience										
Countries with arrears and/or rescheduling during 1994–98										
Total debt	**577.8**	**618.4**	**663.7**	**702.9**	**725.5**	**749.8**	**803.1**	**817.7**	812.3	824.2
By maturity										
Short-term	73.5	92.7	88.0	100.1	111.0	157.6	159.0	95.1	66.5	66.5
Long-term	504.3	525.7	575.7	602.8	614.5	592.2	644.1	722.6	745.9	757.8
By type of creditor										
Official	305.1	330.0	353.1	373.8	434.8	406.9	427.3	440.7	431.5	433.0
Banks	167.1	166.7	136.2	174.9	197.3	206.3	207.6	196.6	194.1	196.0
Other private	106.8	122.0	174.6	154.4	93.6	136.7	168.4	180.5	186.8	195.3
Other net debtor countries										
Total debt	**719.8**	**801.1**	**878.5**	**973.7**	**1,012.9**	**1,057.3**	**1,117.7**	**1,144.3**	1,178.5	1,234.6
By maturity										
Short-term	117.9	127.9	132.1	159.0	167.6	189.2	180.1	166.8	166.9	173.2
Long-term	601.9	673.3	746.3	814.7	845.2	868.1	937.6	977.5	1,011.7	1,061.4
By type of creditor										
Official	320.7	340.7	374.8	395.5	386.6	373.2	398.8	410.1	420.3	430.0
Banks	159.5	173.2	197.2	234.8	243.2	288.3	302.5	295.7	303.2	317.2
Other private	239.7	287.2	306.4	343.5	383.1	395.7	416.4	438.5	455.0	487.4
Other groups										
Heavily indebted poor countries										
Total debt	**180.0**	**191.8**	**202.3**	**210.3**	**205.5**	**202.1**	**204.4**	**209.8**	207.9	214.9
By maturity										
Short-term	9.2	10.5	11.0	11.8	10.5	9.4	6.1	6.1	5.3	5.6
Long-term	170.8	181.3	191.3	198.6	195.0	192.7	198.4	203.7	202.6	209.3
By type of creditor										
Official	148.9	157.4	168.7	173.6	167.5	158.7	162.7	165.5	161.1	163.9
Banks	15.8	15.6	17.2	17.5	19.3	19.4	16.2	16.9	17.0	18.0
Other private	15.3	18.7	16.4	19.3	18.8	23.9	25.5	27.4	29.9	33.1
Least developed countries										
Total debt	**133.4**	**143.2**	**151.2**	**156.5**	**155.4**	**156.8**	**163.6**	**167.0**	164.7	171.1
By maturity										
Short-term	6.8	6.8	7.8	7.6	4.7	3.9	5.0	5.3	5.7	6.3
Long-term	126.7	136.3	143.4	148.8	150.7	152.9	158.6	161.8	159.1	164.8
By type of creditor										
Official	121.4	128.5	136.5	140.7	138.8	135.3	139.9	141.6	136.9	139.8
Banks	6.5	6.5	6.1	6.6	6.6	6.3	6.7	7.0	7.1	7.5
Other private	5.5	8.2	8.6	9.2	10.0	15.1	17.0	18.5	20.7	23.8
Middle East and north Africa										
Total debt	**213.8**	**219.1**	**236.7**	**236.7**	**250.6**	**251.3**	**267.9**	**269.6**	265.6	265.3
By maturity										
Short-term	47.0	55.2	47.7	45.4	49.3	61.5	68.1	67.6	67.1	67.9
Long-term	166.8	164.0	189.0	191.3	201.4	189.8	199.8	202.1	198.6	197.4
By type of creditor										
Official	112.7	120.0	129.9	149.2	145.8	132.9	132.2	127.9	126.0	122.5
Banks	73.1	66.8	69.8	68.3	84.9	93.8	107.2	111.2	108.8	109.3
Other private	29.2	32.6	37.2	19.4	20.0	24.8	28.6	30.7	31.0	33.7

Table 41. Developing Countries: Ratio of External Debt to GDP[1]

	1992	1993	1994	1995	1996	1997	1998	1999	2000	2001
Developing countries	**35.1**	**33.2**	**36.5**	**37.2**	**35.3**	**34.7**	**38.1**	**38.9**	**36.0**	**34.7**
Regional groups										
Africa	64.5	70.7	78.1	74.9	70.2	67.6	70.2	71.3	67.7	65.8
Sub-Sahara	66.0	73.8	80.6	75.8	72.1	69.4	73.5	76.4	74.1	73.7
Asia	31.1	31.0	33.2	30.3	28.4	29.2	31.6	29.6	27.9	26.4
Excluding China and India	45.9	47.2	46.7	44.7	42.7	46.3	57.4	49.9	46.0	41.3
Middle East and Europe	32.4	34.8	39.0	34.1	34.4	34.7	39.2	39.8	36.7	38.0
Western Hemisphere	31.8	27.0	30.3	36.7	35.3	33.6	37.5	42.7	38.6	37.2
Analytical groups										
By source of export earnings										
Fuel	38.9	44.5	47.9	41.1	38.7	36.6	41.3	39.6	33.9	34.4
Manufactures	27.2	24.4	28.1	30.6	29.1	28.9	31.5	33.0	30.0	28.9
Nonfuel primary products	72.7	70.0	66.5	58.2	51.3	44.7	44.2	43.6	40.8	37.4
Services, income, and private transfers	68.4	61.4	65.1	59.2	52.7	47.4	45.3	43.6	39.2	37.5
Diversified	38.6	40.7	41.1	42.2	42.6	45.2	54.6	54.9	55.7	53.7
By external financing source										
Net creditor countries	15.9	16.7	15.8	11.0	16.3	19.3	26.9	26.5	21.5	22.2
Net debtor countries	36.3	34.0	37.7	38.7	36.4	35.6	38.6	39.6	36.9	35.4
Official financing	77.0	81.3	98.3	91.4	82.6	78.6	79.5	78.4	71.5	67.8
Private financing	30.8	27.8	30.8	32.6	31.1	30.8	33.8	34.8	32.3	30.7
Diversified financing	75.7	81.5	79.5	76.2	71.6	69.7	74.8	76.3	73.2	73.4
Net debtor countries by debt-servicing experience										
Countries with arrears and/or rescheduling during 1994–98	44.7	37.2	43.5	46.3	42.8	42.4	49.2	54.7	48.8	45.6
Other net debtor countries	31.5	32.0	34.3	34.6	32.9	32.0	33.5	33.1	31.6	30.8
Other groups										
Heavily indebted poor countries	92.2	92.2	91.4	82.8	69.9	59.7	55.2	52.0	46.5	42.5
Least developed countries	71.4	70.8	67.3	61.3	53.2	46.4	44.2	40.9	35.7	32.8
Middle East and north Africa	39.7	42.2	45.1	41.8	40.1	38.8	42.5	40.5	35.8	36.2

[1]Debt at year-end in percent of GDP in year indicated.

Table 42. Developing Countries: Debt-Service Ratios[1]

(Percent of exports of goods and services)

	1992	1993	1994	1995	1996	1997	1998	1999	2000	2001
Interest payments[2]										
Developing countries	**8.5**	**9.7**	**8.8**	**8.9**	**8.5**	**7.8**	**9.1**	**9.1**	**8.3**	**8.3**
Regional groups										
Africa	1.0	9.5	9.6	9.4	8.2	8.1	8.5	8.0	6.6	7.4
Sub-Sahara	8.4	8.1	8.6	8.3	7.0	7.1	7.4	7.2	6.1	7.2
Asia	7.8	6.9	6.4	5.9	5.9	4.9	5.6	6.1	5.4	5.4
Excluding China and India	6.7	6.1	6.0	5.9	6.0	6.4	7.2	6.9	6.3	5.6
Middle East and Europe	5.7	6.0	4.7	5.7	5.0	4.7	6.7	5.6	4.7	5.8
Western Hemisphere	16.9	18.1	16.6	17.2	16.6	16.2	17.8	18.3	18.0	16.6
Analytical groups										
By source of export earnings										
Fuel	−0.3	5.2	4.7	5.3	4.3	4.2	5.3	4.5	3.4	4.3
Manufactures	11.5	11.2	9.6	9.6	9.1	7.9	8.8	9.1	8.7	8.5
Nonfuel primary products	11.2	10.3	9.0	8.3	7.2	7.0	8.1	7.4	8.0	7.4
Services, income, and private transfers	16.6	13.3	8.4	5.5	6.1	5.1	5.4	5.3	5.4	5.2
Diversified	10.0	10.5	11.3	11.8	12.4	12.7	14.9	15.9	14.7	13.9
By external financing source										
Net creditor countries	1.6	1.7	1.7	2.3	1.6	1.9	3.0	2.7	1.9	2.6
Net debtor countries	9.7	11.0	9.8	9.8	9.4	8.6	9.7	9.8	9.2	9.0
Official financing	−8.7	11.6	12.5	9.1	8.9	8.6	9.0	7.5	7.3	6.8
Private financing	11.8	11.5	10.1	10.2	9.9	9.0	10.3	10.8	10.2	9.8
Diversified financing	9.5	9.1	8.6	8.0	7.6	6.5	6.8	6.0	5.5	6.5
Net debtor countries by debt-servicing experience										
Countries with arrears and/or rescheduling during 1994–98	7.4	12.5	11.1	11.8	12.0	11.7	13.7	13.7	11.7	11.0
Other net debtor countries	10.8	10.4	9.4	9.1	8.5	7.5	8.4	8.5	8.3	8.3
Other groups										
Heavily indebted poor countries	11.0	10.6	12.0	8.8	8.9	6.8	7.1	5.6	5.7	5.3
Least developed countries	7.1	6.3	5.8	7.6	7.0	3.9	5.2	3.6	3.7	3.5
Middle East and north Africa	0.5	6.0	4.5	4.6	4.4	3.9	5.1	4.1	3.0	3.4
Amortization[2]										
Developing countries	**14.7**	**13.8**	**13.5**	**14.7**	**16.4**	**16.9**	**17.7**	**19.3**	**14.8**	**13.7**
Regional groups										
Africa	18.8	18.4	17.7	17.6	16.7	12.8	13.4	12.6	10.9	15.2
Sub-Sahara	13.1	11.2	10.7	11.8	13.9	9.9	10.9	10.6	9.4	12.7
Asia	11.0	10.6	10.3	11.5	9.7	9.9	12.5	12.9	9.3	8.8
Excluding China and India	12.5	11.5	11.5	13.1	10.5	12.6	17.5	18.0	12.3	11.6
Middle East and Europe	7.3	8.3	9.6	10.4	14.1	10.8	12.0	11.5	9.0	7.7
Western Hemisphere	25.3	22.0	20.7	22.9	30.9	37.5	33.5	41.4	32.5	27.5
Analytical groups										
By source of export earnings										
Fuel	8.0	9.6	11.3	13.6	16.9	13.0	13.1	10.0	6.7	9.3
Manufactures	16.7	12.8	13.0	13.5	16.1	17.1	16.9	20.5	16.2	12.4
Nonfuel primary products	13.4	15.1	12.1	21.9	14.4	11.3	11.6	13.3	10.6	14.7
Services, income, and private transfers	18.1	17.7	10.0	7.6	7.6	10.3	7.7	7.1	6.5	6.7
Diversified	18.3	19.8	18.6	18.0	19.7	24.3	28.8	31.3	25.3	25.2

Table 42 *(concluded)*

	1992	1993	1994	1995	1996	1997	1998	1999	2000	2001
By external financing source										
Net creditor countries	0.7	1.5	5.0	4.2	7.9	4.0	4.7	4.0	2.4	3.4
Net debtor countries	17.1	15.8	14.7	16.0	17.5	18.6	19.0	21.1	16.6	15.0
Official financing	25.5	25.6	23.7	33.4	15.9	12.8	11.5	11.5	8.5	14.0
Private financing	16.5	15.2	14.1	14.2	16.6	18.9	19.5	22.8	18.1	15.3
Diversified financing	20.1	15.3	15.6	16.3	17.9	13.3	14.3	11.9	9.1	12.6
Net debtor countries by debt-servicing experience										
Countries with arrears and/or rescheduling during 1994–98	20.2	19.9	18.4	23.7	23.7	27.6	32.5	40.2	26.2	22.8
Other net debtor countries	15.8	14.1	13.3	13.3	15.3	15.2	14.3	14.3	12.9	12.1
Other groups										
Heavily indebted poor countries	13.8	14.3	12.9	25.1	16.8	8.8	9.3	10.1	10.2	15.1
Least developed countries	11.4	9.8	10.7	13.5	18.9	7.5	7.3	9.0	6.1	16.5
Middle East and north Africa	9.6	11.4	12.1	13.5	16.3	12.3	12.7	10.4	6.8	8.2

[1]Excludes service payments to the International Monetary Fund.
[2]Interest payments on total debt and amortization on long-term debt. Estimates through 1999 reflect debt-service payments actually made. The estimates for 2000 and 2001 take into account projected exceptional financing items, including accumulation of arrears and rescheduling agreements. In some cases, amortization on account of debt-reduction operations is included.

Table 43. IMF Charges and Repurchases to the IMF[1]

(Percent of exports of goods and services)

	1992	1993	1994	1995	1996	1997	1998	1999
Developing countries	**1.1**	**0.9**	**0.7**	**0.8**	**0.7**	**0.7**	**0.5**	**0.9**
Regional groups								
Africa	1.2	1.2	0.8	2.1	0.7	0.9	1.1	0.5
Sub-Sahara	0.9	0.7	0.4	2.4	0.7	0.7	0.8	0.2
Asia	0.6	0.3	0.5	0.4	0.4	0.2	0.1	0.2
Excluding China and India	0.5	0.3	0.2	0.2	0.2	0.2	0.1	0.2
Middle East and Europe	—	—	—	0.1	0.1	—	0.1	0.2
Western Hemisphere	2.8	2.7	1.7	1.5	1.7	1.9	1.2	3.2
Analytical groups								
By source of export earnings								
Fuel	0.5	0.6	0.4	0.5	0.4	0.4	0.6	0.5
Nonfuel	1.2	1.0	0.8	0.9	0.8	0.7	0.5	1.0
By external financing source								
Net creditor countries	—	—	—	—	—	—	—	—
Net debtor countries	1.2	1.1	0.8	0.9	0.8	0.8	0.5	1.0
Official financing	1.9	2.2	1.2	4.2	1.2	0.9	1.3	1.0
Private financing	1.2	1.1	0.9	0.7	0.7	0.8	0.5	1.2
Diversified financing	1.2	0.8	0.9	0.9	0.8	0.6	0.3	0.4
Net debtor countries by debt-servicing experience								
Countries with arrears and/or rescheduling during 1994–98	1.4	1.4	0.7	1.3	0.6	0.4	0.5	1.1
Other net debtor countries	1.2	0.9	0.9	0.8	0.8	0.9	0.6	1.0
Other groups								
Heavily indebted poor countries	2.1	1.7	1.0	4.7	1.3	0.5	0.5	0.3
Least developed countries	1.7	1.3	0.8	6.5	1.5	0.2	0.4	0.3
Middle East and north Africa	0.3	0.4	0.3	0.3	0.2	0.3	0.4	0.3
Countries in transition	**0.4**	**0.3**	**1.1**	**1.4**	**0.8**	**0.6**	**0.9**	**2.4**
Central and eastern Europe	0.7	0.6	2.0	2.3	0.8	0.4	0.6	0.7
Excluding Belarus and Ukraine	0.8	0.7	2.3	2.7	1.0	0.4	0.5	0.4
Russia	—	—	0.1	0.2	0.8	0.9	1.7	5.9
Transcaucasus and central Asia	—	—	—	0.1	0.3	0.4	1.1	2.0
Memorandum								
Total, billions of U.S. dollars								
General Resources Account	8.192	7.503	8.669	11.857	9.892	9.926	8.442	18.194
Charges	2.423	2.184	2.123	1.898	2.661	2.140	2.142	2.494
Repurchases	5.768	5.319	6.546	9.960	7.231	7.786	6.300	15.700
Trust Fund	0.001	0.060	0.017	0.015	—	0.007	0.001	0.001
Interest	0.001	—	0.003	—	—	—	—	—
Repayments	—	0.060	0.014	0.015	—	0.007	0.001	0.001
PRGF[2]	0.051	0.148	0.331	0.584	0.736	0.865	0.880	0.855
Interest	0.018	0.022	0.025	0.031	0.033	0.038	0.039	0.041
Repayments	0.033	0.126	0.306	0.552	0.703	0.827	0.842	0.814

[1]Excludes advanced economies. Charges on, and repurchases (or repayments of principal) for, use of International Monetary Fund credit.
[2]Poverty Reduction and Growth Facility (formerly ESAF—Enhanced Structural Adjustment Facility).

Table 44. Summary of Sources and Uses of World Saving
(Percent of GDP)

	Averages		1994	1995	1996	1997	1998	1999	2000	2001	Average 2002–2005
	1978–85	1986–93									
World											
Saving	23.3	22.9	23.1	23.5	23.4	23.9	23.3	23.2	23.8	23.7	23.8
Investment	24.4	24.0	23.8	24.3	24.0	24.1	23.4	23.2	23.7	24.1	24.6
Advanced economies											
Saving	22.0	20.9	20.9	21.4	21.5	22.1	22.1	21.7	21.9	22.1	22.5
Private	21.6	20.4	20.9	21.1	20.7	20.1	20.2	18.9	18.7	18.8	18.8
Public	0.4	0.5	—	0.3	0.9	1.9	1.9	2.8	3.2	3.3	3.7
Investment	22.8	21.8	21.3	21.5	21.6	21.9	21.7	21.9	22.4	22.6	22.9
Private	18.3	17.8	17.3	17.5	17.7	18.1	18.0	18.1	18.6	19.1	19.4
Public	4.5	4.0	4.0	4.0	3.9	3.7	3.7	3.8	3.7	3.6	3.5
Net lending	−0.8	−0.9	−0.5	−0.1	−0.1	0.2	0.4	−0.2	−0.5	−0.5	−0.4
Private	3.3	2.6	3.6	3.5	3.0	2.0	2.2	0.8	—	−0.3	−0.6
Public	−4.1	−3.5	−4.0	−3.7	−3.1	−1.8	−1.8	−1.0	−0.5	−0.2	0.2
Current transfers	−0.5	−0.3	−0.4	−0.3	−0.3	−0.3	−0.3	−0.4	−0.3	−0.3	−0.3
Factor income	−0.3	−0.5	−0.5	−0.3	−0.2	−0.1	0.1	0.2	0.2	0.1	—
Resource balance	−0.1	−0.1	0.4	0.4	0.4	0.6	0.7	−0.1	−0.4	−0.3	−0.1
United States											
Saving	19.7	16.9	16.4	17.0	17.3	18.1	18.8	18.5	18.2	18.4	18.6
Private	19.9	17.9	17.0	17.1	16.5	16.2	15.7	14.4	13.4	13.7	14.0
Public	−0.2	−1.1	−0.6	−0.1	0.8	1.9	3.2	4.0	4.8	4.7	4.7
Investment	21.2	18.9	18.8	18.7	19.1	19.9	20.8	21.1	21.9	22.1	22.1
Private	17.7	15.2	15.6	15.5	15.9	16.7	17.6	17.7	18.5	18.8	18.9
Public	3.5	3.7	3.2	3.2	3.2	3.2	3.2	3.3	3.3	3.3	3.2
Net lending	−1.5	−2.0	−2.4	−1.7	−1.8	−1.8	−2.0	−2.6	−3.6	−3.7	−3.5
Private	2.2	2.7	1.4	1.7	0.6	−0.6	−2.0	−3.3	−5.1	−5.1	−5.0
Public	−3.7	−4.7	−3.8	−3.3	−2.4	−1.3	—	0.7	1.5	1.5	1.5
Current transfers	−0.4	−0.4	−0.5	−0.5	−0.5	−0.5	−0.5	−0.5	−0.4	−0.4	−0.4
Factor income	0.3	0.1	−0.4	0.1	—	−0.1	0.4	0.8	0.4	0.1	−0.2
Resource balance	−1.4	−1.7	−1.4	−1.3	−1.3	−1.3	−1.9	−2.8	−3.6	−3.4	−3.0
European Union											
Saving	20.7	20.4	19.8	20.6	20.4	21.0	21.3	20.9	21.3	21.7	22.2
Private	20.9	21.2	22.4	22.7	22.0	21.1	20.4	19.5	19.2	19.6	19.7
Public	−0.2	−0.8	−2.6	−2.2	−1.6	−0.1	0.8	1.4	2.1	2.1	2.5
Investment	21.5	21.2	19.7	20.0	19.4	19.6	20.5	20.7	20.9	21.1	21.3
Private	17.6	18.0	16.9	17.4	16.9	17.3	18.1	18.3	18.5	18.7	18.8
Public	3.9	3.3	2.8	2.6	2.5	2.4	2.4	2.4	2.4	2.4	2.5
Net lending	−0.8	−0.8	0.1	0.6	1.0	1.4	0.8	0.2	0.4	0.6	0.9
Private	3.2	3.2	5.5	5.3	5.1	3.8	2.3	1.1	0.7	0.9	0.9
Public	−4.1	−4.0	−5.4	−4.8	−4.1	−2.5	−1.5	−1.0	−0.3	−0.3	—
Current transfers	−0.7	−0.4	−0.4	−0.2	−0.4	−0.3	−0.4	−0.4	−0.4	−0.3	−0.3
Factor income	−0.9	−1.1	−0.8	−0.8	−0.5	−0.4	−0.5	−0.6	−0.4	−0.4	−0.4
Resource balance	0.8	0.6	1.4	1.6	1.9	2.1	1.7	1.1	1.2	1.3	1.6
Japan											
Saving	31.2	33.1	31.5	30.7	31.5	31.4	29.9	28.6	29.0	29.4	30.1
Private	27.5	24.9	26.0	25.9	27.0	26.8	31.9	28.2	30.1	29.2	28.3
Public	3.7	8.1	5.5	4.9	4.5	4.5	−2.0	0.4	−1.1	0.1	1.7
Investment	30.1	30.4	28.7	28.6	30.0	29.1	26.7	26.1	26.2	26.6	27.6
Private	21.3	23.4	20.0	20.0	21.2	21.3	19.1	18.1	18.9	20.1	21.9
Public	8.8	7.0	8.6	8.6	8.7	7.8	7.6	8.0	7.2	6.5	5.8
Net lending	1.0	2.7	2.8	2.1	1.5	2.3	3.2	2.5	2.9	2.8	2.4
Private	6.1	1.6	6.0	5.8	5.8	5.5	12.8	10.2	11.2	9.1	6.5
Public	−5.1	1.1	−3.1	−3.7	−4.2	−3.2	−9.7	−7.6	−8.3	−6.4	−4.1
Current transfers	−0.1	−0.1	−0.1	0.2	−0.2	−0.2	−0.2	−0.3	−0.2	−0.3	−0.3
Factor income	0.1	0.7	0.9	0.8	1.3	1.4	1.5	1.2	1.5	1.5	1.5
Resource balance	1.1	2.2	2.1	1.5	0.5	1.1	1.9	1.6	1.6	1.6	1.2

Table 44 (continued)

| | Averages | | 1994 | 1995 | 1996 | 1997 | 1998 | 1999 | 2000 | 2001 | Average 2002–2005 |
	1978–85	1986–93									
Newly industrialized Asian economies											
Saving	...	35.6	33.6	33.7	32.8	32.7	33.3	32.8	32.3	31.5	31.0
Private	...	27.9	26.1	26.5	25.8	25.9	25.8	25.6	25.2	24.5	24.3
Public	...	7.6	7.6	7.3	7.0	6.8	7.5	7.2	7.1	7.0	6.6
	...										
Investment	...	29.9	31.9	32.7	32.2	30.8	23.3	25.2	26.8	27.0	27.3
Private	...	23.8	25.0	26.0	25.5	24.2	16.2	17.8	19.8	20.5	20.9
Public	...	6.1	6.8	6.7	6.7	6.6	7.1	7.3	7.0	6.6	6.4
Net lending	...	5.7	1.8	1.1	0.6	1.9	10.1	7.7	5.5	4.4	3.6
Private	...	4.2	1.0	0.5	0.3	1.7	9.6	7.8	5.4	4.0	3.4
Public	...	1.5	0.7	0.6	0.4	0.2	0.5	−0.1	0.1	0.4	0.3
Current transfers	...	0.1	—	−0.3	−0.3	−0.3	0.2	−0.1	−0.2	−0.4	−0.4
Factor income	...	0.5	0.6	1.1	1.1	1.7	1.6	1.9	2.1	2.1	2.0
Resource balance	...	5.0	1.2	0.3	−0.2	0.5	8.3	5.9	3.5	2.8	2.0
Developing countries											
Saving	22.4	23.5	26.7	26.9	26.6	27.2	26.0	25.8	26.7	26.4	25.9
Investment	23.9	25.4	27.9	28.8	27.8	27.6	26.5	25.7	26.2	26.6	27.1
Net lending	−1.5	−1.9	−1.2	−1.9	−1.2	−0.4	−0.5	0.1	0.5	−0.3	−1.2
Current transfers	0.8	1.0	1.1	1.1	1.1	1.3	1.1	1.3	1.3	1.3	1.2
Factor income	−1.0	−1.4	−1.0	−1.5	−1.2	−1.3	−1.3	−1.7	−1.8	−1.8	−1.8
Resource balance	−1.2	−1.5	−1.4	−1.5	−1.1	−0.4	−0.3	0.5	1.0	0.3	−0.6
Memorandum											
Acquisition of foreign assets	1.1	0.9	3.0	2.5	3.2	4.2	2.4	3.0	3.5	3.3	2.4
Change in reserves	0.3	0.6	2.1	1.7	2.1	1.5	0.1	0.8	1.2	1.5	1.1
Regional groups											
Africa											
Saving	21.0	16.9	16.3	15.7	16.5	16.0	16.2	16.4	18.8	18.4	20.0
Investment	23.0	19.3	19.8	19.7	18.4	18.4	20.4	20.3	20.1	20.7	22.0
Net lending	−2.1	−2.4	−3.5	−3.9	−1.9	−2.4	−4.2	−4.0	−1.3	−2.3	−2.0
Current transfers	1.3	2.9	3.5	3.0	3.0	3.0	3.2	3.1	3.2	3.1	2.8
Factor income	1.0	−3.6	−4.0	−3.7	−4.3	−4.5	−3.2	−4.0	−4.6	−4.4	−3.4
Resource balance	−4.4	−1.6	−3.0	−3.2	−0.6	−1.0	−4.2	−3.0	0.1	−1.0	−1.4
Memorandum											
Acquisition of foreign assets	−0.4	0.7	1.5	1.3	2.9	3.2	0.4	1.6	3.6	2.1	1.8
Change in reserves	—	0.1	1.6	0.7	2.2	2.2	−0.3	0.4	2.9	1.6	1.5
Asia											
Saving	25.1	28.7	33.5	32.9	32.5	33.5	32.7	31.5	31.9	31.5	30.2
Investment	26.1	30.0	33.8	34.6	33.5	32.4	30.1	29.6	30.1	30.4	30.3
Net lending	−1.0	−1.3	−0.3	−1.7	−1.0	1.1	2.6	1.9	1.8	1.1	−0.2
Current transfers	1.3	0.8	1.2	1.1	1.2	1.5	1.2	1.3	1.3	1.3	1.2
Factor income	0.3	−0.5	−0.2	−1.0	−0.5	−0.6	−0.8	−1.2	−1.0	−1.1	−1.3
Resource balance	−2.6	−1.7	−1.4	−1.8	−1.8	0.2	2.2	1.9	1.5	0.9	−0.1
Memorandum											
Acquisition of foreign assets	2.7	1.5	4.7	3.0	3.5	5.6	4.0	4.3	4.2	4.4	3.2
Change in reserves	0.8	0.8	3.6	2.0	2.2	1.7	0.9	1.4	0.9	1.8	1.3
Middle East and Europe											
Saving	24.5	19.1	22.4	24.4	21.8	21.4	18.0	21.0	23.7	22.7	22.3
Investment	24.2	23.3	21.7	24.4	21.4	21.8	22.3	21.5	21.9	22.6	24.5
Net lending	0.3	−4.2	0.7	0.1	0.4	−0.4	−4.3	−0.4	1.8	0.1	−2.2
Current transfers	—	—	−0.7	−0.7	−0.4	−0.3	−0.5	−0.2	0.1	0.1	0.1
Factor income	−0.8	0.8	1.0	1.5	0.9	0.9	1.0	—	−1.0	−0.5	−0.3
Resource balance	1.1	−5.0	0.4	−0.7	−0.1	−0.9	−4.8	−0.3	2.6	0.6	−2.0
Memorandum											
Acquisition of foreign assets	2.7	−1.2	1.4	1.3	2.4	3.0	—	1.4	4.2	2.9	1.1
Change in reserves	0.8	0.2	1.0	1.6	2.6	0.9	−1.8	0.8	2.5	1.9	0.6

Table 44 *(continued)*

	Averages		1994	1995	1996	1997	1998	1999	2000	2001	Average 2002–2005
	1978–85	1986–93									
Western Hemisphere											
Saving	18.9	19.2	18.6	19.0	19.3	19.3	17.5	17.3	17.9	18.0	18.7
Investment	21.5	20.9	21.5	21.3	21.2	22.6	22.2	20.1	20.6	21.2	21.7
Net lending	−2.6	−1.7	−2.9	−2.3	−1.9	−3.2	−4.7	−2.8	−2.7	−3.2	−3.0
Current transfers	0.4	1.0	0.9	1.1	1.0	1.0	1.1	1.2	1.1	1.1	1.0
Factor income	−3.6	−3.2	−2.3	−3.0	−2.8	−2.7	−2.8	−3.0	−3.1	−3.2	−3.1
Resource balance	0.6	0.5	−1.6	−0.5	−0.2	−1.5	−3.0	−1.1	−0.8	−1.1	−0.9
Memorandum											
Acquisition of foreign assets	1.3	0.9	0.7	2.5	3.0	1.9	0.3	0.9	1.4	1.2	1.1
Change in reserves	0.2	0.6	−0.2	1.4	1.8	1.0	−1.0	−0.7	0.5	0.5	0.5
Analytical groups											
By source of export earnings											
Fuel											
Saving	27.9	19.5	21.9	24.2	24.6	23.6	17.8	21.6	28.3	25.7	24.3
Investment	25.0	22.8	21.3	23.6	19.6	21.0	23.1	21.4	21.3	22.2	24.5
Net lending	2.9	−3.3	0.6	0.6	5.0	2.6	−5.3	0.2	7.0	3.5	−0.1
Current transfers	−2.6	−2.8	−2.4	−2.4	−2.0	−1.9	−2.2	−1.9	−1.5	−1.5	−1.1
Factor income	0.1	0.7	−0.7	0.2	−0.5	−0.8	0.1	−1.6	−2.7	−2.0	−1.5
Resource balance	5.4	−1.2	3.6	2.9	7.5	5.3	−3.2	3.7	11.2	6.9	2.4
Memorandum											
Acquisition of foreign assets	3.6	−1.6	3.3	0.7	5.4	5.1	−0.8	1.0	6.9	3.9	2.1
Change in reserves	0.7	−0.7	−0.1	—	4.3	1.9	−3.0	−0.7	4.7	2.3	1.1
Nonfuel											
Saving	21.4	24.0	27.3	27.2	26.9	27.6	26.9	26.2	26.5	26.4	26.1
Investment	23.7	25.7	28.7	29.4	28.7	28.3	26.9	26.1	26.7	27.0	27.4
Net lending	−2.4	−1.7	−1.4	−2.2	−1.8	−0.7	—	0.1	−0.1	−0.6	−1.3
Current transfers	1.4	1.5	1.5	1.5	1.5	1.6	1.5	1.6	1.6	1.5	1.4
Factor income	−1.2	−1.7	−1.0	−1.7	−1.3	−1.3	−1.4	−1.7	−1.7	−1.8	−1.8
Resource balance	−2.5	−1.5	−1.9	−2.0	−2.0	−1.0	−0.1	0.2	—	−0.3	−0.8
Memorandum											
Acquisition of foreign assets	0.5	1.2	3.0	2.7	3.0	4.1	2.7	3.2	3.2	3.3	2.4
Change in reserves	0.2	0.7	2.4	1.8	1.9	1.4	0.4	0.9	0.8	1.4	1.1
By external financing source											
Net creditor countries											
Saving	33.1	14.7	17.0	21.2	22.9	23.8	14.3	20.4	27.4	24.5	23.4
Investment	25.3	19.9	20.1	20.6	19.1	20.8	22.4	20.7	19.2	20.1	22.8
Net lending	7.8	−5.2	−3.1	0.5	3.8	2.9	−8.1	−0.3	8.2	4.4	0.7
Current transfers	−7.5	−10.3	−10.4	−9.1	−7.8	−7.2	−8.1	−6.8	−5.7	−5.8	−5.4
Factor income	0.7	5.7	3.1	5.3	4.4	4.4	5.2	3.8	0.8	1.0	1.9
Resource balance	14.6	−0.7	4.1	4.4	7.1	5.8	−5.2	2.7	13.1	9.2	4.2
Memorandum											
Acquisition of foreign assets	7.8	−3.1	−0.7	1.0	6.0	5.1	−5.0	0.9	8.6	6.2	3.8
Change in reserves	1.5	−1.0	−0.4	—	4.1	3.6	−4.6	−1.3	3.6	2.4	2.2
Net debtor countries											
Saving	21.9	23.8	27.1	27.1	26.8	27.3	26.4	25.9	26.7	26.4	26.0
Investment	23.9	25.6	28.2	29.1	28.1	27.8	26.6	25.9	26.4	26.8	27.2
Net lending	−2.0	−1.8	−1.1	−1.9	−1.3	−0.5	−0.2	0.1	0.3	−0.4	−1.2
Current transfers	1.2	1.4	1.5	1.4	1.4	1.6	1.4	1.5	1.5	1.5	1.3
Factor income	−1.1	−1.7	−1.1	−1.7	−1.4	−1.5	−1.5	−1.9	−1.9	−1.9	−1.9
Resource balance	−2.1	−1.5	−1.5	−1.7	−1.3	−0.6	−0.2	0.5	0.6	—	−0.7
Memorandum											
Acquisition of foreign assets	0.7	1.1	3.1	2.6	3.1	4.2	2.6	3.1	3.4	3.3	2.4
Change in reserves	0.2	0.7	2.2	1.7	2.1	1.4	0.2	0.8	1.1	1.5	1.1

Table 44 *(continued)*

	Averages		1994	1995	1996	1997	1998	1999	2000	2001	Average 2002–2005
	1978–85	1986–93									
Official financing											
Saving	14.2	13.5	14.8	14.8	15.8	16.9	15.3	16.9	19.5	19.9	21.2
Investment	20.8	18.8	21.8	23.1	21.7	20.5	21.6	22.5	22.3	22.9	23.9
Net lending	−6.6	−5.3	−7.1	−8.3	−5.9	−3.6	−6.3	−5.6	−2.8	−3.0	−2.7
Current transfers	4.2	4.2	5.0	4.6	4.5	4.2	4.6	4.7	4.7	4.4	3.7
Factor income	−5.2	−4.1	−3.9	−4.8	−4.0	−3.4	−4.2	−5.0	−4.3	−3.6	−2.4
Resource balance	−5.6	−5.3	−8.2	−8.0	−6.5	−4.5	−6.8	−5.2	−3.2	−3.7	−4.0
Memorandum											
Acquisition of foreign assets	0.6	0.7	1.0	1.4	1.2	2.2	0.3	1.2	3.1	1.8	1.6
Change in reserves	0.1	0.3	1.4	0.8	1.7	2.2	−0.5	0.6	3.1	1.7	1.6
Private financing											
Saving	23.0	25.8	28.9	28.9	28.6	29.2	28.2	27.4	27.7	27.5	26.8
Investment	24.7	26.9	29.4	30.3	29.5	29.2	27.7	26.8	27.4	27.7	27.9
Net lending	−1.7	−1.2	−0.6	−1.4	−0.9	—	0.5	0.5	0.3	−0.2	−1.0
Current transfers	0.8	1.1	1.1	1.0	1.1	1.2	1.1	1.2	1.1	1.1	1.0
Factor income	−1.3	−1.7	−0.9	−1.6	−1.3	−1.5	−1.5	−1.7	−1.6	−1.8	−1.9
Resource balance	−1.2	−0.6	−0.7	−0.8	−0.7	0.3	0.9	1.0	0.8	0.4	−0.2
Memorandum											
Acquisition of foreign assets	0.8	1.4	3.4	2.8	3.4	4.8	3.2	3.2	3.4	3.5	2.5
Change in reserves	0.3	0.7	2.3	1.8	2.0	1.7	0.3	0.7	0.8	1.4	1.0
Diversified financing											
Saving	18.1	14.1	16.2	15.6	15.6	15.7	18.0	17.7	19.6	19.4	20.6
Investment	20.6	18.7	21.7	20.2	20.1	20.8	20.8	19.5	19.8	20.9	22.2
Net lending	−2.5	−4.6	−5.4	−4.6	−4.5	−5.1	−2.8	−1.9	−0.3	−1.4	−1.7
Current transfers	2.2	2.7	3.4	3.2	3.0	3.3	3.3	3.1	3.2	3.1	3.2
Factor income	1.8	−2.1	−1.5	−0.4	−0.8	−0.6	—	−2.7	−3.2	−2.2	−1.6
Resource balance	−6.5	−5.2	−7.4	−7.3	−6.8	−7.9	−6.1	−2.2	−0.3	−2.3	−3.2
Memorandum											
Acquisition of foreign assets	0.4	−0.8	1.0	0.6	3.5	1.0	0.1	3.6	2.4	2.2	1.7
Change in reserves	0.4	0.3	2.0	0.8	2.9	−0.2	0.8	1.7	1.3	1.7	1.4
Net debtor countries by debt-servicing experience											
Countries with arrears and/or rescheduling during 1994–98											
Saving	18.7	19.6	21.6	21.2	20.3	19.8	17.2	17.6	20.3	19.9	20.2
Investment	21.4	22.2	23.7	24.7	23.1	23.3	20.2	19.1	20.3	21.4	22.5
Net lending	−2.7	−2.6	−2.1	−3.5	−2.8	−3.5	−3.1	−1.5	—	−1.5	−2.3
Current transfers	0.6	1.2	1.6	1.4	1.4	1.3	1.4	1.6	1.5	1.5	1.3
Factor income	−2.1	−2.3	−1.9	−1.8	−1.5	−2.0	−1.6	−2.9	−2.9	−2.7	−2.3
Resource balance	−1.2	−1.4	−1.7	−3.0	−2.6	−2.8	−2.9	−0.2	1.3	−0.3	−1.3
Memorandum											
Acquisition of foreign assets	0.8	0.2	1.8	1.5	1.8	1.6	0.2	1.1	2.8	1.7	1.0
Change in reserves	0.2	0.3	1.0	1.5	1.5	0.6	−0.2	0.3	2.3	1.5	0.9
Other net debtor countries											
Saving	23.7	25.8	29.2	29.5	29.3	30.2	29.7	28.8	28.9	28.6	27.9
Investment	25.3	27.2	30.0	30.8	30.0	29.6	28.9	28.2	28.5	28.6	28.8
Net lending	−1.6	−1.4	−0.7	−1.3	−0.8	0.6	0.8	0.6	0.4	—	−0.9
Current transfers	1.5	1.5	1.5	1.4	1.5	1.7	1.4	1.5	1.5	1.5	1.3
Factor income	−0.5	−1.4	−0.8	−1.6	−1.4	−1.2	−1.4	−1.5	−1.5	−1.6	−1.7
Resource balance	−2.6	−1.5	−1.5	−1.1	−0.9	0.2	0.8	0.7	0.4	0.1	−0.5
Memorandum											
Acquisition of foreign assets	0.6	1.5	3.6	3.0	3.6	5.1	3.5	3.7	3.5	3.8	2.8
Change in reserves	0.3	0.8	2.7	1.8	2.3	1.7	0.4	1.0	0.7	1.5	1.1

Table 44 *(concluded)*

	Averages 1978–85	Averages 1986–93	1994	1995	1996	1997	1998	1999	2000	2001	Average 2002–2005
Countries in transition											
Saving	. . .	. . .	24.4	23.8	21.9	21.3	17.9	22.3	23.8	22.3	22.7
Investment	. . .	. . .	24.9	24.6	24.4	24.0	21.2	20.5	21.2	22.0	24.4
Net lending	. . .	. . .	−0.6	−0.9	−2.5	−2.7	−3.3	1.8	2.6	0.3	−1.6
Current transfers	. . .	. . .	0.9	0.8	0.8	0.9	0.9	1.1	1.0	1.0	1.1
Factor income	. . .	. . .	−1.1	−0.8	−0.8	−1.0	−2.0	−3.4	−3.0	−2.3	−2.1
Resource balance	. . .	. . .	−0.4	−0.8	−2.5	−2.6	−2.2	4.0	4.6	1.6	−0.7
Memorandum											
Acquisition of foreign assets	. . .	. . .	2.1	3.6	1.8	4.8	3.2	8.8	6.7	4.3	2.5
Change in reserves	. . .	. . .	0.9	3.7	0.2	1.2	−0.4	1.0	3.5	1.9	1.4

Note: The estimates in this table are based on individual countries' national accounts and balance of payments statistics. For many countries, the estimates of national saving are built up from national accounts data on gross domestic investment and from balance-of-payments-based data on net foreign investment. The latter, which is equivalent to the current account balance, comprises three components: current transfers, net factor income, and the resource balance. The mixing of data sources, which is dictated by availability, implies that the estimates for national saving that are derived incorporate the statistical discrepancies. Furthermore, errors, omissions, and asymmetries in balance of payments statistics affect the estimates for net lending; at the global level, net lending, which in theory would be zero, equals the world current account discrepancy.

Notwithstanding these statistical shortcomings, flow of funds estimates, such as those presented in this table, provide a useful framework for analyzing development in saving and investment, both over time and across regions and countries. Country group composites are weighted by GDP valued at purchasing power parities (PPPs) as a share of total world GDP.

Table 45. Summary of World Medium-Term Baseline Scenario

	Eight-Year Averages		Four-Year Average					Four-Year Average
	1982–89	1990–97	1998–2001	1998	1999	2000	2001	2002–2005
	Annual percent change unless otherwise noted							
World real GDP	**3.6**	**3.0**	**3.7**	**2.6**	**3.4**	**4.7**	**4.2**	**4.3**
Advanced economies	3.4	2.5	3.2	2.4	3.2	4.2	3.2	2.9
Developing countries	4.3	5.8	4.6	3.5	3.8	5.6	5.7	6.0
Countries in transition	3.1	−5.1	2.6	−0.8	2.4	4.9	4.1	5.0
Memorandum								
Potential output								
Major industrial countries	2.9	2.7	2.6	2.5	2.5	2.6	2.7	2.7
World trade, volume[1]	**5.0**	**6.6**	**6.8**	**4.3**	**5.1**	**10.0**	**7.8**	**6.9**
Imports								
Advanced economies	6.4	6.1	7.9	5.7	7.6	10.3	7.9	6.6
Developing countries	1.2	9.2	4.7	0.3	—	10.0	9.0	8.7
Countries in transition	2.7	−1.4	4.9	2.5	−2.9	12.4	8.4	7.8
Exports								
Advanced economies	5.3	6.9	6.5	3.9	4.8	9.9	7.6	6.4
Developing countries	4.3	8.7	5.7	3.7	3.5	8.8	7.1	8.4
Countries in transition	2.8	−0.8	6.9	6.5	5.0	10.1	6.0	6.4
Terms of trade								
Advanced economies	1.3	−0.2	0.2	1.3	−0.1	−1.0	0.7	0.4
Developing countries	−4.2	0.6	0.3	−4.6	2.7	4.6	−1.4	−0.4
Countries in transition	−0.1	−2.4	0.3	−4.8	1.1	7.0	−1.6	−0.3
World prices in U.S. dollars								
Manufactures	3.5	1.0	−1.7	−1.2	−1.2	−5.3	1.1	1.0
Oil	−8.1	0.9	4.5	−32.1	37.5	47.5	−13.3	−2.1
Nonfuel primary commodities	1.3	0.7	−3.8	−14.7	−7.1	3.2	4.5	3.6
Consumer prices								
Advanced economies	4.9	3.3	1.8	1.5	1.4	2.3	2.1	2.0
Developing countries	41.9	37.6	7.0	10.1	6.6	6.2	5.2	3.7
Countries in transition	6.6	167.4	23.6	21.8	43.8	18.3	12.5	6.8
Interest rates (in percent)								
Real six-month LIBOR[2]	5.7	3.0	4.5	4.3	4.0	4.6	5.1	5.1
World real long-term interest rate[3]	5.5	4.0	3.2	3.0	3.2	3.1	3.6	3.9
	Percent of GDP							
Balances on current account								
Advanced economies	−0.3	0.1	−0.4	0.2	−0.5	−0.7	−0.7	−0.7
Developing countries	−2.1	−1.9	−0.6	−1.8	−0.5	0.4	−0.5	−1.3
Countries in transition	0.4	−1.0	−0.8	−3.3	−0.6	0.9	−0.4	−2.0
Total external debt								
Developing countries	36.5	35.6	36.9	38.1	38.9	36.0	34.7	31.7
Countries in transition	8.4	34.4	47.6	43.8	52.2	49.3	45.0	39.3
Debt service								
Developing countries	4.4	4.7	6.1	5.9	6.8	6.0	5.6	5.0
Countries in transition	2.0	3.6	6.8	6.3	7.6	7.0	6.3	5.7

[1]Data refer to trade in goods and services.
[2]London interbank offered rate on U.S. dollar deposits less percent change in U.S. GDP deflator.
[3]GDP-weighted average of ten-year (or nearest maturity) government bond rates for the United States, Japan, Germany, France, Italy, the United Kingdom, and Canada.

Table 46. Developing Countries—Medium-Term Baseline Scenario: Selected Economic Indicators

	Eight-Year Averages		Four-Year Average					Four-Year Average
	1982–89	1990–97	1998–2001	1998	1999	2000	2001	2002–2005
	Annual percent change							
DDeveloping countries								
Real GDP	4.3	5.8	4.6	3.5	3.8	5.6	5.7	6.0
Export volume[1]	4.3	8.7	5.7	3.7	3.5	8.8	7.1	8.4
Terms of trade[1]	−4.2	0.6	0.3	−4.6	2.7	4.6	−1.4	−0.4
Import volume[1]	1.2	9.2	4.7	0.3	—	10.0	9.0	8.7
Regional groups								
Africa								
Real GDP	2.5	2.0	3.3	3.1	2.2	3.4	4.4	5.1
Export volume[1]	5.1	2.7	4.2	0.5	2.2	7.9	6.4	5.5
Terms of trade[1]	−3.3	0.8	0.7	−8.3	6.9	11.0	−5.4	−0.6
Import volume[1]	3.9	2.8	4.7	3.0	3.4	7.0	5.5	5.0
Asia								
Real GDP	7.2	8.0	5.8	4.1	5.9	6.7	6.6	6.9
Export volume[1]	7.3	12.8	5.7	2.7	3.4	8.6	8.2	10.1
Terms of trade[1]	−1.5	0.3	0.4	2.5	−1.8	−0.6	1.5	0.6
Import volume[1]	5.1	11.7	4.9	−5.5	3.4	10.2	12.5	12.0
Middle East and Europe								
Real GDP	3.0	4.0	3.2	3.1	0.8	4.7	4.1	4.6
Export volume[1]	2.1	6.3	4.1	4.2	0.1	9.4	2.7	3.2
Terms of trade[1]	−7.0	—	0.2	−15.7	12.6	11.5	−4.7	−1.2
Import volume[1]	−2.2	5.1	2.7	2.2	−3.0	7.3	4.8	4.0
Western Hemisphere								
Real GDP	1.7	3.5	2.8	2.2	0.3	4.3	4.5	4.6
Export volume[1]	4.6	8.3	7.8	6.6	6.6	9.2	8.9	9.7
Terms of trade[1]	−3.8	1.3	−0.6	−5.9	0.1	5.9	−2.1	−1.4
Import volume[1]	−2.2	12.7	5.9	7.7	−4.2	12.9	7.9	7.4
Analytical groups								
Net debtor countries by debt-servicing experience								
Countries with arrears and/or rescheduling during 1994–98								
Real GDP	2.9	3.6	2.5	−0.8	2.1	4.2	4.6	5.1
Export volume[1]	6.5	4.1	3.0	1.4	−1.8	6.3	6.3	8.9
Terms of trade[1]	−4.5	0.5	1.0	−2.8	2.3	6.3	−1.4	−1.3
Import volume[1]	1.0	6.3	1.0	−0.9	−10.8	6.7	10.1	7.5
Other net debtor countries								
Real GDP	5.3	6.7	5.4	5.1	4.5	6.2	6.1	6.4
Export volume[1]	6.1	10.9	7.2	5.3	5.8	9.2	8.4	9.0
Terms of trade[1]	−2.5	0.5	—	−2.1	0.7	1.5	−0.1	0.3
Import volume[1]	2.3	10.8	6.7	1.0	4.5	11.9	9.7	9.8

Table 46 (*concluded*)

	1989	1993	1997	1998	1999	2000	2001	2005
				Percent of exports of good and services				
Developing countries								
Current account balance	−6.6	−16.1	−4.6	−8.1	−1.9	1.4	−1.9	−5.3
Total external debt	201.0	194.7	150.2	172.7	163.5	139.5	135.6	114.1
Debt-service payments[2]	22.2	23.5	24.7	26.8	28.4	23.1	22.0	17.5
Interest payments	10.0	9.7	7.8	9.1	9.1	8.3	8.3	7.5
Amortization	12.2	13.8	16.9	17.7	19.3	14.8	13.7	10.1
Regional groups								
Africa								
Current account balance	−8.6	−11.8	−5.8	−16.9	−13.1	−2.3	−5.7	−5.3
Total external debt	243.3	272.6	220.2	248.6	237.0	192.9	189.8	162.2
Debt-service payments[2]	19.2	27.9	20.9	21.8	20.7	17.5	22.5	17.1
Interest payments	3.5	9.5	8.1	8.5	8.0	6.6	7.4	6.2
Amortization	15.8	18.4	12.8	13.4	12.6	10.9	15.2	10.9
Asia								
Current account balance	−12.3	−11.4	1.6	8.6	7.8	6.0	3.3	−2.5
Total external debt	169.2	153.7	114.2	122.9	116.2	104.2	98.6	77.6
Debt-service payments[2]	21.1	17.5	14.8	18.1	19.0	14.7	14.2	11.1
Interest payments	8.8	6.9	4.9	5.6	6.1	5.4	5.4	4.9
Amortization	12.3	10.6	9.9	12.5	12.9	9.3	8.8	6.2
Middle East and Europe								
Current account balance	−1.8	−16.7	2.5	−14.1	1.6	13.7	6.9	−0.8
Total external debt	133.0	120.7	101.4	134.6	122.5	94.3	99.7	100.7
Debt-service payments[2]	14.9	14.3	15.5	18.7	17.1	13.7	13.5	13.3
Interest payments	6.7	6.0	4.7	6.7	5.6	4.7	5.8	6.5
Amortization	8.2	8.3	10.8	12.0	11.5	9.0	7.7	6.9
Western Hemisphere								
Current account balance	−3.6	−25.8	−22.2	−31.4	−19.0	−17.1	−17.8	−14.2
Total external debt	278.9	292.9	228.8	262.6	257.9	225.3	214.5	180.9
Debt-service payments[2]	32.5	40.1	53.6	51.3	59.7	50.5	44.2	33.9
Interest payments	18.5	18.1	16.2	17.8	18.3	18.0	16.6	14.0
Amortization	14.0	22.0	37.5	33.5	41.4	32.5	27.5	19.9
Analytical groups								
Net debtor countries by debt-servicing experience								
Countries with arrears and/or rescheduling during 1994–98								
Current account balance	−10.2	−15.9	−16.4	−21.6	−8.1	−2.4	−7.6	−7.5
Total external debt	292.8	320.6	250.5	296.1	275.8	224.0	214.6	169.0
Debt-service payments[2]	24.8	32.4	39.3	46.2	53.9	37.9	33.8	23.5
Interest payments	9.1	12.5	11.7	13.7	13.7	11.7	11.0	9.0
Amortization	15.7	19.9	27.6	32.5	40.2	26.2	22.8	14.6
Other net debtor countries								
Current account balance	−7.5	−17.2	−2.6	−1.8	−0.4	−1.6	−3.0	−6.0
Total external debt	190.1	178.4	132.5	144.1	139.7	126.7	121.7	102.4
Debt-service payments[2]	25.3	24.5	22.7	22.7	22.8	21.1	20.4	16.6
Interest payments	12.3	10.4	7.5	8.4	8.5	8.3	8.3	7.5
Amortization	13.0	14.1	15.2	14.3	14.3	12.9	12.1	9.2

[1]Data refer to trade in goods and services.
[2]Interest payments on total debt plus amortization payments on long-term debt only. Projections incorporate the impact of exceptional financing items. Excludes service payments to the International Monetary Fund.

WORLD ECONOMIC OUTLOOK AND *STAFF STUDIES FOR THE WORLD ECONOMIC OUTLOOK,* SELECTED TOPICS, 1992–2000

I. Methodology—Aggregation, Modeling, and Forecasting

II. Historical Surveys

V. Fiscal Policy

VI. Monetary Policy; Financial Markets; Flow of Funds

VII. Labor Market Issues

VIII. Exchange Rate Issues

IX. External Payments, Trade, Capital Movements, and Foreign Debt

X. Regional Issues

XI. Country-Specific Analyses

***Staff Studies for the
World Economic Outlook***

World Economic and Financial Surveys

This series (ISSN 0258-7440) contains biannual, annual, and periodic studies covering monetary and financial issues of importance to the global economy. The core elements of the series are the *World Economic Outlook* report, usually published in May and October, and the annual report on *International Capital Markets*. Other studies assess international trade policy, private market and official financing for developing countries, exchange and payments systems, export credit policies, and issues discussed in the *World Economic Outlook*. Please consult the IMF *Publications Catalog* for a complete listing of currently available World Economic and Financial Surveys.

World Economic Outlook: A Survey by the Staff of the International Monetary Fund

The *World Economic Outlook*, published twice a year in English, French, Spanish, and Arabic, presents IMF staff economists' analyses of global economic developments during the near and medium term. Chapters give an overview of the world economy; consider issues affecting industrial countries, developing countries, and economies in transition to the market; and address topics of pressing current interest.
ISSN 0256-6877.
$42.00 (academic rate: $35.00); paper.
2000. (Oct.). ISBN 1-55775-975-8. **Stock #WEO EA 0022000.**
2000. (May). ISBN 1-55775-936-7. **Stock #WEO EA 012000.**
1999. (Oct.). ISBN 1-55775-839-5. **Stock #WEO EA 299.**
1999. (May). ISBN 1-55775-809-3. **Stock #WEO-199.**

Official Financing for Developing Countries
by a staff team in the IMF's Policy Development and Review Department led by Anthony R. Boote and Doris C. Ross

This study provides information on official financing for developing countries, with the focus on low-income countries. It updates the 1995 edition and reviews developments in direct financing by official and multilateral sources.
$25.00 (academic rate: $20.00); paper.
1998. ISBN 1-55775-702-X. **Stock #WEO-1397.**
1995. ISBN 1-55775-527-2. **Stock #WEO-1395.**

Exchange Rate Arrangements and Currency Convertibility: Developments and Issues
by a staff team led by R. Barry Johnston

A principle force driving the growth in international trade and investment has been the liberalization of financial transactions, including the liberalization of trade and exchange controls. This study reviews the developments and issues in the exchange arrangements and currency convertibility of IMF members.
$20.00 (academic rate: $12.00); paper.
1999. ISBN 1-55775-795-X. **Stock #WEO EA 0191999.**

World Economic Outlook Supporting Studies
by the IMF's Research Department

These studies, supporting analyses and scenarios of the *World Economic Outlook*, provide a detailed examination of theory and evidence on major issues currently affecting the global economy.
$25.00 (academic rate: $20.00); paper.
2000. ISBN 1-55775-893-X. **Stock #WEO EA 0032000.**

International Capital Markets: Developments, Prospects, and Key Policy Issues
by a staff team led by Donald J. Mathieson and Garry J. Schinasi

This year's *International Capital Markets* report assesses recent developments in mature and emerging financial markets and analyzes key systemic issues affecting global financial markets. The report discusses the main risks in the period ahead; identifies sources of, and possible measures to avoid, instability in OTC derivatives markets; reviews initiatives to "involve"the private sector in preventing and resolving crises, and discusses the role of foreign-owned banks in emerging markets.
$42.00 (academic rate: $35.00); paper
2000. (Sep.). ISBN 1-55775-949-9. **Stock #WEO EA 0062000**
1999. (Sep.). ISBN 1-55775-852-2. **Stock #WEO EA 699.**
1998. (Sep.). ISBN 1-55775-770-4. **Stock #WEO-698**

Toward a Framework for Financial Stability
by a staff team led by David Folkerts-Landau and Carl-Johan Lindgren

This study outlines the broad principles and characteristics of stable and sound financial systems, to facilitate IMF surveillance over banking sector issues of macroeconomic significance and to contribute to the general international effort to reduce the likelihood and diminish the intensity of future financial sector crises.
$25.00 (academic rate: $20.00); paper.
1998. ISBN 1-55775-706-2. **Stock #WEO-016.**

Trade Liberalization in IMF-Supported Programs
by a staff team led by Robert Sharer

This study assesses trade liberalization in programs supported by the IMF by reviewing multiyear arrangements in the 1990s and six detailed case studies. It also discusses the main economic factors affecting trade policy targets.
$25.00 (academic rate: $20.00); paper.
1998. ISBN 1-55775-707-0. **Stock #WEO-1897.**

Private Market Financing for Developing Countries
by a staff team from the IMF's Policy Development and Review Department led by Steven Dunaway

This study surveys recent trends in flows to developing countries through banking and securities markets. It also analyzes the institutional and regulatory framework for developing country finance; institutional investor behavior and pricing of developing country stocks; and progress in commercial bank debt restructuring in low-income countries.
$20.00 (academic rate: $12.00); paper.
1995. ISBN 1-55775-526-4. **Stock #WEO-1595.**

Available by series subscription or single title (including back issues); academic rate available only to full-time university faculty and students. For earlier editions please inquire about prices.

The IMF *Catalog of Publications* is available on-line at the Internet address listed below.

Please send orders and inquiries to:
International Monetary Fund, Publication Services, 700 19th Street, N.W.
Washington, D.C. 20431, U.S.A.
Tel.: (202) 623-7430   Telefax: (202) 623-7201
E-mail: publications@imf.org
Internet: http://www.imf.org